LÉON BLUM

LEON BLUM

JEAN LACOUTURE

Translated by George Holoch

HM

HOLMES & MEIER

Publishers, Inc.
New York London

First published in the United States of America 1982 by
Holmes & Meier Publishers, Inc.
30 Irving Place
New York, N.Y. 10003

Great Britain:
Holmes & Meier Publishers, Ltd.
131 Trafalgar Road
Greenwich, London SE10 9TX

English translation copyright © 1982 by George Holoch.
Originally published in French as *Léon Blum* by Jean Lacouture.
© Editions du Seuil, 1977.

Library of Congress Cataloging in Publication Data

Lacouture, Jean.
  Léon Blum.

  Translation of: Léon Blum.
  Bibliography: p.
  Includes index.
  1. Blum, Léon, 1872–1950.   2. France—Politics and
government—20th century.   3. Statesmen—France—
Biography.
DC373.B5L3313   1982   944.081'5'0924   [B]   81-20083
ISBN 0-8419-0775-7   AACR2
ISBN 0-8419-0776-5 (pbk.)

Manufactured in the United States of America

I do not admire the overabundance of a virtue such as valor unless I see at the same time an overabundance of its opposite. Otherwise, it is not a gift but a fault. We do not reveal our greatness by being at one extreme or the other, but by encompassing them both simultaneously, and all that is in between . . .

Pascal

CONTENTS

Part II
THE TESTS OF POWER

Part III
DEFENSE OF FREEDOM

A selection of photographs follows page 276

ACKNOWLEDGEMENTS

Would I ever have dared to undertake such an ambitious project had I not received from the very beginning the encouragement of the family of Léon Blum? I want to thank first Jeanne Blum who, from 1943 to 1950, from Buchenwald to their home in Jouy-en-Josas, shared the trials and the life of the French socialist leader with me. Her generosity and confidence helped me overcome my apprehension about the immensity of the task I had set for myself. The son and daughter-in-law of Léon Blum, Robert (who died in 1976) and Renée, aided me without reservation and with friendship, efficiency, and tolerance. Their daughter Catherine and their grandson Antoine Malmoud offered their help both with difficult research problems and indispensable corrections; Mme. Lancrey-Javel, the daughter of Léon Blum's older brother Lucien, had the courtesy to meet with me and share her precious memories; and their nephew Jean-Pierre also helped me with his advice.

Thanks to Pierre Nora, La Fondation Nationale des Sciences Politiques has collected a great many documents concerning Léon Blum. Under the expert direction of Mlle. Geneviève Chevignard, these archives are the most useful sources for those who wish to study Blum's life and work (his personal archives were seized by the Gestapo in 1940 and probably destroyed). The collected works of Blum have been published by Editions Albin Michel between 1954 and 1966 in nine monumental volumes, carefully edited under the direction of Robert Blum.

Many others helped to make my investigation of Blum's life much easier than it would have otherwise been. Foremost among them,

Mmes. Vincent Auriol, Léo Lagrange, and Paul Grunebaum-Ballin; Annette Vaillant, the daughter of one of Blum's closest friends; Drs. Bernard (son of Tristan) and Laporte; and other friends and colleagues of the first head of a socialist government in France: President Pierre Mendès France, Professor Charles-André Julien, Mme. Pierre Cot, Jules Moch, Daniel Mayer, Edouard Depreux, Louis Vallon, Gaston Cusin, Hubert Deschamps, Pierre Juvigny, Robert Verdier, Alain Savary, Pierre Viraben, and Ambassador René Massigli. Though late in life they parted ways with Blum, Germaine and Georges Monnet nevertheless contributed much to my research, as did Blum's "loyal opposition" on the question of France's role in the Spanish Civil War— José Bergamin, Jean Rous, Gilles Martinet, and David Rousset. Some of the best historians of French socialism, Madeleine Rebérioux, Charles Morazé, Jacques Julliard, Georges Haupt, and René Girault, assisted me with their advice and criticism (not to mention their own work); so did Daniel Blumé, on the policy of "non-intervention." Finally, my good friends Michel Winock and Pierre Nora took the trouble to track down those errors and inaccuracies in the text which escaped me; as did my superb colleague Charles Ronsac. From the beginning to the end, he has been closely involved with this work.

Charles Kiejman participated in this project as a research assistant. Liliane Cravagnolo, Claude Lemaître, Simone Lescuyer—and, as always, Simonne Lacouture—carefully checked the manuscript. I don't know how to thank everyone sufficiently—especially M. Esmenard, the general director of Editions Albin Michel, who had the graciousness to consider the abundant use I made of his edition of Blum's work within the limits of normal quotation and reference. (All references to the Albin Michel edition of *L'Oeuvre de Léon Blum* appear in the notes as *Oeuvre,* with the date of one of the nine volumes.)   J.L.

Part I
APPRENTICESHIP FOR SOCIALISM

A YOUNG MAN
OF THE CENTURY OF
LES MISERABLES

"We were living in the condition that Victor Hugo had foreseen, the entire world was afflicted with insomnia."

(Léon Blum, *Esquisse d'une biographie de Jaurès*)

People of Alsace

The Republic was a hundred years old. Twice overthrown, reestablished in 1870 on the ruins of the Empire, it had finally succeeded in firmly establishing its secular and communal ideology.

For three years the Eiffel Tower had stood on the banks of the Seine as a proud symbol of the triumph of technology and industrialism. Stocks were secure, bourgeois dynasties prospered, but trade unions, legalized eight years earlier, were attempting to establish their position and their rights within the framework of French democracy: the Congress of the *Fédération des Bourses du Travail* in Sainte-Etienne had just demonstrated the vitality of the movement. Gambetta had been dead for ten years, Marx for nine, Hugo for seven. Jean Jaurès had just announced his conversion to socialism, and he was to return to Parliament as a socialist deputy from Carmaux.

During the preceding year, General Boulanger, who had nearly been king in 1889, committed suicide in a Belgian cemetery; Paul Gauguin left for Tahiti; and the Natanson brothers founded *La Revue blanche.* Colonel Alfred Dreyfus, the most discreet of men, moved from the War College to the Central Command. Barrès published *L'Ennemi des lois,* and while Ravachol's bombs terrified Paris the Panama scandal shocked Parliament and its hangers-on. Taine and Renan, the mentors of the generation in power, were about to die. The century's balance sheet was being composed. The year was 1892.

In its July issue—the second of its career—*La Revue blanche* published an article by a young man whose work had earlier appeared in minor journals but who was still obscure. He was twenty; his name was Léon Blum. Until then he had published only slight poems and sketches for romantic girls. The article, published in July 1892 and entitled "Les progrès de l'apolitique," demonstrated the gifts of a writer barely past his adolescence. It was dedicated "to M. Maurice Barrès, deputy from the second district of Nancy"—an indication of the fascination that the novelist-legislator held for the young Blum. But the article published by *La Revue blanche* was nevertheless a barely veiled attack on what Barrès represented for the young at the time: a strange compound of aristocratic egotism, capricious anarchism, and social anxiety.

> The unjustifiable repression by the Versaillais[1] failed to provoke an instinctive community of action or thought among even the most sensitive of Parisians. . . . Public life is of no concern to the nation. Is this because of the frequency of revolutions in the past century? Every movement initiated by the people has produced the opposite of what they expected from it. . . . The people have the illusion of omnipotence, while in fact they haven't the slightest control over their government or their lives. Is public opinion all-powerful? In reality, it plays no role. . . . In this state of torpid languor, the consciousness of the nation is gradually dissolving. Antipolitics has broken the link between the individual and society. . . .
> This is why the future belongs not to socialism but to anarchism. The socialists can produce infinite variations on their mathematical constructions of human happiness and their pompous insistence on distributive justice: they will always come up against the impossibility of unifying individual thoughts and desires, or subjecting them to a unifying principle. Anarchism, on the other hand, provides a concrete and truly practical formulation for the state of mind whose progress we have attempted to demonstrate. Will antipolitics become a politics?

Is this praise of anarchism? Several of Blum's biographers and interpreters have suggested that this is the case.[2] On the contrary, by presenting anarchism as an escape into individualism and indifference, the young Blum, already sensitive to the demands of justice, was denouncing it as a symptom, if not a cause, of decadence. What Barrès propounded as a superior attitude of mind Blum presented as a symptom of collective enervation. There remains the skepticism with which the young man considered the perspectives then available to the socialists, who were making vigorous progress in Germany and who, six months later, were to triple their representation in the Chamber of Deputies.

This is why this early example of Blum's analytic thought is particularly interesting. This "slip of the pen," in which Freud would have discovered evidence of a repressed desire, functions as a foil to an entire political existence in which the typical youthful pessimism of the intellectual spectator was replaced with the optimism of the militant, the leader, and the statesman.

The Blum family came from Alsace, from the town of Westhoffen, southwest of Strasbourg. It seems clear that Abraham Blum, the husband of Sarah May, was Léon Blum's great-grandfather. In 1808, an Imperial Decree had obliged the Jews to choose both a last and a first name. The Blums adopted the family name chosen by Elias Blum in the 18th century, and gradually changed their first names from Baruch and Moishe to Georges and Marcel. However, it was only after he settled in Paris—which seems to have been shortly before 1848 and before his marriage to Marie Picart—that Abraham Blum changed his name to Auguste.

A photograph taken about 1950 shows the Westhoffen house of Abraham-Auguste's childhood in a state of dilapidation. It is the house of economically marginal peasants and artisans, confined to the edge of the village. That may help to explain why the eldest son, Abraham Blum, though attached to Alsace, left at the age of sixteen, first for Amsterdam, then for Paris. In 1869, he married an Alsatian woman, Marie-Adèle-Alice Picart—a seemingly Christian name that was, however, widespread in Jewish communities, at least after the decree of 1808.

The Picart family came from Ribeauville, but Marie was born in Paris. They were more "bourgeois" than the Blums, or rather they had pretensions to gentility, although they were economically worse off. A year before his marriage, Abraham-Auguste Blum had succeeded in becoming an independent businessman—in partnership with one of his brothers—as president of a "silk and velvet" company founded and directed by Moïse Léon. He could thus provide a relatively comfortable existence for his young wife. Married in 1869, Marie and Auguste Blum moved into an apartment above the "Blum frères" shop, 243, rue Saint-Denis. Their five children were born there: Lucien (1861), Léon

(April 9, 1872), Marcel (1874), Georges (1876), and René (1878). The apartment was in a Paris that Léon Blum later defined as "more populist than working-class" but "haunted by memories of working-class insurrections," a very "republican" neighborhood—a word that meant much more then than it does today. Many Jewish merchants had settled there, all the more attached to Jacobin ideology, because before the Empire, the Revolution had offered them the possibility of egalitarian assimilation, and had made France the most apparently welcoming country in Europe for the victims of racial persecution in central and eastern Europe. The synagogue on the rue des Victoires was nearby, and many food merchants, Jews and non-Jews alike, sold kosher products.

This is not to imply that the Blums were noted for ostentatious worship or strict adherence to ritual practices. It must be noted at the outset that Léon Blum's relationship to Judaism was not obsessive or even decisive. Although his parents (particularly his mother) were undoubtedly attached to their religion—Léon and his brothers were all bar mitzvahs, and they said their prayers in Hebrew through adolescence—the education the children received never took the form of conditioning. Neither Blum's son nor his niece remembers regular religious observance in the family setting. Their grandchildren remember eating kosher food in the Blum household only very rarely, and if there was anything special about the cooking, it had more to do with the Alsatian, not the Jewish, dishes that were served.[3] But on the anniversaries of their parents' deaths the five brothers faithfully attended synagogue.

Auguste Blum, whom some of his son's friends described as "an old picturesque Alsatian"[4]—meaning that he didn't look very Parisian and spoke with a strong accent—was rather tall, with narrow eyes, and a strong, straight nose. He wore a pointed beard and dressed rather carefully, like a provincial notable, and his good nature charmed his friends and acquaintances. His five sons loved him enough to visit him every day until the very end of his life. His business sense assured a growing success for the "Maison A. Blum et frères: ribbons and velvets, silks, tulles, and crapes, fashionable articles" and enabled his family to rise from the discreet comfort of the seventies to real wealth in the nineties.

Marie Blum had a more clearly discernible influence on her sons than did her husband. She was possessed by one passion, the passion for justice and she pursued it, according to the striking expression of her second son, "to the point of melancholy." Raised in a climate marked by this "intensity of scruples," Léon Blum could confide to a friend forty years later: "My revolt against injustice is as old as my consciousness.[5]

Early Schooling

Léon Blum was a student at the *lycée* Charlemagne from October 1882 to July 1888. He constantly received the award for excellence and all the prizes in classical literature and in history. It is questionable whether he was more unbearable for his precocious self-assurance than he was touching for his passion for knowledge. At five, he was quoting La Bruyère; at ten, Tacitus; at fifteen, he is said to have noticed a mistake in one of his professor's lectures. But all this pretentiousness was accompanied by an irresistible charm.

In 1888, Léon Blum informed his friend René Berthelot, who was to become the oracle of French diplomacy between the wars, that he was about to realize his dream of leaving the *lycée* Charlemagne and joining him at the *lycée* Henri IV, where they would do the year of philosophy together and prepare for the Ecole Normale entrance exam. At Henri IV, Léon Blum was also to meet several young men who became his friends, for varying reasons and for different periods of time—first of all, André Gide. Under the aegis of Kant and, at a more modest level, Lachelier and Renouvier, his studies there were successful enough to win him second prize in the General Examination in Philosophy. His essay has been preserved, and it reveals some aspects of his character: "If all men are the playthings of an external determinism, we should have the deepest and most loving compassion for the whole human race. We should not be angry at the criminal, but pity him because a whole series of causes independent of his will has made him sink so low." A month later, the corrector of the essay on "happiness" that he wrote for his *baccalauréat* in philosophy declared to a colleague: "If a seventeen-year-old child wrote this, he is a monster."

Léon Blum devoted 1889–90 to preparing for the entrance exam to the Ecole Normale and for a *licence de lettres*. On July 7, 1890, he wrote to Berthelot: "I've signed up for my last exam. We'll have to work like dogs this week." Two weeks later he was accepted at the Ecole Normale, but he had failed his *licence*.

Blum's first year at the Ecole Normale was to end in failure, however. He was not happy as a *normalien,* and his failure and departure from the Ecole Normale must be attributed to this lack of happiness; his intellectual gifts qualified him only too well for success there. Even though he shared a *thurne* with his friend René Berthelot, even though he met Emile Chartier (the future Alain), Célestin Bouglé (the official philosopher of public education), and especially Lucien Herr, eight years his senior and then librarian of the school, the young man rebelled against the "cloister." The surviving picture of Léon at the Ecole, the traditional class photograph, shows a young man with bangs peering over his glasses, standing comfortably with his hands in his pockets and his feet apart, and looking at the world with a rather arrogant air. This is the only image we have of him that shows him at all hostile to others.

After a second failure to obtain the *licence de lettres* in October 1891, the director, archaeologist Georges Perrot, irritated by Blum's fantasies and his half-real nonchalance, and prompted by a routine letter from the Minister of Education,[6] dismissed the young man.

Léon Blum was nineteen and free. His father did not demand that Léon earn his living by joining the family business. But neither did Léon envisage leading the life of a rich young man in the world of literature, like Marcel Proust or André Gide. He signed up at the law school and the Sorbonne, determined to overcome his failure at the *licence de lettres*. But these two programs were not ones that chained a student to his desk. Léon wanted to write, and to publish. He had already met, at the *lycée* and in society, some of the young geniuses of the day. Along with them, he would become a writer.

Among Léon's early friends, according to Lucien Blum, was Pierre Louÿs, "an elegant young man with an oriental look, who smoked expensive cigars and used to say, a little pompously, that he had 'broken with the Parnassians.'" André Gide had introduced Blum to Louÿs; Louÿs was looking for contributors to a little poetry magazine he was thinking of starting, *La Conque*. On December 29, 1889, Louÿs wrote to Blum: "If you are, as Gide has told me, a Wagnerite, if you like Hugo, and if you like Schopenhauer while hating the false pessimists who have so badly understood him and the 'fin de siècle' types who interpret him equally badly, then I think we will understand each other without difficulty."

Fifteen months later, in March 1891, the first issue of *La Conque* appeared; graced by a sonnet by Blum, the issue included texts by André Gide, Paul Valéry, and Marcel Drouin (Gide's uncle). This poem was the first one Blum published. We will cite the two quatrains and not return to it; Gide wasn't the only one who thought (though he may have been the only one who wrote) that Blum had "the most antipoetic mind in the world."

> La nuit l'eau calme des bassins
> au reflet des lumières vagues
> forme d'imaginaires vagues
> et de fantastiques dessins
>
> Ce sont de bizarres coussins
> brodés de colliers et de bagues
> des chevaliers dressant leurs dagues
> des fleurs larges comme des seins[7]

A dozen or more like that appeared in *La Conque* throughout 1891; the reputation of the magazine, however fragile, no doubt owed more to a few texts by Swinburne and Valéry. And Blum's versifying ceased when *La Conque* ceased publication. The magazine that in some sense took up where *La Conque* left off, *Le Banquet* (founded by Fernand Gregh; Marcel Proust and Henri Barbusse were among its contributors) published only Blum's essays. Three were signed, notably a "Fragment on Friendship," praised by Gregh for its "rather dry precision about the wanderings of feeling."[8] Another was anonymous, and with good reason. It was a "Conversation with Schopenhauer," translated from the German by René Berthelot. Fernand Gregh tells us that it was "entirely apocryphal. I was told about it later. I wouldn't be surprised if one of the authors of the joke turned out to be Léon Blum." In fact, it is a fairly safe bet that, five years before publishing his *Nouvelles Conversations de Goethe avec Eckermann,* the young man had found it amusing to try his skills as a writer of pastiche on a philosopher he admired above all others, and Berthelot's name tends to support the hypothesis.

Though he danced well and was very attentive to women, Blum nevertheless remained an intellectual impassioned by literature. As a frequenter of salons, he preferred those where people talked of poetry or the spirit of the age, politics as well as aesthetics: he was a welcome visitor to the Berthelots, the Créanges, and to José-Maria de Heredia, the then-famous poet whose three beautiful daughters were to marry writers. The youngest, Marie, had established the "académie canaque," to which Blum, along with Proust and Valéry, belonged.

He was already a passionate devotee of the theater, and of any kind of peformance. "At the Créanges, where we met several composers, there were often theatrical presentations," says Lucien Blum. "I remember a performance of *Les Plaideurs* with Léon in the role of the defendant, as well as a performance of *Amphitryon* in which he played Sosie and spoke the famous line: 'Je suis, messieurs, l'ami de tout le monde.' "

La Revue

"It is at the time he joined *La Revue blanche* that you can get a sense of the man," wrote his friend and colleague on *Le Populaire,* Jean Texcier, in the preface to the first volume of *L'Oeuvre de Léon Blum* (1881–1905). When he submitted his first piece to the Natanson brothers' magazine, the son of Marie and Auguste Blum was a few months past twenty. He had just left the Ecole Normale; his brother Lucien had, to his great chagrin, been obliged to leave the world of poetry and the arts in order to work alongside his father; *La Conque* had just ceased publication. Too attached to his family to feel isolated, the young Blum was nevertheless confused, in search of himself and his future. He had begun to try out the law, though he wanted to be a writer. Many magazines were available to him—*Le Mercure de France,* which had just been founded, or *L'Ermitage,* for example. He chose to submit his articles to Alfred Natanson not only because social and familial relations had brought them together, but because *La Revue blanche* from the outset in spring 1891, proclaimed its intentions to be not only a literary magazine. Though Gide presented it, with mock enchantment, as "the rallying point for all differences of opinion," it was a publication with a politics; and because of that it is tempting to see it as an ancestor of *Les Temps modernes* rather than a precursor of *La Nouvelle Revue française.* A "politics"? One might rather say a political current, that of the libertarian spirit embodied in the assistant editor Félix Fénéon's pallid complexion, piercing eyes, and aggressive beard—"an astonishing character with imperturbable calm, and sarcastic courtesy as convoluted as an arabesque."[9] Fénéon had recently been released, like his comrades Jean Grave and Zo d'Axa, after a trial against the anarchists. (Neither the word nor this kind of connection was entirely comfortable at a time when Vaillant and Ravachol were throwing their bombs in the name of Bakunin.)

Whom did one encounter in the magazine? Barrès, yes—but he was still vaguely disreputable—and Mallarmé, Gourmont, and Claudel. And "Verlaine, at the end of his teetering life, would be there writing a sonnet at the corner of a table."[10] But most of the contributors, for one reason or another and with varying degrees of vehemence, were rebels: Zola, Péguy, Mirbeau, Apollinaire, Charles-Louis Philippe, Jules Renard, Jarry, Tristan Bernard, Julien Benda, Bernard Lazare. The foreigners: Tolstoy, Ibsen, Stuart Merril, Björnson, and even Kropotkin. The painters, who were at the time the greatest anathemas to official art: Lautrec, Bonnard, Vuillard, Vallotton, Maximilien Luce, Pissarro, Signac, Redon. Claude Debussy published ferocious articles under the signature "M. Croche, antidilettente," in anticipation of the first public performance of *L'Après-midi d'un faune,* organized by Misia Natanson, a student of Fauré. When the Dreyfus Affair exploded five years later, this odd constellation found its meaning and its cause, and it armed for the great common struggle, though that meant breaking with illustrious companions, beginning with Barrès.

Blum very soon affirmed his mastery. His article on "anti-politics" quickly demonstrated his talent for analysis; soon confirming that talent were "First Paradoxes on Renan," "Fragments on Glory," "On Prayer," "Classical Taste," and a "Review of Reviews" in which he attacked with unusual audacity such well-established publications as *La Revue des deux mondes* and the academic criticism of Brunetière, Lemaître, and Faguet. This law student who had barely reached his majority was by 1894 already a personage in the republic of letters. It was at this period, according to Thadée Natanson, that you could hear Anatole France say in the course of a discussion: "That's what I think about it. But let's ask Blum for his opinion."[11]

Not everyone at *La Revue blanche* liked him. Julien Benda, who sketched him in *Jeunesse d'un clerc,* wrote, "None of the 'leaders' I met there made a strong impression on me. I should however say a word about one of them, who had a great political future: Léon Blum. His lack of reserve and of intellectual severity, his lack of doubt, his habit of speaking out immediately on the most varied and serious subjects, his belief in the necessity of what he said, his attitude of authority, his conviction of the infallibility of Jaurès and the genius of Porto-Riche, his acceptance of passing for a great thinker in the eyes of ignorant bankers (like the directors of *La Revue blanche*) or purely literary types, his willingness to play a literary role in judging operettas or vaudevilles, and his need of immediate successes all made him antipathetic to me. At the same time, I was struck by what was both intelligent and weak in his writing, his incapacity to enclose his thought within some solid structure, his notable lack of temperament and inventiveness, his pallid writing. He represented for me exactly what Nietzsche calls the reflected man. One thing however seems undeniable to me: the great sincerity of his political faith and his honesty. Today I can add to that his courage."[12]

It would be impossible to understand anything about Blum if one dissociated aesthetic concerns from the awakening of his political consciousness. From the beginning, the critic, the moralist, the aesthetician, and the political thinker were one. A few hesitations, a few "blunders" in judgment, or revealing "lapses" do not contradict this fundamental convergence: passionately avid for justice, sensitive to the irrationality of a social and economic organization based solely on profit, convinced that the will of men is capable of modifying the realities of public life if only they become conscious of their power, Léon Blum was in a state of "socialist incubation" even before his meeting (or rather his renewed contact) with Lucien Herr, in the spring of 1893.

We should note in passing his state of mind at the time. Thirty years later, he told how, at the age of fourteen, in 1886, in the library of the *lycée* Charlemagne, he experienced a revelation of social injustice.[13] It was produced by a line in *Les Effrontés,* a play by Emile Augier: a journalist, Giboyer, angrily replies to a rich and prominent man: "Wealth may be hereditary, but intelligence is not."

Six years later, Blum's studies had become more sophisticated thanks to the influence of his school friend Louis Révelin, who had become a socialist before him, and who was later his comrade with

Jaurès. He had also broadened the scope of his reading: he had read Fourier (he was apparently introduced to his work by the economist Charles Gide, the uncle of his friend André), investigated Proudhon, and, in the library of the Ecole Normale, skimmed through Marx. When, toward the end of summer 1892, on the train to Enghien where they were spending the vacation with their families, Fernand Gregh asked him what career he intended to follow, he calmly answered "politics."[14]

To be sure, it was with Barrès, the deputy from Nancy, in mind that he made this surprising answer. The author of *L'Ennemi des lois* clearly showed that politics was not simply opportunistic manipulation in the manner of Grévy, or the pattern of sordid compromises whose cynicism would be revealed by the Panama affair. Politics, according to Barrès, claimed to be an elevated struggle. But Blum, for his part, did not confuse style with meaning, elevation with a cause; as we shall see, he knew how to choose his examples, his teachers, and the meaning of his struggles.

Under the Sign of Goethe

Between 1894 and 1896, in a series of anonymous essays published by *La Revue blanche* under the peculiar title *Nouvelles Conversations avec Eckermann,* Blum, at the ages of twenty-two and twenty-three, before meeting Jaurès and before the Dreyfus Affair, revealed himself as he would remain for the rest of his life. This precocious appearance is quite astonishing.

In 1957, his friend Olga Raffalovich collected and published texts written by Blum between 1894 and 1942, under the title *Des "Nouvelles Conversations de Goethe avec Eckermann" à "L'échelle humaine."* By setting the texts out in parallel, she demonstrated their unity; the significance of the essays in *La Revue blanche* can therefore not be overestimated. They were collected and published as a book in 1901, with numerous additions and a few changes, still anonymously; then again in 1909 by Ollendorff, signed this time, but without any essential change in the author's flexible and consistent way of thinking. It should be further noted that in the editions of 1901 and 1909 the first conversations are dated 1897, which is surprising, since *La Revue blanche* published the greater part of them in 1894. Perhaps Blum wanted to avoid playing the role of child prodigy, to present himself as older in order to impress establishment critics, or perhaps he simply meant to indicate carefully the date of a creative or final rereading.

It would seem to be a strange device to put his ideas and judgments in Goethe's mouth. Was it pride? In his diary Jules Renard reports this conversation with Blum: "Should I sign my work, I mean put my name on the cover with Goethe's?" Renard answers, "Why not? The audacity is not in signing the book, but having had the idea of writing it." (In his preface to the 1909 edition Blum was honest enough to adopt this formula as his own, substituting for "audacity" the more ferocious word "impropriety.")

The choice of dialogue as a form of expression is consonant with what we already know of the temperament of the young writer, who was passionately attached to the exchanges of friendship, attracted to pastiche, and had remained enough of a *normalien* to have a taste for the traditional "school joke" in all its forms. Wearing a mask to puzzle the reader and to remain free, choosing a famous name to give more weight, a broader perspective, to his criticism—these are some of the reasons for the curious enterprise.

But Goethe? Why not Montaigne or Pascal, Diderot or Stendhal, avowed masters of the young Blum? In her penetrating essay devoted to the socialist leader, Colette Audry proposes the following hypotheses: "The patronage of Goethe meant first of all that [the author] was laying claim to universality in all domains of thought. Further, he claimed to dominate problems with the serenity of thought of a Goethe. And finally, he asserted the preeminence of the exemplary individual. This provides a definition of what has been called Léon Blum's egotism. Transcendental, indifferent to biographical particularities, and almost impersonal, it resembled an introjection of universal morality."[15]

The work of a man who was primarily a literary critic, *Nouvelles Conversations* is chiefly concerned with aesthetic judgment, a kind of panorama of the literary production of the 1890s, accompanied by a treatise on literary health. Léon Blum's Goethe is also, and very fully, a *moraliste,* a political thinker, and, more precisely, a socialist. Indeed, speaking at the beginning in the tone of a Renan or an Anatole France of the 1880s, the protagonist of the "conversations" brings them to a close in the spirit, if not the style, of Jaurès. (In the course of writing, a significant event intervened, in 1897: the explosion of the Dreyfus Affair and the simultaneous entry into the conflict of Jean Jaurès and Léon Blum.) It may seem ridiculous today that the young man had the great man of Weimar discourse seriously on the respective merits of Paul Hervieu and Romain Coolus, or Brieux and Porto-Riche. What is more interesting is the audacity with which this twenty-three-year-old critic, badly disguised, took on three of the most established reputations of the time: Bourget, Loti, and Barrès, with whom he had grown somewhat distant even before the break brought on by the Dreyfus Affair.

We must, however, guard against seeing this Eckermann only as a dynamiter prudently protected by anonymity. Blum's criticism more readily takes the form of admiration—for France, Renard, Zola, Gide—than of denigration. His finest praise is for authors who were unfamiliar to the French: Tolstoy ("we should rejoice that we live in a time when the earth can offer the tribute of such a man to God"), Kipling, Hardy, and Jane Austen.[16] The criticism is nevertheless marked by the fashions of the day, of course, and by the author's natural kindness, his exuberant sociability, and his friendships. Blum willingly admits this and explains it with disarming grace.

Here is an example of Blum the *moraliste*. Taking up the subject of the family, he approaches it with a boldness that looks forward to *Du mariage:* "It is not at all true," says Goethe,

> that family life is by itself a good moral school. It rests essentially on reciprocal respect, confidence, and admiration. This condition is of no value for anyone. Parents develop, on a small scale, the same confidence in their infallible authority as absolute monarchs. As for children, it is hard to imagine anything more pernicious for their moral progress . . . than a life whose very basis is the lack of mutual clairvoyance. . . . It is dangerous to get used to not judging."

Then there is the political thinker. It required courage—and some criticism made this clear to Blum—to speak about Bismarck in this tone:

> He was a man free of prejudices and resentments, who was never limited by dogmas, who always penetrated things with direct, impartial, and practical vision, but who nevertheless remained *human*. He was a man of *peace*. He was moderate in victory. The evolution of his will was admirable in its constant correspondence to the movement of life. No one surrendered more piously than this brutal master of history to reality and its necessities and laws.

In another part of the *Conversations* there is a passage that already provides a full definition of the political leader and statesman of 1920–50. Goethe defines his own conception of revolution quite differently than Hegel:

> In the formation of the physical world as in the establishment of societies, results of exceptional significance have never been obtained by regular and quiet evolution, bit by bit, advance by advance. What is needed is a sudden eruption of latent energy, the upheaval, the terrible uproar of revolutions. To be sure, revolution has always blown up a ground that was already mined. Evolution prepares for it but cannot take its place.
> What is true is that revolution does not save time as opposed to

regular evolution. The movement of 1789 seemed to perform in a few years the work of an entire century. But for an entire century, French society has been given over to a kind of balanced oscillation, which took away, then restored, then took away again the conquests of the Revolution. *Natura non fecit saltus.* A revolution seems to suppress intermediate stages, which return *after the revolution,* through a retroactive response of the laws of history. Thus, revolutions are necessary and therefore legitimate. But a revolution is not necessarily cruel and bloody, which is something our children should think about.

Finally, in epic form, there is the great "set piece" of the book, the project for a "third Faust" which Goethe reveals to his friends, and which resembles a socialist manifesto. In a preamble, Goethe confides to his friends that if, at the beginning of the century, freedom was the great theme of revolutionary inspiration, the fundamental questions are now:

> How is it that some men lack bread? Why do others eat bread they have not earned by their labor? In order to be free, first of all you have to be. Any society that claims to assure men freedom must begin by guaranteeing their existence. Schiller and Beethoven were greater men than we are, and Beethoven was perhaps the greatest man of all. Freedom was their dream. Their eyes were not open to the obvious.

Then Goethe develops his idea, which is to make his third Faust "a socialist agitator. I have given Faust everything noblest and purest that the human soul can offer. He is an optimist. He believes that man is just, and that only poverty and advanced civilization have corrupted him . . . [he] does not want propaganda to appeal to the violent instincts of the people. He wants to instruct and persuade." Confronting this hero, whose model is obviously Jaurès, stands his rival, Mephistopheles, who is also a socialist leader—and clearly a caricature of Jules Guesde, then Jaurès's implacable adversary. Contradictions arise, grow, and lead to conflict. But if, Goethe adds, "each of Faust's actions brings him in the present nothing but disappointment and sadness, each one begins to develop fruitful results for the future. Faust understands this, and in spite of his suffering never doubts his task. He would not even exchange his suffering for another kind of happiness."

The strangeness of the idea, the ambiguity of the message, and the partisan and polemical character of the allusions to Guesde—whom Goethe-Blum in another passage accuses of being "like Robespierre, a priest"—do not diminish the great interest of this declaration of socialist faith. The fact that Goethe was a Jaurèsian—if not Jaurès himself, or a synthesis of Jaurès and Lucien Herr—only makes him more attractive to us, and makes Léon Blum's text more eloquent.

The conclusion of the book is even more peculiar. In a final conversation, Goethe and Eckermann agree in wishing that the future of the world be entrusted to an elite group of men, those they call "critics," who have "acquired an almost universal faculty of judgment," and whom they also characterize as "men of the race of Herder"—the great German philologist of whom Jean-Paul Richter said "he did not produce a perfect masterpiece, but he was himself one of God's masterpieces".[17]

As Georges Lefranc has pointed out,[18] the real model for Blum here, the man "of the race of Herder," was Herr himself, who in this case cannot be separated from his first inspiration, the Russian exile Peter Lavrov, a true socialist who nevertheless often emphasized the historic role of exceptional individuals, men of the avant-garde. Had Léon Blum, the "critic" who was blossoming into a "political thinker," already assigned himself a place among these wise and learned men devoted to the cult of reason and justice, children of the Encyclopedists? The book ends abruptly. The reader is free to ask himself the question.

The book was received very favorably, indeed enthusiastically. Critics pretended to wonder about the identify of the author, but not about the quality of the work. "Fame awaits him," wrote Michel Bréal. "An admirable style, firmly classic," assured the demanding Fernand Albalat. And Norton Sullerton of the *Times,* an experienced observer of French intellectual life, decreed: "There are only two critics in France: Blum and Gourmont."

Law as a Profession

We have scarcely any information on the unfolding of Blum's parallel studies of literature and law, both of which were thrown into the background by his entry into *La Revue blanche* and by his new friendships. In between an article on the sensibility of young women and one on the ideas of M. Renan, and while simultaneously outlining the first sketches for the *Conversations avec Eckermann* and taking courses on Ronsard and Beaumarchais, he prepared his *licence en droit* from 1892 to 1894. He received his degree in June 1894; as his literary verve could be freely expressed in *La Revue blanche,* it was from the law, for which he had quickly developed some passion, that he would earn his living. He thought of the bar, of course. He seemed destined for it by his charm and his talent for persuasion.[19] But he seems to have preferred a more disinterested activity, one freer from the pursuit of profit.

The *Conseil d'Etat* attracted him, first because it embodied the idea of public service, and furthermore because, as the son of a middle-class merchant, he would thereby give evidence of the social advancement and respectability of the family unit, the full attainment of republican "nobility," and finally, perhaps because his beloved Stendhal had followed the same path before him. How intoxicating to follow the footsteps of the author of *Le Rouge et le noir*.

His candidacy was registered in 1894. The archives of the *Conseil d'Etat* have preserved a "confidential note" devoted to M. Blum, candidate for a position as *auditeur*. Signed by the prefect of the Seine, M. Poubelle, whose name was to be remembered by posterity for other reasons, this note indicates that "M. Blum is not actively engaged in politics," but that "his family and himself have the reputation of being republicans." After failing in his first attempt—the examination for the *Conseil d'Etat* was then the most pretentious of the exhausting competitions forced on twenty-year-old Frenchmen—Léon Blum was ranked second on December 14, 1895. He had treated the following subject: "Provisions for the recruitment of men and cadres (commissioned and non–commissioned officers) for the army, the navy, and their reserves." Blum wrote this examination paper at the time of the first phase of the Dreyfus Affair. For the oral, the young man had to discuss "the legislative power and its relations with the executive," a subject which, one would like to believe, allowed him to shine.

In January 1896, he thus became *auditeur* second class in the *Conseil d'Etat,* a member of the disputed claims section, with a salary of two thousand francs a month; coming one month before his marriage, the salary was enough to set up a household in untroubled comfort.

Léon Blum's career in the *Conseil* was successful, brilliant, though without entirely corresponding to the talent he demonstrated. Less than ten months after joining the *Conseil,* Blum had already attracted the attention of his superiors by preparing a report (which has remained a classic) on an electoral dispute in Fouronne (Yonne). The judgment handed down on November 28, 1896 has been preserved. Transcribed in the hand of its author, the clarity of its exposition, the firmness of the writing, and the lucidity of its conclusions make it a model. Quite obviously, the author of this text gave himself to this work with the fervor and lucidity he devoted, at the same period, to reading and analyzing a narrative by Gide or Renard. From that point on, the legal thinker in Blum was constantly to accompany the critic and the militant. His professional career was in complete harmony with his aesthetic tastes and political convictions. His intellectual equilibrium was assured at the very time when marriage promised long-lasting serenity in his private life.

The Fascinators

> He appeared among us like a new man, like a stranger. To a very coldly skeptical society, which Renan and Taine had trained either for the calm investigation of facts or for the rather detached manipulation of ideas, M. Barrès brought a way of thinking that was dry in appearance, but dry like the hand of a fevered man, a way of thinking charged with metaphysics and provocative poetry, trembling with pride and domination. He spoke with categorical assurance, simultaneously haughty and childlike, and with complete disdain for indifference or lack of understanding! A whole generation, seduced or conquered, breathed in this heady mixture of triumphant activity, philosophy, and sensuality. Deceived by its surprise and by the perennial joy of admiration, since M. Barrès was a master, it thought it had found its master, its model, and its leader.

Blum wrote that in 1906, nearly ten years after his break with Barrès which was provoked by the Dreyfus Affair. But every word of this article from *En lisant* admirably situates the nature of the relationship that was established around 1890 between the author of *Sous l'oeil des Barbares* and a little later of *L'Ennemi des lois,* and the young people of the time, who were seeking someone to admire. We can provide a measure of the fascination in which Blum was held by the author of *Sous l'oeil des Barbares* (which the young man read shortly after its publication at the end of 1890) by quoting from a letter to Renè Berthelot written in the summer of 1890: "Write to me in Charmes (Vosges), in care of M. Salmon. I will have the signal honor of breathing for a week the same atmosphere as M. Maurice Barrès."[20] In *Souvenirs sur l'Affaire* Blum's memories of Barrès are kind:

> I can see the proud and charming grace of his welcome, that natural nobility which allowed him to treat the timid beginner who just crossed his threshold as an equal. I am sure that he felt true friendship for me, almost the solicitude of an older brother. Many years later, after the long separation brought about by the "Affair," when we met in the Chamber, he said to me one day: "You loved my young self, and it responded in kind. . ."

Barrès's influence was strong, but even before the moral and political break of 1897, Blum had been able to assert his independence. In 1896, for example, in *La Revue blanche,* Blum clashed with his master over a book by Georges Clemenceau, *Le Grand Pan,* which Barrès had attacked. A few months later, in a half-mocking, half-impatient tone, speaking about a book by Boylesve, he agreed that in this generation "no one has escaped from the influence of M. Barrès, even in spite of himself." And, on the eve of the break, on November 22, 1897, there is

the long passage that the Goethe of the *Nouvelles Conversations* de-
votes to *Les Déracinés*, "the most important book to appear in France
for a long time." But the tone remained very critical, and Blum vigorously attacked *Les Déracinés*, having his Goethe say: "I cannot believe
it is a bad thing for all young men to leave their native roots. . . [if]
everyone stays in the place where Providence has set him down, the
world will remain the way it is. But it has to change, and Barrès's book
itself is nothing but a long example, a long proof of that necessity."
Even more penetrating was his critique of *Au service de l'Allemagne*,
in which Blum, as political thinker and sociologist, took apart the
mechanisms of Barrès's determinist and ethnocentric system with a
kind of light-hearted cruelty.

The relationship between Barrès and Blum survived even the
difficult tests of the "Affair." In 1913, Barrès was still able to inscribe a
copy of *La Colline inspirée* for Blum with his "friendly memory." And,
on the evening of July 31, 1914, Léon Blum, sitting with the body of the
assassinated Jean Jaurès, saw Barrès approach him with his hand out-
stretched and tears in his eyes which, he wrote fourteen years later just
after the writer's death, "erased many things."

A youthful fascination? It was a little more than that, a lasting admiration and nostalgic tenderness from which even Gide, militantly anti-
Barrès, could not entirely free himself. He noted in his *Journal*, the
evening of Barrès's admission to the Académie in 1907:"Of us all, he is
the one who has changed the least. How I love his thin face, his straight
hair, and even his vulgar accent." Barrès the man and the writer is at
the center of a chapter of Blum's life, a moment in his biography. This
is how he ought to be viewed. But we must look for a major influence
elsewhere.

Léon Blum and his brothers had been brought up in an atmosphere
of reverence for what was not yet called "a certain idea of France," for
the Republic that had been revived in 1870 by the speech and action of
Léon Gambetta. He too was of Jewish extraction, from a humble family, and was bound to the ideology and the legend whose contemporary
prophets were Hugo and Michelet. But the organizer of the national
defense of 1870 was not the bearer of a powerful enough system of
thought nor the practitioner of a coherent enough politics to capture
the attention of Léon Blum at the end of the century, impatient as he
was to discover his own path.

Political life in France, in the hands of men who artlessly called
themselves "opportunists," repelled him at first. One figure, though,
fascinated him at the time, because he brought together and expressed
his own diverse aspirations: Benjamin Disraeli. Blum admired much
less the Jew recognized by gentiles as the most eminent British subject

than the writer who was also a man of action capable of making politics into a noble art. At twenty, Blum often quoted Disraeli's novel *Lothair*.

But in his eyes the most accomplished, the most "classical" writer, and therefore the most worthy to be imitated, was Anatole France. When Blum began his literary career around 1890, France was the reigning writer. Barrès was the half-subversive prince of the young: the author of *Le Crime de Sylvestre Bonnard* was a kind of sovereign. And Proust, like the others, recognized him as such. Fascinated by *L'Ennemi des lois,* Léon Blum nevertheless proclaimed his fundamental attachment to everything Anatole France represented: a certain tradition of moderation and irony, of "taste" and balance, and a decorous Voltaireanism in which the element of pastiche would not discourage the author of *Nouvelles Conversations*.

> He is an epicurean, not a skeptic. Renan seeks the probable, France the intelligible. He is concerned with both the divine and the human. In both the man and the writer, we find the sensibility of Pascal—the most penetrating vision of man by man. In Anatole France there is a union of Voltaire's freedom, Diderot's intellectual inventiveness, and Fénelon's grace.

This was written when Blum, eighteen, was at the Ecole Normale. Three years later in *La Revue blanche* (May 1894), speaking of *Le Lys rouge* (which nevertheless disconcerted him at first), he proclaimed France "the most perfect writer of the age." Blum might have admired from a distance, and seen in France only an inaccessible model. But, in fact, by 1895 they had become friends. After the young critic's first article on him in *La Revue blanche,* the writer sent him his *Puits de Sainte-Claire* with this inscription: "To Léon Blum, from the author of this little book, very grateful and very flattered by an article that is both indulgent and penetrating."

To be sure, certain reservations may be expressed about Blum's devotion to France; it can be seen as a kind of aesthetic "conformism" with a touch of the obsequious. France's influence, longer-lasting than that of Barrès, helped to shift the taste of this sensitive and penetrating critic in the direction indicated by the very conservative article of 1894 on "classical taste," which he decided to include, with almost no revisions, in the *Nouvelles Conversations*.

Blum also greatly admired Georges Clemenceau. When Blum discovered the political realm shortly before 1890, it was neither Guesde nor Jaurès who embodied the left, cried out with the voice of the oppressed, and expressed the demand for a social revolution. It was Georges Clemenceau, the mayor of Montmartre, who had understood, if not supported, the Commune; who as early as 1876 had called for amnesty for the *communard* victims of Versaillais repression; who argued for the right to strike and for the workers massacred at Four-mies; and whose editorials in *La Justice* clearly reflected what he later called "the social fray."

Clemenceau was an incomparable orator. But, in Blum's eyes, he had two other qualities that made him dear to his heart and close to his manner of thinking: politics for him was not a laborious profession but the activity of a "dilettante" (like Disraeli), solicited as he was by innumerable other tastes, passions, friendships, and hatreds; and, sec-ondly, in his style, his ideas, and his actions, he expressed the desire for a completion, a continuation, or a new beginning of the 1789 Revo-lution. The year 1789 had remained incomplete, and 1848 had vainly tried to accomplish the social promises which the price control laws, the activities of Jacques Roux, and the "conspiracy of equals" had attempted to impose against the wishes of the majority of the great Jacobins. We have to take up the torch, continue Robespierre, make the political revolution blossom into social reform: this is what Clemenceau meant for Blum in his twenties.

Four Friends

We continue to search for a major influence on Blum. Who, after Lucien Blum and René Berthelot, was his first friend? The title cannot be given to Pierre Louÿs who had drifted away from Blum even before the Dreyfus Affair, nor to Marcel Proust who was much less involved with Léon than with his younger brother René. Several figures stand out from a crowd of friends, each one so different from the others as to make one hesitate to join them together, but they were all close com-panions.

Fifteen years older than Blum, Georges de Porto-Riche was for nearly forty years, until his death, the best, the most constant, the most faithful friend of Blum and his family. He had come from a Jewish family in Bordeaux, and had attained a kind of notoriety at twenty with a verse play entitled *Un Drame sous Philippe II*, and then waited nearly fifteen years before presenting the famous *Amoureuse* in 1891. In those years, at least until Rostand's triumph, he was considered the greatest man of the theater of his time. Blum frankly used friendship as a justification for finding that certain people had genius. The friendship he felt for Porto-Riche was so strong that it led him to write: "The greatest of contemporary French authors, Porto-Riche, has not yet been granted the recognition he deserves" (June 1900).

Paul Bernard, known as Tristan—who did not choose the name out of "Wagner-mania," a widespread passion among young Parisian intellectuals of the day, but because it was the name of a horse he thought beautiful—was five years older than Blum. Bernard's reputation, which was once immense, has declined. One could almost reduce it to a beard, a hat, and a few witty remarks. Nevertheless, Blum the critic showed a lively admiration for the author of *Le Chasseur de Chevelures.* Writing about *Amants et Voleurs,* he called Tristan a "great writer." He perceptively characterized Bernard's humor as "insidious," then "slow and quiet," contrasting it boldly with the more painstaking and explicit humor of Dickens.

What gives an exceptional character to the friendship between Tristan Bernard and Léon Blum is the fact that they regularly wrote and signed together a rather unexpected department in *La Revue blanche*—sports. Not unexpected as far as the author of *Triplepatte* was concerned but seemingly so in the case of the slender Blum, with a carnation in his buttonhole and badly fitting eyeglasses. The two writers saw fit to explain themselves about this shared taste—which they carried as far as writing alternately, for two or three years (1893-95), the "critique of sports," in which a "hippic note" followed a "velocipedic note" and an "athletic note"—in the inaugural article published in 1893: "It is possible that this department will be surprising, that our serious friends will be disturbed." They developed several arguments: sport could not be a matter of indifference to minds interested in their own time, once it was recognized that sport mobilized "great popular feeling," as Disraeli had pointed out; sport could not fail to affect those who were concerned with social truth, since it was in some sense an "idealized struggle for life"; and, finally, through the beauty of movements and bodies, sport is also an integral part of "the aesthetic we dream about."

Blum met André Gide in October 1889, at the *lycée* Henri IV. In an article published a half-century later,[21] the author of *Paludes* called to mind his memories of their first encounters:

> I can see us, Léon Blum and me, infatuated with literature, passing from hand to hand unpublished sonnets by Heredia that had been transcribed by our classmate René Berthelot. That day, we were walking down the Boulevard Saint-Michel having a very animated discussion; for there was one point on which Blum and I could not bring ourselves to agree: Blum allowed himself to prefer Marivaux to Molière! That seemed shocking to me, and I was so involved in protesting that I was paying no attention to the people we were walking by. Suddenly Blum turned around and went back a few steps. Had he recognized someone? No; I simply saw him approach one of those poor devils who hand out advertisements or handbills. Blum took two and handed me one when he caught up with me, saying: "It's his living. He feels less humiliated when you take his papers." I was rather startled.

In Gide's *Journal,* Blum's name is mentioned for the first time in January 1890. Comparing his friend's attitudes to his own, which he believed to be unique because of his enthusiasm, Gide wrote: "Léon Blum does not know; he is seeking, feeling his way; has too much intelligence and not enough personality."[22] Twelve years went by before the name of the author of the *Nouvelles Conversations* reappeared in his friend's *Journal.* In the interval the two friends had seen a good deal of each other, read each other's work, offended each other, quarreled, and worked together. When Blum received *Paludes* in 1895, he found the inscription rather cold: "To Léon Blum, very cordially, André Gide." But two years later, he wrote one of his most astute critical essays on the book—which had been completely ignored—for *La Revue blanche:* "M. Gide believes passionately in himself and his work. There is no doubt that one day he will be among those whose thought has an effect on universal thought. . . . *Paludes,* a gay novel about boredom, an intimate and difficult narrative, could be the *Werther* [of] this generation."

Gide wrote in his *Journal:*

> Two o'clock at Léon Blum's. The pleasant thing with him is that he always greets you as though he had seen you the day before. Conversation flows without difficulty between us. The artist in him is of no great value and his sentences, like those of Stendhal, are indifferent to everything but the very moment of his thought, which springs immediately from his mouth or his pen, simultaneously rich and clear—clearer indeed than it is rich—with a beginning and an end, and always presented in proper order. One cannot imagine a more correct, clearer, more elegant, or easier presentation than one of Léon Blum's improvisations about an event, a book, or a play. What an excellent 'briefer' he must be for the *Conseil d'Etat.* Ah! if politics did not govern his thoughts so much, what an excellent critic he would be! But he judges things and people according to his opinions, not according to his taste, which he believes to be less certain than his opinions, and he perfers to go against his taste rather than to seem inconsistent to himself. One is not always completely certain that he likes everything he says he likes, but rather that he believes he likes it and knows why."[23]

Why does Gide seem to have taken so much pleasure in pointing out Blum's weaknesses in the theater and the novel, while he preferred to mention only the successes of his other friends, Valéry and Martin du Gard? But even more unjust, and thoroughly nasty, is the famous passage in the *Journal* of 1914, which was seized upon by rightwing critics in 1936 to use Gide against Blum:

> Blum has the kind of precise mind that freezes mine at a distance, and its lucid brilliance maintains it in a state of constriction.

I cannot deny his nobility, generosity, and chivalry (although, to apply to him, these terms have to change substantially from their true meanings). It seems to me that his sort of determination continually to foster the Jew above all, to find that he has talent, even genius, comes first of all from the fact that a Jew is particularly sensitive to Jewish qualities. It comes especially from the fact that Blum sees the Jewish race as superior, called upon to dominate after having long been dominated, and he believes it is his duty to work for its triumph. He has an intelligence that is marvellously organized, organizing, clear, classifying, and which could, ten years later, find each idea again exactly where it had been set by his argument, as you would find an object in a closet. Although he is sensitive to poetry, he has the most anti-poetic mind I know; I also believe that, in spite of his merits, he overestimates himself a little.

Finally, there is a passage whose racist venom is startling:

It is enough for me that the qualities of the Jewish race are not French qualities; and even if the French were less intelligent, less enduring, less courageous in every way than the Jews it would still be true that what they have to say can only be said by them, and that the contribution of Jewish qualities in literature, in which nothing is valuable but what is personal, does not so much provide new elements, that is, enrichment, as it interrupts the slow explanation of a race and seriously, intolerably, falsifies its meaning.

It took many years and cruel tests—those undergone by Blum—before Gide, referring to his anti-Semitic remarks of 1914, in the *Journal* of January 8, 1948, finally wrote: "He disregarded it and never talked to me about it. . . . I have rarely encountered in a Christian such personal disinterestedness and such nobility . . . after so many deaths, he remains the only friend of my generation."

Friendship—this is the key word of a letter Blum wrote Gide the following April: "You are grateful to me, you say, for never having spoken to you about certain passages of the published *Journal*. But do not think that I was insensitive to them. They caused me pain, one in particular, but for a single reason, because they gave me the impression that they were written without friendship. Mine was not changed by it, but I am nevertheless deeply touched by these recent passages from your *Journal*. It is sweet and precious to me to think that you have developed a higher opinion of me as we have both grown old."

Blum certainly experienced and expressed all these admirations, as a young man for Barrès, as a pupil for France, as a friend for Porto-Riche, and as an aesthete for Gide. But the writer of his time whom he perhaps loved and understood the best, and for whom his intelligence most successfully guided his outbursts of friendship, was probably Jules Renard. The slightly dry quality of Blum's taste and the very

analytic cast of his intelligence were more at home with writers like
Renard, whose emotions were restrained by a clockwork-like mechanism than with an oceanic writer like Zola.

> I find in him first of all not what I would call a love of analysis,
> but a love of decomposition. There are many feelings and expres-
> sions that we accept ready made. Renard takes a particularly ironic
> pleasure in unrolling them, unfolding them with meticulous deli-
> cacy, as one would open a fragile and carefully wrapped package.
> That is not analysis, which would consist of looking for causes and
> constituent parts. Renard is content with slowing down and bring-
> ing back to their original states those rapid successions which we
> are in the habit of seeing as unities. He reduces natural but com-
> plex gestures to what would be called in gymnastics their decom-
> posed moments. . . .
> And it is in the decomposition of expressions, movements, and
> feeling that lies the hidden force of his irony. Notice by the way
> that Renard is thereby led to introduce spaces into what is in
> reality continuous, to note intervals which are not in nature. The
> same habit of mind leads him also to enlarge what he isolates; and
> if we have the impression that he sees through a microscope, or
> rather through a magnifying glass constantly brought closer, this is
> not because he exaggerates, but because he distinguishes. . . .
> This procedure, or this talent, is of purely poetic order. I also
> notice in Renard—besides the gift of bringing the image and the
> object together tracing one from the other—another entirely poetic
> faculty; it is the art of mixing several images, without confusion,
> but on the contrary infusing them with reciprocal reflections. Some
> of his most accomplished pieces even depend entirely on an exten-
> sion or a development of images. One might therefore wonder if
> Renard is not above all a poet, a withdrawn and laconic poet.[24]

Jules Renard, who was eight years older than Blum, knew the young
critic from meetings at the Natansons. But the penetration of this short
essay startled him. Although he was so "withdrawn," he could not
refrain from writing a letter of acknowledgment and recognition:

> The twenty-five lines you have written about my "manner" . . .
> seem to me worthy of being called a record. What an invaluable
> pamphlet you could make with the contributions of *good* writers
> by asking them to explain as clearly as they see them *their little
> methods*. If someone, trying to flatter me, asked for mine, I would
> refer to your article. And I would borrow this title from you: "The
> Love of Decomposition" . . . You are younger than I, and perhaps
> I should remain on my guard. All the same, without hesitation, I
> shake your hand with affectionate gratitude.

Six months later, Blum returned to the subject with an essay on
Histoires naturelles, this time in *La Revue blanche,* their common
home. He hailed ". . . a new masterpiece. It also represents the perfection of a manner, which is simultaneously the newest, the most closed,

and the sharpest of the time. . . . I will never tire of talking about M. Renard, because no one has more love, devotion, respect for literature than he—and it is a happy love, a devotion that is always requited."

Jules Renard's reactions were warm, even affectionate:

> 19 July 1897
>
> I'm annoyed to have to write. I would like to talk in a low voice to an extremely sensitive friend [Léon Blum] and correct a daydream a little with the help of his reason.
>
> We are at the dawn of our friendship. You ask me if our friendship has distracted me, what feelings I experienced. It's very complex. It would take a little treatise, with annotations. How many times have I repeated to myself this lugubrious phrase: I feel nothing, I feel nothing. In fact, I was experiencing ideas and not feelings.
>
> 16 April 1898
>
> Your letter of 15 May 1897, how nice it is, how good it is to reread this letter of affectionate admiration. I owe you a few moments of sweet joy, and of sadness.
>
> My very young friend, love your dear wife well and work a good deal, as much as you can, by her side.
>
> I swear to you that all the rest is insignificant.
>
> 17 June 1898
>
> My dear friend, pages (oh! they are rare) like those you have written on the *Bucoliques* in the R. B.[25] fill me with confusion. They give me a kind of joy with which I am not entirely happy. Where do you want me to hide when you talk about me with such confidence and seriousness? . . .
>
> My dear Léon Blum, I see your face clearly. You are sitting on the other side of my work table. You have the smile I know so well which you constantly show, like a delicate light on things. You are amused by my embarassment, but you must be extremely good and must have, for those whose happiness depends on you, a constant and delicate concern.

Yet in the *Journal* one discovers again that, as with Gide, Blum had in Renard a very strange friend. We find hardly a single reference to Léon Blum—and there are many—which is not in some way malicious:

> February 13, 1895:
>
> Léon Blum said to me: "I wouldn't like you to misunderstand what I think about you. But I cannot, without beating around the bush. . . But there I go doing it!"

> November 1, 1895:
>
> Léon Blum, a young beardless man who, with a little girl's voice, can recite for two hours by the clock Pascal, La Bruyère, Saint-Evremond, etc.

February 20, 1896:
   Yesterday, in the synagogue on the rue de la Victoire, Blum was smiling, too much. *La Revue blanche* was showing its collective wit.

December 30, 1897 (right after the première of *Cyrano de Bergerac*):
   At Léon Blum's. A circle hostile to Rostand.
   "You should," said Blum, "since you have influence over Rostand, prevent him from doing anything but theater. Especially, keep him from publishing. It's self-destructive. The disillusionment is too strong."

All the same, when it came to the Dreyfus Affair which, as with Anatole France, strengthened their bonds in struggle, Jules Renard set Blum in a good light, quoting a witticism which he must certainly have envied:

February 18, 1898:
   This evening at *La Revue blanche*. The Dreyfus Affair fascinates us. One would give up wife, children, and fortune for its sake. "Last night," said Mallarmé, "I had dinner with Poincaré who is for Zola without being for Dreyfus, and who said sadly: 'I smell war!'" "Let him be decontaminated!" said Léon Blum.

The "Affair" drew Renard out of his retreat and the reticence of his feelings. For a few months, a real fraternity united the open friend to the reserved one. There remain favorable and sometimes friendly notations in the *Journal,* after 1900, and a few letters which present a sunny side of their relations. In February 1902, Renard wrote a very emotional and friendly letter to Blum on the occasion of the birth of his son Robert. In February 1903, there was a charming note to Mme. Blum: "One of these days you will be Madame President of I don't know what, but you will always be Madame Léon Blum, and that is your highest title! It is even Léon Blum's greatest accomplishment." In November 1903, referring to an image used by his friend in an essay he had sent him, Renard instructed:

   No, the sentence is not very good. You are making a *new* observation. It has to appear *new* to the reader. You want to tell him that snow makes noise. Then tell him: snow makes noise.
   Rewrite, my dear boy, rewrite. It's worth the trouble. But forgive me!

September 17, 1908:
   I have liked nothing better this year than the articles I've read by you.

August 10, 1909:
   I have just lost my mother, who fell by accident, I think, into the well.

December 16, 1909:
   Do not fear your intelligence. It does not interfere with your
artistic gifts.
   I love you dearly.

The Master

   A giant. Everyone who knew him or approached him—except the
Péguy of the *Cahiers de la Quinzaine* from 1906 on—described Lucien
Herr in those terms, because of his muscular and intellectual size and
strength, as a mountain-climber and a man of culture. Since 1888, Herr
had been the permanent librarian of the Ecole Normale—the only position he had ever sought (at the age of twenty-four). There he had
transformed himself into a kind of lighthouse keeper, illuminating the
social and cultural landscape of France and Europe for generations of
young men. When Léon Blum met him for the first time upon entering
the school in 1891, Herr was twenty-seven. He too was Alsatian, born
in Altkirch to a Catholic family that had chosen France after 1870. His
grandfather was a peasant, his father an elementary school teacher.
The Herr family settled in Vitry-le-François, where the father taught.
When he was very young, Herr traveled through Germany and visited
Russia. When he settled in to the chair of librarian of the Ecole Normale, he had already become a socialist: he had read Proudhon, Marx,
and especially Lassalle, and had met Peter Lavrov, in exile in Paris.
But his studies had been concentrated on Hegel, and, though according
to his plans they should have led to a monumental treatise, they
amounted instead essentially only to a long and masterful article for *La
Grande Encyclopédie* of 1890. But his biographer and friend, Charles
Andler (himself a specialist in German philosophy), places it at a lower
level than the sketches for the book or the oral commentaries on it that
he was able to hear.
   Lucien Herr led a very discreet and retired life. He saw few friends,
most of whom he met at the home of Mme. Marillier, the great-
granddaughter of Manon Roland, a salon "of the left" where the historian Charles Seignobos presided. But his essential intercourse was
carried on with books, and he turned the library of the Ecole Normale
into an incomparable tool for research. A contemporary of Blum's
described Herr in his natural surroundings:

   When you entered the library, a huge rectangular room which
   occupies the entire second story of the eastern quarter of the
   school, you were seized, on the right, in the back of the room, by
   the dominating eyes which, from a great distance and a great

height, crossing the long, wide, elevated, massive desk, ruled over the books and their visitors. . . . These eyes were blue, pale, with little golden flames. . . . His eyes looked directly out, with a power of immediate penetration and total analysis, from beneath heavy brows and an immense forehead which made them seem sharper and smaller. He had a powerfully shaped face, a straight nose with its arc slightly flattened and its end slightly turned up, prominent cheekbones, a chin that was strong without being large, a pale complexion, and a blonde mustache drooping in Gallic style over expressive lips, a mobile mouth. His hair was casually divided on either side of his domed forehead, which was balding and creased by deep wrinkles, and long, delicate curls fell around his ears and above his collar. You found yourself with a sudden jolt in the presence and under the influence of a Titan. . . .

Lucien Herr was seated, very high up, before piles of books and journals which formed barricades along the sides of the desk. And when he got up, he seemed very tall, very strong, vigorous, active, powerful, and agile in his invariable dark blue suit, whose vest revealed a little of the white shirt under the wing collar which was always very white. . . . He got up, and you were afraid of being approached, not for a reprimand (which he did very seldom), but for rapid and imperious questions (what do you need? what book are you looking for? what work are you doing?) which were obviously to the point and obviously appropriate, and always demanded an answer. . . . The great librarian, the great socialist almost always, at every time of day, had visitors, friends, comrades around him to distract, excite, and amuse him. They were well known and important figures, or unknown, original, strange, sometimes mysterious people, who were known, or said, or supposed to be smart, very smart, with sharp tongues and demanding, severe, and malicious minds. He towered over them all in height, strength, brilliance, and authority, and they formed around him a redoubtable circle of admiration and deliberation that was both defensive and aggressive. Beware of touching them.[26]

"For nearly three years, the same timidity . . . kept me apart from this prestigious man," concludes Hubert Bourgin, whose dithyramb is all the more significant because it was written forty years later, when he had broken with socialism to join the extreme right. Was it a similar timidity that kept Blum apart at first, or was it the young man's dilettantism which expressed itself in an irritable disdain for everything to do with the Ecole, its ceremonies, or its teachers? The fact is that during the year he spent on the rue d'Ulm Blum was one of the rare students who was not under the influence of Herr. It was only two years later, because of a chance encounter, that he experienced the sort of instant attraction that tied him to Lucien Herr more than to any other man who enriched his life.

It would not be unduly harsh to the young Léon to say that between

Gide and Louÿs, Tristan Bernard and Porto-Riche, he was not a young man very aware of social realities. The experience of crowded neighborhoods, which came to him from his childhood, was becoming blurred. His "socialism" remained very abstract, unlike that of Lucien Herr, in whom we must not see, then or later, simply an intellectual charmed by socialist ideas and orienting the thinking of his listeners or disciples in that direction. Without being a militant in the full sense of the term, Herr chose to belong, ten years before unification, to one of the socialist organizations of the time, and to contribute to its newspaper. The organization was the POSR (the Revolutionary Socialist Workers Party) of Jean Allemane. Why that one, and not the more important POF (French Workers Party) of Jules Guesde and Paul Lafargue? Because the Marxism of the leaders of the POF seemed to Herr to be simplistic, badly assimilated, and dogmatic. As for the Blanquist movement of Edouard Vaillant, it seemed to him outdated. Allemane had in his view the advantage of being an authentic proletarian, of agitating in favor of the workers, and of advocating above all what seemed to him essential: the right to strike, including the general strike.

Thus the articles that Herr wrote regularly for Allemane's newspaper, *Le Parti ouvrier,* were based less on his encyclopedic knowledge than on his will as a militant. Witness an editorial of May 27, 1890 which could have been written by a "permanent" leader of a cell. Pointing out that in 1890 there were twice as many manufacturers' associations as there were trade unions, he wrote: "The workers are heading for defeat if they remain isolated and defenseless. They are certain of victory if they close ranks and if they have numbers on their side. In the battle that is beginning, what is at issue is no longer simply the outcome of a strike. The cause of the whole working class is at stake. In order to bring decisive pressure to bear on the government, the unions must be socialist."

Blum met Lucien Herr again in April 1893. It was a dual "revelation," of friendship and of political and philosophical clarification. Léon Blum told of this chance encounter,[27] on a spring afternoon in the place de la Concorde, which began, "Well, Blum, what's become of you?" Beginning on this banal note, the conversation lasted for several hours as they strode along the Champs Elysées, and it was decisive for the young man. The impressive guardian of the treasures of the rue d'Ulm had at one stroke become a guide and friend, the "diviner" of the subterranean socialist current that already existed in Blum.

> In order to understand clearly what my thinking was like before the meeting with Herr, consider what Clemenceau was like at the time, vacillating between socialism and anarchy. All the negative work

had already been accomplished in me. It was a question of finding
an already prepared form. Herr brought me the idea of organization, collectivism. It was an operation on a cataract.[28]

Just as Claudel discovered that he was a Christian behind a pillar in
Notre Dame, so Blum, thanks to Herr, realized, at the age of twenty-
one, beneath the chestnut trees on the Champs Elysées, that he was a
socialist.

From that point on until Herr's death in 1926—from the Dreyfus
Affair (in which Herr's influence over Blum was as decisive as in the
ideological enterprise) to the struggles for unity from 1899 to 1905,
from the socialist publication society of the rue Cujas to the wartime
debates on the *union sacrée* and participation in government, and then
finally during the great schism in 1920—the lives of the two men were
fraternally intertwined; from 1897 to 1914 they joined with that of
Jaurès.

The friendship between Blum and Herr went well beyond political
and social cooperation, however close that may have been. Blum owed
his taste for sports, and the display he made of it, not only to Tristan
Bernard but also to Herr, who had an inordinate passion for walking,
mountain climbing, and bicycling. He used to arrange to meet a group
of cyclists—Victor Bérard, Maurice Loewé, and Léon Blum—in the
early morning in the Bois de Boulogne, and with caps on their heads
and wearing baggy trousers, the whole assembly would travel through
the Chevreuse valley or toward Enghien, until they collapsed.

The intellectual complicity between the two men was even more
intense and went so far as to be a kind of interpenetration. When he
received the *Nouvelles Conversations avec Eckermann,* Herr wrote to
Blum: "Before writing to you, I wanted to look again at your book, *my*
book. I am proud of it and will live a little more through it. Opening it, I
felt the same upsurge of feeling, gratitude, and tenderness that I had
when you told me of your plan."[29]

When, as he approached fifty, the "giant" felt a kind of weakness and
doubt assail him, when the colossus realized with anguish that his life
was in a sense a "failure" because he had dissipated his creative energy
in the service of others, and that he had been only a prodigious diffuser
of culture, it was to Blum and his wife that he wrote on September 21,
1907: "I'm not whining; I don't complain that my career has not been
good. In large part, it is what I wanted it to be. If I had it to do over
again, I would no doubt do things differently, in part, not because I
have been mistaken, but because I conceive things today more accurately and exactly than in the past."[30]

One can imagine what the death of this tutelary genius (from cancer
in May 1926) meant to Blum. Herr was sixty-two. Overcome, Blum

could not even speak the eulogy which he had been asked to give by several mutual friends: "Those who were there, huddled around the grave, will never forget the despairing gesture, the silence, and the tears of Léon Blum who, desolate and unspeaking, expressed better than he could by words our heartfelt sorrow."[31]

1897. Léon Blum was twenty-five. He was soon to throw himself into the furnace of the Dreyfus Affair, to forge there his weapons and his armor, and to attach himself to the greatest of the men who helped to make him what he was: Jean Jaurès. But he had already woven around himself a network of friends and men he admired, which—except for Barrès—would be changed only by death. He had already chosen his masters: Retz and Saint-Simon, Pascal and La Rochefoucauld, Diderot and Marivaux, Hugo, Stendhal, Flaubert, France and Renard, Shakespeare and Goethe, Tolstoy, Jane Austen, Thomas Hardy. He had already forged his style, characterized by a rather dry lucidity, without musicality, but extremely clear, flexible, and didactic.

In photographs he is beardless; his upper lip is covered with a thick brown mustache; his eyes seem tender behind his glasses; his hair is well-groomed. His clothing is elegant but without Proust's affectation or Gide's deliberate strangeness. A flower decorates his buttonhole. The slightly blurred, charming face, and the slender, stooped, delicate figure could be those of many young men of the time, especially of his circle. If his intellectual and moral character "was already fully formed by 1895," as his friend Bracke (Desrousseaux) wrote sixty years later, his physical style and the projection of his personality were still uncertain.

Breaking with a delicious and frivolous life of sentimental flirtations, which is evoked in his earliest stories in *La Revue blanche,* and which seems to have been marked by no real passion, he was married in February 1896 to Lise Bloch (a cousin of his friends the Bréals) whom he had known for years. She came from a well-to-do family, one branch of which had converted to Catholicism, and which had given the Republic generals, magistrates, and a number of high officials. The marriage coincided with his entry into the *Conseil d'Etat,* and the young couple moved into a rather spacious apartment at 36, rue du Luxembourg.[32] Lise Blum was a little short and not pretty. But she had the charm of an intelligent and cultivated woman, she was vivacious and passionate. A friendly and very open group gathered around her and Léon among whom Tristan Bernard and Porto-Riche, soon joined by Herr and Jaurès, were the most assiduous visitors. It was a life full of excitement, friends, books, and debates, a life he loved.

Léon Blum at twenty-five was not only sociable. It should be repeated that he was already a socialist. This was more than an inclination, but not quite yet a commitment, still less a form of militancy. He needed the two searing experiences of the "Affair" and of Jaurès's words before he could move from early convictions and the dazzling lessons of Lucien Herr to the commitment that made him, from 1898 on, one of the most passionate and effective advocates of the unification of French socialism. But a definitive commitment to social-ist unity required a severe test.

AN AFFAIR OF JUSTICE

"An Average Jew"

Dreyfus. There can be no question here of relating the "Affair," even in summary form, but only of evoking the phases in which Léon Blum was directly involved and of attempting to discover how his personality and his world view were transformed by it. I have taken the essential outlines of this presentation from two texts, one written when he was a young man, the other when he was a political leader. They are among his finest and most enlightening writings. The first is an article for *La Revue blanche* dated March 15, 1898, signed "a lawyer," and entitled "The Trial" (the trial of Emile Zola which had just taken place in February); the second, *Souvenirs sur l'Affaire,* a book made up of seven articles written for *Marianne* in 1935, after Blum had been leader of the Socialist Party for fifteen years.

Justice had been Blum's earliest ideal. Then he had made it his profession. It finally became, in the strongest sense of the word, his passion. In *Souvenirs sur l'Affaire* he wrote:

> I had spent the vacation of 1897 in the country, very near Paris.
> During the month of September Lucien Herr got on his bicycle to
> come to see me practically every afternoon. One day he said to me,
> point-blank, "Do you know that Dreyfus is innocent?"
> Dreyfus? Who's Dreyfus? Almost three years had passed since
> Captain Dreyfus had been arrested, convicted, stripped of his
> rank, and deported. The dramatic event had violently stirred
> public opinion for a few weeks, but it had been very quickly forgot-

> ten, swallowed up, abolished. An effort of the memory that was
> already difficult was required in order to reconstitute the events
> that his name recalled. One finally remembered that an artillery
> Captain had been accused of high treason and that the evidence on
> which the accusation was based was a *bordereau* or itemized list of
> documents he had supplied to Germany. There was no reason to
> suppose that the proceedings had been affected by any legal irregu-
> larity nor especially that the judges had arrived at a decision with-
> out convincing evidence. Besides . . . Dreyfus had confessed to his
> crime. . . . When I questioned my memory, that was the reply I
> received, and since then nothing had troubled my thinking or my
> conscience.

And yet, Blum has the honesty to recall various warning signs he had
seen. For example, his relative and old friend Michel Bréal, a renowned linguist, had said to him shortly after the verdict: "I reject the
hypothesis of a human action to which it is impossible to ascribe motives." He also recalls a visit to *La Revue blanche* by Bernard Lazare,
the "first of the Dreyfusards" (after Mathieu, the Captain's brother),
accompanied by Major Forzinetti who denied having received the condemned man's confession when Dreyfus was confined in the Cherche-
Midi prison. Blum recognized in Lazare "a Jew of distinguished
stock," in the line of the prophets, one of those who say "a just man"
when others would say "a saint." But he had listened to him with a
mixture of skepticism and irony about which, thinking of it again, he
was "not proud." A third "warning" came at a dinner in the home of his
friend and neighbor Arthur Fontaine (at which Blum was not present),
when a certain Colonel Roget,[33] attempting to justify Dreyfus's conviction, related the sequence of events of the "Affair" in such a way that
one of the guests objected: "If what you say is true, Dreyfus is innocent!" The two men had had to be separated.

But these "signs" over the course of nearly three years had not been
enough to alert Blum, the young lawyer hungry for justice. Why—at
the worst—this indifference? More than any other people, observes the
author of the *Souvenirs* with sarcastic penetration, "the Jews had accepted Dreyfus's conviction as definitive and just. Far from bringing up
the subject, they avoided it." According to him, "the majority of Jews
even greeted the beginnings of the campaign for review of the trial with
a good deal of circumspection and mistrust [thinking that] it was something in which Jews should not get involved." Blum writes that this was
the effect of a "very touchy patriotism" and a deep respect for the
army, but it was also "egotistical and timorous caution." They did not
want people to believe in some "racial solidarity," nor did they wish to
provide "food for anti-Semitic feeling. The Jews of the age of Dreyfus,
from the same social class, after having excommunicted the traitor,
repudiated the embarassing zeal of his defenders."

This is why, Blum continued, when Herr came to inform him that "an average Jew like me, unconsciously subject to family patterns and ordinary social intercourse, had no stronger vocation than anyone else to become an inspired Dreyfusard."

Léon Blum an "average Jew"? This is saying too much or too little. An intellectual of a high order, a lawyer belonging to the most elevated institution in the nation, already a socialist at heart, he was in addition of Alsatian origin, and should have recognized how improbable, even unthinkable, it was that this first Jewish officer admitted to the general staff, that this Alsatian who had chosen France in 1872 and who was blindly devoted to the uniform he had chosen, could have committed treason. Everything, including his nonconformist inclinations, suggested that Alfred Dreyfus was psychologically, even biologically, incapable of being the author of the *bordereau*.

A Traitor out of Melodrama

Herr, along with Lucien Lévy-Bruhl, had already convinced Jaurès of the innocence of the convict of Devil's Island. And in Lucien Herr, Blum recalls, "conviction became fact"—a conviction, to be sure, which was based on solid ground. In a pamphlet published a year earlier, Bernard Lazare had established that the handwriting of the *bordereau*, the single piece of evidence which had convicted the Captain, belonged not to Dreyfus but to Esterhazy, a notoriously corrupt and vicious officer.

In 1897, Colonel Picquart, who had succeeded Dreyfus's accusers at the head of the Intelligence Service, had discovered that Esterhazy had sent a *petit bleu*[34] to Schwarzkoppen, military attaché at the German embassy; thus three years after the deportation of Dreyfus the game of treason was still going on. This had led Picquart to reconsider the file and to his discovery of the absurdity of the charges that the very diligent Lieutenant-Colonel Henry had accepted against the convicted man. Duly informed by Picquart, his superiors had first put him off, then threatened him, and finally transferred him to southern Tunisia. Before leaving for his post, he had alerted his friend Leblois, a noted lawyer, who passed on this cry of alarm to the Vice-President of the Senate, Scheurer-Kastner, an Alsatian.

It was in October 1897, three years after the arrest of Alfred Dreyfus, that the campaign for review began—on two grounds, Blum recalls. On the "formal" level, "the sentence was judicially invalid, the rights of the defendant [having] been outrageously violated, [for] in order to extract a guilty verdict from the hesitant judges, they had been shown pieces of evidence so 'secret' that neither Dreyfus nor his defense counsel had seen them." Substantively, Blum recalls, "we could name the really guilty party! . . . When have men who have undertaken to correct a judicial error been favored with such good luck? Dreyfus could not have written the *bordereau* if its author was named Esterhazy."

Hence the confidence of the "Dreyfusards": "The nation had been unanimous in abhorring the crime; it would be unanimous once again in proclaiming and rectifying the error." This is why, Blum recalls, "the Dreyfusards had a rude awakening. To their great stupefaction, the resistance had immediately been organized."

The author of the *Souvenirs* recognizes that many tactical mistakes were made by those who were or became Dreyfusards. For a long time they refused to blow Colonel Picquart's "cover"; he had of course been excluded and harassed by his peers, but he was still a soldier and therefore particularly vulnerable. For a long time they believed in an understanding, in the service of a review of the trial, among former "Gambettists": Méline and General Billot in the government, and Scheurer-Kastner and Reinach among the Dreyfusards. They also imagined that it was for them to operate through veiled revelations, innuendos, and allusions in the press; Esterhazy, terrified of being unmasked, could not fail to take flight, and by that very act would establish Dreyfus's innocence.

> We did not have the slightest suspicion that Esterhazy had been warned and prepared long beforehand. He would not have taken the train for Brussels or Berlin the next week or the next month. He was determined to brazen it out because he knew that the most powerful protectors were determined to brazen it out for him. Since Picquart's investigation and his departure from the Ministry of War, the defense had supplied its arsenal with all the necessary weapons. There was a reply to every argument, to every fact, to every document. The forgery in which Dreyfus's name was spelled out was already filed under his name in the Intelligence Service's safe. . . . How was it possible to imagine that the honor of the army was stubbornly attached to the safety of an Esterhazy? . . . There we touch what remains mysterious in the Dreyfus Affair. The reason for the initial and even preventive position taken up by the "general staff" becomes clear in part only in the light of a single hypothesis. There had to have been a traitor, no longer simply in the criminal sense of the word, but in its melodramatic sense.
>
> One has to suppose that this traitor out of melodrama was simultaneously very clever, very powerful, and very self-interested. A single figure matches these characteristics; it is not Esterhazy, a brutal trooper who had no authority . . . over the army leaders, it is Colonel Henry. He was lodged at the very heart of the general staff; he was the old functionary through whose hands everything had passed; all the authorities had used him, and the confidence he inspired in all of them was limitless. Now, from one end to another

of the "Affair," we find Colonel Henry's presence and his decisive action. . . .

What was called the "general staff" was in reality a man who was deep enough, determined enough, and adroit enough to have projected the collective interest and even the collective honor as a screen for his own safety. It is important to note that, undaunted throughout the whole crisis, insolent, swaggering, counterattacking in the worst situations, Esterhazy suddenly collapsed and fled after Henry's confession and suicide. Only then.[35]

The Dreyfusards and the Others

Blum's *Souvenirs* are fascinating not only because of the atmosphere he recreates and the hypotheses he formulates, but also because of his description of the forces and the men which the "Affair" set in motion. Those who gathered around the "general staff" were first of all the anti-Semitic and Boulangist "avant-gardes," for, Blum writes, "although the Jews had been reluctant to defend Dreyfus because he was a Jew, the anti-Semites did not hesitate to assume his guilt for that very reason."

Eight years earlier, General Boulanger's supporters had not been able to install him as president, nor had they been able to bring down the parliamentary Republic on the occasion of the Panama scandal. "They breathed nothing but revenge. . . . Fate offered them once more the Joseph Reinachs and Clemenceaus who had been allowed to 'pass through' Panama and who fearlessly presented themselves as targets. . . . The 'Affair' was to solidify the alliance of the nationalist party with the army."

But behind these "avant-gardes," Blum discovered the "broad masses, Catholics and men of the 'old parties,' those who continued to consider the Republic as an ephemeral accident in French life [and had] the ultimate aim of destroying, by means of well-directed nationalist feeling, the secularized Republic, or of overthrowing the Republic altogether." Thus, "the system of resistance, once transposed into the popular imagination, was able to create the anti-Dreyfusard legend which it took so many years to dissipate. The original Dreyfusards and their earliest recruits became 'the Syndicate,' and more precisely 'the Jewish Syndicate.' The 'Affair' became a carefully organized plot paid for by the gold of the Jewish Syndicate and of Germany, the Jews wanting to save their brother Jew, and Germany wanting to save the traitor who had rendered it such precious service. All the proofs of innocence were turned into proofs of the conspiracy. Millions of men believed in this legend."

Dreyfusards, anti-Dreyfusards? The choices were not self-evident. Léon Blum expresses his astonishment at finding in the ranks of the "antis" Henri Rochefort whose "dominant inclination was to take the opposite side on every accepted opinion, to reverse anything that had already been judged, who had gone through a court martial and who had experienced his own Devil's Island." Blum cound find no reason for his attitude but "Boulangist solidarity."

He also speaks of his sorrow of having numbered Barrès among the enemies of justice, Barrès in whom he saw at the time "not only a master but a guide, around [whom] we formed a school, almost a court." He had taken on the task of receiving Barrès's adherence to the "party" of review with enthusiasm and assurance:

> He answered neither yes nor no. He did not hide his distress from me. "I am pretty well informed," he said. "I have never seen Zola more frequently. I had lunch with him again a few days ago. Zola has courage. He is a man. But why doesn't he say everything he knows, and, at bottom, what does he know?" He was silent for a moment and went on: "There is a memory that obssesses me. Three years ago I witnessed Dreyfus being stripped of his rank. I wrote an article, for *Le Journal*,[36] you remember. Well! I wonder if I was not mistaken. I realize that every attitude, every expression of the face which I interpreted as a sign of villainy could be the mark of a stoic, a martyr. I no longer know anything about it." I remember his words, not mine. No doubt I tried to exploit the advantage, but he cut me short: "No, I am troubled and I want to think some more, I'll write to you."
> Barrès wrote to me a few days later: in a state of doubt he chose nationalist instinct as a rallying point. This letter fell on me like a bereavement. Something was broken, finished; one of the avenues of my youth was blocked.

Blum was not surprised to find Jaurès among the Dreyfusards; he was "a man whom I did not yet know [but] to whom I was to be so attached during his life, and who was to renew my own after his death." Jaurès, after having believed Dreyfus guilty and having been surprised that he was not shot, was a Dreyfusard, "naturally, as one breathes," writes Blum, "even if Lucien Herr's authority had not influenced his judgment." Jaurès's commitment or that of Péguy the fighter were much less surprising to him than the courage and the eagerness for combat of Anatole France, "the sage, the artist." And he considers that Zola's "heroism" has not been put in its true place. But Clemenceau?

> He had been the leader of a nationalistic, even chauvinistic Radicalism. He was the one who had made Boulanger. This Jacobin was an extreme embodiment of the idea of reason of State. What did a human life mean to him? Logically, he should have taken the head of the resistance and, twenty years in advance, in the midst of the Dreyfus Affair, play the role of the Clemenceau of the war.

> [But] I think he was touched by the close and curious resemblance between Dreyfus's history and his own recent troubles.
>
> For he, too, had just been the victim of a judicial error; he, too, had been condemned on the production of a note he had not written. He, too, had been stigmatized as a traitor by forgers. He had been denied by his friends, abandoned by his electors, expelled from the Chamber where he had held the highest position, because his accusers had brought before the court and spread in profusion throughout the country inept and clumsily fabricated documents which denounced him as an agent of a foreign power.

The left for "review," and the right for "resistance"? Blum's very sharp and equitable analysis goes well beyond that hasty and even false generalization. Although, in the time of Waldeck-Rousseau and Combes, from the turn of the century on and under the banner of "defense of the Republic," almost all the Dreyfusards came together in the Radical and socialist "bloc," at the beginning of the "Affair," a majority of the "left" was opposed to review.

It was, rather, among the moderates, the "opportunists," that Blum discovered those open to the campaign for review, indeed inclined to support it: from Casimir Périer (head of State at the time of Dreyfus's conviction—an event, it was said, that had contributed to his resignation) to Barthou, from Arthur Ranc to Poincaré, from Ribot to Trarieux: it was in this group that the Dreyfusard "syndicate" was best received. Not to mention the "crowned heads," from the Empress Eugénie to the duc d'Aumale; Blum points out that, informed by Rome and Berlin, "all the courts of Europe were Dreyfusards, and perhaps also the Pope and the highest dignitaries of the Roman Church." (Which did not prevent the vast majority of French clergy and right-thinking people from holding the "traitor" and his confederates in contempt.)

On the left, reflexes of a Jacobin type entered into play and, according to Blum, they ought to have led Clemenceau to anti-Dreyfusism. Although a few Radical leaders like Léon Bourgeois and Henri Brisson were able to resist, men such as Pelletan, Berteaux, Doumer, and especially Cavaignac campaigned against Dreyfus. And the socialists? Naturally, the author of *Souvenirs sur l'Affaire* is particularly concerned with defining their behavior rejecting the convenient antithesis: "Jaurès for Dreyfus, Guesde and Vaillant against."

If it is true, Blum recalls, that the most passionate of those who formed an alliance around Jaurès were Allemane,[37] Rouanet, and Sembat (Vaillant's lieutenant and a future "patron" of Blum who was then very hostile ideologically to Guesde), it is nonetheless true that "Vaillant was a Dreyfusard, and Guesde hesitated no more than he did over Dreyfus's innocence. The divergence of their views had to do only with socialist tactics." Guesde and Vaillant were afraid that "Jaurès, entirely preoccupied and as it were inspired by the task he had undertaken," might draw the movement, in alliance with class enemies, into what was not "the proper and specific mission of socialism," while Jaurès, on the other hand, considered that by "making the victory over injustice its own victory, socialism would gain new and greater influence. An optimism which was only partially justified by events."

In fact, during the "Affair," Jaurès had less cause for complaint about desertion with rival factions than he did with the "independent" socialists who were supposed to be his followers: "Millerand and Viviani remained aloof from every debate that had to do with the 'Affair.' On the day of Cavaignac's speech, Millerand published an article which said in effect: 'That's enough: now the "Affair" is over, over for us.' Those moments were bitter for Jaurès. One evening, after leaving the Chamber where he now sat in the gallery of former deputies,[38] he told me that some comrades of the socialist group had surrounded him and led him toward the Champs-Elysées. One of them, who is dead and whom I will not name, had taken him to task, almost abused him: 'Well, Jaurès, how long are you going to keep it up? Don't you see that you're ruining all of us, that our voters will see us as your allies.' Jaurès had answered: 'Your voters will soon know the truth; and then they will accuse you of weakness and cowardice, and you will come and ask me to justify you to them.' And Jaurès had added, with his broad smile: 'I know myself well, I'll go.' "

In Defense of Zola

For Blum, there were two great moments in the "Affair", one in which he was directly involved and another which, because it revealed the full force of Jaurès's character and genius, was no less important to him.

The first episode began with Esterhazy's acquittal on January 11, 1898, and ended with Zola's conviction on February 23. The second began with the speech by Cavaignac, the Minister of War, in the Chamber on July 7 of the same year—answered decisively by Jaurès's series of articles entitled "Les Preuves" in *La Petite République*—and ended with Colonel Henry's suicide.

In November 1897, the Dreyfusard press (in this case *Le Figaro*) had denounced Esterhazy. The government and the general staff responded by bringing him before a court martial. In *Souvenirs sur l'Affaire* Blum writes:

> The juridical position was thus reversed. We understood clearly that the "general staff" had just made a gamble, was playing double or nothing. But not for an instant did the idea even enter our minds

that Esterhazy's acquittal was possible. It was understood that Esterhazy would be tried *in camera* as Dreyfus had been four years earlier. But this time public opinion was aroused and critics were watchful; the judges were informed and would not allow themselves to be entrapped or duped like Dreyfus's judges. The specimens of handwriting would be there, evaluated by other experts and providing obvious proof to the court martial. . . . Above all, Picquart would be there, for it was unthinkable to avoid his testimony, and he had in fact been recalled from exile. . . . Finally released from his vow of secrecy, he would speak freely, face to face, to military judges who were his comrades, and he would bring the truth to light.

We were secretly delighted that the decision by Méline[39] and the "general staff" was bringing about so simply the result we had vainly struggled for: to project Picquart into the heart of the "Affair." Some of us, the incorrigible ones, concluded by saying solemnly: "You see. Why go on about the 'top leaders'? They are perfectly aware that Esterhazy will be convicted, and that conviction is what they want. They have chosen this indirect way to prepare quietly for review." . . . Esterhazy's acquittal, unanimously, without discussion, came as a crushing blow to us.

What was to become of us, what were we going to do? Esterhazy's innocence had been juridically recognized; Picquart's testimony had been discredited; review had become impossible. From now on it would confront a closed, complete, perfect system of resistance. We stood there appalled, in despair before the ruins of our work that had crumbled in our hands. It was one of those moments when all belief withdraws, when one feels isolated and lost in a world forever hostile, when the universe itself seems to become depopulated, empty.

Like all men, I have known in my life a certain number of moments similar to that one. For me there are a few striking expressions conveying that desolation which mechanically come to mind every time such a gaping abyss opens up between reality and the constructions of my thought or my dreams. They certainly have that value for me alone, but I will set them down nevertheless. There is a sentence in *War and Peace* which I had read as an adolescent: "Everything was so strange, so different from what he had hoped."

"Suddenly," Blum continues,

an energetic fist [was to] break the windows of the locked room in which the cause of review was condemned to asphyxiation: *L'Aurore* published Zola's "J'accuse. . . !"

I was living at the time on the rue du Luxembourg. At the corner of the park fence there was a wooden newspaper stand run by old man Granet. Until then I hadn't known that my newspaper seller was a Dreyfusard, but I remember perfectly that Winter morning when old man Granet knocked on my shutter from outside and woke me up shouting: "Quick, monsieur, read this. It's an article by Zola in *L'Aurore*." I hastily opened my window and took the paper old man Granet handed to me. As I read, I seemed to be drinking a powerful tonic; I felt confidence and courage returning. So! it wasn't over; the defeat we had suffered was not irremediable; we could still fight, we could still win. The Resistance would not survive the massive blow Zola had delivered.

For Blum, that is the "masterpiece of Dreyfusard literature," along with the famous passage in *Sodome et Gomorrhe* in which Proust tells how the prince de Guermantes wants to have a mass said for Dreyfus, only to discover that his wife the princess has had the idea before him. Zola's "J'accuse. . . !" is an extraordinary work of polemic:

> A court martial, acting under orders, has just dared to acquit an Esterhazy, a supreme insult to all truth and all justice. And it is over, France bears this stain on its face. Since they have dared, I too will dare. For a year now Generals Billot, de Boisdeffre, and Gonse have known that Dreyfus is innocent, and they have kept this fearful thing to themselves. And those people sleep, they have wives and children whom they love! The first court martial may have been unintelligent, the second is inevitably criminal. . . .[40]
>
> I accuse Lieutenant-Colonel du Paty de Clam[41] of having been the diabolical artisan of judicial error . . . and of having then defended his nefarious work, for the past three years, by the most preposterous and guilty machinations.
>
> I accuse General Mercier[42] of complicity, at the very least through mental weakness, in one of the greatest iniquities of the century.
>
> I accuse General Billot[43] of having had in his hands definite proof of Dreyfus's innocence and of having suppressed it; of crimes against humanity and against justice for political ends and to save the compromised general staff.
>
> I accuse General de Boisdeffre and General Gonse[44] of complicity in the same crime, one no doubt from sectarian passion, the other perhaps because of the *esprit de corps* which makes the War Office the unattackable ark of the covenant. . . .
>
> I accuse, finally, the first court martial of having violated the law by convicting an accused man on the basis of secret evidence, and I accuse the second court martial of having covered that illegality, under orders, by committing in its turn the crime of knowingly acquitting a guilty man. . . .
>
> Let them dare to bring me before a criminal court, and let the investigation take place in broad daylight.
>
> I am waiting.

What is astonishing today is not the magnificent audacity of the tone, but that the authorities could have hesitated to respond to this incredible volley of challenges. Albert de Mun had to enjoin the government and the general staff before they brought themselves to "defend the honor of the army" by prosecuting Emile Zola. Here we must give the floor to Léon Blum, who then made his entrance. While the defense of the newspaper *L'Aurore* was given to the Clemenceau brothers—

Albert, a lawyer by profession, and Georges who, though not a member of the bar, had obtained the authorization to defend the newspaper he directed—the famous Fernand Labori had been charged with the defense of Zola. But was Labori really a Dreyfusard? Blum (and his friends) decided to assist him:

> At the time I was a passable lawyer, although I was specialized in another branch of the law; I belonged to a high judicial body; I could therefore take on some useful work, and I immediately put myself at Labori's disposal. Many mornings I travelled from the rue du Luxembourg to the apartment on the rue de Bourgogne where he had just moved. My task for the moment was given to me, sometimes by him, sometimes by one of his colleagues, Hild or Monira. I was charged with studying certain contentious points of criminal law, with preparing in advance responses to some of the objections that the court or the prosecution would not fail to raise . . .
>
> I thus collaborated, though in obscurity, in the technical preparation of the trial; I was present at almost every session . . .
>
> The spectacle was dramatic, grandiose, but in the end, it was not the spectacle that really affected me. No doubt I perceived it and it got through to me. I participated in the movements of the crowd which, at every point of conflict, set the men of Review face to face with the men of Resistance, threatening physical violence. . . . Like my friends, I was seized by the sudden movements that ran through the courtroom and its environs . . . by those irresistible waves whose like I have seen since then only in the great moments of popular passion.
>
> I still find in myself, barely changed by time, the powerful pathos of certain scenes: the appearance of Picquart, his first appearance in public; the terrible interrogation by Albert Clemenceau of a silent Esterhazy; General Pellieux's interjection to the jury: "Do you want us to lead your children to slaughter?" . . . But the trial, for me, was not that. What I stuck to with my entire presence, with all my attention, what my intelligence and my soul were entirely fixed on, was the development of the evidence, the logical progression of the truth.
>
> Would it or would it not create a kind of obligation in favor of Review, the rational necessity for which the forces of Resistance would sooner or later be obliged to submit? I studied the proceedings like a scientist scrutinizing the crucible in an experiment. . . .
> The real drama was there, not in any particular turn of events in the courtroom, nor in any full-blown confrontation, but in that march of the truth, advancing step by step, then suddenly seizing an unforeseen and decisive advantage, overthrowing the machinations of falsehood as a sortie from a fortress overturns the work of sapping and mining.
>
> Zola was convicted by the jury, but that didn't matter; we were convinced that the Zola trial had decided the "Affair"! I was the one who wrote a report for *La Revue blanche*. I do not wish to reread my article.

Then let us reread it for him. And in moving from the work of the

seasoned statesman and serene historian to that of the young Dreyfusard lawyer in the thick of the battle, we can recognize an astonishing
continuity in thought and action, and above all the analyst's lucidity
and the fighter's courage. It is important not to forget that the trial had
provoked an incredible upsurge of feeling: Jules Guérin's anti-Semitic
gangs combed the neighborhood around the Palace of Justice and the
left bank; Zola and his friends lived under a permanent threat of physical violence. Nor should it be forgotten that in March 1898 Blum was
only a very young civil servant, an *auditeur* at the *Conseil d'Etat* who
had entered public service less than three years earlier. He signed his
article "a lawyer," but there is no doubt that the police on the one hand
and Blum's superiors on the other very soon learned to whom this
fighting article was to be attributed. He bore witness, he acted with full
knowledge of the consequences. Hence the great value of this analysis,
written in the days immediately following Zola's conviction.

> We are now freer from the poignant emotions of the trial, and
> one feels the fever of those two weeks subsiding. But a necessary
> task remains for all of us, that is to review the reports of the
> proceedings, to draw the substance and the truth from each deposi-
> tion, to formulate and disseminate the propositions demonstrated
> by the public proceedings.
> It is clear that the most rudimentary political wisdom counselled
> against prosecuting M. Zola. But when we heard the official an-
> nouncement of the trial from the floor of the Chamber, we did not
> wonder: how will the jury of the Seine decide? What we anxiously
> asked ourselves was this: what will come out of the Zola trial? And
> the only thing we should remember is that it produced more light
> and more truth than anyone could have dared hope. It doesn't
> matter that M. Zola has been convicted, for *M. Zola has entirely
> proved his case:* this is what has to be shown, what has to be
> repeated, endlessly repeated. We cannot permit the predictable
> monosyllable of the verdict to make it possible for anyone to lose
> sight of the unprecedented effort of the fifteen sessions of the trial
> in which, in spite of all resistance, the case for review was pre-
> sented.
> . . . It is established that the *bordereau* is the only evidence law-
> fully brought against Captain Dreyfus. This fact is attested to not
> only by the deposition of Maître Demange,[45] but also by the Bes-
> son d'Ormescheville report. . . .
> It is established that one or more pieces of evidence were pre-
> sented to the judges without having been communicated to the
> accused or his lawyer. This fact, which is enough to vitiate the
> proceedings radically, is clear not only from the silence of General
> Mercier and M. Salles,[46] but also from the explicit affirmations of
> Maître Demange and of M. Stock, who has offered to identify as
> many as four secret items presented to the court martial. . . .
> It is established that Dreyfus has never confessed: we can find
> proof of this not only in his letters but also in the cross-
> examination of Major du Paty de Clam.[47]
> It is established by the correspondence of General Gonse and

Colonel Picquart that in 1896 it appeared probable, or at least possible, that the *bordereau* would be attributed to an officer other than Captain Dreyfus. . . .

It is established that on 17 February General de Pellieux uttered the following words: "There has been a lot of talk about review. Review . . . leaves us completely indifferent. But, gentlemen, the court martial did not wish to put an innocent man in Dreyfus's place, whether he is *guilty or not*."

It is established that the next day General de Pellieux asserted that there was in existence an "absolute proof" of Dreyfus's guilt, and this proof consists of a letter sent to the Ministry of War at the beginning of the Autumn of 1896, *two years after Captain Dreyfus's conviction.*

It is established that the *bordereau* was written by Major Esterhazy. . . .

. . . I will not convince the good, naïve citizens who hoped to see the trial produce some astounding revelation, those who thought that M. Zola, too, had in reserve his "crushing blow," and who expected the appearance at the final session of that notorious irresistible and portable proof that had already been demanded from M. Scheurer-Kestner. Did they believe that M. Zola was going to exhibit at the last moment the written order from the minister to the court martial, intercepted in the mail by one of the syndicate's henchmen? Or that Maître Labori had in his pocket a declaration from General de Boisdeffre attesting to the innocence of Dreyfus? It is clear that M. Zola has not yet provided this proof.

But, in complex events, in which the incidents are intricate and the participants numerous, proof is never so rudimentary. I have attempted to reconstruct the sequence of this argument for honest, reflective, and sincere minds. And I think they will be forced to conclude as I have that everything M. Zola has asserted . . . has been proven. His article is already, in substance, historical truth.

What neither the "lawyer" of 1898 nor the political leader of 1935 wished to describe, the extraordinary atmosphere of the "Affair"—one which certainly had a profound influence on Labori's young colleague—we can find admirably presented in the notes written by Zola himself a few weeks after the trial, in preparation for a book he never wrote:

> Bring out clearly the pressure on the jury, the packed courtroom, the picturesque surroundings, the audience, the lawyers before the bench, the artists, the grim faces, the silent, unquestioning jury. . . . The evening when Trarieux[48] testified as night was falling, with the strains of *La Marseillaise,* shouts coming from outside: the Convention. Our arrivals and departures too; my anger each evening to leave like that. They embraced Esterhazy while they jeered at me. The crowd, artificial anyway, the thousand demonstrators, five hundred paid and five hundred from Jesuit seminaries. The police knew it and did nothing. I refused the offer of those who wanted to bring revolutionaries.
>
> On the other hand, the aesthetic manner in which the sessions formed as it were so many acts in a poignant drama, constructed

by a great artist. The beginning, Mme Dreyfus who was not questioned.[49] Esterhazy's silence, demanded by Maître Tezenas, who was afraid that his client would ruin himself. . . . After the sessions, our wives and children entered, the group alone in the courtroom where night was falling.

All the congresses, all the parliaments, all the committee debates in which Blum later participated were there in germ in this first battle, in those feverish sessions which he lived through beside Zola, Labori, Clemenceau. But we have seen that he did not allow himself to become intoxicated; the lawyer and political analyst constantly dominated the lover of theater and of sensations. The transformation was in process which led him from adolescent sighs to public responsibilities. But however sharp his lucidity and however firm his convictions may already have been, he still needed to acquire, under fire, more resolution.

Jaurès Proves Himself

Less than six months after Zola had thus "entirely proved his case," at the time when Proust's Swann declared to a friend who was worried about his health that "it would be annoying to die before seeing Dreyfus cleared and Picquart a Colonel," a new blow was struck against the Dreyfusards. Godefroy Cavaignac, Minister of War in the new Brisson cabinet (which was thought to be in favor of review), had decided to speak. In front of the Chamber, he opened his file, set forth what had been the "secret file" of the "evidence" and the convicted man's "confessions," finally and above all bringing up the notorious "decisive piece" of evidence, the letter from the Italian military attaché to his German colleague Schwarzkoppen, signed "Alexandrine," which clearly accused Dreyfus. Everything was once more clear: the argument for review was reduced to nothing.

This is what Cavaignac had said or implied to an enthusiastic Chamber, and no one could speak to it in this way with more authority. As soon as he had been named Minister of War, he had decided to find out for himself. He had done the work himself; he had brought a fresh and impartial judgment to bear on the file, for, whatever his instinctive inclinations, he had never taken a position. His irreproachable, almost professional integrity, the austerity of his life, the seriousness of his speech, everything including his "scientific" education and habits, made him the least challengeable of judges. Son of an exile, grandson of a regicide, nephew of a hero of Republican insurrections, no one could suspect him of complicity with the reactionary leaders of the Resistance or the clerical leaders of the "general staff." The new Chamber, just elected in the month of May,[50] had turned the matter over to him in advance, and now the verdict had been rendered. We were no further ahead than at the beginning of the campaign. As on the day of Esterhazy's acquittal, Dreyfus had been convicted for the second time.

I was not present at the session of the Chamber. Herr was with me at home late in the afternoon when the news was immediately brought to us by a friend of his named Félix Mathieu. . . . We listened to him without at first grasping the meaning of his words. We too had trusted Cavaignac. . . . And here he was declaring Dreyfus guilty. He had made himself a guarantor of Dreyfus's guilt and of the authenticity of the evidence he had read.

I can still see that summer evening with great clarity, Lucien Herr and Mathieu sitting with me in the room where I worked. We sat there with our heads in our hands, silent and motionless. Were we crying? I no longer remember. I search in vain for words that might communicate the depths of our depression. Suddenly the bell rang and Jaurès opened the door. We turned toward him in a gesture that meant: "Sit down and cry with us." But on the contrary he started to attack us with a voice I can still hear, in which there was vehemence, anger, but also something triumphant and radiant:

"What's this? You too? Just now, leaving the Chamber, I had to struggle against a group of comrades who gathered around me and bombarded me with arguments. They think everything is over, the fools, and they begged me to end my campaign. But don't you understand that now, and now for the first time, we are certain of victory? Méline was invulnerable because he kept quiet. Cavaignac speaks, argues, therefore he is beaten. Our only dangerous enemies were mystery and silence. Now that Cavaignac has set an example, we'll have to publish everything, exhibit everything, the 'general staff' will have to exhaust its reserves. They can no longer whisper to us: 'But, you know, there is secret evidence which . . .' We'll inspect everything, we'll verify what is authentic and what is forged. The pieces of evidence Cavaignac referred to just now—I swear to you they're forgeries. They smell of forgery, they stink of forgery. And besides they're stupid forgeries, fabricated to cover up other forgeries. I'm certain of it just from hearing him, and I'll prove it. The forgers have come out of their hole; now we've got them by the throat. Stop looking like you're at a funeral; do as I do, rejoice."

We listened to him; from his very first words we had a revelation that he was right. I felt inundated by the same joyful feeling of resurrection as on the morning when I read "J'accuse. . . !" Jaurès added: "Even so, silence, acquiescence, a unanimous vote, it's sad. It's sad there wasn't a single . . . For the first time I regretted my defeat at Carmaux. Well, I still have the newspaper." In fact, soon thereafter *La Petite République* began the series "Les Preuves." After the second fall came the second miracle.

"Les Preuves," Blum recalls, played the same role in opposition to Cavaignac's speech as "J'accuse. . . !" and Zola's trial had played in opposition to Esterhazy's acquittal. In article after article, Jaurès carried out a huge and total process of "review" with a sort of joyful, ferocious fury. Forgeries! Fabrications! Faked documents! Compared to Cavaignac's speech, his dialectical irony, Blum notes, "took on a genuinely Pascalian ring" or sometimes the "delightful playfulness, in Ciceronian style, which was one of the charms of his mind." Blum continues:

> If the forgers had really carried their audacity so far as to take their minister himself for their dupe and victim, then a veritable abyss of felony and villainy was opened before us. Cavaignac had said: "What interests could have driven the Dreyfusards to save a guilty man at any price?" Jaurès answered: "What interests could have driven the men of the Intelligence Service to accumulate crimes in order to prevent the exoneration of an innocent man?" The entire fate of the "Affair" was thus concentrated on a single point: was the military attaché's letter authentic as Cavaignac had asserted, or was it a forgery as Jaurès had demonstrated? . . .
>
> In the very last days of August 1898, I was spending my vacation in Switzerland. Around ten o'clock in the evening, a Zurich newspaper telephoned the news to the hotel porter who came and knocked on my door to inform me. Colonel Henry, summoned by Cavaignac, had been obliged to confess to him that the military attaché's letter was his work. He had been immediately arrested and taken to Mont-Valérien where had cut his throat in his cell. I don't think I have ever, in my entire life, experienced a more profound emotion. What seized me, invaded me, was not the dramatic emotion produced by sensational news. I was no more sensitive to that than I had been to the twists and turns of Zola's trial. No, the immense, infinite joy that seemed to flow over me had its source in my reason. The truth had triumphed. I was no longer witnessing only its certain progress, but its victorious arrival.
>
> Cavaignac's argument had collapsed at a single blow. Jaurès's demonstration had just been verified in every detail, and Henry had certified it with his bloody signature. Besides, wasn't it Jaurès who had instilled the first doubts in Cavaignac? If [he] had asked a trusted officer, Captain Cuignet, to verify the authenticity of the document, this was because Jaurès's arguments had disturbed him, half persuaded him.[51] In any case, no force in the world could any longer place an obstacle before review and, in fact, a few days after Henry's suicide, Prime Minister Brisson opened legal proceedings. The "Affair," the real "Affair" was over.

To be sure, further disappointments lay in store for the Dreyfusards: they had to wait patiently for more than seven years before the *Cour de Cassation* erased Dreyfus's conviction, although he had returned from Devil's Island in 1899. In Rennes that year, there were still (military) judges capable of convicting Dreyfus with extenuating circumstances! Hundreds of Frenchmen[52] contributed to a monument built for Henry the forger. There were also thousands who attempted, with Déroulède, to bring a halt to review by overthrowing the Republic. The Senate of the Republic even took the vice-presidency away from Scheurer-Kestner who had saved the honor of Parliament. Years had to go by before Dreyfus and Picquart resumed their offices and the course of their careers.

Then began what has been called the "Second Affair," the one that gradually replaced the defense of Captain Dreyfus with the defense of the Republic itself, and replaced Zola with the "bloc of the left." It is true that during the course of the "Affair," both in the euphoria of victory and in the bitterness of defeat, the monarchist, anti-Semitic, and Boulangist right, embodied by Déroulède, Jules Guérin, and Drumont, had constantly been preparing a putsch. A futile attempt had been made from the Reuilly garrison in 1899. In response there had been a demonstration of the left in the Bois de Boulogne; it was then, in June 1899, that the young Blum, beside his friend Lucien Herr, grappled for the first time with the *camelots du roy* and other conspirators of the extreme right.

Hence the strategy of "defense of the Republic," largely inspired by Jaurès, and sponsored with an increasingly secularist emphasis by Waldeck-Rousseau and then by Emile Combes. It was this operation, this "reprise" of the Dreyfus Affair, extending the conflict of 1897–99 to the question of the form of government, which Charles Péguy— refusing to assimilate the Republic to Combes's secularism— denounced in a famous expression as a "coarse corruption of a mystique by politics."

Thirty-five years later, reflecting on both "affairs" in the conclusion of the *Souvenirs,* Blum recalled that the Dreyfusards had vainly tried

> to transform the coalition for review into a permanent army at the service of human rights and justice. From the injustice suffered by an individual, we attempted, as Jaurès had done from the very first day, to move to social injustice. [But] we had not succeeded in bringing about a revolutionary change. . . . The crisis may have created violent and long-lasting disturbances on the surface, it had not shaken the country in its depths. Once the cyclone had passed, France found itself almost identical to what it had been before. . . . As the agitation of the waves subsided, the same ocean reappeared under the same sky. . . .
>
> Then, must we look for the explanation in the materialist philosophy of history? If, after the "Affair" or the war, society silently returned to what it had been, is it because social classes had not been changed, because nothing had affected the "human condition,"[53] jobs, salaries, social security, the way people housed, fed, and clothed themselves, or the manner in which wealth was acquired, exploited, and transferred? This is what has to be touched, as the Revolution of 1789 had done. Then the motionless layers will be shaken, then from the depths of the great ocean will arise the great movements of water which will permanently transform the surface. Is that why historic crises like the "Affair" and the war have left fewer traces in the world than a simple crisis of industrial "overproduction"?

This is Blum in 1935, on the eve of the "Popular Front" victory. This tone, this questioning with a Marxist flavor, is not, as we know, characteristic of his assertions in the 1898 *La Revue blanche* article. But if socialist maturity developed in him only through successive sedimentations or slowly ripening contradictions, from the time of the battles at the end of the 19th century to those of 1935–36, it is legitimate to question the correctness of the diagnosis formulated by the great clinician. Was France as little changed as he asserts by the "Affair"?

Without going as far as Gilbert Ziebura,[54] who says that the crisis replaced "a government of the elite with mass democracy," we must nonetheless note that while in 1896 and 1897 power was in the hands of "opportunists" and conservatives like Méline, Dupuy, and Félix Fauré, beginning in 1899 it passed into the hands of true "Republicans," and thence into those of the Radicals, from Waldeck-Rousseau to Combes and Clemenceau. Whatever assaults they may have suffered, the Dreyfusards had certainly won their two battles: the defense of law and the defense of the Republic.

What counted for the young man who came through the affair was the profound reevaluation of his vision of the society in which he lived, of its mechanisms and its values. The aesthete, meditating on the behavior of his mentor Barrès, came to question not only the man but the validity of his work. The lawyer, considering the attitude of the courts, not only military but civil (those which convicted Zola and took so long to erase the injustice of 1894), questioned the bonds that tied an institution to the society of which it was one of the superstructures. The rationalist and more or less hedonist bourgeois who spent his evenings at the theater and his weekends in the country had, during Zola's trial, seen blind powers unleashed and had recognized that social life and its various manifestations were moved by strange impulses. The journalist had discovered that reporting was first of all neither a technique nor a sacred calling but often a mirror image of power relationships.

As for the socialist who was coming to life in him, he could very well write later that "only the socialist party, thanks to the foresight of Jaurès, had attained unity and increased its power"; at the time, he had in fact observed that although the deputy from Carmaux had been able to associate his comrades and his party with the victory of justice, such a pure and clear cause as that of an innocent man wrongfully convicted had created constant divisions among the leaders of the various factions of French socialism. Nevertheless, it was certainly not an accident that in 1899 the young Dreyfusard lawyer joined an organization that called itself socialist. But it was also not an accident that he chose for the purpose a movement whose principal objective was unity, around Jaurès the just.

THE PATH OF JAURES

Socialism as a Culture

The battle for justice and the victories carried off one by one by the "Dreyfusards" did not play the pedagogical, really healing role that had been assigned to them by Herr, Jaurès, Péguy, and the best militants for Dreyfus's cause. But it brought about the formation of what was thereafter to be called "the party of the intellectuals"; it assured the insertion of this shapeless and powerful current into the socialist movement as a whole, which until then had been chiefly led by proletarians, militants, and vulgarizers; and it forever tied together the lives of two men: Jaurès and Blum.

We have noted, in the course of the incidents of the "Affair," the meetings and the cooperation between the two men, reported by the younger man with consistent fervor. With the storm over, we have to judge the effect on Blum. Was he only, on that occasion, what Julien Benda maliciously termed a "mirror-man"?

Jaurès, since his two re-elections at Carmaux, in January and then in August 1893 after a campaign that had made him the spokesman of the struggling glass workers,[55] had become, by the turn of the century, the central figure in French socialism, and was soon to take on the same position in European socialism.

His articles in *La Petite République, La Dépêche de Toulouse,* and *La Revue socialiste,* his speeches in Parliament which prompted everyone to hail him as the greatest orator since Mirabeau, his controversy of 1894 at the University of Paris with Paul Lafargue, the spokesman of orthodox Marxism, his improvised lawyer's philippic in the *Cour d'Assises* against the President of the Republic Casimir Perier who was prosecuting a left wing journalist for libel, the campaigns he conducted everywhere for workers' rights, for a truly egalitarian democracy, for secularization, and for nationalization of the principal means of production—all this helped to make him toward the end of the century both the founder of a *unanimiste* socialism and one who was carrying on the work of the French Revolution. Rather than a successor, we would say he was a protagonist of the revolutionary "deepening" of Robespierrism for which Blum had called. It was not an accident that in 1899 Jaurès undertook his *Histoire socialiste de la Révolution française*.

Testifying at the trial of Jaurès's assassin in March 1919, Blum declared: "For him, socialism was the republic of things extending the republic of persons." And when, thirty-four years later, Blum attempted to explain at the Conférences des Ambassadeurs, to an audience made up largely of socialites, who Jaurès had been, how he had adopted socialism, and what the nature of that socialism was, he noted, "according to the confidences" of his friend and not neglecting the guiding role played by Lucien Herr in this development, that "it was on the basis of the historical phenomenon of the French Revolution and its essential contributions, political freedom and equality later expressed through universal suffrage, that Jaurès had come to search for true freedom and equality. Now, this freedom and this equality are, in the end, economic in nature. The political republic remains incomplete and illusory if it does not blossom into a social republic . . . which makes the wage-earner a free producer, an associate with equal rights in the economic community."[56]

Jaurès himself had attempted to broaden the slightly simplistic economism of this explanation—as reductive of Jaurès's thought as of Blum's—by placing the *Histoire socialiste de la Révolution française* under the patronage of Michelet and Plutarch as well as under Marx ("my history," he writes in the preface, "will be materialist with Marx and mystical with Michelet"), and by specifying in a lecture on "Idéalisme et matérialisme" delivered in 1898 his agreement "with Marx that every future development will be nothing but the reflection of economic phenomena in the mind, but on condition that we say that there already exist in the mind, through the aesthetic sense, through imaginative sympathy, and through the need for unity, the fundamental forces which affect economic life. I do not agree with Marx that religious, political, and moral conceptions are nothing but reflections of economic phenomena."

Blum broadened this gap between Jaurès and Marx still further a few months later by writing in *La Revue blanche* on January 1, 1900: "No thoughtful socialist is unaware that Marx's metaphysics is mediocre, nor that his economic doctrine breaks one of its links every day." But in order fully to appreciate this sentence—which Blum withdrew a few months later when he published the bulk of the article in the *Nouvelles Conversations avec Eckermann*—we have to take into consideration the fact that it reflects the polemical climate in which it was written: on the occasion of the socialist conference of the Salle Japy, in the course of which Jaurès and his supporters came up against the powerful Marxist faction intolerantly and heavy-handedly led by Jules Guesde.

The mistrust the young Blum felt for the geometric and massively doctrinal character of Marxism as it was interpreted by French Marxists was the same feeling he found in Jaurès—the Jaurès whom Trotsky was to call an "eclectic of genius," the fluid, sentimental, various, and lyrical Jaurès, tempestuous and unconfinable, the "synthesizing, symphonic genius" about whom Blum asserted, following Pascal and with as much delight as his friend André Gide might have felt, that a virtue is admirable in a man only in so far as one discovers in him the opposite view.

For neither Jaurès nor Blum was socialism a science. They would readily say with Durkheim that socialism is first of all "a cry," a cry of suffering, even though both had been led to it rationally—should we say "converted"?—by the Hegelian Lucien Herr. But it is very significant that, in search of doctrinal elaboration, in the space of a few years (1897–1899), one wrote a thesis on "the origins of German socialism" which identified the precursory role played by Luther, Kant, and Fichte, and the other organized an essay around Goethe in which the territory was certainly German, but the eras were pre-Marxist and the models scarcely materialists.

For both men, socialism was at once a culture, a morality, and an art, the art of harmonizing, rationalizing society. In his lecture at the Théâtre des Ambassadeurs, Blum admirably summed up the nature of Jaurès's fruitful originality in relation to Marx: for him, "the establishment of a new social order would not simply be the logically ineluctable result of a law, but the response to the demands of moral consciousness. Jaurès moralized, idealized necessity." What was a law for Marx was for Jaurès a craving. The young Blum was conscious of the law but was especially eager to quench his thirst.

Jean Jaurès possessed a charismatic ascendancy over Blum as over almost everyone who met him. But the intimacy of their friendship and the closeness of their collaboration can only be explained by the spontaneous and fundamental convergence of their minds and their visions of the world. Blum recalls, "I saw him for the first time in 1897, in the little apartment at 27, rue Madame, near Saint-Sulpice, where he had moved."[57] Blum's location of their first meeting varied. In a lecture delivered at the Ecole Normale in 1947, he asserted that he had met Jaurès in the library of the Ecole, next to Lucien Herr's desk; sometimes he said that their mutual friend Lucien Herr had introduced them to each other in his apartment on rue de Val-de-Grâce. What is important, however, is the date, 1897—Jaurès was thirty, Blum twenty-five—the presence of Lucien Herr (the mutual "midwife") and the mutual impact of the first encounter. Here we should let Thadée Natanson speak, for, armed with the confidences of his three friends, he was able to evoke the scene, its effects and its later consequences with penetration, although his imagination sometimes embroiders the facts:

> There were the two men face to face. They had been expecting each other. They knew almost everything about one another, except what one was to make of the other. At first Léon Blum saw only the head with its prominent square beard, as powerful as the head of a Roman legionnaire, but a blond Roman, a head growing directly out of the shoulders of an athlete whose strength was gathered in the rest of his body which was stocky and too short not to seem pudgy. He didn't hear the famous ringing tones but a voice which would have been ordinary were it not for the sonority with which he hammered out words with an accent from Castres—he seemed less to have come from there than never to have left.
>
> One observes badly when one is listening intently. His face would have been more pleasant if tics did not trouble his lips and eyelids interfering with his smile and his gaze, a smile which nevertheless expressed kindness, and a gaze so penetrating as to be frightening. What was surprising was an unexpected power of attentiveness. Gestures more like those of a peasant than a foreman pulled unsuccessfully at his trousers, gestures constantly repeated. His trousers ended up as naturally crumpled over his elastic-topped boots as Blum's in a neat fold above his spats.
>
> The room where the socialist leader worked was overflowing with printed matter, and there were as many pamphlets on the floor as on the chairs, for there was no more room on his deal table. . . . A strength with something of fire and wind in it, giving more value to his gentleness. . . . The young man who listened, laughed with pleasure and paused to repeat in a low voice passing expressions. All the dread produced by the harsh odor of garlic which had seemed intolerable . . . had given way before the succulence of a leg of lamb.
>
> Léon Blum presented himself before the older man as a disciple, a disciple who would agree to be completely ignorant in order to have the pleasure of learning everything from such a master. There was approximately the same age difference between Socrates and Alcibiades when Alcibiades had shown himself so eager for the philosopher's teaching and his favors.[58]
>
> Jaurès's external appearance was as casual as that of Socrates; he had the same look of a boor until he spoke. Both Jaurès and Socrates expressed the same delighted surprise from the moment someone was able to "open" them. . . .

He [Jaurès] found that he had not been told enough about this young lawyer-writer and his elegance . . . the delicacy of a thoughtful intelligence which charmed him. The visionary took pleasure in building his future and imagining the services that a young man full of ardor, who was aware neither of everything he knew nor what he was capable of, could render the party, for he didn't doubt for a moment that he would make Blum the most active of militants. It was already an excellent sign that he was so sensitive to all the rhythms dancing in poetry. The flame that inspired him seemed to burn through every doctrine in order to collect its essence. At the very moment a problem was posed, his lucidity presented a deliciously concise solution for it, his subtlety free from any ponderousness. Jaurès paused to smile at his visitor's knowledgeable air, with his flourish of tenderness. Was it not one more attraction that he could allow himself a little affectation while remaining natural?[59]

Whether this bouquet of reactions was the result of the first meeting or of several, it is certain that a fraternal affection very quickly bound the young man to the socialist leader, reinforced for the former by boundless admiration. He said later that in the course of a life in which he "had had the privilege of being in contact with many truly great men, he had met no one—except perhaps Albert Einstein—on whom the seal of genius was so clearly, so obviously imprinted."[60]

"As long as Jaurès lived," Thadée Natanson adds, "Léon Blum never stopped listening to him. He never thought that he had anything better to do, [for] this mentor had done more than give him faith, he had made him see that he already had it. From the day when Jaurès enveloped him, I might almost say that he entered a monastery. He cloistered only the best part of his mind." "I am among those," said Blum, "who have lived in his shadow."[61] And he went so far as to confess to André Gide: "For that man I have been a faithful dog."[62]

Even contradictions deepened the complicity between the heavy tribune from the Tarn—"that peasant of genius," said Vandervelde—with sauce stains on his clothes and full of strong odors and harsh sounds, and the impalpable Parisian with his social graces. Both men, though, were very modest, very sparing of personal confidences. Little by little, Blum tamed Jaurès to the point where he could bring him home or to visit his "Parisian " friends. Herr rebuked Jaurès: "What's this, now you go into society? Don't forget that once there was a man named Ferdinand Lassalle!" In fact, this "society" never went further than the Blums' table in the rue du Luxembourg, in the company of Tristan Bernard, Porto-Riche, Edouard Vuillard, or Jean Perrin, or the very political salons of Mme. Ménard-Dorian, Mme. Caillavet, or Mme. Strauss, Egerias of the left.

"To be a socialist," wrote Charles Andler, "is to have gone through a total internal regeneration and a reconstruction of the entire spirit."

Jaurès and Blum, awakened, "enlightened" each in turn by Lucien Herr, submitted themselves to that process. It led them, one following the other less as a disciple than as a fellow student of an inventive, brilliant older man, toward a socialism in which many analysts have identified the religious character (the word can be found in a famous text by Blum) and of which the founder said in 1898: "The socialist movement wishes to break up all systems of ideas and all social systems which interfere with the development of the human individual, who is the measure of all things, of the nation, of the family, of property, of humanity, of God himself. That is socialism."

This Jaurèsian socialism took the essence of its economic apparatus from Marxism—the theory of value and profits. It held that the class struggle was the fundamental but not the only motor of history, human will and effort carrying on and directing the obscure, buried, and permanent play of material contradictions; it asserted that "the social revolution will be accomplished when a given system of property, a system of production and distribution of wealth, has been replaced by another." But it claimed to be, in addition and above all, an ethical and aesthetic doctrine, which could be realized, beyond the establishment of justice and equality, only in a kind of universal harmony, the models for which were proposed as much by Goethe, Hugo, and Tolstoy, as by Marx.

This Jaurèsian socialism, this *unanimiste,* collectivist, and combative rationalism, in which it would be tempting to see a "deepened democracy" rather than an "advanced democracy," could be summed up in a threefold synthesis: between materialism and idealism, between reformism and revolution, between patriotism and internationalism.

As we know, Jaurès was to stumble on the third part of the triptych, even though it was the one to which the author of *L'Armée nouvelle* had made the most original and convincing contributions. The two other attempts remained in fragmentary state; what his symphonic, synthesizing imagination had not been able to accomplish, Blum spent thirty years of his life seeking passionately and honestly, but in vain.

It would have taken an extraordinary philosophical imagination to demonstrate that idealism can broaden and complete the progress of materialism as the lyrical peroration of a speech crowns its difficult rising argument or as the fraternal song of the harvesters gives beauty and meaning to the harvest, and to demonstrate that between reform and revolution there are only differences of quantity, occasion, and opportunity, that revolutionary action is only the complement of the slow maturing of reform.

Was Blum taking into full consideration the personal influence of Jaurès, his effect on the masses, when he defined socialism, at the time of the struggle for party unity, like this?

Socialism is the result of a purely rationalist conception of society. Not only does it dismiss all the uncertain and confused notions accumulated for centuries by human ignorance and docility, but it tends to reduce more and more, in man himself, the old instinctive ground, the obscure and evil forces which escape from the light of consciousness and the influence of the deliberate will. Socialism wants to bring social justice into harmony with reason, and positive institutions into harmony with rational certainty.[63]

In order for this to be totally Jaurèsian, it would have had to leave room for a certain emotion. Such in any case was the interpretation—a little reductive, a little "radical" in the sense that one was radical at the beginning of the century, at the time of the struggles against clericalism—of the disciple.

Battles for Unity

This socialism composed of positivist rationalism and revolutionary humanism cannot be seen simply as a sign of the times, a somehow banal product of the end of the century which began with the Revolution, fired by romanticism, tempered by scientistic optimism, and haunted by the rise of the masses. There were already many other ways of being a socialist in France, and when Blum was anointed by Jean Jaurès and joined his "crusade," the immediate objective of the leader—then leader only of the "independents"—was to unite the many factions of French socialists.

Why the factions? Why was French socialism still so fragmented, when German social democracy, although affected by very diverse currents of thought, had apparently achieved unity? For at least two reasons. First, French society was still three-fifths rural; second, industry itself was very fragmented (83 percent of the firms employed five workers or less; only 4 percent employed more than fifty workers).[64] This dispersion of manpower helped to split organizations, to encourage a dispersion which also had ideological origins. While German socialism was dominated by the titanic personality of Marx, its French counterpart could refer to seven or eight more or less divergent sources (Babeuf, Fourier, Proudhon, Cabet, Louis Blanc, Barbès, Blanqui, Malon, Marx). Moreover, each faction was led by an original, sometimes powerful personality who was hardly inclined to accept a common discipline.

To simplify: at the top there were two powerful and antithetical leaders: Jules Guesde "the Marxist" and Jean Jaurès "the humanist." Around these two poles were a handful of strong personalities: Edouard Vaillant, a companion of Blanqui and the fighters of the Commune; Jean Allemane, a former typographer and a communard as well; Paul Lafargue, Marx's son-in-law and Guesde's lieutenant; Jean Longuet, Marx's grandson and director of the journal *Mouvement socialiste* whose line was essentially syndicalist; Marcel Sembat, an intellectual with leanings toward Jaurès but tied to Vaillant; Alexandre Millerand (who in 1896 proposed a minimum common program known as the program of "Saint-Mandé", which served for several years as a political charter for the movement) and René Viviani, both lawyers and more Radical than socialist by conviction and temperament; and Aristide Briand, the theoretician of revolutionary syndicalism so tempted by power that he was to become the one-man band of the Third Republic. Also involved, because of the more or less substantial influence of their writings, were Benoît Malon, director of *La Revue socialiste* and a warm supporter of a "total socialism" which greatly influenced Jaurès and Blum; Hubert Lagardelle, founder of *Le Mouvement socialiste,* who was hostile to legal means; the brilliant and unpredictable Georges Sorel, his mentor and ally; and of course Lucien Herr.

Guesde's party, the POF (French Workers Party) was the solid pivot of this configuration. It was founded in 1879, armed with Marxist doctrine which it wielded like a bludgeon, and inspired by the triumphant faith of a disinterested, uncompromising, and tireless leader, and the verve of Paul Lafargue, a Gascon with a ready tongue but limited knowledge (his name will survive chiefly as the author of an ingenious essay on idleness). Solidly established in the Nord, the Pas-de-Calais, the Aube, the Isère, the Gironde, and the Gard, representing the majority of the coal fields, the POF—which contained the strong and active personalities of Bracke, Pressemane, Cachin, and Compère-Morel—constantly proclaimed its virtues of seniority, doctrinal rigor, and mass following.

The PSR (Revolutionary Socialist Party) of Edouard Vaillant was the heir to the Blanquist movement, and was defined less by a doctrine than by its strategy of a break with bourgeois order, the pursuit of a radical seizure of power by any means available. In fact, since the death of "the captive," the eternal prisoner who had experienced the supreme disgrace of being unable to participate in the battles of the Commune, Blanquism had faded. Vaillant was a very sincere, courageous, and honest socialist, but his movement, less solidly established and less disciplined than the POF, often discredited itself by irrational shifts between rigor and opportunism.

The POSR (Revolutionary Socialist Workers Party) emerged from a split in the FTSF (Federation of Socialist Workers of France), itself the outcome of a schism set off in the POF in 1882 by Doctor Paul Brousse, who was exasperated by Guesde's dogmatism. This is why his supporters were more often called "possibilists" than "Broussists." Because he in turn was exasperated by Brousse's opportunism, Jean Allemane seceded from the FTSF in 1890 and founded his POSR, which soon took shape as the third party of French socialism, the only one that could boast an authentic working-class leadership. This was the reason why Lucien Herr gave it his support, thereby serving as a permanent link between Allemane and Jaurès. The "Allemanists" indirectly influenced by Proudhonism and opposed to parliamentary government, hoped to decentralize socialist development by encouraging the creation of regional federations. Allemanism, like *Le Mouvement socialiste,* served as a bridge between syndicalist socialism (the CGT and trade unionism) and political socialism (Guesde and Jaurès).

The Jaurèsians formed the fifth group, known as the "independents," which had assembled pell-mell in a kind of progressive sedimentation, Millerand, Viviani, Briand; then Renaudel and Thomas; and of course Léon Blum and his friends of "socialist unity." Brought together as well as could be expected by the glowing personality of Jaurès and having a common allergy to the doctrinaire authoritarianism of Guesde, the "independents" supplied the largest numbers of socialist legislators: thirty of sixty deputies by the end of the century.

At the fringe of all of this, if not completely outside the play of ambition, there was the solitary figure of Charles Péguy. He too had been a student at the Ecole Normale (after Jaurès and Blum), but he had been less strongly affected than his predecessors by Lucien Herr. But he too had been led to the socialist path by the librarian of the rue d'Ulm before becoming a leading "Dreyfusard." In the heat of the "Affair," on May 1, 1898, he opened a bookstore at the corner of the rue Cujas and the rue Victor-Cousin, a few steps from the Panthéon and the law school. He named it after his friend Georges Bellais, its chief financial backer. In the heart of the Latin Quarter, which was then dominated by anti-Dreyfusards of every stripe, Péguy wanted to create a bastion of socialism by producing and selling militant books and pamphlets. He also published and distributed two of the most serious periodicals of the time, *La Revue socialiste* and *Le Mouvement socialiste.*

A year later, he was on the verge of bankruptcy. A group consisting of François Simiand, Mario Roques, Charles Andler, Hubert Bourgin, and Léon Blum, set up at Herr's urging and based at Péguy's Bellais bookstore, founded the "Société nouvelle de librairie et d'édition." Herr had found the money to bail out the bookstore; Blum also made a significant contribution and played a continually useful role in the management of the risky enterprise. Around the bookstore gravitated the founders of the French school of sociology—Durkheim, his nephew Marcel Mauss, and Lucien Lévy-Bruhl—and economists and historians such as Charles Rist and Seignobos.

This socialist circle published among other things a periodical edited by François Simiand entitled *Notes critiques* (to which Blum contributed an article), and a "Bibliothèque socialiste" consisting of pamphlets by Anatole France, Emile Vandervelde, Millerand, Albert Thomas, and Blum, whose short work on "French workers' and socialist congresses" (numbers 6 and 7 of the collection, published in 1901) reveals a remarkable knowledge of the history of French socialism.

Finally, the Société nouvelle d'édition founded the first "Université populaire socialiste" located on the rue Mouffetard; it lasted for only two years (1899–1900) though its faculty included Herr, Andler, Blum, Longuet, Mauss, and Lagardelle. In a curious passage in *Nouvelles Conversations,* Blum justifies the creation of the popular university not because of the instruction provided for the masses, but because of the commitment of the teachers who, compromised by what they said in front of a public audience, would be at least "hostages" of the revolution. Were the "men of the race of Herder," therefore, in the end merely braggarts trapped by their own words?

The Société itself had a brief and stormy existence. Péguy, however great his genius and his courage, was not a man to forgive anyone for having saved him: he was determined to make Herr and Blum pay for the temporary financial rescue. He was also angry at Blum who, as spokesman for the board of directors, had rejected the publication of *Jean Coste,* a book that he thought admirable but that Blum considered "boring" and pessimistic about the condition of school teachers in the countryside. "The point of view of a bourgeois who has never known poverty!" Péguy justly complained. He founded his own *Cahiers de la Quinzaine,* thereby creating powerful competition for the group that had been formed to save him.

From this there developed a long and painful quarrel between Herr (and his friends Jaurès and Blum) and Péguy, whose socialism gradually "turned" from the mystical and libertarian inspiration of the final years of the century to the neo-Barrèsian nationalism of 1912–14. By the end of the "Affair," the poet of *Jeanne d'Arc* had already set himself outside the socialist movement; he reported on the congresses for the unification of the various parties in a sardonic tone, jeering at the naïveté of Blum and Jaurès.

But at the moment when Léon Blum's socialist consciousness was taking form, and even though the two men were never united in friendship, Péguy was one of the fires at work purifying the metal, shaping the form, fusing together the materials of the movement. Almost always negative, he constantly warned against complacency and conformity and the decadence and the risks involved in what was already called opportunism—"ministerialism" and its compromises. Without this Cassandra in wooden shoes, Blum might have played a different role twenty years later at the Congress of Tours.

In any case, it was on the rue Cujas, under the influence of the Société nouvelle d'édition, that the group called *unité socialiste* was created. Jaurès and Herr were its sponsors to be sure, but not members; the former stuck to his role as unifier, and the latter stayed with Jean Allemane's POSR (Revolutionary Socialist Workers Party). *Unité socialiste* was the first organization that Blum joined, and he was permanently affected by the group's task of unifying the socialist factions.

The question was on the agenda in 1899. Rumors of a military putsch, at the moment when the Waldeck-Rousseau government was preparing to review the Dreyfus trial, made the Jaurèsian theme of "defense of the Republic" a general slogan of the left. The staunchest supporters of revolutionary purity and the fiercest adversaries of the opportunism attributed to Jaurès decided to attempt a union of the socialist movements. Thus was convened the congress held in the Japy gymnasium on the boulevard Voltaire where, from December 3 to 9, 1899, several dozen organizations calling themselves socialist came together to attempt to unify the factions running from Paul Brousse's "possibilism" to Paul Lafargue's doctrinal Marxism.

The Japy congress was for Blum not only a great battle for unity; it was also something like a baptism of fire. He did not preside over any session of the congress as a delegate of the PSR (as the catalogue of the Bibliothèque Nationale exhibition would wrongly lead one to believe because of a confusion with a Blanquist militant also named Blum.) However well informed he may have been of the doctrine and history of socialism, it was the first time that the friend of Gide and Tristan Bernard was really present in a militant crowd.

To be sure, he had lived through the burning episodes of the Zola trial alongside the protagonists. To be sure, he had marched with the republican demonstrators in the Bois de Boulogne and had confronted the anti-Semitic gangs there. But these episodes had the flavor of a fringe adventure. At the Japy congress, Blum moved from his study to a meeting, from books to speeches. Hence the extreme importance for him of a meeting which he described with vigor in a long article for *La Revue blanche* (January 1900) and republished the following year, with many judicious omissions and revisions in the *Nouvelles Conversations avec Eckermann.*

Referring to the Japy congress, Daniel Halévy speaks of the opposition "between the two great families into which men are divided, the doctrinaire Jacobins, rigid in their faith, a compact mass voting with its leaders, and the lively and disorganized crowd of the sons of Danton and Diderot." Even though he was involved in the debate and deeply attached to the group of the "sons of Diderot," Léon Blum was more aware of nuances and convergences. He described the huge smoke-filled room, the broad platform, the thousand delegates arranged in the shape of a fan, their attitude, which was "simultaneously familiar and almost religious, which expressed an unconstrained faith free of formalism" and the remarkable quality of the speakers who, extraordinarily enough, "answered each other, thinking about the question more than about their success." There were the spectators in the galleries, "ready to dictate to their representatives the demands of socialist France," thus evoking "a new Convention, with groups carrying pikes and Hanriot's cannons pointed." Then Blum described the speakers, the leaders:

> Lafargue and Vaillant present a curious contrast. One is a white-haired old man, jovial and blustering, who unleashes carefully prepared sarcasms in a bizarre accent; [65] the other a red-faced and bent old man who, murmuring, and with his head lowered, spouts short sentences with such rapidity that they seem to fall over one another. Vaillant is a very clever party leader, but a bad speaker. I liked Viviani's face: a youthful African mask, a rugged jaw below broad and very prominent cheekbones. He has beautiful, steady eyes, and speaks in a sharp and singing voice.
>
> But it seemed to me that three men dominated the congress: Guesde, Allemane, and Jaurès. Guesde is a model of the romantic orator. He spoke with his head thrown back, as though to lift his periods aloft, and his long hair flowed around his neck. He seemed to project his thrown-out chest toward his adversaries, and he extended his arm with broad flourishes in gestures of prophetic warning against them.
>
> Allemane suited me better. He is a rather small man with thick black hair and a beard that stands out sharply against his pale face. He spoke softly, pacing the platform with small steps, gesturing with a small white hand with which he seemed to choose the most appropriate words and the subtlest arguments. All of his speeches were effective because they were full of tact and relevance. As for Jaurès, his friends . . . had never heard him in more favorable conditions. The obligation to compress his thought into a short space of time no doubt forced him into richer concision, more urgent and more sustained strength. He spoke slowly at first, in a simple manner, which grew and swelled little by little, effortlessly creating words and images, adding to his thought, to use Schiller's expression, the melodic ornament of his lyricism.

However noble the common objective of unity and however serious the tone in which the subject was treated, the Japy congress was poisoned by what was called the "Millerand case." Six months earlier, this talented lawyer, a former Radical leader who had moved to socialism and had become the parliamentary leader of the movement (after the electoral defeat of Jaurès and Guesde), had joined the Waldeck-

Rousseau government, which was center left and Dreyfusard but whose Minister of War was the General the Marquis de Gallifet, the "executioner of the Commune." Hence the indignation of men like Vaillant, an old comrade in arms of Blanqui and the communards.

Jaurès had discreetly given his personal support to Millerand's participation in Waldeck's cabinet, for he saw the leader above all as a defender of justice in the Dreyfus Affair and a defender of the threatened Republic. In *Nouvelles Conversations,* Blum was to characterize Millerand's joining the government as a "revolutionary act . . . which has opened a sequence which history will soon complete." But it was the Millerand affair that provoked the deepest conflict in the congress. On one side were the Marxists and the Blanquists, supporters of Guesde's motion which condemned under any circumstances the participation of a socialist in a bourgeois government; on the other, Jaurès's supporters, known as the "independents," the "Allemanists," and the "possibilists" who maintained that, in exceptional circumstances, for the defence of democracy, such collaboration was admissible. It was well known that, under the influence of German social-democracy, the International was rather opposed to Jaurès's theses. But Jaurès himself had so much prestige.

An incident brought the crisis to a head: Guesde had promised Jaurès that, while he himself would present a "hard" amendment to the congress, he would argue for a compromise motion among his comrades. Although he performed the first action, he neglected to accomplish the second. Beside himself, Jaurès rushed to the rostrum proclaiming: "Jules, Jules, it's a betrayal! Guesde, you have a duty to speak! If not you are dishonored. If it's not a misunderstanding, it's a felony!" Reporting this still famous scene, Blum gives a rather soothing interpretation of it, followed by a very realistic conclusion: for him, Jaurèsians and Guesdistes had "not even had to come to agreement, they agreed already. . . .So this was not the real question. It was a matter of determining whether Jaurès would take advantage of the Millerand case to have unity decreed, despite Guesde, or whether Guesde would take advantage of it to undermine Jaurès's authority."

So it was that both motions were passed, one condemning the principle of participation as contrary to the class struggle, the other approving the entry of a socialist into a bourgeois government, given certain circumstances. Contradiction? Opportunism? Jaurèsian synthesis? Péguy snickered, and most historians have followed suit. But what congress has not practiced this kind of successive sincerity? Everything was finally subsumed by the decision to create, to the strains of the *Internationale* and with red flags unfurled, the PSF. Established on such shifting ground, it had an ephemeral existence.

At the very next congress, also held in Paris, in the Salle Wagram at the end of September 1900, under the influence of Karl Kautsky—who, during the congress of the International held in the same location, had just solemnly opposed all forms of ministerial participation—the Guesdists used the pretext of a bloody incident to secede and to hold their own congress simultaneously at the Salle du Globe.

Was Blum naive or prophetic? Commenting on this secession in *Les Congrès ouvriers et socialistes français,* published the following year, he pointed out that in their final motion the Guesdists "were no longer speaking of union but of unity. In spite of mistakes, rancor, and violence, socialist unity was on the march." Jaurès, disconcerted for a while by Guesde's dogmatism and impressed by his Marxist references, had finally found a counterthrust, a letter from Friedrich Engels to Bernstein: "Marx often declared that it would be blind and absurd to look at all groups outside the proletariat as a homogeneous reactionary mass. This is the position, very complicated, very *nuanced,* at the same time very revolutionary, and very inclusive, it is this truly Marxist position which prevails in present-day socialism."[66]

But in the following year, at the Third Congress of the party held in Lyon (May 1901), the Blanquists of the PSR stormed out, and later joined with the Guesdists in August to found the ephemeral "Socialist Party of France" (known as the PS de F). And in January 1902, it was the turn of the Allemanists to resume their independence: the great momentum that Jaurès and his friends thought they had got under way at the Japy congress had quickly subsided. At the congresses of Bordeaux in 1903 and Saint-Etienne in 1904, the French Socialist Party was practically reduced to the forces of the "independents" alone, and to cut short the drift to the right Jaurès had to admonish harshly those who, like Millerand, wanted to make the PSF a simple electoral mechanism. Before Jaurèsism could once again gather the scattered forces of French socialism under its broad mantle, the deputy from Carmaux would have to put an end to collaboration with bourgeois parties.

L'Humanité

The Dreyfus Affair had occupied Blum for nearly two years, from September 1897 to August 1899. Thereafter, beginning in the summer of 1899, the struggle for socialist unity absorbed a large part of his energies. But there was less fever, less passion. It was no longer total devotion and the alternating intoxication and dejection he had described. A mission had turned into a function. He found the time to diversify his activities, to think, and to write. He worked on the final version of the *Nouvelles Conversations avec Eckermann* which were published in book form by *La Revue blanche* in March 1901, first under that title, then a few weeks later as *Nouvelles Conversations de Goethe avec Eckermann;* it was reprinted by Ollendorf in 1909 and finally signed by Léon Blum. He published a great number of literary articles in *La Revue blanche*. He wrote various political and social studies, notably the *Congrès ouvriers et socialistes français* in 1901 for the Société nouvelle de librairie et d'édition. The work is rather colorless and laborious, an exercise in scholarship he ascetically imposed on himself, but its serenity and fairness are admirable, given the circumstances in which he was embroiled.

Whether composing for *La Revue de Paris* in April 1902 a remarkable analysis of the coming legislative elections in May[67] which returned Jaurès and fifty socialists to the Palais Bourbon, or contributing a series of studies on "Les Monopoles" to *La Petite République,* Blum gives the impression of going through a period of research, intellectual acquisition, and growth. It is as though he were in a gymnasium, developing his muscles and his talents.

Then an opportunity arose to make his service to the socialist cause more useful and more resounding. For years, the idea of founding a real socialist newspaper, directed and edited by Jean Jaurès, had been in the air. There had been talk of it at the Bellais bookstore. Its urgency was felt during the "Affair." It had taken shape also because Gérault-Richard's *La Petite République,* which had accepted the celebrated "Preuves" by Jaurès in the summer of 1898, had turned sour. This was not only because the director, who called himself a socialist, was a politically dubious man, but also because he was mixing the newspaper business more and more with that of another company of his, "100,000 Coats" which sold "Le coquet," a suit for automobile drivers, at the low price of six francs.[68] There was an uproar among neighborhood merchants. Jaurès's enemies asserted that the company could sell at such low prices because it was supplied by prisons and convents! Jaurès had to be spared that kind of affront.

Herr and Blum began a campaign. With the help of Lucien Lévy-Bruhl they collected about 850,000 francs, enough at the time to start a major daily newspaper. It was Herr who suggested the title *L'Humanité,* the most Jaurèsian of words. At Jaurès's invitation, all the illustrious figures of the political and intellectual left (except for Jules Guesde and Paul Lafargue who remained aloof) agreed to contribute to the new newspaper: Jean Allemane, Aristide Briand, Francis de Pressensé, Jean Longuet, Charles Andler, Lucien Herr; the literary writers would include Anatole France, Jules Renard, and Léon Blum; Daniel Halévy would be in charge of news.

"We have the finest talents in Paris!" proclaimed Jaurès. "But where are the journalists?" asked Briand. "And we have seven *agrégés* on the staff!" "Then you should call your paper *Les Humanités!*" Gustave Téry said sardonically.[69]

No one described better than Jules Renard the atmosphere of febrile and slightly naive enthusiasm that greeted the birth of Jaurès's *L'Humanité* at 143, rue Montmartre. The first issue, which published among other things a short story by Jules Renard, "La Vieille," sold, it was said in Paris, 138,000 copies. Said Jaurès:

> The professionals have high hopes for our paper. We are publishing 140,000 copies. There will be enormous waste, but we have room to maneuver: if we sell 70,000, the paper will break even.

Blum, active and feverish, resembled the nymph Egeria. He would watch Jaurès write a note and say "Perfect!"[70]

Blum's column, written in alternation (at his request) with Jean Ajalbert, Gustave Geffroy, and Eugène Fournière, was entitled "La Vie littéraire." With front page leads, it invariably attracted attention. Blum, who wrote two articles a month for *L'Humanité,* followed two principles: "demonstrate the close relationship in the present day between literary movements and social evolution" and "ignore fleeting and mediocre diversion in order to consider only the works which raise the level of discussion." He kept his word.

Very soon, however, the literary critic had to give way to the watchful friend of Jaurès and the financial backer. For, despite its astonishing beginning, *L'Humanité,* badly managed and perhaps too lofty in tone for the majority of its readers, was in distress one year after its creation. In a long letter to Lucien Herr in July 1905, Blum evoked the crisis with verve and feeling:

> Jaurès arrived at my house and said that he finally saw things clearly: the debts are larger than he supposed. He is determined not to suffer much longer through this kind of torment. He has decided to stop publication on 31 July. . . . There are still 40,000 francs to be found so the debts can be liquidated and the paper offered to the party. In favor: Thomas, Longuet, Landrieu. Opposed: Briand and Viviani. According to them, the creditors would not understand this free gift to the party. Guesde continues to refuse to cooperate. Bracke remains in disagreement. . . . I am for a relaunching. You should contribute! Write an editorial on foreign affairs every week. If you refuse, Jaurès will be alone. Save *L'Humanité!*[71]

The paper was bailed out, and Jaurès was able to publish nearly 1800 further articles in it. Blum, however, had stopped being a contributor a few months earlier. Why? To understand, we have to return to the struggle for the unity of the socialist movement.

On May 27, 1905, at the socialist congress in Rouen, "citizen Léon

Blum" delivered his first speech, on a theme that was fundamental for him—one might almost call it his only theme—socialist unity. It would be unwarranted to say that this speech was the origin of the reunification which had been pursued for so long and dreamed of with such ardor. But it can at least be said that it took its place in the direct line of the movement, which had been made irresistible by the genius and democratic spirit of Jaurès.

While Guesde, five years earlier, had refused to bow to the prescriptions of the congress of the International of the Salle Wagram, Jaurès had just decided to conform to the final resolution of the August 1904 Amsterdam congress, which denounced as vigorously as Kautsky had in 1900 any socialist participation in a bourgeois government, and urgently called on the French socialist groups to reunite. Characterized by Guesde at the beginning of the congress as "ex-comrade Jaurès," the deputy from Carmaux had chosen both to break with the bourgeois parties—he prevented Briand from entering the current government—and to effect a reconciliation with the PS de F. Thus the various socialist families met together from April 23 to 25, 1905, in the Salle du Globe in Paris.

Prepared, from the moment the Amsterdam congress ended, by a bipartite commission made up of equal numbers of representatives from the PSF and the PS de F, unification was proclaimed after three days of debate from which, as if by magic, all passion seemed suddenly to have disappeared. Blum spoke again, saluting reestablished unity but expressing some reservations about the form that it took—the socialists' break with the parliamentary "bloc of the left." The basis of the unification agreement was in fact rather Guesdist—a restatement of the incompatibility of class struggle with governmental activities, and emphasis placed on the "conquest of power." But unification itself was an essentially Jaurèsian operation, for Jaurès had succeeded in identifying his name with the word and the idea. It is true that the new party did not fully recognize Jaurès's authority until 1908 at the Toulouse congress, which was a triumph for him. But in 1905 uniting meant uniting around Jaurès, for only he, from that point on, was capable of assuring that unity would be brought about and maintained. The words of the song were Guesdist, but the melody and the music were Jaurèsian.

The party that came out of the 1905 congress was called "French Section of the Workers' International (SFIO). Another Guesdist formulation, but there, too, we shall see a gap between words and deeds. Several of the leaders who were most hostile to Marxism—Millerand, Viviani, Briand, Augagneur, Gérault-Richard, Clovis Hugues—refused to join the new party, which nevertheless prospered, in terms both of rank and file membership and parliamentary representation (51 deputies in 1906, 64 in 1910, 102 in 1914).

As for Blum himself, he withdrew from the life of the party for almost ten years, although he continued to follow some of its debates, participate in section meetings (the fourteenth, directed by his friend Bracke, a fervent Guesdist), and render services to the organization as a lawyer, a journalist, and a man with innumerable connections. And, above all, he continued to see and to offer fraternal advice to Jaurès. In fact, since the Blums' apartment on the rue du Luxembourg was much closer to the Chamber than Jaurès's little house in Auteuil—allée du Chalet—where he had moved in 1903 from his cramped apartment on rue Madame, the socialist leader often came there for lunch between sessions of the Chamber. But Blum nevertheless refused his friend's request that he be a candidate in the 1906 elections, as he had already done in 1902, and, from 1905 to 1914, he turned away from the SFIO, an organization which he had helped to create and with which his name was later to be totally identified.

Why? This is one of the secrets of Blum's political life which, strangely, very few observers have tried to penetrate. The unification of 1905 was partly his victory too. Why, once the work was accomplished, did he turn away from it? Because the result had been attained, and because he was among those who participate in battles but not in the fruits of victory? Because "what is attained is destroyed," because his vocation led him, as in the Dreyfus Affair, to take part only in the struggles? (We have pointed out that the "Affair" and his role in it seemed to him to be over with Henry's suicide.)

Blum's Jaurèsian ardor, his friendship for the man, and his socialist convictions were such that his attitude cannot be explained only by an aesthetic and ethical taste for retreat from victory. This is why it is tempting to accept, in any case to quote, the hypothesis proposed by Madeleine Rebérioux at the conference on "Léon Blum et la culture."[72] She suggests that Blum's estrangement originated in

a latent but profound disagreement not about socialist unity, but about its meaning and its inevitable consequences. The so-called 'insurrectional' and 'antipatriotic' campaign, begun by Gustave Hervé[73] and supported to a great extent by the revolutionary syndicalist faction which was in the majority in the CGT, came up against an irrepressible rejection by a certain number of the members of the French socialist party and some of those close to it. Some, like Viviani and Briand, broke more or less violently with the SFIO. For his part, Jaurès succeeded, in the name of the general interests of the proletariat and the primary necessity of combating war-mongering capitalism, in maintaining, in a dynamic way, the fragile unity of the party. The spontaneous anxiety he felt in the face of a challenge to the concept of the nation gave way as early as the summer of 1905, when he discovered that the most militant sectors of the working class, those without whom there would be no hope of holding off war, applauded Merrheim,[74] were

swayed by Gustave Hervé's vehemence, and challenged nationalism rather than the nation.

But other socialists wanted neither to go as far as a break nor to
accept actively the consequences of unity at the time it was
brought about. . . . Intellectuals brought to socialism by the Dreyfus Affair, and often personal friends of Jaurès, they preferred to
retreat to their tents while continuing to contribute to the party.
They were waiting for the problems to become clear. It was the
union sacrée of 1914 that allowed them to return comfortably to
the SFIO. It seems to me that Léon Blum was among them.

Present in the audience when it was formulated, Blum's son Robert
dismissed this hypothesis. "Herr and my father," he said,

had thrown themselves into the battle for unity. They had succeeded. Once the battle was won, the reserve troops, as they considered themselves to be, withdrew. There was no political
disagreement between Jaurès, Herr, and Léon Blum, neither then,
nor before, nor afterward. Don't forget that, although he was involved in the great debates of the time together with Jaurès, Léon
Blum was then by no means a militant. The atmosphere at home
was not one of lived socialism, everyday militancy. The friendship
with Jaurès and Herr was always evident. But not political commitment.

The question remains open. We should not forget that, more "political" and responsible than Blum, Jaurès accepted that unity be based in
1905 on Guesdist grounds. For he was profoundly convinced that unity
pointed in the direction of his own strategy: secularism, republicanism,
pacifism, and deepening democracy; toward the spirit of what was later
called the Popular Front. Blum, less involved, more abstract, perhaps
had difficulty in accepting that the strategy was accomplished in heavily Marxist language.

Rather than participating actively in a ritual formulated in those
terms and accepting such a constraining dogma, why should Blum not
have directed most of his attention to his career as a lawyer which, if it
flourished, could make him one of the "specialists" which Goethe (of
the *Nouvelles Conversations*) says are basic to the survival of a party?
Blum thought it was for lack of "specialists" that the "opportunists"
and Radicals had failed to establish themselves. The socialists, he felt,
should not make the same mistake. Besides, he could combine a legal
career with literary criticism, politics, and journalism.

A Critic by Vocation

The cessation of *La Conque* and certain conversations with André
Gide led Blum to the conclusion that he was not a poet. He also knew
that he was not a novelist, and he soon gave up his *Raisons du coeur*. It

took him a few more years to admit to himself that he was not a dramatist either; around 1910 he finally set aside a sketch for a comedy entitled *Le Fil d'Ariane*. Earlier, in 1901, he had almost finished a play entitled *La Colère*. He had read the first act to André Gide (who, as we have seen, made a snide remark *in petto* about his friend), then finished it and showed it to his friend Romain Coolus a year later. Coolus spoke about it to Jules Renard, who noted: "Blum has written three acts[75] on anger. Coolus has told me that his hero does not speak like an angry man, that he doesn't swear enough."[76]

Nothing else of *La Colère* has survived. It would have been better if the same were true of *Le Fil d'Ariane,* which exists only in the form of a sketch, a banal series of scenes between actresses, fashionable young men, and rich theater angels. One wonders how the sharp critic of *La Revue blanche* and *Comoedia,* the friend of Herr and Jaurès, the dazzling talker whose profound and judicious aphorisms were often quoted, could have wasted time scribbling this idle chatter. It demonstrates once again that the capacity to judge and even to make others appreciate has little to do with the power of creating fictions.

Blum was a critic not out of spite or resignation or for want of something better. He was a critic by choice, because his penetrating intelligence, his broad culture, his openness to others, his gift for "sympathy," and his benevolence made him the archetype of a certain kind of critic: one who believes that love is a necessary, but not sufficient, condition for understanding. Better than anyone else could, Blum specified his critical attitude and defined his "job as a critic" in the preface he contributed in 1913 to Edmond Stoullig's *Annales du théâtre et de la musique.* Although he unwarrantedly claims "never [to have been] involved in the theater as a reviewer or judge of others' plays," this excellent, lively text, written with typical simplicity, provides a very accurate image of the man and his profession: "I am a critic by profession," he proclaims, "and, I dare say it, by vocation." And, with a kind of joyful abnegation, he emphasizes the imperious duties of the critic and the constant self-examination he must impose on himself.

Blum exercised first the profession of literary critic, and later of theater critic, but the second activity never diverted him from books. "He never thought he was wasting his time in the theater, but he had only one regret, that he had not been able to realize his ambitions as a writer," his son Robert said to me one day. But it is appropriate to distinguish between the two activities, as he does himself in the preface to *Annales du théâtre.* The whole of his criticism as a reader, directed by very personal choices, is coherent. But his theater criticism, guided only by the requirements of topicality, suffers terribly from the mediocrity of theatrical production which did not give him the opportunity of discovering a Beaumarchais or a Musset. He was nevertheless able to place accurately Henry Becque and Jules Renard, to anticipate Claudel's greatness, to discover the scattered qualities (rather than the heavy defects) of d'Annunzio, and to keep himself from being too easily and naïvely dazzled by the artifices of Rostand. But, as we know, he was among those who compared Porto-Riche to Racine.

Where and for whom did he write? We can distinguish two broad periods in his work: from 1892 to 1905 he was essentially a literary critic, though he wrote a theatrical column beginning in 1903; from 1903 to 1914 he was essentially a theater critic. He contributed notes on his reading essentially to three publications: *La Revue blanche* (1892–1901), *Gil Blas* (1903–04, 1908, and 1911), and *L'Humanité* (1904–05). The theater articles were published for the most part in four places: *La Renaissance latine* (1903–04), *Comoedia* (1908–11), *Excelsior* (1912–13), and *Le Matin* (1911–14).

We have already described *La Revue blanche* and mentioned Blum's too brief association with *L'Humanité*. His presence in *Gil Blas* continues to be astonishing. It was in fact a Parisian rag in the worst sense of the word, a place where off-color stories mixed amiably with discreet social blackmail. But a new director, Antonin Périvier, who had in the recent past led *Le Figaro* into the camp of Dreyfus's defenders, wanted to restore to the paper the better reputation it had enjoyed in the past. Hence—an alliance between Dreyfusards—Blum's contributions, which were excellent and durable, but still not capable of elevating the newspaper's shaky status.

Comoedia, a daily he began to write for in 1908 at the insistence of Porto-Riche and Jules Renard, and after a rather long period of semi-retirement from criticism which he devoted instead to the writing of *Du mariage,* was noted for nothing but its apparent refusal to take any political position: it only discussed art and literature. *Excelsior,* the first daily that made systematic use of news photographs (the first page was entirely given over to them), was financed by Basil Zaharoff, the famous arms merchant. *Le Matin,* one of the three principal Parisian dailies, was directed by a big businessman of the extreme right, Bunau-Varilla, who forced his contributors to adopt as pseudonyms the names of the railway stations on the way to his country house. But Blum escaped from this railroading and signed his short pieces "Guy Launay."[77]

In this cauldron, it wasn't easy to maintain one's freedom, one's personality, one's outspokenness. Blum was able to avoid alienating his freedom: in 1905 he preferred to stop contributing to *La Renaissance latine* rather than rewrite a harsh review of a play by Paul Hervieu, an influential figure in the journal. As far as his personality and his outspokenness are concerned, we have to understand Blum's general critical attitude. His criticism can be characterized first of all by its benevolence—which sometimes verges on lack of standards—and second by its psychological subtlety. We should point also to his concern with the social dimensions of a work, or rather what he called its social "equilibrium," but—an apparent contradiction—the absence of any strictly ideological reference, any socialist "line," in his own critical practice.

Blum's benevolence is legendary. It is not disturbing that it was exercised in favor of a failure by Georges Clemenceau like *Le Grand Pan:* the man and the work had high aims. But it is saddening that it was at the service of the vaudevilles or the most indecent dramas of Hennequin and Mouézy-Eon. Probably we should see this as nothing but a form of amused contempt, which did not exclude sharp attacks. The one he launched against his former friend (who was also Tristan Bernard's brother-in-law) Pierre Veber, author of *La Gamine*—whom he had perhaps not forgiven for being the only member of the staff of *La Revue blanche* (except for Lucien Muhlfeld and Pierre Louÿs) to betray the cause of Dreyfus—was cruel enough to bring the two men to fight a duel. Their duel, early in March 1911, was a great Parisian event. The press sent several special correspondents to the Parc des Princes, where "with a serious air below his large black felt hat, M. Blum hit his adversary with a direct shot near the liver, coming very close to killing him." All benevolence, it appears, has its limits! Pierre Veber had slapped the critic from *Comoedia* and he also, bleeding, refused to shake Blum's hand. A period scene.[78]

Blum's psychological subtlety was the critical virtue that most struck his contemporaries, even (or especially) when he used it to show the limits of a "specialist" like Paul Bourget. Does his predilection for Marivaux and Stendhal derive from this inclination? He often pushed this kind of analysis to a sort of loving casuistry, by which one could too often sum up his reviews or even his *Du mariage* or parts of *Stendhal.*

But what enables some of Blum's criticism to be reread today is his constant pursuit of "meaning." Perhaps we should see this as the reason for his gradual shift from literary to dramatic criticism. In the theater, which he thought decadent in 1892 but considered to be "in the midst of a renaissance" fifteen years later, he discovered the "social art par excellence."

His relations with the theater were not always those of a mere spectator. In the course of a lecture on Ibsen at the Odéon on March 15, 1912, he smilingly recalled that he had "appeared on stage otherwise than as a lecturer, fifteen years ago, with the young men from the little magazines and the painters' studios, to play a walk-on role in *An Enemy of the People.*"

In any case, according to him, the critic ought preferably to devote himself to this form of cultural production, not only to guide the public, but because "the resurrection of the theater is bound up with the busy life of great cities, a source of impatience and the desire for diversion, in short with the sudden industrial growth which began at the end of the nineteenth century." He added: "This application of historical materialism may appear to be a paradox or a caprice. But it is merely a sure and simple exercise, since once again writing the history of the theater always means writing the history of manners and morals." It was not an accident that he chose as a general title for his column in *Excelsior* "Le Théâtre et les moeurs."[79]

However attentive he may have been to the links between artistic creation and the social climate in which it is born, Blum was nevertheless not a "socialist" critic, in the sense in which Jean Jaurès, who was then writing the history of the French Revolution, was a "socialist" author. Not only because he refrained from practicing what he called a "sure and simple exercise" on a play by Lavedan or Brieux, which would consist of giving an interpretation of it based on historical materialism, but because—without going as far as his friend Marcel Proust who asserted that a work which displays its opinions is "like a gift that still has a label"—he seems to be particularly careful not to let his opinions constrain his aesthetic judgment.

This attitude obviously allowed for exceptions. Speaking of Barrès in May 1899, a few months after the author of *L'Ennemi des lois* had taken an anti-Dreyfusard position, Blum wrote that such a choice was revealing and that the work of the writer he had admired above all must certainly not be as great as had been thought. ("We must have been wrong," he concluded. He later recovered a completely fair attitude toward Barrès.) From Pierre Veber to Marcel Prévost, his judgments were for a long time guided by the attitudes of the writers toward the "Affair." This led Gide to note in 1906: "Léon Blum's *thought* has lost all interest for me; he is now nothing but a nimble tool at the service of the requirements of *his cause*."[80] And, a year later: "Ah! if politics didn't burden his thought so much, what an acute critic he would be!"[81]

In fact, Blum's criticism does reflect an attitude of mind, which Madeleine Rebérioux, defining the position of the intellectual left at the beginning of the century, describes as follows: "For them, socialism was another name for Durkheimian sociology directed toward the study of the weight of society and the constraints it imposes on individuals."[82] An analytical attitude, the attitude of an observer, not a militant, hardly a partisan—*pace* Gide. It might be said that the subjects treated hardly ever involved the appearance of a proletariat for which the critic of *Gil Blas* or *Comoedia* could have broken lances. But even when he devoted himself, with a marvellous understanding of the heart, to analyzing the sentimental debates of the heroes of Porto-Riche or Bataille, it never entered his mind to establish a parallel between this kind of problem and those—probably very different—which Jean Jaurès's electors in the Tarn had to resolve day after day.

Another lack. In December 1911, Emile Fabre, an honest drudge of the stage who specialized in adaptations of great novels (his *Rabouilleuse* adapted from Balzac remained in the repertory of the Théâtre-Français, where he was an administrator), produced a drama entitled *Les Sauterelles,* which describes the pillage of Indochina by colonization. It was a mediocre play, but a subject of great audacity, in a time when, between the proconsulate of Doumer and that of Sarraut, the imperial system was considered beneficial by almost the entirety of the French intellegentsia. Did Blum seize the opportunity to bring up the colonial problem and to praise an author who was bold enough to approach it? Not at all. The critic of *Comoedia* was content to judge M. Fabre's work as indigestible, which it is. But for all its clumsiness it is appetizing for any observer of the evolution of the human condition. It may be said that this is an anachronistic remark. Perhaps. In 1911 a man of the left, even a socialist, did not react to the "colonial question" or to the proletarian question as his grandson would in 1950. But Jaurès, following Lenin, Hilferding, and Rosa Luxemburg among others, had already raised the problems of imperialism, notably over Morocco, not to mention Félicien Challaye, already an active anti-colonialist. Blum later became a very penetrating critic of colonialism, but his "neutrality" as a spectator of the theater is rather disappointing.

Perhaps it should be said in his defense that French socialism, which was so vital amidst its very confusion on strictly political and union matters, had very little to say in the domain of criticism, which was playing a significant role in popular education and the training of elites in central and eastern Europe and in Italy. It is as though Blum, like a number of other socialist critics of his time—Eugène Fournière, Gustave Geffroy, and even, earlier, the Jaurès who signed his articles in *La Dépêche de Toulouse* "the reader"—had no really socialist way of reading because culturally the "Republic," the republican ideology of the public school system, filled his horizon and blocked his vision.[83] If Blum was not a socialist reader or spectator, this was because he was too completely a *republican* reader and spectator, whose culture was shaped by Hugo and Michelet and who saw in socialism only a deepening of those fundamental values *plus* a grid with which to explain the operation of socio-economic forces.

There remains in Blum the literary and dramatic critic a mixture of courage; he attacked without hesitation some of the most established powers of the day: Bourget and Barrès, Loti and Brunetière, Lemaître and Faguet, the Comédie Française and the Conservatory. His penetration led him not only to situate Gide, Renard, Zola, and Ibsen in the first rank, but to glimpse, with a touch of timidity, the genius of Proust and Claudel as well as the value of the work of Copeau and Antoine. He may be reproached for not having praised more clearly *A la recherche du temps perdu,* the bulk of which appeared after Blum had exchanged his critical platform for political responsibilities. (It seems that Proust did not find Blum's encouragements substantial enough. He wrote on the flyleaf of a copy of *Sodome et Gomorrhe* he sent Blum in 1921: "Dear Friend, have you received my *Côté de Guermantes,* my letters? I have the impression that we are not in contact, although— almost dying and incapable of writing a dedication—I feel so much gratitude and friendship toward you.")

Independent, penetrating, modern in his tastes and his method, Léon Blum proved himself in the end to be more an essayist in criticism than a real discoverer, in the sense that Léon Daudet, for example, who was so inferior to him in generosity of mind and spirit, showed himself to be by immediately recognizing the real value of Proust, Céline, Bernanos, and Malraux. Blum did not "miss" any of the great creators of his time. But, except for Gide, he discovered no entirely original talents who without him would have remained long unknown. Perhaps his most original critical contribution was his reinterpretation of Stendhal (to which we will return), or his recognition of the importance of *L'Education sentimentale,* which came a half century before general critical recognition.

Marriage and Happiness

At the time he left *L'Humanité* and detached himself temporarily from the socialist struggle (but not from its fraternity), Léon Blum was thirty-three. Let us watch him live, write, work, this tall figure with tender and sparkling eyes always veiled by glasses, his head covered with a huge black hat which he never gave up, his graceful silhouette enveloped in a dark overcoat with a velvet collar, a rattan cane in his hand, his feet molded by pearl gray spats. One thinks of Swann whom Marcel Proust was in the process of "polishing." Swann was not based on Blum, nor even on Blum's brother René, a close friend of Proust's, but rather on Charles Haas, a mutual acquaintance.

The Blums left the apartment on the rue du Luxembourg for a larger one at 126, boulevard du Montparnasse, where Léon had a large office-studio decorated with two large Vuillard paintings loaned to him by Alfred Natanson. Lise and Léon Blum's only child, Robert, was born in 1902, and the future author of *Du mariage* devoted passionate attention to his education. He even planned to write for him a treatise inspired by Montaigne, "De l'institution des enfants" (the first edition of Stendhal later carried a notice of its expected publication), but he gave up the project. He contented himself with applying educational theories largely derived from those of Montaigne—which placed primary importance on not overburdening children's minds.

This is why the militant supporter of the public school system did not send his son to the local elementary school until he was eleven, and to the *lycée* until he was thirteen; he wished to spare him until then from the painful contact with grammar and spelling. Robert Blum has recounted how long it took him to correct his spelling, but by the age of ten he had a taste for reading that was rare among his schoolmates. Raised outside any religious tradition, he entered the Ecole Polytechnique and became a civil aeronautics engineer.[84]

Lise Blum, who was very warm and affable and a bit of a "blue stocking," had a passion for the theater. She was not content with accompanying her husband to the premières where he was one of the augurs. She participated in the writing of the articles in *Au théâtre;* and in some cases she replaced him. She frequently wrote theater criticism for a fashion magazine, *Le Bon Ton.* Her friend and cousin Clotilde Bréal, daughter of the great linguist Marcel Bréal, shared her passion. (After having been the first wife of Romain Rolland—who seems always to have blamed the Blums for the breakup of his marriage—Clotilde married Alfred Cortot.) "Lise Blum and Clotilde Cortot, well read, *précieuses,* agreeable, and ardent bridge players, confess that they would have liked to act together in *A quoi rêvent les jeunes filles.*"[85]

But especially they played music in the apartment on the boulevard du Montparnasse. Alfred Cortot often came with his friends Jacques Thibaud and Pablo Casals, with Gabriel Fauré, and also Reynaldo Hahn, who was personally very close to Blum. Blum and his brothers, especially Georges the doctor, had sung a good deal: Schubert lieder, sung in chorus around the piano in the old apartment on the boulevard de Sébastopol, were the favorite pieces of Auguste Blum and his sons.

"Short, knowing how to wrap herself in stoles and shawls, with thick dark blond hair,"[86] Lise was not liked by everyone. Some accused her of a certain snobbery, others of authoritarianism toward her family, husband included; still others reproached her for her "blue stocking" side. But what Jules Renard says of her shows that she had choice admirers: "I said to Léon Blum that his wife is one of those women who make us feel our usual vulgarity. One is respectful and disconcerted. One makes a joke: they don't answer, they hardly smile, and one is ashamed."[87]

For vacations, when they were not staying at the country house their parents rented in Enghien, they were seen at Val-Changis. Often there were also Suzanne Pereyra, the future Mme. Paul Dukas, and her sister Thérèse who was Blum's great love and second wife, the Cortots, the Casals, the Thibauds, Laure Meyer and her daughter Colette, the Tristan Bernards, Misia and Thadée Natanson, Alfred Athis (Natanson), his wife the actress Marthe Mellot, and their daughter Annette, a playmate for little Robert Blum.

A beautiful portrait of Blum at thirty was written by Simone Le Bargy, who was the star of the first production of Rostand's famous *Chantecler* and who later moved from theater to literature and changed her name to simply Simone:

> When I met Léon Blum he was approaching thirty. He was thin, with a good figure, brown hair, milky skin, and a slight mustache drooped in Chinese style over his soft, red mouth with its bright teeth. His straight nose continued the line of his forehead with a kind of absolute rectitude and introduced among his kindly features a more rigorous element that pointed to will, tenacity, and courage, indomitable courage. But the glory of his face, beneath brows raised as though in surprise, were his blue eyes with large black pupils. Those eyes, full of delight and wonder at life, revealed a mystical good will and an enormous faith generously granted to his companions in conversation. They flitted from one person to another, as tender and warm as a ray of sunlight refracted by a fanciful mirror. . . .
>
> When he spoke he folded his long, sensitive hands, the hands of a miracle-working rabbi, on his chest, in a slightly suppliant gesture which indicated the tenderness of his heart and his wish to convince his listener gently. The tenderness which he expressed so forcefully toward his friends was an emotion he felt with even more force toward suffering humanity.
>
> The secret of his change of direction and of his great accomplishments lies there. He repudiated an existence full of ease for the harsh life of a leader and an apostle only because of that generosity, that prodigality of feeling, which suddenly demanded a complete reassessment. . . . Indulgent, optimistic, he loved the world, travel, and the pleasures of an easy life. Lacking any religious belief, without the slightest hope of an immortality, even of the vaguest kind, which would preserve some memory of our passage on earth, he nevertheless followed a mystical belief, the entirely humanitarian belief inspired by the voice of Jaurès whose disciple he had chosen to become. Like that prophet, he believed in progress: boldly in man's progress, calmly in the progress that greater justice would bring to the living conditions of the majority of humanity. Overflowing with good faith, he assumed that everyone he spoke to, even his enemies, possessed the same virtue. . . .
>
> I don't remember ever, at the time, hearing a pessimistic view or a desperate judgment from him about the human condition. Happy, charming, he went on, having succeeded in making pleasures of all his duties. He said to me: "I try to arrange my day as though it were the last day of my life, to include, in however small a way, everything I love."[88]

The Blums were strongly attached to family. Not only did Léon, like his brothers, visit his parents every day (after his mother's death he saw his father daily until his death in 1921), but he was also concerned about more distant relatives. Jules Renard noted: "He is touching, Léon Blum, with his old blind aunt; gracious like Antigone, he serves her, identifies the dishes, cuts her meat."[89] Lise and Léon Blum brought the old lady to Italy. Tristan Bernard, to whom Jules Renard told the story, said to him: "They are meritorious. It would be so easy to take her on the suburban railway and have people call out the names of Florence and Venice."

Blum was prodigal in the expressions of the affection he felt for his brothers, especially for René, the youngest, delicate and nonchalant, whom his friends sometimes called "le Blumet," and sometimes, in order to point to his graceful melancholy, "Infortunio." René was often flanked by his dearest friends, Marcel Proust and Jacques Bizet, the whimsical son of the composer of *Carmen* and the brilliant Mme. Strauss, who was one of the models for Oriane de Guermantes and whose salon had been a citadel for the Dreyfusards.

Were it not for his constant contact with Jaurès and Herr, Blum, from 1905 to 1910, could hardly have been distinguished from other distinguished intellectuals of the day—France or Gide, for example—who also sympathized with the left. His criticism was not very committed politically, and his exemplary conduct at the *Conseil d'Etat* did not differ much from that of his colleagues.

A bourgeois intellectual? Perhaps. But the gentle Alcibiades with his large hat and vague smile was not content with writing critical notes whose publication might involve some risk, singing Fauré songs with Alfred Cortot at the piano, and preparing model legal reports. While his colleagues on the *Cour de Cassation,* for want of something better, finally restored to Alfred Dreyfus recognition of his integrity and the insignia of his rank, Blum was preparing to mount the ramparts once again to criticize the society in which he comfortably but not complacently lived.

In May 1907, he published what has remained his most controversial book, *Du mariage,* with the following prefatory note:

> If the reader disregards the excessive generalizations into which I was no doubt led by the desire to prove, this book may not seem entirely useless. I have thought about it for a long time and, rereading the completed work, I am more than ever convinced of its fundamental truth. To those of my readers whom the work may shock, I plead this conviction.
>
> I ask permission to make public my dedication of the book to my wife, intending thus to show that neither disappointment nor rancor entered into its conception, but, on the contrary, a feeling of gratitude, and that it was written by a happy man.

These few lines clearly express the author's sincere conviction; he was not indulging in a provocative parlor game but intended to write a "useful" book. They indicate that this is the work of a man whose ultimate objective, in matters of private morality as in public life, was indeed always happiness, for happiness and justice were to his way of thinking inseparable, as they were for Socrates—and for Jaurès.

An essay? A novel? A pamphlet? *Du mariage* has been presented as a kind of long preface to the literary production that occupied the chief attention of the critic of *Comoedia* at the time, and which was flourishing in the early years of the century: the "theater of love" which André Gide, in a peculiar metonymy, called a short time later the "Jewish theater," in particular the theater whose symbol and standardbearer was Georges de Porto-Riche. The link between Blum's book and his friend's plays is clear: the central theme of the book is adopted from a line in *Amoureuse* in which the heroine suggests that, like men, women too should be able to indulge without constraint in premarital affairs.

Can we then consider *Du mariage* as a kind of introductory essay about contemporary theater? Blum's ambition, demonstrated by the preface already quoted and by many aspects of the book, was greater. He did not wish simply to explain and illuminate the works of his friends, nor to publish a mere report. He thought of himself, if not as a social reformer, at least as a precursor of possible reforms.

> Considering it obvious that marriage, or legal monogamy, is a badly functioning institution, I wondered if it should be radically abandoned in favor of modern forms of polygamy. It took some courage on my part to overcome the prejudice I felt in favor of free love. Men and women are originally polygamous, and then, in the vast majority of cases, once they have reached a certain degree of development and a certain age, they tend toward and reach fulfillment in monogamy [of which] marriage is the natural form— stability, unity, and the repose of feelings.[90]

Scribbled in the margin of the manuscript was this note:

> My entire reform: tolerate and organize the freedom of women before marriage. All incidental quarrels come from this and would disappear if my notion were accepted. I separate marriage from love, but by organizing love before marriage. I grant to marriage the place that had been forgotten because of lack of thought and the irrevocable drift of morals. I restore to the compromised institution its only chance for survival and duration. I am not reforming it but setting it on its feet.[91]

The idea of "reform" is certainly present, as is the wish to have an effect on morals. Of course, Blum was then above all a man of letters, and his book hardly resembles the work of a contemporary socialist leader like August Bebel who, a few years earlier, had written the treatise *Woman and Society,* essentially a history of the alienation of women seen from an economic perspective. What is more surprising is that Blum in writing his essay relied to such a small extent on scientific research, a reliance that was beginning to be fashionable. It is not so much that he did not refer to Freud, none of whose works had been translated into French (both Blum and Herr knew German), but that he mentioned Metchnikoff only once although he had written a review of Metchnikoff's *Studies on Human Nature: an Essay in Optimistic Philosophy* for *Gil Blas,* and it was a book which supported on physiological grounds Blum's own psychological theories.

There is a moment in the book when something other than a rather monotonous psychologism comes through: the story of a woman in whom the author discovers the full expression of sexuality through her manner of eating strawberries "with a slight trembling of her moist lips, and gestures that were both greedy and protective of her hands." A typical example of the "correspondences" which, according to Blum, insure that a "change in the sexual sphere has repercussions in one's entire being."[92] It is surprising that this suggestive observation of psychopathology remains an isolated remark.

The only political (in the broad sense) source for *Du mariage* was Fourier. Blum praises *Théorie des quatre mouvements* and *Théorie de l'unité universelle* for their prophetic formulations. He hails the audacity Fourier demonstrated by advocating the liberation of woman "from the economic yoke of man" through education, by making her mistress of her own body, and finally by describing marriage as the last step in a progression through which "loving couples rise only with the passage of time." Blum nevertheless differentiates himself from Fourier "in so far as he did not conceive of the organization of love separately from social organization"; the author of *Du mariage* believes that "this partial reform is entirely self-sufficient and one cannot expect perfection solely from the progress of manners and morals."[93] Is it surprising that the more "socialist" and even the more modern of the two is Charles Fourier?

But Blum's three real inspirations, more than the scientists or the precursors of socialism, much more even than the dramatists of the time, were Balzac, Stendhal, and Tolstoy; especially Balzac, whose *Physiologie du mariage* seemed to haunt Blum to the point that one might almost find the origin of *Du mariage* in this passage from *Physiologie du mariage:*

> The freedom which we have boldly demanded for young people is a remedy for this mass of evils. Let us grant the young passion, coquetry, love and its terrors, love and its sweetness. In the springtime of life, no wrong is irreparable, and love will be justified by useful comparisons. With this change in our morals, the shameful scourge of prostitution will disappear by itself.

An even closer source is the passage in which Balzac sums up "the essential periods of women's sexual activity":

> During the ten years after the honeymoon, the woman has to fulfill her "physiological or diabolical obligations," and even the most decent will have at least three lovers. Then there will come, between husband and wife, the treaty of reconciliation, "the matrimonial restoration," which bridges the gap opened by revolution.

And Blum points out: "Balzac appropriately defines the condition created by this treaty with the expression conjugal peace."

Blum is surprised that Balzac did not carry his argument further and, obsessed by his real preoccupation (to avoid the deception of husbands), did not suggest that "war" or "revolution," rather than being integrated into marriage, should precede it, making "conjugal peace" not a remedy but a goal in itself.

Blum differs from Tolstoy in that he sees nothing perverse in sensuality. Like Tolstoy, Blum considers one of the reasons for so many wrecked marriages to be the inequality between the "experienced" man and the woman confined to virginity. But for the Russian the answer lies in mutual innocence. Blum shares many of the perspectives that led Tolstoy to describe the loves of Katya or Anna Karenina as failures, but he writes of the latter:

> Where Anna surrendered, who could claim she would resist? No woman was more scrupulous or more decent than she. But the opportunity for love came to her too late; although made for marriage, she had entered upon it too young. Her misfortune was to be a lover when she was already a wife and mother. She ought to have loved first. The same passion which led her to despair and suicide would not have conflicted with any duty. She would have preserved only a delicious memory, for one forgets the tears love exacts, and one remembers only living boldly and fully. Then, after loving the Vronsky of the time, and no doubt other lovers after the first, she should have been, without distress and without regret, the wife of Karenin.[94]

If the author of *Du mariage* was so burdened with literary references, this is not because he lacked others; his book teems with anecdotes. But he remained a man of letters who probably thought of publishing a novel when he undertook the writing of *Du mariage* in 1904. (His sketch for a novel, *Les Raisons du coeur,* was never carried on with much enthusiasm.) In 1906 he contributed a short story entitled "Elisabeth Masson" to *Les Lettres,* a journal edited by Fernand Gregh, and it was published separately under the same title a month later.[95] This story about a marriage which fails because the heroine experiences the disordered awakening of her senses instead of fulfillment, was reproduced in *Du mariage*.

Blum's choice of the "anecdotal" critical essay form may have led to his abandonment of *Les Raisons du coeur,* in which the same material would have been used in an openly novelistic form. We may sometimes regret the decision. Some passages of *Du mariage,* notably the story of the narrator's pursuit of an unknown woman who offers herself to him with angelic simplicity, are worthy of Jules Renard. It was not an accident that Octave Mirbeau proposed him for the Prix Goncourt, and only the resolute opposition of his colleague Léon Daudet prevented him from openly campaigning for granting the prize to Blum. Who can say what the prize might have changed?

It is not enough to say of *Du mariage* that it was courageous for its time; it still remains a "modern" work. In 1907, his tone, his ideas, and his nonchalant audacity could not fail to provoke violent reactions. In *Le Gaulois* René Doumic went no further than to call it "a joke in rather bad taste." In *La Revue latine* Emile Faguet, who had on other occasions expressed high regard for Blum as a literary critic, wrote: "Léon Blum tends toward the development of the instinct of the prostitute among young women. He is not serious. I ask the public's pardon for having discussed his theories seriously. I even think there are grounds to ask him for forgiveness."

There were also the political opponents, the anti-Dreyfusards and the anti-Semitic fanatics. A certain Jean Livry, in an article in *Le Peuple français* entitled "La pornographie au Conseil d'Etat," denounced "the swine, the criminal . . . [author of this] book which shouldn't be touched without asbestos gloves. Zola, in his most abject works, never reached the corrupt level of this Jew." While an Alsatian weekly spoke of "a Jewish-Masonic and secularist" plot "to dishonor all the women of France," others attacked Aristide Briand, then Minister of Justice, for having given the Légion d'Honneur to this "immoral public servant" a few weeks before publication of the book.

Nevertheless, the critics in general were sympathetic and often admiring. *Le Temps* spoke of a "revolutionary" theory, but also of the "calm" and the "logic" with which it was presented by "an author too sensitive not to feel pity for the Vestals." *Le Figaro* hailed "this bold, courageous, generous book." And *La Revue de Paris* praised its "penetrating observations, and its sober, vivid, elegant, delicious style." *La Petite République* declared itself in favor of "this courageous work, entirely stamped with sincerity and conviction." *Les Annales sociales et politiques* asserted that it was a "book of the day which will be the book of tomorrow." And *L'Humanité:* "Women will like this book which may frighten many men but in which can be found no less good faith than courage."

Strangely enough, Blum did not have great support among women. Marcelle Tinayre, who was something like the Simone de Beauvoir of the time, was favorable but unenthusiastic. Many of his women friends thought he was too bold a feminist, which distressed him. But even more distressing in the circumstances were the reservations of his friend and mentor Jean Jaurès, whose sensibilities, which were "very bourgeois on this point," were shocked by the relaxed theories and tone of his young friend.[96]

Du mariage is nevertheless, in its way, a socialist book, that is, in Jaurès's manner, liberating, optimistic, aiming for the happiness of the greatest number through reasonable harmony. This is why, in this case more Jaurèsian than Jaurès, Blum decided to republish it thirty years later in 1937, while he was in power and had taken on all the responsibilities—moral as well as others—that power entails. He knew that this publication would bring him mountains of abuse; one has only to refer to back issues of *Gringoire*.[97] In a short preface he wrote simply: "This book, written thirty years ago, contains some important truths. The reader should be assured of the serious spirit in which it was conceived and written."

The Lawyer and Life

For nearly twenty-five years, from 1896 to 1919, the tall gentleman with his glasses glittering under his broad-brimmed hat crossed the Seine every morning, from the rue du Luxembourg and then from the boulevard du Montparnasse, to his office at the *Conseil d'Etat*, the noble building next to the Comédie Française at the Palais Royal. Thus there was a symbolic juncture of the places in which he carried on his professions of both theater critic and lawyer. Late in the afternoon, leaving the high-ceilinged, panelled chambers of the *Conseil*, *Monsieur le maître des requêtes* was a short walk from the theaters (except for the Odéon and the Vieux-Colombier) where he exercised the publicly known facet of his wisdom. Rarely have two such diverse careers been so harmoniously intertwined—in a sense, they fed each other.

But we have to qualify this judgment. The rise of the critic of *La Revue blanche* to the first rank had been astonishingly rapid. His progress as a public servant was more normal. "Second class" *auditeur* in 1896, "first class" *auditeur* in 1900, *maître des requêtes* in 1907, government commissioner in 1910—he left the *Conseil* when he was elected as a deputy from Paris in 1919—Blum's legal career was successful but not exceptional. Neither Blum's Jewish origins nor the very visible forms taken by his political commitment contributed in any way to slowing his advancement. His legal career merely developed at the conservative pace set by the administration.

That Blum was remembered at the *Conseil d'Etat* as a remarkable professional, armed with solid knowledge, bold in his hypotheses but serene in his decisions can be evidenced in the praise of his younger colleague Pierre Juvigny or in the favoring of his still classic "conclusions" in a certain Lemonnier affair by the editors of *Les Grands Arrêts de la jurisprudence administrative.*[98]

We should not be unconcerned with Blum's technical competence, even his fame, as a lawyer, because on various occasions it affected his positions or his treatment of some crisis. Someone less certain about the law and less capable of articulating it would have confronted adversaries differently than Blum, for example, did in 1924 and 1938. In 1936, a socialist head of government less impeccable as a lawyer could have experienced even greater difficulties. A former premier confronting the court of 1942 would have used other arguments and would perhaps have foundered had he not retained his legal mastery. For Blum the law was not simply an honorable and original means of livelihood, it was a central fact of his consciousness, his mental structure, and his public image. This was so much the case that it would not be ridiculous to say that, for this socialist, socialism was the application of the law—the fundamental law, of course.

Commentators on Blum's judicial work, which consists of a few dozen judgments of principle rendered between 1910 and 1919, all emphasize his constant concern to harmonize law and life, even if this meant challenging, by going beyond, the current state of the law. At the same time that *Du Mariage* raised psychological and sociological questions about the validity of the institution of marriage and dared to propose a new theory of marriage, Blum the lawyer was conducting a reexamination of the relationships between the individual and the state. Uncompromising on the rights and freedoms of individuals, he was also enormously eager to provide new responsibilities, activities, and perspectives for collective groups. Thus in dealing with the Armentières strikes in 1910 and the Cotton Affair in 1912, he opened up the barely explored territory of social law, the representative character of unions, and their relations with the government. Again, in the case of two priests, he presented the passionately debated question (particularly important for his friend Jaurès) of the relationship between Church and State in a new light.

"Even in contentious and apparently technical affairs one can perceive Léon Blum's deepest inclinations. The primacy of the *general interest* is always present in his conclusions," writes Pierre Juvigny.[99] We should recognize that the nonspecialist reading these texts today is particularly struck by the concern for the defense of the rights of the citizen against the excesses of governmental power. We can in fact notice in this Blum's "deep tendencies"; for him, the progress of collective responsibility and initiative could not be achieved at the expense of the individual.

In order to illustrate these attitudes briefly, we will quote a few excerpts from Blum's judgments in three cases: the *Compagnie générale des tramways* (1910); the municipality of Mesle-sur-Sarthe (1911); and the Lemonniers (1918).

The trolley passengers in Marseille asked for an increase in service. The holder of the franchise refused, arguing on the basis of the stipulations of a contract more than fifty years old. Government commissioner Blum decided clearly in favor of the interests of the community of Marseille and against the inviolability of the contract:

> The needs which a public service must satisfy, and consequently the requirements of its operation do not have an invariable character. Franchise contracts are necessarily entered into for extended periods of time. However judicious the conditions of the original contract may have been, they may be and almost always are superseded or contradicted by events occurring over that long period of years. And since the essential obligation of the franchise holder is above all to assure sufficient operation of the service in question, it follows that the initial charges may grow with the needs of the service. . . .
>
> A franchise represents a delegation of authority, that is, it constitutes an *indirect form of management;* it is not equivalent to abandonment or renunciation. The State remains the guarantor of the performance of the service for the citizenry as a whole. The State will therefore necessarily intervene, if the case arises, to impose on the franchise holder greater expenditures than those that were strictly foreseen, in order to stretch one of the terms of the financial equation, which every contract is in a sense, using not the powers granted to it by the contract, but the power that belongs to it as the public authority.

This decision by the young *maître des requêtes* made Blum, as Pierre Juvigny points out, a precursor of the famous "theory of the unforeseen" from which his colleague Chardonnet and Professor Gaston Jèze created, six years later, a new element of administrative law in the "Bordeaux gas" case. By challenging the idea of the inviolability of contracts, which was the basis of the entire market economy, Blum did not claim to threaten the foundations of the capitalist temple. Emile Durkheim, who was, as we have seen, one of the sources of French socialism, had contributed to this challenge as early as 1893, in *De la division du travail social*.[100] But to establish a legal foundation for the sociologist's critique was to initiate a revolution.

A second decision provides a clearer definition of Blum's juridical ideas. The municipality of Mesle-sur-Sarthe in association with a private citizen owned and operated an electrical factory for which it refused to pay the licence fee, arguing that since the activity provided it with no profit, it was not commercial. Was it a "public" or "non-public" municipal service? If this distinction were accepted and the first alternative chosen, the municipality could have its request for exemption accepted. But Blum decided differently; what was important as far as he was concerned was the expansion of the activities of collective bodies, thereby avoiding fiscal exemptions which would provoke the opposition of all private commerce and industry to municipalization and the various other forms of collectivization. Hence this significant decision:

> We do not think that one can distinguish between public municipal services and non-public municipal services. We believe one can distinguish only between obligatory and optional municipal services, and in our opinion only the first should be granted exemption from the licence fee. . . . Every time a municipality's activity takes the form of actions which come under the authority of fiscal laws and charges, we believe that the municipality must be subject to them, however general the interests to which those actions correspond may be. We are convinced that a solution of this kind is in conformity with the true interests of municipalities, and that, far from impeding the extension of municipal services, it would on the contrary help to develop something which, as far as we are concerned, seems infinitely desirable, that is, the gradual municipalization of the greatest possible number of services in the public interest.
>
> In this sense, it is in the interests of municipalities that, once the distinction on which your jurisprudence has been based until now is abolished, it will become infinitely more difficult to distinguish, among the various municipal enterprises, those which the general principles of the law authorize and those the law intended to prohibit. The notion of lawful municipal activities will become broader by the very fact of being less precisely defined. It will no longer be possible to rely upon fiscal distinctions to restrain the spirit of enterprise and initiative in the municipalities.[101]

Should we see this as the expression of a veritable "municipal socialism," as Pierre Juvigny suggests? In a period when great trusts like the Mercier group[102] dominated most public service franchises, a decision of this kind in any case opened new perspectives. "Gradual municipalization" and the "development of initiative in the municipalities," were not socialism in action, but they did challenge a kind of development based on the economic and political omnipotence of private business.

A third component of Blum's juridical practice was his defense of the rights of citizens against the authorities. In 1910, M. and Mme. Lemonnier visited the town of Roquecourbe, near Castres, on the day of the local festival. As they were walking along the banks of the Agout, a bullet from a nearby shooting gallery—whose dangerous character had already been pointed out to the mayor—very seriously wounded Mme. Lemmonnier; she remained disabled. The Lemonniers therefore appealed against the town and the mayor, and Blum sustained their appeal, accompanying his decision with striking comments:

> For more than a century we have been a people subject to ad-
> ministration. But it is still necessary that the citizen, if the case
> arises, be able to obtain reparation, equitable compensation when
> his rights have been violated by the fault of the Administration. . . .
> This requirement becomes more and more pressing as the demo-
> cratic spirit, or simply the spirit of justice, further permeates the
> body of our laws. . . . Jurisprudence left the citizen completely
> unarmed in this respect. A juridical evolution which is to your
> credit [is leading] to the recognition of responsibility in principle
> not only on the part of the State, but on the part of all administra-
> tive bodies, for wrongs committed by public bodies.[103]

These cases outline a juridical stance which was already entirely
Blum's: development of community initiative and corresponding responsibilities; growth of the arbitrating power of the State and its interpretation of the "general interest"; respect for individuals and
uncompromising defense of the citizen against any "abuse of power,"
personalized or not. We can add a fourth element: a very clear
awareness of the evolutionary nature of the law as a product of social
life, and the necessity of maintaining, by means of jurisprudence, harmony between law and fact. This was the goal Blum sought as a companion of Jaurès, a socialist intellectual, and a literary and dramatic
critic. Was it because the law was more embedded in socio-economic
life than the fiction or theater of the time?

Did he ever believe, according to Joseph Caillaux's formulation, that
"the *Conseil d'Etat* will make the socialist revolution"? Probably not;
he knew its composition and social base too well. But Blum saw the
revolution as the fruit of a long process of maturation followed, or
interrupted, by sudden mutations, and the slow work of jurisprudence
could and even should serve as preparation for the profound socio-
economic changes he desired.

Law, as practice or as theory, never lost its hold on him. Although
he left the *Conseil d'Etat* after his election to the Chamber in 1919, he
joined the bar in Paris in 1921 and argued cases for several years in the
civil court. Pierre Juvigny has told how, after his return from imprisonment in 1945, from his retirement in Jouy-en-Josas, Blum

> continued to inspire, simply on the basis of his moral force, his
> culture, his legal knowledge, and the influence all this produced,
> the best side of the actions of the current leaders of government.
> When, as a member of the Minister of Labor's cabinet in 1948, I
> had prepared a draft law leading to the complete restoration of
> collective agreements, Léon Blum did me the honor of going over
> it with a fine-tooth comb. The conversation lasted for more than an
> hour. He had at his fingertips all the jurisprudence of the Superior
> Court of Arbitration (1938–39), all the legislative and regulatory
> texts promulgated in the area of social and professional relations.
> The young *auditeur* I was then, thinking myself very competent in
> matters of social law, felt infinitely humble.

It remained for the brilliant interpreter of the law to become a legislator himself; only then would the collectivist coloration of his mind truly ripen into socialist practice.

In Defense of M. Beyle

Blum was forty. His son Robert was ten, and the education of the intelligent, attentive, and delicate child took up a good deal of his time. As his duties as government commissioner and *maître des requêtes* at the *Conseil d'Etat* proliferated, he published less and less. He soon gave up his articles in *Comoedia* and *Excelsior;* the only continuing evidence of his literary activities were the short pieces in *Le Matin* signed Guy Launay.

His large study at 126, boulevard du Montparnasse had become a gathering-place where Tristan Bernard met Jaurès and Lucien Herr rubbed elbows with Porto-Riche. And, in a café on the rue de l'Ouest, the militants of the fourteenth section of the socialist party sometimes heard, between two speeches by the stormy Bracke, the delicate voice of the elegant "citizen Blum." At the Toulouse congress in 1908, he had seen the triumph of Jaurès's unifying and parliamentary strategy. The unchallenged ascendancy held from then on by his friend over the party he had helped to unify was a factor in removing him from active participation. From the moment that efficacy and justice were assured of victory, what good would it do him to take on responsibilities in the party? It can be said that, around 1912, Blum was looked upon as a notable figure of the intelligentsia of the left whose responsibilities as a lawyer kept him apart, if not from literature, at least from the social struggle.

It would take extraordinary events to propel him again into the midst of the struggle. But, for this very reason, literary creation became more necessary to him. The author of the *Nouvelles Conversations* could not possibly be content with the role of hurried journalist. A work was waiting for him, a work he had to write. He had realized that he lacked a powerful novelistic, poetic, or dramatic imagination. But he also knew the kind of essayist he could become, and that he ought to put his admirable intelligence and his sensitivity to work on one of the great creators. Of the authors he loved, he chose Stendhal. Why?

We know that, unlike his friend Gide, he venerated Hugo, and that he had a particular fondness for *Les Misérables,* "that sublime book, the masterpiece of French prose of the last century, which enriched my childhood. I cherish with all my heart those beautiful young men who died on the republican barricades singing songs of love." At a time when literature and the intellectual climate were so strongly marked by the monarchist and nationalist intelligentsia, from Daudet to the new Péguy, pleading for what Hugo represented in French sensibility was not a sign of modest ambition.

We also know that, anticipating present-day criticism, Blum considered *L'Education sentimentale* the masterpiece of the novel in the nineteenth century, until *War and Peace* in any case. And his admiration for Balzac was second to none: we have seen how enthusiatically he referred to *Physiologie du mariage* in *Du mariage*. During the conference on *Léon Blum et la culture* (March 1975), Robert Blum pointed out that when his father started searching for a subject around 1912, he thought at first of writing on Balzac. But, he explained, the excessively "reactionary" character of the author of *Une ténébreuse affaire* held him back. Thus he chose Stendhal, to whom he was tied by more hidden and profound affinities.

For Blum, forty, a friend of Jaurès, advocate of an aesthetic which today would be called "progressive," the devotion of his first substantial literary essay to Henri Beyle, known as Stendhal, instead of the legitimist Balzac pointed to something beyond an ardent and mysterious intellectual complicity. Two clues can be found in the book itself.

"Stendhal is the man of confused moments, of social mixtures, of disordered periods . . . when through the natural development of history, social classes are muddled on the surface and dispersed at their foundations." In the author of *Le Rouge et le noir,* Blum the essayist could look for a witness to the conflict-laden history that had given birth to the doctrines and debates of the twentieth century, which everyone felt to be charged with the promise of astonishing upheavals. In a man shaped by the Revolution, the Consulate, and the Empire, he was free to discover a precursor of the struggles of nationalities and classes in his own century.

But his purpose was more precise, as this second quotation indicates: "Until very recently, literary nationalism tried to claim possession of this writer who treated his compatriots approximately as Nietzsche treated his and who, more often than not, following M. Suarès's expression, was a European against France." In fact, a year earlier there had appeared the famous *Enquête d'Agathon* on French youth. The pseudonym concealed two authors, Henri Massis and Guillaume de Tarde who, by publishing the results of an investigation that made it appear that young Frenchmen were above all thirsting after action, order, and religious faith, tended to demonstrate that the youth of the country wished only for "revenge" against Germany. And the investigation emphasized the role of Stendhal as a "professor of energy," to use Barrès's expression.

Blum wished to fight against this co-optation of his beloved Stendhal by the nationalistic right, from Paul Jacquinet (a professor at the Ecole

Normale who had been the first to "rediscover" him, in 1851, and had communicated his passion to Taine; later Jacquinet became the leader of the extreme right faction in the Ecole) to Barrès and Bourget. But before presenting the argument with which Blum opposed "Agathon," Barrès, and Bourget we should indicate the circumstances surrounding the publication of Blum's most successful essay in aesthetics.

Stendhal et le Beylisme first appeared in *La Revue de Paris* from February to May 1914, and was later published by Ollendorff in July. In the preface to the second edition, published in 1930, Blum evokes the strange birth of his book:

> I remember that the day it was put on sale was the day the Caillaux trial began.[104] Two weeks later came mobilization and then war. If books have a fate, it is clear that this one was not born under favorable auspices. The publisher was prepared to "launch" it as books were launched at the time, with favorable comments from writers. Henry Bataille, René Boylesve, and Robert de Flers, to mention only those who have died, had promised prominent articles ("premiers-Paris") in the leading newspapers. I need not say that none of the promised articles had the time to appear.

Blum notes a few favorable pages by Faguet and the "sober praise" of Paul Souday. But it is not too much to say that *Stendhal* was a victim of the war. When he republished it in 1930 and again in 1947, Blum confessed that with this book he seemed to be "exhuming the posthumous work of a dead brother."

Blum did not want to produce a work of erudition, or to multiply the biographical details that so enchant the faithful members of the Stendhal Club and constitute the richness of studies like Martineau's and Del Litto's. Blum defined his aim as follows:

> The only aim I proposed for myself was to study a literary case using the techniques of a novelist studying a living character, to penetrate to the systems of feelings and ideas which shape the particular characteristics of the model and which may reveal its secret, as a formula reveals the secret of a perfume, and then, holding the key to a work which resembles no other, to search for the laws of a destiny which was equally remarkable.

Blum thereby placed himself in the tradition of Sainte-Beuve. But what distinguished him from the author of the *Lundis* is the fact that his enterprise was inspired by sympathy and even tenderness. For him, there was no access to "Beylism" except through the heart, and Stendhal's reputation, created by Taine (who had presented him as "the greatest psychologist of modern times and perhaps of all time"), had something artificial and overblown about it. Finally, if we had to summarize the argument around which the book's five chapters are organized ("Stendhal's Character," "Stendhal and his Characters," "Theoretical Outline of Beylism," "Stendhal and Romanticism," "Sketch for a History of Beylism"), it would be that this work, entirely shaped at the end of adolescence, at the moment when he was invaded by all the impressions out of which he made his books, was above all a hymn of praise to sensitivity, to youthful feelings, and to happiness, a happiness founded on passion and "in which action plays no role."

For him, the characters of Stendhal and those of Balzac have nothing in common. "Stendhal advocates energy, but energy in *feeling* rather than in action, and action itself is energetic to his mind only when it is *disinterested,* when it expresses, without any hope of recompense, a full emotion or a strong passion. . . . A lover is more energetic in his eyes than a soldier, and the idea he created for himself of Italian passions has more to do with his theory than do Napoleonic memories."

Lucien Leuwen is pitiful as an ambitious man, repelled by petitions, intrigues, and accommodations. His only ambition is directed toward love; that is the great, the only affair in his life. If Julien finally understands that he has wasted his life, this is because he discovers that the love of Mme. de Rênal was for him the supreme happiness. In a paper he presented on the conference on Blum and culture in March 1975, Roger Pagosse noted the penetration and originality with which Blum brought out "the moral system implicit in the Stendhalian *pursuit of happiness:* you have to know yourself, determine your sensitive points and your weaknesses in order to cure them, and that presupposes an independent mind and a vigorous will." But this will is not a will to power.

In fact, explains Blum, "the only energy he ever advocated was the energy of the heart, and in his eyes, action had the inexpiable fault of diverting us from art or from love. The land he chose to explore was the Italy of 1820, an Italy without political life, without an army, without social distinctions, but [of] museums, theaters, musicians, and poets who seemed to him the finest in the world, of women who were not afraid to love, where the only possible ambition was to be a seducer or an artist, where everything spoke of passion and nothing distracted from passion."[105]

Did Blum center his argument around *La Chartreuse de Parme,* which obviously lends itself better than any other of Stendhal's works to the support of his thesis? No. He was bold enough to base his argument mainly on *Le Rouge et le noir* and on the character of Julien Sorel. A "beast of prey" as all interpreters of Stendhal, except Zola, had maintained? For Blum, Julien is

> only a wild child turned in on himself . . . who has constructed a
> dream of happiness out of a few sentences in books, too sensitive,
> too completely possessed by the idea of happiness not to be a

preordained victim. The perennial charm of this figure, his original truth, his poetry come precisely from the fact that the writer seized him at the moment when all the credulity and all the demands of youth still survive, when contempt for men expresses more inexperience than cynicism, when calculation and intrigue only disguise the delicate tenderness of the heart, when even malice is passionate, at the moment when the aspirations born from the earliest sense of oneself and the first hostile contact with the world are still permeated with the fresh naïveté of youth, with its disinterested ardor, with its enthusiasm in the face of grandeur and beauty."[106]

This goes rather far. Not that we wish to challenge this seductive interpretation of Julien Sorel, or that of another of Stendhal's characters in whom "political calculation is only a disguise for the delicate tenderness of his heart." But what does seem excessive is the systematic glossing over of the political dimension of the work. It has been pointed out that Blum considered his model a privileged witness for troubled times, for periods of class struggle. But, having noted this fact, he seems determined to discover nothing of Beyle's early experience—so profoundly marked by the troubles of the last years of the eighteenth century that haunted his adolescence and from which all his work springs—in the characters and plots of his novels. This is understandable for *La Chartreuse* which, as he brilliantly demonstrates, owes hardly anything to the conditions of the time and place, and borrows its structure, plot turns, and atmosphere from the Italian courts of the Renaissance. But what of *Le Rouge et le Noir* and *Lucien Leuwen?* Is there such a slight link between these books and the political history of the Restoration and the July Monarchy? He goes so far as to consider Julien's final polemical harangue to the Besançon jury negligible.

Although he perceives the revolutionary dimension of Stendhal's characters very clearly, Blum seems to refuse to discover this dimension in the aesthetic structure of the work, whose autobiographical character he nevertheless recognizes. For him, the conclusion is clear: "Stendhal does not teach public activity." This is indeed true. But does he reflect it so little? This probably unconscious evasion has already been explained. Léon Blum is thinking only of tearing from Stendhal the mask of pre-Nietzschean superman that a school of interpreters has imposed on him for the last half century. His entire effort tends to adorn Beyle with the "gentle and tender" characteristics which were for so long, and so erroneously, attributed to Racine.

Was this a minor argument, the argument of an aesthete or of a fanatic? Not at all. What strikes us above all in this passionate and often masterful plea for a Stendhal stripped of his strong man's robes, restored to his youthful vocations and to the outbursts of his passion, is that it is first of all a confession by Blum himself. It has been said, wrongly, that Blum's *Stendhal* is autobiographical. But nothing bears less resemblance to Beyle's bitter childhood than the happy and settled childhood of Blum. The interpretation he gives of the life and the work is not so much an act of memory as a confession. *Stendhal* was both a new stage in the search for happiness and Blum's moving farewell to this youth.

July 31, 1914

"In every respect—in terms of his profession, his social status, and his love affairs—his life seemed stable and organized."[107] What he wrote about the Henri Beyle of 1810–11 could be said of himself a century later, with the difference that his ties to various groups—family, friends, and ideological, national, or international associations—were substantially more vital than those the mature Stendhal maintained with the society of the late Empire.

A photograph of the time shows Blum beneath an immense Vuillard canvas; he is leaning with studied nonchalance against a shelf in his handsome library, and wearing a soft lounging jacket and very light slippers, with his head thrown slightly back. He was then at the height of what could be called the arc of his *embourgeoisement*. A highly ranked lawyer, a famous drama critic, the author of a book which, from the moment of its impending publication, would place him in the first rank of the essayists of the time, the friend of everybody who counted in the republic of arts and letters—and of almost everybody in the Republic itself—he was also a happy man.

Although the recent death of his mother, who had sunk into a strange apathy in her last several years, had deeply affected him, he strove for happiness. The literature and the art which he loved and defended were attaining success: Marcel Proust had just published *Du côté de chez Swann* and André Gide *Les Caves du Vatican;* his friends Vuillard and Bonnard were recognized outside the circle of *La Revue blanche;* Ravel's *Ma mère l'oye* and Stravinsky's *Le Sacre du printemps* were performed. The Republic that he had seen threatened until the final days of the Dreyfus Affair continued to consolidate its bases and seemed to have become indestructible. Even the conservative aspects of the secularist fervor of the Radical Republic at the beginning of the century seemed to have been challenged. After the success of the parties of the left in the legislative elections of April and May 1914, the "republican-socialist" René Viviani, a former comrade of Jaurès who had remained his friend, became head of the government and put through an income tax law, an old objective of the left, in July.

Since the Toulouse congress in 1908, Jaurès had been unanimously recognized as the head of the socialist movement in France. Although most of his positions were frequently challenged by leftists in favor of "social war" and the CGT, his influence ranged far beyond the borders of the country. During the Balkan conflict of 1912, on the occasion of the Basel congress in particular, he appeared as the leader of an international peace.

But he was also the man who, in 1911, had published *L'Arméee nouvelle* to answer his own question: "How can we increase, to the greatest extent, the chances for peace in France and in the unsettled world around it? And if it is attacked, in spite of its efforts and its desire for peace, how can we increase, to the greatest extent, the chances for safety and the means of victory?" Blum remained very close to Jaurès, seeing him often in his apartment on boulevard du Montparnasse, and preparing for him files, figures, and arguments.

The success of the parties of the left on May 10, 1914—the socialists won 103 seats, thirty more than in the previous assembly, and 1,400,000 votes—seemed to open the way for a government in which Jaurès would take on high responsibilites. But the socialist leader gave absolute priority to the unity of the workers' movement in which the conciliatory influence of the new confederal secretary of the CGT, Léon Jouhaux, was undermined by prestigious militants like Merrheim, Bourderon, and Mouatte, who were opposed to participation in government.

Furthermore, Jaurès was not willing to assume the responsibilities of power alongside Radical leaders like Messiny, who had voted for a law increasing military service to three years—a law Jaurès had fought with all his might. Nor was he willing to do so until there arose some initial challenge to a system which practically excluded workers and peasants from economic growth; women and young men in those classes often had to be satisfied with a salary of one franc a day,[108] and almost everyone was trapped in housing no different from that described by Zola.

Who could identify the chief preoccupations of Léon Blum, this forty-two-year-old epicurean at the beginning of the summer of 1914? Was it the confident excitement preceding the publication of *Stendhal?* Was it the joy of having seen his socialist friends triumph in the legislative elections in the spring? Was it the anxiety created around Jaurès by the violence of the campaign conducted against him by the leaders of revanchist nationalism?

One June 28, Archduke Ferdinand of Austria and his wife were assassinated in Sarajevo by a student connected with the Serbian secret service. No one, not even Jaurès, saw in it initially more danger than in one of those Balkan crises that excited Europe every year. The investigation of the murder of Gaston Calmette, director of *Le Figaro,* by the wife of Joseph Caillaux, Minister of Finance, diverted both the public's attention and the attention of the political elite. But the tone of the Austrian notes to Serbia and of the warnings of the Czarist government to the Central Powers became so heated that Jaurès called a special congress of the SFIO in Paris, July 14–16. In order to impede the escalation of threats crossing from Vienna to Belgrade and from Saint-Petersburg to Berlin, the French socialists came out in favor of the general strike proposed by Edouard Vaillant in case of war. But that strike, explained Jaurès would have to be *"simultaneously* and *internationally* organized."

Did Léon Blum, who had not participated in the congress, approve the strategy whole-heartedly? Like Lucien Herr, he was affected by the argument of Jules Guesde, who maintained that it meant "the risk of surrendering the most socialist country to the least socialist country."[109] But Herr and Blum both had so much faith in Jaurès, and the militarists' campaign against him became so vile and criminal, that they could not fail to feel complete solidarity with his actions.

A few examples of this campaign against the deputy from Carmaux will aid our understanding of the event of July 31. Hatred was not the only motive; there was also greed. The violence of the insults and the precision of the threats were not always proportional to the funds contributed by the Russian Ambassador Iswolsky—*L'Action française* received less than *Le Journal des débats, Le Temps,* or *Le Matin.* But the calls for murder arose especially from that soil "watered" by Russian manna.

In *Le Matin* on July 16, Urbain Gohier, a former socialist, wrote: "If there is a leader in France who is a man, M. Jaurès will be put against the wall simultaneously with the mobilization posters." In *Paris-Midi* on July 17, Maurice de Waleffe went further: "The general who ordered a firing squad to provide citizen Jaurès with the weight his brain lacks would only be doing his duty. And I would help him!" On July 23, after a series of articles by Daudet screaming for death, Maurras in turn wrote in *L'Action française:* "We would not wish to persuade anyone to commit political assassination, but M. Jaurès should be trembling with fear!"[110]

Finally, and most horribly, because the words were written by a man of genius who in other ways was worthy of respect, Charles Péguy demanded for his former friend Jaurès "a tumbril and drumroll until the guillotine delivers us from him!"

From July 23 on, the date of the Austrian ultimatum to Serbia calling upon it to accept humiliation and vassalization, conflict between the two systems of alliances—Austria-Hungary and Germany on one side; Serbia, Russia, France, and England on the other—increased.

Poincaré and Viviani, respectively chief of State and leader of the government in France, left for Saint-Petersburg to strengthen their ties with the Czarist Empire in exchange for some prudent counsel. On July 28, Vienna declared war on Serbia.

Jaurès succeeded in arranging in Brussels an emergency meeting of the committee of the Socialist International, in anticipation of the congress which had been scheduled for August 9 in Vienna and would have to meet in Paris. On July 29, at the moment his friend was preparing to leave for Belgium, Blum rushed to *L'Humanité*. Suitcase in hand, Jaurès asked him to accompany him to the Gare du Nord where he was to meet their comrades Guesde, Sembat, Vaillant, Rappoport, and Longuet, who were going to Brussels with him. It was then, in the uproar of a railway platform, that Jaurès and Blum parted, never to meet again.

The evening of July 29, in the Cirque Royal in Brussels, Jaurès's great voice hypnotized and summoned the immense crowd for the last time: "Attila's horse is still stumbling. It is up to us to use the opportunity to save the peace. The only treaty we know is the one that binds us to the human race! For the absolute rulers, the ground is mined; the revolution that has been unleashed will say to them: begone, and ask forgiveness of God and men!"[111] Before leaving Brussels, the leader of French socialism spoke urgently to his Belgian colleague Huysmans: "If war breaks out, preserve the International. If friends beg you to take sides in the conflict, do nothing of the kind; at all costs preserve the International!"[112]

But the prophet had not reduced the leader to inaction. As soon as he had returned to Paris, on the evening of July 30, Jaurès reached an agreement with Jouhaux for action against the war: a joint meeting was decided on for August 2. Then he wrote his editorial for *L'Humanité*, his last: "All chances for a peaceful arrangement are not lost. The greatest danger is not in events themselves, but in rising tension, in sudden impulses born of prolonged fear, uncertainty, and anxiety." Finally going down to the nearby café, "Le Coq d'or," he declared to his comrade Amédée Dunois: "This war is going to reawaken all the bestial passions. We must expect to be assassinated on street corners."

On July 31, 1914, Jaurès got up early. He received successive visits at home from Lucien Lévy-Bruhl, Charles Rappoport, and Pierre Renaudel. Then he called a meeting of the socialist group in the Chamber, and met with Minister of Interior Malvy. Resignation to the inevitable was already everywhere. He asked for an audience with his former comrade Viviani, the leader of the government, who could not receive him but sent in his place Secretary of State Abel Ferry, whose posthumous *Carnets* give an account of this famous conversation.

Jaurès, accompanied by Longuet, Renaudel, Cachin, Bracke, and Bedouce, spoke sharply to Jules Ferry's nephew: "You are the victims of Iswolsky and a Russian plot. We will denounce you, you light-headed ministers, even if we're shot for it!"

"What are you going . . . to do now?"

"Continue our campaign against the war!"

"You'll be shot on the street."

And as the dejected socialist delegation withdrew, Ferry took Bedouce by the arm and whispered to him: "It's all over." Jaurès heard and could not suppress a kind of tremor of physical suffering.

It was nearly eight in the evening. Back at *L'Humanité* Jaurès feverishly read the dispatches. He hoped especially for an initiative from London. He was also waiting for the arrival of Hermann Müller, delegate of the German social democrats, who was to report to his French comrades on the efforts undertaken in Germany to stop the war. But it was learned that the (revealing) congestion of the German railway network had delayed the messenger from Berlin for several hours. Then, before starting to compose his article which, according to several friends (Longuet, Rappoport, Renoult), was to be a new "J'accuse . . . !" Jaurès accepted an invitation to dinner with several friends—Renaudel, Longuet, Landrieu, the general secretary of the party Dubreuilh, Amédée Dunois, Daniel Renoult, and the deputy from Alsace, Georges Weill. They decided to go, as they often had, to the café du Croissant opposite the newspaper offices. It was the closest place and frequented almost entirely by journalists; they would be among friends. No one paid any attention to the pacing of a blond, weak-looking young man loitering in the area with a little pistol in his pocket. Jaurès seated between Renaudel and Landrieu ate with less appetite than usual. His back was to the window, which opened onto the street; it was very warm. At 9:30, Marius Viple rushed in from the nearby office: the British government had delayed until Monday the statement of its position. Now where could they place their hope? At 9:40 there were two shots: the first, almost point-blank, went straight through Jaurès's head. He sank softly on his right side, like a child going to sleep. It took him five hours to die.

When did Blum learn of the death of his friend? We do not know whether he was immediately informed by a witness, perhaps Renaudel or Longuet. We can find no trace of his presence in the hour following the attack and the arrest of the assassin, the mental defective Raoul Villain. Everything suggests that he went directly to Jaurès's home in the allée des Chalets, where the body was transported around midnight. When Barrès arrived before dawn to present to Jaurès's daughter Madeleine the letter which his admiration for his titanic adversary had compelled him to write, it was Blum who greeted him.[113] Barrès approached the man who had been his disciple twenty years earlier and said: "Your grief is also mine."[114]

Blum felt at first a void, of course, along with the most poignant sorrow. The morning of August 2, he went to see his friend and neighbor the diplomat Philippe Berthelot, from whom he knew he could obtain the most reliable information. Mobilization notices had been posted. Jaurès had died before seeing the collapse of his hopes. Blum's old friend from the Ecole Normale, Philippe's brother René Berthelot, whom he had not seen for years, was there: "The men embraced, overcome with grief. Blum was in a state of deep depression. Jaurès was dead and war had arrived. The two catastrophes were more than a man could bear."[115]

But at the meeting of Jaurès's friends organized the next day by Renaudel, Herr, and himself, Blum and his friend Louis Révelin persuaded the group not to try to secure exemplary punishment for the assassin.[116] They could refer to a hundred statements by Jaurès to justify this appeal for clemency. This was still the prevalent state of mind five years later at Villain's trial, in March 1919, and it lay behind the speeches for the defense by Duclos de la Haille and Paul-Boncour, and behind Blum's own deposition.[117]

To be sure, confronted with Jaurès's murderer (whom the jury acquitted, ordering Mme. Jaurès to pay costs!), Blum could not restrain himself from expressing a kind of astonished reproach: "There is something that would almost make one despair of everything, and that is that a man like Jaurès could have created hatred around himself." But he turned very quickly from resentment to tell the nationalistic instigators of the assassin what the man who was shot down on July 31, 1914 represented for the country, and he recalled that it was in speaking to Barrès that Jaurès, in one of his most justly famous expressions, had attempted to define socialism: "One is faithful to the tradition of the great workers of the past not by arbitrarily reversing the course of history, but by continuing their work; it is by flowing toward the sea that the river remains faithful to its source."

ORDEAL BY FIRE

The *Union Sacrée*

"**W**hat would he have done if he had been here among us? What would he have been during the war?" Léon Blum quickly raised this question, which continually haunted him, on July 31, 1917, in a lecture delivered at the Palais de Fêtes on the rue Saint-Martin on the third anniversary of Jaurès's death. He answered with an assurance which, coming from him, could not fail to be disconcerting:

> About his attitude in the beginning, the days following the assassination, there is no possible doubt. He hated war. All of his activity for the preceding fifteen years had been directed toward preventing it. . . . He would thus have carried out to the end the effort for peace. He would have needed to be completely sure that, on our side, everything that it was possible to do or to attempt to prevent universal catastrophe had really been done or attempted. Those who lived with him during the last days know how imperious, how troubling was this need of his conscience. But they also know that the need had been satisfied.
> Confronted with certainty, with the irreparable, he would not have doubted for a single instant that war had been unleashed by others, and that the German government was indeed a criminal government that had to be overthrown by war, from the moment that it was not overthrown by the revolutionary struggle of the German proletariat. . . . He would have done what we have all done. He would have cooperated in the national defense . . . and would have become its leader.

This is a strange presumption, hardly "Blumian," and it can be explained only by the violence of the conflicts then dividing the socialist movement, in the midst of which Blum and his friends needed to justify themselves. His description of what Jaurès's attitude would have been in August 1914 and afterward is possible, even probable, but it is not so certain. We have quoted Jaurès's violent remarks, a few hours before his death, on "light-headed ministers" and "Iswolsky's plot." Would he have been satisfied, as Blum asserts, with the few prudent warnings formulated at Petrograd by Poincaré[118], or with Viviani's gesture of withdrawing French troops ten kilometers from the border, as grounds for concluding that "the need [for peace] had been satisfied"? Another companion of Jaurès's final hours, Rappoport, made a different forecast and believed that the founder of *L'Humanité* would have carried his war on war much further. To begin with, wouldn't he have exploited better than Sembat, who saw him on August 1, the visit of the spokesman of the German social democrats, Hermann Müller? Wouldn't he, at least, have provided a powerful echo for Liebknecht's struggle in Berlin against imperial policy?

The adherence of socialists to the war effort was instantaneous and massive. As early as August 1, *La Bataille syndicaliste*, an organ of the CGT, had adopted the patriotic tone of the press as a whole. On the fourth, at Jaurès's funeral, while Viviani brought greetings from the government at war, Jouhaux launched a call to arms. On the same day, the socialist group in the Chamber voted unanimously for military appropriations. On the sixth, in the Salle Wagram, the socialist federation of the Seine applauded an ultra-nationalist speech by Edouard Vaillant (the man who had made the famous motion on July 14, 1914— three weeks earlier!—"insurrection rather than war"). Vaillant was "hailed as usual with the cry 'Vive la Commune!' but this time it was to show that the Commune was the patriotic reaction of the Parisian working class against the defeatists."[119]

They were all rivals in patriotic fervor, from Guesde to Sembat, from Cachin to Gustave Hervé—ex-champion of the most thundering antimilitarism. "The social-democratic brothers had become nothing but 'Boches,' and everybody was ready to deal with them with the bayonet, *à la francaise*."[120] *La Bataille syndicaliste* spoke of "race wars against the Germans with tainted blood," and, "realistically," launched an idea: "Let us use the war to seize markets from Germany: export!"

Dissonant voices, however, were soon heard in some sections of the union movement, notably in *La Vie ouvrière*, where Merrheim, Mouatte, Bourderon, and Rosmer (some of whom had been drafted, others of whom were freer to act) expressed the earliest warnings. By the end of 1914, the leader of the socialist federation of the Ain, René Nicod, and those of the Haute-Vienne, Adrien Pressemane and Paul

Faure, were warning the party against the draft and the madness, especially since they had learned that the German social democrats had resisted more firmly than the French party against the patriotic passions of August and that the socialists in the Reichstag had voted against military appropriations.

But when, at the end of August 1914, the leadership of the SFIO was offered participation in the government, it did not consider it worthwhile to debate before agreeing to designate Guesde (for a Ministry of State) and Marcel Sembat (for the Ministry of Public Works). Instead, it contented itself with asserting, in the "29 August manifesto," that once it was no longer a question "of ordinary participation in a bourgeois government . . . [but] of the future of the nation . . . the party did not hesitate."

Nor did Blum, apparently, when Sembat proposed that he become head of his cabinet office. Declared unfit for service because of myopia, and at forty-two no longer eligible for conscription, he still wished to "serve." Nothing was more standard than his invitation by a Minister to a member of the *Conseil d'Etat,* a body from which immediate subordinates of executive authorities were often recruited. As a socialist and a noted lawyer, Blum seemed natural for such a position, even though he was not an intimate of his new "patron."

Marcel Sembat was a lawyer, an aesthete particularly passionate about painting, and like Clemenceau, a friend of the great Impressionists. He had written some art criticism and had married Georgette Agutte, a sculptress of some talent. A former Blanquist, in 1905 he had become a Jaurèsian, although Jaurès did not like him. In 1911, when Caillaux headed the government, there was talk of Sembat's participation. "If Caillaux had offered me a portfolio," he proudly announced, "I would have kicked it away!" Jaurès, informed of the remark, laughingly said: "The scoundrel didn't say what he would do with his hands."[121]

Elegant, witty, very courageous, slightly skeptical, Sembat was nevertheless a man who could reach an understanding with Blum, flattered as he was to have a colleague who was both a famous critic and a highly reputable lawyer. Their work together, which lasted for more than two years—from August 1914 in the Viviani government to December 1916 when Briand, who had succeeded him, reorganized his cabinet and broke with his Minister of Public Works—seems to have been untroubled, at least in part because Sembat, who was rather nonchalant, relied on the strenuous work that Léon Blum would provide.

If the post accepted by Guesde—who had become if not the leader, at least the most prestigious figure in the party—was essentially symbolic, Sembat's post as Minister of Public Works, in contrast, was a principal element in the war machine. In spite of the efforts and the capacities of Blum, it is not certain that Sembat's ministerial management was adequate. It is possible that, when he reorganized his government in December 1916, Briand broke with his old comrade Sembat because the Minister had been violently criticized for several months, even by the socialists, for delays in the coal supply. Moreover, at the beginning of the painful winter of 1916, made gloomy by the great massacre at Verdun, someone had to be found "guilty."

The role of "chef de cabinet" is one of the peculiar features of the French political system. It is in part responsible for the combination of irresponsibility and sanctification of the ministerial function under which the public life of the country labors. Behind this figure, who is both screen and illusionist, scapegoat and public relations agent, the minister can put himself forward or retire into the background. Was this the case for the Sembat-Blum combination?

In this case, there can be no doubt of the exceptional role played by Blum. He had to overcome the mistrust that Marcel Sembat felt toward everyone around him except his wife,[122] and the mistrust with which the government treated the socialists—they were often deprived of information and therefore unable to participate in certain essential decisions. Blum was better able to recognize the injustice of this treatment than most; in the course of several missions to London, he noted that the ministers of the Labour Party were not held in suspicion by their colleagues in the cabinet of Saint James.

Nevertheless, "Léon Blum literally fascinated the leading public officials. His intelligence, his abilities as an organizer, and his legal knowledge allowed him to exercise his influence everywhere without the slightest difficulty, first of all over his boss himself,"[123] whom he ended up replacing in all matters concerned with internal debates in the party matters toward which Sembat expressed a detached and ironic judgment.

One of the rare documents of the time which provides evidence of the work Blum did for the Sembat cabinet was the draft of a law which it was the task of others to get through the legislature. Blum considered Louis Loucheur the official sponsor of this law, which was passed under Clemenceau's government and which changed the mining regulations of 1810 by increasing the rights of the State. Written by Blum in 1916 and very carefully annotated in his delicate and precise handwriting, this text[124] proposed an increase in state responsibility, and, in consequence, "the precariousness of franchises, profit sharing, and clauses providing for purchase by public authorities." The author was thus conducting himself as a consistent socialist.

The attempts he made to convert civilian factories to military purposes gave Blum the opportunity to increase his contacts with the most important industrialists of the time, and in doing so, to acquire a knowledge of economics and a sense of efficiency that was later to surprise his opponents in the Chamber and the other participants in the Matignon negotiations.

Independently of these contacts and the problems that they posed for him, what Blum learned in the twenty-seven months he spent at the head of Marcel Sembat's cabinet were not only the mechanisms of power, but also the destructive nature of participation in the government for a revolutionary party, the impotence of the socialist ministers, and the growing division of the party on the problem of participation. The leaders of the SFIO were also divided on the question of whether the party, by bringing down Ribot (Viviani's successor at the head of the government), could become the leaders of the ministerial coalition. This was the argument of the "right," Albert Thomas and Pierre Renaudel, against which Herr and Blum protested, denouncing these maneuvers as potential weakeners of the war effort.

A new debate opened in the party in November 1917, when Clemenceau, who had not been deterred by such scruples from his permanent pursuit of power, and who (with Sembat's help?[125]) had finally succeeded in bringing down Painlevé, was designated to form a new government and offered participation to the socialists. Herr and Blum were once again in agreement, this time that the SFIO should participate in the government, which represented for them nothing but national defense.

As *chef de cabinet* to one of the three socialist ministers (Albert Thomas joined Guesde and Sembat in the government on May 1915 as Secretary of State for Armaments), Blum was intimately involved in party debates, which went on throughout the war on two questions: the struggle for Jaurès's succession and the conflict between advocates (a majority until July 1918) and opponents (more and more numerous from 1917 on) of the *Union sacrée* for national defense. The second question was particularly prominent and appeared decisive, while the first was constantly present, but somehow muffled, latent; no one openly attempted to impose himself, to strengthen his advantages, to assert his pretentions, except Albert Thomas. This must be seen as one of the most peculiar historical phenomena of the time: Jaurès was gone, but no one declared his candidacy to succeed him, as though no one could dream of replacing him. But each one of them was involved in this undeclared struggle.

Immediately after Jaurès's assassination, French socialism should have been led by the man who had been his rival, double, and opposite, Jules Guesde. But the deputy from the Nord was old and sick. He accepted the ministry offered him by Viviani, but he did not attempt to impose personal ascendancey over Jaurès's orphans. We can note, however, that his influence in the party remained considerable through his supporters, who were the most prestigious men in the party:

Bracke, Cachin, Lafargue, Lebas, Pressemane, Rappoport, Paul Faure, Mistral. But this influence operated in various directions, for the first two were the most fervent advocates of adherence to the *Union sacrée* while the last four were among the most active opponents of this nationalistic policy, which was in fact directly inspired by the old leader.

With Guesde keeping himself aloof, like Vaillant (who was little more than a red Déroulède and who died in 1916), who could emerge as the head of the party? The Jaurèsists lacked prominent figures. Renaudel? Georges Pioch defined him in a cruel phrase: "He is Jaurès's feet." Albert Thomas? He had also been on the right of the party, and his "bitter end" policy during the war carried him to the fringes of the movement; early in 1918 some members called for his exclusion. Jean Longuet? Karl Marx's grandson, who was perhaps the only true Marxist in the party, had the disadvantage of having appeared too much a pacifist at the beginning of the war—he was one of the first, in the federation of the Seine, to oppose the *Union sacrée*—and not pacifist enough from early 1918 on. Moreover, this generous, learned, and wise man, who had founded *Le Populaire du soir* in 1917, had neither a taste for power nor the temperament of a leader. The party's conscience, yes, but not its leader.

Marcel Sembat? Had he wanted, he could have claimed the inheritance. He had the eloquence, the tact, and the talent—although his writings, and particularly "Faites un roi, sinon faites la paix!," a little pamphlet published in 1913, are rather disquieting—but he did not have the true will to lead. In the end he was a dilettante, an amateur; this is perhaps why he got on so well with Blum, who sometimes placed himself in the same category.

Blum, who was in no way *papabile,* who was a member of no important party body, who had a kind of halo created by his friendship with Jaurès, who maintained a discreetly marginal, "non-competitive" position, and who shared Jaurès's passion for unity, suddenly seemed likely to emerge as a possible candidate. He was only the *chef de cabinet* of one of the socialist ministers, but it happened that his office in the ministry on the boulevard Saint-Germain was, from 1914 to the end of 1916, a gathering place and a forum for debates. Thus he made his apparently technical office into a political forum in which he gradually established himself as an arbiter, a mediator.

Was all this without his seeking? There is at least one witness who maintains the opposite, who presents this period in Blum's life as a kind of permanent plot—his former comrade in the Librairie socialiste on the rue Cujas, Hubert Bourgin, who had become an absolute nationalist and who observed Blum without benevolence from his position on Albert Thomas's cabinet beginning in May 1915.

The few pages Bourgin devoted to Blum in *De Jaurès à Blum* formed the basis of the anti-Blum polemics that continued for the next thirty years. Bourgin talks of encountering Sembat's *chef de cabinet* in a corridor of the Chamber: "His eyes glittered prodigiously, throwing out Dantean flames, his face was pale and tense, and below his mustache his sensual lips seemed to be savoring some delectible prey. This living image of political passion, this symbolic figure, agitated and tormented, was terrifying, but he had a kind of restrained beauty. I seemed to be discovering a strange and superior being in whom were mingled messianic beliefs, a prophetic faith adapted to modern times, Asiatic frenzy, European, French, and Cartesian intelligence, and refined aestheticism. This apparition one winter evening in 1916 allowed me to understand Léon Blum."

It might almost be a pastiche. Blum terrifying, Blum Asiatic. Bourgin's passion—which was certainly "European, French and Cartesian"—was such that he went so far as to see a proof of messianic Machiavellianism in the fact that in 1915 "Blum was jubilant in telling [him] of Italy's entry into the war on the side of the allies," news at which he could not fail to rejoice in his dual role as patriot and as member of the SFIO (the SFIO had sent Marcel Cachin on a special mission to Mussolini, then a leader of the socialist party, to convince the Italian left to join the fight).

During this entire period when he was, along with Sembat, both a significant cog in the war machine, and a very influential adviser in the internal debates of the socialist party, Blum carried a great deal of weight. This was recognized by only a few careful observers, among them Lucien Herr, whose opinions were still very influential in the upper reaches of the movement, and who favored active participation in the national defense.

But, as early as summer 1915, the policy of "patriotism" began to provoke very serious opposition within the party, where Romain Rolland's cry of alarm in November 1914 had been heard. *Au-dessus de la mêlée* was well designed to sow some doubts in the minds and hearts of intellectuals and humanists who had been shaped by German culture like Herr and Blum. It is disconcerting, even disappointing, that this warm appeal did not have more impact on men like them. Had Jaurès been alive, it is hard to believe that he would not have responded to the warning.

Confronting Pacifism

The great challenge to the *Union sacrée* began in December 1914, when the CGT refused to participate in a conference organized by various neutral workers' movements in Copenhagen, and Pierre Monatte indicated his disapproval by resigning. On January 17, 1915, Jean Longuet dared to congratulate the participants in the Copenhagen conference in *L'Humanité,* but he added: "But let us not forget that German imperialism is the chief culprit!"

At the same time, the English socialists of the pacifist group led by Keir Hardie were denouncing "militarism and capitalist imperalism."

In France, the newspaper *La Vie ouvrière* under the influence of Monatte and Rosmer, the metal-workers' union led by Merrheim, the federations of Haute-Vienne (Pressemane), Ain (Nicod), and soon thereafter Isère (Mistral), intellectuals like Raymond Lefèvre and Marcel Martinet, a few socialist personalities like Daniel Renoult and Amédée Dunois, and then Jean Longuet, organized opposition. They were supported by Russian émigrés whose Paris newspaper *Nache Slovo* was directed by Martov and later by Leon Trotsky after he had been expelled from Zurich in 1916.

In March 1915, several of the best known leaders of German socialism—Rosa Luxemburg, Clara Zetkin, Ledebour, and Liebknecht—launched an appeal for peace. In France, they evoked a favorable response only in the organ of the metal-workers' federation, *L'Union des métaux,* which defied the censors by publishing a surprise edition on May 1, 1915. It was becoming more and more difficult in the SFIO to look only along the sight lines of machine guns.

On July 14 and 15, a year after the congress in which Jaurès had supported the motion "insurrection rather than war," the first National Council of the party was held in Paris. It adopted a resolution that called on the government to "bring forth, in the face of the horrors of war, the light that will lead the world to peace." But two months later, when the Swiss socialist Grimm and his Italian colleague Morgari invited the various parties of the International to Zimmerwald, near Bern, to talk of peace, Renaudel, in the name of the SFIO, refused to participate in a German social-democratic delegation. The organizers had hoped for his refusal.

Only two union representatives, Merrheim and Bourderon (supported in the party by Pressemane), went to Zimmerwald (September 5-8, 1915) where, under the influence of Lenin and Trotsky (who composed the document), a manifesto was published denouncing the *Union sacrée* and calling on "proletarians of all countries" to unite against imperialism. The report presented soon thereafter by Merrheim to the militants of the federation of the Seine led to broad approval for the Zimmerwald texts. Renaudel was booed. Longuet presented a balanced point of view. The unanimity of August 1914 was forgotten.

We have no documents revelatory of Blum's state of mind in the face of this evolution. Indeed, the very official position he occupied forced him to be reserved. None of his friends or comrades of the time have suggested that this scrupulous man had the slightest hesitation about continuing his activity in the war cabinet, where he worked until December 1916. On the basis of certain confidential statements Jean Longuet made to his close companions, it may be inferred that, for the "pacifists" in the party, Blum, like Sembat, remained one of the firmest supporters of social-patriotism. This was true even though, at a congress held in London in 1916, Blum's "boss" expressed very severe criticism of the allied czarist regime, which provoked shocked remonstrances from the Quai d'Orsay. It is legitimate to think that this philippic expressed a point of view shared by the two men: although they were entirely absorbed by their task, they could not forget that they were socialists, and the czarist government was, to say the least, an awkward ally.

In April 1916, the second wartime socialist conference, at Kienthal, did not provoke a much more favorable reaction among the leadership of the SFIO than had the Zimmerwald conference. But three deputies were present: Blanc, Brizon, and Raffin-Dulgens (the last two had shown their hostility to the Party's policy for a long time). On their return, they voted against military appropriations. From that point on, the change of direction accelerated. At the National Council in August 1916, the majority led by Renaudel and Thomas confronted an opposition consisting of more than a third of the militants. At that time there were established, one after the other, a "Committee for the defense of international socialism," a "Union Committee," and a "Committee for the resumption of international relations," which was later radicalized and became a "Committee for the Third International."

Jean Longuet, Pressemane, Paul Faure, and Mistral led the opposition, but without approving the positions taken at Kienthal, which were modeled on those of the Bolsheviks (to transform international war into civil war), and from which the three "pilgrims" of April dissociated themselves. At the end of December 1916, the SFIO congress concluded in a kind of statement between those who were just barely the "majority" and the "minority," who were already preparing to impose their militant pacifism on the whole party.

But as early as the beginning of 1917, this left was divided between a Longuet-Pressemane-Paul Faure faction and a more radical "Kienthal" group in which the school teacher Loriot and Louise Saumoneau were prominent, as were the first French Leninists, for instance André Ferrat. They came together to acclaim the anti-czarist revolution which broke out in Petrograd in March, and to approve sending a delegation to the international socialist conference to be held in Stockholm. But the Poincaré government refused to grant any visas for Sweden; it was imperative not to "undermine the morale of the army."

At the moment when the Leninist revolution of October 1917 was about to erupt, and when the SFIO was in the process of shifting from reformist nationalism to revolutionary pacifism—as witnessed by the rise in the party of men like Loriot, Verfeuil, Ferrat, and Guilbeaux—what was Blum's position?

He had left the ministerial cabinet in December 1916 and rejoined the *Conseil d'Etat*. But this was not in order to recover the security of the lawyer, nor was it a retreat into technicalities. He had been too involved in the life of the party, from his watchtower in the ministry, not to have seen and appreciated the magnitude of the movement that was taking shape. From the end of 1916 on, it was no longer a matter of a quite normal debate between majority and minority, but of a veritable ideological confrontation which carried with it the risk of a schism. The unity of the party was at stake from the moment the opposition was no longer made up of men like Longuet who were viscerally attached to the SFIO, but of men like Loriot animated above all by ferocious hostility to the massacre.

For a man like Blum, this risk of a schism was anathema. He threw himself into the struggle to revive the movement for unity, a movement that seemed to him to be the part of Jaurès's legacy that fell more to him than to anyone else. Three years later, at the Congress of Tours, he said that he became involved in the public life of the party on only two occasions, in 1905 to work for unity, and in 1917 to attempt to save it.

But before launching this crusade he proclaimed, with a kind of violence, the basis of his thought. After publishing an article in *L'Humanité* of April 8, 1917 in which he maintained that the future of the Republic was inseparable from the "victory of right," he seized the opportunity of the third anniversary of Jaurès's assassination to deliver a speech in the Salle des Fêtes on the rue Saint-Martin. Blum was not afraid to align himself with those who had learned from Jaurès that patriotism was compatible with internationalism. Blum evoked Jaurès's memory on July 31, 1917, while the first phase of the Russian Revolution had been under way for four months, after the "miracle offensive" of the new supreme commander, Nivelle, had failed amid rivers of blood, and while American troops were beginning to land:

> We decreed the *Union sacrée* . . . out of whch only Jaurès could . . . make an ardent, effective, and all-powerful force, free and active as fire. The spark was in him. He alone would have been able to establish and maintain permanent contact between the soul of the people and the leaders of the war. He alone would have been able to maintain the enthusiasm of the early days which has slowly subsided for lack of nourishment. He alone would have been able to show us—always present, always luminous—the true reasons, the just reasons for the war.

The just reasons for the war, the soul of the people and the leaders of the war—Blum was here thoroughly committing himself, and boldly calling on Jaurès for help. Where is the Blum of legend, sinuous and fragile? It was not as a tepid middle-of-the-road advocate that he entered the struggle; but it was as the inventor of an elusive socialist "center." For three long years he worked to bring together the divided army of Jaurès's heirs.

His activity in this direction took three forms: the struggle within party organizations, notably congresses and national councils; the parliamentary campaign which brought him to the Chamber in autumn 1919; and finally the writing of doctrinal works. By the end of 1920, Blum—the partial, crippled, and contested heir of Jaurès's enormous legacy, one of the leaders of a party which was only a minor remnant of the great socialist movement—had nevertheless become one of the essential men of postwar France.

For a Reform of the Government

Blum was incapable of keeping to himself the experience he had gained at the head of Marcel Sembat's cabinet. He had been carefully considering the course of public affairs in France for more than twenty-five years; he knew the political theater as well as he knew the theater itself. But in those two years, beside a minister who had given him free rein and had entrusted him with enormous responsibilities, he had learned a good deal more from the inside. Although he had given up the idea of replacing the dramatists whose work he criticized, he did not think he ought to be silent on matters concerning the national community. Thus, at the end of 1917, less than a year after he was obliged to leave the ministry, he published in *La Revue de Paris* "Lettres sur la réforme gouvernementale," which were collected and published as a book at the end of 1918 by Bernard Grasset.[126] The book was published anonymously, but its author was recognized even more quickly than he had been for *Conversations avec Eckermann*.

One model, two vices, and three ideas haunted the writer and inspired his essay. The model is British democracy, slightly retouched in the spirit of a passionately republican Montesquieu; the vices are party inconsistency and governmental instability; and the ideas are first, restoration and consolidation of the authority of the president of the Council of Ministers who, freed of any other ministerial responsibility, would be given a permanent staff of advisers and decision makers similar to the British "war cabinet"; second, a revitalization of the parliamentary mechanism, freed from the unwarranted rule of committees; and finally, the adoption by the government of the methods of work and management of industrial or commercial companies. (We should add the wish for electoral reform based on proportional representation, but the idea was formulated only in passing and not forcefully.)

Let us consider the third point, the most curious and unexpected (although we have already pointed out the extreme interest Blum took as *chef de cabinet* for the Ministry of Public Works in his discussions with the great managers of the time). There is this very significant passage:

> The leading idea which has guided me and ought to inspire them in turn is that the management of a modern nation does not present itself as a task apart, unique in its nature and essence, but on the contrary, the rules of action are the same everywhere, and a large country is not led by different methods than a large industry or a large commercial establishment. To specify the notion of governmental leadership—which was my particular object—I have multiplied suggestions and parallels taken from what are called, sometimes quite inaccurately, "industrial methods." One may perhaps proceed further on the same path and gradually define, on the basis of empirical observations, a kind of Taylorist method of government and administration. This path is the right one. If we do not immediately enter upon it, large industry will soon usurp government.

As though it had not done so already in 1917. And the argument provoked very strong reservations on the left. In an article in *La Lanterne* on January 11, 1918, Max Rivière denounced the danger constituted by the introduction not only of the methods, but of the realities of industrial power, into the heart of the governmental system. In saying this, was Blum's critic less innocent than the essayist himself?

What is striking, even astounding, in this intelligent essay—so modern in its tone and ideas that it was quite easily republished twenty years later without appearing at all dated—is the complete absence of even the slightest reference to socialism. While he was preparing to enter the great battles from which the SFIO would emerge torn and defeated, Blum spoke here with the voice of the most neutral, or at least detached, expert. And although he evoked the disorganization, irresolution, and weakness of the parties, he did not attempt to set apart the SFIO of which he was a member, nor even to save his sharpest barbs for it. He was holding himself outside, above the parties, his own included.

Deploring the absence of men with wide experience in matters of State, he writes of the Radical Party:

> It represented the current opinion of the country; it held the majority in both houses; it was in a position to assure its leadership

of the country for a long period of time. But its leaders failed to create and to renew around themselves a ministerial staff, and we have seen its authority decline from day to day, as its governmental capacity decreased. There is no doubt that the history of the radicals will be the history of the socialists tomorrow; whatever their electoral successes, their effective grasp on the course of events will finally depend on the potential ministers they have been able to recruit. This will be a great lesson for political parties, when we have any worthy of the name![127]

The most significant aspect of "governmental reform"—which the author understands in the strictest, most technical sense—is the call to strengthen the powers of the president of the Council of Ministers, according to a "centralist and autocratic conception" [sic] which is in no way "contrary to republican doctrine," even though Blum speaks of the heads of government of the Third Republic as "kings." All the words and images point in the same direction: whether he speaks of "rudder," "commander," or "leader," Blum is asking for a ruler.

Unlike those (like André Tardieu) who suggested the same thing in the following two decades, Blum was a true democrat who had remained an ardent parliamentarian, and, he was careful not to aim simply at strengthening the executive.

> . . . the dual role of a head of government becomes clearer, or rather the dual nature of his function, for at bottom it is a single function. Leader of the Executive, leader of the Legislature, he assures the harmonious and complementary operation of the two governmental organisms. Constantly bending ministerial work in the direction of the popular will formulated by Parliament, and parliamentary work in the direction of ministerial accomplishments, he directs each one as a function of the other, and like a drive shaft or a transmission belt, he maintains their reciprocal correlation. . . .
>
> It is incumbent on the President of the Council of Ministers, leader of Parliament as of the government, placed at the summit of the two powers, to assure their harmony through the community of ends and the permanent correspondence of their rhythms of movement. Classical philosophy posed an analogous problem when it attempted to explain the relations between the soul and the body. Given two substances of different nature, how could their exactly parallel operation be assured? My solution is the solution of Descartes's God: uninterrupted action on each of the two substances, permanent adjustment of the two clocks, continuous creation.

A strong government, organized parties (and better established as specific entities through proportional representation), and management and administration run according to the methods of modern industry. The Republic according to Blum certainly shows the effects of the period when it was constructed, the time of the war and the first days of the Clemenceau government[128]—in which, as we have seen, he would have liked the socialists to participate—dominated by the requirements of arms production and the provision of supplies. In short, what is troubling in the recipes proposed is not that they are hardly socialist, but that they seem to anticipate the wishes of a head of government, Clemenceau, who had grasped power with a kind of carnivorous and gluttonous greed, in order to "make war," he said, which meant for him to struggle against any other form of pursuit of national safety. What is troubling, then, is that the author of the "reform" could be seen, in the immediate situation, as a kind of Machiavelli rewriting *The Prince* for the use of the angry Caesar who intended to make power not only a machine for war, but the tool of permanent revenge. Joseph Caillaux, treated as a traitor for having evoked the possibility of a compromise peace, was the first to pay the price.

It is clear that this is not what Blum wanted and that his essay had higher and broader aims. But every work is written in particular circumstances, and there are times when praise of authority can only be received as praise of authoritarianism, and praise for efficiency as praise of cynicism. Would Tocqueville have published a pamphlet against anarchy on the eve of the "Trois Glorieuses"? Would Rosa Luxemburg have denounced the Meansheviks on the day of Martov's arrest?

There remain some very judicious criticisms of "technicity"—the word "technocracy" was not yet in use—in political matters: a prophetic satire of the cabinets of the Vichy regime and of "synarchy." The *Réforme* is a good work, useful in other times, and its author himself found inspiration in it twenty years later, at the moment when he confronted the longed-for storms of summer 1936.

The Center and Unity

Blum did not undergo the ordeal by fire physically. But the comfortable, one might even say cosy, intellectual who, after the battles of the "Affair" and of the congresses for socialist unity, had settled into a double life as a critic and lawyer was, from the moment of the death of Jaurès, pushed into perpetual competition.

There was Sembat's cabinet. There were the debates inside the party, and the articles for *L'Humanité* justifying the policy of national defense, or preparing an economic strategy of State intervention and price control, or calling attention to Wilson's "fourteen points." Blum had become a public man, a man in the fray. He was involved in all the debates of the country at war, in all the battles of the divided party. His first life, as an intellectual "in contact" with politics, was coming to an end. With the last months of the war, his second life began: as an intellectual "in" politics.

Within the socialist party the policy of the *Union sacrée* had been demolished. As early as the 1915 congress, Adrian Pressemane, referring to Belgian documents, had raised the question of the responsibilities for the outbreak of war. The direction was shifting. At the December 1916 congress, the majority gathered only 52 percent of the votes. In 1917, Jean Longuet and Paul Faure, who had just established *Le Populaire du Soir* (whose literary page was edited by Henri Barbusse, leader of a vigorously pacifist current of thought), challenged the orientation of the majority supported by Herr and Blum.

The Russian Revolution, the disastrous conclusion of Nivelle's offensive, the advances made by the court of Vienna to Briand in view of a separate peace, the social crisis which was brewing and overflowing frontiers (Abel Ferry wrote at the time in his *Carnets* that "peoples everywhere threaten to make peace against their governments"), even the resistance of some German socialists against the war—everything contributed to a reexamination of the resolutions made in August 1914.

Blum refused to undertake it. But he nevertheless did not resign himself to being imprisoned in the right-wing coterie which then led the party, under the iron hand of Renaudel, Thomas, and the secretary-general Dubreuilh. His great dream was already of a center which would reconcile the nationalist faction, oriented toward power and the direction of the war effort, and the pacifist faction, which was first led by Longuet, after Zimmerwald and Kienthal had radicalized it, and was later to be led by Loriot and Ferrat, supporters of Bolshevism and of real "defeatism" in the war. But Blum had allowed himself to be carried too far from the second group by his own patriotic fervor and by the weight of his friendships to be capable of playing the role of conciliator.

The first reexamination attempt was made at the party's national congress, held in Bordeaux from October 6 to 9, 1917, a month before the seizure of the Winter Palace by the Bolsheviks. In the center of the room, symbolically, was a small group—Sembat, Auriol, Sellier, Moutet, Lafont, Blum, and, with them for the last time, Marcel Cachin, who had been elected in Bordeaux. To do what? They had on their side only a few militants, notably those from the fourteenth section of the Seine. Charles Andler, a "social-patriot" if there was one, ridiculed them, saying they formed less a center than the "geometric point of every indecision."[129] Blum only spoke in passing from the rostrum, but he attempted to work out a compromise resolution, which fell flat. The majority had very little room to maneuver. It allowed itself to be affected by the conciliatory attempts of the Blum group, but the end result was a final resolution of extraordinary incoherence.

The press was not sparing with its sarcasms. Although *La Petite Gironde* of Bordeaux said it was relatively satisfied that "for the majority, the safety of the fatherland remains the supreme law" and that "above class feeling and working class internationalism opposed to national defense, it places the claim of France and its allies to be in the right," *Le Temps* was harsher, especially on what Blum represented and pursued:

> The Bordeaux congress was to the very end a demonstration of incoherence. It succeeded in saving the unity of the socialist party only in appearance. As long as it persists in the equivocation born from the desire to reconcile, at all costs, what are by definition mutually exclusive positions—national duty and the pretention of revolutionary internationalism to control the entire political life of the world—socialism will in fact misjudge the deep feelings of the peoples struggling for right and freedom, and will struggle impotently.

Things were clarified but not in the way Blum wished. As early as the session of the National Council, which met in July 1918 to prepare the October congress, the "minority" was victorious. On August 19, in *L'Humanité,* he again attempted to gain support for the idea of unity at any price. But Jaurès's paper was already escaping from the control of Renaudel and the right wing. Marcel Cachin was preparing to succeed him, and he carried off the *tour de force* of making people forget that he had been the most exalted herald of the *Union sacreé.* Frossard took the place of Dubreuilh as secretary-general. It was more and more difficult to practice "centrism." The left finally gained victory at the October congress, where Longuet appeared a moderate, amidst Verfeuil, Loriot, Bourderon, and Louise Saumoneau. And when Blum proposed at the close of the congress to replace the vote "by tendency" with a "resolution of synthesis," he was laughed down. He was forced to take note of the weakness of the cohort that followed him (7 percent of the votes) and the rather narrow victory of the pacifists of the left and the extreme left.

However, he was not disarmed. Indeed, it is perhaps from those months of his apparent political defeat that his vocation to exercise essential responsibilities can be dated. If he did not give up then, if he stubbornly struggled against the faction which had become the majority, if he still attempted to win support for his ideas of compromise though he felt that he had been abused, that the determined opponents of the war were largely right, that the propaganda for "national defense" was surrounded by lies and deceptive silences—it was because there had arisen in him a vocation to act, to direct, to exercise a form of power.

When the opportunity to impose himself arose, he seized it with a keenness that stupefied all those who knew him as the acute, clever adviser, the discreet partner. In January 1919, a commission was set up in the party to formulate a program. After all, the war was over. The question of national defense, over which the party had split and which had reversed the majority, was outdated. The question of the Russian Revolution had already arisen, and it would provoke the great schism. But in the meanwhile, what was to be done? Divided, weakened by the war and by the nationalistic fervor which continued for a while to stir up the majority of former soldiers, the party was seeking the path of recovery on the eve of the legislative elections that were to redraw the face of the nation in November 1919.

Strangely enough, while the German party had moved from the Gotha program to the Erfurt program,[130] the French party had no program, properly speaking, at all. It had lived from and in the inspiration of Jaurés until July 31, 1914. Since then, it had lost itself in controversies over the *Union sacrée* and participation in government. The commission chosen to fill this astonishing gap was made up of representatives of every tendency, from Renaudel and Thomas on the right to Bracke, Cachin, and Auriol in the center to Frossard, Dunois, and Longuet on the left. It chose Léon Blum as president and spokesman. Of course, he was elected as a lawyer and writer but also because he was, as a disciple of Jaurès, a conciliator. For Blum it was a stunning promotion.

To be a Socialist

On April 21, 1919, Blum mounted the podium of the special congress. Within an hour and a half he conquered it. Never since Jaurès had this confederation of opposites heard a speech that was so unifying, stirring, and positive. Redefining the concepts of "democracy," "revolution," and "dictatorship of the proletariat," in order to make them the headings of the SFIO's "program of action," Blum was once again a socialist of reason and passion, qualities which both he himself and others had perhaps forgotten because of the role he had played during the war. After recalling the depth of his attachment to militant socialism, he came to his conclusion, which is both a call for and a very astute and appealing redefinition of unity:

> In a party like ours, what does unity mean? We all believe that a different social system must replace the existing one and that justice demands it. We also believe, or have come to believe relatively recently, since this is the contribution of Marx and his friends to socialist doctrine, that this transformation is prepared by the internal development of capitalist society itself, perhaps not

with absolute fatality, but at least with a certain logical rigor. These are the two things we believe, and this twofold declaration of faith makes us socialists.

With the exception of these two points, do you not realize that everything is changing, variable, in perpetual motion, not only in our tactics, but in our doctrine? . . . The Party is continually changing and evolving, between two points, two fixed poles: one is the future society which we foresee, which we predict, which we wish to bring into being; the other is the present society, from whose womb we wish to draw that future society.

Well, comrades, if this is true, is it not a completely logical necessity that among us socialists there exists a constantly renewed variety of thoughts and tendencies, and within this constantly renewed variety of thoughts and tendencies, two essential currents? There is the current that leads certain men, according to the nature of their minds, their affinities, or their professional qualities, toward one of the poles, toward the present, the real world; a second current leads the others toward the second pole, toward the future ideal society. Comrades, this has always been true, and it is necessary that it be true. It is not a contradiction between the various tendencies in our party: it is a division of labor, nothing else.

You must realize that if some of us did not maintain this more precise and solid connection with the real world, socialism would be only a religious dogma, a philosophy. And if, on the other hand, some of us were not more persistently turned—like the Moslem toward his holy city—toward the future, the ideal, toward the mirage outlined by the anticipated shape of the future City, then our party would be nothing but a party of democratic reform, and no longer what it is: socialism. These two currents are necessary, so necessary that I would go so far as to say that I would personally consider it a great misfortune if our Kienthalian comrades[131] were to leave us tomorrow. Why? Because, to my way of thinking, they represent in a particularly precise way the force turned toward contemplation of the future and the ideal which is a necessity of socialist life and development.

Unity, at every moment of the evolution of the socialist party, is simply an equilibrium between the divergent movements, the determination of a kind of vectorial sum. Unity implies a search for formulas which, according to the immediate state of tendencies, doctrines, and surrounding circumstances, can provide governing outlines for the party's activity, the common, collective activity of socialism.

At every moment, Jaurès's activity consisted precisely in determining that equilibrium, calculating that vectorial sum, tracing for all our comrades that governing outline. Is this immobilism? Not in the least, because the party is constantly in progress, because, in the passage from the real boundaries of the present society to the ideal boundaries of the future society, it is in constant movement. But, comrades, it must move as a whole, as a stellar system moves, according to the laws of gravity, carrying everything at once in its transformation, not only the star, but all its satellites.

More a clarification than creative thinking? Of course. This is often true for Blum. But in this divided assembly, tormented by violent fevers, shaken by rancor and mistrust, these clear, judicious, and attractive remarks were received like fresh spring water. The orator was warmly received. Although the left—a third of the votes—refused to approve this too–balanced text, a vote was immediately taken to print the speech and publish it as a pamphlet. The next day in *L'Humanité* Marcel Cachin wrote: "Blum attained the highest eloquence, and it was a joy for the mind to hear this simple, luminous, emotional, elegant, and profound language."

A leader had been born. After April 21, 1919, the life of Léon Blum could no longer be the same, nor could the life of the party. From then on, his voice was awaited, even if, as at Tours, it was rejected or ridiculed by many. The adviser, the expert, the civil servant, the *éminence grise* had given way before the valued, admired, and vilified champion of one of the essential currents of French socialism. For better or for worse.

The same Léon Blum who, at the end of 1917, offered French political society a program of "governmental" reform entirely lacking in socialist content, eighteen months later published a little pamphlet which was more a defense and illustration of Jaurès's doctrine: it was a kind of breviary. Had the author of *Lettres sur la réforme gouvernementale* been criticized by his friends because of his neutrality? Had he accused himself of detachment, or even of being an objective supporter of Clemenceau, proposing a program for a Caesar? The shift from the very technical tone of the *Lettres* to the almost devout one of *Pour être socialiste* can be better explained by Blum's entry into the political furnace, more specifically his participation in the electoral campaign of 1919.

The little pamphlet entitled *Pour être socialiste* was written during the summer of 1919, just after Blum's "entry into active politics"—the speech at the special congress in April 1919—contemporaneously with the July congress which voted for the "Bracke resolution," excluding any electoral agreement between the socialists and any other political body, including the Radicals. In those feverish weeks, while he was still attempting to prevent a split in the party (foretold by the creation of a new "International," the third, proclaimed at Moscow in March), and when he had just agreed to be a candidate in the legislative elections scheduled for November, Léon Blum had finally become a militant. He had to define and assert himself on the doctrinal level.

His speech on April 19 had made a place for him, but more in the realm of speech-making, the art of persuasion than anything else. He also had to express socialist ardor. This was the object of this brief text written for the Fédération National des Jeunesses Socialistes and dedicated to his son Robert, who was then seventeen.

Is this manifesto naive? Yes, and it is even sometimes boyscoutish. For example, when he deals with the question of transferable capital in a manner that might be accepted by the *vicaire savoyard* or a timid precursor of Christian Democracy, Blum, in attempting to address young people too clearly and simply, became patronizing. But it is hard to resist the fraternal warmth and the stirring passion of this hymn of love to socialism.

Referring to some undefined innate sense of justice, to the fundamentally moral and almost religious quality of socialism, denouncing social inequality and the immorality of capitalist appropriation, warning against the illusions of scientism and the danger of unsocialized technical discoveries, emphasizing the necessity and even the urgency of an international nationalization of the production of wealth, Blum expressed with touching loyalty the very essence of Jaurèsism.

He did not have Jaurès's compelling voice, his sometimes pompous but formidable presence. But if he lacked imagination (and training in economics) he was capable of formulating in a few sentences a subtly didactic summary of a situation or an historical development. There is this connection made between war and socialism:

> I have come to the end of these few pages without speaking to you about the event from which we have barely emerged, whose shadow still hovers over us. From the war I have derived only subsidiary arguments; I have made infrequent and indirect allusions to it. On the contrary, I could have taken from it the essential grounds of my argument. It would have been easy for me to show you that there is a kind of necessary connection between war and capitalism, that these two evil powers are born from one another and will only disappear together. Continuing the analysis, I could have made you grasp, in the very unrolling of the war, the growing conflict between capitalist interests and common interests, the growing necessity for methods of collective organization. I could have shown you capitalism's incapacity to resolve the crushing problems which are the legacy of the war. Its impotence is obvious to everyone. We are seeing it gradually collapse under the weight of the responsibilities it has itself accepted. There is no further doubt possible that, by allowing this war to break out, it signed a certificate, which would sooner or later come due, of its decline and death.
>
> The war projected a kind of brutal and expected light on the basic vices of bourgeois society. It suddenly shattered the mask covering the reality of events. But that reality existed before the war, and this is why we were socialists before the war.
>
> We do not wish to make you socialists of pure feeling. We need something more than a movement of revolt against the hideous spectacle that the human race has just witnessed. We need your

thoughtful and complete adherence. Thus I have attempted to present to you not the current arguments for socialism, but its fundamental reasons, those which were no less true yesterday than they are today, and will remain true tomorrow, until the inevitable transformation.

What is true is that the war has, in an extraordinary way, brought closer the moment when the fundamental ideas of socialism will be incorporated into the universal consciousness.

Deputy from Paris

The first edition of *Pour être socialiste* appeared in the socialist party bookstore in September 1919, at the beginning of the election campaign—Blum's first, in the second district of the Seine. Asserting his growing authority, he delivered the speech on general principles at the special congress held in Paris from September 11 to 13, and assured passage of the "Bracke resolution." In Blum's mind, as Gilbert Ziebura has acutely pointed out, what was important at the moment was less loyalty to the principle of class struggle than concern for party unity, which would have been broken by an agreement with a "bourgeois" organization. The new leadership of the party, although in disagreement with him on fundamental questions, considered him, since the April congress, one of the most valued leaders of the SFIO. It showed its esteem for him by choosing him to contest the election in the "safe" district including the 1st, 2nd, 3rd, and 4th *arrondissements* (those of his youth), and the 11th, 12th, and 20th (Faubourg Saint-Antoine, Belleville, and Ménilmontant)—working-class neighborhoods which had already been won over to socialism.

In his memoirs, Blum's fellow candidate Paul-Boncour recalls the 1919 campaign: "The unity of the socialist party was complete. Moderates like myself headed lists which included supporters of the extreme left wing of the party who were soon to leave us. Meetings were crowded and warm. Enthusiasm was widespread and hopes were enormous. We expected from the elections not the seizure of power, but a means to direct the coming legislature toward a bold group of political and social reforms and a democratic organization of the peace."[132]

Blum campaigned on three issues: defense of the unity of French socialism, a demand for profound and radical social reform, and denunciation of the Treaty of Versailles, in which he saw not a means for establishing the "just peace" he had called for, but the *diktat* of a conqueror carrying out his revenge and laying the basis for counter revenge. Besides, the National Council of the party had rejected the Versailles Treaty the preceding July 16. What is more, these attacks against the treaty allowed the former *chef de cabinet* of Sembat to

separate himself from his wartime "social-patriotism" and to recover a
Jaurèsian voice:

> The National Council has correctly said that it is up to us, mem-
> bers of the old majority, to express with the greatest force the
> lament of Justice denied. . . . We believed that this war would
> really be a war for Justice. Even if I am the only one left today, I
> believed it with all my heart.
> And this idea of the war determined our idea of victory. Victory
> was not material primacy or the assertion of superior force, it was
> the superiority and primacy of a moral idea, of a system of Justice.
> And that idea of victory determined our idea of the Peace. Peace
> was not the establishment of a new balance of powers, it was
> Justice, the full realization of Justice.
> Today we can no longer surrender that attitude. This is why, if
> there remains in the peace a single trace, a single threat of violence
> and iniquity, France can no longer seem to us victorious. This is
> why the treaty of Versailles strikes us as an act of denial and
> treason!

Blum was elected after his fellow candidates Pierre Dormoy and
Paul-Boncour. (The latter had just argued the case against Jaurès's
assassin at the long-delayed trial in March 1919, which had ended with
Villain's acquittal and Mme. Jaurès's being ordered to pay costs, a
scandalous verdict which provoked a huge popular demonstration.)
But the SFIO suffered a defeat which had serious consequences for its
future. The party increased its vote in the country as a whole by about
250,000, but it lost 34 seats in the Chamber (from 103 to 69), including
those of leaders like Longuet and Renaudel.

Why? The nationalistic fervor that swept the country had operated
against those who denounced the Versailles treaty and Clemenceau's
arrogance. Social unrest had just been expressed in a series of workers'
demonstrations which had been easily contained and repressed by the
authorities, giving the masses the impression that the party, preoccupied with internal arguments, was allowing them to be crushed by
the bourgeoisie. Finally, the electoral system—proportional representation by department, except in cases when the winning list obtained an absolute majority—encouraged coalitions. By applying the
"Bracke resolution" and isolating itself from the Radicals, the SFIO
had knowingly condemned itself to defeat. Blum nevertheless maintained, in an article in *L'Humanité* on November 22, 1919 pompously
entitled "La victoire," that the increase in votes and the preservation of
the party's independence from bourgeois forces were well worth a
temporary loss of parliamentary strength. The notion might have been
more acceptable had it been presented in a more modest tone.

In any case, he was in the Palais Bourbon where he was soon elected
secretary of the SFIO parliamentary group. Having been in turn a
mediator, the presenter of the socialist program at the April congress,

and then strategist and spokesman of the September congress, Blum became one of the most visible party figures. Objectively enhanced by the electoral defeat of Longuet and Renaudel, by the premature aging of Sembat, and by the isolation of Albert Thomas at the extreme right of the movement, Blum's position was at the head of the center-right confronting Frossard and Daniel Renoult, the new men of the left.

His duties as a deputy were incompatible with the office of *conseiller d'Etat*. He had to leave the great establishment where he had forged his talent and his reputation; on the advice of his friend Thadée Natanson, he registered at the bar. In a few months he became one of the most renowned civil lawyers in Paris, thus assuring himself a larger income than he had received both from his work as a higher civil servant and as a theater critic. (Naturally he gave up criticism; newspapers like *Le Matin* could not call for contributions from a socialist leader.)

Blum was forty-seven when he entered professional politics. The dilettante of the beginning of the century and the participant-observer during wartime had suddenly in 1918-19 become a thoroughly responsible figure committed to political and parliamentary battles.

The year 1920 was for Blum the year of his début in the Chamber. The first speech he delivered there was devoted to the subject that was most familiar to the former *chef de cabinet* of the Minister of Public Works: regulation of the railroads. Arguing against the raise in fares proposed by the government, he denounced the principle of private operation and the incoherence created by the multiplicity of networks, suggested an extension of the notion of public service, and concluded with a demand for nationalization. On this matter of public law, he displayed his mastery and dominated the Assembly. What is particularly worthy of attention is the very political conclusion to his speech:

> I know we are not here to teach you lessons. But I really don't look like someone trying to teach his colleagues lessons. I will even tell you very frankly—and you will have occasion to experience this often in the course of the legislature—that we are not here to prevent you from committing what we think are mistakes, when they injure only yourselves and your party interests.
>
> But when we are convinced, as we are today, that what we think a mistake touches on the interests of national productivity and vitality, then we, who are not bloody and destructive sectarians, address the entire Chamber, and we urge it not to commit a mistake which could damage the general interests of the nation of which we are responsible co-leaders with the same right as all of you, and which we fully and entirely hope to govern one day.

A proclamation of optimism, an affirmation of the concept of "responsible co-leadership," an attempt at seduction, a fierce denunciation—Léon Blum was asserting himself entirely and powerfully.

The SFIO Turns Left

More troubling battles lay ahead. The problem of participation in the war effort, which had so cruelly divided the party since the beginning of 1915 and ended up replacing the nationalist majority (Renaudel, Thomas) with the pacifist minority (Longuet, Paul Faure), was continued and amplified by an even more burning question: whether to join the Third International, founded by the Bolshevik victors of Petrograd in March 1919. Because it had been incapable of preventing or even interrupting the war, the Second International had collapsed at the outbreak of conflict between working classes. The question was whether they should attempt to revive it, or whether they should fall back on Lenin's organization, or whether some attempt at synthesis should be made.

Three hypotheses, three factions. The first, which considered the Second International alive and aimed only at rejoining it, was embodied in Renaudel and Thomas, the "patriotic" right. They relied on the vigorous efforts of Camille Huysmans, secretary of the Second International, to revive it by calling congresses in Bern and Lucerne. But the final blow to the Second International came from Switzerland, from the independent group of the German social-democratic party, the USPD of Haase, Eisner, and Bernstein, who had courageously dissociated themselves from the nationalistic policy of the official party. In agreement with a certain number of French and Italian socialists, they proposed to "reconstruct" an International with the best elements of the old one, instead of simply joining the Third. This strategy allowed for negotiations with Lenin about a fusion on more or less equal terms.

This was the policy adopted by the "Committee for the Reconstruction of the International" established in December 1919, whose supporters were called the "reconstructors." Jean Longuet, Paul Faure, and Daniel Renoult were its founders; they confronted the loyal members of the old organization gathered around Renaudel and advocates of unconditional adhesion to the Third International like Fernand Loriot, director of the "Committee for the Third International." Called for February, the national congress in Strasbourg would have to choose among these three tendencies, and settle for a long time the party's future and its doctrine.

What was Blum's position? By tradition, temperament, and a sense of loyalty, he felt close to Renaudel. Having supported the policy of "social-patriotism" during the war, he was in no position to determine that the old organization, still marked by the memory of Jaurès and of the "bells of Basel," had really been unworthy. But he was too acute not to sense that this was a lost cause, and he was above all too passionate a believer in unity not to attempt once more to set himself in the center, that is, with the "reconstructors." In any case, the federation of the Seine delegated him to the Strasbourg congress on this basis.

It was a tumultuous conference. Once again, Blum was seated in the center. But he constantly placed himself in confrontation with the left, attacked as he was, along with the whole parliamentary group, as a "reformist." After not speaking for a long time, he broke his silence to propose the addition of an amendment to the resolution of the "reconstructors" with a view toward eliminating the passages denouncing participation in government in war time. How could he have not made the attempt for his friends, for himself? He was defeated; the atmosphere of the congress ruled out such refinements.

To disconcert and isolate the extreme left, Renaudel quoted Lenin: "In case of war, one must help to defeat one's government!" Turning toward the left, he added: "Let the French socialist who is ready to support such a statement stand!" Loriot arose at his desk: "*I* stand to approve Lenin's idea." A great shudder of amazement ran through the assembly. In vain, Mayéras (close to Blum) evoked the country's "sensitivity," the "anguish" that had seized it; several voices were raised in turn to support Loriot—those of Raymond Lefèvre, Louise Saumoneau. The progress of Bolshevism within the SFIO was astounding.[133]

The votes provide evidence of this. The right was crushed: the congress decided to leave the Second International by a vote of 4,330 to 337. The left advanced: 1,660 delegates proposed immediate adhesion to the Third International. 3,040 supported the "reconstructors" who argued for a conference with the delegates from Moscow with a view toward "action on the basis of the traditional principles of socialism." It was a prudent formulation. But simultaneously a decision was made to send two delegates to Moscow where the second congress of the Third International was under way: Marcel Cachin, who had already made a journey to the USSR (he had returned dazzled) and Jean Longuet. But the leader of the "reconstructors" was unable to leave, and the secretary general L.-O. Frossard, who had joined the strongest side, went with Cachin in his place.

This development, the slide toward the extreme left, soon accelerated. Blum had joined the "reconstructors" to uphold the centrist line and to serve as a mediator. But the debate soon entered the very heart of this group. The French neo-Bolsheviks—Loriot, Ferrat, Sadoul, and Souvarine—concentrated their efforts against its "right wing." At a meeting of the party's National Council held on July 4, Blum and his friends succeeded in passing a declaration that the party had not joined the Third International, and that Cachin and Frossard were attending the congress of the International in Moscow only as "observers." But it was a rearguard battle. Around him and Longuet there was already a whiff of excommunication.

Nevertheless, he continued to plead desperately for unity and compromise. In a series of articles he published during the summer in *L'Humanité* (whose editorship he assumed during Cachin's absence from May to August 1920), he attempted to demonstrate that nothing was irremediable, that the party's sovereignty was intact, and that the congress scheduled for the end of the year would decide in complete freedom.[134] The serenity was superb, but artificial.

The return of Cachin and Frossard from the USSR, their immediate transformation of *L'Humanité* into a propaganda organ for joining the Third International, and especially the publication of the famous "twenty-one conditions" that Lenin and his friends had set for joining,[135] unleashed Blum's wit and polemical verve. The surprising thing in this affair is not that Blum the democrat reacted in the way he did, but that, in a party of democrats schooled by Jaurès and led by Longuet and Paul Faure, he was for so long (nearly three months) the only one to do so! Let us take an example. On September 19, 1920, analyzing the documents that had just come to him from Moscow, he outlined a prophetic critique of a half-century of applied Leninism in contrast to the tradition of Jaurès:

> One single preoccupation predominates everywhere: to bring together under one command, for an act of war, with all the weight of hierarchical authority required by a state of war, the "avant-garde" forces of the proletariat. . . . But how does communist doctrine conceive the seizure of power itself? The communist avant-garde, intentionally limited in numbers are obviously insufficient for armed victory over all the forces of resistance of the modern state. The doctrine in fact assumes that victory will be due to the participation of the "broad masses" of the proletariat, masses who are not yet communists, not yet organized, but whom, when the day comes, the avant-garde will be capable of carrying with it through the power of impassioned propaganda. An armed attack but also a surprise attack. We are familiar with this theory in France, and it is hard to resist the definitive judgment of Rappoport on this "Blanquism with tartar sauce."
>
> The compromise of the revolution by premature and abortive attempts at insurrection, or assuming the best, the seizure of power in such conditions that the revolution, that is, social transformation, cannot follow within a sufficiently short time, these are the practical dangers into which this doctrinal error would lead us. And we are called reformists, and even counterrevolutionaries, we who are protecting the true interests, the true nature of the Revolution!

Blum was attempting to roadblock the "putschism" behind the Moscow documents and the sectarianism of Zinoviev, president of the Third International, who was already visibly preparing for the expulsion of Longuet and his "reconstructor" friends. With Bracke, Blum established a "Committee of socialist resistance to adhesion." But he succeeded in attracting mostly rightists, and the majority of the "reconstructors" stayed away. When the federation of the Seine met in November in order to prepare for the Tours congress in late December, the man who had won acclaim for the common "action program" eighteen months earlier was put on the defensive.

"Will I be expelled, and when?" Blum asked Frossard, who hedged. His stubborn resistance was impressive. But the advocates of joining the Third International that evening had fourteen times as many votes as he did.

An Angry Proletariat

It is impossible to understand the depth of this ground swell and the extent of the irremediable defeat of the "resisters," if one does not consider the troubled situation of the working class at the time in all of Europe—in Vienna, Turin, Munich, Hamburg. One must also consider the stormy relations between the men who had returned from war and their governments, especially those relations in France.

French society at the end of the war was schizophrenic. After four years of equality in the face of death, citizens returned to a world that was more inegalitarian than ever; superprofits gained during the war had accentuated economic injustices.

At the very moment when France was drawing up an account of its losses—a million and a half dead (one third of them men between twenty and twenty-five), three million wounded (one fourth of whom were permanently handicapped), ten departments laid waste and ten others forever paralyzed by the exodus of young workers—at that very moment, the French working class, resuming the everyday bitterness of its condition, witnessed what Jules Romains called "the great light in the East," the establishment of a socialist government in Russia.

In France, the forces of the left seemed to be moving from failure to failure. To be sure, the membership of the CGT increased in a few months from 300,000 to one million. This led Clemenceau to grant the eight-hour day to the working class in April 1919, thereby blocking the first general strike of the postwar period, which had been scheduled for May 1, 1919, following the outrage after the acquittal of Jaurès's assassin. But the legislative elections of November 1919 resulted in a decline in socialist representation and the defeat of some of the best known socialist leaders. Confronted with stagnation in France and revolutionary progress in Russia, the working class felt the right to ask questions. There followed a radicalization of demands in the workplace.

The very powerful federation of railway workers (more than 300,000) began a strike in January on the Paris-Lyons-Marseilles line, whose nationalization Blum had just called for in the Chamber. Gathering support among miners, dockers, metal workers, and masons, the situation was moving toward the explosion of a general strike on May 1, 1920. By the end of April, Clemenceau foresaw (hoped for?) a real test of strength between the working class and the government.

The government was that of the president of the Council of Ministers Alexandre Millerand, the former socialist who had become a strongman for the bourgeoisie. With the cooperation of the large railway companies, and the mobilization of reservists, managerial staff, and students from the *grandes écoles,* the head of government recruited strike breakers everywhere;[136] by the end of May the movement was defeated. More than 18,000 railway workers were fired, and the members of the national board of the CGT were arrested and imprisoned, along with several leaders of the extreme left, Loriot and Souvarine, for instance, who had called for the strike.

This severe defeat for the revolutionary movement served only to bolster it. The militants had felt their strength, and they attributed their defeat less to the adventurism of their leaders than to the divisions among the leaders of the official left, to the prudence of the "politicians," particularly the legislators, and to the repressive ferocity of a government which had passed into the hands of one of the former "social-patriots" whose conduct during the war was considered by many a betrayal.

These more or less obscure feelings were clarified and exacerbated by the election of this same Alexandre Millerand as President of the Republic in autumn 1920. Not content with having broken the May strike with unprecedented brutality, he intended to lead France in a military crusade against the Soviet Union by sending an expeditionary force to Poland. There was a climate of class struggle in France and an atmosphere of Holy Alliance in Europe. At the end of the year 1920, the working class was not inclined toward moderation.

Its central political organization, the SFIO, inevitably experienced the repercussions of these storms. All the more because the components of the organization founded, or rather unified, by Jaurès in 1905 had been transformed from top to bottom since the armistice. At the moment when the congress of Tours was about to convene, it was estimated that less than a third of the 90,000 prewar members of the party had survived; taking into account lasting defections to nationalism, like Gustave Hervé's, less than a quarter had rejoined. On the other hand, there were more than 100,000 new members since 1918. This meant that, in the party about to hold its congress six years after Jaurès's death, less than a tenth of the militants had been taught and inspired by the assassinated leader. It had become difficult to argue for the lessons given and the methods defined in 1908 at the congress of Toulouse against this post-Jaurès, post-massacre body.

Another element in the transformation was the attitude of the peasantry. Kept under the thumb of semi-feudal and clerical conservatism until just before the war—except in a few departments like Haute-Vienne, Drôme, and Ain—the French peasantry had been rudely awakened by the experience of mobilization, trenches, exchanges of information, and close contact with fellow soldiers. They returned in an almost drunken state. As soon as the left spoke to them of transformation, they moved toward the most extreme and fundamental change. The names of the prewar leaders meant nothing to them. In the entire period leading up to the congress of Tours and during the sessions of the congress, the peasants and their delegates continually gave massive support to the most radical speakers. The first French deputy to proclaim formally his adherence to Russian-inspired communism was a peasant, Renaud Jean from Lot-et-Garonne.

But we have to qualify the notion that the Bolshevik revolution immediately aroused general enthusiasm among the French proletariat, as well as the notion that the sudden shift to the left of French socialism is to be attributed to the massive entry of peasants and young soldiers returning from the war. On the last point, Annie Kriegel is cautious: "The statistical data invalidate the idea that the new followers of socialism brought with them the revolutionary ferment that was to transform the party. If one compares the increase in membership with the evolution of the relative strength of the various factions in each socialist federation, it is not possible to demonstrate a positive correlation between the influx of new members and the socialist party's movement to the left."[137]

As for judgments made about Lenin's government, we have to take account of the anger that the Brest-Litovsk treaty of March 1918 had provoked in France, not least among a substantial number of workers, because it had allowed the German command to transfer the bulk of its fighting troops to the French front, creating the gravest danger for Paris since September 1914. Moreover, Bolshevik methods and the arrogance of the victors of October were even then broadly criticized in the French socialist press. But the factor that shifted the balance, and made a scrupulous democrat like Jean Longuet into a passionate advocate of the Bolshevik revolution, was the launching of the anti-Soviet crusade, the recognition of the White Russian "government" of

Wrangel, and the dispatch of an expeditionary force (of which Captain de Gaulle was a member) against the Red Army—in short the veritable counteroffensive that Millerand launched in 1920.

In *L'Humanité,* from November 1919 to August 1920, Blum also constantly denounced this attempt at "restoration," which he compared to the Bourbons' war in Spain in 1823. Quoting Béranger, who had called on French soldiers to desert, and referring to Colonel Fabvier who had turned his forces against the monarchist troops, Blum suddenly found himself upholding a revolutionary line of proletarian internationalism. But Lenin was not to show him much gratitude.

The great congress of Tours approached, but nothing could be decided there because the real turning point had come in February at Strasbourg, and the department federations had voted; the adhesion of Jaurès's party to Lenin's International was practically guaranteed. The only remaining question was along what lines the split would take place and whom the center and the right of the "reconstructors" would join, Loriot's "Committee for the Third International" which was already solidly in the majority or Blum's "Committee for socialist resistance to adhesion." The left wing of the faction, which had been in the majority at Strasbourg, had already followed Renoult and Verfeuil and joined the victors.

There were thus three principal "lines": the "left," made up of both avowed Bolsheviks like Loriot and Souvarine and pro-Soviet "politicians" whose nominal leaders were Cachin and Frossard; a "center," led by Jean Longuet, Paul Faure, and Adrien Pressemane, which was still fighting for conditional adhesion, somehow hoping that the unacceptable conditions set by Moscow could be attenuated; and finally, a "right," which, with the combined voices of Blum, Bracke, Mayéras, and Paoli, had chosen to resist out of principle, without hope.

To understand clearly the debates that were about to begin in Tours, we should recall that, within the majority in favor of adhesion, not only was there a split between Cachin, Frossard, and Renoult ("Guesdists" before the *Union sacrée* and the center-left and left of the "reconstructors") on the one hand, and Fernand Loriot and Boris Souvarine, leaders of the "committee for the Third International" (considered by Lenin his best supporters) on the other, but that the latter were rivals in extremism with syndicalists who had already established a "communist party" (which Moscow distrusted). Another sign: the most renowned French socialist, the aged Jules Guesde, kept from the congress by ill health, six weeks before the debates published an article in *Le Cri du Nord* that was extremely hostile to the Bolshevik leadership. And he said this about them to Frossard and Cachin: "They assassinated Plekhanov! Marxists, Bolsheviks? Come now! You can't create socialism in the most backward country in Europe."[138]

Among the factors operating at Tours that favored adhesion, we should not neglect two events that charged the atmosphere of the congress. One was the recent accidental death of three pro-Soviet militants returning from a trip to the USSR: Raymond Lefèvre, Vergeat, and Lepetit, who were made "honorary presidents" of the congress. The second was the fact that two of the most ardent advocates of adhesion to Bolshevism, Loriot and Souvarine, had been arrested for "conspiracy" seven months earlier, after the May strikes, and they were still in prison. What speech by either of them could have made more of an impression on the congress than this telegram from the prisoners read from the podium by their lawyer: "We regret nothing, except our inability to participate directly in the historic struggle which will be resolved at the congress of Tours. As [bourgeois] repression grows more cruel, the communist idea gains strength."

No words could more strongly persuade the delegates that France, like Russia four years earlier, like Germany two years earlier was on the eve of revolution, and that the moment of "boldness," commandos, and avant-gardes had come. This makes it a bit easier to understand the curt brutality of Moscow's tactics and demands, reflecting the state of mind of Lenin and Trotsky who foresaw a rapid advance of revolution throughout Europe. Even better, this progress would not take place in "backward" Poland—where the nationalist regime, rescued by Western intervention, seemed to be enjoying a reprieve—but in Germany, where the multiplicity of Marxist movements seemed to point to great revolutionary fertility rather than to the risk of division. Even the split decided on at the close of the social-democratic congress of Halle strengthened Russian hopes. Not to mention the strikes and occupations of factories in Italy, which ended on December 24, 1920 (the day before the opening of the congress) with a working-class victory, a "Matignon" before the fact that was apparently more decisive than the victory of 1936. (But it was also a Pyrrhic victory, paid for by the unleashing of the great fascist wave.)

If the revolution was here, from Budapest to Berlin, from Turin to Munich, why hesitate? What the International needed were shock troops and disciplined avant-gardes, not committees of intellectuals; the Comintern would take care of that. Did Lenin or Trotsky need Kautsky, Longuet, or Blum?

This mistaken analysis, this prediction by the men of October, led to the authoritarian character of their behavior in the debates at Tours.

Appointment in Tours

In the gray, smoke-filled Salle du Manège in Tours, [139] 285 delegates representing 89 of 95 socialist federations met on the morning of December 25, 1920. It was Christmas Day, but that was of no concern to these secularist militants. Full beards, salt and pepper mustaches, bald heads: there was a good deal of talk about "young people" during the five days of the congress, but the majority of the delegates were over fifty. The passionate Paul Vaillant-Couturier, who was not yet thirty, stood out all the more, and beside him, barely older and much more surprising, was an Indochinese with an emaciated face and burning eyes whose name was said to be Nguyen Ai Quai (or Quoc)—he did not choose the name Ho Chi Minh until twenty years later.

The banner dominating the platform bore the famous phrase, "Workers of all countries, unite!" In his speech, Longuet was sadly ironic about the use being made of his illustrious ancestor's words. The two chairmen were Marcel Cachin, whose mustache was still black and who looked like a mature Vercingétorix, and Ludovic-Oscar Frossard, who had strong, cold eyes behind his glasses. Facing them were the large and noisy left where Vaillant-Couturier, Renoult, and Rappoport were particularly noticeable, the center solidly grouped around Longuet, and the right where Blum, flanked by Bracke and Sembat, feverishly prepared his speech of severance and farewell.

On Frossard's suggestion, and over the objections of Blum, the question of joining the International was to be treated first, and the spokesmen of the federations would be heard on the subject. Frossard was counting on the litany of the majority to discourage the "resisters."

This took the whole day. Strangely enough, one of the cities supposed to be the "reddest" in the Midi, Toulon, was one of the four dominating the majority for the Longuet motion (conditional adhesion). Indicating that in his federation the most recently created sections were the ones which supported most massively the Cachin motion (unconditional adhesion), the delegate from Saône-et-Loire, Nouelle, wondered if "the enthusiasm for Moscow's positions were not inversely proportional to socialist education."

On Sunday December 26, Marcel Sembat mounted the platform. He had a jetblack beard and a pale complexion, and wore glasses, a morning coat, and a white tie. His argument came down to a rather powerful objection, but one that was very badly received: by forcing the parties which joined the Third International to create clandestine organizations, weren't they giving the government weapons for all kinds of later repression? "Our old comrades[140] also had conspiratorial traditions, but good lord! we did not put that on display as you do in the Moscow conditions!" There were shouts that he was attempting to frighten the audience in order to disguise his own cowardice. The first of the insults that were to spring from the left's benches later appeared in the pages of *L'Humanité*. Sembat was already expelled, defeated.

The next day, Marcel Cachin and Paul Faure confronted one another. The first presented a hymn of praise for the Russian Revolution, "an essential stronghold against imperialism" and for the strategy of seizing power through insurrectionary violence as Guesde had so long advocated. Faure, with biting but desperate wit, expressed his refusal to accept the twenty-one conditions imposed by Moscow, so humiliating that the most fervent supporters of adhesion did not dare even to refer to them.[141] He pointed out, not without courage, that:

> These decisions from Moscow oblige you to conduct clandestine propaganda in the barracks. I would like to ask you if you will sign that and in that case, if you will personally carry out your decision. At this congress, it is easy. But I, for one, confess with complete sincerity that I do not feel capable of carrying out, in the conditions in which I am asked to do it, clandestine propaganda in the barracks. If I had a son, I would tell him not to do it. . . . I do not want to sign this commitment . . . because I only sign those I honor.

Most of Paul Faure's speeches hardly seem to justify his reputation as an orator. But the conclusion of his speech at Tours is masterful:

> We are being subjected to what has been called, in a story by Villiers de l'Isle-Adam, the torture of hope. This torture was inflicted on poor devils condemned to death by the Inquisition. Since they had been imprisoned for a long time and seemed willing to accept death, out of a refined sense of cruelty and in order to make them experience more strongly the regret of leaving this life, they were made to suffer the torture of hope. At a given moment, a sliver of light appeared beneath the door; they pushed and the door opened. They went on. Under another door, they saw light again; the door opened again. They continued on in this way and approached the exit, where they could see the horizon, open space, life. Suddenly, at the moment when they felt a mad hope return and revive their spirits, the sinister laughter of monks and executioners echoed from all sides and they were brought back to prison to await torture. This was the torture of hope. This is how you have been conducting yourself in this business of the twenty-one conditions for the last three months.
> Someone whispers to us: "Frossard will give his interpretation, you'll see that these twenty-one conditions are easy to swallow. It's a little medicine, a nothing: you close your eyes and it's over." For my part, I cannot accept it. I will not join your side if you do not say formally, in clear terms, as honest men, as we all should be, what you think of us and what you intend to do with us.

"When Léon Blum stood up," according to his friend Thadée Natanson, "first he confessed to his exhaustion. It was no longer simply nerves, it was almost anguish." What could he hope for? The most solid arguments by adversaries of the move to join Moscow were over; the majority in favor of joining was all the more obvious, massive, undeniable.

If he spoke at all, it was first out of obligation to defend the positions of the "Committee of socialist resistance" which he had founded. But it was also because he possessed indomitable courage and even a certain love of challenge, and perhaps also because through Lucien Herr he had access to information (scarce at the time) about conditions in the USSR and the internal practices of the Bolshevik party. He spoke because he was familiar with Lenin's dictum: "To unite, we must first define what divides us." A good dialectician, this passionate supporter of unity attempted to outline the field of differences, so that it would one day be possible to bridge them. Was he speaking too late, or too soon? No matter; he had to speak.

His very beautiful speech[142] was constructed like a symphony. In the first movement, *allegro ma non troppo,* he described the incompatibilities in structure, organization, and even conception between the party he had helped to found fifteen years earlier and the party that was to follow the model established in the USSR. In the second, *largo,* he pointed out, with a power and precision to which his friend Herr had contributed, the doctrinal contradictions between the socialism the Jaurès and his Proudhonist companions had derived from *Capital* and the amalgam of Blanquism and Marxism created in exceptional circumstances by the genius of Lenin and Trotsky. In a concluding *scherzo* he spoke ironically about those who claimed they were joining this powerful Church only to transform it from within.

Blum did not dispute the facts: the organization which Moscow asked the foreign socialists to join in unity was "a doctrinal whole whose powerful and even majestic character it is impossible to deny." But it was totally "new," a radical break with the traditions of French socialism, as far as the composition, the structure, and even the objectives of the party were concerned.

> This new socialism . . . rests upon a kind of vast factual mistake which consists of generalizing, for the whole of international socialism, a certain number of notions drawn from a particular local experience, the experience of the Russian Revolution itself, and establishing as a necessary and universal rule of action for international socialism the experience of those who had carried out and brought to life the Russian Revolution, an experience that was perhaps open to question but was gradually derived from the facts themselves.
>
> The constitution of our party is above all popular in character. According to the excellent formulation in our statutes, the leadership of the party belongs to the party itself. It was in the rank and file of the party, among the mass of militants and dues-payers that collective will and thinking were shaped. This will and this thinking rose from level to level, from the section to the federation, from the federation to the National Council, from the National Council to the Congress. There has been talk of leaders. There were no leaders, and there are none, in the socialist party. Control was

exercised over those who are called leaders where it could be exercised: it depended, and it still depends, on the militants. Those whom you call leaders were only interpreters, representatives of the collective will and thinking developed by the rank and file of the party.

Socialism is not a party confronting other parties. It is the entire working class. Its object is to bring together, through their common class interests, the workers of all countries. Our party was therefore a party with the broadest possible membership. As such, it was a party of freedom of thought, for the two ideas go together and one derives necessarily from the other. If you wish to assemble in the same party all the workers, all the wage-earners, all the exploited, you can bring them together only by using the simplest and most general statements. You will say to them: "Socialists are all those who want to work for the replacement of one economic system by another, all those who believe, for it is the basis of Marxism, that there are ineluctable connections between the development of capitalism and the development of socialism. If you are with us to carry on this work, your act of allegiance is complete, you are socialists." The activity of this party was in popular education and public propaganda.

What will the new party you wish to create be like? Instead of the popular will taking shape in the rank and file and rising from level to level, your system of centralization entails the subordination of each organism to the organism hierarchically above it; at the top, there is a central committee on which everything must depend, a kind of military command formulated on high and transmitted from rank to rank, down to the militants and the sections. What of the autonomy of groups and federations? These positions tell you that that is a pure and simple heresy. Beside the public organisms, there are clandestine organisms. . . . An error in translation in the documents, a kind of shifting between the word illegal and the word clandestine, has led a certain number of comrades to believe that we, the adversaries of the Third International, were by the same token opposed to illegal action. There is not a single socialist who would consent to allow himself to be confined to legality. I said it in my electoral campaign, I will say it on the floor of the Chamber at the first opportunity, I will say it everywhere that it has to be said. On illegal action, we are all in agreement. Not on clandestine organization. . . . The proof that the two notions do not coincide is that at the present moment the French party recognizes the legitimacy of illegal action and does not yet have a clandestine organization.

The communist arguments will impose on us, on the one hand subordination at every level with a central committee at the top, and on the other clandestine organisms which you are compelled by the arguments and the statutes to establish. The executive committee of the Third International even reserves the right to impose this activity on you directly, should you show any weakness or delay in fulfilling this requirement. And when there is a juxtaposition of public and clandestine organs, where does real authority lie? By force of circumstances, in the clandestine organism. Your secret central committee cannot be created by deliberation in your congress, it will have to have a different origin. Its constitution will have to be brought to you from outside. That amounts to saying that in the party you are trying to change us into, central power will finally belong to a secret committee designated . . . under the control of the executive committee of the International itself.

Until today the unity of the party was a unity based on synthesis and harmony, a kind of vectorial sum of all the forces, and every tendency was involved in establishing and determining the common axis of action. You are no longer seeking unity in this sense, but absolute uniformity and homogeneity. In your party you want not only men who are inclined to act together but men who have committed themselves to think together: your doctrine is fixed once and for all! *Ne varietur!* Whoever does not accept it cannot join your party; whoever no longer accepts it will have to leave. I do not wish to examine the question of expulsion from the point of view of any particular individual! It is of little importance to me if you wish to draw the line of division in one place rather than another, if you wish to keep one person and not another. The documents are serious in another way.

Moscow demands the complete and radical purge of everything that the socialist party has been up to now. This is why you say: whoever does not accept the arguments, in letter and in spirit, will not join the Communist Party and the Third International; whoever votes against joining and has not completely submitted within the established time limit, will be expelled from the Third International. Is this the party we have known? No! The party was an appeal to all workers, while the one you want to establish is the creation of small, disciplined avant-gardes, who are homogeneous and subject to rigorous control. Their size is of little importance, as you will find in the documents, but they are all to be tightly controlled and ready for prompt and decisive action!

The applause that erupted on the left at this point made a mockery of Blum's argument. He responded by exclaiming: "We remain in the party as it was, we cannot accept the party you want to create!"

Blum had thus already shown that in party composition, organization, and methods, everything distinguished the SFIO from the organization predetermined by Moscow's "twenty-one conditions." He continued his discussion of the doctrine, pointing to the unbridgeable gap between the two visions. He applied himself to demonstrating that, as far as the very concepts of revolution and dictatorship of the proletariat were concerned, it was he and his friends who continued the tradition that ran from Marx to Jaurès:

The debate is not between the reformist and the revolutionary idea, but between two revolutionary ideas which are in fact radically and essentially different from one another. Reformism, or more precisely revisionism—I prefer that word—no longer exists in national or international socialism since the Amsterdam congress and the unity agreement. If someone has failed to follow the party's doctrine, it is up to the militants, the federations, and the congress to apply the sanctions provided for in the regulations. But, for my part, until now, I know of only one socialism in France, the one defined by the statutes and mentioned on our membership cards, which is a revolutionary socialism . . . a movement of ideas and action leading to a total transformation of the property system. Revolution is, by definition, this very transformation. Then where is the point of disagreement, the point of conflict between us?

Revolution means, for traditional French socialism, transformation of an economic system based on private property into a system based on collective or common ownership. A change [which] will not be made by imperceptible modifications and continuous evolution. At some point . . . whatever changes and attenuations have been won beforehand, there will have to be a break in continuity, an absolute and categorical change. This break in continuity which is the beginning of the revolution itself has as a necessary but not sufficient condition the conquest of political power. That is at the very root of our doctrine. We think, we socialists, that the revolutionary transformation of property relations can be accomplished only when we have won political power.

If a delegate to a socialist congress, who must be a member of the party for at least five years, can reach the point of disputing assertions like those I have just made, no further discussion is possible! That means seizure of the central authority, which is now called the State, by any means, excluding neither legal nor illegal means. That is socialist thought.

THE PRESIDENT: Our comrade is tired. And it is very difficult to speak in this atmosphere!

BLUM: International socialism and French socialism have never limited the means they would use to seize political power. Lenin himself has agreed that in England power might very well be won by electoral means. But there is not one socialist, however moderate he may be, who has ever condemned himself to wait for the conquest of power from electoral success. On this point, no discussion is possible. The motto for all of us is Guesde's, which Bracke repeated to me not long ago: "By every means, including legal means!" . . . This revolutionary idea which was that of Jaurès, Vaillant, and Guesde, has always had to defend itself against two opposite deviations, and has always made its way with difficulty between a deviation of the right and one of the left. The former is precisely the reformist deviation. The basis of the reformist argument is that, if not the totality of social transformation, at least the most substantial benefits it is to provide for the working class, can be won without a prior crisis in political power. This is the essence of reformism. But there is a second error of which I am obliged to say that it is essentially anarchist. It is the error which consists in thinking that the conquest of political power is an end in itself, while it is only a means. Open your party card. What is the objective the socialist party has set for itself until now? The transformation of the economic system. Open the statutes of the

Communist International. Read the article in which the International defines its goal. What is this goal? Armed struggle against bourgeois power. For Lenin's thought, which has deeply penetrated the minds of the writers of the statutes and which constantly recurs in them, is that, before the seizure of political power, it is impossible to carry on an effective campaign of propaganda and working-class education. Which amounts to saying that the conquest of political power is not only, as we have always said, the condition for social transformation, but that it is even the condition for the earliest efforts of propaganda and organization. I can conceive of this when you are confronted with a proletariat like the Russian proletariat and a country like Russia where no effective large-scale propaganda had been carried out before the seizure of power. One can imagine in that case that it is first of all necessary to destroy bourgeois power for this progaganda even to become possible. But is the situation the same in our Western countries? I refuse to concede that, until this conquest of political power, which you will no doubt accomplish tomorrow, there has been no socialist propaganda in this country. I refuse to say that all the past work has been for nothing, and that everything remains to be done. No, a good deal has been done, and you do not have the right to deny and betray yourselves today!

My friends and I do not accept this tactic of the unconscious masses led without their knowledge by avant-gardes, this tactic of the conquest of political power by a surprise as well as an armed attack, we cannot accept it. We believe it would lead the proletariat to the most tragic disillusionment. We believe that, given the current state of capitalist society, it would be madness to count on the inorganic masses. We know what the inorganic masses are like in France. We know they follow one man one day and another the next. We know that one day the inorganic masses were behind Boulanger and another day behind Clemenceau.

You have chances of taking power in this country through vast working-class movements of an organic character, which presuppose that education and other forces have been carried as far as possible. You will not make the revolution with gangs that run after any man on horseback. You will make it with millions of organized workers who know what they want. Your party's enterprise is condemned to failure in advance!

We are so much . . . supporters [of the dictatorship of the proletariat] that the idea and the theory of [it] were included by us in an electoral program. We are afraid of neither the word nor the thing. I might add that I do not think, although Marx wrote it, that the dictatorship of the proletariat is bound to preserve a democratic form. The very essence of a dictatorship is the suppression of all constitutional prescriptions.

Then where is the disagreement? It is not in the fact that the dictatorship of the proletariat is exercised by a party. In fact, in Russia, the dictatorship is not exercised by the Soviets but by the Communist Party itself. We have always thought that, in France, after the seizure of power, the dictatorship of the proletariat would be exercised by the groups of the socialist party itself, becoming, by virtue of a fiction in which we all acquiesce, the representative of the entire proletariat. The difference lies, as I have told you, in our divergences on organization and on the idea of revolution. A dictatorship exercised by the party, yes, but by a party organized like ours, not like yours. A dictatorship exercised by a party based on the people's will and the people's freedom, on the will of the masses, consequently an impersonal dictatorship of the proletariat. But not a dictatorship exercised by a centralized party, in which all authority rises from level to level and ends up concentrated in the hands of an open or secret committee. The dictatorship of a party, yes; the dictatorship of a class, yes; the dictatorship of a few individuals, known or unknown, definitely not!

Just as the dictatorship must be impersonal, so must it be temporary, provisional. We accept dictatorship if the conquest of power is not pursued as an end in itself. But if you imagine, against the entire Marxist conception of history, that it is the only way to bring about that transformation on which neither capitalist evolution nor our own propaganda work has had an effect; if as a consequence, too great a distance, an almost infinite space of time were to intervene between the seizure of power (condition) and revolutionary transformation (goal), then we are no longer in agreement. Then, we say to you that your dictatorship is no longer the temporary dictatorship which will allow you to carry out the final construction work on your society. It is a stable system of government, almost legitimate in your eyes, behind whose shelter you wish to do all the work. That is Moscow's system.

The last point of Blum's speech, devoted to the problem of national defense, did not have this prophetic power. Today it seems more dated. But it was a problem that aroused passion at the time. In a debate among him, Cachin, Longuet, and Renaudel, how could he not deal head-on with this question which for three years had carried more weight than any other? Once again Blum showed that he was much less "subtle" than he was rash.

> None of use has ever said that the duty of national defense was an absolute and unconditional duty. But we have said that refusal of, abstention from national defense was also not an absolute and unconditional duty for socialists. We assert it again: there are circumstances in which, even under capitalist rule, the duty of national defense exists for socialists.
> A VOICE: Be specific!
> BLUM: No. I don't want to wrestle with a way of thinking which, at bottom, is Tolstoyan or neo-Christian rather than socialist. . .
> A DELEGATE: Give an example! a hypothetical case!
> BLUM: That's very simple: suppose there is obvious aggression, an attack by any nation at all.

There was noise, crying out, tumult, singing of *l'Internationale*. It only remained for Blum to take his leave. He did so in a few phrases

that have remained famous, too famous; some have used them to wrap
this vigorous political speech in a mantle of confused nostalgia:

> There is a categorical opposition, a contradiction, between what
> has been socialism and what will be communism tomorrow. . . . I
> know very well that some of you, who are with us in spirit, are
> joining the Communist International only with the ulterior motive
> of changing it from within, of transforming it once you have pene-
> trated it. But I believe this is a pure illusion. You are confronting
> something that is too powerful, too coherent, too stable for you to
> be able to dream of changing it.
>
> I also believe it is not a very noble attitude. One joins or one
> does not join. One joins because one wishes to, or one does not
> join because one's reason accepts or does not accept. I know that
> in a party shaped by the people, in essence a people's party, like
> ours, the leaders are only voices to speak more strongly in the
> name of the masses, they are only hands to act more directly in the
> name of the crowd. All the same, they have a duty. They are the
> servants of the collective will. But they have the right to try to
> recognize and interpret that will. They have the right to ask them-
> selves if what they see before them is only a whirl of conflicting
> eddies drifting toward the banks, or if it is the real current, deep,
> slow, and majestic, flowing down the river. And then they main-
> tain, in spite of everything, an individual conscience. And there are
> moments when they have the right and the duty to say to them-
> selves: "Can I or can I not follow?" This is the point we have
> reached today. I repeat, a majority vote will change nothing in this
> cry of our conscience, which is strong enough to dominate the
> concern for unity which has always guided us.
>
> We are convinced, in our very depths, that while you go off on
> your adventure, someone must stay to guard the old house. We are
> convinced that at this moment there is a more pressing question
> than knowing whether socialism will or will not be united. It is the
> question of knowing whether socialism will or will not exist. To-
> morrow, we will perhaps be divided as men who understand in
> different ways the interests of socialism and socialist duty. Or will
> we be divided as enemies?
>
> Are we going to spend our time in front of the bourgeoisie treat-
> ing each other as traitors and renegades on the one hand, madmen
> and criminals on the other? Will we not grant each other the pre-
> sumption of good faith? I ask: Is there anyone here who believes I
> am not a socialist?
>
> A VOICE: You're a confusionist!
>
> BLUM: In this moment, which is for all of us a moment of tragic
> anxiety, let us not add that too to our sorrow, and our fears. Let us
> be able to refrain from words that hurt and wound, from acts that
> wrong, from everything that would be fratricidal division.
>
> I say this to you because this is no doubt the last time I will
> speak to many of you, and nevertheless because it must be said.
> Let all of us, even separated, remain socialists; in spite of every-
> thing, let us remain brothers, brothers separated by a cruel quarrel,

but a family quarrel, and whom a common home may once again bring together.

The impression created, less by the sentimental peroration, than by the argument as a whole, was very powerful. Daniel Renoult could speak of "provocation" all he liked, call Blum a "schismatic," assert that "true revolutionaries can no longer live with him," but many voices asked for the speech to be printed. Raffin-Dugens, one of the "pilgrims" of Kienthal who obviously belonged to the majority, had the courage to declare:

> You were born in the bourgeoisie; like Jaurès you came to socialism. You brought to the proletariat in which I was born, like all those I have loved—father, mother, brothers, sisters—the contribution of your knowledge and your devotion. Very well! I say that when one sacrifices, as Jaurès did, all one's connections to struggle with the proletariat, one has a right, the right to be respected. You will leave. But I am sure that on the floor of the Chamber you will help, without thinking of tomorrow, to defend what you defended when you were in our ranks, and I will continue to hold you in affection.

But the votes in favor of adhesion were too numerous and too constraining. The next day, Bracke attempted to resume Blum's argument with the help of quotations from Marx:

> Since the various sections of the working class have reached different degrees of development, it follows that their theoretical opinions which reflect the movement are also divergent. . . . Taking into account the differences in institutions, customs, and traditions, the means by which the workers will seize power could not possibly be identical from one country to the next. There are some where the workers may reach their goal by peaceful means. . . . Karl Marx may have been mistaken about some things; but he was not mistaken when he said that, along with men who thought differently from the way he did, he had his place in the organization. I beg you, comrades, do not expel Karl Marx from your International!

The Great Schism

Wasted efforts. The case was closed. The leaders of the Third International wanted their victory to take on a violent, an imperious, even an offensive character for the losers. The day after Blum had so passionately pleaded for the avoidance of insulting polemics, the administrative secretary of the party, André Le Troquer, read from the rostrum the text of a telegram he had just received from the president of the Third International, Zinoviev, which was nothing but an insult hurled at the group of "reconstructors":

> Longuet and his group have been and remain determined agents of bourgeois influence on the proletariat. The Communist International can have nothing in common with the authors of such resolutions. The worst service that can be rendered to the French proletariat in the present circumstances is to dream up some vague, confused compromise which will later be a millstone for your party. We are deeply convinced, dear comrades, that the majority of thinking workers in France will not accept such a ruinous compromise with the reformists and that it will finally create at Tours the true Communist party, one and powerful, freed from reformist and semi-reformist elements.

An obvious provocation. Why? Why did Lenin and his companions seek to humiliate Longuet in this way? Wasn't he Karl Marx's grandson? Hadn't he fought against militarism during the war with more courage than Cachin and Frossard? Wasn't he, after Jaurès, the most well known and respected Frenchman among the socialists of the entire world? Precisely, writes Annie Kriegel,[143] it was this prestige and popularity which brought him the Bolsheviks' ostracism: there could be no center of interest or attraction except Moscow. Not only organisms and doctrine, methods or thought, but men as well had to be concentrated. No popularity, no prestige, no personalities could be permitted outside the high command sitting in the USSR.

It was because he was respected that Longuet had to be rejected. It was the "banality," the doctrinal flabbiness, and the vulnerability to criticism of Cachin and Frossard that made them valuable in the eyes of Lenin and his lieutenants. Those who might cause difficulties inside the International, Longuet in France, like Kautsky in Germany, were cast into outer darkness.

The debate continued for almost three full days, and the dialogue between Longuet and Frossard (he, at least, was capable of paying tribute to "plague-carriers" like Blum and Bracke) took place at a level worthy of the stakes. But nothing could stand in the face of the thunderbolt hurled from Moscow, the effect of which had been further reinforced by the pathetic speech of Clara Zetkin, former companion of Rosa Luxemburg and Liebknecht. She arrived in Tours unexpectedly, appeared on the platform while Frossard was delivering his speech, and proceeded to call on the French workers to "carry out revolutionary acts."

The schism took place on the last night, December 29 in two stages, one right after the other. First there was the defeat of the Longuet-Paul Faure motion (adhesion "with reservations") by the Cachin-Frossard motion (adhesion with no significant reservations except the preservation of union autonomy), by a vote of 3,028 to 1,022. Thus three quarters of the French socialists submitted to the ukases of Moscow after Zinoviev's telegram, after the numerous humiliations of the masters of the Third International.

Frossard made a final effort for some motion toward synthesis:

> At the congress of the Communist International we were asked to expel Longuet and the centrist faction. We left the congress rather than accept a condition which would have dishonored us, and we returned to France convinced that thereafter no one would insist that we dissociate ourselves from comrades at whose side we had fought bitter battles in our party, with complete agreement in our thinking. [Turning toward Longuet and Pressemane] I do not agree with Zinoviev. No, you are not servants of bourgeois influence. When we voted for our party to join the Third International, we did not intend to surrender forever all critical spirit, all freedom of discussion, and we intend to maintain our right to examine freely both documents and men.[144]

But Vaillant-Couturier was already speaking with the voice of the prosecutor Vyshinsky. Addressing Longuet and his friends, he threatened as prophetically as Blum: "You are moving toward them [the right], you will be led to deny a large part of your politics. If not today, then tomorrow, you will no doubt justify the most terrible criticisms of Zinoviev and the communist International!"

The schism was consummated by the rejection of a motion proposed by Mistral and Pressemane, old friends of Longuet, which called both for the refusal of the expulsions demanded by Zinoviev's telegram and for the maintenance of "the present unity of the party" (1,398 votes for, 3,247 against). In the meantime Blum had withdrawn his motion, which could have counted on only about 350 votes. A crushing defeat.

But before leaving the hall, the group of "Socialist resistance to adhesion" which he led announced:

> A vote in a congress does not have the power to transfer to tomorrow's party the commitment that still binds us to the party of today and yesterday. Nor does a vote in a congress have the power to interrupt the life of socialism in France or to prevent the participation of the French proletariat in an International that can contain all organized workers. We therefore let the first Communist congress hold its meeting here. The congress of the socialist party (French Section of the Workers' International) will continue its work in the Salle du Démophile, 72, rue de Lariche, tomorrow, Thursday, at 10 o'clock in the morning. All delegates who do not accept the resolutions of the congress of Tours transforming the party into a Communist Party are invited.
> THE PRESIDENT: The Communist Congress continues. Frossard has the floor.

"The renewed socialist party cannot in any way represent a right-wing deviation." This was the assurance of Léon Blum as he began the rival congress with the "reconstructors" in the Salle du Démophile the next day.[145] Right-wing? The speech delivered in Tours by the author of *Pour être socialiste* would certainly have created a scandal for its "leftism" at the twenty-second congress of the PCF in 1976. In fact, he would not have been allowed to deliver it.

In any case, his activity during the three months preceding the Tours meeting, his general performance at the congress, and the collapse of the "Longuetists"—all pointed to Blum as leader of the party, the man who had first opposed the commands of Moscow and whose speech had forcefully "legitimized the ideology of the minority."[146]

The qualities which he had just demonstrated—his perspicacity, his strong convictions, his feeling for pluralism, his decisiveness—allowed him to reach the top in an organization "whose structure prohibited the presence of a powerful party leader at its head."[147]

But the role he was about to assume did not distract him from the old dream of unity. He was primarily responsible not for the schism, which was engraved in the Bolsheviks' "twenty-one conditions," but for bringing it into the open. It was he who had proclaimed "The king is naked!"—which did not mean that he had lost hope in a later synthesis. As he was leaving the Salle du Manège, he encountered Charles-André Julien, a historian he respected, who had chosen the majority side[148] because "the time," as he said later, "was not propitious for analysis. We were surrounded by the enthusiasm provoked by the creation of the first workers' state."

Blum said simply: "Au revoir, Julien!"

Part II
THE TESTS OF POWER

SFIO

The Ruins of the "Old House"

L ate in the morning of January 1, 1921, when Jean Longuet, Paul Faure, Léon Blum, and their friends found themselves in Paris, on the platform of the gare d'Austerlitz, their baggage was nothing but shadows. After their expulsion from the congress, they had held a single session at the Tours city hall, in the course of which they had proclaimed that they were "the socialist party as it was unified by Jaurès, Guesde, and Vaillant," and expressed the hope of "bringing the Communist dissidents back" into it. At the congress, three quarters of the delegates had voted against them. In the country at large, the situation seemed even worse: the wind of defeat could only sweep more violently across the political landscape where these refugees would pitch their tent. All the power of the party was in the other camp, which had the unreserved support of a Great Power and of the International.

"It was against our fanaticism that the Communist wave broke at the time," Blum wrote a few years later. This is accurate, but one wonders about his state of mind that evening, surrounded by men whom he had led on and associated with his resistance. He knew very well that they were even more dispirited than he by the break—Longuet especially, Longuet the internationalist, the true Marxist, the most insulted, the one who had suffered the greatest defeat.

Blum was certainly more optimistic than his companions, and he remained that way. He believed deeply that the legitimacy of the minority—that is, their fidelity to the tradition of Jaurès—guaranteed their survival and their ultimate triumph. This disastrous congress was also the one in which he had asserted himself, or had been seen, as at least the partial heir of Jaurès. The kingdom had been destroyed, but the "little king of Tours" had been consecrated by his talent, his courage, and the faithfulness of his speech to the thought of the founder (a faithfulness more obvious than at the time of the *Union sacrée*).

Of course, we should not carry the assimilation of Blum to Jaurès too far. Jaurès had a capacity to be in spontaneous harmony with the people, a feeling for the masses, and a revolutionary sensibility that was often lacking in Blum. He was equal in courage to Jaurès but not in imagination, comparable in intelligence but not in the vital energy and communicative power that make one wonder what the assassinated leader would have made of the speech delivered by his friend in Tours.

Spoken, proclaimed, roared, enacted by Jaurès, with the prodigious spiritual and physical power that hypnotized Barrès as well as the glass workers of Albi, what effect would have been produced by this fundamental warning? Would French socialism thus proclaimed ever have fallen into the hands of those who were to make it a pathetic reflection of the regime engendered in the USSR by the violent genius of Lenin, the passivity of the masses, and the corruption of absolute power?

But, with or without Jaurès, what was left of the "old house" of which the resisters had proclaimed themselves "guardians"? The parliamentary group of which only twelve out of sixty-eight had chosen the Communist camp, some mayors, about fifteen federations, about 30,000 out of 180,000 militants (the police at the time estimated their number at less than 10,000), and *Le Populaire* of Jean Longuet, a paper on the brink of bankruptcy. The party installed itself in the paper's little offices on the rue Feydeau. In Seine, especially in Paris, the situation was disastrous. In Vaucluse, Corrèze, Drôme, Lot, Loire, and Dordogne, they were annihilated.

Nevertheless, here and there, certain strongholds remained: Nord, which was still substantially Guesdist, Pas-de-Calais (where the majority of Tours soon shifted in favor of the SFIO), Bouches-du-Rhône, Gironde, Haute-Garonne—in short, the developed regions where the party had been established for a long time, where it was organized and vital and had had the time to establish a framework of loyal followers and notables. Where the movement was young, spontaneous, recent, or inorganic, it had moved at a stroke to the side of the maximalists. What could be more natural? In *Entre deux guerres,* Paul-Boncour himself, epitomizing the right, recognized that at Tours the party had been "emptied of its most fervent elements."

Apart from the Paris area, where the collapse of the socialists was almost absolute, urban centers everywhere were stronger than rural areas. The proletarians were more "socialist" than the peasants, which was "analyzed as an advantage"[1] at the time by the SFIO. The majority of mature and experienced men remained attached to "what had been their work, the work to which they had devoted their time, their lives,"[2] while the younger men "chose adventure," fascinated as they were by the great light from the East and the instant methods that were held up before them. They thereby "deprived the party of a membership that was more significant because of its dynamism than because of its size, and created the risk, which it did not always avoid, that the party would fall into bureaucracy and electoralism."[3]

Bureaucracy, electoralism? The SFIO of 1921 was both structured around central bodies—the annual congress, the National Council (which met several times a year), the CAP (permanent administrative committee) whose secretary-general, Paul Faure, was the real director of the party—and decentralized in departmental federations, each of which contained local sections. The mayors who remained members of the party were a sign of power in the rank and file. At the top the prestigious "head" represented by the parliamentary group spoke and acted amid constant challenges.

The system was deliberately complex in order to avoid authoritarianism, although it contained a risk of bureaucratic stagnation. At Tours, Blum had recalled that his system subjected the "leaders" to the control of the militants. This was still the case: in the days after the split, the SFIO was in the hands of a triumvirate composed of Paul Faure, in charge of the party apparatus, Jean Longuet, director of the press and source of the ideological "line", and Léon Blum, the parliamentary leader. Longuet soon retired, and Blum took over from him everything except what had to do with the functioning of party mechanisms. The duumvirate Faure-Blum remained in place for almost twenty years without threatening the various personalities and the very diverse currents within the SFIO, from Renaudel to Zyromski, from Paul-Boncour to Pivert, from Mistral to Auriol.

In the disarray of the twenties the various factions avoided the conflicts that divided the victors of Tours, conflicts which would once again challenge the victorious SFIO in the thirties. At the very first meeting in the Tours city hall, a proposal to exclude the extreme right—Varenne, Paul-Boncour— was rejected by Longuet himself. And although Mistral recommended "screening out the right," his comrades agreed that it would have been ruinous; eliminating Renaudel, for example, would have reduced the party's power of resistance.

The only significant conflict which arose within the SFIO in those years had to do with the orientation of *Le Populaire*, which Renaudel and Paul-Boncour wanted to open to a broadly republican and democratic, rather than strictly socialist, public, while Longuet wanted to radicalize it by emphasizing class struggle in rivalry with *L'Humanité*. Longuet, for the most part, got his way, not only because he was the ideologue of the party as well as the founder of the paper, but also because the faction he symbolized, the "reconstructors," was very influential in the party as a whole. After all, although it was Blum who had delivered the most powerful speech at Tours, he was a bit marginal. The exclusion, the split, had been the rejection of the "reconstructors" by the movement. It was around them as a base—even though they did not wish to limit so narrowly the meaning and implications of the term that designated them[4]—that the SFIO had to be "reconstructed."

Blum was in complete agreement. He had been the man of the hour, of resistance to the Bolshevik faction and the veto. But, as he had pledged to Paul Faure, he did not want those who had been excluded to form a "rightist faction." It turned out that his parliamentary work at the time, in opposition to the "National Bloc" and Millerand, with their repressive class policies and chauvinistic diplomacy, constantly pushed him toward the left; he therefore unreservedly supported the direction given to the party by Faure and Longuet. Moreover, he was encouraged to do so by the two friends he admired most, the old Guesdist Bracke, who had recovered, like Blum, from the fever of the *Union sacrée,* and Lucien Herr. From this point on, then, Blum set himself on the center-left of the party, closer to Longuet and Faure than to Renaudel or Varenne. He now left the centrist position that he had so long dreamed of occupying during the war (when he was solidly on the right) to his friends Auriol and Pressemane.

This relative cohesion, in spite of the diminished resources available to the men who had been defeated at Tours, seems to have allowed them to carry out what Blum called the "heroic effort of 1921" and to play an increasingly important role in electoral contests. As early as July, in the working-class stronghold of Saint-Denis, the socialist Chrétien came close to defeating the Communist mayor Goguet. In Colombes and Lyon socialist candidates defeated their Communist opponents. When the unions, echoing the politicians, split in July 1921, the new pro-Communist CGTU was far from a majority over the CGT of Jouhaux, who had remained close to the minority of Tours. So, the first socialist congress after the split met at the cooperative restaurant on the avenue Philippe-Auguste in Paris on November 1, 1921 in an atmosphere of surprising euphoria. Paul Faure, with his striking Périgord accent, could tell his comrades: "We are saved, we are freed from despair!"

Let us see what had "held." At the congress Hubert Rougier reported a membership of 55,000. The parliament included 56 members, and Blum had already established himself as their leader in the course of the past year. Two socialists held Senate seats. Some mayoralties of large cities remained in the hands of the SFIO—Lille, Strasbourg, Grenoble, and Brest, and even in the Paris region, Puteaux, Montreuil, and Alfortville. Some influential newspapers continued to publish the arguments of the losers of Tours: aside from *Le Populaire,* there was *Le Cri du Nord* of Delory and Salengro in Lille (it soon disappeared, but was replaced by *La Bataille), Le Droit du peuple* of Mistral in Grenoble, *Le Populaire du Centre* of Pressemane in Limoges, *La Montagne* of Alexandre Varenne in Clermont-Ferrand, *Le Combat social* in Montluçon, and in Toulouse *Le Midi socialiste* where Vincent Auriol was the dominant voice.

But what became of *L'Humanité* and the assets of the party before Tours? From January to April 1921, a socialist delegation led by Bracke and Faure attempted to convince its Communist counterparts, led by Frossard and Dunois, to divide influence over the newspaper and to share the assets. Wasted effort. Opposing "socialist legality" to "bourgeois law," and accusing their opponents of having misused 60,000 francs belonging to the party—which had in fact gone to establish a cooperative—Frossard and Dunois refused to give in on anything, which left the SFIO in the greatest poverty, at the moment when a Soviet agent named Zalewski, whose presence at Tours had been denounced by the minority, was distributing checks so imprudently that he was arrested by the police and provoked a scandal which the right-wing press fully exploited against the whole working-class movement.

The Tribune of *Le Populaire*

For this fragmented party, along with the mayoralties and its parliamentary "stars," *Le Populaire* remained the best weapon. Founded four years earlier by Jean Longuet, and having remained the organ of his faction, in March 1921 it became the official organ of the party that had taken refuge in its cramped quarters on the rue Feydeau, near the Bourse. The list of its administrators was identical to that of the party, and Blum was associated with Longuet in its political committee. A morning daily, *Le Populaire* had four pages and sold for 15 centimes. Toward the end of 1922 there were 20,000 regular readers, 7,000 subscribers, and the deficit was about 20,000 francs a month, which meant that it was vegetating. While the party was constantly strengthening itself from 1921 to 1924, finally achieving great electoral success in the framework of the *Cartel des gauches,* the paper declined to such an extent that its administrators were forced to suspend publication in June 1924, after their victory. Until 1927, *Le Populaire* was only a bimonthly newsletter for militants.

This weak newspaper nevertheless played an essential role, and it will survive in the history of French political life because between 1921 and 1924 it published some three hundred articles by a great journalist named Léon Blum. His editorials against the crushing of Germany and the occupation of the Ruhr, against Millerand's attempts to increase his personal power, and especially the admirable "Rosa Luxemburg et le Bolchevisme" (April 18, 1922), which I cannot refrain from quoting, helped to shape social consciousness:

> Rosa Luxemburg does not at all attack the Communists for seizing power in October 1917 by an act of brutal violence.[5] According to her the act was necessary because it was in conformity with the logic of revolutionary processes. A moment always comes, according to her, when great revolutions are given the choice between life and death: either go forward with a very rapid and resolute impetus and overturn all obstacles with an iron hand, or be thrown back past their points of departure and crushed by the counterrevolution. Nor does she dream of questioning for an instant that the dictatorship of the proletariat was on the one hand in conformity with Marxist doctrine, and on the other demanded by circumstances. But how should it be exercised? In what conditions? Does it imply, as the Russians thought, suppression of all democratic institutions, restrictions on every kind of public life, prohibition of all exchanges of ideas and opinions? Rosa Luxemburg protests the Russian conception with an abundance of theoretical, historical, and psychological arguments, with emotion, eloquence, and revolutionary fervor that have never been surpassed. It is in the name of the Revolution itself, in the name of its interests, its very life, its success, that she attacks the theory of Trotsky and Lenin.
>
> It is during the revolution, she says, that the governing political organs and elected bodies can and should experience, in the most direct and constant way, the influence of the life of the nation. To suppress all democratic institutions under the dictatorship is to dry up the vital source from which the dictatorship itself must draw nourishment, "the active, unhindered, energetic political life of the broad masses of the nation."
>
> Rosa Luxemburg shows that "without unlimited freedom of the press, without a life of meetings and associations freed of all restrictions, it is entirely impossible to conceive of rule by the popular masses." It will be argued that bourgeois dictatorship was established by the same procedures, but that ignores the essential difference. "Class rule by the bourgeoisie had no need of training and political education of the whole people (quite the contrary). For proletarian dictatorship it is the vital element, the air without which it cannot exist. . . . Faith in the creative force of the people is the idea of which democracy is the essential affirmation and Bolshevism the flagrant negation. To think and to act as the Bol-

sheviks have done is to substitute utopian for scientific socialism and to perpetuate the terror and moral corruption it creates. This is the original flaw and these are the necessary consequences of this socialism which has been decreed, granted from a conference table by a dozen intellectuals."

We, at least, have the right to reread Rosa Luxemburg's pamphlet with some pride. I imagine that she is not suspected of half-hearted attachment to the revolution and secret complicity with the bourgeoisie. She gave everything to her socialist beliefs, including her life.[6] And yet, before Tours, at Tours, we thought as she did, we wrote and spoke as she did. Her fundamental objections are ours. Like her, taking a Marxist point of view, we denounced the utopian character of Bolshevism.

Another of Blum's editorials from the same period, read today, takes on a strange resonance. Commenting on an article by a certain Sarraute, a close friend of the President of the Republic, which maintained that the head of state, far from being a symbolic or ornamental figure, had the duty to "act" and that, "if he is not the man of a party, he is the man of a politics for seven years, unless, of course, during that period, universal suffrage, in the form the law provides for the expression of its sovereign will, that is, in general elections, rises up against the policies it had theretofore approved," Blum wrote acidly:

If M. Sarraute's style is a little murky, his thought is clear. Universal suffrage will have to pronounce a verdict on the policies embodied in the person of M. Millerand in two years,[7] and if it comes out against those foreign and domestic policies, M. Millerand will leave the Elysée Palace. This is what M. Sarraute bluntly declares in the name of M. Millerand. The President of the Republic is in the Elysée Palace to assure the continuity of certain political directions, foreign and domestic. He does this for seven years, unless in the interval these political directions are disavowed by the country, in which case the President leaves. For he can obviously not remain in place like a classic pillar, while he is in fact claiming the role of an active political figure. And, of course, he can remain even less to assure, during the tail end of his seven years, political directions opposed to his own.

There is thus a single possible conclusion to this hypothesis: the President's resignation. We have all been clearly warned. We all know the directions of his domestic policies. If M. Millerand is the man of a politics, he is the man of the National Bloc set up around his name. If the National Bloc is defeated in two years, universal suffrage will have condemned M. Millerand's politics, and the defeat will touch M. Millerand himself.

No ambiguity: we are now well and duly warned. If the Bloc is defeated in two years, M. Millerand will resign. If we succeed in cleaning out the Palais-Bourbon, the Elysée will be cleared out at the same time. Bravo! The stakes of the battle are doubled! To work, comrades, to work![8]

Parliamentary Storms

But it was in the Chamber, whose work he sometimes discussed in *Le Populaire* with ferocious power, that Blum essentially established his reputation. Barrès, his former "mentor" and current political adversary, wrote of him: "I am touched that the revolutionaries have chosen Blum and Boncour. These intellectuals . . . elevate the tone of the gangsterlike discussion and constantly divert brutal demands in the direction of culture. They are civilizers as well as destroyers."[9]

The tall gentleman had just doffed the broad-brimmed black hat around which journalists of every stripe gathered on the steps of the Palais-Bourbon. His gaze glittering and tense, his mustache silky, his nose long and straight, this gentleman who looked like an orchestra leader or a magician, slipped through the corridors into the gallery of the *Quatre Colonnes* and then into the Chamber, where he sat on the front benches of the extreme left, usually between Bracke and Auriol.

He attended the sessions faithfully, in part as secretary of the socialist group, but also as a legal expert constantly consulted by his party on the texts of laws, always on guard against the extreme measures which the massive majority of the National Bloc in the *Chambre bleu-horizon* felt authorized to take. The tall gentleman with glasses was always there, watching and replying, his hand on Vincent Auriol's shoulder, reading out of the corner of his eye a file showed to him by Bracke. When he asked to speak, the Chamber would fill up again. Sometimes there was an uproar, sometimes he was greeted with the tense silence of a criminal court.

Let us take two examples.

On January 11, 1923, three weeks after Blum, in a long and passionate speech, had warned Poincaré against the occupation of the Ruhr as a means of "making Germany pay," an exercise of armed force that he thought could only lead to the rebirth of German militarism and to the isolation of France, the socialist leader once again took the floor. It was the very day that French troops entered the Ruhr. The benches of the Assembly were full, the atmosphere tense. Blum knew that this time he was confronting a passionately nationalistic bloc enflamed by anguish and the certainty that action was necessary. It was worse than at Tours:

> LEON BLUM: If the Chamber, in obvious agreement with the government, intends to let pass in silence a series of events that are dangerous. . .
> LEON DAUDET: Indispensable!
> MAGNE: Dangerous for international bankers!
> LEON DAUDET: For Jewish bankers! . . .
> LEON BLUM: If its silence, following the applause of a mo-

ment ago [during Poincaré's speech], means acquiescence, tacit or explicit assent. . .

MARCEL HABERT: Explicit!

LEON BLUM: We, at least, can neither wait nor be silent.

FROM THE CENTER: Who's "we"?

MAGNE: There is room here only for Frenchmen!

LEON DAUDET: To Jerusalem!

LEON BLUM: I am addressing the Chamber to assert, in the name of my friends, against the policy that has just been presented to you, a total refusal. . .

MARCEL HABERT: You are on the side of Germany!

LEON BLUM: I declare that we protest with all our strength. . .

YBARNEGARAY: The Jewish Protestant!

LEON BLUM: . . . against the military occupation of the Ruhr.

LIEUTENANT-COLONEL JOSSE: In the name of Germany!

LEON BLUM: We mean to protest especially in the name of the national interest.

LEON DAUDET: In the name of the Jewish International!

LEON BLUM: I hear people speaking of Jews. . . Is that, in your minds, an intimidation or an insult?

THE PRESIDENT: These perpetual interruptions are intolerable, gentlemen, but I have heard nothing insulting directed toward the speaker.

(This President was named Raoul Péret. His name could appear in an anthology of parliamentary hypocrisy.)

Eleven months later, the "operation" in the Ruhr had borne the fruits which Blum had predicted. He took the floor to draw the conclusions from the episode:

The putsch by Hitler and Ludendorff failed in Munich, of course, but do you see a great difference between Hitler and von Karr, or between Ludendorff and von Losow? . . . Even without an emperor, the military empire has been reestablished in Germany. I could reread to you the protest which we formulated last January 11 at the moment when the Premier announced, amidst your acclamations, that French troops had just entered Essen. You would see in that protest that the occupation of the Ruhr, by over-heating nationalist feeling, could only benefit the parties which, in Germany as in France, professionally exploit nationalist feeling. . . . Engaged in this absurdly prolonged resistance, I know, and the German social-democrats have constantly repeated, that [Germany] could sustain it only by ruining its finances and its public treasury, by imposing more and more severe hardships on all its citizens, and by placing greater obstacles in the way of private interests. In these conditions, how could nationalist feeling in Germany not take on the most intense, malignant, and dangerous form, that is, the form of hatred against France, considered as an implacable enemy, to which all the hardships and all the privations they suffer are attributed? This is how nationalism has developed in Germany, since the beginning of this year, and as a direct consequence of French policy.

This time, the Chamber listened to him in silence. Very few were willing to recognize that he was speaking the truth. But who could avoid observing that the enterprise of January 1923 was turning into a disaster? And who was not secretly grateful to Blum for triumphing so discreetly, so sorrowfully, when it was a question of revealing ten years in advance the mortal enemy of the future?

Electoralism, parliamentarianism? When such a use is made of an electoral mandate, when a militant expresses himself like this against his class enemies, blending moral resistance with intellectual education, is he engaged in "class collaboration" or revolutionary instruction?

At the Head of the Party

A great parliamentarian, and on that level an obvious leader of the SFIO; a great journalist, and thus the almost daily inventor or adaptor of the ideological "line" of the socialists, was Blum also head of the party? Reliable observers have denied that this was true, at least until the early thirties. Tony Judt, for example, the latest historian of this period, writes that

> Léon Blum was then a newcomer. Between 1921 and 1926 he could never claim the role of head of the socialist party. During this period nothing permits us to say that he was anything but the secretary of the parliamentary group. Within the party, his role was secondary. Having no experience as a militant, he had strained relations with militants. His speeches and articles, marked by technicality and intellectuality, were off-putting. Assimilated by many militants to Auriol or Paul-Boncour, he was considered a parliamentary specialist, and his friendship with Jaurès was not enough to attach him to the original SFIO.[10]

There is not one of these assertions which, in the light of research, seems to us correct, including the assimilation to Auriol and Paul-Boncour. But this description has the virtue of encouraging investigation of temporary and regional realities.

To situate Blum in the party in the course of the twenties, we must keep in mind the crises and tensions that preceded and followed the split of December 1920 and the role he played in them, the climate of the France of the National Bloc and the *Chambre bleu-horizon,* the divisions in the working class and those that were tearing apart the party of the victors at Tours, the structure and the make-up of the socialist party, the figures in the SFIO who then occupied the front of the stage and had a claim to lead the party, and finally the personality of the author of *Pour être socialiste.*

Let us consider this last point. Blum was of bourgeois origin. He was from the "petty bourgeoisie," if one considers the economic substratum and the nature of the activities that were the basis of his start in life, as well as the milieu of his childhood; from the "grande bourgeoisie" if one emphasizes the cultural background of his adult life, his relations since Jaurès's death, and his aesthetic tastes. And this was true although he had never been rich.

At the time of which we are speaking he was a lawyer at the Paris bar. Even though, according to his friend Thadée Natanson, he was more than scrupulous in the matter of fees,[11] his exceptional talent and his specialty in civil law made him a man without financial worries. (This was how he wished to live, unconcerned with accumulating stocks, bonds, or real estate. When he decided to help *Le Populaire* he had to take most of the money from the legacy of his father, who had died in 1921.)

His closest friends were not, as has sometimes been said, the fashionable people of Paris, the heroes of *A la recherche du temps perdu*. To be sure, there were the Cortots and Reynaldo Hahn, who evoke Mme de Verdurin's salon or summers in Cambremer; and Vuillard and Bonnard, who make one think of Elstir. Until 1924, there was Anatole France and the salon of Mme de Caillavet. Blum's closest friends were the Auriols, Alexandre Bracke, his colleague at the bar André Blumel, Alfred and Thadée Natanson, the diplomat Philippe Berthelot, and of course the man who had remained his mentor, Lucien Herr, whose death in 1926 was one of the most profound losses in his life.

If the real framework of his significant activity was made up of professors and civil servants, this was still hardly a proletarian milieu. But was it an exception? A bourgeois intellectual can lead a socialist party. What were Marx and Engels, Guesde and Jaurès, Lenin, and even Trotsky? What were Vandervelde and Huysmans, MacDonald and Attlee, Turati, and even Gramsci? Victor Adler, Pietro Nenni? Except for Stalin, Bevan, Caballero, and the leaders of the second generation of the Third International, it was rather common.

But neither his economic well being nor his bourgeois, if not aristocratic, intellectual milieu helped bring Blum closer to rank and file militants. There was also something more serious. He was Parisian, intensely, ardently Parisian. In a party which, since 1920, was reviving only through its provincial connections (in Lille, Marseille, Grenoble, and Toulouse) Blum's Parisian roots and his Parisian style were not assets.

The fact that he was a Jew operated neither for nor against his rise in the party; Marx's nearly anti-Semitic assimilation of Judaism and capitalism (in the middle of the nineteenth century, and in the Rhine region of Germany) had little influence. The SFIO remained the party established by the most powerful of Dreyfus's defenders, Jean Jaurès. It remained the French political organization that was the most open to exiles, dissidents of every origin, and it had more Jews in the middle and upper levels of its leadership than any other party—men who were often Blum's sharpest party adversaries.

Blum was also, even fundamentally, a "man of parliament." And this was perhaps the greatest obstacle to his being accepted as the real leader of the party. Even though Jaurès had ennobled the function of representative, the activity (or better the activities) of a frequenter of the Chamber always inspired a kind of mistrust on the left, symmetrical to the rising suspicion in rightist circles. At the congress of Tours, when the future Ho Chi Minh, denouncing the misdeeds of colonization, was interrupted by Longuet, the best arguments he could find to silence him was: "Quiet, Parliament men!"

To be sure, in this period of resistance to the National Bloc, the performance of Blum and his group in Parliament offered little ground for challenge from the rank and file. The excerpts from speeches we have already quoted are clear enough on this point. But from 1923 on, beginning with the campaign of the *Cartel des gauches* in alliance with the Radicals, and especially after the election in the framework of this bourgeois alliance, suspicions were renewed, and Blum's "star" quality that made him the favorite target of cartoonists of the bourgeois press did not always help him in the opinion of the rank and file militants. Assimilated, then, to Paul-Boncour? No. But as suspect as a worldly preacher of Notre-Dame would be in the eyes of a curate in a working-class suburb.

Blum's handicaps as a candidate for leadership of the party— supposing that he had been one, like Guy Mollet, for example, in 1946—were numerous. Moreover, the SFIO of the early twenties was inspired and directed by the "reconstructors" of 1919–20. Blum had of course appeared in their ranks at the Strasbourg congress of February 1920. But he was not part of the "family"—followers of Guesde and Longuet—still immersed as he was in the climate of the *Union sacrée* of 1914–17. He was thus ideologically (or historically) out of phase with the "general line." But he had been able to radicalize his positions in response to the political situation. Besides, what "Guesdist" could find anything to criticize in any of his major speeches, at the congress of April 1919, or the congress of Tours?

If we set aside his past, his milieu, his way of life, and his incurably aristocratic style, we can situate Blum only in the center of the SFIO of the twenties, even in the center-left, in the very middle of the "reconstructors," whose fight he supported, whose worries he shared, and whose aspirations he expressed. Ideologically, he was perfectly placed—at the intersection of the strictly Marxist current embodied by Longuet and the neo-Jaurèsian current of Renaudel and Sembat—to assume the highest responsibilities.

Was there anyone more suited than he? In 1922, both Jules Guesde and Marcel Sembat died. Since the congress of Tours, Sembat had moreover shown all the signs of "disinterestedness," and was nothing more than a moving and sarcastic witness to battles already old. Pierre Renaudel remained the breathless guardian of Jaurès's legacy: a virtuoso in the manipulation of congresses, a clever calculator, but with no ideas. Who would have dared seriously to oppose him to Blum?

Albert Thomas, on the other hand, was a warm and noble figure, of working-class origin, with Jaurèsian power, and a sharp intelligence. But from the period of the *Union sacrée* on, deprived of the enlightened counsels of the great man, he revealed himself as a democratic technician, if not a technocrat, a man who dreamed of fusing the proletariat and middle managers into what had not yet been named an "historic bloc." He was certainly an honest man, with great human resources, but entirely foreign to Marxism, and above all preoccupied with productivity, in the popular, even "populist" style adopted by certain Communist ministers twenty years later at the time of reconstruction. The story is told that when he visited the USSR during the summer of 1917 accompanied by Kerensky, the crowds, seeing this huge bearded man with golden hair and a ruddy face next to the pale, thin head of the revolutionary government, cheered him: he was the one who ought to be the Russian.

But even before Tours, Albert Thomas had felt himself a loner in the SFIO. The rise of Marxist or *Marxisant* ideologues in the party apparatus, the minority position of the "patriots" after the summer of 1918, the refusal of the party to support his own aspirations to play an important role in the government—everything distanced him from the party whose hope he had been on the eve of the war. He drew his own conclusions with dignity; rather than follow the example of the renegades Millerand and Viviani, he left for Geneva, where he had been offered the directorship of the International Labor Organization, in the framework of the League of Nations. He had removed himself from the debate.

Jean Longuet was only forty-four at the end of the war; but he remained indelibly marked by the attacks of the Bolshevik leaders at the end of 1920. He was the one who had extended his hand to the International: and he was the one who had then been attacked. He was not, like Blum, a resister who had chosen his camp. Despite himself, he had been rejected and insulted, called an "agent of the bourgeoisie." He did not get over it. Not that he was embittered; he struggled sincerely to keep "his" *Populaire* alive, he welcomed Blum on the paper and shared editorial duties with him. He never recovered from his defeat at Tours. He was only a survivor, for nearly twenty more years; he died at the time of the Munich agreements.

Finally, there was Paul Faure. George Lefranc's formulation, "If Léon Blum was the head of the SFIO, Paul Faure was its heart," is not without wit. But how can one really compare the author of *Pour être socialiste* with the man who was, for twenty years, the party's chief engineer, with passion, patience, drive, and meticulous dynamism, but without very often being capable of rising above manipulations of the apparatus? Reading the articles Paul Faure provided almost daily for *Le Populaire* is a chore. His few speeches in the Chamber never evoke his superb peroration at the congress of Tours.[12] His most famous *bons mots* place him alongside Balzac's *illustre* Gaudissart.

A native of Périgord, he had vigor, but not the kind one might attribute to Fénelon. A Guesdist, he was ardently attached to socialist principles, but he had only a smattering of Marxism. Of bourgeois origin—his father was a lawyer—he nevertheless had the gift of mixing with people; and his name, his face, his wit, the campaign meetings he held, his correspondence, and his tours in the provinces were, from 1920 to 1940, irreplaceable energizing elements in the life of the party. In the minority during the war, along with Longuet and Pressemane (one of the founders with Faure of *Le Populaire du Centre*), he had remained deeply pacifist.

In fact, pacifism was the sum, the dead-end of his thought. His pacifism made him incapable of distinguishing resistance to Nazism from the 1914 conflict. Beyond pacifist blindness, we must also speak of cowardice. Edouard Depreux reports in his *Souvenirs d'un militant* that, questioned by an investigatory commission during Blum's trial at the court of Riom about the nationalizations carried out by the Popular Front government, Paul Faure was satisfied with answering: "As Minister of State in the government of 1936, I had no involvement with nationalizations."

Until 1940, however, he was a leader of great power. His title of "secretary-general of the party" was not mentioned in the statutes, which established only a secretary-general of the CAP (permanent administrative committee). But his activity—one would say his magnetism if the word did not presuppose virtues and talents which Paul Faure lacked—his "presence" in short, had become personalized, and when he met with the rank and file, the federations, and the sections, he was not only the delegate or the emissary of the central organism, he was felt as the real head of the party. It was his name that appeared at the bottom of all the circulars, it was he who appeared at difficult moments.

He was gracious, easy to approach, and had a facile mind. The heart of the party? His impact might be located a little lower, closer to the stomach. If one insists on speaking of the heart, one might say, adapting a cruel expression of Gide about one of his colleagues, that he spoke from the heart as others speak through the nose.

But with his handsome features, his tender smile, his warm eyes beneath bushy black brows, he had a good deal of charm. He was omnipresent, devoted, cordial. He led, inspired, controlled. However dazzling Blum's reputation may have been, for the rank and file of the party Paul Faure was the visible man. In 1926, when one of the best known journalists in the party, Louis Lévy, decided to compile a little book of interviews with SFIO personalities entitled *Comment ils sont devenus socialistes,* he noted that he spoke first of all to Paul Faure (and he added "obviously").

Political leadership, though, is not shown and exercised only from the inside. From the point of view of the rank and file, Paul Faure was at the helm. But the SFIO was also a cultural entity, a national current, a counterstate, and the center of an international constellation. In that case, it was impossible not to recognize Blum's preeminence. The militants found him too Parisian, too parliamentary? That is quite possible. Too intellectual, too difficult to follow? Nothing proves that this was true. On the contrary, his powerful intelligence charmed and attracted, and many militants felt pride in having a writer of his stature speak to them without at all "popularizing" his style.

The fact remains that, whatever their differences, Paul Faure and Léon Blum cooperated on apparently equal terms for nearly fifteen years. The balance was upset in 1934, when the entry into "high" politics and the approach of power concentrated all attention on the statesman, throwing the political operator into the shadows. *Entente cordiale?* Mutual tolerance? The prestige of the "prima donna" certainly annoyed the mechanic.

Paul Faure never forgot that he was already one of the leaders of the left of the party when Blum was still immersed in the troubled waters of the *Union sacrée.* He knew that without his industriousness, his communicative drive, his intimate knowledge of the militant rank and file, Blum, with all his talent, would not have had the support of a great party, but of a mere parliamentary clique. The right-wing press shrewdly pointed out the numerous signs of discord between the secretary-general, head of the "house," and the intellectual leader.

Until 1938, however, it is impossible to find evidence of any major disloyalty between them. Blum knew all that the party—and thus he himself—owed to the multifarious activities of the man who had in the end deserved the title of "reconstructor." His natural elegance reinforced the dictates of his conscience on this point. Their relations could not but suffer from the extreme disparity of their talents, their ways of life, their concerns, their aesthetic tastes. But "party patriotism" carried the day. A basis of understanding was found to save *Le Populaire,* to defeat a candidate of the National Bloc, to revive the Vaucluse federation, to help elect Jules Moch in Sète. An accommodation was made between Paul Faure's slightly sectarian, down-to-earth, programmatic vision, and Léon Blum's overly relaxed and wide-ranging vision.

It is tempting to compare the relations between the two men to those established between Jean Jaurès and Jules Guesde after the congress for unification of 1905. This would be a disservice to Guesde. And the comparison doesn't lead very far. To be sure, Faure was as much a Guesdist as Blum was a Jaurèsian. But between the "founding fathers," whatever Jaurès's intellectual superiority, relations were based on equality. The deputy from the Midi never forgot the pioneering role of his comrade from the Nord and what his activity as introducer and vulgarizer of Marxism in France had contributed to the party. Guesde the sectarian, the "priest," the secular preacher, had authentic grandeur. There was nothing comparable in Paul Faure. It is impossible to speak of "dual leadership" by the two heirs, which implies community of nature and of depth. At most we can speak of complementarity.

Perhaps we should add that these comments and descriptions involve shifts in time. Are we superimposing images and facts of the late twenties and early thirties on the more diffuse realities of the immediate postwar period? The important thing is not that these power relationships between Blum and Faure, between the two men and their chief comrades, and between them and the rank and file were established in 1921 or after 1928. But the curve, the tendency, was certainly in this direction, and at times of great decision—formation of the *Cartel,* refusal of participation, resistance to the "single front," acceptance of "popular union"—our description of the kind of relations that existed is accurate.

Moreover, we should not dwell too long on the notion of "head" of the party. We know how energetically Blum had argued at Tours against any kind of hegemony, and how he had contrasted the egalitarian and controlled leadership of the SFIO to the hierarchical and militaristic system of the Bolsheviks. Later, when his authority had been recognized, he constantly refused to be called "head" of the party; he preferred the word *animateur,*[13] until the day in May 1936 when he fervently claimed the responsibilities of leader on the eve of assuming power.

It was one of Blum's schoolmates, Louis Révelin,[14] who had outlined the structures of the party leadership in 1905. At the congress of

Limoges in 1906, he declared: "The congress is the head, the federations are the locations of movement and life, the National Council is the natural organ of leadership" (article 27). Gradually, this function passed from the National Council to a mere executive organ (article 39), the famous CAP (Permanent Administrative Committee), a natural organ of the bureaucratization which is the fate of every institution which is not shaken, churned, or overthrown at regular intervals by a cultural revolution or a rebellion of the rank and file. With Faure controlling the CAP (Blum did not join until 1927) and the federations, Blum's role became significant during National Councils and especially congresses. Not to mention the parliamentary group, where his influence, supported by that of his closest friends, Auriol, Bracke, Lebas, and Moutet, was unrivaled.

But if the personal relations between Blum and Faure were for the most part positive, the same cannot be said of the relations between the CAP and the parliamentary group which, especially after 1924 and during the periods when the SFIO followed a policy of support for center-left governments, was the target of caustic criticism from those outside Parliament. Deputies and senators were presumed to be carrying out "class collaboration" in a more reprehensible way than locally elected officials (mayors and local councillors), journalists, lawyers, or other party intellectuals. In January 1930, Faure had to remind the members of the CAP that members of parliament could also act as militants.

None of the congresses of the SFIO, between the great schism of 1920 and the congress of 1933 at which the split of the "neo-socialists" began, led to any decisive innovations, either in structure or in doctrine. At most, we can point to the 1923 congress in Lille which, through the ambiguity of its decisions, discreetly opened the way for the strategy of the *Cartel des gauches*. The strength of the reactions of the opponents of alliance with the Radicals, notably Longuet and Pressemane, made it apparent that despite the resistance of all the federations, the opening that would permit the formation of the *Cartel* had been made. This was the coalition that would win the election and eliminate the National Bloc, which had been taken over by Millerand with such voracity that he identified it with his career as President of the Republic and was obliged to resign on its defeat—as Blum had predicted in 1922.

But it was not until the congress of Marseille in January 1924, that the decision which led to electoral victory was finally taken. This congress was also the congress of decisive recovery. Faure declared that the party already had 80,000 members (growth of 150 percent since the beginning of 1921) and that 78 federations were represented. In more than half, the SFIO had more sections and members than the SFIC (French Section of the Communist International, as the rival organization was often called). From that time on, the minority of Tours had reestablished equilibrium with their conquerors.

But perhaps the most interesting congress of the period was the one in Lyon (April 1927) where, after the failure of the *Cartel* policy, and against a dual challenge—the left, in the person of Jean Zyromski, criticized him for not taking enough account of the "growth of class antagonisms" in order to radicalize the party's action; the right reproached him with systematically refusing to share the responsibilities of power—Blum provided a dual response, doctrinal to the left and strategic to the right. This constituted a decisive renewal if not of the doctrine, at least of the "line" of the movement. The response to Zyromski points to a whole series of investigations and movements which were to take shape in the succeeding years:

> It is true that, for all sorts of reasons, new forms of capitalism have appeared, and to borrow one of your expressions with which I completely agree, forms that have taken on a more and more dictatorial character. It is true that the excessive concentration of industrial enterprises and as a corollary the introduction of new industrial methods, and beyond industrial concentration, the creation and development of what you call financial superconcentration, all this has indeed given the new capitalism a new form; and this capitalism is now imposing its dictatorship even on States, even on political institutions, and every day we see it commit new usurpations of sovereignty.
>
> . . . Well! What I mean is that the phenomena pointed out by Zyromski have the peculiar character of not weighing only or especially heavily on the working class.
>
> . . . Does excessive concentration, financial superconcentration weigh most heavily on the proletariat? It has more effect than the proletariat believes, and we have great difficulty in making this understood because the repercussions are so indirect. But the repercussions are more direct, and more clearly visible, on a large part of the capitalist class, on commerce, on small-scale production, on a large variety of members of the bourgeoisie. And in the end what it weighs on most heavily is the political form of bourgeois democracy; for if we take, for example, the battle that marked the two years after 11 May,[15] against whom was the oppression of high finance particularly directed? It was much more against a political conception than against the proletariat itself.
>
> What I would like to say to the congress is that my own fear is that these new forms of capitalist evolution, far from increasing the consciousness of class antagonisms in the working class, far from accentuating those class antagonisms, as the Amsterdam motion said, will on the contrary create, between this modernized and strengthened capitalism and the working class itself, apparent communities of interest, precarious of course, but nevertheless

perceptible enough that class consciousness, consciousness of the class struggle, far from being intensified, will on the contrary be somehow obscured.

As for the response to the "participationists" of the right, it already sounds like a prelude to June 1936:

> From now on we will engage only in battles that we inspire and lead. . . . We have all searched our consciences after the three difficult years we have gone through. I want to make a confession to you. It is that, after Herriot's fall, when we had vainly called for the fight to continue and not to give in to the Senate, when we had called on the other parties in the Chamber to reconstitute the Herriot government against the Senate and to stand for no other government, and after all these efforts had failed, I did not ask the party group for authorization to take the floor to say: "Well! As far as we are concerned, something is over. We are ready to continue the fight, but we will no longer accept the leadership of others. We gave you all our strength, all our support; you tried and you did not succeed. We are ready to begin again whenever you like, but this time *we* will hold the reins, and *we* will lead the fight!"

The vigor of these two stands—one which dared to question the inevitability of the aggravation of class struggle, and the other which, opening the way to "direct" exercise of power, made accession to power more difficult than ever—resulted in the hardening of opposition against Blum from both sides, from Zyromski and Renaudel. But nevertheless, it is from the Lyon congress, at the end of which he joined the CAP, that can be dated the beginning of his "reign" over the SFIO. It was then that the man who was still considered the "conscience of the party," Jean Longuet, who had remained essentially the spokesman for the left of the party, declared that "Léon Blum has made a place for himself because of his competence and his talent."

The Second International Survives

The SFIO in which the deputy from Paris thereafter assumed major responsibilities was far from the disorganized band of exiles from Tours. Beginning in 1921, it had even undertaken a counterattack by working toward the reconstitution of an International along the lines dreamed of by the "reconstructors" around Jean Longuet in 1919.

In February, when the party barely knew whether it would survive, it sent a delegation to a meeting in Vienna to which the Revolutionary Socialist Party had invited the SFIO, Keir Hardie's Independent Labour Party, the Italian Socialist Party of Turati, and the USPD (the minority German Socialist Party, Ledebour's group, which had broken from the Party three years before.

"The Vienna union of socialist parties" was immediately denounced by Karl Radek as "International two and a half," a nickname which put an end to the hope the Austrians entertained of fusing with the International founded by the Bolsheviks in 1919. Less clearly than Radek but in a heavy-handed way, Renaudel also helped to muddy the waters by the summary, almost aggressive, manner with which he attempted to impose the French point of view over the loyally internationalist suggestions of Bauer and Adler.

The "International two and a half" nevertheless survived for two years. When the principal spokesmen of the French party—Longuet, Bracke, and Blum—had made it know that their most pressing concern was the resumption of contacts with Moscow, the outlook became more promising. The SFIO congress of November 1, 1921 having given its leadership authorization, a conference was called in Paris in February 1922, to which were invited the Labour Party and the Scandinavian socialists as well as the parties of the Third International. The Communists rejected the invitation, so that the conference finally brought together only the English, the Belgians, and the French.

A second meeting, in Frankfurt, was scarcely more promising. But in April 1922, the USSR sent Karl Radek to Berlin. In spite of violent confrontations with the social-democratic leaders, he agreed to the establishment of a "Committee of Nine" consisting of three representatives of the three "internationals"—the Second, "two and a half," and the Third. A surprising *de facto* recognition! But a month later, Radek broke off discussions on the understandable pretext that while the Committee of Nine was meeting, a delegation of the SFIO headed by Renaudel was participating in a conference of the Second International in Brussels.

The hope of the "great reunification" was annihilated. On October 14, 1922, a few weeks before his death, Jules Guesde made a final effort: he published an article in *L'Echo du Nord* in favor of having the SFIO call an international socialist conference with the Soviets. It was a waste of effort. The socialists had to resign themselves to the "small reunification" between the old International of 1889 and the Vienna International.

This was accomplished in May 1923, at the Hamburg congress, where Friedrich Adler resigned himself to a fusion which fell far short of the Austrian hopes of 1921 and subordinated the revolutionary socialist movements to the social-democratic majority, since the IOS (Socialist Workers International) was under the control of the Labour Party, German social democracy, and the Belgian workers party. But the Hamburg conference was the scene of a significant demonstration of internationalism.

Recalling his party's opposition to the treaty of Versailles, Blum, spokesman for the SFIO, solemnly declared on May 24, 1923, that the article of this "imposed" treaty which, to him,

> appears particularly [wounding] is the one in which Germany is forced to recognize its exclusive responsibility for the war. For this recognition of responsibility could have the slightest value only to the extent that it was voluntary and freely given. Constraint seems to me even more serious, less acceptable, in the case of a moral affirmation like that than for any material obligation.

After denouncing once more the methods used to make "Germany pay," above all the occupation of the Ruhr, Blum concluded in a typically Jaurèsian vein:

> True internationalism, for us, consists first of all in the acquired habit of submitting international relations, and the facts of any kind that can influence those relations, to a spirit of exact observation, impartial criticism, and objective reasoning, free from any kind of prejudice or passion. It consists in the firm and resolute determination to apply to states as to individuals the rules of Justice, Morality, and Law, and for states as for individuals, to resolve differences and conflicts of any kind by the peaceful procedures of Law. It consists, finally, I would even say that it consists essentially, for us socialists, in the conviction, which is continually confirmed by experience, that in the current state of the world economy there can be no contradiction between the real, long-range interests of any particular nation and the real, long-range interests of all the others.
>
> There have been times when the grandeur of a state could be based on the defeat and subjection of others; there have been times when the wealth and prosperity of a state could be supported by the ruin and the poverty of others. Those who would believe that this past History can be repeated are harboring the most senseless and fatal of illusions. All the nations of today, whether they wish it or not, are in a position of solidarity in good or evil fortune. The ruin of one nation is a cause of poverty for all the others; the prosperity of one nation—even a victorious one—presupposes the prosperity of all the others, even the defeated. It is this inevitable solidarity of one country with all other countries which constitutes the unshakable foundation of our international socialist action. In this sense, internationalism and the most clear-sighted patriotism are identical.

The stenographic report of the congress indicates that several times while Blum was speaking, "thunderous applause" overwhelmed his voice. It was not so much the ideas he expressed or the remarks he made that were hailed as it was the courage required for a French representative to rise up so boldly against the chauvinistic currents that were flowing on both sides of the Rhine at the moment when the violent occupation of the Ruhr was going on. The president of the session, Crispien, who had been (on the German side) one of the protagonists of the *Union sacrée,* was deeply moved and rose to declare:

> Our comrade Léon Blum has spoken as a representative of the France with which the German proletariat, in spite of everything, feels solidarity. Comrade Blum's courageous speech reminds us of the greatness of spirit of many of our predecessors in the battle; it reminds us of Jaurès. We thank comrade Blum for his courageous speech, filled with the purest spirit of internationalism![16]

The Shadow of Government: The "Cartel"

As he took on more responsibilities and increased his national and international audience, the question of power became more insistent for Blum. The SFIO was recovering and consolidating. The right-wing governments of the *Chambre bleu-horizon* accumulated mistakes and disappointments. A change in the majority became plausible from the beginning of 1923 on. Soon thereafter, a sure sign, the Radicals abandoned Poincaré and made less and less discreet advances with a view toward a reversal of electoral alliances. What would the SFIO do as the elections, scheduled for 1924, approached? At the Hamburg congress, Blum tried to get the International to take a position that might enlighten or direct him. A wasted effort.

The doctrine of the SFIO, since its establishment in 1905, shortly after the 1904 Amsterdam congress, was clear on participation in a bourgeois government, tolerable only in case of "exceptional circumstances." Hence the participation of Guesde, Sembat, and Thomas from 1914 to 1917 (although that "tolerance" provoked a great deal of criticism). The doctrine was much less simple on the question of electoral alliances. The famous "Bracke motion" of 1919 was a warning against alliances with bourgeois parties—if not against arrangements for the second round of elections. But as early as 1922, Paul Faure, an opponent of electoralism, declared: "Attack bourgeois candidates first! Then attack the worst bourgeois candidates!" Which introduced a nuance useful to tacticians.

At the time, Blum was as suspicious as his friend Bracke of any electoral alliance. He expressed his longing for a system of "proportional representation" which—every man for himself—would solve the problem. But since that solution was rejected by the majority, he raised the questions reflected in the motion of the Lille congress (February

1923), on the basis of which suggestions and distinctions would proliferate, ending up with the *Cartel* strategy. It was not Blum, as has often been said, but the Guesdist Compère-Morel who, "with a heavy heart," gave the signal for the acceptance secretly hoped for by many socialists, by distinguishing between electoral alliance (acceptable) and participation in power (inconceivable). From that point on, the current swelled. Its opponents, like Jean Longuet, who were supporters of the formation of a "workers bloc" (rejected by the Communists), still attempted to distinguish the situation in the Midi—where the alliance with the Radicals was necessary—and that which prevailed in the Nord—where it was imperative to persist in the attempt to reach an understanding with the PCF.

All the same, at the Marseille congress, it was Blum who won agreement for the solution of a "restricted" *cartel* or *"cartel* of one minute"—the minute one places one's ballot in the box—surrounding it with very severe restrictions: each federation could conclude local alliances with the Radicals or the Communists only with "the express authorization" of the CAP and in cases where the alliance would clearly operate against the National Bloc. This first of the major motions inspired by Blum bears the full imprint of its author: the principles are strongly emphasized, but loyalty to an intangible past does not exclude tactical initiatives in all directions.

It is quite characteristic of the "manner," the style of Blum, that on the eve of this experiment, which he clearly felt would lead him and his party down paths where they would find all too many opportunities to compromise, he published in a distinctly "bourgeois" journal, *La Revue de Paris,* a long article entitled "L'Idéal socialiste," which was in a sense a way of tying his hands, of explaining to those with whom he was going to have to live what he was and what his loyalties were. Pointing out that he was writing on the eve of an election, he emphasized the following, which would not win over his centrist allies:

> More than any other party, the socialist party detests violence and bloodshed. We hope that social transformation—which is the real meaning of the word revolution for us—can take place through legal processes, through an electoral victory, for example. But in this respect, the lessons of history have made us somewhat skeptical.
> We are not very certain that legality, on the very day when we might call upon it for our benefit, will not let us down. We are not very certain that the representatives and leaders of present society, at the moment when its essential principles appear too seriously threatened, would not themselves go outside the bounds of legality to enter the realm of what would appear to them the Right. It happened on 2 December; it happened much more recently, very close to us. A putsch which protects the social system is generally

the beneficiary of a good deal of sympathy. If socialism were definitevely bound by sworn respect for legality, it would risk playing a fool's game. Who can reproach us for this?

The republicans, even the moderates, have not forgotten, I think, the origins of the Republic in this country. The Republic was never proclaimed in France by virtue of a legal vote delivered according to constitutional forms. On 10 August 1792, in February 1848, on 4 September, it was established by the will of the people in revolt against existing legality. Today we have universal suffrage, but it existed on 4 September, it existed, or very nearly so, on 10 August. Then it was only a fiction; but is it a full reality today? Doesn't the influence of the boss and the owner weigh on the voters, along with the pressure of financial powers and the press? Is every voter free in the vote he casts, free through the development of his mind, free because of his personal independence? And to liberate him, isn't it precisely a revolution that we need?

The author of *Pour être socialiste* was reelected on May 11, 1924 in the very working-class second district of Paris (the first, fourth, eleventh, and twentieth *arrondissements*). Ninety-eight other candidates of the SFIO were elected at the same time. With the support of the small group of "socialist-communists" of Georges Pioch, they held 105 seats in the new Chamber, compared to 140 Radicals and 44 "republican socialists." It was not a triumph, but it was a success. It is legitimate to ask that electoral association with the center had contributed to the socialists that they would not have been able to gain themselves. Forty of them were elected without an agreement with the Radicals, and the largest margins were won in districts where no alliance had been made.

But one must also note that the isolated Communists, with 8 percent more votes than their rivals of Tours, held only 26 seats. Along with the right, they were the great losers: in less than three-and-a half years, undermined by constant division (Frossard left the SFIC on February 1, 1923), they had lost the initiative on the left, and for the next ten years were to play the role of a mere extremist sect—until the moment when they returned to a strategy of unity.

The electoral strategy of the *Cartel* had thus "paid off." But at the very moment when the leaders of the SFIO had to accept interruption of publication of *Le Populaire,* this success opened the way to an even more redoubtable and more classic debate, the debate on "participation." On June 1, Edouard Herriot, the Radical leader called on to form the government by the new President Gaston Doumergue (successor to Millerand who had been obliged to follow the National Bloc in defeat), wrote to his socialist colleague a letter whose first three words have remained famous because of what the right saw as a sign of complicity:

"My dear Blum" (an automatic formula for former comrades at the Ecole Normale) "The clear will of the country is that this [electoral] cooperation continue in the councils of government. I therefore ask, in the name of my party, for complete support from the socialist party. The people have done their duty; it is up to us to fulfill ours!"

From the first meeting between delegations of the two parties, the plan of socialist participation was excluded, by mutual agreement, as it was again the next day when Herriot returned to the attack with the kind of program which presupposed socialist cooperation. In the meanwhile, a special congress of the SFIO had voted for support without participation. Did Blum argue, as has often been said, for the entry of socialists into the government, attempting to overcome the opposition of the CAP and the Seine federation? No. Blum, like his friends, Bracke and Lebas, was opposed to participation in the government. With this ruled out, he declared himself in favor of support for this government of "reforms." But however reformist the Radical leader may have considered himself, his cabinet nevertheless followed financial and military policies (despite the evacuation of the Ruhr) that put the good will of its socialist allies to the test.

From the beginning of 1925, in the Seine federation (led by Zyromski and Bracke), Blum and his parliamentary friends were put in the minority. The national congress which was held in Grenoble in February was an opportunity for Blum to explain himself, with the loyal support of Paul Faure who, hardly suspected of sympathy with the Radicals, was, like Blum, concerned with maintaining party unity. Blum's speech in Grenoble was "completely frank and clear," in the judgment of Ziebura.[17] He concealed nothing. The support given to a government which, by carrying out the Dawes plan [18] and opening the way to détente with Germany, was essentially serving the cause of peace and democracy, was still justified. But the position adopted by the party, forced either to ignore its own program or to abandon the government to its fate and thereby risk returning the right to power, was a dead end. Ideology or politics? March toward socialism or priority given to the defense of bourgeois democracy? Short term or long term? Blum continued to ask his comrades and himself the painful questions of Grenoble.

The socialist parliamentary group attempted to reconcile ideology and support. On March 25, in a letter to Edouard Herriot, Léon Blum expressed the strongest reservations about his government's disastrous economic and fiscal policies and, considering the "really dramatic danger," revived his cherished notion of a tax on capital.

The government, wrote Blum to the man he addressed as "My dear Herriot," must undertake a broad operation of financial reform and stabilization of the currency, making the Treasury truly secure, definitively freeing the State from the help of, and consequent domination by, the banks, quickly restoring its true value to the franc, permitting the preparation on more favorable grounds of definitive stabilization of the currency, and thereby, in the long run, obtaining for the country a benefit greater than the momentary sacrifice it would be asked to make. This operation, in our opinion, can consist only in a tax on capital, set at a moderate enough rate not to distort its true character, but high enough to free at one stroke the State, the Treasury, and the country itself from the difficulties oppressing them—for such an operation can only be carried out once: from 12.5% to 10%.

The Minister of Finance in the Herriot cabinet, Clémentel, appalled by this demand, resigned on April 2. The Radical leader, who cooperated with Blum, was defeated on a vote of confidence in the Senate. Called to succeed him, Briand once again attempted to secure the participation of his former socialist comrades, with no success. He gave up the attempt. Paul Painlevé, for his part, was content with asking for the support of Blum, who obtained agreement from his friends. But new Minister of Finance, Joseph Caillaux, in whom a number of socialists (including Blum) had confidence because of his pacifism, his role in introducing the income tax, and the hatred with which he was viewed by the right, deeply disappointed them by rejecting any fiscal attack on capital and the establishment of a social insurance system.

In May, the SFIO won significant victories in the municipal election, notably mayoral contests in Bordeaux, Toulouse, Nîmes, and Rennes. The opponents of support for the government, like Zyromski and Faure, were all the more encouraged to contrast the growing strength of the party with its incapacity to direct the government's policies. At the special congress held on August 15 in the Salle Japy (site of one of the historic meetings of French socialism in 1899), Blum accepted without reservation the arguments of Faure in favor of withdrawing the party's support from the Painlevé government.

The leaders of the SFIO did not simply feel frustrated by the contradiction between their consolidation and the role they were made to play as the Saint Bernard of exhausted Radicalism. The outbreak of rebellions in Morocco and Syria placed them in an intolerable position—caught between the repression carried out by their Radical allies and the bold anticolonialist campaigns conducted by the Communists, led by Jacques Doriot and Maurice Thorez. It was at this point that the acceptance—without consulting his comrades—of the position of governor-general of Indochina by Alexandre Varenne, socialist deputy from Puy-de-Dôme, turned an uncomfortable situation for the party leaders into a scandal.

The "colonial" doctrine of the SFIO was imprecise, although Jean Longuet had already taken public positions strongly in favor of the emancipation of Morocco and Syria, and obtained direct aid for North African nationalist militants. Blum, too, had argued for Tunisian freedom in 1920. But his positions on this question took shape only at a later date. In any case, the colonial crises accentuated the discomfort within the SFIO and contributed to a stiffening which led to the break with the Painlevé government and its successors.

On the "Conquest" and the "Exercise" of Power

But the contradictory implications of the *Cartel* policy continued to trouble the SFIO. In fact, it was toward the end of 1925 that the most serious crisis since the Tours split began, and it came close to destroying the unity that had been so dearly obtained and defended. A tactical maneuver of the socialist parliamentary group whereby Blum declared that, in order to carry out its financial program, his party was ready to assume "power alone," provoked strong feeling in the party and a brutal reaction from the CAP. In fact, it seems that Blum wanted to set in motion a broad debate on basic problems, both in the Chamber on the government's economic strategy, and in the party on the perennial question of power.

He thereby risked calling into question the socialist unity for which he had always been—except at Tours—a passionate advocate. But, as at Tours, he gave priority to his demands for clarity, logic, and reason. It was in this context, in the congress known as the congress of la Bellevilloise, in January 1926, that he delivered a speech which is quoted almost as often as the Tours speech. In it, he carried out what Henry Kissinger would call fifty years later a "conceptual breakthrough," by establishing the famous distinction between the "conquest" and the "exercise" of power.

To a party which was struggling with the permanent contradiction between a hypothetical revolutionary seizure of power, the official objective of the French socialists, and reformist or revisionist participation in bourgeois power, Blum proposed a third solution. According to him, the socialist party, which sooner or later, before the revolution, would be forced to assume governmental responsibilities, should do so only on the condition that, alone or in coalition, it had control of the situation.

This "exercise of power," which presupposes the acceptance of democratic and parliamentary rules in the framework of the capitalist system, "is and always will be a particularly difficult and painful experience for socialist parties," Blum admitted. Painful less because of the obstacles the law would put in the way of the realization of a bold program than as a result of the "revolutionary disappointments" that this legalism would provoke among the rightly impatient masses, and perhaps also because of the "loss of originality" it would bring about for the party. But on the other hand, this exercise of power would allow the socialists to accelerate the pace of reforms, because a government under socialist leadership would act "with energy, resolution, and decisiveness that would not [allow] it to be stopped by the obstacles that other governments find insurmountable." Blum concluded with these words:

> Although I am not a legalist as far as the conquest of power is concerned, I am when it comes to the exercise of power. I think that if the course of parliamentary activity calls upon us to exercise power in the framework of present institutions, we should do so legally, fairly, without committing the kind of swindle which would consist of taking advantage of our presence in the government to transform the exercise of power into the conquest of power.

It was a remarkable speech which prefigured with striking accuracy the future of the Popular Front, a mixture of bold reforms, "revolutionary disppointments," legalistic scruples, and that disarming and disarmed honesty that made up its greatness and its weakness. To each man his own *Mein Kampf*. It is legitimate to prefer Blum's to Hitler's. In any case, friends and enemies knew from then on what to expect from the man and his essentially *contractual* vision of power.

Critics of this speech have spoken of "subtlety," "ambiguity," and even "illogic"—even writers predisposed in Blum's favor like Gilbert Ziebura. But having paid this tribute to the usual clichés, the German historian seems to us to see things very sharply when he writes: "In fact, the subtlety of Léon Blum's conceptual distinction was a response to a concrete situation: his aim was to allow the party to follow, for as long as possible, a policy of self-preservation, to spare it difficulties and responsibilities that its numerical weakness and its fragile structure would prevent it from taking on. It was necessary to maintain the party 'intact' for the day when the 'exercise of power' would become necessary."

Blum presented an assessment of the experience of the *Cartel,* from the point of view of the SFIO parliamentary group, in a report delivered at the Twenty-third Congress, which was held in Clermont-Ferrand a few weeks later. He knew that the CAP and the "left" federations, including his own Seine federation, were preparing to subject his activity to a veritable trial. He argued:

> We now know the difficulties of a policy which is neither support nor opposition. A decisive turn toward reaction tomorrow, by placing us in opposition, could restore all our tactical ease. But we do not wish for it. Our duty is to consider not our comfort or difficulties as a party, but the national and international interests of the working class. We prefer to think that our difficulties derive above all from our strength, and that, if we had less influence in the country and less authority in the Chamber, we would be freed from most of our hesitations and scruples. The difficulties of political parties increase with their responsibilities, and their responsibilities with their power. This is why we willingly agree to see ours grow still further.

Was Blum "subtle" or "spurious"? Who has ever spoken to his comrades in clearer terms? He knew that he was speaking to men haunted by the demon of division, and that their rightful demand for ideological rigor might lead to decisions that would end up destroying the socialist movement. The May 1926 congress in Clermont-Ferrand continued to follow Blum and confirmed his approval of the "principle" of support for "reform" governments.

Herriot's return to power in July 1926 seemed about to exacerbate the problem fully once more, and to revive arguments whose sharpness and violence were continuing to grow. But the Radical leader was soon voted down, and his party turned to the right, assuring Poincaré's triumphal return in a climate of dramatic financial crisis. Fourteen years after the *Cartel* Chamber, that of the Popular Front would go even further in the art of self-destruction.

Between Radicals and Communists

The unity of the SFIO had been saved. The moral cohesion of the socialists was established against Poincaré and his new Radical allies. The "tactical ease," which Blum had declared he did not wish for six months earlier, had been restored. It was the moment for reflection and assessment. *Le Populaire,* driven by the necessity of battle, was about to be revived, and, as he was elected director, Blum devoted the greater part of 1927 to the composition of two long series of articles on the relations between socialism and Radicalism on the one hand, and between socialism and Bolshevism on the other. These are key texts.

In response to an interview given to *La Revue de Paris* by Maurice Sarraut (brother of the future head of government and real "boss" of the Radical party), in which socialist "non-participation" was cited as the principal cause of the failure of the *Cartel des gauches,* Blum undertook an explanation of the relations between the SFIO and its former allies. On the question of responsibilities his argument is not very convincing. We did not participate, he says, because, preferring to govern alone, you did not really ask us to; this is a very narrow interpretation of Herriot's letter of June 1, 1924. Blum is much more interesting when he examines how far understanding can go between vague Radical reformism and the "revolutionary" will of the socialists.

What is the meaning, he asks, of the old Radical projects for the "elimination of the wage system" if M. Sarraut's party remains attached to present forms of property? The Socialist Party, conscious of class antagonisms, tends toward an essential transformation of the property system.

> This is what M. Maurice Sarraut characterizes as a "cataclysm" or a "miracle." It is what socialism names the Revolution. The socialist theory of the dictatorship of the proletariat derives logically, necessarily, from our conception of the revolution. History teaches us that every political revolution, that is, the passage from one political regime to a different one, has *almost* always involved what I will call a suspension of legality, when the old institutions have been overthrown and the new institutions are not in a condition to function. These periods of suspension of legality[19] are, by definition, periods of dictatorship. The republican revolutions of the nineteenth century had their instruments of dictatorship, which were called provisional governments. We foresee that a social Revolution would find itself confronted with the same practical necessity, and this is why we see in the dictatorship of the proletariat an *almost* inevitable corollary of proletarian Revolution.

There would be a good deal to say about those two "almosts" which we have italicized. One might find there a definition of "Blumism," usefully completed by the conclusion of Blum's letter to Maurice Sarraut:

> Because, in our eyes, revolutionary transformation presupposes a period of preparatory work, which will have sufficiently penetrated, molded, and adapted capitalist society, and will have insured the adequate development of socialist realities and socialist ideas; because we know that this preparatory work is dependent domestically on the protection and extension of political freedom and externally on peace, we can support the Radical program in these three areas: political freedom, peace, and social reforms. We cannot support it as useful and beneficial in itself; we can support it as contributing to our own efforts. In this sense, according to the now classic expression, we and the Radicals can "go part of the way together." If the Radical Party vigorously undertakes the action that corresponds to its role, it will remain possible to find a sufficient number of common objectives for our concerted energies. For the Radicals, this will be the end and the goal; for us, it will be the beginning and the means.

But it was especially with reference to the Communists that Blum had to clarify his socialist and revolutionary ideas. He hesitated for a long time, finally deciding to do so a few days after his dialogue with the Radicals. He was careful to reiterate his apprehensions:

> I don't feel sure of myself. I have taken too much part in our struggles. Too many poignant memories are still present in my mind. Although I believe myself, with complete good faith, indifferent to personal attacks and insults, I am not indifferent to the bitterness of broken friendships and the misunderstanding and sabotage of work accomplished together. What will nevertheless help me to preserve my freedom of judgment is my complete conviction that, in all of Europe and consequently in France, working-class unity must one day be reestablished. None of us has ever given up that hope. The words with which we separated at Tours were not spoken by us in a half-hearted way.
>
> Bolshevism broke off from socialism as some heresies broke off from religions to form new religions. . . . [It] came out of socialism, even if it was by reaction or contradiction. It was inevitable that, in spite of the divergence of their development, common notions . . . would persist within the two doctrines.
>
> On the incoherence of the capitalist system, on the chronic disorders created by the anarchy of production and free competition, on the ways in which workers are exploited, on the injustice of the division of wealth, Bolshevism professes the same ideas we do, because it has remained, if I may say so, within the orbit of our thought. The real problem is to determine how, under what conditions, and by what means the passage from one society to another will take place. It is precisely at this point that appears the fundamental opposition between Bolshevism and socialism. . . .Because Bolshevism has confused the seizure of power with the Revolution, the means with the end, it directs all its tactics toward the conquest of power without considering the moment, the circumstances, or the consequences, and for the same reason the entire will of the Soviet government is today still directed toward the maintenance of absolute power, even though it knows itself to be incapable of bringing about social transformation.
>
> We socialists continue to think that the seizure of political power, considered in isolation and in itself, is not the Revolution, that on the contrary it creates the Revolution, becomes the Revolution only in so far as the proletariat, having seized power, can use it to establish a new system of property. We therefore conclude that true preparation for the revolution consists in preparing for the transformation of the social system rather than arming for military coups, and we warn the working class against imprudent or premature attempts.

Is this faint-heartedness? No, Blum maintains, it is the "preservation of the sacred trust that was placed in our hands: revolutionary faith and hope." Without seeming troubled by the idealist element in this argument, the director of *Le Populaire* continues:

> Socialism will not wait to begin revolutionary transformation of the social system for the day when present society has come so

close to the new society that one can glide from one to the other without a jolt—as one travels on a ferry from one bank to the other without leaving the railway car or the tracks. It knows that that day will never come, that a great distance will always remain between the two lands and that the crossing will always be something of an adventure. But socialism does not want to waste the limited number of chances available to the working class. . . .

If, knowing that the crises bound up with the very system of production and distribution are not presently susceptible to any satisfactory solution, it proposes palliatives, partial and temporary remedies, inspired by its own thought, directed toward its own solution, it is aware that it is preparing the Revolution. It is preparing it materially by erecting in the present chaos something like a foundation for socialist order.

Blum contrasts this work of bridge-building to "the state based on tyrannical dictatorship and terror, the price for the premature seizure of power out of harmony with real conditions, which indicates in reality the failure of revolutionary transformation. By maintaining oppression and tyranny in order to hold power, one gradually returns, by surrender after surrender, concession after concession, to the very capitalism one had claimed to annihilate. Bolshevism knows this history, I think. We know it too, and it is because we know it that we do not want to repeat it."

Finally, describing the differences in practices and methods between the SFIO—open to debate, freely approachable, publishing all its documents—and the SFIC—secret, closed, and as it were permanently prepared for attack and assault, for civil war spontaneously arising out of international war—Blum concludes with a poignant meditation:

These dissensions have not only made common action between the Bolsheviks and us extremely difficult, they have created a kind of incompatibility of feeling and morality between the two parties. I will repeat and reorganize the themes and the words that have constantly flowed from my pen in the course of this study. They are discipline and military hierarchy, permanent mobilization of shock troops, preparation for a putsch, fomentation of civil, religious, and racial hatreds, internal war, colonial war, foreign war. Everywhere there is a call to violence, everywhere a hope in force.
. . . We feel pain when our daily experience informs us of the feelings they seek to propagate in the working class: duplicity, the spirit of informing or betrayal, hatred, systematic calumny! And no assistance to propaganda, no passing advantage against opponents could compensate in our eyes for this corruption of the workers. We remind you of Guesde's declaration: "How will we go about building the new society if, on the day of victory, you have corrupted all our human resources?"

When he wrote that, Blum had not yet experienced the electoral defeat against Jacques Duclos after a campaign in which he was spared nothing. But he had already carried on coexistence with the PCF for seven years, in the course of which the electoral battles of the *Cartel* were only minor episodes.

We will refer several times to an article by Annie Kriegel on the relations between the leader of the SFIO and the Communists, "Léon Blum vu par les communistes."[20] In particular, she analyzes Maurice Thorez's famous polemic against Blum in *Les Cahiers du bolchevisme* ("repugnant reptile, jackal, lackey of the London bankers, fink, furious warmonger")[21], and she considers some of the reasons which constantly provoked Communist hostility to him.

In Blum, suggests Kriegel in *Aux origines du PC français,* the militants saw a bourgeois, an intellectual, and a Jew. On this last point, it is obviously not a question of assimilating the attitude of a party in which Jewish militants and leaders were numerous and influential to that of the anti-Semitic right. But it seems that the militants of the PCF saw Blum very clearly assuming his identity as a Jew, rather than attempting to blend his Jewishness totally into revolutionary fraternity, that is, "not expecting the simple victory of socialism to resolve the Jewish problem."

An intellectual? The PCF did not lack adherents in that category. But if Communist polemics placed the literary activities of the author of *Stendhal* in such an unfavorable light, this was because they saw him as a writer both of a certain style ("equivocal prose," "venomous casuistry," "indecent self-analysis") and especially, as Annie Kriegel emphasizes, of a certain *type:* while the party readily honored "the scientist," "the poet," or "the teacher," it "abominated the kind of unclassifiable intellectual who quietly stirred up ideas about the reform of society," whom the concept of the "human sciences" had not yet allowed to be integrated into a reassuring category. Wasn't the basis of the problem the fact that intellectuals of that kind tend, by the multiplicity of their points of view and the diversity of their research, to "create doubt that the party is the source of all science"?

A bourgeois? The Communists had had with them men who were richer and "better born" than the son of Marie and Abraham Blum. But, observes Annie Kriegel, they were men of faith or order, bound to a system of established values, while the leader of the SFIO was a typical "independent," the product of social and cultural success, "from whom it seemed impossible to expect the upsurge of revolutionary energy." Foreign to the working class? Yes, in a sense, Blum was. Benoît Frachon later expressed this with a good deal of force and rather heavy-handed disdain in an interview in the film by Harris and Sedouy, *Français, si vous saviez!*

But perhaps we should be simpler. What exasperated the Communist leaders was perhaps especially the fact that this social-democrat was a man of unassailable moral integrity. He was essentially "unco-optable," a man over whom they could have no "hold," for electoral, financial, or ideological reasons. How they would prefer a Guy Mollet! Author of the great anti-Bolshevik indictment of Tours, responsible in large part for the rebirth of the SFIO which was first despised and then envied, spokesman of the only force on the left which could command a national audience, Blum was the target of a good deal of rancor from the extreme left. Among a thousand examples of anti-Blum polemic (one of the most constant features of Marcel Cachin's *L'Humanité,* which Blum himself had founded twenty years before) we will quote one that provoked one of the rare responses of the director of *Le Populaire.*

On December 5, 1928, two notorious swindlers, Mme Hanau and Lazare Bloch, were arrested. The director of *Le Populaire* (which was conducting an investigation against them) decided to interrupt the campaign because they were "now only under indictment." The next day in *L'Humanité* Paul Vaillant-Couturier made a double accusation against Blum, first that he had conducted a campaign against the swindlers to serve the interests of another bank, and second that he closed the investigation because he had "other friends to consider." Blum exploded:

> You wrote that, Vaillant-Couturier, you signed that? I say it without any pride, for there is no reason to be proud of it; Vaillant-Couturier knows me well enough not to have misjudged me for a minute. He knows as well as anyone how much he is slandering me, how he is lying.
>
> But there is the habit he has developed over the years of degraded propaganda. There is the repeated order from Moscow: defile, tarnish, dishonor. Vaillant-Couturier doesn't believe a single word of what he says. But he obeys; he carries out the infamous job. He carries it out like so many others who have lived close to us, who were our friends, who still glance at us in passing with friendly complicity, who dare to offer us their hands. I, who have maintained respect for that past and never despaired of the future, I have always kept silent, and if it weren't Vaillant-Couturier, I would still keep silent. A piece of filth more or less, whether it comes from *L'Humanité* or the fascist press, doesn't count.

The Most Insulted Man in France

"It doesn't count." It took a certain stoicism to write that when he was the most insulted man in France, more than Clemenceau, Jaurès, or Caillaux had ever been. It took a large measure of serenity not to respond like that every day, either to *L'Humanité* or to the hounds of the press of the right and the extreme right.

The attacks were surprisingly monotonous in their vulgarity. We can get a sense of what the "intellectual elite" of the French right was like between the wars from the fact that Charles Maurras wrote of Blum, "There is a man who should be shot, but in the back"; or from the remarks of Pierre Gaxotte, who called Blum a "Palestinian mare" and suggested that he be sent "with the dregs of the European population streaming into our country to concentration camps in Madagascar." An excerpt from a contemptible book entitled *Les Trois Ennemis de la France: les francs-maçons, les Juifs et les métèques* by a certain Gibelin claims, "The abominable kike, the treacherous Léon Blum—leader of the socialists (capitalists) in rabbit fur—has renounced the social and French directions of Jaurès. The unassimilable Jew Léon Blum has dishonored socialism with his plans for the suspension of legality—his hope for a Blum dictatorship! For Léon Blum dreams of one day becoming the 'Bela Kun' of France!"

We have already quoted a few fragments from reports of parliamentary debates, torrents of abuse hurled against one deputy by others who had also been elected by the French people—abuse directed less against what he did or said than against what he was. The attacks to which he was subjected must have become intolerable one day in November 1924, when this man who was so courteous, so open to all forms of thought, so careful to say or do nothing that could be turned against his party, used, in the National Assembly, a word that became a powerful element in his legend: "hatred."

If historic words have one thing in common, it is that they were never spoken. This is true for the notorious "I hate you!" of Léon Blum—in so far as one can consider the analytic record of the Chamber a reliable source. If you plunge into this jungle of print today, you find something rather different. It is hardly probable that it was corrected later: the "analytic" is prudish, readily eliminating scatological abuse or attacks on the private lives of honorable members, but it remains faithful to strong feelings, and hatred is among them.

On November 13, 1924, four months after the victory of the *Cartel,* with Edouard Herriot as Premier enjoying the support of the SFIO without its participation in government, the National Assembly was discussing the budget of the Ministry of the Interior, and more specifically its secret funds. Blum, speaking for the socialists, who were ordinarily opposed to approving this kind of appropriation, indicated their support for Herriot's requests. Jeers started:

> LEON BLUM: Do you think I am so naïve as to mistake the sense of your jokes and your sneers? You're saying to yourselves: now the poor socialists are really in trouble.
> M. GUERIN: We don't say poor!
> LEON BLUM: Do you mean by that that I am a rich socialist?

Please, let's drop these petty personal references. I don't think I'm the one they diminish the most. You are saying to yourselves that we are in an embarassing position, as has already happened in the last few months in our policy of support. It is true that the socialist party is often in difficult situations and that this is the case today. Why conceal it? What is so comic about it? In effect, the socialist party has party traditions to maintain, and at the same time, it hates you so much, you and the politics you represent, it is so convinced that for four years you have brought disaster on this country.

M. LAMAZERE BETBEDER: It is you who have brought disaster! We have had enough of hearing you speak like this!

LEON BLUM: Just now I used a word I regret and which I withdraw, because it is not a question of personal hatred. For my part, I feel none. But our party hates your politics so much, it fears its effects on the country so much, it knows so well what would happen tomorrow if you took power again, even insidiously, even by slow and insidious erosion . . .

M. LEBRUN: You are the greatest profiteer from the workers!

LEON BLUM: . . . Once again the country would be under the dual threat of ruin and war!

Blum sometimes commented on this famous exclamation. The strange thing is that by dint of being criticized for it in its legendary form, he believed he had said "I hate you!" and he criticized himself for the remark in this form, adding with a sigh: "I did it for Herriot." Whoever the beneficiary may have been, it was the tone of the remark that was important. If one adds the corrective which he immediately introduced, one hears something different from a passionate, hysterical "I hate you!"

It is nevertheless true that it is in the form of "I hate you!" that the remark has remained, that it has entered history, and that it has often been quoted as proof of Blum's "racism," "sectarianism," and "class fanaticism."

His friends and his family had to beg him during the Popular Front before he finally decided to respond to the innumerable campaigns, conducted by *Gringoire, Charivari, Le Matin,* and *Je suis partout,* about his villas on the shore of Lake Leman and his golden dishes. (The campaign was so effective that, encountering him in the concentration camp at Dachau in April 1945, the Austrian chancellor Schuschnigg spoke to him naïvely and admiringly, of these notorious dishes.)

All his close friends agreed: Blum never cast a glance at the press that made a specialty of insulting him. But who can say that a certain amount of hatred did not in the end condition his consciousness, undermine his courage, penetrate the depths of his unconscious, and thus create obstacles and anxieties? Who can say that this long litany did not in the end wear down the internal resistance of this intrepid man and provoke in him, when he had assumed great responsibilities, attacks of self-accusation?

The First Defeat

Until 1926, Blum's political career, much as his previous careers as writer and lawyer, unrolled in a kind of jubilant euphoria. Not that tragedies were lacking: the murder of Jaurès, the split at Tours, the failure of the *Cartel* in 1926. But almost in spite of himself, events had always nourished Blum's optimism. At the moment when his second term as Deputy came to an end, with the end of the legislature of the *Cartel,* he seemed carried by the spirit of Jaurès and his own talent toward some unknown democratic and socialist heaven. He had many friends and a multitude of enemies.

But in 1926 he lost a friend, his best friend since the assassination of Jaurès: Lucien Herr. This death came like a cruel warning. As long as Herr had lived, Blum had felt guided in some way, supported in his convictions: not only was socialism wise and just, but it was wisdom and justice, and it was enough to make sure that the temporary disorder of things come to an end for hope to be finally accomplished. But for several months, the inextricable political tangle in which he was caught and the harsh calls to order from the CAP and the Seine socialist federation made him recognize how rectitude can follow tortuous paths. Herr's death left him very much alone. A legislative session which had begun just at that time in hope was being overcome by disappointments.

Was the result a failure for the *Cartel des gauches?* Must we see in public life nothing but a matter of budgets? It is true that, coming up against what he himself called "the wall of money," Edouard Herriot presided over an unprecedented slide in the value of French currency and that, on the pretext of restoring public finances, Joseph Caillaux, who embodied the financial policies of the left (the prewar income tax), imposed an extreme right financial strategy. It is true that the purchasing power of the working class had collapsed in the course of three years. It is true that colonial conflicts had just broken out in Morocco and Syria. It is true that anti-Communist repression had taken on intolerable forms; several leaders of the party, including André Marty and Jacques Duclos, had just been arrested.

But if, on these points, the policy of socialist support for the *Cartel* governments had turned out to be a trap, we must not forget that this was also the time when France, breaking with Poincaré's idiotic German policy—occupation and humiliation, according to Blum "the barbaric system of imprisonment" which sowed the seeds of Nazism—

rediscovered a diplomacy worthy of the name, began the evacuation of the Ruhr, helped to restore Germany to the concert of nations, reconciled Paris with its Anglo-Saxon allies, accepted the Dawes plan, and finally recognized the Soviet Union which M. Millerand had attempted to destroy.

If we agree that, in order to break with the rule of the *Chambre bleu-horizon* and the National Bloc, the SFIO chose to support a government which restored democratic exchanges to domestic politics and reason to international affairs, then it had not been on the wrong track. Moreover, what other attitude could they adopt in the system which prevailed in France, taking account of the social and economic power relations in the mid-twenties? The end result of the *Cartel* was disappointing. But the government had moved toward some socialist objectives (peace, democracy). The SFIO could not refrain from "going along," even though Blum was obliged to temper somewhat his natural optimism and gird his loins for fiercer battles.

During these four bitter years he had nevertheless been able to formulate and persuade his comrades to accept the two axioms on which his political strategy would be based from then on: 1) Support is not participation; 2) Between the conquest of power (the temporarily inaccessible revolution) and participation (parliamentarianism dissolving their program), there was a third way, *the exercise of power* in the framework of the bourgeois system, with socialists in control, not to *replace* the system, but to *change* it—not to make the revolution but to prepare the way for it and to educate its protagonists. It was on precisely these grounds that the man who, since the congresses of la Bellevilloise and Lyon, was the real leader of French socialism, would act, in and out of power, from 1928 to 1940.

In 1928, the *Cartel* legislature, which had become the legislature of neo-Poincarism, came to an end. The election caught the SFIO in a state of disarray; the economic failure of the *Cartel* might be attributed to it. Many in the party wanted to replace the opening to the right toward the Radicals with an opening to the left toward the Communists, without however committing themselves to a "single front" or a "workers' bloc," advocated by only a small minority of militants. This was also the time when Bukharin had won support in the International for the leftist policy of the struggle of "class against class," which was reflected in France (where anti-Communist repression was increasing) in the form of an accentuation of the sectarianism of the PCF, and consequently of the SFIO. The time was so unpropitious for a union of the movements of the left that the Political Bureau of the PC decided to maintain its candidates in the second round of the elections against the socialists, except for those who explicitly declared themselves in favor of the "workers' bloc" and adopted a minimum "common program," which made any alliance impossible 99 percent of the time and played into the hands of the right. Once again, Blum was indignant:

> Who can be made to believe that the Communist workers of France, if they had had to decide for themselves, if they had simply been consulted, would have been in favor of the maintenance of their candidates in the second round? Who can be made to believe that *their* preference, *their* wish, was to send a reactionary majority to Parliament?
>
> Le Troquer's presentation to the Seine Federal Council has in any case removed all doubt. The Political Bureau of the French Communist Party was the first to realize that the order from Moscow corresponded neither to the thought nor to the interests of its militants. It understood this so well that it sent one of its members to Litvinov, the people's commissar. He tried to obtain an attenuation, some exceptions. Litvinov answered the ambassador, who, it appears, was none other than Raymond Jean: Don't discuss; obey!
>
> French workers who follow communism are subject to that kind of military discipline. The Third International displaces and maneuvers them like pawns on a chess board. If they were maneuvered for the benefit of "World Revolution," that would be one thing. But Moscow does not believe in World Revolution. They are maneuvered according to the accidents or caprices of internal Russian politics. What dominates those politics for the moment is the struggle of the current leadership against the Trotskyite opposition. Trotsky accuses Stalin of surrenders and deviations. It is a question of proving to him that the current communist leaders have remained pure revolutionaries, and since the proof is difficult to provide in Russia, French workers will pay the price for the demonstration.
>
> This is why France must have a reactionary majority, a reactionary government. With this majority, this government, there is every chance that working-class conflicts will proliferate and intensify. Repression can only spread, and as an inevitable consequence, it will foster popular rebellion. The French party will thus provide for international communism the revolutionary flavor which is somewhat lacking in Russia. And Stalin will be able to answer triumphantly: We, traitors to the Communist cause! Communism has never led a more bitter and resolute struggle against capitalism.
>
> This is the role given to the French workers. That this struggle involves the risk of losing some of the advantages they have so laboriously conquered at such a price, that the progress of their organizations and the movement of reform will come up against all-powerful reaction, all that is of little importance. Such petty considerations carry little weight with the great leaders of the Third International. *They* have nothing to lose.[22]

At the special congress held by the SFIO toward the end of December 1927, Blum won agreement for the tactic of free choice by the federations for establishing alliances in the second round, either with the Communists or with "progressive republicans." He himself was subjected to a strong challenge: in the second district of Paris (Ménilmontant) which had elected him twice (the method of voting had been changed and the boundaries redrawn so that the middle classes were better represented), he ran against Jacques Duclos. His sentencing *in absentia* to thirty years in prison "for anarchist activities" (!) had just multiplied his popularity. The fervent campaign he conducted against this conviction in *Le Populaire* was of no help to him; Duclos was the martyred revolutionary, and Blum the ally of bourgeois repression. Moreover, the right had presented two candidates, one of whom described himself quite simply as a "reactionary," and the Radical Party was good enough to propose another candidate against Blum!

Strangely enough, Blum seems to have underestimated the risks involved. Until the eve of the vote of April 23, 1928, he considered his success a certainty: the articles in *Le Populaire* are evidence of this. And yet the campaign had been terrible. What he had experienced in 1924 was nothing to what his Communist opponents made him endure in April 1928. Here we should quote Jacques Duclos, evoking his campaign as a secret candidate in his *Mémoires:*[23]

> Since the police were looking for me in the twentieth *arrondissement,* I spoke in the theater of Saint-Denis. I took my place on stage in the dark, and when the lights went up, the excited audience, wild with joy, recognized me in spite of the beard I had grown, and I spoke carried by their enthusiasm. When, to wild applause, I concluded my speech by saying that while I was speaking in Saint-Denis, Maurice Thorez was speaking in Lille, and Jacques Doriot in Valenciennes, the lights went out again and I disappeared. . . . Pierre Sémard[24] was conducting the campaign [for me] in the twentieth *arrondissement,* and he told me of Léon Blum's confusion when he debated against him. The argument he developed about his behavior in the face of repression could be summed up like this: "You know, Blum, that there is a tradition in the working-class movement. You are never a candidate against a victim of capitalist repression. By opposing Duclos, you are providing justification for the scandalous accusations against him." And when Blum answered that if he was elected one of the first things he would do would be to present a proposal for amnesty, Pierre Sémard explained: "That changes nothing. On the contrary; you're making your position worse, for by announcing a proposal for amnesty, you recognize the injustice of the accusations made against the Communists, and by presenting yourself as a candidate against one of the accused, you have become the ally of the government which wants him to be beaten."

Jacques Duclos as Robin Hood received 1700 more votes than Blum in the first round, but the party maintained Blum's candidacy in the second round in spite of very strong resistance from the Seine federation and the CAP.[25] The socialist leader benefited from the official withdrawal of the Radical candidate, but many of these votes were lost, and the following Sunday Blum still had 1200 fewer votes than his communist rival. Invited by *Le Temps,* which was jubilant to see him eliminated from Parliament, to comment on his defeat Blum wrote in *Le Populaire* on May 6:

> In November 1919, the two neighborhoods of Père-Lachaise and Charonne, the twentieth *arrondissement,* chose me to succeed our great and beloved Vaillant, and at the time there was hardly a safer seat in all of France. The twentieth *arrondissement* trusted me without knowing me very well. I have thus always considered myself their representative. Ties of unalterable affection have matured and increased between its militants and me. How could I have thought of abandoning them to present myself elsewhere when the single-candidate electoral system was reestablished? I had no illusions about the risk I was running.

A curious assertion, if we refer to his April articles. But, we are told, optimism, even tactical optimism, is revolutionary. And he proceeds to recount the campaign, its maneuvers, and its violence:

> Personal attacks everywhere replaced political debate; systematically organized slander was propagated from door to door, by word of mouth, by a swarm of fanatics or mercenaries: my millions, my châteaux, my valets, my servile contacts with foreign powers, with international finance, with the government. The order was given from the very beginning among the merchants and the petty bourgeois: above all, defeat Blum; better Duclos than Blum, and since we could answer only with words, our meetings were sabotaged by obstructions whose violence and disgracefulness are impossible to describe.
>
> In the first round, in order to assure Duclos's advantage, the most notorious reactionaries of the area voted for him by the hundreds, some of them with open ballots. In the second round, while we recaptured a substantial number of votes from the Communists, the majority of M. Fieschi's voters (Radical) shifted to M. Gautrat (the "reactionary"), and a new wave of a thousand votes flowed to Jacques Duclos for more certainty. It should be said in passing that had my candidacy not been maintained, M. Gautrat, and not Duclos, would have been elected.
>
> Perhaps some of my comrades in the party will criticize me for boldly taking such a great risk. . . . I did not foresee that my personal defeat, although it was almost inevitable in the conditions under which I entered the struggle, would be published and proclaimed everywhere as a symbolic defeat of the party. I blame myself and ask forgiveness for having exposed the party to this defamatory campaign. And yet, if I had it to do over again, I think I would do the same thing.

We have to make allowances for bitterness here. It was his first defeat. But it was attenuated by the performance of the party, which received 1,700,000 votes nationwide, as many as before the Tours split, and 600,000 more than the Communists—who lost 13 of 27 seats, while causing the socialists to lose about twenty with their tactic of maintaining candidates into the second round to lose about twenty.[26] The definite consolidation of socialist positions was qualified, however, by an observation: these positions were certainly reinforced in the rural areas of the Midi; but they collapsed in the industrialized regions where the Communists once again took the lead.[27]

Blum was not exiled from Parliament for long. Everyone in the party was intent on returning him to the Chamber. After the first round, several leaders, among them Jean Longuet, had proposed that his candidacy be withdrawn and shifted to the neighboring constituency, where the old syndicalist militant Alexandre Luquet, who had come in first, offered to step down for him. Blum had refused.

While waiting for the opportunity to return to Parliament, he devoted himself, in *Le Populaire,* to deepening his role as mediator between the factions of the party, in which the right inspired by Renaudel had strengthened its positions during the election. Released from his obligations as leader of the parliamentary group which bound him to the moderate wing, he could approach the debate in the Toulouse congress (May 1928) from a more detached position. He rejected any collusion with the Radicals whom he considered permanently attached to Poincaré's new majority. As for alliance with the Communists, Blum maintained that the battle they had imposed on the SFIO ought not to preclude a return to the "working-class tradition," as soon as the practices that had brought about his own defeat were abandoned.

A Parisian in the Vineyards[28]

"In March 1929, a few days after the death of the socialist deputy of Aude, the wine grower Yvon Pélissier, a group of young militants from Narbonne and I met in the Café de la Poste, and we asked ourselves: 'Why not offer the seat to Léon Blum?' It was a safe district. But Eugène Montel seemed the logical candidate: he was a school teacher who had travelled from farm to farm on his motorcycle and built the Aude socialist federation stone by stone. He had a heart of gold, a husky voice, and southern eloquence. Somebody gave him the idea, or he had it himself. The next day a telegram was sent from Narbonne to Paris: 'Your place is in the Parliament. Narbonne offers you its seat.' The answer was immediate: 'I'm coming.'

"We were stunned when we saw a *montparno* get off the train, with his big hat, his pocket handkerchief, and light-colored suit. He dazzled us. We knew him less from photographs than from Sennep's drawings, which showed his delicate, society side, not at all the strength and enthusiasm of the man. And as soon as he spoke, we were under a spell. He moved into the Grand Hôtel. The landlady, Mme Dora, was very pretty, but Léon Blum, without being a puritan, 'behaved' very well, unlike a lot of southern politicians! But he was terribly disorganized, always looking for what he called the 'wandering flock' of his affairs.

"His public meetings—one of them was superb, in the Salle des Synodes, the most beautiful room in the town hall which is the old archbishop's palace, where he was perfectly at ease—his meetings surprised us: he never attacked his enemies personally. He simply spoke about politics, with the tone he used in the Chamber or in his articles in *Le Populaire*. That was a change for us! But once he used a personal argument. Cachin had come to debate him. 'Marcel'—his voice was breaking—'Marcel, you were a guest in my old house!' "

—Did the audience follow? Wasn't it disoriented?

"Not at all. I won't tell you that everyone understood everything. But people were flattered that one of the great 'stars' of the time came to speak to them, and that he was their deputy. 'Think of that,' they said, 'a leader.' And his arguments were so sharp, so logical that he made himself heard, and he used his weak voice very cleverly to obtain silence. What always struck me was that he never 'talked down' to his listeners, he was always completely himself."

—His fellow candidates and his entourage spoke in a different way. I've heard that one of his friends proposed to build a pipeline for wine across France. Another suggested an armed attack on Toulouse, the fortress of the Radical Sarraut.

"Yes. But he never played local games, never tried to make himself into a *méridional*. He stayed the way he was when he came, for three legislatures: distinguished but warm, friendly, and rational. He got angry when his supporters made an uproar: 'But let my opponent speak!' Once, in 1936, he made an ironic remark about a right-wing candidate named Leroy-Beaulieu: 'Why choose a Jesuit novice to oppose me?' But he never jeered at his perennial competitor, the 'independent socialist' Sabatier, who was known as 'Paul Faure's cuckold' and who, whether or not he had been cuckolded by the secretary-general of the SFIO (a famous charmer), tried to make Blum pay for his misfortune."

—He was elected in the first round on April 14, 1929, against the Radical Gourgon, and always easily reelected. Did he come often to Narbonne?

"No. About three or four times a year, but then it was a delight. He received a lot of visits, he asked carefully about local conditions. He had made a study of wine questions, the problem of prices, insurance against hail, distribution. He spoke with ease about barrels, about marketing Corbières and Minervois, he was interested in the prospects of the 260 wine merchants in Narbonne."

—Admirable for a teetotaler.

"A teetotalar? No. He drank moderately—one or two glasses a meal, like me—but as a connoisseur. I won't say that he didn't prefer Burgundies to the wines of Aude."

—Was he interested in strictly regional civilization, the Cathars, the Protestants of the Midi, the centers of Jewish culture in Languedoc, Catalan civilization?

"No. He came for too short a time, and he was too busy. You know, *occitanisme* was not yet fashionable. And yet, Eugène Montel was interested in the Cathars, the role of the Inquisition.

—But would you say he had found the right way to speak to the people of Languedoc, that a real understanding had been established?

"Yes. Or almost. But in 1932, a campaign poster for Blum (but who had made it?) shocked me. It started like this: 'I have added some brilliance to these three words: deputy from Narbonne.' That was true. But the people of the Midi don't like to be told that they are honored by your being involved with them. Aside from little mistakes like that, you can say that Léon Blum had gained widespread respect, which went beyond our socialist circles. Just as they had supported Ferroul in 1907, our bourgeoisie had more or less adopted him."

—It is moving, and out of the ordinary, that a square in Narbonne is named after him and his second wife: "place Thérèse et Léon Blum."

"Yes. Thérèse Blum came only once or twice, but she made quite an impression with her vivacity and enthusiasm. A kind of Gavroche. Besides, she was a militant!"

—So Blum's electoral position was very solid in Narbonne?

"If it hadn't been for the war, he would have been deputy for life. The major parties had even given up presenting serious candidates against him. When Jean Mistler made gestures toward beginning a campaign in Aude in 1932, the Sarraut brothers, speaking for the Radical party, dissuaded him. But in 1936, the Radical committee of Aude put up a poster right before the elections calling for a vote against Blum."

—When he left for Narbonne in 1929, Poincaré said to him: "Watch out: you're going to come up against Radical fascism!" Which was a bit thick. But *La Dépêche de Toulouse,* to discredit him, spoke of Marxism as a "Teutonic concept," while *Le Télégramme* called the socialist leader a "cold doctrinaire man from the North."

"Yes, I remember that kind of attack. Blum's elegant cordiality was a better answer than argument. People also appreciated his courage. In 1935, he came here to defend a group of young *gauchistes*—the word wasn't yet in use at the time—who had demonstrated the preceding November in front of the monument for the war dead with cries of 'Soviets everywhere!' In order to get into the court, Maître Blum, decked out in a robe that only came to the middle of his thighs, had to confront excited right-wing demonstrators and a squadron of mobile guards on horseback, sent by the sub-prefect Voizard on the pretext of maintaining order. He went through the crowd and the police cordon with a calm that I didn't share."

—His real triumph in Narbonne was obviously as head of the Popular Front government, wasn't it?

"Yes. On October 25, 1936, we had an unforgettable banquet in what we called the 'wooden hut.' Why was it unforgettable? Because we saw the general, the prefect, and the notables paying court to the socialist deputy from Narbonne!"

—War was raging in Spain. It must have been a particular preoccupation here, 80 kilometers from the border, in a territory with strong Catalan influences.

"Of course. But Léon Blum, although I know he wanted with all his heart to aid the Republic, never talked about it."

—In the end, can you say that, during the period of serious economic crisis between 1931 and 1935, when wine prices collapsed, he substantially helped the region, distributed the government largesse that his voters must have hoped for? The important laws on the *Office du vin* were the work of the neighboring deputies from Hérault, Barthe and Baylet. And although in 1930 he helped to defeat a bill which would have established a tax of 7 francs on each hectoliter of wine sold; although, in the same year, he obtained significant help for flood victims among the peasants; although he helped pass a tax favorable to wine growers in 1932, he did no more than his colleagues in the region. If Montel had been elected in his place, he would have done no less. Can you say that he was really a deputy from Narbonne? Or rather a deputy in Narbonne?

"Yes and no. A people like this one can't help benefiting from hearing words like his, so disinterested, so instructive. Perhaps it's among the young socialists in Languedoc today that you can measure the influence, the signs of the time Jaurès's heir spent with us."

"The Fear of Responsibilities"?

Blum's analysis of the situation of the Radical party in 1928 had one weakness: it did not grant sufficient weight to the movement of the left embodied in the young deputy from Vaucluse, Edouard Daladier, whom circumstances were to project into the limelight. In July 1929, the Chamber placed Poincaré in the minority, and because of his disappointment and his illness, he was definitively eliminated from public life. Three months later, Briand in turn was beaten by an opposition made up on this occasion of an alliance between the right led by Louis Marin and the left by Blum. The Assembly made an about face, like the *Cartel* Chamber, but in the opposite direction. Once again, one-third of the way through, it was at the disposal of those who had been in a minority at the beginning, following another shift in the balance of power in the Radical party, which had become more than ever the arbiter—or the curse—of parliamentary equilibrium.

Called on to form the government, Daladier revived the great debate among the socialists. Much more clearly than his elder Herriot had done four years earlier, he offered the SFIO the famous, unacceptable, tempting, detestable, irresistible participation. This time it was on the basis of a genuine program of the left, providing for reductions in military spending as well as a lowering of sales taxes, and the evacuation of the Rhineland as well as paid vacations for certain categories of workers. The socialists were offered four ministries, including Finance, and Justice which, along with the post of Deputy Premier, would go to Blum.

The way had never been so open before him. At its meeting the next morning, the SFIO parliamentary group leaned toward participation. Even Faure did not dare to go against it. Only Blum was opposed, but he was placed in a smaller minority than ever before: 36 to 12. Were the socialists going to enter the government against the advice of their principal leader? Meeting in turn on the next day, the National Council, after a passionate debate, voted against participation: "provincial" rigidity had barely won out over "Parisian" flexibility, 1590 to 1450. It has been calculated that if the Guesdist Nord federation, controlled by Jean Lebas, had not cast its votes in a "bloc" and had counted the 72 votes in favor of participation separately, everything would have been different.

In short, Daladier's "breakthrough" was turned into a failure, which opened the way for a Tardieu government "militantly reactionary," explained Blum. Who was to blame? Some observers contrasted Jaurès to Blum, holding up the master, the bold strategist of republican union, as an example to the disciple. But in 1929 the threats against the "Republic" were no longer, or not yet, what they had been in 1902. Everything leads one to conclude today that socio-political conditions in the France of 1929 were not ripe for substantial socialist participation in the government—even if "participation" could at any time be the basis of a healthy politics for them.

Although it did not contradict a doctrine he had long before expressed and justified, Blum's eloquently negative attitude in the affair earned him severe criticism, within the party as well as in large sections of "republican" public opinion. We must quote here the answer he gave to this indictment. Under the title "La peur des responsabilités," he wrote in *Le Populaire* on December 26, 1929:

> I have been told so often in the past ten years that I was a juggler of ideas absorbed by the play of their interaction, a "subtle dialectician," that is, a hair-splitter, that I have almost come to believe it, or fear it. What reassures me a little is that I have recently become a dense, perhaps benighted, sectarian, fanatically attached to the letter of dogma, and wishing to impose at any cost my immutable ritual catechism. And these two conditions of mind fit very badly together; all my "dialectical subtlety" could not succeed in reconciling them.
>
> I confess that I am more touched by another reproach. Opposing polemics readily attribute the attitude I have maintained for the last five years in this great debate to what is called "the fear of responsibilities," and I have sometimes had the impression that this feeling was shared by some of our comrades. Is it true that the prospect of power throws me into some undefined state of timidity? One never knows oneself well, but in all sincerity, I think I am more guilty of boldness than an excess of prudence or temporizing. Our beloved Marcel Sembat criticized me for it more than once: "You know, Blum," he said to me, "your mistake is that you always burn your bridges behind you."
>
> Why should power frighten me? I have the advantage over almost all of my opponents of having already experienced it. I "participated in a participation" for two and a half years, and I can certainly say that confidence and friendship made that "participation" a real "sharing."[29] It is entirely possible that my memories of that time have something to do with my current convictions, for, in spite of general conditions which made it necessary to take account of our ultimatums or vetos, I was able to verify how every determined and innovative undertaking came up against the "framework of capitalist society" which restricted us. Nevertheless, I went through the experience, and having done so, power does not frighten me. I will even say that I don't consider myself in any way unsuited for power. Without excessive vanity, I grant myself a vision of the whole of things, and a speed of judgment and decision which do not make me incapable of power. And I am not afraid of risking my reputation(!) because I think I am free of vanity. So what am I supposed to be so afraid of? It certainly would not have taken a great deal of courage for me to accept the post of Deputy Premier and the Justice portfolio in a Daladier cabinet!
>
> I ask your pardon for this tone of self-justification and personal apology. I have not often been guilty of this failing and I definitely intend not to be caught in it again. At one stroke, I have gotten rid of a certain number of bitter impressions that have been accumulating in me for weeks, and even for years. Now I am purged,

and it's over. It is not in my nature to ascribe personal motives to any of my comrades, whatever their nature. Perhaps from now on I will be granted similar credit.

This is a piece that should be kept in reserve and reared in connection with 1936. For several weeks, the leading opponent of participation continued his campaign in *Le Populaire* on two fronts, showing that entering the government would lead the SFIO into the risk of "confusion" with the Radical party, all the more dangerous because of its closeness and because there was apparently no clear boundary between them; while, from the Communist side, "the delays, insufficiencies, and fits and starts of governmental action will be watched with the greatest avidity and exploited with the greatest harshness. Since the working class in France is more sensitive, more critical, and quicker to anger, because of the existence of communism, its reactions would take place in a skeptical atmosphere, with all the risks of inflammatory disorders that may follow from that fact."

We can see that no argument was neglected. In any case, this need to argue is evidence of the opposition provoked in the party by Blum's choices. He who had invented so many formulas to win support for his views now had to fight against Paul-Boncour's suggestion of "sharing" power, the meaning of which was certainly more equalitarian than that of "participation." For Blum, the question was not the distribution of ministries but "preponderance in action." The SFIO should refuse power not only when it does not assume control ("participation"), but even when control (Paul-Boncour's "sharing") is based only on easily revoked compromises not backed by a stable parlimentary majority, the presumed source of what he called "preponderance in action." Even at this early date, only the possibility of a "Popular Front" (did he glimpse it?) opened the way, in his mind, to the "exercise of power" which he wished for, while waiting for the distant "revolution."

Blum was so aware of having said everything, of having argued through the entire question, that for the first time in many years he refused to speak at the January 1930 congress in Paris—much like Waldeck-Rousseau in the Palais-Bourbon, who left the Chamber as soon as he had finished his speech, convinced that he had answered all the possible arguments of the opposing party. It was a serous mistake: deprived of his incomparable art of compromise, the party was closer to a split than it had ever been since the congress of Tours. Of course, the silence of the great conciliator was not the only cause for these profound stirrings. There had just appeared on center stage the first "evil angel" capable of calling into question Blum's moral and intellectual ascendancy. This was the source of a rebellion that was to occupy the life of the party, and the life of Léon Blum, for three long years, leaving them traumatized, confronting the worst.

THE CHALLENGES OF
FASCISM

The Torment of Tantalus

He was named Marcel Déat, and he was from a peasant family. He had a slightly Mongol face resembling Lenin or Clemenceau. A *normalien,* an incomparable dialectician, he was the only member of the party capable of standing up to Blum on doctrinal as well as general cultural questions, and on electoral tactics as well as financial management. He made an immediately powerful impression with his dark, sharp, tense, watchful gaze, his prominent cheekbones, the jet-black tuft of his mustache below his pointed nose, his savage jaw and curt gestures, his harsh remarks, sarcasms, and oratorical flights. From his first appearance he was seen by everyone as the heir, the dauphin.

For an ambitious man he had at first placed himself a little too far to the right of the party. Desiring to make a place for himself, he had chosen to run in Marne in 1924 in tandem with a Radical, without consulting the CAP. He thus exposed himself to a number of difficulties. He probably acted out of a combination of defiance and impatience. He had an acute awareness of his strength and thought he was under Blum's protection. It is true that the leader of the party showed great consideration for him; aside from Bracke, the parliamentary leader found himself rather isolated culturally in a party dominated on one side by opportunists like Renaudel and on the other by sectarians like Zyromski. The young philosophy teacher charmed and even fascinated him. However little he agreed with his views—the most boldly in favor of participation in the whole SFIO, along with Renaudel and Paul-Boncour—Blum perhaps gave way to his attraction by resolving in a way relatively favorable to the rebels the conflict that had broken out at the Paris congress: Déat and his friends demanded proportional representation for their minority faction (two-fifths of the votes) in the CAP, *Le Populaire,* and the secretariat of the party.

The conflict was resolved at the 1930 congress in Bordeaux, where the SFIO was the guest of Déat's boldest lieutenant, Adrien Marquet. Blum covered significant concessions to this right wing with his authority: the "Déatists" entered the CAP in force, being given 12 of 25 seats—more than their representation in the party—while the parliamentary group was granted greater decision-making maneuverability. Blum would later regret these concessions.

The elections were approaching. In the Parliament, coalitions of the right and arrangements of the extreme right succeeded one another—Tardieu following Laval, and Laval, Tardieu—except for the brief interlude of the Steeg (Radical) cabinet supported by the socialists. France was beginning to feel sharply the effects of the world crisis, and the growing anxiety in the country seemed to be working in favor of the SFIO, which carried off success after success in by-elections.

In May 1931, the Socialist Party was bold enough, ten years after the great struggle, to hold its congress in Tours, where in fact the least dramatic meeting of its history took place, though a long debate on national defense stirred some excitement and set the stage for later crises. While Faure boasted of a substantial increase in membership—it was about to pass 135,000—and of the return to the "old house" of a number of disenchanted communists (an observation that had a certain sting in Tours), Blum imprudently announced that in the general elections of the following year the party would increase its vote by 25 percent and its parliamentary representation by the same percentage.

A few months later, on April 10, 1932, speaking to the voters of Narbonne, he even took the risk of asserting that the SFIO would attract "hundreds of thousands of new voters" and would become the largest party in the Chamber. From this he naturally drew a conclusion in conformity with his doctrine: the SFIO would then be unable to shirk its responsibility to assume power. In what form? Coalition, sharing, hegemony? The orator of Narbonne, usually so clear, and in this case so imprudent in his predictions, was careful this time not to speak openly. He confined himself to speaking of the necessity for an agreement between parties in a coalition on only three points: the development of social insurance (including unemployment insurance), nationalization of insurance and railroad companies, and reduction in military spending. In short, a more modest program than the one offered by Daladier two years earlier when he had attempted to bring the socialists with him. But the essential point was Blum's prediction of success.

This time "responsibilities" were approaching. Blum offered to accept them with the boldness he had attributed to himself at the end of 1929. But his optimism had once again led him astray. The SFIO did make progress on May 1 and 8, 1932, gaining 200,000 votes (not the 750,000 predicted by the deputy from Narbonne) and increasing its parliamentary representation from 113 to 130 deputies. Blum once again placed the blame for his disappointment on the Communists who, to his astonishment, continued the tactics of "class against class" that had brought them the disaster of 1928, made still worse in 1932: they had lost 300,000 votes in four years and now had only ten deputies (one-thirteenth the number of the minority of Tours). But the SFIO was no longer measuring the gap between the two branches of French socialism; they were more concerned with calculating the distance between the party and power.

On May 8, 1932, Blum wrote in *Le Populaire:*

> While the Communists, in the name of the tactics of 'class against class,' served the capitalist class against the working class, by standing down for the Communists in better positions than our candidates, we really carry out the tactic of class against class; we re-establish for a moment in the electoral domain the political unity of the working class against which communism has been continuously working for twelve years.

Futile attacks. The SFIO remained outside the gates of power, but still close enough so that the old insistent problem was posed once again. A door should be opened or closed. This one was ajar, and by delivering his jubilant speech in Narbonne, Blum had helped to give arms to participationists like Renaudel.

On May 29, 1932, the Socialist party met again in a congress under the high arches of the Huyghens gymnasium, not far from the café where Blum had attended in the past the meetings of the fourteenth socialist section as a simple militant at the side of Bracke. The game was not over.

In a series of articles for *Le Populaire,* Blum had just pointed out that there were two possible formulas for the inevitable Herriot government: "concentration" (Radicals and the center with the support, it was whispered, of some socialists) and the old *Cartel* which Renaudel now called the "conjunction of the left" (Radicals and socialists). The socialist leader violently rejected the first possibility. On the second, curiously coming close to the policy he had so long and fervently fought against, he wrote:

> If the party had been called to power by the majority of voters, it would have carried out the entirety of its own program. It is not its fault, but that of the voters, that it did not win a majority, or even a majority within the majority. The problem which it now confronts is how to carry out the maximum portion of the program it cannot execute completely. Ministerial participation cannot be excluded *a priori*.

Blum was retreating, and maneuvering. Principles gave way before "realities." In this spirit, the May-June 1932 congress gave birth to what has been called "Les cahiers de Huyghens," a veritable government program which included a series of propositions in which can be found the beginnings of the program of 1936:

1. Consolidation of peace through arbitration (a typically Jaurèsian word) and disarmament.
2. Reduction in military expenditures and prohibition of the arms trade.
3. Control of the banks and protection of deposits in savings accounts.
4. Creation of a regulatory commission for grain.
5. Unemployment insurance.
6. Nationalization of the railroads.
7. Forty-hour week.
8. Amnesty for political offenses.

Presenting this program in *Le Populaire* on June 4, Blum began by asserting that "in the current state of national and international relations, the party does not think it possible to reject propositions that may be made to it. It does not oppose to them reasons 'of principle,' reasons deduced from the law of class antagonism." He further explained that the plan did not have the status of an "ultimatum." But this time it was the Radicals who created difficulties. There was a certain degree of anger in Blum's comments the next day, on the reception granted the socialist proposals by the neighboring party. On unemployment insurance (the socialists spoke of "general protection," the Radicals of "charity") as well as the reduction of military expenditures, and the nationalization of insurance and railroad companies, Blum noted that "the opposition of views is complete."

Once again "responsibilities" receded. The SFIO moved very quickly from the support which it had nevertheless granted Herriot to opposition provoked by the brutal deflationaist policy of this very timidly Radical cabinet, which was soon defeated. In January 1933, again with the "complicity" of the Socialist party, which he had left a few months earlier just before becoming one of Herriot's ministers, Paul-Boncour was removed from power. Paul-Boncour's defection, followed by his defeat at the hands of the party in which he had symbolized participation, were the prelude to and the occasion for the gravest crisis experienced by the SFIO since the congress of Tours.[30]

The crisis had been brewing for a long time. Frustrated ministerial ambitions, in this party constantly on the verge of power, had grown bitter. Who could go through this torment of Tantalus with impunity? The latent rebellion of the impatient lacked a leader bold enough to confront Blum and sweep aside his virtuous arguments. This leader, whom we have already glimpsed, was already present in the person of Marcel Déat, who had suitably surrounded himself with a young pretorian guard—Marquet, Montagnon, Bonnafou, and Cayrel—as well as a benevolent cohort of notables like Renaudel and Compère-Morel.

Edouard Daladier, leader of the Radical left, was again called on to form a government. As in 1929, he immediately offered the socialists an impressive degree of participation from which Blum was at the outset excluded: Auriol would have Finance, Compère-Morel Agriculture, Renaudel Commerce, Déat Aviation, etc. Quite naturally, the Socialist Party delegation recalled its program, "Les cahiers de Huyghens." Daladier refused to commit himself clearly, but he did not express the reservations which, coming from Herriot a year earlier, had resulted in the failure of the project. Blum, Bracke, and the left chose to make the "cahiers" a condition, a prerequisite, an "ultimatum,"[31] while Déat and Renaudel fought to present them only as the formulation of a general orientation.

Once again, the opponents of participation were victorious. But at the congress of Avignon in April 1933, the parliamentary group which he had so long represented violently opposed him when, in what was called the "Avignon resolution" he recalled the absolute supremacy of the National Council and the congress over any other body. The rebellion was so violent that Séverac, Faure's assistant, declared: "A split is inevitable. We might as well do it immediately."

The rebellion had become much more pugnacious since the firebrand Marcel Déat had taken over from the ponderous Renaudel. It was certainly a coincidence, but nonetheless striking: the days in early 1933 when the young leader of "socialism of action" finally rose up directly against Blum were the days of Hitler's rise to Chancellor. We should also note, with Gilbert Ziebura, that the events of Berlin had scarcely any immediate effect on the decisions of either side.

"I am appalled!"

Hitler had been in power for several months when the special congress demanded by the circumstances met on July 14, 1933 in the Mutualité. On June 21, Blum had published its preface in Le Populaire:

> It depends on the party itself to maintain its unity. Where then does its distress come from, and what can it fear? On one side it is said "they" are trying to push us out by force. "Their" secret plan is to cut off the "right" of the party to facilitate fusion with the communists. On the other side it is said "they" are only looking for a pretext to leave. All "their" plans have already been made. "They" no longer accept party discipline. . . . The danger would appear only if the congress, instead of exercising its judgment with serene impartiality, were to give its decision a tone of primitive harshness, mistrust, or suspicion. Then there might be a question of "indirect exclusion."

But was it a question of discipline, of relations between the various party organisms, or was it simply a question of personalities, rivalries, and jealousies? Obviously not. The hostility toward Blum that men like Marquet or (on another level) Compère-Morel could not hold back, the personal ambition of Déat, and Renaudel's long-frustrated ministerial ambitions all carried little weight in the face of what was at stake as it had been in 1920: the very meaning, direction, and future of socialism in France.

For Blum, the doctrine he had inherited from Jaurès was simultaneously a deepening of the republican spirit of the Revolution, a social aesthetic, and a charter for the liberation of the proletariat—a morality as well as a vision of the world. It was this morality, this vision, this "heritage" of hope that had to be preserved and made fruitful, but only in the most favorable conditions for the working class—and in this "favorable," the very detailed and analytic mind of Blum perhaps included too many conditions and saw too many parameters, to the point that he was led to a kind of historical scrupulosity, a political Jansenism.

For Déat, for Marquet, for Montagnon, socialism was "efficacy." It was a plan and the means of the state to carry it out. It was authority through state power and for the nation, and not social democracy. It was action for action's sake or rather the means for an action whose end could not be openly expressed (the book Déat published in 1930, *Perspectives socialistes,* is reticent precisely on the prospects) and which would be revealed only in the course of a later congress, drawing from Blum in a kind of outraged sob the word "fascism."

It was clear that it was hardly a matter of the relations between the parliamentary group and the CAP, or even of participation! However cleverly Blum at first attempted to camouflage things under words, discipline, arbitration, or internal relations, as at Tours, what was at stake was the SFIO's *raison d'être,* the legacy of Jaurès, and the future of the working class.

For four violent days at the Mutualité, from July 14 to 17, 1933, those who were later called "neo-socialists" unleashed several attacks against Blum. On Friday, Déat presented a review of the crisis; Saturday, it was Montagnon's turn; Sunday morning, Marquet's; on Sunday evening, Déat spoke again, in conclusion.

Bracke had opened the debate by speaking sharply to the minority: "Who will dare to initiate a split?" Déat had replied by raising the question of efficacy: "You will finally have to choose between opposition and intermittent support. Your dialectic cannot console those who are now being martyred by Hitlerism and fascism!" (The good disciple, the better to save the German anti-Fascists, was going to invent French fascism.)

But the "neos" were not content with arguing. They attacked the leader of the party in terms that might have been taken from the right-wing press, aggravated by the personal frustrations of young and ambitious men impatient under the "tutelage" of the great man and his "orthodox verbalism." Thus Déat attacked the "sterility" of Blum's politics and the "Byzantinism" of his doctrine. While Marquet called him, in the style of Léon Daudet, a "mandarin of decadence," Marcel Déat dared to speak to him without attempting to conceal an anti-Semitism without precedent in the history of French socialism: "I, who know you well, know the extent of your Oriental passivity."

Beyond abuse, the "neos" were revealing their intentions. What they were proposing was heard elsewhere in Europe at the time. Thus Montagnon: "The strength of fascism comes from the necessity which seems obvious everywhere for a strong state, for a powerful state, for an ordered state. It is in the middle classes that revolutionary ferment exists today. You have noticed it especially in Germany, now they are arising in France. What must we do? Regenerate our parliamentary system, that great decrepit machine, make a strong state, master of its currency, capable of controlling the economy and finances, of imposing certain regulations on big capital." Thus Marquet: "The working class feels that the time has come to use for its sake the governmental powers that until today have been put to work against it. It has itself incorporated the notion of authority in a socialist action which it would like to be logical, coherent, and strong. . . . Must we base the organization of the world on freedom and justice? The nations are in the process of moving into the domain of a new national reality."

Blum was stirring in his seat, making gestures, and Marquet shouted rudely to him: "Allow me! Everyone here has the right to express his opinion." It was at that point that Blum let fall the famous "I am listening to you with an attentiveness you can imagine. But I confess to you that I am appalled!" It was not only Marquet's words (which might have come from Germany or Italy) that provoked this "confession" (a witness, David Rousset, told us that it was delivered with consummate art and heart-rending tones that stirred the audience) it was also the

almost benevolent attention that he felt coming from all the benches of
the congress, and not only from the small kernel of Déat's supporters.
Thus, thirty years of the life of the Party, the great refusal of Tours,
and his constant teaching had made French socialism, whose scattered
fragments he had succeeded in bringing together, into a culture in
which the bacilli of fascism were developing at the instigation of the
man in whom he had perhaps seen, a short time before, the heir of
Jaurès's legacy.

He rose to his feet. He fought for two hours from the platform to
secure the vote against these "neos" already infected by fascism, of a
motion armed with the "punitive harshness" that he had wanted to
spare them a few days earlier. By nearly 2,200 votes against 752, a
violent resolution by Paul Faure struck the necks of the rebels like a
guillotine. But it was still only a censure.

It took another parliamentary crisis, when, on the pretext of saving
the unstable Daladier cabinet, the 28 "neo" deputies dared to vote for a
law reducing the salaries of civil servants (obviously rejected by all
levels of the Party) for them to be excluded. Would it not have been
more fitting for Blum and his friends to have rejected the rebels for
disloyalty to the democratic spirit than for reasons of discipline?

The "neos," whose chief appeared to be the stolid Renaudel (who
soon died, in despair at having gotten involved in this adventure), while
their real leader was of course Déat, thus seceded. With 28 senators
and 7 deputies, they were a force to be reckoned with. But they took
with them barely more than 20,000 militants, particularly a significant
group from Bordeaux (Marquet, Bonnafous, and Cayrel were deputies
from Gironde). They played no significant role[32] until Vichy and the
occupation gave free rein to their appetites.

For Léon Blum the 1933 split was a personal drama. Of course, as at
Tours twelve years earlier, he had set up the roadblock, since he was
the only one who foresaw the deep implications of a totalitarian mode
of thought. But he still had to explain, first to himself, and elucidate,
persuade, denounce, and purge. The virus was too pernicious. He
therefore wrote a long series of editorials, from July 19, 1933, to January 3, 1934, which indicated the depth of his sensitivity to the perver-
sions of fascism. The following excerpts give some idea of the just
passion that inspired him:

> At the Sunday morning session of the Congress, I interrupted
> the speech by our comrade Marquet from my seat, by letting fall
> the exclamation: "I am appalled!" My shock has not lessened on
> reflection. On the contrary, it has only grown by my reading of
> press commentary. The feeling has now been created among the
> public at large that, in the midst of the congress of the French

Section of the International, the manifesto of a national socialist party—not to say National-Socialist—has just been brilliantly presented. . . .

By attempting to block fascism's road to power, by attempting to take power before fascism does, one more or less consciously follows in its footsteps. By attempting to steal fascism's possible clientele, one ends up offering to the same public, with the same publicity techniques, a functionally analogous product. By proceeding, as fascism does, to bring together confused masses, by calling, as it does, on all the categories of the impatient, the suffering, and the greedy, one smothers the class action of the socialist party under that mass of adventurers—adventurers often because of poverty and despair—who have one by one supported all the dictatorships of history.

You cannot destroy fascist ideology by plagiarizing it, you can only strengthen it. . . . For socialism as we have always understood it and continue to understand it, these are really questions of life or death. Will the party remain the political tool of the working class, urban and rural, or will it become the representative of confused and heterogeneous masses? Will it be the interpreter of the workers' demands or of what is called the "general interest," a class party or a party of the declassed?

Does the party still intend to bring into being a social democracy conceived as the condition for and the completion of political democracy, or will it allow itself to be drawn toward the construction of the state based on force, on a Caesarist model? Will it be a party of freedom or a party of authority?

Finally—I am inclined to say especially—does the party still have as its objective the international organization of workers and the establishment of a collectivist system of property and production which, by its very nature, can only be international, or must its action be circumscribed, even temporarily, within the national framework? Will it be a national socialist party or the French Section of the Workers International?

As a counter to all this, on August 17, 1933, Blum had the courage to publish, next to his own article and three days after a threatening philippic by Déat, Marquet's answer:

For more than a week, no doubt in the name of the friendship you offered us at the end of the congress, you have been trying to demonstrate in *Le Populaire* that I have become a fascist.

Thus, before 500 delegates from the federations of the French Section of the Workers International and 2,000 militants from Seine, three fascists[33] were listened to and applauded in the course of three days?

You are vainly attempting to cushion the shock our speeches produced on the congress, the party, and the country.

The working class and democracy felt that the declarations which you condemn came in time to protect France from a fate

identical to that of Italy and Germany. For we had reached that
point.

Subtly, by means of Byzantinism, you are leading us to fascism.

When Blum learned that, the better to defy him and his comrades,
the "neos" had decided to establish themselves as "Jean Jaurès
groups," he could not refrain from replying:

> It is the worst enemies of socialism who repeat: there are two
> socialisms, one good, the other bad; one is living, generous,
> humane, the other rigorous as a calculation or a logical construc-
> tion; one is really French, right-thinking, a "native" growth, the
> other is German in origin and international by nature. Jaurès never
> for an instant agreed to situate socialist action outside the class
> action of the proletariat. He proclaimed it in terms whose clarity
> cannot be surpassed; for him as for Marx, socialism and the work-
> ing class were indistinguishable. The realization of socialism and
> the victory of the proletariat were in his eyes two sides of the same
> fact. What would he have thought of those men for whom the
> notion of class is an outmoded concept, and the existence of the
> proletariat as a class a fact no longer true or an invalid observa-
> tion? He could only have repeated: "You have necessarily placed
> yourselves outside socialist life and thought." How heavily his
> judgment falls on those who dare to cover themselves with his
> name.
>
>   . . . To oppose Jaurès to Marx is nonsense, Jaurès was a Marx-
> ist. In the present state of things, an anti-Marxist socialist would
> no longer be a socialist and would soon become an anti-socialist.
> Besides, how could we extricate ourselves from this identity be-
> tween socialism and Marxism, when it is our most furious or most
> cynical opponents who use it against us? Marxism is the name, in
> France and elsewhere, which has always been given to socialism
> when the aim is to fight it, vilify it, eradicate it. When Le Temps
> seeks to fill honest French Radicals with disgust and horror at our
> maleficent party—that is, five or six times a week—it calls us
> Marxists and not socialists. It was against Marxism that Mussolini
> declared war. It is Marxism that Hitler, Goering, and their gangs
> claim to be ripping from German soil. Whoever attacks socialism,
> whoever wants to ridicule it or make it an object of hatred, calls it
> Marxism.
>
>   All the more reason, like the Tramps of William of Orange, to
> assume proudly the name with which they want to mock us or
> condemn us. Yes we are Marxists, yes we are internationalists. We
> know perfectly well to what this profession of faith exposes us. We
> know that the enemies of socialism will continue, as in the past, to
> denounce us as men without a country, traitors, advocates or
> agents of Germany. That doesn't matter, provided that no social-
> ist, through his imprudences, provides them with involuntary sup-
> port.

The argument was not closed. It continued with weapons in hand,
before the tribunals of Vichy, and against the harbingers of Nazism.

Seven Days in February

The neo-socialist crisis was not only a caricaturized "revolt of the angels" and the sudden appearance of a dark, ambitious figure. It was an expression of something very powerful in French society: the crisis of the middle classes in the early thirties—classes which Déat attempted to enlist, as Hitler had done in Germany ten years before. But the French had not yet had the "opportunity" of defeat nor the enormous wave of unemployment which assured the Nazis of support among certain sectors of the proletariat as well as the middle classes.

France in 1934 was nonetheless deeply troubled by the disappointments provoked by the regime's use of the sacrifices of the war, the disorders of the political system, public demoralization, and (a more verifiable fact) a fall in income affecting several social categories. With the exception of a small well-off social stratum, the decline in living standards between 1930 and 1934 has been evaluated at 20 percent (although Alfred Sauvy is more cautious about the figure).

"The crisis seemed to affect most of all small individual owners of land, shops, small industry, the category of worker-bosses, owners of their tools and their fields, which made up the ideological model to which the third Republic aspired under the influence of the Radical Party, after as well as before the First World War. This is why the difficulties that struck them affected the deepest foundations of the regime."[34]

The regime was first of all, on the surface, the Parliament. It was in the Assembly, among the "deputies," that very broad currents of opinion saw the source of the evil, the weakness from which the country was suffering, the hecatomb of governments fruitlessly succeeding one another, at the mercy of crisis and the economic forces attempting to organize it for their profit. Whether they came from the right like Poincaré and Tardieu, or from the left like Caillaux and Daladier, the men who succeeded one another in power seemed caught in an inextricable network of contradictions and impotence.

Many held the Socialist party responsible for this paralysis, because it was a pillar of the parliamentary system but absent from governmental action, which is its corollary and continuation. The very peculiar game that the SFIO parliamentary group played on the fringes of power distorted the representative system, clogged the machine, and did a great disservice to republican order.

Blum was well aware of this. His thought evolved in those years in response to the rise of the Fascist threat, which he had perceived early and had firmly denounced. Since Tours, he had always given priority to the purity and cohesion of the party, the "sacred trust" which had to be preserved from opportunist temptations and short-term missions so that it would be ready for larger tasks—either the conquest or, more probably, the "exercise" of power. But now he began to wonder whether the demands of the defense of democracy should not take precedence over any other concerns. What would be the use of a fine Socialist party, quite pure and quite united (in so far as it was either in 1933), if it were to be caught in the trap of a coup d'état and dictatorship, like the German Social Democrats?

Blum saw clearly that this question led to another. The SFIO might be (would be?) led to take on responsibilities—this was the meaning of the Narbonne speech in 1932 and of "Les cahiers de Huyghens." Could it do so without having tried everything to re-establish working class unity, in whatever form? Unity was necessary for action, particularly in the labor unions. Unity was also needed to prevent democratic socialism from losing itself in a muddled and isolated operation from which only the totalitarian current would derive arguments and benefits. As much out of concern for the democratic Republic as for self-protection, the SFIO, in those months and years, had simultaneously to prepare for its entry into the government and restore its links with the PCF. It was a battle on two fronts that was awaiting detonation.

While Blum and the SFIO were seriously heading toward the responsibilities of power and while the leaders of the International in Moscow, instructed by the disaster their policy of hostility toward social democracy had provoked in Germany, a strategic revision to open the way to a coalition of leftist movements, French political life was being deeply disturbed by three factors which were not new but had recently been revived: antiparliamentarianism, anti-Semitism, and anticommunism.

Anticommunism had hardly changed since 1917. Connected to the old resentments created by the "betrayal" of Brest-Litovsk, fed by the tragic news from Moscow—liquidation of the "kulaks," Stalin's first purges—inspired by the campaigns of a press (which was sometimes joined by Le Populaire) which grew hysterical at any mention of "the man with a knife in his teeth," kept alive by the vulgar violence of L'Humanité, anti-Communism found its way into nine-tenths of what was published in France.

Anti-Semitism, temporarily devalued by the Dreyfus Affair and discredited as a bourgeois value by the impeccable solidarity of the French Jewish community during the Great War, was revived by the arrival in France of many Central European refugees from Nazism and their accession to leading positions in business, the administration, and politics. Hitler was then demonstrating that anti-Semitism could be a "profitable" policy, in the strictest sense of the word: the confiscation of Jewish fortunes and the expulsion of Jewish managers provided the state and individuals with large profits and new jobs. French anti-Semitism had found, in Maurras, Gaxotte, Vallat, and Céline, its theoreticians, practitioners, spokesmen, and users. A section of the press was devoted to it. A path was open before it. It had become one of the cards in the French political deck.

As for antiparliamentarianism, born during the Panama scandal, revived by the campaigns of Clemenceau (the victim of Panama) against the war policies of his rivals, sharpened by the failures of the *Cartel* in 1926, it had grown stronger since the early thirties when the vices of ministerial instability had been openly displayed. It was only necessary that the specter of corruption haunt Parliament for this general hatred of "the deputies" to break out. The combination of these fantasies and refusals led to the appearance of the "leagues," more or less paramilitary organizations whose common ambition was to "restore order," "clean out the Augean stables," "re-establish French power," and "restore morality" on the basis of the "veterans' spirit." There were a number of leagues, each with its own style, but a single overall project. The general tone was provided by the three "antis," but anti-Semitism was muffled by the leaders of the largest organization, the *Croix-de-feu,* who were very reticent on this point.

A typical example of this state of mind is this appeal by Gustave Hervé, the old leader of socialist antimilitarism before 1914, who had converted to extreme nationalism and launched a campaign in *La Victoire* to call on Marshall Pétain: "Who will cleanse Marianne's stables of the filth the parliamentary regime has deposited there in the last fifty years? Only a great popular wave can wash them clean. We hear people groaning on all sides: 'How can we get rid of this impotent and corrupt regime? Who is the leader who will emerge in France like the leaders of Italy and Germany?' "

Among the rank and file, in the *Croix-de-feu, L'Union nationale des combattants, Solidarité française, Jeunesses patriotes,* or *L'Action française,* we can find an old tradition, the endless parade of Déroulède, Boulanger, the generals of the Dreyfus Affair, Jaurès's assassin, Joseph de Maistre, Drumont, M. de Charette, and General de Galliffet of 1871. It was the perennial party of the Whites, the Chouans, the Restoration, the coup of December 2, and the Versaillais. The old civil war kindled in 1789 continued. From Herriot to Cachin and from Daladier to Blum, the Girondins and Montagnards of 1934 confronted the party of the great revenge.

This multifarious clan, well equipped, endowed with an ideally simplistic "ideology" ("France for the French"), and financed by the largest capitalist group in France (directed by Ernest Mercier), was given at the end of December 1933 the profitable issue of outraged virtue. The Crédit Municipal of Bayonne had issued counterfeit bonds;

mixed up in the affair was an adventurer well known in Parisian "society," Alexandre Stavisky, who had connections with the councillor Pressard, brother-in-law of the Radical Premier Chautemps, and with one of his ministers, Dalmier, also a Radical. About to arrest the swindler at Chamonix on January 8, 1934, the police found him dead. A suicide? Killed before he talked? The scandal led to the collapse of the Chautemps cabinet.

In *Le Populaire* of January 10, Blum wrote that the "affair" certainly contained

> titillating and striking peculiarities: a certain technical perfection, a powerful element of the picturesque, particularly because of the contrast between the extraordinary casualness of the swindler and his judicial record, the massive size of the sums involved, and the quality of the major victims. But, all things considered, the Stavisky affair with all its ins and outs is a normal product of the regime which it characterizes. The revulsion and anger of public opinion are defensive reflexes of human morality against the absurdities and monstrosities produced by the social system, and we should therefore encourage them. We should not identify ourselves with certain dispensers of justice as corrupt as the guilty men. We must seize this weapon, like all the others, for our own purposes of demonstration, of human liberation and purification.

The right-wing press, for its part, began to exploit the affair politically. Henri de Kerillis, its most typical representative, wrote that since Stavisky had been a financial backer of the Radicals, the party was "no longer qualified to control the fate of the nation." Nevertheless, it was Edouard Daladier who was asked to form a government on January 29: he was to all appearances honest and had a reputation for being energetic. But the enemy had already unleashed the great movements of harassment against the regime. As early as January 9, *L'Action française* sent its militants into the streets around the Palais-Bourbon, with cries of "Down with the thieves! Down with the assassins!" They enjoyed the support of the population (in this "fashionable" neighborhood in any case), and extraordinary tolerance on the part of the police (whose head, Jean Chiappe, was notoriously connected to the parties of the right, if not the extreme right, although he had suppressed a document damaging to Stavisky in 1933).

These were two sufficient reasons for Daladier to dismiss this strange prefect of police on February 3. It was said that there was a third: as a price for its support of the Daladier cabinet, the SFIO had demanded the dismissal.[35] Blum, who had already announced, in *Le Populaire* on January 28, the vigorous intervention of the SFIO in the crisis, denied on February 5 that a bargain of that kind had been struck between his group and the head of the government. But he "did not rule out" the possibility that Chiappe's dismissal might contribute to his group's support.

On the right, there was an uproar: Daladier was handing Chiappe's head to Blum to assure socialist votes and to cover up the suppression of the affair! "It is a Jacobin coup d'état! Tomorrow the socialists will ask for the head of General Weygand.³⁶ Will M. Daladier grant it to them?" asked Taittinger, the leader of *Jeunesses patriotes*. On February 5, fifteen right-wing deputies called on the people of Paris to come out into the streets the next day, while Maurras, announcing in *L'Action française* that the government was preparing to assassinate certain members of the opposition, proclaimed: "Person for person, head for head, life for life!"

It was at this point that the most active of the "leagues," *Solidarité française*, put up the following poster:

> Daladier is leading you like a herd of sheep to the Blums, the Kaisersteins, the Schweinkopfs, and the Zyromskis, whose very French names are a whole program.
> Patriots, these are your masters!
> People of France, this is the dictatorship that awaits you!
> Your Parliament is corrupt.
> Your politicians compromised.
> Your country abandoned to the mud of scandal.
> Your security threatened.
> Civil war rumbles.
> War is waiting in the wings.
> Peasants, you are threatened with ruin—look at the grain scandal.
> Workers, intellectuals, your jobs are threatened by foreigners.
> None of you is in your own country any more.
> France for the French.

All the leagues called their "troops" to the Champs-Elysées for the late afternoon of February 6. Everyone came, including ARAC, the organization of Communist-leaning veterans (led by Jacques Duclos), which did not want to give the right a monopoly on virtuous indignation.

The riot, which was started at five on the Champs-Elysées by the *Camelots du roy* and the militants of *Solidarité française*, spread onto the pont de la Concorde toward the Palais-Bourbon, and was barely contained by the mounted mobile guard, when Blum rose to speak in the Chamber. It was a little past seven on February 6, 1934.

Edouard Daladier, designated Premier, read his declaration amidst a torrent of abuse, nearby gunfire, yells of "Assassin!" by Georges Scapini and Philippe Henriot. Xavier Vallat openly went back and forth between the Assembly and the rioters. A delegation from the Municipal Council of Paris came to demand the government's resignation. Cautious deputies were seen sneaking out the back door; separating those who stayed at their posts and the furious mob crying for death was little more than a few police cordons.

Blum's voice reached his colleagues only through a barrage of insults. That evening, Edouard Herriot admired in him a "republican hero."

> We do not bring you a vote of confidence but a vote of combat. The parties of reaction, who were defeated two years ago and who have looked for revenge first in financial panic and then in moral panic, are now attempting a violent seizure of power. It is no longer just dissolution they are aiming for but brutal oppression of the civil liberties which the working people have conquered, which they have paid for with their blood, which are their possessions, and the guarantee of their ultimate liberation. The people, who made the Republic, will know how to defend it. As interpreters of their will, we are determined, in the domain of parliament as in every other, to block the path of the outrageous offensive of Fascist reaction.
>
> If the government leads the struggle with enough energy, with enough faith in the popular will, it can count on us. If it fails in its duty, then we will launch throughout the country a call to republican forces and to the masses of peasants and workers.
>
> All of public opinion must be convinced, by prompt and resounding proof, that no consideration of any kind whatsoever will halt or restrict the repression of scandal. The national atmosphere must be purified and renewed. The deep causes of distress are unemployment, present suffering, anxiety for the future, and the grave apprehension provoked by foreign events. . . .
>
> Civil liberties only survive because of the confidence and enthusiasm of the popular masses. They are compromised from the moment they no longer guarantee a life of security and peace. We are determined to repeat that too to the country if we are not heard in this Chamber. In the battle that has now been joined, we demand our place in the first rank. Fascist reaction will not pass.

Daladier received 360 of 580 votes cast. The riot had united behind him the entire "republican" left. But after a lull in the evening, violence redoubled after midnight. There were rumors of twenty, of fifty deaths (there were in fact fifteen, only one among the police). Daladier and his Minister of the Interior, Eugène Frot, went to the Elysée where, in spite of his weakness, President Lebrun seems to have encouraged them to act firmly; then they held a veritable council of war at the Ministry of the Interior. Should the government hand in its resignation? Should it declare martial law? Should they present an indictment for conspiracy against national security and arrest the most outrageous rebels, particularly the leaders of *L'Action française?* Should Parliament be suspended?

On all these questions, Daladier and Frot confronted delaying tactics of delay and passivity on the part of most senior civil servants and military authorities. Was this the reason or the pretext for the resignation of the Premier and the Interior Minister? Daladier's courage was obviously dissolving. On the morning of the 7th, he received Blum, who was perhaps the only one to advise him to "remain and struggle." The leader of the SFIO went so far as to offer substantial socialist participation in the government.

> DALADIER: "I will have to proclaim martial law, suspend Parliament . . .
> BLUM: "A republican government must fight the mob with the constant support of the Assembly by keeping it informed of its decisions. It is up to Parliament to approve the proclamation of martial law. You do not have the right to suspend it."

Petty legalism? For Blum, legality was all the more a whole when it was under violent challenge. Could the cabinet be saved? Did it deserve to be? The scruples of the author of *La Réforme gouvernementale* helped to resolve Daladier's final doubts, and he pathetically handed in his resignation to the head of State. The way was clear for a coalition covered by the name of former president Gaston Doumergue, a timid Radical, who would be under the thumb of Minister of State André Tardieu, the right-wing leader who was most involved with the rioters of February 6, and for whose benefit the whole operation had been conducted. The Minister of Labor was André Marquet, and Marcel Déat held the portfolio of Aviation. Beside them could already be seen the képi of the Minister of War named Philippe Pétain, who had been in the minds of many of the demonstrators at la place de la Concorde.

But for the moment, the "leagues" had gone too far, or not far enough, and the left prepared a great counter-attack. And yet, things had begun badly. On the morning of February 6, in *L'Humanité,* Marty had accused the socialists of "complicity with the system." Nevertheless, that evening, the Seine socialist federation proposed a counter-demonstration with the Communists. A strike? A march? They were not even received by their Communist comrade. The next day *L'Humanité* breathed fire:

> A regime of blood and filth! In the rapid decomposition of the capitalist system, they are displaying all their iniquity. They are all involved in scandalous corruption, deputies and senators, judges and police, ministers and dignitaries of the bourgeois state. The indignation of the masses is mighty, irresistible, and yesterday the Fascist cliques which assembled with the prior knowledge of the government were able to attract a large contingent from the petty bourgeoisie. The 'democratic' government, its 'left-wing' Cham-

ber, its socialists whose pitiful collapse contributed to the birth and development of these militarist groups, are the ones who are really to blame.

On February 8: "The bloody Daladier-Frot government, supported by the Socialist Party, have helped the *Union nationale* to come to power. They have just given way before it. This is how the Radical and socialist parties pave the way for fascism!"

That evening, the PCF called on its militants and "the people of Paris" to demonstrate the next evening at seven in la place de la République. A substantial number of young socialists joined the Communists in confronting the police, who attacked as brutally as on the 6th: in two hours, between the gare du Nord and the gare de l'Est, eight people were killed and dozens were wounded. Once again, the working class paid the greatest price.

That day, Blum had published in *Le Populaire* an alarmist and militant analysis:

> For the second time, the formation of a National Bloc has sanctioned the revenge of reaction in spite of electoral defeat. In 1926, the weapon was financial disorder and panic, both provoked by those who exploited them. In 1934, the blow against the will of the electorate was planned under the cover of scandals, Tuesday's riot, and its dramatic consequences. But the situation is more alarming than in 1926. The forces that have been unleashed cannot be controlled at will. The royalist and Fascist shock troops have felt their strength, and they will grow bolder. Behind the National Bloc which covers the stage, we have a further attack to fear. Therefore, more fervently and more methodically than ever, the masses of workers and peasants must organize their resistance.

"The masses of workers," without distinction? The day before, the CGT (whose leadership was close to the SFIO) had already called for a general strike and demonstrations on February 12. The pro-Communist CGTU had replied with a similar appeal. An attempt to outbid, or an expression of solidarity? Serge Bernstein[37] answers the question a little too definitely perhaps: "outbidding." He bases himself on the attitude of the Communist leadership, at that time violently hostile to the SFIO. But how could solidarity be "avoided" when the two appeals converged? Unless it was a challenge with the objective being a real confrontation—though that was highly improbable, given the underground development among certain supporters of the Third International, and the Second as well.

In general, the strike of February 12 was widely observed and considered a victory for working-class organizations. But the day was especially significant because of the (competitive, complementary?) demonstrations. The SFIO had called its militants to the cours de

Vincennes for a march to the place de la Nation. The PCF had done the same, obviously intending to carry out a "co-opting" maneuver in the rank and file with the slogan of a "single front." According to reports of the national police, when the socialist contingent got under way at three in the afternoon, it included 300,000 people marching behind socialist elected officials, headed by Blum. But another contingent also advanced toward the place de la Nation, singing the *Internationale* and *Le Jeune Garde,* and chanting the slogan: *"Front unique!"* "Ferrat, a member of the political bureau of the Communist party, mounted the bandstand where the boulevard Diderot enters the place de la Nation, delivered a speech advocating a single front. But the demonstrators, at the insistence of some of their number, resumed their march and, behind their red flag, joined the socialists."[38]

It was this fraternization among the rank and file that gave meaning to the "historic" events of February 12. While the two parties' newspapers continued to tear each other apart, the Communist militants "joined the socialists." In an article published in February 1950, a few weeks before his death, Blum described in *Le Populaire-Dimanche*

> the conjunction, the combination of a twenty-four hour general strike ordered by the CGT and a great public demonstration in the place de la Nation, organized by the Seine and Seine-et-Oise federations of the SFIO. How did the idea take shape? In rue Victor-Massé, in the offices of *Le Populaire* which Oreste Rosenfeld and I hardly ever left, the leaders of the Seine federation—particularly Jean Zyromski and Marceau Pivert—and those of Seine-et-Oise—Descourtieux and Germaine Degrond—maintained constant contact with us. We proposed the idea to the CAP. The general secretariat, represented by Paul Faure and Jean-Baptiste Séverac, was not very enthusiastic.

Daniel Mayer later described how Blum, supported by Vincent Auriol, had to exercise all his authority to convince Faure: "If the general secretariat does not call for a demonstration, my dear Paul, *Le Populaire* will do it."[39]

We have to make allowances for a certain taste for "dramatic embellishment" in the rest of the narrative when Blum evokes the meeting of the socialist and Communist marches in the cours de Vincennes: "The heads of the two columns were now face to face, and the same cries were heard on all sides. Songs were sung in chorus. The leaders of the march came together. It was not a collision, it was fraternization. Through a kind of ground swell, the people's instinct and the people's will had imposed the unity of action of the organized workers for the defense of the Republic."

More moving and stronger still is the story of the meeting in the cours de Vincennes told by the privileged witness Charles-André Julien in the film by Françoise Verny and Claude Santelli, *1936, ou la mémoire du peuple*. The old militant historian evokes the two armies marching toward each other, at each other, Blum at his side in anguish, and suddenly arms opening, eyes meeting, voices mingling. He cannot recall this outburst of popular feeling, this "true birth of the Popular Front, imposed by the rank and file, by the masses," without breaking into tears. Had Michelet witnessed the fête de la Fédération or the arrival of the Marseille volunteers in Paris, would he have been able to evoke those moments coolly?

Did this mean unity? It took four more months for it really to get under way, on the essentially pacifist grounds developed two years before, not without ulterior motives, by the Amsterdam-Pleyel Committee directed by Romain Rolland and Henri Barbusse. It was further promoted by the fiery and brilliant Gaston Bergery, an independent leader of reformed radicalism who launched *La Flèche* and inspired the "Common Front"; and, in his rather disturbing and adventurous way, by Jacques Doriot who, from his base in Saint-Denis, multiplied militant pre-electoral initiatives for a union of the left. Thus, the future leader of French fascism, although he had half-broken with the PCF and the International (he was expelled in June 1934 after refusing to go to Moscow in April to explain his activities), helped to push Stalin's decisions in a clearly anti-Fascist direction. Thorez, duly informed by an important delegation from the International in June, obeyed. It was in this same month of June that the PCF offered unity of action to the SFIO and the CGT, given concrete form, as a first step, by a meeting of delegations of the two parties in the cité Malesherbes. This took place on June 14, 1934, five months after the riot of the "leagues."

In an editorial on the same day, Blum explained that the principle of unity of action was established, provided that the "insulting attacks," which came as usual from *L'Humanité,* stopped. The next day, he published an analysis (which turned out to be prophetic on a number of points) of the reversal of Communist strategy under the title *"Défense internationale contre le fascisme"*:

> The Fascist riot of 6 February and its repercussions among the masses in France have allowed the Communist International to carry out a change of front whose necessity it had no doubt sensed since Hitler's rise to power in Germany. The Nazi victory has confronted the Russian Revolution with the gravest danger it has encountered for the last thirteen or fourteen years. The target of Japanese aggression in the Far East, forced to contemplate the imminence of a war which its courageous desire for peace has been able to forestall only with great effort, the Soviet government now feels behind it the additional threat of Hitler.
>
> There is no need to look for other causes of this diplomatic version of the NEP, the signing of non-aggression pacts, Lit-

vinov's travels, and Russia's coming entry into the League of Nations—which is also, we might note in passing, a change or reversal of attitude. The Soviet government wants to guarantee the "security" of its European front with a system of international agreements if possible, with the support of particular foreign powers if necessary. Nothing is more logical or more legitimate. But, in the case of both general agreements and particular support, France has become the key piece on the chessboard. It is in France that the essential conditions for Soviet Russia's "security" are located.

If community of action in France could help to protect the Russian Revolution against racism in the international sphere while blocking fascism in the national context, it would acquire in my eyes a double value.

Pacifism and/or Antifascism

This concluding sentence, in fact the whole article, shows that few other public men of the time were capable of analyzing with consistency both domestic conditions and foreign affairs, and showing the connections between them. Careful reading of his articles in *Le Populaire* and analysis of his activities as leader of the SFIO reveal that he was most frequently concerned with questions that, in appearance at least, determined the evolution of French society and the condition of the working class. But his study of diplomatic and strategic problems, especially after Hitler's rise to power, and his participation in foreign socialist congresses and contacts within the International show that he was passionately concerned with what he called *Les Problèmes de la paix*—the title of a book published in 1931 which collected some of his articles from *Le Populaire*.

Jean Longuet, who liked and admired Blum enough to have remained in the background while Blum led the party, readily said to his associates that his friend was less competent in foreign than in domestic affairs. It would be easy to agree with him on this point if it did not seem preferable to replace the notion of competence with something that called into question not so much his knowledge and capacity to understand and judge, as his freedom of thought and his detachment from ideological constraints.

The same Blum who, until the tragic events of 1934, based his domestic strategy on an idea and a word—"non-participation," a kind of permanent holding of the SFIO in reserve for the "exercise of power" which was to come about only on a healthy and solid basis, the party not having been previously compromised, distorted, or divided by participation in the workings of managing the bourgeois state—based his entire foreign strategy on a still more central and obsessive idea—disarmament. In the light of what happened in 1936, some commentators may ridicule the "non-participation" which perhaps contributed to the lack of preparation and the failures of the members of the Popular Front government. Others, myself among them, would rather challenge the virtues of disarmament in such circumstances.

One might say that it amounted to confusing a policy with its results and forgetting that the rise of Nazism was connected to the feverish armaments policy of the victors of 1918, who, by imagining the danger of German rearmament, had ended by creating it. In 1930, Count Bernsdorf, representative of the Weimar government in Geneva, demanded to know on what grounds one could continue to enforce disarmament in Germany, when all the other countries rejected it. Of course, at that point the war had been over for only twelve years. But that period had included the occupation of the Ruhr, which German public opinion had unanimously seen as a French war of aggression.

It is impossible to deny the boldness and coherence of Blum's reasoning about diplomacy, directly inspired by Jaurès's thought, until the early thirties. Its first element, in 1919, was criticism of the Versailles treaty, about which Bainville said that it was "too soft where it should be harsh, and too harsh where it should be soft." Blum accepted only the second half of the description. For him it was a primitive treaty looking toward the past rather than the future and reflecting the rancor and the appetites of the victors more than what was needed to build peace. A second element in Blum's diplomatic doctrine was the adaptation of reparations to the real current capacities of Germany, in order to make them a contractual procedure directed toward the combined economic rebirth of both countries, rather than an instrument to pauperize the vanquished.

A third theme was the violent denunciation of Poincaré's strategy of occupation of the Ruhr in which Blum saw nothing but a cynical and usurious proceeding, a resurrection of militarism, and a provocation of the most dangerous German nationalist demons. A fourth idea was more directly derived from Jaurès: every conflict should be settled by arbitration. This procedure should be made obligatory, and a state would or would not be recognized as an aggressor according to its acceptance or refusal of arbitration. If it refused, the socialists themselves would be justified in armed resistance against it. Finally, the fifth idea was disarmament, which was to "purge" every urge to warfare.

To the same degree that the first four positions seem hardly subject to challenge, the fifth raises questions, more related to the historical context than the source or rigor of the idea. The idea of disarmament is very attractive, and very few, except for Jaurès, developed it as well as Blum. But what seems extremely open to criticism in Blum's diplomatic behavior is that disarmament held the same place in his thought and writings no matter what happened. It was unaffected by Mussolini's plotting to arm pro-Fascist and revanchist movements in Central Europe—in fact Blum attacked with a great deal of lucidity his supplying of arms to the Hungarian right in 1926—by Japan's invasion of Manchuria in 1931, and even by the rise of Nazism in Germany.

It is essential to be precise about this point. The diagnostic errors committed by the socialist leader about the future of Hitler in 1930, and especially in 1932, are famous, and have given rise to much sarcastic commentary. We must quote excerpts from various articles of the period. If they are compared to the majority of contemporary predictions, they demonstrate the complexity of Blum's thought and his ability to consider many facets of the truth, rather than his naiveté or incompetence.

In *Les Problèmes de la paix* (1931), the director of *Le Populaire* wrote:

> Hitler is further from power today than General Boulanger was on the evening of 27 January 1889. Should we fear his rise to power? Not according to me. I believe that Hitler's star has already risen to the highest point in its course, it has already reached its zenith.[40] I think so for reasons I expressed long ago chiefly because of the fundamental incoherence of his gangs and the necessary dissociation of the heterogeneous elements that made them up. But let us ignore probability and imagine Hitler in power.
>
> First of all, nothing indicates that once installed as Chancellor, the absurd wandering apostle of racism would not feel a heavy mantle of prudence and circumspection fall on his shoulders; on that day, his program would become very embarassing both domestically and in foreign affairs, and we have seen many such opportunisitc metamorphoses. Nevertheless, let us continue to adopt extreme hypotheses and admit that Hitler in power would remain the Hitler of today. What would happen then? . . . Neither the power nor the military reputation of Germany is such that it can gather half of Europe in its shadow, as it did fourteen years ago. It is impossible to attribute even to Hitler, even to Mussolini, such absurd and lunatic intentions. And, what is more, it is up to us to make them permanently impracticable.

But how? Faced with this madness, Blum still saw no path to follow but disarmament. He fully recognized the fundamental qualitative difference between the "absurd wandering apostle of racism" and his predecessors, Brüning and Streseman. Yet, he did not make the qualitative jump from the strategy toward Wilhelm II and Bethmann-Hollweg defined by Jaurès, which he himself redefined toward Weimar Germany, and the strategy called for, made necessary, so it seems to us today, by the appearance of the Nazi phenomenon.

On the floor of the Chamber, in the commission on Foreign Affairs of the National Assembly, and in his articles for *Le Populaire,* he continued his calls for disarmament for five more years. But he cannot be faulted for his campaigns against the chauvinism of the majority and against the lamentable general staff which, under the immediate aegis of Weygand and the more distant protection of Pétain, enclosed the French army in the most routine abdication of intelligence. We must also add that a man whose strategic realism and authority are more acknowledged than those of Blum, Franklin Roosevelt, revived the great disarmament negotiations with MacDonald and Herriot as late as 1937. And a man who had left the SFIO in 1931 to be better able to devote himself to national defense, Paul-Boncour, still made partial disarmament an article of his "constructive plan" of 1932.

But it remains puzzling that a man like Blum, with such an undogmatic intelligence and obvious courage could harbor, apparently unconsciously, the contradiction between the militant antifascism which governed his action and the aspiration for disarmament which continued to dominate his writing. Perhaps it is necessary to have lived through the years 1938–45 to feel all the absurdity of such an attitude which throws a distressing shadow over the behavior of the leader of the SFIO in this area from 1930 to 1936. Confronted with a phenomenon like Hitlerism, was he incapable of revising a strategy, however intimately connected it may have been to his education, to the memory of Jaurès, and to the impulses and pressures of his party? In 1914, he had been able to silence the echoes of Jaurès's voice in order to enter the *Union sacrée* cabinet. Although he was so courageous, from an intellectual and civic point of view as well as on the physical level (as he showed particularly in 1936), he was incapable at that point of reorienting his diplomatic and military doctrine. Blum had been able to move from the religion of "non-participation" to the ideas of "les cahiers de Huyghens," and to the offers made to Daladier on February 7, 1934. But on the question of disarmament, Hitler's assumption of the Chancellorship in 1933 was not the decisive revelation that February 6, 1934 was for him.

But it cannot be said that he had underestimated the importance of the Hitlerian phenomenon. The picture he drew of it remained vague, and he mingled a kind of contemptuous incredulity with his fear. Nevertheless, immediately after the Nazi accession to power, at the end of January 1933, his tone became more dramatic, more in tune with gloomy reality. On February 9, Blum was still attempting to doubt the worst:

> Hitler is governing in shameless violation of the spirit of the Weimar constitution, but he is not exercising complete and open dictatorship. Will this partial exercise of power in the framework of feudal and business Germany help Hitler to achieve next month the absolute majority which would transform the exercise of power into revolutionary conquest? It is possible; it is natural to fear it; it

is wise to prepare for it. But excellent judges of German affairs doubt it.

Three weeks later came the Reichstag fire, and his tone sharpened:

> This is the beginning of racist terror. Our comrades in Germany were indeed right to fear as the supreme danger the combination of the racist organization and the government apparatus in the same hands. And we were also right to declare that if Hitler were to take power, the destruction of proletarian forces would become the single article of his program, in any case the only one whose execution he could not postpone. We have reached this point today, thanks to the anti-worker fury over big business and to the still unexplained plot of Hindenburg and Papen. The history of Mussolinian fascism is repeating itself. With the same inspiration, the same episodes, and the same goal, but with something still darker and more ferocious.

Two weeks later, the same Blum who foresaw "racist terror" and wrote, with profound insight, that the war against the German left could from one day to the next turn into a war against the Soviet Union, the same Blum waxed indignant against the *"Soyons forts"* campaign launched at the time by Henri de Kerillis:

> The arms race does not prevent war, it makes it unavoidable. The more alarming the ascendancy of Hitlerian racism becomes, the more non-rearmament of Germany becomes the essential condition for the security of France. And the non-rearmament of Germany is practically impossible without a general program of arms reduction and control.

For months, Blum continued on these two paths. When the British press announced at the end of 1933 that Hitler was reportedly ready to accept arms control, Blum wrote on December 12 that it was inconceivable that the Nazi dictator was acting "in good faith," and that there was no question of agreeing to negotiate with him, even on these terms; but he added that this was a further reason to reopen the Geneva disarmament conference "with Germany's presence if possible, in its absence if necessary." Dealing with an individual devoid of good faith, and therefore of an attitude of reciprocity, Blum was proposing to organize global disarmament. A strange inconsistency, which it took Blum many months to overcome; he didn't do so in practice until he had access to government files and responsibilities.

There remains his very keen awareness of the Fascist menace and the need to unite against it. No one—in the areas of civic, political, and ideological struggle—had more successfully related the domestic and foreign aspects of the problem than Blum. No one called more constantly for vigilance, persuaded as he was that internal enemies—

whom he was the first, in 1935, to dare to call the "French Hitlerites"— were abetting with terrible efficacy the danger that the various forms of Nazi blackmail posed for France and Europe.

This suggests a surprising "division of knowledge," a surprising incapacity to go beyond the assumptions of his political and strategic thought. From the late twenties on, Blum saw better than anyone the extent of the Fascist phenomenon, its implications, and its connections. But until 1935, he was never capable of drawing the simplest and most natural conclusions from this knowledge. Against self-confessed assassins who assert themselves by acts of death, is there any choice but to give oneself the means of defense? It is a basic reflex. But the basic was not his strong point.

Toward Popular Union

In any case, his campaign against fascism, like those conducted by the Communists, the Committee of Vigilance of Anti-Fascist Intellectuals (CVIA) founded by Paul Rivet, Alain, and Paul Langevin (unofficial representatives, respectively, of the socialists, the Radicals, and the Communists), and Gaston Bergery's efforts to create a "common front" are responsible for whatever progress was made toward unification of the forces of the left.

Certain fears came to light within the Socialist party. By agreeing to work with the Communists, weren't they opening themselves to attempts at infiltration, seduction of the rank and file, and the risk of defection? The question was raised by a number of important leaders of the party, notably in the Nord. There was hardly anyone of note in the SFIO who did not remember the famous phrase of Albert Treint, whom Moscow had installed in 1923 as successor to the too flexible Frossard as Secretary-General of the SFIC because of his exemplary sectarianism: "We are close to the socialists, as a hand is close to a chicken to be plucked."

Taking account of these various currents of thought, Blum wrote on July 14, 1934:

> No doubt prudence is necessary. But I am convinced that our party will find the means to reconcile the two feelings that animate it: it does not want to be duped, and at the same time it does not want to let an opportunity to prepare for the unity of the working class go by without seizing it. The movement of spontaneous enthusiasm which we feel developing may recall by some signs that of the autumn of 1930. But in 1930 the movement was toward division and today it is toward reunion. It is not carrying the working class toward Moscow, but toward proletarian unity.

Neither the signature on July 27, 1934 of the "unity of action agreement," according to the terms of which the two parties agreed to "struggle against fascism, war and preparation for war, seditious leagues" and "for the liberation of Thaelmann and other political prisoners in foreign countries" (the case of Stalin's prisons was not mentioned in any other way), nor some common campaigns in the local elections, nor the participation of Blum and Marcel Cachin shoulder to shoulder at a meeting for unity in September 1934, relaxed the vigilance of the socialist leader toward an organization whose intolerance and brutal sectarianism he had often experienced. When André Marty, commenting on the work of the non-communist International in *L'Humanité* in November 1934, added that the delegation of Russian "Mensheviks" could lay no claim to a representative role, Blum replied sharply in *Le Populaire* and added:

> Unity of action between us and the Communist party is now solidly enough established to have nothing to fear from such a debate. Without apprehension, we can articulate in public thoughts that sear our lips. . . . [S]ince it legitimately feels strong, since no fear can stop it, does the Communist party not think this is the moment to extend to Russia the spirit that animates it in the rest of Europe? The unity of action agreement was signed in France for the defense of democratic freedoms. Does Russian communism not think it possible to apply to Russian socialism the principles of what I would call workers' democracy? Does it not feel that it would thereby impart a truly irresistible force to the movement toward international unity of action and the organic unity of the proletariat?

During the discussions between the two parties provided for in the July 27 agreement for the purpose of developing a "common program," in late 1934 and early 1935, Blum did not fail to point out contradictions and unmask Communist responsibilities. On January 20, 1935, the day after a large meeting for unity held in the Salle Bullier with the spokesmen of the two parties and several representatives of the Radical left, he announced the suspension of negotiations and contrasted the views of the PCF, which wanted to stick to a catalogue of social demands aimed at improving the condition of the workers, to those of the SFIO, which wanted the problem to bear the "seal," the "stamp" of socialism. "For them," Blum wrote,

> it was simply a matter of articulating themes of action around which a vast popular movement could be united, going beyond the limits of our two parties and the masses grouped around them. This is why they dismissed reforms like Public Agricultural Offices, the confiscation of failing businesses, and socialization, even socialization of the arms industry and the arms trade. While accepting the

necessity of "gathering" and attaching to the anti-Fascist bloc a large zone of popular elements, we replied that for every movement there has to be a designated goal. We insisted on proclaiming before the "united" masses that we want to lead them toward socialism which is the only path to their salvation.

But wasn't it Blum himself who, at the SFIO congress in Toulouse in May 1934, had called for a "union between ourselves and the entire country"?

No matter. Divergent views, tactical discords, and ulterior motives could not check the powerful movement toward unity, which was spurred by the fear of fascism. The sixth of February had awakened latent forces, that were held spellbound by the increasingly provocative actions of the dictators—Mussolini in Abyssinia, Hitler on the left bank of the Rhine, in Austria, and against German democrats and Jews. Thanks to these madmen vigilance was maintained, while the Soviet change of direction facilitated alliances between the various factions of the French "left."

By going to Moscow in May 1935 to sign a military defense agreement with Stalin, who declared that he "understood and approved" French military policy, Pierre Laval intended among other things to place the French Communists in a position that was inconsistent with their antimilitarist stance. In fact, he helped to create the Popular Front by facilitating contracts between the PCF, which had at one stroke become "defensist" and Jacobin, and the traditionally patriotic Radicals. Only the socialists—Blum first of all—detected in all of this an excessive flavor of military bravado.

The most significant prefiguration of the Popular Front can be found in the municipal elections of May 12, 1935. In the fifth *arrondissement* of Paris (Saint-Victor) the municipal councillor Lebecq, president of the *Union Nationale des Combattants* (UNC), one of the key men of the 6th of February, had been forced into a run-off. To attempt to block him, the organizations of the left, particularly the Communists whose representative, Nedellec, had come in second, withdrew their four spokesmen and replaced them with a common candidate, Paul Rivet, a left-wing socialist who was the creator of the Musée de l'Homme and a friend of Blum's. Rivet's victory over a figure like Lebecq was considered an exemplary test: he became the first elected candidate of the Popular Front.

On July 14 the enthusiasm for unity was expressed in all its force in an emotional and symbolic "representation." The *Comité du Rassemblement populaire,* established in June under the presidency of Victor Basch, professor at the Sorbonne and president of the *Ligue des droits de l'homme,*[41] called for an assembly of "all the forces determined to defend freedom" and "the great revolutionary tradition." The Radical party decided to respond to the invitation along with the SFIO, the PCF, the CGT, the CGTU, the *Comité de vigilance des intellectuels antifascistes (CVIA)*, the *Association des ecrivains et artistes révolutionnaires* (AEAR), the *Comité Amsterdam-Pleyel*, the *Association réblicaine des anciens combattants* (ARAC), and others.

That morning in the Buffalo stadium—where in one row an already very famous and still revolutionary writer, André Malraux, sat next to an obscure foreign militant, Josip Broz, who had not yet taken the name Tito—there was a "meeting for peace and freedom." From the platform, the great physicist Jean Perrin reminded the audience, in the style of Michelet, that most French revolutionary traditions are also patriotic traditions. At the conclusion of the afternoon march from the Bastille to the cours de Vincennes, Victor Basch read the "oath" which Blum, Daladier, and Thorez, standing side by side on the platform, took along with hundreds of thousands of other participants:

> We pledge to remain united to defend democracy, to disarm and dissolve seditious leagues, to place our freedoms out of the reach of fascism. We swear, on this day which reincarnates the first victory of the Republic, to defend the democratic freedoms conquered by the people of France, to give bread to the workers, work to the young, and to the world a great and human peace.

The Popular Front did not yet exist, but it had already found its style, its images, its "festival." Blum entitled his editorial on July 15 *"Vive la Nation et vive la Révolution,"* giving in to the collective jubilation: "We will sing the *Marseillaise* with exaltation." With exaltation, but not yet with confidence.

Negotiations for the development of a "common program" of the left were nevertheless revived. But it was not until September, after the August congress of the International in Moscow where Thorez had been congratulated for his unitary attitude, that the SFIO and the PCF succeeded in reaching an agreement. Seven months later, Maurice Thorez revealed that the Communists had succeeded in removing from the text of the agreement references to nationalizations that were too specific, "in order not to foster illusions." This was of great benefit to those Radical leaders like Daladier who were in favor of a broad alliance of the left, a new *Cartel* including the Communists. They pointed out that in the May municipal elections the Radical Party had performed best in areas where it was allied to the socialists.

Thus, supported by Radicalism's "young Turks"—notably Pierre Cot, Jean Zay, Pierre Mendès France, and Jacques Kayser—the president of the party, Edouard Daladier, who was called by *L'Humanité* "the executioner of the sixth of February" only a few weeks earlier, succeeded in having the Nantes congress (October 1935) approve the entry of the Radicals into what Maurice Thorez had just named the "Popular Front for work, peace, and freedom." In Communist meetings, cries of "Daladier to power!" suddenly replaced "Death to Daladier!"[42]

The Radicals thus participated in developing the "common program" in which, since Communist prudence had supported their own inclinations, there remained only one nationalization—the arms industry—the reform of the credit system, and particularly the Banque de France, and the creation of a Grain Office. For the elections, the leadership of the three parties agreed that each one would present its own candidates and its own program in the first round. In the second round, the "platform" of the Popular Front would become the common program in the name of which the best placed candidate would be supported.

If this program is analyzed in terms of the power relations between the two major parties of the left, it can be said that the Communists had won the battle of the program and the socialists the organizational battle. The PCF had succeeded in avoiding the affirmation of a "socialism" which would have embarrassed their principal allies, the Radicals; the SFIO had avoided the creation of unified rank and file organisms which would have allowed their allies to "raid" them.

Thus, after its style and its flavor, the Popular Front had finally found its charter—rather vague—and its procedure—more precise. Blum, the cautious but effective artisan of this convergence, discussed it prudently in *Le Populaire* on January 11, 22, and 26, 1936, and in a meeting held during the same period. Presenting the common plan as "a program for cooperation in the second round of the elections, for a parliamentary majority, for a government" (a minimal interpretation), he continued, heightening the tone: "By our attitude, we have launched and made popular in France the two ideas from which have come, on the one hand proletarian unity, and on the other, the Popular Republican Front." He pointed out in conclusion that it was "an attempt to govern together and to act quickly in order to relieve the poverty and injustice which are the breeding ground of fascism."

"To govern together"? The Radicals offered to do so by breaking with the Laval government, a gesture which Blum considered indispensable: what would elections conducted by a figure like Pierre Laval have been like? "To relieve poverty"? The two union federations, the CGT and the CGTU, were putting the finishing touches on a unification which "opens the way," wrote Blum, "to political unification." The building blocks had been brought together. What was still lacking for the Front which was to present itself before the electorate in a few weeks? Perhaps an outburst of collective feeling.

Until He Bleeds

Late in the morning of February 13, 1936, Blum left the National Assembly to return to his home on the Ile Saint-Louis. He got into the car (a Citroën B-12, the quintessential mass-produced car) belonging to his friends Germaine and Georges Monnet. Monnet, socialist deputy from Aisne, was one of his favorite disciples—he was even called his "dauphin"—and was soon to become Minister of Agriculture.

Monnet, at the wheel, entered the rue de l'Université, and then turned onto the boulevard Saint-Germain. He should have thought—the press had talked about it that morning—that the boulevard would be obstructed by the crowd waiting for the appearance of the funeral procession for the historian Jacques Bainville, one of the intellectual leaders of *L'Action française*.

Maurras and his supporters naturally wanted to make the funeral a symbolic demonstration: the crowd was made up of a majority of young people and students, many of whom were *camelots du roy*—themselves, it was later learned, infiltrated by *cagoulards*. The crowd was tense if not aggressive.

When Monnet recognized his mistake, it was too late to turn back: he tried to make his way through, but the car angered the crowd. It had a deputy's identification sticker, increasing their exasperation. Who was it? Monnet, a socialist? Yes, but who was that in the back seat? It was Blum! Blum! For months, for years, their masters Maurras and Daudet had called on them to lynch him, to "shoot him in the back," to slit his throat "with a kitchen knife," this "public enemy," this "human garbage who should be treated as such!" And there he was within reach, cornered in the back of the car! What luck! "Death to the Jew!" Blows started to fall, first on the back and side windows of the car, then on Blum's neck and head. (He was sixty-four). "Women in fur coats watching the scene, their eyes glowing, shouted: 'Kill him.' "[43]

Georges Monnet and his wife attempted to intervene, pulling Blum off the seat and out of the car. A passer-by and two policemen finally appeared. They were jostled but managed to place the wounded man on the pavement, where he was kicked several times. Men working on the façade of the nearby Ministry of War rushed up and carried the socialist leader covered with blood into the courtyard of a building on the rue de Lille. From there he was brought to the Hôtel-Dieu by the director of the municipal police, Guichard, who was noted for his right-wing opinions and who had appeared more than a half-hour after the beginning of the attack. Stitches were sewn. A bandage surrounded the wounded man's head. He was asked if he wanted to bring charges. "No." "But it's serious, an artery is cut." "No, not an artery, just a vein."

The "delegation of the left" (a memory of Jaurès's days), like the "Victor Basch committee," a permanent organ of the Popular Front, immediately met in the Chamber to demand a response from the government. The new Premier, Albert Sarraut, took the floor around three, not only to "condemn the iniquity of such an act," but to add: "Repression will be carried out where these attacks are premeditated." Almost the entire Chamber, including the professional anti-Semite Xavier Vallat, applauded. But the next morning *L'Action française* surpassed itself. Maurras's and Daudet's daily published this "report" on the affair of the boulevard Saint-Germain:

> While the ceremony was taking place in the dead man's house, a magnificent car dashed into the crowd. Protests were raised against this rich, reckless driver undeterred by respect for the dead. But one of the passengers declared that he was a deputy and that he intended to pass.
> A deputy? This is not a very attractive word for the Parisian crowd. Protests multiplied. At one point, according to some witnesses, the deputy called the people blocking the way "hoodlums." People looked and recognized Léon Blum in person, accompanied by the socialist deputy Monnet. Immediately, the crowd, which was already incensed at his insolence, burst into a unanimous roar of anger. The car windows were shattered. The socialist leader could have been severely hurt if, at that moment, the *ligueurs* and the *camelots du roy* who were present had not intervened.

Three days later *Le Canard enchaîné* carried the headline "The odious attack of M. Léon Blum against M. Charles Maurras has failed pitifully!"[45]

The dissolution of the *Ligue d'Action française*[46] and of the *Camelots du roy,* preceded by a search in which the police found on Maurras's desk a cup filled with coins with the inscription: "Product of the sale of Baron Blum's glasses," did not satisfy the left. They wanted more eloquent testimony to what they felt and what they were planning. They had to demonstrate it.

"Fine! But let there be as many tricolors as red flags!" answered Albert Sarraut to the delegation of the left that had come to ask him for the right to march on February 16. It was the people's response to aggression. Blum, of course, was absent: he was being treated at home before being sent to his friends the Auriols in Muret where he stayed until the end of March, weak and distant from public affairs. But the entire leadership of the Front was present, on February 16 at 10 o'clock, at the approaches to the Panthéon. They were to go over the pont Sully, along the boulevard Henri IV, toward the Bastille, and from there to the Nation. At the head of the procession came the socialists— Paul Faure, Salengro, Zyromski, Pivert, Léo Lagrange, Victor Basch, Paul Rivet (the man who had been elected on May 12, 1935); then most of the Communist leaders, with Thorez at their head, and the Radicals, notably Daladier. For five hours, half a million demonstrators crossed Paris, in a majestic calm.

What Brasillach was to call "the Popular Front's expiatory procession" was also and especially a prophetic march, a peaceful assault. Maurras, for his part, saw in it only "numbers, barbaric Asia, escaped prisoners, jailbirds, criminal weaklings, real scum, dregs of the slums, from Russia, the half-wild Levant, in which the Jews and the wogs have no trouble in standing out." But it was this immense underworld, this people of wogs, this scum of the earth who were in two months to decide the fate of the country.

At the moment when the procession passed the Île Saint-Louis, not far from the socialist leader's house with its closed shutters, Madeleine Lagrange, Léo's wife, shouted: "Blum to power!" The slogan was obvious. But her friends silenced her. It wasn't the moment! But February 16, 1936 was also the day when Spain elected its new assembly and sent to the Cortes a strong majority for the *Frente Popular*.

A Man and a People

The day was approaching.

Blum had long passed the age of sixty. His silken mustache and his long hair were beginning to gray. His height and his build, as well as his slightly studied elegance, made him stand out in a political world made up of plump notables, stocky men with pot bellies. His mildly annoying aristocratic air aged well. Behind the glasses that made them glitter, his gray-blue eyes maintained their sometimes satiric gaiety. The voice which he treated every summer, during his cure in Cauterets, remained fragile, but sometimes, when emotion did not make it crack, it took on surprising depth. He had given up sports a long time before and seemed no longer interested in them, even though he was the deputy of one of the capitals of rugby.[47] Despite the flat feet that gave him a duck's walk, his appearance remained relatively lively. His health was practically intact; this Proustian type was never ill.

Consider him first of all on his bench in the Chamber. Flanked by the genial Auriol and the grumpy Bracke, he rests his very white face, divided by the bridge of his Modigliani-like long nose which makes a sharp angle with his jutting chin, on his very long and delicate hand which surrounds his face like a cloth of a Pietà. He listens with a kind of selective delectation.

For him, as for Jaurès, all human speech counted. The important thing was to know how to respond and to transform raw material often made of stupidity and ignorance into pure gold. It was only low abuse that he had difficulty hearing, or didn't listen to. The 1932-36 Chamber did not particularly delight him. It had no Clemenceau, Briand, Poincaré, Caillaux, or Barrès, opponents of distinction. Herriot was worn out, Tardieu snarled more than he spoke, Daudet choked on his hatred. What could be said of the "young talents" of the right, Ybarnegaray or Philippe Henriot? Could he even hope to be listened to by them?

He spent almost every evening at *Le Populaire* on rue Victor-Massé, with Oreste Rosenfeld who had succeeded Jean Longuet as director of foreign affairs, Daniel Mayer, the young man in charge of social affairs, and Georges and Charles Gombault, whom he affectionately called "Gombinet." He worked long and hard on his articles, sometimes rewriting them as many as five times. He attributed to them a strictly pedagogical importance; nor did he neglect his courses at the Ecole Socialiste through 1935.

Blum loved the newspaper and those who made it, perhaps even Compère-Morel, his administrator, who detested him and constantly made him feel it, from one congress to another. He loved the paper, the lead, the smells. He loved his pen gliding on the paper, the friends who gathered for a first reading of the editorial which they passed from hand to hand, and the criticisms they made. He could be stubborn, but liked to be contradicted. He never alluded to the fact that the newspaper was triply his—because he gave it the prestige of his articles, because he was its essential link with the party, and because, between 1921 and 1930, he poured into it most of what he owned.

It was there, more than in the Chamber, more than at home where he was caught up in a climate of bourgeois intellectualism, comfort, and "success," that he lived his life as a militant. There were also the congresses and the meetings, which he loved in spite of the outbursts of rancor and jealousy of which he was the target. But in the smell of ink and paper of the old *Populaire,* between Bracke's rages and Rosenfeld's cold outbursts, Daniel's anecdotes, and Paul's witticisms, he was at home, with them *chez nous.* Some of them, with a bit of mockery, called him "the general." This absolutely civilian man was amused. He ruled with the lightest possible touch.

His working methods reflected both his deep-seated fantasy and his sense of efficacy. Here is a description by one of the people who knew him best:

> For a speech, an article, a book—whether he was on a train, in a car, at his desk in the Chamber, or very often at night—he noted the idea as soon as he had it on the back of an envelope or in the margin of a newspaper. Pieces of paper were stuffed in his pockets or piled haphazardly on a corner of his desk under a large key that his friend Porto-Riche had given him. When he wrote, he sifted

through them, crumpled them and threw them in the waste basket (not without a certain pleasure), or filed them carefully. Then he had only to dictate to himself, sometimes so quickly that his pen had trouble keeping up with him.

In the spring of 1936, Blum was more than ever the parliamentary, intellectual, and above all moral leader of French socialism.

Intellectual leader, of course, because he had been able in some way—better than anyone else in any case—to preserve Jaurès's three great syntheses: between idealism and materialism, reformism and revolution, and patriotism and internationalism. Because, through the undistinguished episodes of public life in the twenties and thirties, he had been able to give life to a "certain idea of socialism" which he had developed, and which he defined as both rebellion in the name of justice and as a demand of reason. Finally, because he had led his party between the reef of parliamentarianism and the abyss of dogmatism, to the threshold of power alongside the two movements which respectively embodied those dangers—Radical and Communist—while establishing distance from them and making the SFIO the center, if not the necessary fulcrum, of the coalition.

By making fine distinctions between participation in power (excluded), exercise of power (desirable), and conquest of power (dreamed of), he had perhaps helped to complicate rather than simplify the road to socialism. This was all the more true when, in 1934, he further burdened the analysis by adding the idea of a defensive "occupation" of power. Since 1932, since the Narbonne speech and "les cahiers de Huyghens," Blum had simplified his doctrine. Opposition to participation was a thing of the past; the hypothesis of revolutionary conquest was hardly plausible in the current state of French society. There remained the exercise or the occupation of power which, by means of reforms, could and must become revolutionary.

He was of course a socialist. Was he a Marxist? We have alluded to his hesitations on this point: they go back to the beginning of the century. From this point of view, the great Tours speech itself is irreproachable. The fundamental questions came later, after 1940. But before then he can hardly be described as breaking with or even toying with the doctrine. From one congress to another, from one crisis to another, he can be seen refining if not deepening his beliefs and his convictions. More than anything else, his battle with the "neos" in 1933 brought him in reaction closer to Marxism. What better way to get a taste for the virtues of the dialectic than through a dialectical operation? We have quoted the July 1933 article in which he proclaimed himself all the more a Marxist because his opponents attacked him as such, wanting to make it an insult or a vice. Even when, after the defeat of Déat's right-wing heresy, he turned toward the left of the party—Zyromski, Pivert, Collinet, Descourtieux, the men associated with *La Bataille socialiste* and *La Gauche révolutionnaire,* and the Seine federation—to warn them of the temptations of putschism or a hasty fusion with the Stalinists, he still spoke in the name of the philosopher of Trier, maintaining that there was more Marxism in Jaurès than in Blanqui.

One can, of course, as Gilbert Ziebura and many others have done, point to the contradiction involved in his activity. If the exercise of power were to be accomplished according to his wishes, following a long and scientific preparation of the masses and a wearing down of hostile powers, if the class struggle were to have been previously abolished or mitigated by the convergent effects of parliamentary democracy and social reform, what would remain of genuinely revolutionary demands. What would be the content of references to the dictatorship of the proletariat?

Wouldn't this lead, through maneuvering, to the ideal strategy of generals of the past who manipulated and conditioned the enemy for the sole purpose of not having to fight—like Napoleon at Ulm? What would remain of that irreducible element of Marxism, the confrontation of classes? Of course, Marx had foreseen the possibility of revolutionary transformation by legal means, in societies like England and America. Guesde proclaimed that socialism should come to power "by every means, even legal means." But Blum's argument tended to transform the exception into the rule and to make the advent of socialism less a break than a mutation (a word that he loved a great deal, according to Robert Blum), and even less a mutation than a *maturation.* Wasn't the plan for avoiding battle by maneuvering at bottom a plan for basic class compromise? Can a society be transformed without confrontation? Doesn't a decisive mutation imply a break?

The socialist in him remained above all the Jaurèsian who wanted to deepen and complete the French Revolution. This is indicated by an article of the period, one of his finest pieces, on the Declaration of the Rights of Man, which he wrote in 1935 for *La Grande Encyclopédie* of Anatole de Monzie. However pious a "republican" and however passionately attached to the work of the "men of freedom" he may have been, he nevertheless saw and admirably denounced their weaknesses: "The Declaration created freedoms, not freedom. In spite of all the rights that are demanded or proclaimed, there is no true freedom for the individual left naked and alone in the presence of the State."

This was written forty years ago. To be able to say that, one must have fought a great deal, from the Dreyfus Affair to the sixth of February, from Tours to the Mutualité (confronting Déat and Marquet), and one must have thought more than a little about everything.

On the eve of the great events that were about to swallow but not transform him, how did he live? Lise Blum died in December 1931. Two years later, Blum married Thérèse Pereyra, his cousin Cécile Grunebaum-Ballin's best friend. She was Paul Dukas's sister-in-law and for years had been part of the group of musicians and painters with whom he preferred to associate. Thérèse had a great deal of wit, enthusiasm, and gaiety. Blum had been attached to her for a long time. She was very involved in the party and participated in his political activities. Moreover, she was an admirable housewife and a tireless factotum. He was entirely happy with her—until she died in 1938 from a spreading cancer.

Outside the party, his friends were still the same, but death had taken many of them from him: Lucien Herr in 1926, Georges de Porto-Riche in 1930—the beloved "Porto" who affectionately criticized his "love of unpopularity." He still saw Tristan Bernard, with whom, among many other things, he tirelessly exchanged Jewish stories; Thadée and Alfred Natanson; Simone Porché, the great actress who like her cousin Julien Benda had become a writer; Georges Boris; Julien Cain; Paul and "Cécette" Grunebaum-Ballin; the distinguished scientist Jean Perrin who entered his government in 1936; not to mention the intelligent banker Horace Finaly, director of the Banque de Paris et des Pays-Bas, who supported him at the time of the Popular Front; nor his amiable fellow-tenant at 25, quai Bourbon, the Radical deputy Yvon Delbos, a devotee of poetry and the theater, who became his Minister of Foreign Affairs. He kept in touch with his Montparnesasse neighbor, Philippe Berthelot, and maintained cordial relations with the American ambassador, William Bullitt. All of this made up a not very "socialist" milieu. It is hardly necessary to add that the household and the way of life of the leader of the SFIO were not very "socialist" either.

As he approached power, the campaigns against his "fortune" and the "luxury" in which he lived proliferated in the right-wing press, and even in certain left-wing circles. But at the end of January 1936, Jean Lasserre, a reporter for *Le Petit Parisien,* which was at the time a "republican" paper, but far removed from socialism, described the man and his surroundings like this:

> He is not nearly as thin as caricatures or photographs would lead one to believe. He has a full face; he is tall and holds himself erect. He lives in an apartment on the quais, which some have depicted as a satrap's palace, but its greatest luxury is its view of the Seine, and the rest is the simple environment that any person of good taste would have created in such a location. In M. Léon Blum's study, which is by the way also his living room—where are the

> rows of galleries and mirrors of the satrap, and his antechambers
> full of chandeliers and candelabra?—I caught a brief glimpse of
> Mme Léon Blum. Did she have knitting in her hand? I'm no longer
> sure, but she might have.

A satrap? The legend of sumptuous silver, golden dishes, and mansions on the shores of Lake Leman had a long life. A few weeks after February 6, 1934, a right-wing deputy, Fernand-Laurent, had announced that he would question the government on "M. Léon Blum's means of existence," and Blum had answered in Le Populaire:

> I don't suppose that M. Fernand-Laurent is doing this with benevolent feelings, but he has nevertheless unsuspectingly rendered me an inestimable service. He has offered me an opportunity which I have been vainly seeking for at least fifteen years. How can I destroy the legend of Blum the arch-millionaire? How can I persuade public opinion that I possess neither a collection of antique silver, nor a gallery of paintings, nor a luxury automobile, nor liveried servants, nor châteaux, nor villas on the Côte d'Azur, nor current accounts in Swiss banks? I have been living for fifteen years in the midst of these rumors, which are idiotic but impossible to dissipate or deny, and M. Fernand-Laurent has come along and given me an unexpected way. He has questioned the government on my "means of existence." At last! I will be able to get rid of my fortune. Thank you, sir, thank you from the bottom of my heart.[48]

This was the character and the way of life of Léon Blum, president of the SFIO parliamentary group in the Chamber, and as such called on to assume the responsibilities of power in the event of an electoral victory for the Popular Front, at the moment when history had given him a rendezvous with the people of France.

What was this people like in 1936, and how did it live? France was a nation of 42 million, with a stable demography[49]—a population of old people, but of sick people as well. Masculine mortality was then the highest of any industrialized country, due especially to alcoholism and tuberculosis.

The active population represented barely 50 percent (approximately 20 million people). Foreigners were less numerous in 1936 than in 1931 (5 percent as opposed to 7 percent five years earlier).[50] Some parts of the country were undergoing modernization, others—the Midi, West and Southwest—impoverishment, and the gap between them was growing. Thus the slippage of Blum's party from its industrial bastions to its rural reserve was a sign of weakness—all the more so because farmers were penalized by the brutal fall in prices of agricultural products between 1931 and 1936. This led to the creation of leagues of protest like the Peasant Front (the "green shirts" of Dorgères).

It was around 1930 that the population of France became urban in its

majority: 52 percent were city dwellers in 1936. The industrial proletariat was the largest group. Their income had fallen by about 15
percent from 1930 to 1936, particularly as a result of Laval's deflation-
ist policies, and unemployment was substantial (almost a million at the
beginning of 1936), but had been declining for several months.

But the condition of the working class was less and less tolerable,
not so much as far as income or even employment were concerned, but
rather the atmosphere of work and human relations:

> Factory society was modeled on military society, with the posi-
> tive and negative aspects of paternalism, multiplied by what was
> called Fordism. This involved strict discipline, rigorous adherence
> to the time clock, the prohibition of smoking, and the lack of any
> relaxation. A highly organized system of spying assured that in
> large businesses every union leader, every socialist or Communist
> militant, every reader of a left–wing paper, even of the moderate
> left, was dismissed as soon as he was unmasked. To bring
> *L'Oeuvre* to Citroën was as imprudent as to bring it to the bar-
> racks, even under the Radical governments of which the news-
> paper was the most representative organ.[51]

The housing conditions imposed on the whole of the working-class
population at the time were just as painful and retrograde. Although the
famous *Aubervilliers* of Elie Lotar, because of its exaggeration of poverty, could not possibly represent the average level of proletarian housing (even though this suburb was the fiefdom of one of the most
influential men of the government, Pierre Laval), it is enough to refer to
Guilloux's books, or better still those of Céline, to measure the "quality of life" imposed on the electors of Thorez or Jean Longuet.

The middle classes, as we have seen on the occasion of the explosion
of February 6, were in decline: heads of middle-sized businesses,
owners of apartment houses, small-scale stockholders were slowly
sinking. But, as Henri Dubief points out, the small shop, the typical
center of the French system of exchange, was growing richer. Noting
"the enormous extension of the network of intermediaries which
weighed on the economy and lowered the standard of living of the
wage-earners," he adds: "The state encouraged it, because the small
shop was a rampart against socialism and communism and because, if
its defense were neglected, it would become the sociological basis of
fascism, out of hatred for the state."[52]

As for the upper levels of the bourgeoisie, the analysis of which was
brutally simplified by the appearance of the (Radical) slogan of the
"two hundred families" (the largest shareholders in the Banque de
France, who because of their holdings had an extraordinary amount of
social control and of ideological influence) they demonstrated that the
France of the mid-thirties was still (or already?) one of the most in-

egalitarian societies of Western Europe. It was also the country in which, in spite of certain appearances—political and social rises of impoverished professors like Edouard Herriot, or the heroes of Jules Romains, or even of Jean Giraudoux—the separation between social classes was the best preserved.

THE POPULAR FRONT

Preliminary Note

I t would be impossible to understand anything about the Popular Front, about that year of experiments that were decisive for France and contemporary Europe, about Blum's failures and accomplishments, or about the relationships between the new government, the working class, and the "revolution" if certain aspects of the situation were not borne in mind.

1. The Popular Front originated as a *defensive alliance* among parties and organizations "of the left" against the Fascist direction taken by the leagues of the extreme right. The victory on May 3 had postponed but not eliminated the danger. The seeds of civil war still existed in France in 1936.

2. The Popular Front was a *coalition of diverse social and political forces,* all of which were indispensable for a parliamentary majority. Without a minimum of support from both the Radicals and the Communists, without the help of the CGT, without the unity of the SFIO, it would have been impossible to govern. Power could only be exercised, (to use Blum's vocabulary) by working toward a basic convergence of all these forces. When the spokesmen of the extreme left criticized the government for restraining the movement of the people, the "spontaneous pressure of the masses," they pretended to be unaware of the real origin of that pressure. They forgot that the masses had begun to move only when control of the police forces had changed hands, that is, when an alliance of political parties, of "corrupt bosses," had enabled a

235

socialist to be named Minister of the Interior. The government did not "co-opt" the revolutionary movement in order to block it; the revolutionary movement co-opted and used the power given to it by the "political" superstructure.

3. The fact that the government of the Popular Front was established under socialist control was a *surprise* for everyone, for Blum as well as for Thorez and Herriot, for Moscow as well as for London and Berlin. What had been foreseen was a government led by the Radicals, under the direction of Daladier or Chautemps, with significant participation on the part of the socialists, and at least the symbolic presence of the Communists. The new government was therefore relatively unprepared and, in particular, ignorant of the real nature of the financial situation.

4. In fact the Popular Front came to power in an *economic and financial climate that had been changed* by a deflationary policy which had devitalized the whole nation. Its remedies—a rise in purchasing power leading to a rise in consumption and in turn an increase in production; government initiatives; large-scale public works—were greeted with crippling suspicion by the men at the centers of economic activity because of the "politics" of the government that wanted to use them.

5. The government came to power in an *extremely dangerous period internationally,* continually menaced by a threat of war that took on concrete form after July 18—the Spanish rebellion, which was supported by the Axis powers. At that moment, any change made too swiftly might have led to a general conflagration: among other consequences might have been the establishment of a truly revolutionary government in France, or even the growth of social agitation that would have been exemplary for the entire European proletariat. From June 1936 to June 1937, the leaders of the first Blum government constantly walked a tightrope between civil war and international war.

6. Finally, and not the least important, Blum constantly spoke about power—of "conquering," "exercising," or "holding" it. These are delicate and useful distinctions. But, completely absorbed by his investigation of the use that could be made of power, he seemed to have forgotten to redefine or even to analyze the content of the concept. If he had done so, he would have been led to ask himself whether he were not *confusing the notion of "power" with "government."* The two are quite distinct. This should have been obvious to him; in the framework of a capitalist society a socialist Premier does not control the real means of power, the monopoly of force.

Of course, by installing loyal and trustworthy men at the head of the two key ministries—Interior and Finance—and by replacing old-style capitalists with a man of the left like Emile Labeyrie at the head of the nationalized Banque de France, Blum had provided himself with rather substantial protection. But really to "exercise" power, he would first of all have needed real control over the army, and he did not have it. As we shall see, this was less important when the question of intervention in Spain vaguely arose in March 1938, than when, on frequent occasions, the possibility of changing the treaty with the Soviet Union into an alliance arose. The police would then have had to become the unequivocal defender of the Republic: the disastrous Clichy affair demonstrated to Blum that this could not be the case. Finally, he would have had to control financial resources beyond those available to the only nationalized bank.

The "Blum experiment" made it possible to see that his ingenious distinction in 1926 between "exercise" and "conquest" had to be further refined. If one can "conquer" real power, "exercise" can only be the business of "government."

This observation, which is not limited to the example of Blum, does not mean that "the exercise of government" based on popular suffrage is a false advantage, or that it cannot be the source of profound social transformations.

A Shared Victory

> I am not describing a Utopia, a dream vision, I am describing a society all of whose elements exist and are immediately available to you. All that is needed to bring this society into existence is an exercise of your will. . . . Have I been able to convince you, or at least to move you?

On April 21, 1936, five days before the decisive vote, Blum, recovered from the wounds that had prevented his campaigning, gave his only speech to the voters of Narbonne; it was the first of his speeches broadcast on the radio.[53] He spoke from the balcony of the town hall, the former archbishopric, an admirable gothic palace; Blum loved its "Consuls" room and its "Synod" room with the polished wood vaulted ceiling. The huge warm crowd strained to hear his slightly quavering voice:

> The Socialist party asks you to grant it power, as it is the right and the duty of every political party to do, in order to put its own program into operation. If, as is quite possible, neither the socialists nor any other party of the left wins a majority by itself, the Socialist party is ready to enter a majority, a coalition government which has adopted the common program of the *Rassemblement populaire*. This is how the situation has changed. The *Rassemblement populaire* exists. Its common program exists, signed by all

the parties and groups that have joined in it. This program is not the specific creation of a particular party, but it contains the constructive demands common to all of them, and it commits all of them.

No party will be able in the future to say that it is too much or not enough. No party will be able to accuse the other parties of confronting it with impossible demands or compromises. The contract exists, and, for our part, we will remain faithful to the obligations it expresses or implies. We will make the common program the standard determining withdrawal from the second round of the elections. We consider it as the criterion which will define the majority. We are ready to apply it in government, in concert with the other parties grouped in the Popular Front.[54]

"Program," "contract," "government": everything was there, and nothing more. Two weeks earlier, the Radical party had made public its adhesion to the *Rassemblement populaire* which had been decided in the month of January. From that point on, the electoral battle was fought over the "common program" published on January 10, which did not abolish those of the four principal parties involved (SFIO, PCF, Radical party, and the group of the socialist and republican union, including the "neos" who had been excluded in 1933), but which, Blum wrote on March 29, would be "the program of action for a Popular Front government," since "the democratic majority which will come out of the next election will necessarily be a coalition majority, grouping all the parties which adhere to the *Rassemblement populaire*."

The program of the Popular Front (this is the name it should be given from now on, since the socialists and the Radicals had gradually adopted this originally Communist terminology), whose preamble pointed out that it had been composed in such a way that "each party, each organization can join in common action without surrendering any of its doctrines, its principles, or its particular goals," was divided into two parts. The first was entitled "political demands," which were subdivided into the "defense of peace" and the "defense of freedom." The second encompassed "economic demands," under three headings: restoration of purchasing power, defense of savings and organization of the credit system, and financial stabilization.

Among the principal "political" demands were the dissolution of the Fascist leagues, the repeal of the statutes restricting freedom of opinion, the equal distribution of broadcast facilities, the application of union rights, the extension of obligatory schooling, an official investigation of the situation of the colonies, and in the international sphere, the consolidation of collective security by sanctions against the aggressor and arms reduction, the nationalizations of war industries, and an increase in defensive pacts like the one between France and the USSR.

The "economic" demands included the creation of a national unemployment fund, the reduction of the work week without a reduction in wages, a plan for large-scale public works, an increase in agricultural prices, support for agricultural cooperatives, the creation of a grain office, a radical reform of the Banque de France which would make it the "bank of France," no longer that of an oligarchy, a reform of taxes in the direction of fiscal relaxation, and control over the export of capital.

In brief, supported by the Communists, the Radicals had succeeded in softening the program, making it as flatly "populist" as their own. André Delmas, a union leader tied to the socialist left, wrote bitterly that "the Radicals and the Communists had agreed to include in this minimum program only measures that did not seriously threaten the privileges of the bourgeoisie."

Had Blum fought much to introduce nationalizations besides that of the arms industry into the program? It is not evident that he did. Most of the articles he published at the time were reserved on the point. Thus, in August 1935, he maintained that nationalizations are only "a moment in the social revolution" and that the objectives of the united left should be above all "to establish in the chaos the rudiments of rules of clarity." In short, in the months preceding victory, "it was as though Léon Blum, conceiving of the Popular Front only under Radical leadership, was intent on warning the Radicals against the weakness of their leaders and on informing them that the Socialist party, in its propaganda, would use that weakness as a weapon against them."[55]

Describing the preparation of the common program, the "founding father" Victor Basch excused its modesty in *L'Oeuvre:* "It was a task of Penelope." The right, not very sensitive to the Greek reference, pretended to see in these innocent *cahiers de doléances* the program for a new October. *L'Ami du peuple* of François Coty covered its face:

> No common doctrine, no common mystique brings together [the allies of the Popular Front] but only a hatred. Hatred of what? They have gone to a great deal of trouble to explain to you that it is the hatred of all forms of fascism, of everything that opposes, in France and elsewhere, democratic freedoms and Progress; it is more simply the hatred of everything which claims allegiance to these words, this thing: the French nation; French feeling; a national way of thinking and acting.

Furiously anti-democratic, Charles Maurras nevertheless called on his friends to "make their vote a barricade which can halt or slow down the barbarian horde." But the general tone was no longer as violent or as passionate as in 1934. As a candidate in Loire, Antoine Pinay was satisfied with ritual denunciation of communism, that "veritable poison with which a society worn out with suffering commits suicide."

As for Colonel de la Rocque, he boldly laid claim to the role of "supreme arbiter." This is why

> the *Croix-de-feu* movement refuses to allow itself to be integrated into a coalition of the traditional right. It is presenting candidates, but on the other hand it will not refuse to support other candidates [who] adhere to the right if they are for the elimination of all financial, internationalist, and masonic influences on the state, against any alliance with the men of the red flag.

And, as always, the most grotesque was M. Frédéric-Dupont, candidate in the seventh *arrondissement,* who plastered the walls of Paris with this poster: "The district which contains the Invalides owes it to itself not to despair. We must dissolve the union of elementary school teachers!"[56]

Ridiculous, panic-stricken, or militant, the right in general had lost its bite. Was this because it no longer had confidence in its strength? Henri de Kerillis wrote in *L'Echo de Paris* in March:

> Is victory impossible? Of course not. But finally the figures are the figures. And with approximately 180 national deputies out of 615 in the Chamber whose term is ending, it seems in the end rather chimerical to hope that there will be 308 of them next April while the 'Popular Front' this time has the benefit of the total contingent of Communist votes, which had in part been denied it four years ago.

While the right, less combative than in preceding years, seemed half-resigned to defeat—had the attack on Blum thrown a veil of shame over the combat tactics of its most frenetic leaders?—on the left the Communists too were conducting a campaign which contradicted from top to bottom the propositions they had put forth at the time of the disastrous "class against class" strategy of 1928 and 1932.

It would be hard to go further in this direction than Maurice Thorez in his April 17, 1936 speech, known as "the extended hand," in which the leader of the PCF proposed a reconciliation not only with the Catholics but also with the most conservative right.

> We are working for true reconciliation of the French people. We extend our hand to you, Catholic, worker, employee, artisan, peasant, we who are secularists, because you are our brother. We extend our hand to you, national volunteer, old soldier who has become a *Croix-de-feu,* because you are a son of our people, because you suffer as we do from disorder and confusion, because you wish, as we do, to prevent the country from sliding into ruin and catastrophe.

And in order to provide itself with support against the irritation which this kind of maneuver produced among its socialist allies, the PCF (no longer called the SFIC, as in 1920) multiplied advances toward the Radicals, who, they thought, like Blum himself, would lead in the first round and would remain the largest group in the Chamber. Jacques Duclos, notably, saluted them at the beginning of April as the "first party in France" and recognized that they represented "the middle classes" who everybody agreed, since the fever of 1934 and the rise of fascism, held the key to political power.

It was to conquer this middle ground or to establish connections with those who dominated it that the Communist leaders initiated what Céline called "Labiche communism," embodied not only in Thorez and Duclos but also in the once and future "leftist" André Marty, whom Lucien Rebatet, observer of the electoral campaign, described in these terms:

> With his old sweater, his pencil mustache, and his Parisian street speech, comrade Marty resembles a little guy who has won in the national lottery. This is communism in slippers sitting by the fire: "Vote for us, comrades. You will pay fifty cents less for gas and electric. You'll have no more foremen or office managers. Ah! it will be a nice comfortable life, free subways, and fishing two days a week! We'll all be petty bourgeoisie." This is Moscow's new slogan for French use.

Today, the best historians wonder whether the confrontations between these "petty bourgeoisie"—who were soon to demonstrate, in Spain and under the occupation, that their *embourgeoisement* had limits—and the militants of *Solidarité française* and the *Jeunesses patriotes* were so rare, whether the campaign, which ran from April 7 to 25, was so calm.[57] As an adolescent in Bordeaux at the time, steeped in Jesuit piety, I still remember the fascinated terror with which I witnessed the few brawls that exploded on the *cours de l'Intendance* at the end of the working day during those spring weeks. Followers of the leader of the Gironde extreme right, Philippe Henriot, most of whom came from the very reactionary law school, confronted with fists and sometimes clubs workers from Bègles and brawny dockers and some young socialist intellectuals, one of whom was to become the greatest critic of his time, a man in whom his friends already thought they saw the Blum of the next generation: Gaëtan Picon.

For someone attempting today to relive and to study, in the light of subsequent history, the themes and slogans that gave it its flavor, the campaign of 1936 seems to indicate that remarkably little attention was paid to the great events stirring Europe. Of course, the decisive factor for change, the formation of the coalition of the left, owed a great deal to the danger of Hitler, and to the entirely new awareness which the Soviet government had developed of that danger. On the right, a man like Henri de Kerillis had clearly recognized the importance of the electoral success of the Spanish *Frente Popular,* and he pointed out the exemplary value of this "grave revolutionary situation. The parallel between the situations and the political structures of the two countries is striking. Spain today is our guinea pig, and everything that unfolds there constitutes a supreme warning for us."[58]

Reduced to the half-silence of a convalescent since February 13, Blum was unable to analyze this parallel at his leisure, and from a socialist perspective. In any case, the study of the behavior of the Spanish "guinea pig" reminded him that a Popular Front could bestow major responsibilities on men of the moderate left like, in Madrid, Casarès Quiroga, Giral, or Azaña. This precedent strengthened his conviction: the victory of the left, in France too, would bring to power a government under Radical leadership, to which the two great working-class parties would furnish a "participation" called for by the circumstances, vigilantly watching over the application of the program of reforms developed by the *Rassemblement populaire.* Thus the "occupation" of power would be assured, against fascism rather than for socialism, until the real "exercise" of power under socialist leadership became possible. At sixty-four, could Blum wait for yet another legislature to provide him with the opportunity?

On April 25, the eve of the first round, from Narbonne where he had been welcomed by his friends Dr. Lacroix, the mayor, and Eugène Montel, Blum sent to *Le Populaire* these reflections, remarkably free of the usual pre-election propaganda and appeals:

> The popular masses have felt that the facts speak for us, that everyday reality testifies in favor of socialist thought and socialist action. They have understood that they can confidently place in our hands the fate of the country and consequently their own fate. I firmly believe that we have instilled this conviction in them. The whole question is whether they will be able to vote in accordance with it, whether the courage of reason will prevail over the routine resistances of habit and resignation. We will know the answer in a few hours. Our duty during these last weeks has been to prepare and enlighten the will of universal suffrage. Our duty in the months to come, once victory has been attained, will be to execute it faithfully and boldly. But between these two duties of the parties is located the duty of the popular masses.

". . . another man in a man"

"I am tired, and not very satisfied with the result. The Radical committee of Narbonne asked for a vote against me on a last-minute (Saturday) poster. I am tarnished by this shame." This is what Blum wrote to his friend André Blumel on April 27, even though he had been elected in the first round.

Forty years later, this reaction of the leader of the victorious left, the man who was going to govern France in the name of the Popular Front, is astonishing. One would have imagined fanfares, sudden triumphal prophecies. Two days later, Blum made his rather morose prudence public in *Le Populaire:*

> I am not blind to the difficulties. I know how certain elections in the first round were corrupted by suspect and odious manipulations, and I need no further example than the one that has temporarily removed from the Chamber a man like Jules Moch.[59] I know what happened in my own district. I know that some of our withdrawals in the second round will benefit only uncertain allies or secret enemies. But if we will it firmly and together, all these flaws will be erased, all these faults will be corrected.

In fact, it was a success, not a triumph, which Blum had not at all been counting on. Then why these ill-tempered remarks? Because the right had not lost much more than 1.5% of its vote, and the left had gained less than 2 percent? Rather it was because, within the "left," the Radicals had receded to such an extent (400,000 fewer votes) and the Communists progressed so strongly that the plans that had been constructed for months collapsed. The possibility of the exercise of power suddenly arose for Blum on an electoral base that he considered inadequate.

Yet it was not: the SFIO (taking into account the votes won by those who could be assimilated—Paul-Boncour, Georges Izard, Pierre Viénot, Paul Ramadier)[60] not only came in first among the parties, with 2,200,000 votes, but could look forward hopefully to the results in the second round in many of the 424 districts in which there was a run-off and in which withdrawals by candidates adhering to the common program would play a role. This is why on April 30, while the four organizations of the left called their voters to join the common battle, the *Comité national du Rassemblement populaire* under the presidency of Victor Basch "greeted joyously the victory in the first round" and demanded that its adherents follow instructions by "transferring their votes to the Popular Front candidate in the best position in the first round."

The grounds for Blum's restrictive analysis of April 27 and 28 were changed first of all by the climate of popular hope which marked the May Day celebrations, and further by various estimates of prospects for the second round presented to him on the same day by his son Robert Blum (a *polytechnicien* adept at figures) and his friends Maurain, Blumel, and Moch.

These estimates indicated that the Popular Front could not fail to win a majority of at least 120 seats, and that the Socialist Party would be by far the largest in the alliance. It was therefore necessary to be prepared for great decisions. Just before the second round of voting, André Blumel went to meet Blum at Limoges, where he was stopping on his way back to Paris from Narbonne. During dinner in a restaurant they received a telephone call from *Le Populaire:* according to Paul Faure, on May 3 the party would have more than 140 seats! The socialist leader was so preoccupied, according to Blumel, that he poured salt on his strawberries.

On May 3, "republican discipline" functioned, except in about fifty districts—in which the socialists and Radicals violated the contract more often than the Communists. But Thorez and his comrades were nevertheless the great beneficiaries of the operation: from 10 they advanced to 72 deputies, while the socialists had 147, the Radicals kept only 116, and the various republican-socialists had 41 among them. Thus the Popular Front brought together 376 representatives in the Chamber against 220 "national" deputies. The SFIO had not increased its vote since 1932. It suffered from the 1933 split, while the "neos" were located on either side of the division between left and right, depending on their electoral interests: Déat, for example, had "joined the camp of fascism," wrote *Le Populaire,* while Marquet, in spite of himself, remained the deputy of the left in Bordeaux.

In the absence of a popular landslide—3 percent of the votes had shifted since 1932—the movement had taken place above all within the left, from the Radicals to the Communists. And accentuation of the leftism of the left seemed to embarrass everyone: the socialists because they found themselves entrusted with unexpected responsibilities, the Radicals because they were deprived of them, and the Communists because their entire plan was based on a Radical government.

No matter: it was a great success for the left which depended on its strategy of unity. Public opinion saw it that way. The night of May 3 was that of "the reconciliation between the people and the government" (Louis-Martin Chauffier). Crowds filled the boulevards; strains of the *Internationale* could be heard in the warm evening air. Clara Malraux has described the euphoria of the winners under the frightened gaze of conservative shopkeepers. The Malraux, the Lagranges, and the Nizans were sitting outside a café, opposite the façade of *Le Matin* where the hoped-for results went up in lights. A stranger approached and, staring at the author of *Les Conquérants,* said: "Are you happy now, Malraux?"[61]

Blum, who had returned to Paris late Sunday morning, had stopped by *Le Populaire,* then closeted himself at home on the quai Bourbon. Toward midnight, when success seemed assured, he prepared an enormous banner headline for the front page: "After electoral triumph, power!" which greeted Parisians at dawn. He went to bed, was awakened at seven, and wrote without revision the editorial which appeared in a special edition of the socialist daily on Monday, May 4, shortly before noon:

> It is not enough to say that the second round has completed the victory. It has given it proportions and a meaning that almost no one dared hope for. The triumph of the Popular Front is crushing.
> Now, we have to act. The French people have indicated their will with shattering force. This will permits no discussion, no quibbling, and it would not stand for any resistance. It must be carried out.
> The Socialist party claims its part and its responsibility in the common action. The government that will present itself before the Chamber is a Popular Front government.
> The Socialist party has become the most powerful group not only in the majority but in the entire Chamber. Moreover, it forms the axis of the Popular Front, it occupies the center between the Communists and the Radicals. We therefore insist on declaring without losing a moment that we are ready to play the role that belongs to us, that is, to form and lead the Popular Front government.

It would be impossible to be clearer. This was not only a cry of victory. One can sense in it a slight threat, an echo of the "conquest of power." Blum firmly pointed out, and he did not write this by chance, that the victory "would stand for no resistance." Did this mean that recourse to other means might be considered if legal means were not enough? In any case, Jaurès's disciple already knew that he was burdened with the responsibility he had not dared to foresee. As leader of the largest party, he was too legalistic not to see himself thus charged. But then his memory was certainly haunted by Vigny's couplet: *"Josué s'avançait pensif et pâlissant,/Car il était déjà l'élu du Tout-Puissant."*[62]

Chosen? He had chosen. Some newspapers[63] had proposed other possibilities: the designation of Vincent Auriol, for example, less an anathema to the Radicals, the neosocialists, and moderate public opinion. Or the choice of a Radical leader, Herriot or Chautemps. Or a reshuffling of the Sarraut cabinet, increasing representation of the left. But he did not waste time considering these suggestions. When André Blumel and Jules Moch visited him on the fourth in his apartment on the quai Bourbon, they found him "alert and fresh," and he said to them: "The President of the Republic will designate me, with a heavy heart, but he will do it, because he respects the Constitution."[64]

Uncertainties proliferated. Not in so far as public order or possible "resistance" on the part of the leagues or the army were concerned: the right seemed stupefied and resigned. But three questions were immediately raised, with reference to the monetary situation, the attitude of the head of government in place (Albert Sarraut), and the participation of the Communists in the government. Not to mention the other "uncertainty," about the capacity for power of the man who had been chosen by the nation.

As early as May 8, Blum broached the three questions one after the other. To the leaders of the PCF he said: "The victory would not seem complete to us if the Communists did not join us in the *exercise* of the power that has been *conquered*." This formulation is remarkable, because for the first time Blum associated the exercise and the conquest of power, the better to convince the ex-majority of Tours.

But when would this power be seized? The editorialist of *Le Populaire* clearly let it be known that Sarraut—he had just informed him of the fact—would remain in power for his full legal term which expired a month later, for that was his right. Was this in the public interest? It was, according to Blum, who provided a weighty argument:

> Stock-market and monetary instability which are presently troubling the Paris market have the direct or indirect aim of damaging the Popular Front majority and the government that will derive from it. It is in the interests of the parties grouped in the Popular Front to calm or to limit any movement of panic. The tactics of our opponents in this case dictate ours. If M. Sarraut were to hand in his resignation, there would be only one possible explanation in the eyes of the public, that is, that the government suddenly found itself confronted with such a serious situation that it admitted itself incapable of dealing with it. This would play into the hands of our opponents. It would set off the stock-market and monetary panic which we intend on the contrary to calm.[65]

The argument is a good one. But it has not been enough to silence the criticisms directed against Blum on this point for the last forty years. Excessive legalism? The constitution is very explicit: the new Chamber cannot take office until the term of the old one has expired. If he had demanded to be named Premier, Blum would have had to present himself before the Chamber of 1932, in which the Popular Front did not have a majority. Should he risk beginning the career of his government by being voted down by the Assembly? Had the vote of May 3 brought about such a "qualitative change" that the old Chamber would have accepted a government of its opponents?

As early as May 5, battle had been joined in the CAP between legalists and activists:

> MARCEAU PIVERT: We have to begin the battle immediately. Gold exports are increasing. The *Croix-de-feu* are counting on our inertia. We have to demand that the Sarraut government give way.

BRACKE: There is nothing to be done before 2 June when the Chambers meet.

MARCEAU PIVERT: Doesn't that allow the enemy a little too much control over the game? Why don't we take the initiative in our hands? For the life of me, I cannot understand why the formation of the government that represents the will of the masses is impossible! In our place, do you think the Fascists would have hesitated for a minute?

LEON BLUM: No! But the point is that we are not Fascists!

It is hard to see, unless they were to have Augereau's grenadiers invade the Palais-Bourbon, how the victors could eliminate the Chamber whose term was expiring. But we have to note that an extremely sober observer like François Goguel, examining this situation during the 1965 conference, wondered whether Blum had not demonstrated at the time "juridical formalism."

Thus began the interregnum which Blum described in these terms: "It was the time when I was the crown prince."[66] Since Albert Sarraut closely involved him in the exercise of power, "he reigned without governing, and I governed without reigning," explained Blum. Was it wasted time? The month of May 1936 was not a static time, neither for Blum nor for the victorious coalition. Three times—on May 10 before the National Council of the party, on May 24 at the *mur des Fédérés*, and on May 31 before the special congress of the SFIO—Blum, by his words or his presence, indicated the meaning of the victory, prepared for the accession to power, and laid the groundwork for future action.

His speech of May 10 is one of the most enlightening—about Blum himself—he ever delivered. It happens that a filmmaker[67] has captured for us his image and his voice on that day of triumphal ordeal. How young this man of sixty-four still seemed! His voice was capable of assuming the strength and the resonance equal to the circumstances:

> In a battle like this one, there must be a leader: command must be exercised, under your permanent oversight, but in its fullness. I have never spoken to you in any other way. You know that whatever faith you or the party may have in me I owe, on the contrary, to a constant effort of conciliation and persuasion. Today, something else is involved. In these new circumstances, another man must be revealed in a man. I know, without any distinctions, that you have complete confidence in me. I deserve it and I will continue to deserve it.
>
> I do not know if I have the qualities of a leader in such a difficult battle: I cannot know it, no more precisely than any of you. It is a test that you will make of me and I will make of myself. But there is something that will never fail me: resolution, courage, loyalty. I want to say to you again that I do not present myself to you today as a man already crushed in advance by the weight of duties and responsibilities, even though, believe me, I know what they are. I

> have not come here to say: "Take this cup from me, I did not wish
> it, I did not ask for it." Yes, yes, I asked for it and I wished it,
> because it is the victory of our party within a republican victory.

These remarks have been harshly criticized, even by admirers of
Blum. Does a leader confronted with responsibilities have the right to
question publicly his capacities and abilities? Isn't that a demobilizing
manner of speaking? Our point of view is different. Blum's grandeur is
tied to the openness which he offered and asked for. We see it rather as
the claim to an authority—something other than and perhaps more than
a power—an anguish before the offered "cup" which he has mastered,
the determination to bring out "another man."

Three weeks later, from May 30 to June 1, the socialists met in
congress in Paris, once again in the Salle Huyghens. On the second
day, after a speech by Faure (who, as an old antiparticipationist,
showed that by accepting power the victorious SFIO would remain
within the framework of "party legality"), Blum mounted the platform
to long and affectionate applause. He pointed out that "since things had
not happened as predicted," the Socialist party, which had become the
"largest element in the Popular Front majority," would, in spite of the
Communists' refusal to participate, assume the tasks of power in the
framework of a coalition.

In response to a slogan launched by Jean Zyromski and his friend
Graziani, demanding "total power," he pointed out that:

> not only did the Socialist Party not win a majority, but even the
> combined proletarian parties did not do so. There is no socialist
> majority, there is no proletarian majority. There is the Popular
> Front majority, whose locus is the Popular Front program. Our
> aim, our mandate, our duty, is to accomplish and execute that
> program. It follows that we will act within the present social sys-
> tem, the same system whose contradictions and iniquity we have
> demonstrated. . . . We have to find out whether, by means of
> action carried out within the present system, it is possible to pre-
> pare minds and material conditions for the inevitable advent of the
> system which remains our aim and our goal. We have to find out
> whether it is possible to assure a passage, a peaceful, amicable
> transition between this society and the society whose definitive
> establishment is and remains our goal.

He then had the boldness to pronounce a taboo word for orators:

> I do not contemplate for a moment the possibility of failure. If I
> speak of failure, if I advance such a hypothesis, it is only in order
> to give my thought logical and complete expression. But if it were
> to happen that we fail, if it turned out that insurmountable resist-
> ances force us to recognize that it is impossible to reform present
> society from within, that it is impossible to carry out at the present
> moment the necessary work of rescue for the entire nation, then, I

declare to you, I would be the first to tell you so. I would be the first to say to you: "It was a chimera, it was an idle dream! There is nothing to be done with this society as it is, we can expect nothing from it, the resistances of egotism, routine, and self-interest are insurmountable," and I would be the first, in that case, to tell you why and how we had failed, and what conclusions you should draw from our failure.

As spokesman for the Socialist party, he reminded his partners in the Popular Front that solidarity was even deeper than they seemed to believe:

> The reactionary press often taunts us with Kerensky preparing the way for Lenin. Although I do not wish to express a hurtful judgment on an exile, I will nevertheless say that I hope the government which the party is about to form will not be the Kerensky government. But even if it were, you can be sure that in present-day France it would not be Lenin who would reap its harvest! The cause is common to all, the interest is the same for all. The danger, should it arise, is equal for all!

But at the very moment that he was warning the PCF against certain hidden aims, he spoke words which disarmed him in the face of his allies:

> I declare to you that, as far as I am concerned, I am determined to confront everything, except for one thing: disagreement with the party, or disagreement with the working class as a whole. That would be the only insurmountable obstacle, insurmountable because, for my part, I would not want to surmount it!

By declaring that a disagreement with "the working class as a whole," was "insurmountable," wasn't he surrendering himself to the discretion of the friends of Maurice Thorez? Of course, he was thereby proclaiming that he would not be a Noske.[68] But he was excluding not only bloody conflict but "disagreement." Some of his companions, like Maurice Paz,[69] saw it as a grave tactical error, a confession of fundamental impotence vis-à-vis partners who, from that point on, by provoking or exploiting a serious problem, would hold the key to his continuation in power.

The position of the Communists was all the stronger because on May 14, in response to a very pressing offer from Blum, their leaders had made it known that they refused to participate in the government. But while in January 1936, at the Villeurbanne congress, Maurice Thorez had asserted that the "tactic of the Popular Front" could not possibly lead the PCF to "a banal policy of ministerial collaboration," because it was "not a bourgeois party" but "the party of the working class" (expressions whose every word seemed chosen to wound his socialist allies), on May 14 the secretary-general of the PCF wrote to Blum in an entirely different tone:

> We are guided by a single and exclusive concern: to assure at any price the success of the enterprise of economic and social renovation, and the preservation of peace and freedom desired by the people of France. We are convinced that the Communists will better serve the cause of the people by loyally supporting, unreservedly and without interruption, the government under socialist leadership, rather than by offering, through their presence in the cabinet, a pretext for the enemies of the people to create panic.

Was this Jesuitical? Probably not. Besides, it is fairly certain that Thorez was in favor of communist participation in the government. In his *Mémoires,* Jacques Duclos speaks of his "magnificent boldness" on this point, but adds that the majority of the political bureau ("of which I was a member") refused to attempt the adventure.[70] It is difficult to uncover the origin of this refusal, and to know why Duclos chose to reveal his opposition to Thorez on such an important matter.

In his indispensable *Histoire du front populaire,* Georges Lefranc quotes an article by the Moscow correspondent of *Le Petit Parisien,* Georges Luciani, dated June 16, 1936, that reported various conversations he had had since May 3 with Soviet civilian and military leaders and from which it appeared that his informants expected from the Popular Front "a strong and united France determined to respond appropriately to Hitler." They also did not rule out the possibility "that the great success of the French Communists might have the effect of a boomerang on Franco-Soviet cooperation." The journalist summed up the results of his investigation a bit too schematically:

> The Soviets are confronted with a dilemma. Either urge on the Popular Front in France and seize control of power, which is equivalent to a revolution, [and] would bring on civil war, paralyze France, and make it an easy prey for Hitler's appetite. Or else the Popular Front postpones the revolution to better times, makes itself the leader of national defense, carries the pacifist bourgeoisie and the antimilitarist people with it, and makes everyone feel the necessity to be strong in order to resist Hitler. Moscow has clearly declared itself in favor of the second line of conduct.

Indeed, the choice was not new. It had sometimes taken more picturesque forms. In 1943, at Vichy, Pierre Laval told the former militant of the socialist left, Georges Soulès (who later adopted the pseudonym Abellio), that during their conversations in May 1935 on the occasion of the signing of the Franco-Soviet pact, Stalin had asked him why he didn't take the leadership of the Popular Front that was in the process of formation in France!

The PCF, however, made it known that it would not be content with the role of noncommissioned officer in charge of production, rearmament, and mobilization. Paul Vaillant-Couturier indicated in a few famous sentences that "the Communist party will carry on outside the government a sort of 'ministry to the masses,' with the most determined elements of the Popular Front, grouped in its committees." In short, as a brake on disorder but an accelerator of demands, a champion of rearmament but an advocate for working-class causes, the PCF would be a government on the fringe of the government, if not a state within the state and a reformist revolution within the revolutionary reform. A comfortable position.

In any case, the socialist leader was therefore forced to rely only upon the allies on his right, the Radicals and the Republican-Socialists. The Radicals were weakened by their electoral reverses and the old dissension between Herriot, who had almost been defeated in his Lyon stronghold and attributed this semi-failure to the compromising alliances of the Popular Front, and Daladier who, as an artisan of the coalition, was bitter that the leadership of the government, which all signs seemed to indicate would be his, had eluded his grasp.

Confronted with the Communist refusal, should Blum have chosen to form a homogeneous socialist government, on a narrower basis but within the ideological framework of the Popular Front? Didn't the withdrawal of his allies on the left decisively unbalance the organism that had been created the preceding January? To reestablish balance, shouldn't he have proposed to the Radicals that they too confine themselves to support without participation, and formed a purely socialist government? This was proposed on May 6 by Marceau Pivert (who did not always demonstrate such good sense) and André Philip. But to do so would be to neglect the fact that, for the Radicals, to be out of power was to languish in exile. It was beyond human strength to keep Chautemps and Herriot, Daladier and Sarraut out of the government. Although Blum the logician must have considered it, Blum the practical politician immediately rejected the possibility.

On Sunday May 24, for the first time the head of a French government marched before the *mur des Fédérés*, spattered sixty-five years earlier with the blood of the fighters of the Commune; it was as though were indicating to the companions of Varlin and Delescluze that their sacrifice had not been in vain, and to the bourgeoisie that the very sources of power were about to change.

Louis Guilloux has warmly evoked that day, as a witness, militant, and novelist, in *Les Batailles perdues:*

> That morning it was reported that the Negus was sailing to London, that the castle of Prince Stahrenberg[71] had been attacked by the Nazis, that Belgium had voted against fascism, that a popular front had just been formed in Chile.

At the corner of the boulevard and the rue du Repos, opposite
the café *L'Excellent,* so well known to the old militants, the head
of the procession was waiting. Delegations from the provinces,
groups of socialist and Communist militants, and union delegations
made their way through the crowd as well as they could behind
their flags.

Fists were raised. A great roar, shouts, and applause burst out:
Léon Blum was approaching from the rue de Charonne, accompanied by citizen Thérèse Blum and surrounded by a small group
of friends.

"It's him! Look! He's with Bracke!"

Breaking through the barriers, a few people managed to approach Léon Blum and his friends to shake their hands.

"Vive Léon Blum! Vive old man Bracke!" . . .

There was another great shout when it was learned that Léon
Blum was leaving the wall, where he had stayed behind a group of
children, to return to his work. He responded to the applause by
raising his fist and smiling.

"To work, Blum!"

Women held their children up to him and shouted: "Vive Blum!"

On the avenue de Père-Lachaise his tall and delicate form appeared again amidst the crowd, greeted with a final shout: "Vive
Léon Blum! Vive old man Bracke!"

Demonstrators had joined the police to make a chain to enable
him to leave, shouting: "Discipline! Discipline!"[72]

This last word could not suffice to reassure the greatly agitated
bourgeoisie; for, since the middle of May it was no longer simply
mulling over its electoral defeat and calculating the risks involved in
the formation of a Popular Front government led by Blum. Its attention
had turned altogether toward what historians have chosen to call "the
social explosion," the immense movement of sit-down strikes which
accompanied the great political shift of May 1936, and gave it simultaneously its framework, its rhythm, and perhaps its historical meaning.

The Fear of the Right

Even before this popular upsurge placed its prerevolutionary seal on
the transfer of political power brought about by the May 3 vote, the
majority of the French bourgeoisie, which for a century and a half had
monopolized the state established on the principles of 1789, had made
its verdict known. It was in general negative. Of course, a significant
fraction of the Radical party, with Daladier and the "young Turks," and
newspapers like *L'Oeuvre* and *Le Petit Parisien* had agreed to place
their confidence in the *Rassemblement populaire.* Further, a strong
intellectual current, which was hardly "popular," including Gide and
Chamson, Alain and Malraux, Berl and Schlumberger, supported the

leaders of the Popular Front. But class reflexes generally operated against this populist–style reformism, though it was the only force capable of saving French society from economic disaster or bloody revolution.

The right was afraid, and the right cried out. Maurras was of course the cruellest. On May 15 he wrote in *L'Action française:* "It is as a Jew that we have to see, conceive, understand, fight, and cut down the Blum." Jean Renaud, the *führer* of *Solidarité française,* joined the chorus: "the country will recover the consciousness of its dignity and its mission, and it will knock the emblematic Blum from his pedestal of clay, the man of sanctions and the coming war." Apparently less brutal, but endowed with higher subsidies, André Tardieu wrote in *Gringoire* on May 15: "M. Blum has denied 'any thought of hostile reprisals.' But it was he who one day, with his fist raised, shouted to half the Chamber, 'I hate you!' M. Blum and his friends, strengthened by their relations with the Bérard bank, M. Oustric, and M. Patenôtre,[73] to the cry of 'Down with the thieves!' oppose the cry 'Long live the thieves!' "

The *Croix-de-feu* were divided between their haste to blame others for the defeat and a kind of pseudo-satisfaction whose foolishness surprised even the well–informed. At the same time that it denounced the Communists who bore "on their hypocritical faces, stamped with a red brand, the Asiatic seal," the "envoys of Moscow," and "the gold lavished by the Soviets," Colonel de la Rocque's organ *Le Flambeau* published this strange profession of faith which provoked laughter throughout France:

> Wolves become shepherds.
> Communist leaders suddenly assume *Croix-de-feu* ideas.
> They preach reconciliation.
> They take an interest in national defense.
> They adopt the tricolor.
> They even repudiate the influence of Moscow.
> Treason? Calculation?
> *Croix-de-feu* ideas come to power through the people.

But the best analysis, from the point of view of the "nationals," was written by Jean-Pierre Maxence, a young Fascist-leaning novelist:

> The right turned itself over to the Leagues, and the Leagues led it into disaster. It placed its hopes in men who not only did not succeed, but went into hiding like deserters. I know otherwise courageous women who, when they passed a picket line and a worker held out a collection box, were seized with cold shivers. I know directors of newspapers who, from May to October [1936] and even in March 1937, had only one thought: not to be banned. . . . Not a considered act. Not a reflex. Especially no

examination of the elements of the situation; no effort lucid enough
to understand the reasons for defeat and the reasons for victory!
Their rout taught nothing to the bourgeois right, momentarily disguised as the revolutionary right. For some, the Popular Front was
one particular minister; for others, it was the Jews. The politics of
the right-wing press remained fragmentary, personal, and divisive.
Violent in words, insufficient in ideas, non-existent in action.[74]

As always, it was François Mauriac, who was to be found on that
side for a few more months, who made the cruellest attack, in *L'Echo
de Paris* on May 8:

> The same government cannot possibly rely on the mob and com-
> bat it with the forces of order. It should be absolutely clear that
> from now on those who take to the streets will do so as
> masters. . . . It will no longer be [a matter] of a demonstration, but
> one of those *journées* whose dates remain inscribed on the tablets
> of History to mark the various crises of the Revolution. In 1929,[75]
> the head of a Radical government and all his ministers escorted
> Jaurès's ashes to the Panthéon. It did not take anything more; the
> crowd became angry and threatening, and from Paris, panic seized
> all of France.
> One cannot simultaneously depend upon the mob and suppress
> it. On the day when, after calling the popular masses to his aid, the
> socialist Premier was reduced to bringing armed force against it, he
> would be swept away and, according to an ineluctable law, other
> leaders would arise from the mob itself, and they would not make
> distinctions between Léon Blum and Pierre Laval or Louis Marin.
> A socialist government has everything to fear from the street, be-
> cause it is unarmed against it.

Victory in the Factories

Unarmed? The Popular Front government was unarmed because it
chose to be vis-à-vis the workers, its constituency; Blum was neither
Noske nor Kerensky. Also because, in spite of the forgeries and the
nonsense of right-wing observers like Jacques Bardoux, or the dreams
of leftist intellectuals like Daniel Guérin, the situation was not really
revolutionary. Because the "seizure of power" was not on the agenda,
neither for Blum nor against him. The vast movement of sit-down
strikes in the spring of 1936 was the consequence of, rather than an
attempt to go beyond, the electoral victory, although it did have the
objective effect of doing so.

"The political explosion took place on May 3, the social explosion at
the beginning of June," wrote Lucien Romier, editorialist for *Le Figaro,* three months later. "The Blum cabinet itself was the result of the
political explosion. It came to power just in time to experience the
social explosion." Emphasizing the contradictory not to say conflict-

ridden, character of this dual movement, two historians, Jacques Danos and Marcel Gibelin, write: ". . . the popular masses, disciplined and confident, were ready to take the offensive. When they did, it was Léon Blum who was the first to feel slapped."[76]

Slapped? No published writings, no remarks made at the time by the leader of the first socialist government, support this assertion. It was when he confronted his judges in Riom, before whom, however dispassionate he might be, the professional lawyer and great debater could not fail to bring out the arguments in his favor, that Blum, quoting Romier's article, let fall the famous expression on the explosion which had "struck in the face"[77] the Popular Front government from the moment it took office. In any case, the "social explosion" of May–June 1936 was, for the Popular Front government and for the coalition as a whole, Communists included, both a decisive preliminary test and a vigorous stimulant.

The best explanations of the working-class movement of 1936 have been given by the exemplary union militant Pierre Monatte, a pacifist in 1914 who had spent some time in the PCF and had become the leader of *La Révolution prolétarienne,* the newspaper in which he wrote, as early as July 10, 1936:

> So much poverty, so much constraint, so much oppression had to result in an outburst of revolt. But when? Slavery in the modern factory, suffering built up for years, everything that the bosses had succeeded in imposing since the workers' defeat in 1919–20, to which had been added the weight of rationalization, followed by the economic crisis, these are the deep causes, the essential causes of the recent strikes. The decisive factor which unleashed them was the coming of the Popular Front government. Finally, the police would no longer be at the bosses' service! Finally, the government would be, if not benevolent, at least neutral! By the same token, they did not have the strength to bear it any longer. Not even to wait until the new government was formed. The great release had taken place.

But Monatte did not content himself with this general justification for the "explosion." He found more circumstantial explanations for it: first of all, "the decisive factor which was provided by the very fact of the birth of the Popular Front government [which] gave the working class more than we dared hope from six months of efforts under its protection" and further, "the intervention of the Communists at the origin of the movement." Of course, Monatte explains, they had "not foreseen the extent of the movement. But the sounding was certainly taken by them. It encountered the underground layer of water, the current of suffering and hope searching for an outlet."

We should not neglect Monatte's suggestion of the possibility of provocation on the part of the bosses. By deciding immediately after May Day to dismiss workers who had really challenged them, they seem to have wanted to embarrass the Popular Front, "to slip a few strikes under its first steps, to create the void of a period without newspapers, therefore fertile in rumors and encouraging panic, and to make it fall into this void as it came into existence. . . . One must admit that it would have been a master-stroke."

In any case, work stoppages were not rare early in 1936 among a working class whose purchasing power had declined by 20 to 25 percent since Pierre Laval had come to power. Investigations carried out by journalists of every persuasion during the crisis brought out a terrifying reality, previously ignored by almost the entire press of the period. In *L'Illustration,* the quintessential organ of the provincial bourgeoisie, Robert de Beauplan spoke of "starvation wages,"[78] while in *Candide,* the extreme right-wing journalist Pierre Villette recognized "the extreme poverty of the working class, insufficient wages, and terrible cases of exploitation."[79]

In February the Marseille longshoremen, in March the Michelin workers, in April the Berliet metal workers in Lyon, even before the electoral success of the Popular Front, had given the alarm by halting work. But it was a few days after May 3, when French workers "became conscious of their poverty at the same time that they realized their power,"[80] that the movement exploded in the novel form of "occupations" of factories.

On May 11, the workers of the Bréguet factory in Le Havre stopped work to protest the dismissal of two workers who had taken May Day off. (See Monatte's hypothesis.) The management agreed to negotiate, but as the discussion continued past normal closing time, the strikers decided to stay where they were. They settled down in the factory. The matter was resolved within twenty-four hours thanks to the arbitration of the Radical mayor Léon Meyer, who brought about the reinstatement of the two workers; but the breach had been made, the precedent created, and the same phenomenon was repeated during the week of May 14 to 20 at Latécoère in Toulouse, at Bloch (later Dassault) in Courbevoie, in Vénissieux, and in the steel mills of Longwy.

Were these "occupations" unprecedented? Of course not. Factories had been occupied in Italy in 1920 (inspiring famous analyses by Gramsci), in Spain in 1933, in the Welsh mining country in 1935, as well as in France, in the automobile factories of Citroën and Simca, and again in Aisne early in 1936. But aside from the Italian incidents, none of these movements had ever been as extensive as the one which, in a second wave beginning on May 26, developed in Issy-les-Moulineaux (Nieuport factory), Levallois (Hotchkiss), Billancourt (Farman), and especially at the Renault factory, where the sit-down strike numbered more than 100,000 by the end of the month, frightening both the owners and the Sarraut cabinet members responsible for the factories on strike, Minister of Labor L.-O. Frossard and Minister of Aviation Marcel Déat.[81] The fear was all the greater because not only industry was affected: agricultural strikes took place in Hérault and east of Paris. At first inattentive (except for *Le Populaire* and then *L'Humanité*), the press, enthusiastic or terrified, finally grasped the enormous importance of the movement around May 25.

Terror? This is what was expressed by the bourgeois press:

> The striking building workers were able to walk the streets of Paris under the folds of the red flag. Strikers from cafés and restaurants did the same. Yesterday morning, they organized a great march along the boulevards. A truck carrying young men brandishing their fists and shouting led the procession which created a traffic jam on the boulevards. All revolutions begin in this way. Paris has the very distinct feeling that a revolution has begun."[82]

Enthusiasm? "When you feel strong in the street, you cannot continue to feel like a slave in the factory. When you have seen tomorrow's Premier raise his fist like a comrade before the wall of the fighters of the Commune, how is it possible not to believe that, this time, the government is no longer on the side of the capitalists?"[83]

There was a third tone, that of sympathetic curiosity, which can be found in a letter from Gide to Martin du Gard on June 14:

> You no doubt suspect that we have just lived through extraordinary days in Paris. You can imagine the appearance of closed stores, and warehouses and factories occupied by workers, more easily than the calm exaltation of the crowd. No jubilation; no shouts; a surprising "sobriety." People greeted each other in the street; you speak with anyone at all; passers-by stop and join in the dialogue; a dense group forms under the amused gaze of the police. Not once have I seen them have to intervene, nor heard a single "Move on."[84]

We have to provide some precise glimpses of these strikes, which left such a powerful imprint on the minds of Frenchmen in every camp, and directed Blum's policies. We will quote excerpts from reports written for their respective newspapers by two of the most brilliant intellectuals of their generation, Emmanuel d'Astier de la Vigerie and Bertrand de Jouvenel.

D'Astier describes one of the first nights of the occupation of Renault:

> One o'clock in the morning. The accordions, the cornets, and the flutes are silent. There is no more dancing. The long hours begin to weigh on one's shoulders. Even card games are dying out.

One workshop is still singing *Sous les roses*. But, curled up in corners, groups of sleepers begin to drop off. In one corner, a last accordion and a last cornet have taken up *Tout va très bien, Madame de la marquise,* and the workers repeat in chorus: "Tout va très bien!"

Nevertheless, the atmosphere in the workshops is full of tension. In spite of the laughter, the games, and the jokes, frayed nerves are barely controlled by discipline. One senses that their spirits are oppressed by the lack of any apparent external resistance, that they are on the lookout for a mysterious provocation from an implacable enemy.

But a striker said to d'Astier:

"We've gambled and won this time. All the conditions for success were fulfilled: surprise; the mass movement perfectly organized and contained within specified limits; communication from factory to factory through well established channels; money, since municipalities are generously supplying us, which is essential for morale; discipline without violence, because our officers are now adequately trained; and finally our tactics: occupy the factory; sustain ourselves whatever the cost, as in a city under siege; protect the stocks and the machines; demonstrate enough passive force so as not to have to use it."[85]

Jouvenel in *Marianne*:

For three days I have gone from factory to factory. I have seen cheerful jostling around baskets of food brought from outside, I have heard falsetto voices and comic imitations applauded. I witnessed no brutality. I have heard of no bad treatment inflicted on anyone, nor of damage to any machine. The sit-down strike is a prolonged picnic. It takes an effort to remember that we are witnessing a battle. Who is the enemy? Where is the enemy?

The door bearing the once fearsome word "Management" is closed. In this office which is respected by the workers, there are account books. By examining them closely, one would see what wage increases are possible without bankrupting the business.[86]

What exactly was this movement which suddenly overturned the social order, production relations, property rights? Who wanted it; when and by what means had it been carried out? What was the origin and meaning of this economic mass mobilization, of this victorious armistice which the French proletariat imposed on the instrument of its exploitation?

The hypothesis of a "plot" has been rejected by all the participants in the drama, beginning with contemporary leaders as little indulgent toward the Communists as René Belin,[87] Edouard Daladier,[88] and Jules Moch,[89] and they reject it both for the Communists and for activist groups. The role played by the Communists seems to us perfectly summed up in the article by Pierre Monatte quoted earlier. It was cardinal in exploiting the movement but not in setting it off.

A second hypothesis, advanced by Daniel Mayer, who was then in charge of social reporting for *Le Populaire* and who was closely involved in the movement, attributes the occupation of the factories to the workers' determination not to let "scabs" break the social movement. (There were more than half a million unemployed at the time.) Just as Blum had agreed to take on the "occupation of power" to keep out the Fascists, so the workers controlled the means of production to keep them from the hands of strike breakers.[90]

There is a third hypothesis, proposed by Antoine Prost at the 1965 conference.[91] Quoting the leftist leader Michel Collinet, who spoke of "saturnalia," he maintains that the 1936 strikes were "the expression, on a quasi-magical plane, the plane of a collective celebration," of the revolutionary ideal. Various writers had suggested this before, notably Simone Weil, who was long a factory worker. Her testimony and her interpretations are incomparable for their penetration and the strength of their convictions:

> I went to see my friends in a factory where I worked a few months ago. The joy of entering the factory with the smiling authorization of a worker guarding the gate. The joy of finding so many smiles, so many words, such a fraternal welcome. The joy of walking freely through the workshops where people used to be riveted to their machines. The joy of hearing, in place of the pitiless roar of the machines, music, singing, and laughter. The joy of walking past the bosses with your head held high. The joy of living in the midst of these silent machines at the rhythm of human life.
>
> Of course, the hard life will begin again in a few days. But no one thinks of that. Finally, for the first time, and forever, there will be other memories hovering around these heavy machines than those of silence, constraint, and submission. Memories which will fill the heart with a little pride and will leave a little human warmth on all that metal.
>
> People are completely relaxed. There is none of that ferociously intense energy, that determination mixed with anxiety which is so often seen in strikes. People are determined, of course, but not anxious. They are happy.[92]

But as was suggested by d'Astier's article and by the research of Georges Lefranc who was a participant in the drama, the movement as a whole was also a bitter fight, and the background remained threatening. After this "vacation of legality," the working class awaited the "return to normal."

How did Blum react to what might appear to him to be, at the moment when he was about to undertake his "exercise" of political power, a rash attempt at the "conquest" of economic and social power?

When the time of serene reflection had come, he had this noble vision of the strikers' behavior: "What contributed the most to the terror [of the owners] was the kind of tranquillity and calm majesty with which they had settled around the machines, like guards and also, in a certain sense, like co-owners."[93]

But in the spring of 1936, how did he feel, what did he say, what did he do? This lawyer who was so concerned with legality reacted first of all as the leader of a working-class party. To the SFIO congress on May 31, he presented this warning:

> Movements like this one must, in every case, remain under the direction and control of the autonomous union organization. Just as we must attempt to provide public opinion with an understanding of working-class movements, it is also our role to turn to the working masses and to show them to what an extent their confidence, their explicit, formal, and constant confidence is necessary to us.

With this clarification made, he set to work to dissuade the government of his predecessor, Albert Sarraut, from using force against the strikers, force to which the Radical leader was no more inclined to resort than his minister Frossard.[94] Then in the days preceding his accession to power (June 4), Blum prepared a two-pronged strategy aimed simultaneously at assuring emergency provision of essential food supplies by relying as little as possible on requisition, and at beginning a process of conciliation.

The new Premier presented the motives and the goals of this peaceful strategy in two speeches, the first broadcast by the radio on June 5th, the second from the rostrum of Parliament on the 6th—in anticipation of the discussions which brought representatives of management and the unions to the hôtel Matignon on June 7, discussions in which he played the role of arbitrator.

On June 5,[95] the day after his assumption of office, Blum declared on the radio:

> To be effective, the government's action has to take place in a context of public security. It would be paralyzed by any breach of the peace, by any interruption in vital services to the nation. Any panic, any confusion would serve the hidden designs of the enemies of the Popular Front, some of whom are already looking for revenge. The government therefore asks the workers to rely upon the law for those of their demands that must be regulated by law, and to pursue the others with calm, dignity, and discipline.

On the 6th, before the National Assembly, he clarified his ideas and his intentions on various points. What were the causes and the nature of the strikes? Was the government going to be content with enduring the movement? What did it intend to undertake?

After explaining that, for him, it was incorrect to speak of "occupation" of factories, since the workers had not come from outside, and they had therefore "taken up residence in the factories," he added:

> The essential cause [of the strikes] is the crisis itself and its continuation, for any prolonged crisis, in particular any unemployment crisis brings about simultaneously a decline in wages, a change in working conditions, and a change in relations between management and labor. . . . I have been asked if I considered these factory occupations as something legal. I do not consider them legal. The occupations are not in conformity with the rules and principles of French civil law.

But, turning toward the right of the Assembly, he proclaimed his determination to rule out any evacuation by force:

> If it is a question of putting police forces into action, then the next day perhaps the army, and who knows, gentlemen, perhaps some of the leagues which at this moment are helping to stir up the movement, if that is what you expect, well, I tell you that you expect it in vain.

He recalled his two-pronged strategy: provision of food and essential services and search for conciliation. The provision of food supplies—health and security services had never been interrupted—sometimes took on picturesque forms. The requisition of the necessary fuel was first considered by Léon Jouhaux, the leader of the CGT. Blum himself accepted, on the condition that the strikers agreed. On the evening of June 5, since Paris had run out of the fuel oil without which bread could not be baked—what a beginning for a "popular" government!—Jules Moch and the union leader Finck, authorized by the new head of government and the leadership of the CGT to obtain fuel, made the rounds of the depots in the Paris region, all of which were "occupied." Everywhere the strikers objected that, since they were responsible for quantities of fuel that were recorded at the time work stopped, they could not possibly divert one drop of it. Moch and Finck had to promise them that the military would soon deliver replacements before they finally agreed to turn over the indispensable fuel.[96]

As for the arbitration, the success of which Blum had taken on as his mission, it took the form of the famous Matignon agreements. This was not the first attempt along those lines. From May 30 to June 3, Albert Sarraut and L.-O. Frossard had attempted a first mediation between unions and management. It had failed and ended with a new outbreak of strikes, sometimes accompanied by the sequestration of managerial personnel (at the Peugeot factory in La Garenne, for example). The employers were so exasperated that, according to one of their spokesmen at the time, the dominant tendency was to "refuse any discussion as long as a single factory was still occupied."[97]

But the initiative for negotiations nevertheless came from the employers. The very day after the formation of the government, on Friday the 5th of June, M. Lambert-Ribot, who had been Léon Blum's colleague at the *Conseil d'Etat* and had become chief representative for the *Comité des Forges,* citadel of large industry, sent word to the new Premier through their mutual friend Paul Grunebaum-Ballin that contact between workers' and employers' delegations under his sponsorship could open the way to negotiations on the basis of a general raise in wages in exchange for evacuation of the factories.

That very evening Blum received Lambert-Ribot and three other leading employers, Duchemin, president of the *Confédération Générale de la Production,*[98] Richemond, president of the Group of Metallurgical Industries, and Delbouze, president of the Paris Chamber of Commerce. Blum said to the employers' delegation that the government ruled out any use of force and that serious events might take place within 48 hours, that they therefore had to act quickly, and that priority was given to the problem of wages. The next day the CGT, informed of the plan by Roger Salengro, the new Minister of the Interior, agreed to negotiations. On Sunday the 7th, at 3 P.M., discussions opened in Blum's office in the hôtel Matignon.

Facing the four spokesmen of the employers were Jouhaux, secretary-general of the CGT, Belin and Frachon, secretaries of the CGT, Semat of the Federation of Metal Workers, Cordier of the building workers, Savoie of the food workers, and Milan of the hat workers. Under Blum's direction, the government was represented by Salengro, Dormoy, and Moch (Lebas, the Minister of Labor, was detained in his district in Roubaix).

The Premier reminded his listeners that the day before the Chamber of Deputies had approved his intention to resolve the conflict peacefully and that, since most questions at issue had to be resolved by law, it was the question of wages that remained to be dealt with. The employers naturally emphasized the necessity of evacuating the factories, while the union representatives demanded wage increases of 10 to 15 percent. During the Riom trial, Blum later told how a member of the CGT delegation had declared:

> We promise to do everything we can;[99] but we are not certain to succeed. When you are dealing with a tide like this one, you have to give it time to subside. And besides, perhaps now you will regret that you took systematic advantage of the years of deflation and unemployment to keep all the union militants out of your factories. They are no longer present to exercise the necessary authority over their comrades in order to have our orders carried out.

His interlocutors were forced to agree that this was true.

It was also at Riom that Blum reported these revealing incidents:

I heard M. Duchemin say to M. Richemond, as he was shown certain wage levels that were frighteningly low: "How is it possible? How could we let it happen? We have failed in our duty by letting things go on like this."
I can still hear Lambert-Ribot saying, while we were discussing wage raises: "You mean you're not satisfied with these rates! But when have French workers ever seen a general raise in wages of this magnitude?" And Benoît Frachon answered: "And when in France have you seen a working-class movement of this scope and this magnitude?"

At the end of the afternoon, Blum asked for an interruption in negotiations so that he could participate in a meeting at the Vélodrome d'Hiver, along with Maurice Thorez, where he calmly declared to an enormous and passionate crowd: "In the course of the conversations, I observed on the part of the representatives of the employers a spirit of conciliation and an understanding of the situation to which I would like to pay tribute. I would be committing an evil action if I did not recognize it." Meanwhile, at CGT headquarters, Benoît Frachon declared to his comrades: "They've given in on every point!"[100]

The agreement was signed one hour after midnight. It stipulated that the employers agreed to collective contracts with the workers providing for freedom of opinion, union rights, and the recognition of workers' delegates elected in the factories. Wages were increased from 7 percent for the highest paid to 15 percent for the lowest (even more for those which were judged to be "abnormally low"). There were to be no reprisals for the strike, and the CGT undertook to ask for the resumption of work and the evacuation of the factories as soon as the employers had begun negotiations on the means of putting the agreements into operation.

On the left, the agreements were greeted with exhiliration. L'Humanité ran a headline: "Victory has been won." Le Populaire proclaimed: "The bosses have capitulated! Which bosses? All of them!" In Syndicats, René Belin, one of the negotiators, wrote more calmly on June 15, 1937: "The Matignon agreements were valuable above all for their psychological meaning. They reduced the divine employers to a human scale. The haughty and distant colossus, who until then had been unapproachable, was deflated. The workers felt that he was within their reach." On the right, however, M. Lambert-Ribot's reaction in Le Temps of June 8 was typical—he spoke of a "forced experiment" and a "dangerous and false situation."

Blum, whose stature had increased because of this quick agreement, was already asserting that the movement was cooling down. But strikes continued in the metal industry, the building trades, and the mines. Between June 7 and 11 the social atmosphere even seemed to grow worse. There were rumors that a "sudden storm"—inspired by the Communists, of course—was brewing.[101] Protests arose everywhere about the increases in "abnormally low" wages. The strike stiffened in the provinces; in Lyon, Bordeaux, and Marseille fights broke out. Another conference between management and unions became necessary; on June 9, Blum brought together Duchemin, Belin, and Frachon, and insisted that work be resumed and the factories evacuated.

Then, on June 11, before an assembly of militants from the Paris region in the Jean-Jaurès gymnasium, Maurice Thorez threw into the balance the weight of his authority as leader of the "ministry to the masses" to bring about détente:

> You have to know when to end a strike once you have obtained satisfaction. You even have to be able to agree to a compromise if all your demands have not been met, but if you have won victory on the most essential demands. If the demands of our comrades the metal workers have been satisfied, we can and we must sign the agreement bringing the present movement to an end.

The next day, June 12, the agreement with the metal workers was signed, specifying without broadening the Matignon agreements. It was this settlement which, in accordance with Thorez's prediction, brought about détente. The passage by the National Assembly of the social laws presented by Blum, the approach of the summer vacation, and also a certain lassitude and the occasional irritation provoked by workers' delegates exercising their new-found authority over their comrades without much tact, all helped bring about the resumption of work. On June 25, Salengro was able to proclaim, with some presumptuousness:[102] "Thus has concluded without a drop of blood the most formidable social conflict in the history of the Republic!" (A statement Blum echoed six years later in the Riom court by quoting Briand: "Look at my hands! Not one drop of blood!")

Had a revolution been betrayed? By forging a compromise, obtaining a "cooling off," returning the popular river to its bed, had Blum and the government which came to power on June 4, 1936 aborted an historical opportunity, the conquest of power by socialism? This is the argument of militants and revolutionary historians like Guérin, and Danos and Gibelin—even of Colette Audry. The argument was already summed up in the famous article which Leon Trotsky had written at the beginning of June 1936, for an issue of *Lutte ouvrière* which was seized by the Minister of the Interior: "The French revolution has begun!" The article contains the prophetic inspiration and the brilliant intuitions of the founder of the Red Army, and at the same time his incurable mania for seeing everything in the light of the incomparable situation of the Russian October, the situation of an empire in a state of complete decomposition, a disintegrating army, and a defeated ruling class.

Nothing of the sort was observable in France in the spring of 1936,[103] where stability reigned in an old and pluralistic state; there was an army rather admired by the people, a disciplined police force, a ruling class which was certainly disconcerted and on the defensive, but which still possessed most of the means of action, the control of credit, strong international support, and a practically intact system of management and constraint. When on June 12, 1936, while a government under socialist leadership which had far from exhausted its progressive possibilities was in place, *Lutte ouvrière* called for the seizure of power by armed committees of "the unemployed, peasants, and soldiers," it was merely a plan naïvely applied to a situation that had no relation to the one in which the Soviets arose from the disintegrating Russia of 1917.

The debate on the revolutionary nature of the situation began *in vivo,* from the end of May 1936. It was opened by Marceau Pivert who published an "opinion column" in *Le Populaire* under the title: "Everything is Possible!"

> Don't try to sing us lullabies: an entire people is now on the march, with a determined stride, toward a magnificent future. In the atmosphere of victory, confidence, and discipline which is spreading through the country, yes EVERYTHING IS POSSIBLE for the bold! . . .
> The masses are much more advanced than one might imagine, they are not troubled by complicated doctrinal considerations, but with sure instincts they call for the most substantial solutions; they expect a great deal; they will not be satisfied with something like herb tea carried on tiptoe to the bedside of a sick mother. On the contrary, the riskiest surgical operations will meet with their agreement, for they know that the capitalist world is on its deathbed. Everything is possible, and right now![104]

To which the PCF opposed this veto formulated two days later in *L'Humanité* by one of its secretaries, Marcel Gitton:

> No, no, Marceau Pivert! There is no question for the new government of "surgical operations" . . . the attempts made by our worst enemies, and also by the Trotskyites, to try to draw us into rash actions which could not have failed to bring about an estrangement between the Popular Front and a significant number of little people have failed miserably. All those attempts came up against the good sense of the socialist and communist workers, and of the laboring masses as a whole.[105]

Of course, there was in the France of spring 1936 the "Great Fear" of the ruling classes, well described by the Communist historian Pierre Vilar in the proceedings of a conference published in 1966 by

Démocratie nouvelle: "Fear among the bourgeoisie was much stronger than has been said. There was such panic that a substantial part of the bourgeoisie was ready to accept anything out of fear of the development of the Popular Front."[106] This opinion was confirmed by Philippe Serre, a deputy of the Christian left, who asserted at the 1965 conference: "I saw the employers suddenly blown away. If the Popular Front program had been ten times more ambitious, it would have been accepted at the time without protest." But in the course of the debate in 1966, Jacques Duclos, like Jean Bruhat at the 1965 conference,[107] and like most analysts of the PCF, vigorously denied that the situation in May–June 1936 was revolutionary.

All accounts agree—except that of Daniel Guérin, who evokes with touching fervor the formation of a "soviet" in the neighborhood of the porte des Lilas—the strikers of 1936 were less concerned with the political content of the movement, or with going beyond its ideology, than with the affirmation of their human dignity, breaking the old relationships, and affirming their class solidarity. All witnesses, from Simone Weil to Daniel Mayer, from d'Astier to Frachon, emphasized the naïveté of the strikers, the particularly conservative character of their behavior, and their ignorance of the political significance of the movement. Even Marceau Pivert, director of *Le Gauche révolutionnaire,* admitted that he had been mistaken at the time about the development of the consciousness of the working class—drawing this distressed admonition from his comrade and friend Daniel Guérin: "So, it wasn't the organization but the class which was mistaken?" Unthinkable!

Pierre Mendès France, Ernest Labrousse, and Annie Kriegel pointed out during the debates at the 1965 conference that a revolutionary situation can develop without awareness on the part of the participants. But if one attempts to define the level of consciousness on which the great movement of the spring of 1936 grew and developed, one may conclude that it was the level of a reasonable class optimism.

The working class felt itself simultaneously united, freed from the threat of repression thanks to the new type of government it had elected, and permitted to assert its rights. But it felt much more that it was carried by the new government—although it might urge it into action—than inclined to go beyond it. It had just penetrated the walls of the state: was it about to destroy that weapon, that resource? With the exception of a libertarian fringe, a revolutionary current, and Luxemburgist groups, the answer is clearly no.

To sum up the atmosphere of those six famous weeks, we will turn again to a quotation from Simone Weil who, under the pseudonym of Suzanne Langlois, wrote in *La Révolution prolétarienne* on June 10, 1936:

People are completely relaxed. There is none of that ferociously intense energy, that determination mixed with anxiety which is so often seen in strikes. People are determined, of course, but not anxious. They are happy. They sing, but not the *Internationale,* not *La Jeune Garde;* they sing songs, quite simply, and that is fine. They laugh for the pleasure of hearing themselves laugh. They are not malicious. Of course, they are happy to make the bosses feel that they are not the stronger. It is finally their turn. It does them good. But they are not cruel. They are very happy.

The Brief Summer of Socialism

On June 4, 1936, the new Chamber of Deputies, the source of the powers of the Popular Front, finally took office. Albert Sarraut, head of the last government of the preceding legislature, resigned. Blum was called to the Elysée Palace at 6 P.M.

Did President Lebrun again communicate his apprehensions and ask again the question formulated on May 8: "Don't you think that a socialist at the head of the government risks frightening public opinion and provoking strikes, and that a Radical—perhaps Chautemps—would be in a better position to reassure people?" In any case, Albert Lebrun could not go as far in this direction as the Chief Rabbi of Paris who had come to see Blum to tell him: "If you do not accept the Premiership, 'someone' promises to provide you, for the rest of your life, with a pension equivalent to the salary of the head of government."[108]

On leaving the Elysée at 7:00, the socialist leader informed the head of state that he would present his cabinet very quickly. This was done at 9:30; the first government under socialist leadership in the history of France assembled in front of the photographers on the steps of the Elysée. In spite of the presence in the government of the first three women ministers, Irène Joliot-Curie, Mme. Brunschwicg, and Suzanne Lacore (the first two were noted intellectuals, the third a simple school teacher from Périgord), the cabinet did not have the stamp of originality that Blum had hoped for.

Entangled in constitutional rules and partisan bargaining, Blum had been neither quick nor ingenious in his choices. Aside from the women, the cabinet did not even include any members who were not deputies, men whose prestige and devotion to the union of the left would have helped to increase confidence—Paul Rivet, Victor Basch, Jean Guéhenno, or Léon Jouhaux (who had refused Blum's offer of the Ministry of Labor).

The government was nevertheless judiciously divided into two major sectors: diplomatic and military affairs were turned over to the Radicals (Daladier, the Deputy Premier, was given Defense, Pierre Cot

Aviation, Gasnier-Duparc the Navy, Delbos Foreign Affairs); economic and social affairs fell to the socialists (Auriol was given Finance, Spinasse Economic Affairs, Bedouce Public Works, Monnet Agriculture, and Lebas Labor). The socialists also held Interior (Salengro), the Colonies (Marius Moutet), and a new position, Sport and Leisure, went to Léo Lagrange. Finally, the Radicals held National Education, which was given to Jean Zay, who was, along with Pierre Cot, Jacques Kayser, and Pierre Mendès France, one of the "young Turks" of the Radical party who had so strongly urged the creation of the Popular Front; Justice was given to the former journalist Marc Rucart, and Commerce to the courtly lawyer Paul Bastid.

Daladier's position as Deputy Premier and Minister of Defense, and those of Auriol as Minister of Finance and Salengro as Minister of the Interior followed the predictions. It was more surprising to find Yvon Delbos, a nonchalant deputy from Dordogne, in charge of Foreign Affairs. In fact, Blum had considered offering the post to Herriot, who was well thought of in London and Washington, and even more appreciated in Moscow. The mayor of Lyon preferred to be elected President of the Chamber. Blum then fell back on his neighbor on the quai Bourbon, Delbos, who had been sent by Herriot to negotiate with the Soviets ten years before, who had since then taken a firm position against Laval's diplomacy, and whose rather colorless personality would allow the head of government to give whatever direction he chose to French diplomacy—although its true inspiration, if not its real head, was the Secretary-General of the Quai d'Orsay, Alexis Léger, who fascinated Blum as a poet as well as a diplomat.

Blum surrounded himself with a coherent group. At the head of his cabinet he placed André Blumel, a socialist lawyer who had been his close collaborator at the Palace of Justice and was a long-time friend; he was cordial, tireless, a good lawyer, courageous, and knowledgeable about the secrets of the SFIO and the Parliament. He was assisted by the sub-prefect Pierre Combes; Hubert Deschamps, a colonial administrator of exceptional intelligence, torn away from his jungle for a few months; Mireille Osmin, a "lively and gay Pasionaria," daughter of one of Jules Guesde's lieutenants; and René Hug, Administrative Secretary of the SFIO. The last two were particularly concerned with relations with the party, which were often difficult. Blum had explicitly expressed the wish that the party lead a life very independent of the government. Even though Paul Faure was a Minister of State, the SFIO lived up to his expectations.

Blum also appointed two under-secretaries of state to the Premier, the amiable Radical François de Tessan (who died in a Nazi concentration camp) and Marx Dormoy, a socialist of the "pragmatic" variety whom he had been able to dissuade from joining the "neo" dissidents three years before. This grenadier of the guards with his salt-and-pepper beard became one of the Premier's confidants, later replaced the unfortunate Salengro, and was assassinated under Vichy.

The only structural novelty of the government, in conformity with the principles set forth twenty years before by the author of *La Réforme gouvernementale,* was not that Blum had given himself no portfolio,[109] but that he had accomplished his plan to create a "general secretariat of the government," entrusted to Jules Moch, who would collaborate closely with him in preparing dossiers, disentangling complex affairs, and would sometimes function as a useful "buffer."

Gathered around Jules Moch at the general secretariat were some of his comrades from the UTS (Union of Socialist Technicians) who had been working for years to prepare the plan of action for the first SFIO government: notably Raymond Haas-Picard, Robert Marjolin, and Roger Renault; intellectuals like the professors, of literature—Yves Chataigneau; political economy—Etienne Antonelli; and history—Charles-André Julien, who became Secretary-General of the Select Committee on the Mediterranean charged with redefining relations between the Republic and the Arab peoples; and political militants like Marceau Pivert. Jean Zyromski, for his part, refused to enter this "sub-government."

The participation of Marceau Pivert, with whom Léon Blum had ties of great affection, had provoked a great stir among his friends of the "revolutionary left." But only one of them, Daniel Guérin, had opposed his acceptance of a post "in charge of radio propaganda" which made him a small-scale Minister of Information, very visibly associated with the responsibilities of power. Guérin tells, with a touch of cruelty, how his leader set to work to promote the personality of Blum as one would manufacture a star, by relying on the services of the celebrated Tchakhotine, author of *Le Viol des foules,* who was known as "Professor Flamm." There is a touch of Groucho Marx in this affair, at least as Daniel Guérin presents it.[110]

Thus covered on his left by the leader of the most revolutionary current, author of the famous "Everything is possible!," and on his right by the amiable Professor Bastid, a very faint Radical, Blum confronted the Chamber on June 6. As we have seen, he was then deeply involved in the question of the strikes, between the first meeting, with the employers' delegation on June 5, and the second and decisive one, with the union leaders on the 7th. He was already in possession of enormous and precarious power. But this meticulous legalist did not consider himself empowered to govern, nor even to move into Matignon (President Lebrun had proposed that he do so on the 4th) until he had been installed by the Chambers.

These scruples seem foolish to us today, and they may have played a negative role. But they indicate what this succession of June 6 represented for him: a republican consecration. The son of Abraham Blum, the disciple of Jaurès, the old advocate of nonparticipation, the ingenious inventor of the "exercise-occupation" of power, found himself on the government bench, backed by a comfortable majority, but menaced by a pack of implacable enemies, conservatives, anti-Semites, and professional patriots. For once, he had a completely prepared speech. He held the pages firmly as he mounted the rostrum where he had so often assailed Poincaré, Laval, and Tardieu. His jaw jutted out more forcefully than usual, and the gaze he cast over the assembly was not his usual affable one.

> The government does not have to look for a majority. It already exists. It is the majority the country wanted. The government is the expression of that majority assembled under the sign of the Popular Front. The government does not have to formulate its program. It is the common program subscribed to by all the parties which make up the majority. The single problem which it confronts will be to transform the program into actions.

Thus Blum presented himself as the executor of a program, the loyal agent of a coalition. However, the mandate which he had received and which he proposed to fulfill scrupulously had already been broadened by the upsurge of the masses. Thus no one was surprised when he announced that among the first proposals he would offer for adoption before the parliamentary recess, within a month, would be not only paid vacations, collective bargaining, the creation of the Grain Office, the reform of the Banque de France, the nationalization of the arms industry, and the extension of obligatory schooling—all measures contained in the common program of the victors—but also the 40-hour week, which was not explicitly in the program,[111] but which had just been imposed, without their being fully aware of it, by two million strikers.

It was on this point in particular that he was harassed by the opposition. The right had had the time to evaluate the disproportion between the cautious program of the left and the strength of the popular movement which it could now use as a lever. Paid vacations, collective bargaining, the reform of the Banque de France, these were all concessions that had long been considered inevitable. Everyone would give in then, from M. Reynaud to M. Flandin. But the 40-hour week, even before the evacuation of the factories had been assured? Four speakers in particular censured the head of government and his plans: Paul Reynaud, who competently and shrewdly reproached him for not announcing the inevitable devaluation of the currency; Louis Marin who, without concealing his long-standing affection for Blum, presented himself as the defender of the property rights challenged by the factory occupations; and two old opponents—why not say enemies?— Fernand-Laurent and Xavier Vallat.

The former was aggressive: "Do you conceive of freedom as the arbitrary sequestration of engineers and supervisors, preventing them from leaving the factories by violence? Yes or no, does property still exist in France?"

The latter chose to be insulting: "Your accession to power, Mister Prime Minister, incontestably marks an historic occasion. For the first time, this old Gallo-Roman country is going to be governed by . . ."

HERRIOT (who was presiding): "Take care, Monsieur Vallat!"

VALLAT: "by a Jew. I dare to say out loud what the country is thinking in its heart; it is better to place at the head of this country a man whose origins lie in its soil rather than a subtle Talmudist!"

Pale, the head of government rose from his bench and began to leave. His friends held him back, while Herriot denounced this miserable attack in solemn oratorical tones. Blum was then able to answer the other speakers, claiming for the government the role of arbitrator— which he was to play on the following day—between the employers and the unions. That evening he won an impressive majority: 384 votes to 220. The 376 representatives belonging to the Popular Front had been joined by a few deputies of the independent left, notably those of *La Jeune République*. The leader of the SFIO was thus installed in power.

Solidly? In parliament, yes. But in the country? It would be impossible to understand anything of Blum's strategy as head of government if one did not consider, in parallel with the extreme left movements and the social upheaval which challenged that strategy, the forces of the right which challenged it more violently, stubbornly, and fanatically. One has to have lived through that time, on the *right* side of the barricades, to have a sense of the bitterness of the resistance which the vast majority of the French bourgeoisie—including a substantial segment of Radical voters—put up against the Blum "experiment." It was almost an immunological reaction. Xavier Vallat was not entirely wrong to present his anti-Semitic ravings at the rostrum of the Chamber as the uncensored expression of widespread but unspoken feelings.

The forces that created obstacles for the new government are to be found much less among the parties of the right and the extreme right, who had been disturbed, disconcerted, stunned by their defeat in May, than in the press, the professional organizations, military circles, and certain currents of the Catholic Church. Of course, since the "leagues" had been dissolved in June, two new parties essentially inspired by anticommunism had been formed: the PSF (French Social Party) which had come out of the *Croix-de-feu,* and the PPF (French Popular Party) which was the creation of dissidents from the PCF led by Jacques Doriot.

By the end of the year, the PSF claimed two million adherents (which is certainly an exaggeration). It brought together and inspired a number of currents hostile to the Popular Front. But the notorious incompetence of its leader, François de la Rocque,[112] and the emptiness of his doctrinal references made it a shapeless and barely active rag-bag. As for the PPF, which had attracted some brilliant intellectuals (Bertrand de Jouvenel, Drieu La Rochelle), it succeeded only fitfully in extending itself beyond its suburban fiefdom in Saint-Denis.

More dangerous in the long run for the Popular Front government was the hostility of the Chambers of Commerce which held a special conference on June 9 and formulated a veritable declaration of war against the Blum cabinet, the 40-hour week, and unionism in general. Most of the professional groups which expressed the opinions and interests of the middle classes reacted similarly. As for the peasant organizations—notably Henry Dorgères's "green shirts"—they constantly demonstrated, sometimes brutally, against the Popular Front and its policy of organization of markets.

The army's prejudices against the Popular Front were evident, even though Daladier's authority was not subject to significant challenge. The influence of Marshall Pétain, a former "republican" who had joined the extreme right in 1934, was very strong, as was that of the very reactionary General Weygand. Although Colonel de la Rocque was hardly taken seriously, and extremist organizations like *francisme* or *Solidarité française* were held in suspicion in the army, *La Cagoule*[113] still attracted disciples, and *L'Action française* maintained an ascendancy to which even men like de Gaulle was on occasion susceptible. General Gamelin, received by Blum on June 10, said that he was "reassured" by the meeting and let that fact be known. But it took the rearmament efforts of the Blum cabinet to dissipate the prejudices of a minority of the officer corps. The majority remained openly hostile.

The Catholic Church hesitated. Of course, the majority of lower- and middle-class clergy and of the faithful were reflexively hostile to the "reds" and their "Jewish leader." But hadn't the Communist leaders, this time, "extended their hand" to the Catholics? The hierarchy did not wish at the outset to obstruct the "experiment." Cardinal Verdier, to the scandal of the right, recommended to the faithful that they subscribe to the first loan floated by the new government. Among Blum's first gestures, one that provoked a great deal of comment, was his visit to the Papal Nuncio during the summer of 1936.

The occasion for the visit was a request that a speech by Pope Pius XI be rebroadcast over French radio. The Foreign Ministry had pointed out that to respond favorably to this apparently inoffensive request would be to risk creating a precedent: since the Pope was a head of state, what was to prevent Hitler or Mussolini from using the authorization as a pretext for demanding the same thing? The head of government settled the question: the request should be denied. But he would do better. The next day the Nuncio gave a reception. It had been thirty years since the head of a French government had visited the Nuncio's residence; Blum attended the reception.[114] André Blumel has told of "the arrival of Léon Blum at the Nuncio's residence, accompanied by his wife, François de Tessan, and myself. Three Jews and a Prot! Some guests wondered why there was no thunderbolt from heaven. But others came up to congratulate Blum, like René Pinon of *La Revue des deux mondes,* and some priests. Blum did not want, as the Comtesse de Noailles quipped, to have the strong-boxes sealed with communion wafers."[115]

But the climate between the government and the Church changed for the worse in the succeeding months. On October 31, the five French cardinals addressed a pastoral letter to the faithful which did not simply point out the "seriousness of the crisis" and the "practical atheism to which the country seems to be resigned," but went further and asserted that "among children of the same fatherland, too often the gesture of a hand extended fraternally is replaced by a closed fist, the unfortunate symbol of violence and hatred!"

The most constant and relentless opponent of the Blum "experiment" was perhaps the press, with the exception, of course, of *Le Populaire, L'Oeuvre,* and *L'Humanité,* weeklies like *Vendredi, Marianne,* and *Vu,* and some serious dailies like *Le Petit Parisien* and *Paris-Soir* which strove for neutrality. But *Le Journal, Le Matin, L'Echo de Paris, L'Epoque, Le Figaro, Le Jour,* and *L'Ami du peuple* (that is, along with most of the provincial press, three-quarters of what was published in France), and even more the weeklies *Candide, Gringoire,* and *Je suis partout* conducted a veritable war against the government.

One quotation from the real leader of the opposition in the country, André Tardieu, indicates the tone of the opposition press: "If a financial crisis or an international complication were to arise, the leader (*duce* in Italian, *führer* in German) which M. Blum claims to be would reassure me neither by his sureness of judgment, nor by his strength of character, nor by the rectitude of his national reactions."[116]

This was the climate in which Blum set to work.

The Contract and the Festival

"The Popular Front is a contract between the working class and the middle class." This luminous formulation, which is so "Blumian," comes not from the head of government of June 1936 but from Maurice Thorez addressing his comrades on July 9. It clearly sums up the nature of the "experiment," the limits it entailed, and the state of mind of the man who presided over it.

André Blumel has recalled Blum in the course of a discussion suddenly referring to the text within reach on his desk: "Is it in the Popular Front program?" All his actions, all his decisions can be referred to two concerns: not to go beyond the limits of a contract which involved divergent loyalties, and not to violate the understanding between the working class (represented in the government by the SFIO, outside the cabinet by the PCF) and the middle class, i.e., the Radical party.

As early as June 9, two days after the signature of the Matignon agreements, the cabinet began the effort to move from the revolution brewing in the streets to a revolution through law in the framework of Parliament. As a first step, plans had to be determined in the Council of Ministers, under the presidency of Albert Lebrun, who did not always conceal his suspicion. Jules Moch has described the first meeting on June 9, one of the most important in the history of the Republic:

> Seated across from Léon Blum, Albert Lebrun looked with gloom and discouragement at the pile of dossiers to be considered. He picked up the one on top: it was the plan reducing the work week to forty hours with a reduction in weekly wages. He pronounced its title in a surly tone. Then he turned to the man on his right, Deputy Premier Daladier; then he looked in succession at every member of the government, ending with those on his left, Ministers of State Chautemps and Maurice Violette, and asked: "Does any one of you, gentlemen, have anything to say about this proposal?" After a prolonged silence, he questioned Léon Blum opposite him: "And you, Mister Prime Minister?" Léon Blum who, like many of us, was sitting for the first time in that solemn assembly, calmly answered: "But I signed that text, Mister President, because it conforms to our program."
>
> Albert Lebrun reflected for a moment, then abruptly picked up his fountain pen, held it in the air, and said: "In those circumstances, gentlemen, I will sign; I sign with a heavy heart; but I sign all the same, since it is my duty."
>
> All the other proposals were approved in the same way, without one minister saying a word, so that this Council, one of the most important because of its social consequences, lasted an extremely short time.[117]

Blum was then in a position to present to the Assembly five proposed laws, three of which—the forty-hour week, paid vacations, and collective bargaining—made his reputation in the country. A thirty-three member committee was created, presided over by the socialist Sérol, in which André Philip played the role of motor and Paul Reynaud that of brake. But the proposals were very quickly discussed in the whole

Assembly and easily adopted on June 11: paid vacations by 563 to 1, collective bargaining by 571 to 5. There was a longer struggle over the 40-hour week.

Paul Reynaud denounced the proposal, accusing it of going "against universal experience. Everyone has always wanted to stabilize costs. The government is going to impose a surcharge on French prices, which are already the highest in the world. If Parliament were to pass a law tomorrow abrogating the law of gravity in France, gravity would continue to operate." To which Blum responded quite calmly that the important thing was to reduce unemployment and revive production: if that is accomplished, "production costs will be spread over a larger number of products." There were predictably 160 deputies who voted against the 40-hour law (to which Alfred Sauvy, who was one of Paul Reynaud's advisors, has since devoted an analysis characterized by detailed hostility in his remarkable *Histoire économique de la France entre les deux guerres*).

In the Senate, Joseph Caillaux—who had not yet unsheathed all his claws—took up where Paul Reynaud left off, comically characterizing Blum's socio-economic policy as "Lilliputian Rooseveltism." But in the Senate as well the government proposals were adopted with large majorities. For the government, this early summer, with its excellent weather, was not a time of difficulties.

The euphoric atmosphere permitted the rapid passage of reform of the organization of the Banque de France—whose council was no longer to be made up of only the 200 largest shareholders, representing the notorious "200 families," but of all 40,000 shareholders—(444 to 7), the extension of obligatory schooling to the age of fourteen (468 to 80), the nationalization of the arms industry (485 to 45), and the dissolution of the "seditious" leagues—some of the major articles of the Popular Front program.

But relations between Parliament and the government began to become strained at the end of June when, expressing Blum's ideas with a certain heavy-handedness, Vincent Auriol declared at the rostrum of the Chamber: "Until now, rigorous balancing of the budget has been seen as the source of economic rebirth. It is on the contrary on the basis of economic rebirth that we hope to establish solid finances." On the contrary? The formulation was not very shrewd. It provoked irritated reactions from the right. Reactions which were to swell during discussion of the law creating the grain office.

The debate began at the Palais-Bourbon on July 3. It took Blum and his skillful Minister of Agriculture Georges Monnet six weeks to overcome the resistance of both chambers and win passage of the proposal in the Assembly (385 to 203), a proposal in which the opposition chose to see a "socialization of agriculture" (*Le Temps*, July 6), a "dictatorial and statist plan," or "the finest monument known of Marxist organization," and which was attacked even by the Radical Henri Queuille, while in fact it was designed to create a system for the stabilization of prices by making cooperatives the only purchasing bodies.

The bitterness of the debate was more clearly reflected in the press than in the Chamber. In *Le Populaire,* the chief ideologue of the SFIO, Bracke, used all his eloquence to help Blum and Monnet:

> You, the reactionaries, scream revolution. So be it! The great French Revolution gave peasants the right to own land. The successful operation of the grain office, as it is developed and improved, will give them the freedom to produce on that land and to protect their product from exploitation by others. Thank you for the publicity you have given to the Popular Front by your plots, your insinuations, your slanders, and your protests. The peasants will understand and will join with those who have opened the path of liberation before them.[118]

Le Temps brought in the very conservative lawyer Joseph Barthélemy:

> This floury construction of the grain office is completely worthless. You assert that it will work to create a minimum price. We fear that it will prevent grain from reaching its normal price level in case of a bad harvest in importing countries. The office will cost money. Who will pay? The farmers. The plan is to bureaucratize agriculture, barely leaving each farmer his bed and board. The plan is for the birds.[119]

But the Blum government was still carried by a wave of popular support, which came to a culmination on Bastille Day. "14 July 1935 had been a militant 14 July. 14 July 1936 was a triumphant 14 July," wrote Victor Basch. A platform was set up in the place de la Nation, and a million Parisians marched past it between 3 and 6 o'clock. It was a large cube draped in white, with an enormous portrait of Jaurès at the back, framed in red with these words above it: "Down with war! Long live peace!"

Blum, planted behind the microphones, confidently sang *La Marseillaise* and *L'Internationale* in turn, his delicate, pale fist raised. Immediately behind him, dark, slender, eyes flashing through his glasses, rejoicing with his whole being, stood Marceau Pivert, the organizer of the spectacle. To the right of the platform were Duclos and Gitton, impassive; to the left, Thérèse Blum (who had grown thinner) with an excited look; Maurice Thorez, radiant, his blond hair tousled, with a triumphant air and singing with a powerful voice, looking like Danton on the evening of August 10, flanked by Daladier who seemed distracted, more sullen and gloomy than usual, and Salengro with his arms crossed trying to appear like a strong man.

The five Blum brothers: Lucien,
Léon (second from the right),
Georges, Marcel, René.

At Enghien, the fragile adolescent Blum
stands at his mother's side.

The mentor: Lucien Herr, librarian at the
Ecole Normale Superiéure.

"Eckermann" of *la Revue Blanche*, a delicate
expression and a flower in his lapel.

Jean Jaurès.

Blum, the lawyer, in his library.

Léon Blum and his wife, Lise.

The men who rebuilt the "old house" ("vieille maison"). Blum, then a deputy in the National Assembly from Paris, is between Bracke (on his left), and Grumbach, Renaudel, Paul Faure and others.

Comrade Blum with Vincent Auriol on his right.

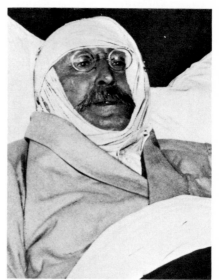

February 13, 1936, the night of the attack on the Boulevard Saint-Germain.

The dawn of the Popular Front. At the *mur des Fédérés*, Blum is flanked by French Communist leader Thorez on his left and Cachin, M. Paz, Thérèse Blum, Bracke, Gitton, Jacques Doriot and Jacques Duclos on his right.

Blum at a rally of the Popular Front. Behind him is Marceau Pivert, the leader of the left wing of the SFIO.

Blum, president of the Council, December 31, 1936.

Blum with his Minister of the Interior, Roger Salengro.

Blum with Minister of Aviation Pierre Cot.

International Women's Day. Blum speaks beneath the three arrows, symbol of the SFIO, and in front of a portrait of Rosa Luxembourg. At his side, Marthe Louis-Lévy; behind him Germaine Moch.

With Catherine, daughter of Robert and Renée Blum, on the eve of the disaster of 1940.

Seated in front of reproductions of his favorite paintings, Blum awaits his accusers at Riom. It was at this time that he wrote *A l'échelle humaine.*

Blum at Pétain's trial.

Blum in New York, April 1946.

Blum reading the Socialist newspaper *le Populaire*, to which he regularly contributed.

At Jouy-en-Josas among his books, some flowers, and "Janot's" garden,
Blum watches the postwar world.

Place de la Concorde, April 2, 1950. Blum's funeral. Robert and Jeanne Blum,
Michelle and Vincent Auriol, head of the French government at the time.

At the head of one column of marchers were Madeleine and Léo Lagrange, Clara and André Malraux, and Jean Cassou. At the head of another Andrée Viollis, André Chamson, and Jean Guéhenno, the directors of *Vendredi,* which published the next day this starry-eyed description:

> We marched and sang with our comrades. The column was twenty people across with arms linked; twenty men whom we know, who live together every day, who share the same labors. And suddenly, a vast crowd showed itself even friendlier to us than our closest friends. . . .
>
> Who said there were cracks in the Popular Front? Never had it felt stronger or more united. A cause of such obvious justice necessarily creates a kind of unanimity. The party leaders were able to see today how great were the unity and the cohesion of their troops. If it were necessary, they would find in such a day support for the necessary boldness.[120]

Unity, cohesion, necessary boldness? Could they know, these poor honest writers, that not one day would go by after the publication of these enchanted lines before the fine unanimity and the warm dynamism of the place de la Nation were struck a mortal blow? On July 18, dispatches that went at first unnoticed were published in the middle of the day in *Paris-Midi* reporting the beginning of the Spanish uprising that was to divide, undermine, shatter the Popular Front, and drive Blum to the verge of resignation and then to the verge of betrayal, an unhappy celebrant of a perverted ritual.

The 18th of July concluded the first phase, the rising and solar phase of the Popular Front. From that point on nothing was the same as before. Until then it had been necessary to navigate cautiously, to compromise, to manipulate, but always within the framework of the ethics on which Blum, following Jaurès, had based his behavior, the ethics of civilizing socialism. It had been necessary to form a government without the Communists, to sign the compromise of June 7, and to contain the popular movement. It had been necessary to adapt to what was possible in order to respect the contract. But the highest celebration, the 14th of July, had been a sincere celebration. A week later, that no longer would have been true.

We reserve complete treatment of the Spanish problem for the following chapter. But we should indicate here the extent to which it created a kind of break, an historical frontier. From the end of July 1936 on, the Popular Front was no longer united and Blum was no longer happy. What kind of celebration can be carried on when next door your comrades are being shot? What kind of happiness can be based on the abandonment—inevitable or not—of the deepest solidarities?

A Changed Life

But the Popular Front operated in France and it was first of all responsible for French society. It had signed a contract to change French society, from which it derived its legitimacy, and that society underwent greater transformations in three months than at any time since the great upheaval of 1914-18.

Better than anyone else, Blum, before the court of Riom, summed up the time and drew lessons from what he had accomplished at the head of the government:

> For my part, I think of that work, to which so many misdeeds and crises are now imputed, with a great deal of feeling.
> I did not often leave my ministerial office during the period of my government; but every time I did, every time I passed through the industrial suburbs of Paris and saw the roads covered with processions of jalopies, motorcycles, and bicycles, with working-class couples wearing matching sweaters—showing that the notion of leisure awakened even in them a kind of natural and simple coquetry—all that gave me the feeling that, through the organization of work and leisure, I had in spite of everything contributed a kind of adornment and illumination to hard and obscure lives, that not only had they been given more opportunities for family life, but that they had been shown a prospect for the future and given hope.

The Popular Front government, more than any other in France, had made a beginning toward the establishment of a "social order less contradictory to man than the present order," to quote Jaurès.[121] Beginning in 1936, a proletariat who "was only encamped at the gates of the city" acquired a feeling of dignity which was half conquered and already entirely possible. Blum said again at Riom:

> I remembered with a certain pride the words spoken by an English statesman who had fallen from power: "I will leave a name which will perhaps be spoken with hatred by monopolists and speculators, but which will perhaps be spoken with a feeling of gratitude in the homes of those whose lot in this world is work."[122]
> For my part, I felt an emotion and a pride of this kind, and I believe I have the right to express it before my judges.

Of all the laws passed between June and August 1936 which reshaped French working-class and peasant society, the most famous remain the 40-hour week and paid vacations, although Blum declared to the Chamber on August 16 that the most important law was the one that established collective bargaining and obligatory arbitration (that is, "democracy in the factory"). The most popular was certainly the law, based on the right to rest and leisure, establishing two weeks of paid vacation, which, an extreme right-wing publicist like Lucien Rebatet admitted, should have been proposed long before by any government worthy of the name.

Testimony abounds of the tie that was thereby created between Blum and the working class, who readily attributed its passage to him. Jules Moch tells that sometimes when he was driving the head of government back from the home of his friends the Grunebaum-Ballins in Mesnuls (Seine-et-Oise), where he often spent the weekend, they were stopped by cyclists or campers who recognized Blum and wanted to shake his hand and congratulate him.[123]

These policies can be summed up in another name: Léo Lagrange.

Léo Lagrange was a Jacobin from Gironde. He was born in 1900 in Bourg, a port and wine-making town near the Bec-d'Aubès. He was a very militant and vehement socialist, not at all inclined toward empty words. Very tall, solidly built, with a fair complexion, a powerful chin, and a sonorous voice, Lagrange had a touch of Jaurès about him—so Blum told a friend. Everything about him seemed to mark him out for a position of power. He was always careful not to abuse that kind of authority, which he held in great suspicion because other leaders of the young had used it so badly. He had joined the Socialist party at the age of twenty (at the time of the congress of Tours). Although he had taken a position as a democrat against joining the Third International, he had remained close to the left-wing faction of the SFIO most favorable to the Communists, Jean Zyromski's *Bataille socialiste*. In 1930 he was elected to the CAP (Permanent Administrative Committee, the government of the Socialist party), and in 1932 he entered the National Assembly as deputy from Avesnes (Nord). His first speech had been devoted to a denunciation of Stavisky's influence, his second to criticizing the direction of Pierre Laval's first government. He knew how to choose his targets.

When Blum was forming his government, he remembered his passion for sport as a young critic on *La Revue blanche* and created the position of Secretary of State for Sport and Leisure, to which he named the thirty-six-year-old deputy, who was not one of his close collaborators in the party but whose boldness he admired. He had in fact to take on a pioneering role. Since Paul Lafargue and Benoît Malon, whom Blum had so admired a half-century before, who had raised the question of leisure? Marxism had contributed so much to the sanctification of work!

Léo Lagrange, his wife Madeleine (both lawyers), and the few collaborators their paltry budget allowed—Bécart, Dolléans, Roux, Bontemps, and Mme. Grunebaum--Ballin—set out first to establish certain principles, then, on the basis of the laws for the 40-hour week and paid vacations, to create the conditions which would make leisure something other than non-work.

On the very day of the formation of the government, June 6, Léo Lagrange declared on the radio:

> The content of what we mean by the expression the organization of leisure is something that ought to be defined. In a democratic country, there can be no question of an authoritarian organization of the leisure, the distractions, or the pleasures of the popular masses, or of transforming clearly distributed amusements into means of not thinking.

And in answer to questions from an American reporter:

> Our aim consists in recreating the sense of joy and dignity. We have to place all kinds of leisure activities at the disposal of the masses, and let each individual choose. We have to open every road so that everyone may participate in the free and equitable functioning of democracy.

It should not be forgotten that Lagrange was entrusted with the role of leader of the young at a time when, from Rome to Nuremberg, others were making perverse use of similar functions. It was the time of the fascist *dopolavoro,* the Nazi *Kraft durch Freude,* and in Spain, of José-Antonio Primo de Rivera. In France, Jacques Doriot had not forgotten that he had been the leader of the *Jeunesses communistes* for nearly ten years, before receiving subsidies from Mussolini and passing to the side of the Axis. There were many poisons to be purged, many ghosts to be exorcised by a single man.

Means had to be found to break down the barrier that had grown up between the universe of concentrated urban work and the external world of nationwide leisure, and first of all the directors of the still-private large railroads had to be persuaded to offer reduced-price tickets.

The scene was picturesque. Lagrange received the four principal directors of the railroads at his brand new desk and very clearly set out his views: he wanted a 50 percent reduction on tickets during paid vacations. The "experts" were dumbfounded. Impossible! Profit margins were too narrow. One of them burst out: "Mister Secretary, what you are asking us is anti-railroad!" At that point, Léo Lagrange could no longer restrain himself. He banged on the table and spoke the harsh language of the state and of power. He wrested from them a reduction of 40 percent and several millions of the people of France benefited.[124] Thus there came about the slightly miraculous and scandalously delayed encounter between the mass of the people and French space, the meeting of the working class with the sea, the discovery of France by those who built it, what Léon Blum called "the reconciliation of isolated and frustrated workers with natural life."

You may believe a young provincial "of good family" who was old enough to have his eyes and ears open: the French bourgeoisie accepted with very bad grace the accession of the working class to its elementary rights. Satirists and cartoonists were prodigal with their sneers about "paid vacationers," those people who dipped their feet in the water so awkwardly on the now-crowded beaches. A cartoon published on August 12 in *Le Canard enchaîné* showed an old biddy sitting in a bathtub at the edge of the waves and clucking: "You don't think I'm going to bathe in the same water as those Bolsheviks!"

In a more serious mode, the extreme right magazine *Combat* spoke of the "rape" of the French countryside by "the filthy paws of the secular monster" which was making the French lose their "final reason for living." "Whoever has not decided to open his veins in a warm bath or to flee to an Egyptian monastery, will have nothing left but to take a rifle and some cartridges and shoot down as many as he can of the tyrants who are as dangerous as German barbarians, to unleash an internal revolution, even if it is bloody."[125]

Even more typical was an article in *L'Echo de Paris* on September 26, 1936, with its belligerent inanity:

> One day last August, near Alençon, around 10 o'clock in the morning, we had stopped at the edge of the superb forest of Perseigne which we had just passed through. A group of school children led by their teacher formed a procession and, under the startled gaze of the few inhabitants of "Le Buisson," took up *L'Internationale* as they went off toward Saint-Pigorner.
>
> The automobile, my four children . . . and our entire group were greeted by the look of hatred one finds almost everywhere today in what was once our lovely France.
>
> It depends on the good people who are still the majority for us to rediscover that lovely France; but they have to wish it, to demand it by any possible means.
>
> This is no longer the time for lamentation or protest, but for action!

L'Internationale and "looks of hatred" or not, life had changed. Another society was taking shape in the warm summer of 1936, a society in which class confrontations were not all eliminated, but had moved to another level and were considered in a new light. Blum could boldly declare in a speech broadcast on December 31:

> Hope has returned, and with it a taste for work and a taste for life. France looks and feels different. Blood courses more rapidly through a rejuvenated body. Everything leads one to feel that in France the human condition has improved. New social relations are being established; a new order is being developed. We can see that equity and freedom are in themselves beneficial and salutary.

The leader of the Popular Front concluded that this new happiness was therefore increasing "the spiritual power of the country."

"Spiritual power"—only Blum could use words like those, words which made political notables and professional nationalists snicker. But it was not for nothing that he spoke of change in the "human condition." The 1936 government was in fact the first to attempt, in parallel with its effort to transform the material conditions of working-class life, to offer the community cultural nourishment as a right.

Of course, it was not because the author of *Stendhal et le Beylisme* had come to power that the year 1936 was so rich in literary creation: it was the year of publication of *Les Beaux Quartiers, Mort à crédit, Journal d'un curé de campagne, Les Jeunes Filles,* and *Les Vraies Richesses* by Giono, *La Vie de Jésus* by Mauriac, *Les Yeux fertiles* by Eluard, *Les Sueurs de sang* by Jouve, and *Le Voyage en grande garabagne* by Michaux.

Of course, these distinguished writers had not postponed publication until one of their colleagues was installed as Premier. But the reigning climate, made up of a mixture of joyful excitement and vague anxiety was more propitious than any other to creative flowering. Martin du Gard published, with admirable aptness, *Eté 14,* and Guilloux *Le Sang noir,* so thoroughly in harmony with the passions of the time. Giraudoux produced *La Guerre de troie* whose hero Hector, caught in the dilemma of choosing between false bravado which encourages him to accept war and true heroism which means rejecting it, reflected Blum's anxieties as he confronted the Spanish conflict.

It was indeed in the theater that the influence of this strange government was felt. Jean Zay, Minister of Education, put the Comédie Française under the direction of an imaginative man, Edouard Bourdet, and stimulated joint activities by the four best men of the theater of the time: Dullin, Jouvet, Baty, and Pitoëff. It was a golden age for the Parisian theater.

Moreover, this cultural ideology had first been expressed in a theater. On the evening of July 14, 1936, after the enormous parade for popular victory, the old théâtre de l'Alhambra was packed with an excited crowd. Naturally they were performing *14 juillet* by Romain Rolland, one of his worst plays, a kind of comic strip for an adult education course. The audience was crowded with what Madeleine Lagrange comically called "the 200 families of the Popular Front." The curtain was designed by Picasso, the music was by Milhaud and Roussel. Roger Désormière, musician and militant, conducted the orchestra. Several times during the performance *La Marseillaise* burst forth, coming alternately from the audience and the stage. When the performers took their bows, *L'Internationale* replaced *La Marseillaise.* The performers from the Comédie Française, led by Marie Bell, raised their fists. (Blum was not present: he did not like Romain Rolland very much, and especially not his theater.)

Was the ideology republican, militant, socialist, revolutionary? Pascal Ory, who has thoroughly studied this aspect of the politics of the Popular Front, speaks rather of *unanimisme*. It is in fact noteworthy that most organizations created at the time—studios, amateur troupes, "agit-prop" companies—were backward in comparison to a company like the *Groupe Octobre* of Blin and Itkine which, having carried on pioneering activity for three or four years under the aegis of revolutionary socialism, was then in a state of decline. The cinema which flourished at the time, from *La Belle Equipe* of Duvivier to *La Marseillaise* of Jean Renoir, reflected a rather mildly committed *ouvrièrisme* or traditional Jacobinism; the government's filmmaker was not Vigo but Carné. Do not break the windows!

What is striking in this cultural policy, which multiplied apparently minor but interesting innovations—like Georges Monnet's "bibliobuses" in the Soissons region, popular choruses and orchestras which sprang up almost everywhere, and organizations for popular art and traditions—is first of all that it provoked few conflicts between "avant-garde" culture and "popular" culture. Everything came under the magic word "popularization." At the same time, there was a sudden development in France toward an "associative" tendency (not characteristically French); Blum, who was so open to Anglo-Saxon civilization, supported this very strongly. The fact that the innumerable associations which sprang up during the summer of 1936 weathered the following seasons rather badly is no criticism of the Popular Front, which gave them constant support. It is only a sign that the French form associations less readily than the Swiss, the Americans, or the Vietnamese.

The ambiguities were obvious, as in every populist undertaking. Pascal Ory is not wrong in finding in that ambiguity the reason why Vichy could co-opt many of the "groups" whose working-class boy-scoutism was barely tinted red. Vichy, and later the Fifth Republic.

But if there was, strictly speaking, no cultural ideology of the Popular Front (and is that so deplorable?), there was a great communal hope that, in the words of Jean Cassou, one of the movement's inventors, "all of life might be common property."

A Day in the Life of the Head
of a Popular Government

Government is also an art of living and often, particularly in France, of living to old age. Blum, coming to power at the age of sixty-four, had

understood that the task he was entrusted with was not one of management, but of decision and arbitration, that it involved above all the
capacity for reflection and the preservation of a certain serenity. Thus
he decided to spend a good deal of time at home, in his apartment at 25,
quai Bourbon where, reading and receiving many visits, he prepared
for the choices he would have to make at the hôtel Matignon.

Let us quote André Blumel:

> He was a man who had the habit of working very quickly and of
> working alone. He was capable of asking for many opinions, a
> great deal of advice, but then he decided by himself. In the course
> of the 1936–37 government, Jules Moch and I were happy to spare
> him a certain number of superfluous visits, so that he stayed home
> in the morning, wearing a bathrobe and slippers, to meditate and
> reflect. A room had been set up for him in the hôtel Matignon
> where he spoke over the phone only with me, so that he would not
> be disturbed.

In May, he had of course given up directing *Le Populaire:* its general
policy was determined by Bracke and day-to-day operations carried on
by Oreste Rosenfeld. But he followed its progress with passionate
concern, often calling both men to visit him. He also received the two
leaders of the party, Paul Faure (who had become a Minister of State
but remained above all the Secretary-General), and his assistant,
Séverac, three times a week.

Blum liked to get up late. Daniel Guérin has provided a picturesque
description, without excessive sarcasm, of the moments preceding the
petit lever of the socialist leader. But we should note that the description dates from a few years before his accession to power and was no
longer true for the period we are discussing:

> That morning, to his visitor's surprise, he was still in bed. Pil-
> lows gave him a sitting position. Around him on the sheets were
> newspapers and memoranda. He was wearing mauve-colored pa-
> jamas flecked with gold. His welcome was warm, almost expan-
> sive. His good will shone through his glasses, a familiar and yet
> distant good will—aristocratic. The charmer immediately put the
> visitor at ease, treating him like an old acquaintance.

From June 1936 on, however, Blum got up almost every day around
eight o'clock. In his study or in his salon whose windows opened to the
Seine ("which," he said, "at that point barely resembles a tributary")
he studied dossiers and received visitors. Thus, from early August on,
he began almost every morning by seeing the man who was charged
with "getting around non-intervention" in Spain in such a way that the
Republic might receive as much aid as possible: Gaston Cusin, a close
collaborator of Vincent Auriol. They spent hours together inventing

the subtlest tricks. From time to time the tall gentleman in a bathrobe would smile and sigh: "The things you make me do! Aren't we going too far, my dear Cusin?" That hour was never wasted, in any case not for the Spanish Republic.[126]

Every Wednesday at 9 o'clock, the Communist leaders—almost always Thorez and Duclos, but sometimes also Cachin and Gitton, never Marty—rang his bell. Jacques Duclos, in his *Mémoires*,[127] presents a good description of these marginal cabinet councils of a sub-government of the left:

> An old house on the bank of the Seine, a beautiful carriage gate which bore nobly and proudly the mark of past centuries, a paved entryway giving on an inner courtyard and an old and beautiful staircase with a handsome bannister led to the apartment. Spacious rooms with very high ceilings. This was the framework of our meetings, made up of both refinement and simplicity. In the study where we were usually received, there was a beautiful library and a very beautiful edition of the works of Stendhal, who was one of Léon Blum's favorite authors—which was by the way a point of agreement between us. Léon Blum was a man of extreme courtesy, even a little mannered, and before we touched on serious questions, we always had a general conversation which he was very adept at carrying on. I had noticed that when he was expecting a rather difficult discussion, because of events, he tried to relax the atmosphere a bit by revealing to us certain "secrets" of ministerial deliberations, secrets which were known by many. But the direction was always the same: he informed us of the difficulties he was confronting, and we often took off from there.

Toward noon Blum went to the hôtel Matignon, where he heard a brief report on the situation from André Blumel or Jules Moch, then usually had lunch with his colleagues, when he was not the host for a large association (the American Club in June, for example) or for some very close friends. The afternoon was devoted partly to Matignon, partly to the Chamber or the Senate, where he was very assiduous, supporting bills that were difficult to pass, especially in the Senate, alongside his colleagues, not all of whom had the oratorical talent of Cot or Monnet. One has to read the texts of Blum's interventions during the summer of 1936 in order to appreciate his great talent as a debater. On August 6, for example, there was this typical skirmish, after a series of philippics from speakers of the right about some factory occupations which were continuing:

> THE PREMIER: The opposition speakers have questioned us about a crisis which is over. You criticize us for a policy which has succeeded.
> M. FERNAND WIEDEMANN-GOIRAN: It has collapsed.
> M. GEORGES ROULLEAUX-DEGAGES: As in Spain!

M. CAMILLE BLAISOT: Such a statement from a government which gives in to force is abominable! Never has a more serious statement been made!

THE PRESIDENT: If you please, gentlemen, listen to the Premier.

THE PREMIER: It is a result about which Parliament, the majority, and the government have the right to be proud . . . because they reached the end of a crisis like this one through conciliation and persuasion.

In reality, it is the success which you are unable to accept. You hoped for continuing disorder. You hoped that disorder would oblige us to use force. In this way, you wanted to damage the government and dissolve the majority . . .

M. ANDRE DAHER: All the rostrum needs now is a red flag!

THE PRESIDENT: Gentlemen, please do not interrupt. No debate is possible if you do not listen to the premier in silence.

THE PREMIER: I ask you on the contrary to have the same feeling that we must all have today, that is, satisfaction that such a serious crisis . . .

M. FERNAND WIEDEMANN-GOIRAN: Which you provoked.

THE PREMIER: . . . could be resolved without irreparable accidents occurring between citizens of the same country.

The best description of the Premier confronting the Chamber in the summer of 1936 is probably the one provided by his opponent Paul Reynaud:

> When I looked at Léon Blum on the cabinet bench, with his languid, elegant air, the white patch of his handkerchief extending from his pocket, his eyes shining through his glasses, his hand placed directly on his long, drooping mustache, tense, ready to reply, I thought: this thoroughbred man is in his rightful place. But my friendship for him made me find his fate unjust when, speaking in a staccato manner from the rostrum which his tall body dominated, he presented his party's arguments. This is why each great debate seemed to me to be like a station of the cross for Léon Blum. And I sometimes said to myself: "He does not deserve that."[128]

At the hôtel Matignon, Blum's office door gave onto the garden. To the right of his office was the cabinet meeting room, decorated with tapestries depicting the adventures of Don Quixote. To the left was André Blumel's office, followed by those of his cabinet colleagues. Jules Moch and the General Secretariat were established on the second floor, along with the two Under-Secretaries of State and their special assistants. They shared the rooms of the Premier's apartment, since Blum continued to live, as we have said, on the quai Bourbon. There was also an apartment for the Premier's assistant, which Blumel moved into in order to take care of night duty and to filter messages, transmitting to Blum only those of the greatest urgency.

"The space is so crowded because of the new organization of the premiership," wrote Jules Moch, "that I have to put writing desks in the corridors and in the luxurious marble bathrooms: we transformed bathtubs into work tables by covering them with boards."

Every evening which the premier did not have to devote to "appearances," he spent with a few colleagues on the quai Bourbon. Around the dinner table presided over by Thérèse Blum were almost always to be found Renée and Robert Blum, discreetly loyal and active; and André Blumel and Oreste Rosenfeld.[129]

Little by little, the relative serenity of mornings and evenings on the quai Bourbon became insufficient compensation for the tension of negotiations, challenges, and decisions. Gradually, Blum's "distance" from events decreased. Gradually, he was more brutally immersed in the whirl of events. Neither Blumel's concern, nor Moch's diligence, nor Dormoy's ingenuity could protect him any longer. Crises proliferated, and he felt their full force directly. From early 1937 on, Blum was a tired and harassed man warned by some of his doctors to avoid any irregularity in diet or hygiene. When he finally gave up power, it was with a kind of physical relief.

Foreign Horizons

Blum took office with the intention of personally assuming responsibility for the conduct of French diplomacy. His tendency to see things in the most open-minded way, his internationalist convictions, and the anxiety that the Axis powers had created in the world, all led him to invest an enormous portion of his talent and concern in international affairs. This is why, although he did not deliberately choose to do so, he easily made do with a minor figure who was amiable and self-effacing, Yvon Delbos, as Minister of Foreign Affairs, rather than a "star" like Herriot or Paul-Boncour.

For several weeks, the new Premier had hardly been able to deal with questions of foreign affairs, even though his first diplomatic voyage, to Geneva, took place at the end of June. The social crisis at first dominated the entire horizon. But as soon as he was able to develop an understanding of the situation of France in the world—every morning he read the most important diplomatic dispatches—he had to recognize that, like the French economy in the spring of 1936, it was "a landscape of rubble" (Pierre Renouvin).

Four basic conditions determined that situation.

First, the apparently irresistible rise of the Axis powers, Nazi Germany and Fascist Italy. Germany had been able to reoccupy the left bank of the Rhine on March 7, 1936 without provoking the slightest serious reaction from France, whose general staff met the next day and lamentably concluded that the country was isolated and impotent.[130] Italy had made it known in Geneva on May 10 that Abyssinia was definitely annexed and that the ruler of Rome should henceforth be considered "Emperor of Ethiopia." This was a double challenge to treaties and to collective security, accompanied by intense and unconcealed rearmament.

A second basic condition was the weakening of alliances among the democracies, not only because Laval had created antagonism between Paris and London, but also because France's inaction in the face of Hitler's challenge on March 7, 1936—partially due to British reserve— had unfavorably impressed its allies in Brussels and Warsaw, and, from Prague to Bucharest and Belgrade, the members of the "Petite Entente." Thus each country was tempted to find, through bilateral negotiations or a resort to neutrality, assurances against the Axis powers (judged by some to be less threatening than the USSR), assurances which French protection seemed no longer capable of providing, and which England seemed less and less inclined to grant.

Blum himself very powerfully summed up the development of these relations. Recounting a visit to Prague in 1937, in the course of which he had been able to establish simultaneous contact with all the representatives of the Petite Entente, he reported the objection that was made to his encouragements of concerted resistance:

> "Now that Germany has again occupied the Rhineland, if we were threatened, would you come to our aid?" Relations remained good. They asked us for arms. They also asked us for money, of course. We did what we could, but something had been broken: a principle, a certain confidence. The direct contact which had existed before March 7 existed no longer.
>
> A nation like Poland which, to be sure, had gotten dangerously close to Germany before 1934, but which immediately after March 7 had spontaneously told us: "If you enter the Rhineland, we will enter Silesia," a nation like Poland itself no longer provided security.[131]

A third reality was the atmosphere of tragic crisis in which the USSR seemed to be enclosed. Since the assassination of Kirov, trials and purges had proliferated even in the army, and the country had drawn around itself a curtain of systematic suspicion which condemned the only power which was openly opposed to fascism to a kind of diplomatic freeze, to isolation and blacklisting. But where else could a counterweight be found against the states inevitably destined to trouble the peace because of their aggressive ideology and their economic instability?

The fourth and final imperative, but not the least, was the sad state of the French economy and currency, which forced the country to resort to international assistance, which in turn involved constraints. The only source of this assistance seemed to be the Anglo-Saxon powers. Hence the orientation, or rather the irresistible "magnetization" which constantly reappeared in the apparent "choices" of Blum, Auriol, and the Foreign Ministry.

Before analyzing "Léon Blum's diplomacy"—a perhaps unwarranted expression, but one which reminds us that this man, who was so eager to seek advice and so respectful of the competence of others, finally made his decisions alone and tenaciously stuck to them—it is important to present those who worked with him to put it into practice.

In the first rank, and much more than the minister in charge, was a man who impressed Blum not only by his competence, but also by his poetic genius. (Might one suggest that had this man not been the great poet of *Anabase,* Blum would not have allowed French diplomacy to be confined within the narrow limits of the alliance with England?) This man, who was named Alexis Léger, had already become famous under his literary pseudonyms: first Saint-Léger Léger, then Saint-John Perse.

Alexis Léger, a disciple of Aristide Briand and of Blum's friend Philippe Berthelot, had been Secretary-General of the Quai d'Orsay since 1933. With the collaboration of some talented professional diplomats (Paul Bargeton, René Massigli, Robert Coulondre, René de Saint-Quentin, Roland de Margerie), he had made it a temple of Anglophilia, not without reason, and thereby anticipating Blum's wishes. Anglophilia is perhaps not the best word, because for Léger the ruling idea was not that England should be considered a trusted friend, but on the contrary, that there was a risk it would fall into a general compromise with Hitler. This preoccupation was justified by the successes won by the Nazi ambassador in London, von Ribbentrop, a confidant of Hitler, who had always dreamt (as *Mein Kampf* indicates) of this reversal of alliances.

It is a fact that in certain serious circumstances—from Spain to Munich—this group's obsession with remaining wedded to the British position weighed heavily on French decisions. Decisions which, even considering the basic community of views with English democracy in the face of the dictatorships, should have paid more attention to the responsibilities and particularities of France, especially in the Mediterranean.

Yvon Delbos was not a man to oppose such views. A convinced anti-Fascist—he had firmly opposed Laval's pro-Italian policy, harbored an unfailing animosity toward Mussolini, and had returned from a journey to the USSR in 1932 with the certainty that an alliance between Paris and Moscow was necessary—he had in addition as head of his cabinet a pacifist democrat with socialist leanings, Henri Laugier, who influenced him very strongly in this direction.

In the play of forces that influenced Blum's diplomatic conduct we must also include the two successive American ambassadors, Jesse Strauss and, beginning in September 1936, William Bullitt, who was not only Blum's neighbor but his friend, as he was a friend of Franklin Roosevelt. (In this connection, it is important to point out how the ascendancy the American president and his envoys held over Blum has been neglected by most historians, who attribute slight importance to American intrusions during this period.)

Blum placed enormous value on personal relations. No one can measure the influence on the course of events of his friendship for Anthony Eden, whom he met just before assuming office. Let us quote the memoirs of the former Secretary of the Foreign Office:

> . . . I stopped in Paris for my first informal conversation with M. Blum on May 15th. This I enjoyed, reflecting ruefully how much it must have advantaged our two countries if he had been our partner in the last two years of missed opportunities. . . .[132]
>
> In a reference to the relations of Signor Mussolini and Herr Hitler, Blum expressed his conviction that it would not be possible to keep the two dictators apart. Sooner or later their policies would converge. He was afraid that British public opinion was at the moment making the same mistake about Hitler as French public opinion had made about Italy; the latter had attempted to secure Mussolini's support against Hitler, and now it looked as though we were attempting to secure Hitler's support against Mussolini. I assured Blum that no such intention was in our mind.[133]

Intentions or ulterior motives? Serious operations had been set in motion, and the "complicity" between the two men and the two powers—confronting the two others—were well-established. It was an essential component of the period.

To these basic facts of the situation, and to the influences that affected Blum, we have to add an intervention which helped give direction to his diplomacy. On May 15, 1936, preparing to take charge of the government and anxious to learn about the economic situation, Blum was visited by one of the best economic experts of the period, Emmanuel Monick, who was then a financial attaché in London. To the questions the socialist leader asked him about the state of the currency and the possibility of a devaluation, this bold expert gave an answer which was to have significant consequences.

There are two possibilities, Monick argued. Either you maintain the currency at any price, you establish exchange controls, you impose a strictly planned economy, you place France on an autarkic footing—and then you risk slipping toward the totalitarianism you are fighting against. Or else you open the borders, you maintain a system of free exchange, depending then on London and Washington to carry out a currency adjustment simultaneously with a coalition of democratic governments. The financial expert of course recommended adoption of the second strategy.

Blum was so impressed by this consultation (known from Monick's memoirs)[134] that he immediately sent his visitor on a "secret" mission to Washington and then to London. Emmanuel Monick returned with encouragements from the two governments—on the condition that a concerted alignment of currencies open the way to the harmonization of economic policies.[135]

Many other factors influenced the choice Blum made, as early as June 1936, of an Atlantic alliance before the fact. But this kind of advice, addressed to a man whose natural tendencies inclined him toward the Anglo-Saxon democracies, who passionately admired the New Deal and Roosevelt himself, and who was moreover rather ill-informed about international financial affairs, can be considered significant.

A final remark. Not only Blum, but several of his interlocutors of the time, reasserted: diplomacy cannot in any way be a reflection of ideological debate. After a conversation with the new head of government on June 10, 1936, General Gamelin, the army Chief of Staff, wrote that "Blum is capable of putting the permanent interests of France above party conflict, and consequently no ideological mystique will interfere with his foreign policy decisions."[136] The judgment has to be qualified a little: it was valid for relations with the Third Reich and the USSR, but not for those with London, which were marked by veritable Anglomania, nor for those with Rome, which were marred by a justified but nevertheless constraining bias against Mussolini.

The treatment of the Spanish problem as a whole will be studied in the next chapter. Whatever twists and turns it may have taken— essential in moral terms, in the consciences of the Popular Front leaders and for their relations with one another, and especially in the conscience of Blum himself—the basic diplomatic options of the June 1936 government did not depend on those vicissitudes. Blum had made beforehand the decisive choice in favor of alliance with England, for the camp of liberalism and classic democracy. In the face of the dictators, the choice is easily understandable, although perhaps it enclosed France too rigidly within the three circles of the League of Nations, the Entente Cordiale, and the Petite Entente, neglecting *a priori* any serious sounding out of Rome with a view to dissociating it from the Axis. But, in any case, what Blum had seen more clearly than anyone else was that the essential line of demarcation passed between totalitarianism and freedom.

As soon as Blum was free to deal with foreign affairs, he left for Geneva in order to define, in the framework of the League of Nations and before the world, the principles of action of his diplomacy. He had already presented its broad outlines to the Chamber on June 23, placing the accent much more on collective security than on disarmament (in this respect the head of government already distinguished himself from the head of the party). It is also noteworthy that he named the countries on whose help he counted to preserve peace in this order: Great Britain, the United States, and the USSR. The language in which he addressed Germany was firm but open to dialogue.

His speech in Geneva on July 1 was certainly not the one he had long dreamed of delivering in a place which was for him sacred and devoted to peace. Nothing could be less soothing, less "pacifist," than the remarks he seemed to hurl in Hitler's face: they brought him torrents of abuse from the right-wing Parisian press which had just encouraged Mussolini's war in Africa but could not tolerate considering armed resistance to fascism:

> Among the most resolutely peaceful peoples warlike traditions, the "warrior virtues" are not buried at any great depth! It would not take too many ordeals to bring them back to the surface. One has the right to speak as I do when one has devoted one's life to the cause of peace. . . .
>
> International agreements are defied or stymied if the powers who have signed them are not determined to go to the very end. Going to the very end means accepting the risk of going as far as war. We must therefore accept the possibility of war in order to preserve peace. The pact imposes this choice on all the powers, without distinction. Our development plans limit it to those which are closest—geographically or politically—to the power which is attacked. But, more or less generalized, the possibility exists, and the risk remains. I declare without hesitation that in the present state of the world that risk must be considered with full awareness and with complete courage.

Blum attempted from that point on to win over his favored allies, the British, to this position of "resistance," while at the same time trying to revive the spirit of Locarno, which would consist of linking Berlin and Rome to Paris and London by a new nonaggression pact. Immediately after his assumption of office, the head of the French government proposed to his British counterpart, the very conservative Stanley Baldwin, that they meet in Boulogne. The British preferred to wait a bit and receive the new French leaders in London on July 23. In the meantime the Spanish storm had broken, and it created serious dissensions between the conservatives of London and the socialists of Paris.

But Anthony Eden, who was so equivocal about Spain, reiterated without ambiguity, on the evening of the July 23 conversations with Blum and Delbos and the Belgian ministers van Zeeland and P. H. Spaak, that in case of aggression, Great Britain "would come to the aid of France and Belgium." Throughout the following months, the British leaders, who had overcome some of their prejudices against the Popular Front, continued to reiterate the closeness and solidity of the commitments that tied them to France—if not to the French system of Eastern alliances—and the excellence of the relations inspired by the spirit of the Entente Cordiale, which had been further strengthened by the proclamation of the Berlin-Rome Axis on November 1, 1936, but somewhat weakened by Belgium's return to neutrality.

That Blum wished to extend the Entente Cordiale to the United States and oppose an "Atlantic" triangle to the extension of the Fascist Axis to Madrid and Tokyo is obvious. The dispatch of a political man of high caliber to the Washington embassy (Georges Bonnet, future head of the Foreign Service), the naming of a personal friend of Roosevelt's, William Bullitt, as ambassador to Paris, Washington's warm welcome of special envoys like Emmanuel Monick—everything seemed to work toward the establishment of special ties between the United States of the New Deal and the France of the Popular Front—including their convergent attitudes toward Spain.

It is difficult to understand why these inclinations did not become realities. In the serious and detailed book by the American scholar J. E. Dreifort on Delbos and the foreign policy of the Popular Front,[137] Franklin D. Roosevelt is mentioned only twice in three hundred pages, and with reference to periods (1937–38) when Blum was no longer at the head of the government.

The excellent biography of Blum by Joel Colton is less reticent on this point. It quotes in particular a picturesque letter from Bullitt to Roosevelt on November 8, 1936, concerning the reelection of the American president:

> Blum came personally to express his congratulations. . . . He entered the front door, flung his broad-brimmed black hat to the butler, his coat to the footman, leaped the three steps to the point where I was standing, seized me and kissed me violently! . . . I listened without batting an eye to as genuine an outpouring of enthusiasm as I have ever heard. . . . Blum himself said to me that he felt his position had been greatly strengthened, because he is attempting in his way to do what you have done in America.[138]

Joel Colton also provides an excerpt from the diaries of Henry Morgenthau, the Treasury Secretary of the New Deal, according to which Roosevelt considered it "very important that Blum remain in power." Morgenthau said he agreed with this wish, estimating that Blum was "the only French leader really determined to carry out social reforms and to fight against fascism." But he was opposed to granting financial aid to France, "which had not repaid its war debts," even in the form of an advance from the American Stabilization Fund, "which would be throwing money in the Atlantic Ocean, given the proportions its war budget has assumed."[139]

It is safe to say that Roosevelt and Morgenthau did not spend a long time regretting that they had not supported the rearmament effort of the Popular Front. But to see Blum condemned by his friends for excessive rearmament seems a bitter irony of history.

Relations between Léon Blum and Joseph Stalin hardly threatened to become idyllic. But the head of the Popular Front government and his Minister of Foreign Affairs spent several months attempting to give life to the pact signed in Moscow in May 1935 by Pierre Laval, which had then been sabotaged by him and his successor at the Quai d'Orsay, Pierre-Etienne Flandin. Blum maintained very regular contacts with the Soviet Ambassador Potemkin who, in parallel with his colleague Maisky in London, fervently played the card of alliance with the democracies, which Stalin had authorized his Foreign Minister Litvinov to pursue for a time. Blum attempted on several occasions to add military agreements to the 1935 pact in the form of technical covenants, which the USSR wanted. He thought he could thereby return, in order to contain Hitler, to the Triple Entente of 1914 between England, France, and Russia.[140]

But he came up against the skepticism of the general staff, which had sent him a memorandum very critical of the USSR as early as June 24, 1936, and particularly against that of the majority of Radical notables, who argued against these attempts both because of the refusal of the Polish and Rumanian governments to allow Soviet troops to pass through their territories (which greatly reduced the scope of the Eastern alliance), and because of the information contained in the report by General Schweisguth, deputy chief of the army general staff. After watching the Red Army maneuvers in September 1936, this officer asserted that it was not capable of confronting the best European armies. This contradicted an earlier report by General Loiseau, which was more optimistic and which Blum trusted.[141] One day at a meeting of the cabinet, when Blum argued for an attempt to establish closer relations with the USSR, President Lebrun said: "But really, haven't you read the Schweisguth report?"

But there was also a faction in the government which wanted to give priority to the alliance with Russia. Its spokesman was Pierre Cot, according to whom it was better to "begin the war with Russia as an ally and England neutral than with England as an ally and Russia neutral." The former Minister of Aviation provides some very interesting information on the subject:

> Léon Blum intended to turn toward Moscow after stopping off in London. The idea was a good one. But its realization required time

which was not granted to the Popular Front. I was familiar enough
with Léon Blum's thinking to be able to affirm that if the Popular
Front had not been broken in 1938, instead of signing the Munich
agreements, [he] would have signed an agreement with Soviet Russia and Czechoslovakia.[142]

Encouraged by men like Pierre Cot, Franco-Soviet military bargaining was in any case carried quite far. It was also accompanied by
strange initiatives. One of them, which offers a curious light on the
mentality of certain industrialists, was reported by Blum before his
judges in Riom:

> Russia had placed a certain number of orders in France, notably
> orders for large artillery to arm battleships which were being built
> in the Black Sea and to which Stalin attached particular impor-
> tance. These orders for large artillery were supposed to be filled by
> Le Creusot, and I was periodically visited by the Soviet Ambassa-
> dor Potemkin, who asked me to put pressure on the chief of artil-
> lery or on Le Creusot so that the orders would be filled more
> completely and quickly.
> Now, one of the representatives of the arms industries, which
> had been nationalized in June 1936, M. de Saint-Sauveur who, I
> think, was particularly involved in relations with the USSR, had
> indicated to Potemkin that if it could be arranged with our govern-
> ment that the nationalization of Le Creusot were to go no further,
> the Soviet orders would be filled with more speed and with good
> grace. Potemkin came to see me one day to report his conversa-
> tion, leaving it to me to draw the appropriate conclusions!

But the Soviets were not satisfied with buying arms from France.
They insisted that the 1935 pact take on a form closer to that of an
alliance. This is what Ambassador Potemkin seems to have said to
Léon Blum on February 17, 1937;[143] and the Foreign Minister said the
same to Yvon Delbos the following May. It was a wasted effort.
Caught between his Anglophilia, his desire for a relaxation of tension
with Berlin, the irritation he felt at the Communist campaigns against
him, and the skepticism of the general staff about the combat worth-
iness of the Red Army, the head of the Popular Front government
resisted these approaches.

Early in the summer of 1936, a new ambassador, one of the best
professionals of the Quai d'Orsay, Robert Coulondre, was sent to Moscow. As he was about to leave for his post, he visited his Minister,
Delbos, the Chief of the General Staff, Gamelin, and the head of government, Blum, to learn the intentions of those who were sending him
to the USSR. What did they expect from his mission? Delbos was
rather negative: according to him, it was important above all to warn
the Soviets that the schemes of the PCF in France risked damaging
relations between the two countries. For Gamelin, the ambassador's

mission consisted of collecting as much information as possible on the strength of the Red Army. Only Blum spoke of the pact in a positive way; he urged the ambassador "to guarantee to the Soviet government the will of the French government to assure its faithful application." Upon his arrival in Moscow, Coulondre said he was impressed by the Soviet colossus, and to his Minister, who urged him to be prudent, he sent this judicious warning: ". . . we have to ask not to what extent the USSR will be with us, but with whom it will be." In April 1937, when the ambassador returned to Paris and suggested that Stalin should be taken at his word in his apparent desire to resume negotiations, Blum expressed his regrets in being blocked from that path by the "reticence" of the general staff. Delbos said approximately the same thing to his Soviet counterpart Litvinov, in May 1937.

Moreover, the Premier had received warnings from Eduard Benes, his Czech colleague (the warning came through Robert Blum, who was visiting Prague in late December 1936) that the chief of the Red Army was in contact with Berlin. Since then it has been argued that this was a deceptive maneuver by the Nazis who, through multiple channels, thereby persuaded Stalin to have Marshall Tukhatchevsky, his best strategist, shot. According to another argument, it was Stalin himself who, in order to get rid of the marshall, forged the dossier of his contacts with Berlin. A diabolical operation in any case that led General Gamelin to say: "How can you expect us to count on an army which executes its leaders?"

If we consider as well the disagreements between Moscow and Paris provoked by the Spanish conflict, there is no reason to be surprised by the stagnation and ultimate failure of Blum's inclinations toward a closer alliance with the Soviets, inclinations that were all the more hesitant because of London's opposition. It is clear that the leader of the Popular Front had long before decided to make the alliance with London the cornerstone of his diplomacy and to give it priority over the alliance with Moscow.

He did not make this choice solely for reasons of personal inclination, but also because it left him freer to take steps toward a relaxation of tension with the Third Reich. There is no doubt that the conclusion of a Franco-Russian military alliance as close as the one of 1911–12 would have pushed Hitler and his allies to extremes. The objection seems pitiful forty years later, but it was not in 1936.

We have seen how Blum, who had vigorously denounced Nazism as leader of the SFIO, was able as leader of the government to alternate warnings and conciliatory gestures in his approach to the Third Reich. In a foreign policy speech on June 23, he declared that he did not want to "question the word of Hitler, a former soldier who went through the misery of the trenches for four years." The Nazi leaders who, curiously enough, had suppressed polemics on their side—one of their organs,

Die Angriff, was called to order for having written about Blum that " in the Middle Ages, the city of Narbonne had been wise enough to expel its Jews"[144]—seized the opportunity they had been offered.

On August 28, Blum received Doctor Schacht, Economics Minister of the Reich and Director of the Reichsbank, who had been sent to Paris to indicate that Hitler had offers to make. It was a remarkable conversation. "I am a Marxist and a Jew," the Premier declared at the outset, "but we can arrive at nothing if we set up ideologies as insurmountable barriers." Nevertheless, Blum explained, it is necessary that Hitler agree to "liberate France from the fear of the German menace." Only in that case would it be possible to move toward an agreement, but not a bilateral one: France intended to remain faithful to its alliances and its commitments. Therefore, they could only discuss a general agreement. Not even ruling out consideration of German colonial claims in Africa, the head of the French government concluded: "I am ready to begin the conversation immediately."[145]

What has been called the policy of "buying peace" consisted in short, of offering economic advantages to the wolves. Would loans, technical missions, economic advantages, and the consolidation of their currencies be enough to calm them, if not to make them silent? In London, men like Chamberlain and Henderson thought so, and they seem to have persuaded Anthony Eden on the one hand and Emmanuel Monick on the other. But the latter two refused to carry the argument as far as Chamberlain, who thought it advisable to feed the wolves not only with loans and butter, but also with the land and the lives of the Czechs.

During the 1965 conference, André Blumel, Blum's closest collaborator, pointed out that negotiations were undertaken "much more seriously than has been said."[146] They came up against two major obstacles. Hitler, for his part, refused to "globalize" negotiations. Since the Nazi leader, as we now know, had the preliminary objective only of dissolving alliances and isolating his opponents, he refused to move beyond the bilateral framework. On the British side—since one cannot consider a French move at the time without simultaneously examining the reactions it provoked in London, source of encouragement or veto—there was a categorical refusal to open the colonial question. Eden dryly informed Blum of the fact a few days later.

Even though the principal territory in question was the Cameroons, where British interests were much less significant than those of the French, the Foreign Office clearly saw that entering on that path would encourage Hitler to go very far. Thus Blum's goodwill (he seemed to have envisaged an African bargain along the lines of the one between Caillaux and Wilhelm II in 1911) came up against the combined refusal of Berlin and London.

Although they refused to consider a formula that challenged the

Empire, the English held to their plan of "buying peace." They further developed the idea in November, and Blum, after studying a report on the subject prepared by Emmanuel Monick (who continued to play the role of prime mover of the strategy in London), delivered an important foreign policy speech on January 24 in Lyon which was based on what he called "the necessary connection of economic cooperation with political settlement and the organization of peace." Although the suggestion was made in the manner that was least likely to offend German sensibilities, the Lyon speech was badly received in Berlin. Meeting the French ambassador François-Poncet the next day, Goebbels declared that he had "found nothing new" in Blum's remarks. In fact, the Nazis thenceforth refused to speak in the global framework of collective security within which the leader of the Popular Front government always situated proposed negotiations.

Another visit by Dr. Schacht to Paris in March 1937 produced no results, even though Blum once again received him. This time the head of the French government pointed out that "one country could not provide economic aid to another in which it could see a possible aggressor." The German press did not even mention this meeting. Moreover, the celebrated miracle doctor of the German economy, whom Hitler criticized for having "rushed into territory that had not been sufficiently explored,"[147] was about to be disgraced. He made another trip to Paris in May, formulating conditions which were equivalent to a notice of breaking off negotiations: the Third Reich demanded the restitution of Eupen and Malmédy and a reexamination by France of the Danzig question. This time, Blum refused to receive him. The two men did not see each other again until seven years later, in the camp at Dachau.

The care which Blum had taken not to allow his feelings or his ideological convictions to interfere with his relations with the Nazi government is less evident in his relations with Mussolini. Did he really answer the associate who pressed him to speak with the Italian dictator: "I have not forgotten that Mussolini is Matteotti's assassin"?[148] Statements like that do not tell all. But we have already noted Blum's conviction, expressed to Eden as early as May: Mussolini is indissolubly linked to Hitler, and it would be useless to attempt to dissociate them from one another—this was the policy advocated at the time not only by the French right, but also by a very broad faction of the Radical party led by the two "pacifists" of 1917, Malvy, who had met Mussolini shortly before and guaranteed his "Francophile" sentiments, and Caillaux.

This was one of the points on which Blum was most constantly and violently attacked by the press and the legislators of the right. This reluctance to sound out the ulterior motives of the Italians was, moreover, attributable to Delbos as much as to the head of government. But was it necessary, for reasons of age, to recall the ambassador to Rome, Charles de Chambrun, a rather excessive "Mussolinian." This gave the Italian dictator the opportunity to demand that his designated successor, M. de Saint-Quentin, present his credentials to the "King of Italy and Emperor of Ethiopia."

By June 1936 France had given up sanctions against Rome. But this again was to fall in with London, and Mussolini was therefore not at all grateful to the French government. André Blumel has reported[149] that, through the intermediary of a banker named Dreyfus, contacts were made during the summer of 1936 with the Italian Minister of Finance, Count Volpi, after which the Italian press published a commentary attributed to Mussolini himself which offered the hope of reconciliation.

The Italian ambassador Cerutti was received by Blum in late January 1937. Cerutti asserted that Mussolini felt an "insurmountable repulsion" toward Hitler and therefore wished to establish "close" ties with France, on the condition that Paris abandon the Spanish Republic, in which case Mussolini would undertake to make Franco a friend of France! Blum broke off there. The plan to send Pierre-Etienne Flandin as ambassador to Rome went no further. Since November 1, 1936 and the announcement by the *duce* of the Berlin-Rome Axis, Blum's skepticism about the chances of dissociating the two dictators had been confirmed.

The failure of the Popular Front government's attempts to revive a front of resistance to Nazism in Eastern Europe, from Warsaw to Belgrade, Prague, and Bucharest, must be attributed to the collapse of France's "credibility" after the retreat in March 1936 when Hitler reoccupied the Rhineland, and not to the steps that were taken later. Also involved was the distrust which the governments of the various countries felt toward the USSR. Most conversations stumbled over the subject of the refusal of the right of passage for the Red Army through the territory of these states, with the exception of Czechoslovakia: only Prague was willing (then!) to welcome Soviet troops.

The only area in the East where the diplomacy of Blum and Delbos appears to have been too timid was Poland where, taking into account the interest demonstrated in favor of a tightening of bonds with France by Marshall Rydz-Smigly, it would perhaps have been possible to remove the very Germanophile Colonel Beck from the center of power. For the other countries, it is hard to see how the Nazi rise and the hasty reactions of accommodation on the part of the small powers of Eastern Europe could have been changed—until Munich, of course.

In short, in foreign affairs, were it not for Spain, Blum's record would be rather positive: he renewed ties with the British—an urgent task which he accomplished with complete success—and built some bridges toward the Americans. But the alliance he sought with the USSR was blocked by the army's biases, and his attempt at accommodation with the Third Reich came up against Hitler's voracity. In Eastern Europe he paid the price for earlier French renunciations. In this "landscape of rubble" he had rebuilt only one structure, the Entente Cordiale with London. Between 1940 and 1942 it was discovered that there indeed was the best ally, until the appearance of the ally in the East which had chosen for a time to cut its losses.

It is impossible to conclude this brief evocation of Blum as the real head of French diplomacy without recalling that, from the moment he assumed office (as the speech in Geneva on July 1 demonstrates), he lived with the fact that war with the Axis powers seemed inevitable, and inevitable in the short run.

What kind of diplomacy could be carried on by an unarmed country? There are certainly few areas in which the exercise of government imposed a more agonizing reconsideration of the bases of his life as a militant and a theoretician. He had been unable or unwilling, as was Jaurès, the author of *L'Armée nouvelle*, to undertake a systematic reexamination of the fundamentally pacifist strategy of French socialism. We have seen that in his editorials for *Le Populaire*, as well as at the rostrum of the Chamber or in the Committee on Foreign Affairs of the National Assembly, he was still an apologist for disarmament in early 1935, two years after Hitler's rise to power.

However, from that point on, his prejudices began to waver. Hitler's threat to the small powers of Central and Eastern Europe, which relied for protection largely on their French ally, became clearer. The entire future of collective security was at stake. And on March 15, 1935 in the Chamber, when Paul Reynaud, urged on by Colonel de Gaulle, advocated the formation of armored divisions (the only ones able to intervene in the event of Nazi aggression against Austria or Poland), Blum turned to one of his neighbors and murmured, "On that point he's right." What could France do for the general peace if it were sheltered behind its Maginot Line? And how could it come out of its protected field without modern, effective, and rapid weapons at its disposal?

As Premier, finally informed of the demands of defense, Blum was encouraged to meet the singular Colonel de Gaulle through their mutual friend Colonel Mayer. Charles de Gaulle finally entered Blum's office in the hôtel Matignon in September 1936.

The two most antithetical figures in the France of that time were face to face. Let us quote Blum's *Mémoires:*[150]

> He entered with calm, even placid, ease, this man whose height, breadth, and build made him seem gigantic. At the first contact, one felt in him a man "all of a piece." This was true for his physical

form, which each of his movements seemed to shift without friction, as a whole. The same thing held for his moral "behavior." The man who thus presented himself, who looked at me so calmly, who spoke to me in his slow and measured tones, could obviously be possessed at any one time by only one idea, one belief, but then he must give himself to it absolutely, with nothing else entering into the balance. Clemenceau is an extreme type of these temperaments who are prevented by an often contemptuous misanthropy from believing in the useful result of any action, and yet who can be deterred by nothing from acting, because action represents for them a vital necessity.

Charles de Gaulle has given his own version of the conversation in his *Mémoires de guerre*. He presents himself as a sarcastic prophet, a good-natured giant confronting the fragile head of government. In reporting this dialogue he obviously attempts to show that a holder of executive power, in the Third Republic, was neither capable of concentrating on a serious matter, nor aware of his power, nor in a position to make himself obeyed. He no doubt weighted the last sentence he spoke to Blum: "National defense is incumbent on the government," with all the irony a military man could use in recalling that truth to a political leader who was, moreover, a socialist.

Blum did his best to convince Daladier of the validity of Colonel de Gaulle's ideas. But Daladier was deaf to persuasion, and those around him even more so. Everyone was in agreement about building tanks and "scattering" them through the French army. But they did not want to make them autonomous divisions, instruments of an original strategy of counterattack with a wide range of action.

In September 1936—in response to Hitler's decision to increase the length of military service in Germany to two years—a plan for rearmament, known as the plan "of 14 billion," was adopted, exceeding the general staff's requests by 5 billion francs. It was even supplemented by a special appropriation for the navy which carried expenditure beyond 20 billion francs. A third series of military expenditures was passed in December 1936. All these plans taken together, whose implementation was to be spread over four years, were to double the capacities of French forces between 1936 and 1940. Referring to the figures presented to the Riom court by Blum, Daladier, and M. Jacomet (the comptroller general of national defense)—figures which none of the military leaders called to testify against them could refute—if France had pursued the effort undertaken in the summer of 1936, by 1940 it should have had 3000 tanks (800 of them heavy tanks) and 1500 combat planes. For armored weapons, this would have placed it on a level comparable to that of Germany. If aircraft production was less advanced, this was certainly not the responsibility of the minister Pierre Cot or his associate Jean Moulin.[151]

We will return to some of these points in our discussion of the Riom trial, which was in particular the trial of the "military" policy of the Popular Front. What has to be said about Blum's attitude toward these questions during his time as head of government is that he really did bring to birth "another man in a man." Belatedly, perhaps. Perhaps also he should have made use of the authority that this new attitude had gradually won for him in military circles—either through Daladier or directly—to free the army of those who were fundamentally and deliberately hostile to republican government and democracy, like Maxime Weygand.

Unlike most of his successors in power, Blum had become aware of the scandal of colonialism. It was obviously not his responsibility that he worked out no definitive solutions, since his attempts in Syria, Algeria, Indochina, and even in Tunisia were one after the other sabotaged by his successors or by Parliament. But it can be said that he established the bases for a change in relations between France and its colonies.

In this area, Blum's choice of associates was exceptional. For the head of the Colonial Ministry, he had named Marius Moutet who was known especially for having defended Annamite patriots in the courts, thereby earning the gratitude of the future Ho Chi Minh. As Secretary of State for Foreign Affairs, with particular responsibility for relations with the Arab world, he had designated Pierre Viénot, a disciple of Lyautey who had been won over to socialism, and an innovative and courageous diplomat. As Secretary-General of the Select Committee on the Mediterranean which he had just created, he had appointed Charles-André Julien, whose name was a program in itself: decolonization through socialism. Finally, as the Vice-President of the Council, there was Maurice Violette, former Governor-General of Algeria, and the only one who had ever attempted to bring about changes in Algerian conditions.

Under Blum's direct supervision, this group of men with similar convictions—Marius Moutet still resembled a true socialist—took a series of initiatives that were audacious for the time.

The first was the opening of negotiations in Syria (still under French mandate from the League of Nations) conducted by Pierre Viénot, which resulted in the independence treaty of the Syrian Republic in September 1936, a treaty which was unilaterally broken by France two years later, thereby undermining its moral standing in the Levant on the eve of the war.

The second was the attempt to change the status of Algeria according to the "Blum-Violette" plan which opened French citizenship to Algerian veterans. This apparently modest reform broke with the old incompatibility between loyalty to Islam and membership in the French political community, and gave Moslems the right to hold public office, notably that of mayor. This prudent step provoked a hue and cry among those whom Charles-André Julien called *les prépondérants*. Delegations of colonizers laid siege to Blum, who had to confess to Jules Moch that he had never seen a face so filled with rage as that of the notorious Abbé Lambert, deputy from Oran and the most racist of priests. The total obstruction of reform procedures, organized by the Governor-General in Algiers and the Radical party in Paris, prevented the bill from coming before Parliament.

Third, Pierre Viénot and Charles-André Julien attempted to avert the crisis that was brewing between France and the Tunisian nationalists, a crisis which Blum had seen coming for a long time, and which was aggravated by the Italian policy of encouraging the movement hostile to the "protectorate." While Viénot went to Tunisia and created a scandal by declaring that "the interests of colonization are not necessarily those of France," Julien received Bourguiba in Paris. In this case too, powerful local interests destroyed moves toward change. But the seeds of a reformist strategy had been sown, and they bore fruit twenty years later.

The policy of the Popular Front was most unobtrusive in Morocco. Blum had been satisfied with replacing the very authoritarian resident-general Peyrouton by an intelligent disciple of Lyautey, General Noguès. But subtle maneuvering was no longer enough to conceal the vices of the system. In discussing Spain, we will return to the timidity of these policies.

It was perhaps in Indochina that Blum's brief period in power left the largest number of traces, not only because political amnesty allowed the various revolutionary movements—the Communists in particular—to express themselves and to be elected to the mayoralty of Saigon, but also because the creation of an office of Labor Protection led to the end of a number of social abuses. For the leaders of the Vietnamese revolution—who later went through other ordeals, first of all the harsh anti-Communist repression of 1939–1940—the years 1936–1937 represented a kind of historical oasis. (I heard testimony to this effect from Prime Minister Pham Van Dong in Hanoi as recently as May 3, 1976.)

Are these meager results? It did not depend on Blum for them to be more significant. Here again, one may suggest that this man of imagination, this "revolutionary through the law," lacked determination. Couldn't he, for example, impose the Violette plan in Algeria by decree? Yet in dealing with Algeria, it was probably impossible to carry out such a reform without the support of Parliament in a society that was so hermetically colonial and dominated by the Radical party. There are cases in which the necessary revolution is outside the realm of law.

Before coming to the betrayals, the decadence, and the agony of the

Popular Front, we must nevertheless point out that this "experiment," which has so often been called a failure, was the source of an immense harvest, and that the summer of 1936, from the flowering of the cherry trees to the gathering of the grape harvest, was one of the great seasons in the history of modern France. A people on its knees had risen to its feet. A hope had been born which could not be destroyed by the fallout. The summer of 1936, even if it were considered to have ended on July 18, could not be forgotten by the "memory of the people."

THE BLOOD OF SPAIN

For Whom the Bell Tolls

On July 18, 1936, in the middle of the afternoon, Blum was meeting at the hôtel Matignon with a delegation of teachers headed by the union leader André Delmas, when he was brought a dispatch from the French ambassador in Spain, Jean Herbette, which indicated matter-of-factly that a military *pronunciamento* had just broken out in Spanish Morocco. Blum seemed disconcerted by the news, which his visitors had learned of a few hours earlier in *Paris-Midi*. They were surprised that the Premier was so belatedly informed of an event already public knowledge, and they heard him sigh: "If we succeed, no one will be able to say that we have been helped by circumstances!"[152]

Blum was all the more cruelly surprised because that morning he had received a visit from Jimenez de Asua, a socialist lawyer, Vice-President of the Cortès and author of the Spanish Republican Constitution; Asua had assured him that the situation in his country was "excellent." It was a particularly optimistic assessment, coming five days after the assassination of the monarchist leader Calvo Sotelo and at a time when Madrid political circles were humming with rumors of a *coup d'état*. American Ambassador Claude Bowers, more attentive than his English and French colleagues, had passed on those rumors to his government.[153]

The news from Spain struck the Popular Front in a period of great euphoria: the strikes were coming to an end in a climate of victory. A week earlier, Maurice Thorez, drawing up a preliminary assessment of the activity of the Popular Front, had declared his confidence in its future and had spoken of a "government that would last until the next legislative elections." The flight of capital was decreasing. On July 14, the celebration had been triumphant.

The leaders of the Popular Front could not fail to feel concerned by the fate of the *Frente Popular.* The two governments, born within a few weeks of one another, were established on the basis of a coalition between the middle and working classes. Of course, the rise of the Spanish left had been accompanied by violence that had nothing in common with the factory occupations in France. The fragility of democratic traditions, the strength of the anarchist movement, the methods of the reactionary right, and the habits of the army south of the Pyrenees explain these differences. But the common hatred in which the conservatives of both countries held the two coalitions of the left— in which the "republicans" of Madrid held the place of the Radicals in Paris, in their case monopolizing ministerial responsibilities to the exclusion of the socialists and the Communists—would suffice to weld the two governments together and guarantee their solidarity.

When General de Castelnau or Henri de Kerillis denounced the *Frente Crapular,* their target was just as much Paris and Toulouse as Barcelona and Madrid. Every blow struck against popular power in Spain was struck against popular power in France as well. When Blum had heard Jimenez de Asua give him "excellent" news from Spain, he had been reassured about his own future. When he received Herbette's dispatch, it was for him that the bell tolled. He immediately recognized the gravity of the situation.

Did he already anticipate what the fundamental solidarity between the two governments involved in the way of risks and responsibilities that had to be assumed immediately? If he had any doubts on that Saturday the 18th or the following day, he was enlightened on Monday, July 20th, upon arriving at the hôtel Matignon, where André Blumel had received an uncoded telegram the night before signed by the new head of government José Giral—who had just replaced Casarès Quiroga—which ran as follows: "Surprised by dangerous military coup, ask you to arrange with us immediately for supplies of weapons and planes. Fraternally, Giral." The fact that the appeal was uncoded surprised the recipients; it was such a serious matter, and in addition Spain's ambassador in Paris, Cardeñas, was known to be in sympathy with the *pronunciamento.* This indicates how extensive the movement had already become.

Giral's request was not at all exorbitant. Not only had international law authorized aid to a legal government fighting against a rebellion, but in 1935 (through the Laval government, and while Manuel Azaña, who had since become President of the Spanish Republic, was Minister of Defense), Madrid and Paris had signed a trade agreement providing for the delivery of French war matériel to Madrid up to the value of 20 million francs.

Blum immediately called a meeting for the afternoon of the 20th with Edouard Daladier, Minister of Defense; Pierre Cot, Minister of Aviation; Yvon Delbos, Minister of Foreign Affairs; and Vincent Auriol, Minister of Finance; all four were directly involved. Everything seemed clear: they had to apply the 1935 agreement and supply the requested matériel. Equity demanded it, and so did ideological solidarity and the national interest: the arrival in power in Madrid of an extreme right junta, inevitably favorable to the Fascist states, was a risk to be avoided at all costs. Everyone reacted along those lines at first, Blum above all.

But on the 21st, when Ambassador Cardeñas came to fulfill his mission by giving details of the "order" of the government he still pretended to serve—twenty Potez planes, a thousand Lebel rifles, a million cartridges, fifty machine guns, and eight 75-millimeter artillery pieces (enough to withstand a local coup, not to conduct a civil war): he was convinced that he would receive a rejection. The immediate acceptance by his French interlocutors was so surprising to him that he handed in his resignation the next day, but not before he had informed the French Ambassador in London, Corbin, and asked him to warn the British government about these exchanges. His military attaché, Colonel Antonio Barroso, who was also on the side of the rebels, alerted the right-wing Parisian press. Papers from *L'Echo de Paris* to *L'Action française* fully supported the military *coup d'état* from Monday morning on.

On the 22nd, Pierre Cot informed Blum and the new Spanish chargé d'affaires, Fernando de Los Rios, that most of the supplies requested could be delivered quickly, particularly the twenty Potez planes. He also informed the Quai d'Orsay, which in principle was supposed to be consulted, saying that since Blum was in agreement, the deliveries would be carried out regardless. This did not fail to provoke a stir in the Ministry, where the all-powerful pro-British clan was quickly aware of the raised eyebrows of the Foreign Office (obligingly conveyed by Ambassador Charles Corbin), and where the very influential conservatives were alarmed by a position of such warm support for the "reds" of Madrid.[154] Thus the services of the Quai d'Orsay published a very acid note on the 24th: "No sale of arms to a foreign country can be made without the formal agreement of the Department."

On the evening of July 22nd, Yvon Delbos left for London, where Blum joined him late the next morning. It was long believed that the French leaders—whose visit to London had been prepared long in advance to consider a tripartite conference with the Belgians on the Rhineland problem—had gone there on Thursday, July 23rd, at the request of the English, who were worried about their involvement in the Spanish affair. Diplomatic documents as well as Eden's memoirs and Blum's deposition before the Investigative Commission of 1947 disprove that notion. For the most part, Blum's stay in London was officially devoted to tripartite relations between London, Paris, and Brussels, and to monetary questions, and subsidiarily to the Spanish question, which is mentioned in no official document. But we know that it is often the problems unmentioned in communiqués that leave the deepest marks, and this was true for the Spanish tragedy on July 23rd and 24th.

This comes out, among many other things, eleven years later in Blum's narrative of the affair to the Parliamentary Investigative Commission:

> When I arrived in London, I received a visit at the hotel where I was staying from Pertinax,[155] who asked me the question: "Is it true that you are supplying arms to Spain for its defense against Franco's military coup?"
>
> I said: "Yes, that's true."
>
> He answered me:"You know that that is not very much appreciated here."
>
> I said to him: "Possibly. I know nothing about it, but in any case we will do it."
>
> Before I left, in the same room in the same hotel, the man who was then Secretary of State in the Foreign Office, Mr. Anthony Eden, with whom I had very friendly personal relations, came to say good-bye to me and asked me the same question: "Will you give arms to the Spanish Republicans?"
>
> I said: "Yes."
>
> Then he said to me: "It's your business, but be careful, I beg you."

In other circumstances, Blum spoke with more clarity about the attitude of his English hosts on July 23 and 24, 1936. In 1946, he spoke to socialist militants of the "great apprehension" they showed about French aid to Spain: "We heard outcries of fear!" As Joel Colton says: "The British conservatives made it clearly understood to Blum, Delbos, and Léger that they would have a negative attitude and that they had no wish to take part in the factional struggle in Spain." This was expressed still more strongly a week later by Winston Churchill in a letter to the French Ambassador Charles Corbin: "If France sends aircraft to the current government in Madrid and if the Italians and the Germans intervene on the other side, the ruling forces here will agree with Germany and Italy, and they will move away from France." One could not sum up a situation more clearly.

Let us continue with Blum's narrative to the Investigative Commission of 1947:

> I left London by plane on Friday 24 July; on landing at Le Bourget airport, I saw Camille Chautemps on the ground (along with some friends who had come to meet me, like Marx Dormoy).
> I said to him: "Hello, you've come to meet me?"
> "Yes," he said, "because I want to tell you about what is happening in Paris; it's serious."
> "What, what is it now?"
> He said: "Well, while you were in London, perhaps you didn't know that Kerillis had started a tremendous campaign in *L'Echo de Paris,* that all the plans that had been prepared have been made public, that all the arrangements that had been made have been revealed in great detail, and that feeling, particularly in parliamentary circles, is running very high."

Blum then decided to contact the highest authorities of the state. He found the President of the Senate, M. Jeanneny, "in a state of extreme agitation."

> He said to me: "How can you do this? No one here understands it. It is not a question of politics, no one is looking for grounds for opposition, but really, the idea that at this moment you can become involved in an enterprise whose consequences cannot be exactly foreseen, the idea that we might be led into war over the affairs of Spain, while on the 7th of March we hesitated and finally gave in when it was a matter of the military re-occupation of the Rhineland and the direct, immediate security of France, that is something that no one here can understand. And under what conditions are you going to get involved there?"
> I saw my cabinet colleagues. What M. Chautemps and M. Jeanneny had said to me was real. There was great agitation. The principal leaders of the Radical party had made it clear to Delbos how much they feared my initiative. I tried to change this position by a direct conversation with Herriot, but I found him, as far as Spanish affairs were concerned, extremely reserved, and he advised me with all his strength to maintain the same reserve: "I beg you, my dear boy," he said, "I beg you, don't stick your nose into it."

The revelations made by the resigning military attaché of the Spanish embassy, Barroso (who was expelled a few hours later, against the advice of the Quai d'Orsay), had done their work. On July 23, 24, and 25, the right-wing press—and the moderate Radical press—came out with extreme violence against the decisions made on July 21 by Blum and his principal associates.

On the 23rd, the sinister Raymond Cartier launched a cry of alarm in *L'Echo de Paris:* "Would the French Popular Front dare to arm the Spanish Popular Front?" Asserting that any aid to the Spanish government would be "a crime against the nation," and that supplies had already been sent through Bayonne, Cartier continued: "In spite of our artillery and our planes the rebels may be the masters of Spain tomorrow. How will we look then?"

The next day, while Henri de Kerillis proclaimed: "It was Blum himself who gave the order to deliver arms! This government is criminal and abominable!" *L'Action française* took the lead in the campaign: "The French forbid the Blum government to give this aid [to the Spanish government]. Because if the 'insurgents' are victorious we have lost the friendship of Italy, and that's enough. Let us not make Spain into an enemy." Maurras concluded: "Blum is leading us to war!"

But, sadly, it was François Mauriac, in *Le Figaro* on July 25th, who indicated the tone of bourgeois opinion with the greatest violence—and, of course, with the greatest talent and persuasive force:

> The Premier must know that there are a few of us who have been trying to resist the wave of hatred which has swept through the French since the advent of the Popular Front. We have striven for moderation. In an atmosphere of civil war, we have attempted to "preserve reason."
>
> But if it were established that our rulers are actively collaborating in the massacre of the Peninsula, then we would know that France is governed not by statesmen, but by gang leaders, acting under the orders of what we must call the International of Hatred. We would know that the Premier of today has forgotten nothing of the old rancor that possessed Léon Blum the partisan. Such an act would risk pushing the wisest into the party of the violent.
>
> We do not wish France to be responsible for shredding a single drop of Spanish blood. Spain is indivisible in our heart: the Spain of El Cid, of Santa Teresa, of San Juan de la Cruz, of Columbus and Cervantes, El Greco and Goya. I believe that I speak for a vast population belonging to all parties, from Guyenne and Gascony to Béarn and the Basque country, when I cry out to M. Léon Blum, who is burning to intervene, who has perhaps already intervened in this massacre: Take care, we will never forgive you for this crime.

(Mauriac's repentance came, and quickly. But who can estimate the evil he did then among his public by this terrible exhortation?)

On the left, the opposing positions were just as clear. But there was less vehemence in support of the Republic and of providing aid. It was rare for anyone to write in *L'Humanité* with as much restraint as Gabriel Péri on July 27: "We are concerned that France may soon have a border to defend on the Southwest." *Le Populaire* was firmly committed to support of the Republic; even the very pacifist Faure wrote: "Perhaps you imagine that our French defenders of law and order are trembling with indignation. Not at all. It seems the treacherous officers and the generals in revolt have taken on in their eyes the status of servants of order" (July 22, 1936). *Le Peuple,* organ of the CGT, was harsher and perhaps more perceptive: "We had the right to expect from the Popular Front government something other than a series of abdications."

In fact, everything was in the process of shifting to the detriment of the Republic. Fernando de los Rios, an old friend of Blum's, who was interim ambassador in Paris until Alvaro de Albornoz assumed the post a few days later, observed in a message sent on the 25th to José Giral, head of the Madrid government, that the promises to send arms and planes made on July 21st and 22nd were beginning to be questioned.

> This morning,[156] when I arrived at the Ministry of Aviation,[157] everything was going well, but when I got to the Potez offices, the difficulties appeared insurmountable.[158] The press campaign and the reproduction of the letter of resignation of the advisory minister[159] have had such an effect that when Blum went to see the President of the Republic this morning he found him disturbed, in a state of mind that made him say: "Delivering arms to Spain can mean European war and revolution in France." The pressure is enormous. From two-thirty until quarter-to-four I met with the head of government. "My heart is torn," said Blum, who is convinced like one of our own people and who knows the European importance of the struggle being waged in Spain. I have never seen him so deeply moved. "I will maintain my position at any price and with all its risks," he said. "We must help friendly Spain. How? We shall see."

There exist two versions, both Spanish, of the consultations between Paris and Madrid during these crucial days. One is from the same Jimenez de Asua who had so inopportunely reassured Blum on July 18 about the immediate future of the Republic, the other from Juan Negrin who was to be the last head of the republican government.

The problem in both cases is to determine whether the discussions took place on July 25, the day on which the French government decided to withdraw, or on August 7, the day on which the so-called "non-intervention" policy was made public. Neither one specifies the exact date of the conversations. Negrin even confesses that he cannot remember.

In an account delivered at the 1965 conference, Jimenez de Asua, assistant to the new ambassador, Alvaro de Albornoz, and to Fernando de los Rios after the departure of the pro-Franco Cardeñas, told of turning over to the purchasing office of the Ministry of War a check for 11 million francs in payment for the arms Giral had requested from Blum in the telegram of July 19. An emissary was to receive the shipment in Bordeaux: he discovered that nothing was ready. At the same time, Vincent Auriol informed Asua that, "because of the English," the arms that had been purchased could not be delivered.

The next day, while Fernando de los Rios in turn met with a refusal at Potez, Jimenez de Asua met Blum at home at seven in the morning:

Léon Blum in pajamas, his eyes full of tears, told me himself what had happened. The English Prime Minister Baldwin, going over the head of his French colleague, had directly contacted President Lebrun and told him in the most formal terms that he had learned of the sale of arms to the Spanish government and that, in case it led to war with Germany or Italy, Great Britain would remain neutral. The news spread rapidly in political circles. The Radical-Socialists[160] informed the head of government that they would resign if he was determined to deliver arms to Spain.

Premier Blum said to me word for word: "We are bastards if we do not keep our promises. And since we cannot, we socialists will leave the government. The crisis is about to begin."

I immediately returned to the embassy and told the news to Ambassador Alvaro de Albornoz and Fernando de los Rios. Both men were convinced that it was absolutely necessary that the Blum government remain in office, and they thought about ways of avoiding its fall. We would take back the check that had already been submitted in payment to the Ministry of War and tear it up in Blum's presence, as a sign of our giving up the purchase.

I energetically opposed this solution and maintained on the contrary that we had to tell Premier Blum that we would in fact consider that the French socialists had failed in their duty if they accepted what the British Prime Minister imposed on them and still remained in the government. I added that the socialist group in the Chamber of Deputies, which was large, could do more for us in opposition than in the government.

Since we could not come to an agreement, we decided to consult Madrid. The Minister of Foreign Affairs agreed with the Ambassador and de los Rios. Very much against my will, I went to the Ministry of War, took back the check, went to see Léon Blum at home, and tore up the document as a sign of our renunciation. I did not fail to tell the Premier what had happened. With a sad smile, and speaking in a very low voice, he answered me: "I think you were right."

It seems to me that, under pressure from England and the Radical-Socialists, Blum had to accept "non-intervention," which did us so much harm. But I should emphasize that the Premier delayed it as long as he could, in order to ship us beforehand some fighter planes, the Dewoitines.

This important account obviously calls for some comment. First of all, of the direct approach Stanley Baldwin made to Albert Lebrun there is no trace anywhere. Is it not, if not an invention, at least a simplification, a "manner of speaking," the epitome of the obvious pressure London was exerting on Paris? Similarly, the threat of the Radical ministers to resign mentioned here seems a little simplistic. We will of course return to this question. Presented in this way, the affair is excessively schematic.

"We are bastards" is not part of Blum's vocabulary, though the circumstances were serious. As for the hypothesis, so justly formulated by Jimenez de Asua, about the role the socialists could and should have played, and the influence they could have had in opposition, we will return to it with all the care an examination of such an idea deserves. In any case, reading Asua, one discovers that the Spanish leaders were not unanimous—as apologists for Blum have sometimes written—in demanding that he remain in power at any price. One also discovers that the head of government was at heart in favor of moving into opposition.

The scene nevertheless has a ring of deep truth, and perhaps better than any other account epitomizes Blum's attitude during this period. In it is expressed that "guilty conscience" so well analyzed by Colette Audry in *La Politique du juste,* and which led the most honest of public men to assemble after the fact so many disordered and contradictory arguments.

This is Negrin's account:

> It was toward the end of July or the beginning of August. From Madrid at least Giral; Barcia, the Minister of Foreign Affairs; and Prieto[161] spoke. In Paris were Fernando de los Rios, Jimenez de Asua, and, I am almost certain, Albornoz. The conversation turned to non-intervention. The Spanish government was informed of the results of a visit by Léon Blum to London[162] and of the demands of the English government which, in case of a refusal to accept the principle of "non-intervention," would consider itself released from any promise of aid to France, if as it feared, the conflict spread as a result of the aid given to the Spanish Republican government. The French also informed the Spanish government that their resignation would depend on what we considered most useful and most favorable for our struggle and our cause.
>
> At the end of the conversation, everyone at both ends of the wire was in agreement on the choice. Not only those who had spoken, but others who were present: Lluhi, the Minister of Labor, the Minister of Justice whose name I no longer remember, and one or two other government ministers.
>
> Afterward, we spoke a long time about the news we had just received and its possible consequences. Everyone—except for me—was convinced that the war would last for a few days, or at the most for a few weeks. Everyone—myself included—believed that the replacement of the Blum government could be fatal for us, less because of the difficulties of obtaining [arms] which we hoped, after all, could be gotten around with this government with more or less difficulty—which, in fact, happened in part—than because of the consequences which a cooling, or worse a reversal of France's sympathetic attitude toward Spain might have on the international situation, which might, in a short time, produce the strangling of the Republic.
>
> Later, when we learned that the solution had been in accordance with our wishes, we breathed freely and commented on *our narrow escape.*[163]

Jules Moch, referring to the second letter, locates this exchange of views around the 8th of August. His memory is generally good. The (probable) participation of Alvaro de Albornoz in the debate would tend to support that date; he had probably not taken up his post on July 25. But the reference to the London conversations would lead one to situate this communication in July. Thus, describing the crisis of July 24–25, Blum wrote: "It was then that I wanted to leave the government."[164]

What remains is the certainty that in the eyes of most of the Spanish Republicans, uncertain friends in Paris were better than opponents.

A Balance of Power and Two Vetoes

"We shall see," Blum had said as he left de los Rios to take part in the special cabinet meeting called for July 25 by President Lebrun after his conversation with Blum. It was a decisive meeting in which the two camps confronted one another: for the first time the Popular Front cabinet was deeply divided. The leader of the "opposition" to aid for the Spanish Republicans was the Vice-President himself, Camille Chautemps. A few minutes before the meeting began, according to Jean Zay, "Chautemps took the young ministers aside, gave them a lecture, and explained to them that the insurgent officers would soon be victorious and that the present government would collapse like a house of cards."[165]

The debate at this cabinet meeting on July 25, 1936 was thus very spirited. The right-wing press the next day spoke of "stormy arguments." Blum seems to have played less the role of leader of the camp in favor of aid to the Spanish Republic—which he was in fact—than that of conciliator attempting to avoid clashes between the most open proponents of support for Madrid—the Radicals Pierre Cot and Jean Zay, the socialists Vincent Auriol, Marx Dormoy, Jules Moch, and Léo Lagrange, and the Republican-Socialist Maurice Violette—and the advocates of prudence, led by the Radicals Chautemps and Delbos. The Minister of Foreign Affairs gave a long presentation of British reservations. Daladier, rather inclined to support aid, did not conceal his apprehensions: military complications might arise. Pierre Cot pointed out, on the other hand, that if the rebellion triumphed in Spain, certain ideas might come to one leader or another in the French army.

One idea came out of these deliberations: the supply of arms to the Spanish Republic, legitimate in principle and consonant with agreements that had been made, involved too many internal and external risks to be carried out openly, on the governmental level. It was therefore important to act discreetly, allowing private firms to operate through the channel of states friendly to both Paris and Madrid—Mexico, for example.

The communiqué published that evening revealed of course only a small fraction of the truth. It indicated:

> The French government, after the deliberations of the cabinet, has unanimously decided not to intervene in the internal conflict in Spain. This position, proposed by M. Yvon Delbos, Minister of Foreign Affairs, was unanimously approved. Finally, on the question of the supply of war matériel which the Spanish government is said to have requested, it was declared in official circles at the conclusion of the cabinet meeting: it is false that the French government has affirmed its determination to follow a policy of intervention.

A strange document, as strange as it is hypocritical. It deals *in fine* with an "intervention" that no one was calling for. There is mention of the only real question, adherence to the agreement of 1935 on arms deliveries to the legitimate government of Madrid, but only in incidental fashion. There is an allusion to the supplies which Madrid "is said" to have requested—which is carrying deceit a bit too far. As for the "unanimity" that came out of the discussion, it is mentioned twice, which is at least once too many! It is technically true that Cot, Auriol, and Violette, like Blum himself, accepted with grave misgivings this retreat which was already a betrayal. But why should it be trumpeted in such a way? To counteract the pro-Fascist press which, not content with forcing these men into humiliation, wanted as well to display their divisions?

This deceptive document was supplemented, though not clarified, by two others which were equally ambiguous and contradictory. The first was a circular from Delbos to the French ambassadors in these terms:

> Certain inaccurate press reports having given to understand that the French government was lending its support to the Spanish government to combat the insurrection, I believe it necessary to [remind] you that this government . . . has made it a rule not to intervene in the internal affairs of other nations. Consequently, any delivery of land or air war matériel is forbidden to the state and to private industry. Nevertheless, following certain precedents, the exportation of unarmed planes, which may be supplied to the Spanish government by private industry, is authorized.

Three days later, Blum and Delbos addressed the Foreign Affairs Committee of the Senate, where undisguised partisans of Franco were at work. They reiterated their denial that any arms deliveries would take place. Although it was false (everyone knew that men like Malraux, for the honor of the country, were violating these "promises" and honoring as individuals the commitment that had been made by the community), this declaration earned them the senators' approval.

The same evening, Delbos declared to the Chamber of Deputies: "We could have delivered arms to the Spanish government, which is legitimate in law and in fact, and is moreover a friend of France. By supplying arms to this government, France would not have violated the principle of non-intervention in the affairs of another country. But we did not do so, first of all out of principle and for humanitarian reasons, and in order not to give a pretext to those who would be tempted to supply arms to the rebels." An elegant sophistry. Who was unaware that the pretext had already been given? Was American Ambassador Bowers the only one who informed his government of the ties that already linked the insurgents to fascist Italy?

These ties came fully to light on the same day that Delbos spoke so blandly to Parliament. On July 30, in fact, news reached Paris from Rabat which was calculated to give heart to the friends of the Spanish Republic: two Italian planes, openly flying through what was then French air space over Algeria on their way to "Spanish" Morocco, had had to make forced landings, one near Nemours, the other at Berkane in "French" Morocco. As soon as he was informed, Pierre Cot sent General Denain, former Minister of Aviation, to investigate. In a few hours this officer was able to establish, thanks to the confessions of Italian pilots, that Rome had already set in motion a vast program of systematic aid to the Franco rebellion. Military aircraft, pilots, and the instructions carried by the men who had crash–landed in North Africa were absolutely clear. Some of their orders were even dated July 17, the day before the uprising!

For Blum and his companions, possession of these documents should have meant gaining an unexpected opportunity to reverse their pitiful withdrawal of July 25. But this revelation gave rise to only a few vague impulses toward reappraisal, from July 31 to August 8, which finally gave way to the unfortunate and definitive decision in favor of non-intervention. Why this resignation, on the part of so scrupulous a lawyer, so sincere a democrat, so loyal a friend, so courageous a man?

Every politics is the result of a balance of power, tempered and modified by will. In this case, the balance of power triumphed without reservation over will. We have already said it, but it is worth repeating: since the Communists had refused to participate in the government, Blum's politics, the expression of the Popular Front coalition, depended on alliance with the Radical party. Thus the "contract between the middle class and the working class," as Maurice Thorez had summed up the 1936 program in exemplary fashion, was demonstrated in everyday affairs and carried out in practice. But the middle class, represented in this instance by the Radical party, the class which had granted its support to the social policies of the Popular Front in order to break with Laval's deflationary policy, which had, without too much bad grace, accepted the increase in the purchasing power of the masses and the equalization of living standards as a condition for economic recovery, fearfully refused the slightest risk in foreign affairs.

Of course, we have seen and will see again Radical leaders in the government advocate aid for Republican Spain, beginning with Pierre Cot, Minister of Aviation, who symbolized that policy more than any socialist minister; and he was supported in this by his colleague Jean Zay; much more discreetly by Minister of the Navy Gasnier-Duparc; and, briefly and partially, until August 8, by Edouard Daladier. If the latter, president of the party, soon changed sides, this was because its electoral base and its apparatus, especially the provincial notables, were terrified by any support of the Spanish "reds."

We have already seen the role played by Chautemps, which was a decisive one. The subtle Vice-President, playing a multiple game, first reprimanded the senators, then used their opposition as a weapon, and made numerous approaches to the Radical press which, except for *L'Oeuvre* and *La Dépêche de Toulouse,* supported non-intervention. Chautemps wrote much later in his *Carnets secrets de l'armistice:* "Shaken by the deep resistance of Parliament, realizing that one could not conduct a foreign action without the support of the entire nation, [Blum] regretfully decided in favor of non-intervention." Admirable objectivity! Camille Chautemps was modest in victory.

But it would be a mistake to hold this wily politician particularly responsible for a Radical policy which was first of all that of the highest authorities in the state. We have seen the reservations, the warnings, and the admonitions of Presidents Lebrun, Jeanneny, and Herriot: the three most prestigious figures in the state were, in various ways, determined adversaries of taking any risk to aid the neighboring Republic.

This was not all. In the Radical party, there was a very powerful faction led by Louis Malvy, the former "defeatist" Minister of 1917 strongly supported by Caillaux, which was betting on Franco's victory. Strongly impressed by Mussolini, knowing the Spanish military leaders from his long stay in Madrid, and presenting them as "true republicans devoted to order," Malvy was the leader of a strong pro-Franco "lobby." He was supported not only by Caillaux, but also by a group of fanatically anti-Communist Radicals whose spokesmen were Emile Roche and Pierre Dominique. If we note further that the dismissal of his son-in-law Peyrouton as Resident-General in Rabat had made him Blum's sworn enemy, one can imagine the effectiveness of this propagandist for Franco within the second major party in the government.

When one considers that the two most influential Radical ministers in the circumstances, the Minister of Foreign Affairs and the Minister of National Defense, became, respectively the symbol and the defender of nonintervention, it is justifiable to say that in the Spanish affair, the Radical party, half the Popular Front (on the governmental level), exercised an invincible force of obstruction. Any policy aiming to provide long-term aid for the Spanish Republic would obviously have led to a cabinet crisis and a breaking of the Popular Front "contract."

We will certainly consider later the consequences of and the justifications for a possible resignation of the cabinet, which Blum envisaged as early as the night of July 24. In the meanwhile, it is legitimate to agree with Robert Blum, who at the time spoke every day with his father and his closest associates, André Blumel and Jules Moch:

> Toward Republican Spain, the choice was not between intervention and non-intervention, but between non-intervention and the fall of the government in Parliament. My father's dearest wish was to leave with the declaration: "I think that we must aid Spain, but I am refused the means, and I resign."[166]

We have seen how Blum made the Madrid government the arbiter of the situation—an illegitimately established arbiter whose involuntary intervention corresponded to the deliberate intervention of London. (Thus Blum made French policy dependent on two foreign attitudes, a Spanish petition and an English veto.)

For, in seeking the reasons which forced Blum to betray himself during those cruel days at the end of July 1936, we must also consider the British attitude. Just as we have seen the Radical party's support for his domestic policy slip away from the head of government, we must also recognize the collapse of the pillar of his foreign policy represented by the alliance with England. Few subjects have given rise to so many lies, explicitly formulated or covered by silence. There is even one man, Charles Corbin, French Ambassador in London, who asserted that in this matter there was "no pressure, diplomatic or otherwise, by Great Britain on France,"[167] which amounts to taking us all for fools.

From the very first, notably after the appeal cleverly sent to London by the pro-Franco Ambassador Cardeñas[168] before he left Paris—this informed man knew what he was doing—all that came from the British cabinet were warnings and threats, first veiled, then direct. Of course, one may say that Eden's "Be careful!" addressed to Blum on July 24 was not an ultimatum. But Eden was intelligent enough to know that this type of discreet pressure was much more effective than a direct threat addressed to as sensitive and proud a man as the socialist leader.

Whether Baldwin's warning to Lebrun which Blum spoke of to Asua was mythical or real, it expresses perfectly what the French delegation encountered in London that day, and on the following day when they met Lebrun, Jeanneny, and Herriot in Paris: a wall of suspicion, vetoes, and warnings. With the difference that the British conservatives barely concealed their sympathy—natural enough—for the Franco forces, defenders of "Christian order" and of the owners of the Rio Tinto mines in which there was heavy British capital investment. While the right-thinking French averted their eyes and evoked the corpses of nuns dug up by the Catalonian anarchists, their English counterparts told each other of mutinies and executions of officers on the ships of the Spanish fleet, ships that sailed in the same waters as those of the Navy itself! The horror of it!

Baldwin, or perhaps Chamberlain—versions differ—confessed to a visitor who passed it on to Jules Moch, who was in London on July 30: "We English hate fascism. But we hate Bolshevism just as much. If there is a country where Fascists and Bolsheviks are killing each other, then that is a great gift to humanity."[169] During that summer, in any case, Churchill, on his various visits to Blum (whom he greatly respected), constantly denounced the Spanish Republicans. When the new Spanish Ambassador to London, Azcarte, was introduced to him, he turned away, muttering: "Blood, blood, blood!"

Then what can Mr. Eden's denials mean? In *Facing the Dictators,* he brazenly maintains that Great Britain had nothing to do with the decisions made in Paris in late July 1936, asserts that "non-intervention" was a purely French policy, expresses indignation that some of the responsibility has been attributed to him, and repeats these strange assertions in the introductory interview published as a preface to Georges Soria's *Histoire de la guerre d'Espagne* in 1976.

What is meant by these rectifications is that there was in fact a distance between London and Paris. The British felt and *wished to be* neutral, that is, not concerned in the Spanish tragedy, while the French, emotionally and intellectually involved, forced themselves into "non-intervention" or "non-interference," excluding active involvement but not "support." When Eden maintains that Paris, not London, invented non-intervention, he is speaking the truth. But it is none the less true that this choice was a kind of middle term between the policy of neutrality which expressed the British point of view (a neutrality rather hostile to Madrid) and the support of the Republic which the Popular Front cabinet wanted to provide. Eden, Baldwin, and Chamberlain did not invent non-intervention. Having urged Blum to neutrality, they were content to see him halt in mid-stream, between their hands-off position and his own intentions of support.

The former Secretary of the Foreign Office alleges that the threats attributed to him—to denounce the Locarno pact, for example, or to renounce any military solidarity with Paris if France intervened in

Spain—were never expressed by him or his services. All the same, in reading a particular dispatch from the British ambassador in Paris dated August 7, we shall see that the pressures were sometimes very precise. But it was above all the attitude of English officials, hostile to the Republic, which hung over all French decisions of the time, all the more so because at the source of the official information used by the two governments were two men—the Ambassadors Henry Chilton and Jean Herbette—spontaneously favorable to the rebels, unlike their American colleague whose sympathies lay with the legal government.

One can certainly disapprove of the extreme docility to their English ally which Blum, Delbos, and Léger had made the alpha and omega of their diplomacy, from the moment at which that docility led them to abandon their friends and even to violate their treaty. But one cannot deny the fundamental nature of that influence in which men as different as the Spanish statesman Manuel Azaña, the American diplomat Claude Bowers, and the French writer François Mauriac saw the key to all the decisions Blum made at the time.

Can it be argued that it was possible for Blum to choose the domestic alternative by relying on the Communist party, and the foreign alternative by boldly playing the card of the Soviet alliance? Internally, the objection does not hold: the working-class parties did not have a majority in the Chamber; the SFIO and the PCF together included only 220 deputies. And even supposing that a split had taken place among the Radicals, and that Pierre Cot and Jean Zay, associated with pro-Spanish Republican-Socialists like Violette and Viénot, had brought some 60 deputies to support Blum in his fight for aid to Spain, then that very slender parliamentary majority would have had the task of carrying with it a state apparatus which was deeply impregnated with the most authoritarian radicalism (particularly in the case of the prefects), and with conservative tendencies (especially the army officers and the diplomatic corps).

We know very little about the state of mind of the army, except that it was under the influence of Marshall Pétain, who later became Ambassador to Franco, and of General Weygand, a strong-arm reactionary. It is true that Daladier's authority was generally recognized in the army. But what would that "authority" have provided if the president of the Radical Party had moved from government to opposition? The air force, in spite of Minister Pierre Cot and his closest associate Jean Moulin, was even more inclined toward the right.

In the last volume of her memoirs, Clara Malraux tells of waiting in the canteen of Villacoublay for the departure of the plane that was to take her husband and her to Spain in early August 1936. She heard hostile remarks from the pilots about the "bastards" who were going to fight with the Republicans, and their eagerness to see an arms embargo proclaimed against Madrid.

As for the navy, in spite of its chief Darlan, who was then a supporter of the Republic, this was the body which was soon to be the framework for the most reactionary regime in contemporary France: Vichy. Like its British rival, it reacted with horror to the mutinies that had taken place on Spanish ships.

The words which the military attaché to the French embassy in Madrid addressed to Blum have often been quoted: "The King of France would intervene." There were precedents, from 1808 to 1823, unequally auspicious. But what a sovereign supported by his party might have done was much more difficult an undertaking for a leader of the left; just as only a leader of the "left" like Cavaignac could suppress a Parisian revolution which would have destroyed a Bourbon or an Orléans; or as de Gaulle could make a peace in Algeria which would have been impossible for Mendès France.

We remain rather ill-informed about the attitude of the military toward Spain (although it is impossible to forget that it was General Castelnau who originated the expression *Frente Crapular* and that Marshall Franchet was a supporter of the most seditious leagues), but we know more of the feelings which prevailed among the diplomats. They were of three kinds.

Among some there reigned a kind of resignation which derived from France's inaction after Hitler's coup on March 7, 1936. For them, among whom was René Massigli, conference director at the Quai d'Orsay, everything seemed useless. Paris had lost the confidence of its allies. How was it possible to take risks for Spain that they had not dared take for the Rhine?

Another current, led by Alexis Léger, was moved only by its pro-British obsession: everything rather than allow the slightest misunderstanding to develop between the Quai d'Orsay and the Foreign Office. In London, Ambassador Corbin was the exaggerated symbol of this obsession; he was known as "the Ambassador of England to the Court of Saint James."

Finally, a third group of diplomats was inspired by the most simplistic anticommunism. Some dreamed of close ties with Mussolini, others were moved by simple fear of the "reds"; thus, the French representative in Spain, Jean Herbette, telegraphed Delbos on the eve of the *pronunciamento* that the Spanish government "did not fear fascism, but anarchism," and at the height of the crisis seemed primarily preoccupied with remaining at a safe distance from Madrid, preferring to reside at San Sebastian (soon occupied by Franco's forces), or at San Juan de Luz, which made this ambassador to the Republic rather an observer of the rebels.

This was Blum's position, scrutinized by a press whose vast majority was in favor of caution if not passivity, and at the head of a divided and unhealthy administrative apparatus which was undermined by pro-

Franco influences. The domestic veto which he confronted from the majority of the Radical party and the foreign veto formulated in London certainly tied his hands.

In his long battle for nonintervention he had occasion to allege that he chose not to run the risks of civil or international war. These arguments are open to discussion. The obstacles to continuous and large-scale aid which we have described seem sufficient to explain—if not to justify—the policy he resigned himself to following. It remains, among other things, to judge whether this policy was the one called for by his life, his role as heir to Jaurès's legacy, the long-term interests of democracy and socialism, and the interests of peace.

"Non-Interference"

The fact that the revelation of Italian intervention, with the forced landing of the two Savoias in North Africa on July 30, 1936, did not change the course of French policy and open the eyes of those advocating abandonment of the Republican government in Madrid, indicates how firmly set that policy was. We have just pointed to the most important of these influences. They operated all the more effectively because, during the last days of July, a framework within which they could freely function had been formed: the so-called policy of "nonintervention."

A surprising and inadequate word. Practically no one in France spoke of "intervening"—as Louis XVI, for example, had intervened in America, or Napoleon III in Italy, or as Mussolini and Hitler had done or were about to do in Spain. To be sure, there was Blum's plan for a raid on the Catalan coast on March 15, 1938, to which we will return. As early as the summer of 1936, Admiral Darlan suggested a temporary occupation of Minorca to oppose the Italian navy. In Rabat, General Noguès considered threatening Spanish Morocco, where a German landing was feared (reported, then denied in January 1937). But these were only short-lived impulses.

What was in question was the possibility of supplying arms to a legal government defending its existence, the simple application of the Franco-Spanish agreement of 1935. This was moreover the argument that Delbos himself had presented to the Chamber on July 30. Blum, as a lawyer, was so conscious of the inappropriateness of the expression "non-intervention" that he proposed to speak of "non-interference," a more modest and slightly more accurate expression. But as always, bad currency drove out the good, and "non-intervention" survived.

This unfortunate—but perhaps inevitable—initiative was the work of Alexis Léger and his group of competent diplomats, notably Massigli and Coulondre. They were all good republicans and in no way inclined to treat Franco gently because of fascist sympathies. Then what led them, between July 25 and 30, to create this murky plan? A paralyzing pacifism? For some of them, yes. But the idea which obsessed Léger— one he had verified in London from July 22 to 24—was the idea we have heard formulated by Winston Churchill: if Paris helps Madrid as Berlin is assisting the rebels, London will lean toward Berlin. An impious possibility!

It was against this possibility that Alexis Léger lived, worked, and formulated his plans. To oppose it was his raison d'être as Secretary-General of the Quai d'Orsay. Anything rather than give a foothold to that threat. Rather betray a promise on what was after all a secondary front than see an alliance between England and Germany come to pass, which would cast France into isolation and place it at the mercy of Nazi militarism. One can imagine the effect of this man of great talent and incomparable charm presenting this argument to Blum and Delbos, and claiming the support of Herriot, Jeanneny, and the man of peace of twenty years before, Caillaux.

In short, on July 30, at the moment when the news of the Italian intervention came out, the Léger plan had already been worked out and fixed in people's minds. It seemed open only to modification of detail and temporary suspensions. For it sadly but astutely expressed the balance of power in France, a fundamental diplomatic choice, and also the reality of the weakness of French armaments at such a precarious time.

But on August 1, during the second of the three meetings of the cabinet which were to bog the Popular Front government down in "non-intervention," Blum, who had been particularly struck by the discovery of Italian intervention, participated more directly and actively than the week before. "Our duty is to aid our Spanish friends," he declared, "whatever the consequences that may flow from that support."[170] But immediately afterward, President Lebrun intervened to advise "prudence," and Yvon Delbos recalled at length the British point of view and the warnings coming from London. He even emphasized the fact that the English conservatives were more sympathetic to the rebels than to the Republicans.

At that point, Blum, who was beginning to feel "abandoned" by several SFIO ministers, like Spinasse and Rivière, spoke again to admit that "the risk [was] considerable for Spain to see Hitler and Mussolini supply more arms to its opponents than we" and that "it might be in its interests if there were a thoroughly policed non-interference agreement."[171]

That afternoon, after this step backward by Blum, only Pierre Cot, Maurice Violette, and Marx Dormoy "held" firmly for aid to Spain.[172]

But after the meeting, Blum confided to Jules Moch—who, on a mission to London, had not been present and was "dismayed" by the cabinet's retreat—that he had not given up carrying out delivery of planes to the Republicans, provided that they were flown by Spanish pilots. This would allow about twenty aircraft to be transported south of the Pyrenees during the first days of August.

In spite of Delbos's warnings, if not his open opposition, during those few days Pierre Cot and Jules Moch organized shipments of matériel officially intended for Mexico and Lithuania but which were in fact sent to Santander.[173] But at the same time, with a view to sounding out the governments concerned, Delbos and Léger sent the first plan for a non-intervention pact to the French embassies. This note clearly suggested an understanding on this formula, and pointed out that, although France had already respected its rule, the delivery of matériel to the rebels might later lead it to resume its freedom of judgment. It was this last proposition that had succeeded in gaining the support of men like Blum and Auriol. Didn't they see that making French non-interference depend on a similar attitude on the part of the Italians was to place on the same footing legal aid to a legitimate government and illegal support for a rebel faction?

In possession of the document on August 2, the Foreign Office responded favorably two days later. It was understood between the two governments that London would use its influence in Lisbon, Berlin, and Rome to persuade those three capitals to accept the plan, and Paris would do the same in Moscow. The Germans and the Portugese declared themselves vaguely in favor of the plan. Mussolini was silent for a while. The Quai d'Orsay considered itself rather well rewarded for these first efforts.

But Blum had not yet given up bringing into effect a procedure that was more beneficial to the Spanish Republicans. On August 1, he had received at home the Labour MP Philip Noël-Baker, a long-time friend, and Jean Longuet, a warm supporter of aid to Madrid. The three men wondered about the chances of changing the official British point of view. Since Parliament and Cabinet were on vacation, Noël-Baker suggested going through the Admiralty, emphasizing that the maneuvers of the Italian fleet in the Mediterranean from Spanish bases threatened the British navy. The Labour MP argued that by convincing the heads of the navy they could change many things in the British cabinet's way of thinking. Blum declared:

> I then took it upon myself to send Admiral Darlan on a mission
> to London, with Daladier's agreement of course. I asked him to get
> in touch with the First Lord of the Admiralty,[174] Lord Chatfield,
> . . . to explain to him, from his point of view, how it was in the
> obvious and urgent interest of Great Britain to oppose, as we our-

selves were trying to do, the installation of the Franco regime in
Spain with the help of Italy and Germany.

Admiral Chatfield answered Admiral Darlan that he could not
take on a commission of that nature, that Franco was a good Spanish patriot, that on the day when he came to power he would be
able to defend himself against the ascendancy of Mussolini or Hitler, and that consequently he would not lend his aid to negotiations
of that kind.[175]

In his account, Blum makes no mention of an idea he had suggested
to Darlan: British mediation between the two parties to the Spanish
conflict, a rather striking idea since it placed the two camps on the
same footing. It might have been useful. Chatfield rejected this suggestion as brusquely as he had the others, maintaining that arbitration was
futile; since the two adversaries "appeared determined to exterminate
one another" (the admiral did not take the trouble to explain that he
was glad of it), any government which tried to interpose "would be
caught between the hammer and the anvil."[176]

In any event, Darlan returned to Paris on the 6th completely down-
cast. The failure of this mission had the most serious repercussions on
the decision taken in the cabinet meeting three days later. But another
event, on the very next day, was even more discouraging for the supporters of Republican Spain: the British Ambassador Sir George Clerk
called on Yvon Delbos to "be more certain" about the French position.

The French minister informed his visitor about the first approaches
toward signing a non-aggression pact. He pointed out that although his
German colleague, von Neurath, had expressed his personal approval,
no official response had come from Berlin, much less from Rome. The
English diplomat then raised the question of France's actual aid to the
Spanish Republic. Delbos admitted that despite the decision of principle made on July 25, Paris could not refuse to send to the legal government of Madrid five aircraft that had been ordered before the war: were
the Italians and the Germans not supplying planes to the rebels—
twenty-eight already from the Nazis alone? Clerk then had the nerve to
declare that he could not be certain that the Madrid cabinet was the
real government of Spain; wasn't it simply a screen behind which the
anarchists were operating? To this Delbos replied that he did not think
Giral and Azaña were extremists.

It is necessary to quote the conclusion of the telegram Sir George
Clerk sent that evening (August 7) to the Foreign Office:

> I concluded the interview by expressing the hope that the
> French Government, even though, pending an agreement of non-
> intervention, they might feel themselves precluded from stopping
> private commercial transactions with Spain, would do what it
> could to limit and retard such transactions as much as possible. I
> asked M. Delbos to forgive me for speaking so frankly and I re-

peated that all I had said was entirely personal and on my own responsibility but I felt that in so critical a situation I must put before him the danger any action which might definitely commit the French government to one side of the conflict and make more difficult the close cooperation between our two countries which was called for by this crisis.[177]

It was said that George Clerk, then a young Secretary in the Foreign Office, was the official who had received the false news of the sailing of the French fleet toward the English coast during the Fachoda affair. The emotion he still felt must have had something to do with the harshness of this ultimatum thirty-seven years later.

John Dreifort, who quotes this important document, sees it as a "serious warning." He adds that, three days later, these purely "personal" remarks (according to Clerk) were entirely approved by the Foreign Office and that Eden himself considered them part of an "official" document.[178] On this basis, Anthony Eden maintained that London had no responsibility for non-intervention, first in a debate in the House of Commons in 1936, then in an exchange of letters with Mrs. Rathbone, a Labour MP, and finally in his memoirs. One of his spokesmen, Col. A. Shuckburgh, denounced in an official note the assertions of those who claimed that London had any responsibility for "the unilateral decision by France" as "journalists' nonsense."

Rather than the late Anthony Eden, whose sense of historical truth—or, to be charitable, whose memory—it later became legitimate to question (notably over the Suez affair in 1956), we will quote the celebrated British military historian Sir Basil Liddell Hart who, with all the sources at his disposal and writing several years after the former Prime Minister, summarizes his country's attitude in the Spanish affair in this way:

> On receiving news of this Fascist foreign aid to Franco, the French Government agreed to the Spanish Republican Government's request to be allowed to purchase French air craft. But after sending a small consignment, the French suspended further ones when the British Government on August 8 delivered a virtual ultimatum that if France did not promptly ban the export of war material to Spain, and a war with Germany ensued, Britain would consider herself absolved of her obligations under the Locarno treaty, to aid France. . . .
> Under such pressure from the British Government, the French pursued the alternative aim of a non-intervention agreement between the powers to prohibit the export of arms to either side.[179]

A Fateful Decision

It is easy to imagine the state of mind of the pusillanimous Anglophile Delbos as he left the Quai d'Orsay on August 7, after Sir George

Clerk's outburst, to go to Blum's cabinet meeting at the hôtel Matignon. They had gone beyond Churchill's grumbling or the "advice" Eden gave Blum on July 24. From Chatfield's rebuff of Darlan to Clerk's admonitions to Delbos, it was indeed an escalation of threats from across the Channel. Let us repeat that one may criticize the docility with which Blum and his companions bowed to British admonitions. It remains the case that these warnings were constant, increasing, and finally determining.

Immediately before the meeting on the 7th, which was to prepare the decision expected at the conclusion of the cabinet meeting of August 8, Blum and those who were urging him to act boldly in favor of Madrid had nevertheless taken a series of steps which the leader of the Popular Front presented in these terms:

> Since we had felt freed by the manifest evidence of the supply of war planes by Italy to Spain, we had brought together a rather large squadron, not by withdrawing planes from our own squadrons, nor even by anticipating on deliveries which airplane manufacturers were contractually required to make, but by buying on the market, in Paris, a certain number of completed aircraft which had not yet been delivered, aircraft ordered by other nations which were not able to accept immediate delivery, or which could be made to wait. This squadron was made up at the time of forty or fifty aircraft, and it was ready to leave.
> We arrived at this solution: have the batch of planes we had ready leave in great haste, and once this expedition had been made, which by the way practically exhausted the capacities of our industry at that moment, try to introduce and to impose on Italy and Germany the system of non-intervention, or, as we said at the time, non-interference.[180]

Jules Moch, for his part, explains that "some of the forty or fifty aircraft" which Blum mentions had already been delivered, and that on August 7 there were only thirteen Dewoitine fighter planes available at the Pau airport. He describes the picturesque circumstances of the departure of these planes in these terms:

> During the cabinet meeting of 7 August, Pierre Cot and I were in constant contact with the Pau airport[181] and we were informed of every takeoff. Léon Blum and Pierre Cot knew that each time one of my assistants gave me a little piece of paper it meant that a plane had just taken off for Spain. The Premier drew out the discussion until I had announced the flight of the thirteenth and last Dewoitine.[182]

But the extraordinary cabinet meeting of August 7 was not only devoted to this theatrical "dispatching." It was also the occasion of the debate in the course of which, by a tiny majority and without Blum taking a clear position this time, non-intervention was decided upon. If we try today to determine the positions of the thirty-four members of the Blum government, on the basis of the memories of the survivors (notably Georges Monnet, Pierre Cot, and Jules Moch, whom I was able to question), we discover that it apparently would have taken little for the Delbos plan to be rejected and the government broken up.

It seems legitimate to say that about a dozen opponents of nonintervention declared themselves: Auriol, Violette, Salengro, Moutet, Lebas, Cot, Zay, Marx Dormoy, Léo Lagrange, Pierre Viénot, and Jules Moch; that about the same number of proponents spoke as clearly: Delbos, Chautemps, Paul Faure, Spinasse, Rivière, Bedouce, Jardiller,[183] Bastid, and, with some reservations, Daladier and Gasnier-Duparc. It has not been possible to determine the attitude of the others, for example, the Minister of Justice, Marc Rucart.

In sum, it seems that what shifted the majority was first of all the vigor with which Delbos, a moderate advocate of prudence who had suddenly been struck by the opinions of London and "primed" by Alexis Léger and his group, argued for the plan with which his name was associated from then on. This was followed by Blum's withdrawal from his position at the meeting on August 1, in which he had emphasized France's obligation to prevent Spain's falling into the hands of the Fascists. He, too, was moved by the increase in English pressure, and he confined himself that evening to the role of a kind of arbitrator—perhaps considering himself morally absolved of his obligations by the flight of the planes from Pau toward Spain. After all, that was a bit more than what the 1935 agreement had provided, and it had already, in fact, been carried out.

Thus the fateful decision not to aid the Spanish Republic was made, and it was simply ratified the next day in the cabinet meeting presided over by Albert Lebrun, who had been informed of the previous day's discussion and sharply reproached the Premier for having (for the first time in history) determined French foreign policy in the absence of the head of state. One can be certain, in any case, that Lebrun's presence would not have changed the decision made on August 7, 1936. It corresponded in every respect to his wishes.

On the 9th, the Quai d'Orsay sent out a directive according to which "the export of war matériel to Spain and its possessions is prohibited until further notice." Thus, even in spite of the revelation of Italian intervention on July 30, this new circular was still more restrictive than the one of July 27: it even prohibited exports by private industry. There was a single reservation: if the agreement on non-intervention was not signed within a short time, Paris "might find it necessary to re-examine the entire situation."[184] The day before, the Quai d'Orsay had sent to the capitals concerned the plan for non-intervention worked out by

Alexis Léger: London gave its agreement on August 10th, Rome on the 21st, Moscow on the 23rd, and Berlin on the 25th. A "non-intervention" committee was created and began meeting in London on September 8. A smooth operation, it demonstrated the diligence and competence of French diplomacy.

However neutral he may have been in the debates of August 7 and 8, however convinced that non-intervention was the only policy that could simultaneously prevent the disruption of the majority, civil unrest, the collapse of the alliance with England, and the risks of very serious international complications, Blum was nevertheless aware that his choice constituted a surrender of principles and a breach of promise. It satisfied neither his nobility of mind nor his heartfelt loyalty.

The decision made on the 7th and announced on the 8th of August had of course received some approval. A lawyer like Georges Scelle, writing in *La Dépêche du Midi,* saw it as "a practical necessity." And Victor Basch in *L'Oeuvre,* without concealing his sorrow, argued that it was a supreme effort in favor of peace. But as a whole the left-wing press was harsh, even sardonic. Even *Le Populaire,* directed in Blum's absence by Bracke and Rosenfeld, two loyal associates, expressed its rejection. Jean Longuet called for application of the 1935 agreement. Bracke spoke of an "immoral" solution, and Rosenfeld considered the situation "tragic." *Le Peuple,* organ of the CGT, denounced the "fateful compromise" even more harshly. But it was Vaillant-Couturier who published in *L'Humanité* the best commentary on the decision:

> To prevent a legitimate and friendly government from trading as it likes is to violate a state's sovereignty, to intervene. Sanctions which no one dared apply to Italy are applied to the Spanish government because it is a popular government. The French masses demand no "intervention" from the French government. But they refuse to allow the friends of France in Spain to be strangled.[185]

The right-wing press demonstrated even more bad faith and sectarianism in the affair than had been expected. While Léon Bailby in *Le Jour* asserted that the Blum government had once more shown itself "incapable of making any sincere and valid commitment," Pierre Gaxotte in *Candide* affirmed that "the imbecilities of the Popular Front have placed France in a difficult position." And *L'Action française* naturally went the furthest in refusing to recognize either the evidence or justice. This policy, wrote Maurras, "goes against the grain of all political prudence [which] says and repeats: we must not intervene. And if others intervene, we must intervene still less. And the more the others intervene, the more France must refrain from any intervention."

In this uproar, Blum could perceive the tragic nature of his situation, caught as he was between the impossible and the unacceptable. But no press commentary, even from Bracke, could make him judge more harshly the unacceptable and painful character of his choice than the dispatch sent to Delbos on August 10 by the new Spanish ambassador, Alvaro de Albornoz. Albornoz was all the more deserving to be heard because he had been so insistent on maintaining the leader of the SFIO in power.

In this brief but eloquent document, Albornoz gave "formal assurance that the French government would find loyal and complete cooperation from the Spanish government in order to prevent the events in Spain from becoming the source of difficulties of an international order." But he added that the suspension of arms shipments, far from being a means of non-intervention, constituted on the contrary "a very effective intervention" in the internal affairs of Spain. "In fact," Albornoz explained, "it could have the effect of making the current abnormal circumstances last longer than if my government were not deprived by this measure of means of action which it normally would have been able to obtain in France without recourse to any exceptional measures."[186]

Aside from a few slightly ridiculous diplomatic formulas ("the current abnormal circumstances"), it could not be said better. Intervention was not selling arms to a friendly legal government in danger, it was decreeing a kind of embargo against it. If it was true that at the moment Albornoz was writing, Paris had applied the agreement of 1935 by delivering approximately thirty planes, including the thirteen that left Pau on August 7 (planes of rather mediocre quality and entrusted to inexperienced pilots, except for the "mercenaries" recruited and led by André Malraux), it was also true that the nearly complete halt of shipments in the following weeks cost the Madrid government dearly—most notably at Irun on September 5.

Blum saw the decision of August 7 challenged not only by the left-wing press and his Spanish friends. The working class which had until then so warmly supported the Popular Front and its leaders indicated its anxiety and disapproval as early as August 8. On that day there was a large festival in the park of Saint-Cloud. It was then that for the first time Blum felt something that had been magnificent come undone, the harmony between the particular man he was and the crowd which heard him speak.

The theme of the festival in the park was an "oath for peace." Spain was obviously on everyone's mind. When the Premier arrived, with his wife Thérèse, he was greeted with cries of "Solidarity with Spain!" The balloons that were released had his face on them as well as those of Jaurès and Cachin, but there was already a certain reserve in the reception of his speech in which he spoke of the situation only in general

terms. The crowd shouted "guns and planes for Spain!"[187] A shout
which Blum was to hear often in the coming years.

The circle of critics tightened around him. Soon his closest associate
(along with Bracke), Vincent Auriol, tried as well to dissuade him from
"non-intervention" as it was conceived in Paris. On August 12, the
Minister of Finance, who in the cabinet meeting of the 7th had been
one of the opponents of the Delbos formula, wrote the following letter
to the Premier, to whom he had offered unconditional admiration and
devotion for twenty years:

> My Dear Premier and friend,
>
> You know the troubled mind and heavy heart with which I re-
> signed myself the other day to the so-called attitude of neutrality. I
> never thought of intervention, no more than you or anyone else,
> but I did think that once the insurgents were substantially aided by
> other nations, which in my opinion are pursuing a long-range pol-
> icy against democracy, France, and peace, there were grounds on
> our side to help a friendly, legitimate, and recognized government,
> to whom we owe, through formal agreements, aid, assistance,
> arms supplies.
>
> I am convinced that if we had been determined to help this
> legitimate government, recognized as such by everyone, England
> would itself have proposed its mediation, and it would have been
> better, in my opinion, for it to take the lead. In any case, the
> decision was made.
>
> But, since last Friday, I have had the impression that Italy is
> using postponements to manipulate us. I know that it is continuing
> to aid General Franco. I have learned from customs offices that
> contraband munitions are reaching the insurgents. . . .
>
> For my part, and I tell you this very frankly, I can no longer
> stand by helplessly in this fools' game. I can do so even less be-
> cause I raised a question which apparently was not thought worthy
> of consideration but which nevertheless seems important to me:
> the protest of the Sultan against the use of Moroccans in a civil
> war. . . .
>
> Obviously, I am not asking for intervention in Morocco, as you
> may well imagine. If the Sultan were to make a vigorous protest
> and if it were brought to the attention of his subjects who have
> been sent by Franco against the sons of Spain, I think that that
> would produce a great effect from the moral point of view and that
> it would embarrass the Fascist general.
>
> In any event, this is a question to be considered: Franco's right
> to act in Morocco, and perhaps a diplomatic initiative by the great
> powers might make him understand that he risks disturbing the
> peace in North Africa. What an unfortunate example, if tomorrow
> an insurgent from Morocco or anywhere else were to indulge in the
> same attitude.
>
> What preoccupies and distresses me is that the diplomats have
> been very active in winning support for their argument for neu-
> trality, but they now seem slow to move when it is time to organize
> that mentality to which we ourselves made the sacrifice of an ab-

stention, at the risk of appearing to abandon a friendly people and
to ignore our national and international obligations toward that
people. . . .
   A great sadness accompanies [my] terrible apprehensions.
   I embrace you affectionately.

                                                    VINCENT AURIOL

   Had he written nothing but that, Vincent Auriol's name would be
worth remembering. Aside from some judicious suggestions—notably
that more active aid would have brought about British mediation rather
than an aggravation of the dangers of the conflict—the future President
of the Republic very appropriately emphasized the Moroccan aspect of
the crisis and the possibilities a diplomacy worthy of the name would
have had to assert the rights of the Moroccan sovereign in the affair. At
the risk of seeing the Sultan use this as an argument for emphasizing his
own rights. It is distressing that a man like Pierre Viénot, responsible
for Arab affairs in the government, who was a firm advocate of aid to
the Spanish Republic and of reformist policies in North Africa, was not
then given a mission to Rabat which might have created difficulties for
Franco.
   Vincent Auriol's letter seems to have had no political effect. There is
no doubt that the Premier was very moved by it, but he was moved so
often that summer. It seems that, paraphrasing Marie Tudor's statement about Calais, he said to Auriol: "If they opened my heart, they
would find there the word Spain."
   Let us try once more to understand Blum's role in this affair. Let us
try to understand why such warnings, coming from such men, seemed
less determining to him than those from London or from the old gentlemen of the Radical party. Among all the reasons already enumerated,
we will put forward the following, which certainly played a decisive
role. First, the certainty that there was a threat of war, a certainty
which apparently dated from his trip to Geneva at the end of June and
from his contacts with Eden at the same time. It was essential to delay
the day of reckoning, for when he assumed office, this pacifist and old
advocate of disarmament discovered with anguish an unarmed France
confronting increasingly armed neighbors. According to Jules Moch, in
a conversation in November 1976, Blum and his government thought at
the time that the dictators would be in a position to start the war in
1941, and that they should prepare for that date. Until then, they could
only gain time.
   Blum was certain of another thing: whatever France did for the
Spanish Republic, the Fascist regimes would do even more, since they
could devote many more efforts and resources to armament and could
draft "volunteers" among their young men at will. In short, to quote a
penetrating judgment by André Blumel, "non-intervention was essen-

tially an attempt to prevent others from doing what we were incapable of accomplishing."

From August 8 on, attention was focused above all on setting up the legal, or theoretical, framework for "non-intervention." From August 12 to 25, the five states most concerned in the affair—Great Britain, Portugal, Fascist Italy, the Soviet Union, and the Third Reich—adhered to the pact proposed by the Quai d'Orsay. But while these diplomatic operations held the attention, at least of French public opinion, the dictators of Rome and Berlin feverishly accelerated their aid to the Franco forces, not only in arms—as France had done from July 29 to August 8—but in men and "advisory" missions. Preparations were made for sending large bodies of troops. The extent of these interventions was revealed on September 30 at the rostrum of the League of Nations by Alvarez del Vayo, Minister of Foreign Affairs in the government of Largo Caballero,[188] who had succeeded José Giral at the beginning of the month.

Is it of any interest at this point to question the dictators' real intentions? We must certainly note that Mussolini became much more deeply involved in the affair than Hitler; he made it a question of prestige and laid the foundations for a permanent base in the Balearics (which explains Admiral Darlan's idea of a raid on Minorca, from which he was hurriedly dissuaded by his British colleagues).

Hitler seems never to have considered the Spanish affair except from the perspective of maneuvers and technology. He saw it first as a means of "trapping" France, drawing its attention to the South, leading it to expend men and matériel, and second as an experimental area for his aviation and his weapons. Thus the role played by the "Condor Legion" and the systematic destruction of Guernica were decided upon in order to measure the military necessary to terrorize a civilian population. But according to a certain "Hossbach document,"[189] as well as from dispatches from the French embassy in Berlin, it seems that Hitler had no desire to see the war end quickly, even with a victory by his ally Franco; he preferred to maintain the festering Spanish sore because it caused division in France and out of it might come at any moment a good pretext for a crisis.

This was also Stalin's point of view, and he too found in Spain a good training ground for his aviators and agents, not to mention (the Zinoviev trial took place in August 1936) the opportunity to liquidate a substantial number of "opposition" figures. This does not mean that the USSR provided insignificant aid to the Madrid government. Apparently indifferent to the affair until early August, then staging demonstrations in favor of Republican Spain from the 4th on, the Soviet government adhered to the non-intervention pact on August 23, the same pact which the spokesmen of the PCF violently condemned.

Unlike the French leaders, however, Stalin was faithful to the agreement only in so far as the other camp respected it; he acted, as Blum should have acted: by responding blow for blow, by providing if possible as much matériel as the enemy. Soviet aid to Madrid—most of which was transported across French territory and with French "complicity"—was relatively late: it did not become substantial until October 1936, the date when the formation of the "international brigades" was authorized by Stalin and then supported by the Communist parties. Had it been earlier and in addition to more substantial French aid, it might conceivably have altered the course of the war. The fact is that it only prolonged the agony of the Republic. But it could justly be offered as an example to French leaders by Maurice Thorez and his comrades.

In France, in fact, the debate was more vigorous than ever. Although some of those who had at first supported Franco had opened their eyes—like François Mauriac who had been pushed to the other side by the massacres perpetrated by Franco's forces in Badajoz on August 15, and Georges Bernanos who had witnessed in the Balearics the manner in which Franco's forces defended "Christian order," the extreme right-wing press and right-thinking people continued to treat Blum as a "war monger." On the left, the CGT, the PCF, and the left of the SFIO—especially Jean Zyromski's *La Bataille socialiste*[190] and the Seine federation as a whole—relentlessly denounced the abandonment of the Spanish people, which is what "non-intervention" amounted to from their point of view.

We have a curious account of the dominant state of mind in France during those violent months of the summer of 1936: the confidences of Portugese Minister of Foreign Affairs Monteiro to Anthony Eden, as the Secretary of the Foreign Office has reported them. After spending a few weeks in France, the diplomat said he greatly feared that France would suffer "an internal conflict" in the course of the next few months. France might be shattered, he said, because, "the hatreds within the country were greater than the hatred of some Frenchmen for the foreign enemy. The *Comité des Forges*, for instance, was so anti-Blum that it had scarcely the time to be anti-German." Eden concluded: "Monteiro and I saw this with regret, Hitler with satisfaction."[191]

There was a lot of talk about "revolution" and "civil war" in France. A note from the head of the Sûreté Nationale to the prefects, dated October 8, 1936, for example, noted that two bishops, of Versailles and Montpellier, had ordered their priests to provide themselves with civilian clothes and passports in order to be able to leave the country in case violent conflict broke out. At the same time, a colonel named Gabet was confined and dismissed for having said, with reference to

Spain: "Similar events might very well take place in France. On that day, I don't know what side I would be on."[192] Was he punished for having formulated the possibility in public, or for not having made it clear that he would be on the side of order?

Also at the same time, the extreme right multiplied demonstrations in support of the rebels. While Pierre Laval sent Franco a telegram of encouragement and support, a kind of congress of the "leagues" which had been dissolved was held during the summer in the Salle Pleyel. Pierre Taittinger, head of the *Jeunesses patriotes,* called for the creation of an "International of national parties" (!) and sponsored sending messages of solidarity and a ceremonial sword to Franco—the sword was blessed by a Spanish bishop. A Toulouse newspaper, *L'Express du Midi,* wrote that the left would have to get used to the perspective of living surrounded by Hitler, Mussolini, and Franco, "a perspective which delights us as much as it distresses those gentlemen."[193]

The Plea of Luna-Park

Challenged in this way from the right, Blum was hardly less criticized or pressed over Spain on his left. On September 3, in the course of a meeting in honor of La Pasionaria, his name had been booed. Two days later, at the hôtel Matignon, he received a delegation of metal workers, who, claiming to support Spain and on the pretext of offering him "complete backing" for this purpose, warned him that they were preparing to call a one-hour strike two days later, a strike which could only appear as a means of making the government give in and redirect its policy toward more effective aid to Spain.

The head of government, ordinarily so benevolent, received this disguised ultimatum with asperity. He dryly answered the union representatives that they might very well go on strike, but that this step would in no way change a political line adopted by the government in the general interest. After dismissing these petitioners, he felt that their action revealed deep anxiety in working-class circles. Learning that the next day the Seine socialist federation was holding a meeting in Luna-Park which would raise the question of aid to Spain, he suddenly decided to attend.

On that Sunday September 6, public opinion was struck by the fall of Irun to Franco's forces. It was a defeat at the very gates of France. Blum, who had spent the night—as he did almost every Saturday night—with his friends the Grunebaum-Ballins in Mesnuls (Seine-et-Oise), asked Jules Moch to come and drive him to Luna-Park, near the Porte Maillot. During the drive, he told his friend that he still wished to aid the Spanish Republic, but that his reason urged him to do everything in order to preserve peace. "His hope remained that violations of the agreement would restore our freedom of action. Nevertheless, he told me, it would be better for our friends if the agreement were respected by everyone."

One can imagine the tension—and the attention—that prevailed in Luna-Park when the tall gentleman with gray hair mounted the platform. The feverish atmosphere helped to make this stirring plea into a battle:

> I was not included in the program for this festival, [but] yesterday I spoke with our comrades from the factories. Afterward, I felt the need to speak with my comrades and friends of the federation. I do not need to give you a long explanation for that. My eyes, believe me, are not closed to reality. I did not wish to allow a cruel misunderstanding to develop between the Popular Front government which I lead and a part, at least, of the working masses without explaining myself, because I want to dissipate that misunderstanding at all costs.

The audience was tense. But Blum had begun to forge the link to which he owed his incomparable authority. The crowd in Luna-Park remained turbulent: the majority, members of the Seine federation, of *La Bataille socialiste,* and of *La Gauche révolutionnaire,* had been joined by many Communist militants. There were cries of "Blum to action!" and "Guns and planes for Spain!"

> Is there a single man here, whether he agrees or not with me about the question I am about to discuss, who believes that I have changed in the last three months? Could three months of the exercise of power have made me a man different from the one you have known for so many years? You know very well that I have not changed, that I am still the same. Do you believe that there is a single one of your feelings that I do not share and that I do not understand? The other night at the Vélodrome d'Hiver you heard the delegates from the Spanish Popular Front; I had seen them that very morning. Do you believe that I listened to them with less emotion than you did? When I read, as you did, the dispatches about the fall of Irun and the agony of the last militia men, could you possibly believe that my heart was not with them? And do you believe, in addition, that I have suddenly been deprived of all intelligence, of every faculty of reflection and foresight, of every capacity to weigh the relations between the consequences of the events I am witnessing? You don't believe any of that do you? Then what?

Blum was gaining ground. The confessional tone, the psychologism, the personalization of politics were appropriate. But the audience was not yet silent. There was still an uproar, mutterings, and cries of "Blum to action!" But also more numerous cries of "Vive Blum!"

Comrades. I know very well what each one of you wishes in his heart. You would like arms to be delivered to the legitimate government and not to the rebel forces. . . . [But] there is no hope that aid can be given to one side without being given to the other! Ask yourselves who will gain the advantage in such a competition! Once an arms race has taken root on Spanish soil, what can the consequences be, the consequences for all Europe, in the present situation? Do not be too surprised, my friends, that the government has acted as it has! I say the government, but I could just as well speak in the first person, because I assume full responsibility. . . . I would not like the words I am about to speak to appear cruel or bitter to my friends in Spain who, I know and I am not surprised, sometimes judge our conduct harshly; that is natural. I would not like to appear to perceive more clearly than they do their own interests and the interests of their country. But, we thought that even for Spain, instead of beginning a struggle and a necessarily unequal competition, the course of action which contained the most real help was to obtain the kind of international abstention which, in spite of the glaring and harmful inequality at the outset, would in the end have allowed national sovereignty gradually to assume its predominance. And we did so in order to avoid international complications whose gravity and imminence were evident to us. . . . If we had not made the offer of 8 August,[194] will you ask yourselves what then would have become of an incident like the *Kamerun?*[195]

This conduct for which we are criticized, which has wounded in you feelings which I more than understand, has perhaps spared Europe from the danger of a general conflagration. I will ask you to take the word of a man who has never deceived you.

He had passed the most difficult point. Next came the moment for confession:

I can say that I did my best to avoid power for a substantial number of years. I am exercising it today in conditions that can hardly make anyone envious, and you know that when *I* say that it must be true! I have two duties to fulfill: a duty toward the Party whose delegate I am in the government and, as head of government, I have duties to the national community toward which we as a party have contracted certain obligations. If the day comes when I can no longer reconcile these two duties, when I can no longer, without failing my disciplined solidarity with my party, provide for the great national interests with which I am charged, then on that day power will become impossible for me.[196]

I will add one more thing. I am in the government not at the head of a socialist government, not at the head of a proletarian cabinet, but at the head of a coalition government whose contract was shaped by the common program of the *Rassemblement populaire.* However, we have not been able to settle everything through the contract. The policy which we have just adopted has met with no objection on the part of other powers. The covenant to which I declare it impossible today to refuse or withhold the signature of

France, bears, for example, the signature of the Union of Soviet Republics. I therefore cannot believe that the course of conduct we have followed is contrary to the principles of the *Rassemblement populaire* and to the general lines of the program it produced.

Now that he had involved the USSR in his argument and that the Communists had had to applaud him, he could go a little further:

> We have friends who call the government's conduct feeble, and dangerous because of its very feebleness. They speak of our weakness, of our capitulations, they say that it is the slack habit of concessions to the bellicose powers that is creating the real danger of war in Europe. They tell us that we must on the contrary resist, that it is through the exaltation of patriotic feeling that peace can now be preserved.
>
> My friends, my friends! I know this language, I heard it twenty-four years ago. I am a Frenchman—for I am French[197]—proud of his country, proud of its history, nourished as much as anyone else, in spite of my race, by its traditions. I will consent to nothing which damages the dignity of republican France, the France of the Popular Front, or the security of its defense. But when we speak of national dignity, national pride, national honor, will all of us forget that for fifteen years, through constant propaganda, we have taught this people that one of the necessary constituents of national pride was the will for peace?
>
> ... I do not believe and I will never admit that war is inevitable and fated. To the utmost limits of my power and with the last breath in my body if I must, I will do everything to divert it from this country—you hear me clearly, everything to avert the coming, the present danger of war. War is possible when it is accepted as possible; fated when it is proclaimed to be fated. And I for one refuse to despair of peace and of the action of the French nation to bring it about.
>
> My friends, I had an almost physical need to speak to you today as I have. I asked myself, seriously, bitterly, at our National Council[198] if I would find in myself the will and the substance of a leader. I have no idea. When I reconsider the history of these three months with some critical severity, there may be many circumstances in which I am not fully satisfied with myself, where someone else would have been able to do better than I have done. Yes, I know what I'm saying, I know it better than you do! Except that there are two things of which I can never be accused: lack of courage and lack of loyalty.
>
> I think that by being here at this moment, and by speaking to you as I have just done, I have given you evidence of courage. My loyalty will not fail either: loyalty to commitments made to the electoral majority, loyalty to the commitments undertaken by the other elements of the *Rassemblement populaire,* loyalty also, let me tell you, to myself, to the thoughts, to the convictions, and to the faith that have been mine all my life, in which I have grown and lived like you, like you and with you!

The audience gave a standing ovation to this astonishing self-parody of "Blumism," so overflowing with both cleverness and sincerity! That evening in Luna-Park Blum carried off a professional victory by almost completely winning over an audience with a hostile majority, or one that was at least rebellious at the outset. But in this case, was it not at the expense of what he had come to believe most deeply in the last few weeks, that is, that the time of pacifism had passed and the time for organizing resistance had come? The dilemma was now clear: democracy or barbarism. References to 1914 and Jaurès sounded a little false. Of course, there was no question of resigning oneself to the inevitability of war. But how could he identify so simplistically the conflict between imperialisms of 1914 with the unilateral threat which Nazism represented?

This celebrated speech—the least convincing of those that made his reputation—allowed him to win over an audience, not to convince the left as a whole, nor even his party. Far from it. Two months later, on November 8, he once again had to argue before the National Council of the SFIO. "Non-intervention? We did not choose it, we accepted it," he argued. "We accepted it in the conviction that the internal situation of this country and the international situation drove us to that step." Blum admitted, of course, that he had underestimated the dictators' duplicity. But he maintained once again that if the pact had not been proposed in early August, "Europe would have run the risk of general war in the second half of August." This was now his principal argument. Hadn't he himself gradually amplified and inflated it?

The fact is that his other argument, the one which had been most constant until then, had dwindled if not collapsed on September 30, at the rostrum of the League of Nations, when Alvarez del Vayo, Minister of Foreign Affairs in Madrid, had presented such a damning account of Mussolini's violations of the pact that the primary purpose of non-intervention, the prohibition or at least the limitation of intervention by others was shown to be fallacious.[199] The preservation of peace through self-discipline, the unilateral refusal to intervene to help friends? The position beame less and less tenable.

On October 30, in the course of a meeting at the Mutualité, Maurice Thorez openly attacked non-intervention. He was freer to do so since Stalin had decided at the end of September to suspend application of the agreement he had signed a month before because of the violations perpetrated by the Italians and the Germans. Moreover, Thorez had just returned from a brief stay in the USSR, and he knew that Moscow was preparing to become more deeply involved in the conflict. Therefore he went very far in denouncing what a PCF speaker had just called "the policy of the bare backside." He denounced "the responsibilities of comrade Blum in non-intervention, that juridical monstrosity which is assassinating our Spanish brothers," and the retreats and the complicities of the government in the face of fascism. Retreats, to be sure. But complicities? The accusation was absurd. In any case, was this the end of the Popular Front?

Blum's answer did not come until five weeks later, in the course of a debate on foreign policy in the National Assembly on December 4 and 5, in which Jacques Duclos and Gabriel Péri, supporting Maurice Thorez on the rostrum, shot holes through the foreign policy of the Blum cabinet. His speech that day, less famous than the one in Luna-Park, was more solid:

> I will accuse no one of wishing to urge us directly or indirectly to war . . . [but] on the most serious and certainly the most moving of current questions, the Spanish question, a mutual desire for peace nevertheless leaves us in practical disagreement with one of the groups of the majority, the Communist party. I agree without hesitation that the establishment in Spain of a dictatorship connected by excessively close bonds of gratitude to Germany and Italy would represent not only an assault on the international cause of democracy, but a source of anxiety—I will not say more—for French security and, consequently, a threat to peace.
>
> I do not deny for a single instant the personal friendship that binds me to the Spanish socialists and to many Spanish Republicans, in spite of the bitter disappointment which they now feel and express about me. To carry this sort of public confession to its conclusion, I will add that, after August 8, a certain number of our hopes and expectations were in fact disappointed. . . . The policy of non-interference, in many respects, did not provide everything we expected from it. Yes. But, gentlemen, is this a reason for condemning it? Here and now all of us must carry our thinking to its logical conclusion. If, in the name of international freedom and French security, we must indeed at any cost prevent the victorious establishment of rebellion on Spanish soil, then I assert that the conclusion of M. Gabriel Péri[200] and M. Thorez is not enough. It is not enough to denounce the non-interference agreement. It is not enough to re-establish free arms trade between Spain and France.
>
> Only a government can really arm another government. To be truly effective, assistance must be governmental. This is so from the point of view of matériel as from the point of view of recruitment. It should involve, in the guise of supplies, a withdrawal of arms from our stocks and, in the guise of volunteer soldiers, a withdrawal of men from our forces. Free trade should become, willy-nilly. . . de facto intervention, intervention that is less and less concealed. This is the logical consequence, and this is the practical consequence. And yet, it has not been proposed to you. And M. Maurice Thorez, at this rostrum a moment ago, energetically argued against it. . . .
>
> It is argued against us that since the end of October, the Union of Soviet [Socialist] Republics, following Germany and Italy, and in

order to restore the balance, has carried out arms deliveries to Spain and yet war has not resulted. . . . I believe that if it were possible for the Russians to respond to the German and Italian deliveries without provoking armed conflict, this is precisely because of the psychological subsidence, the kind of lowering of the European temperature which the non-interference agreement permitted to come about.

What can we be accused of? Of having feared war too much, of having done too much for peace? If there were a mistake on our part, gentlemen, it would be that one. Well, we can live with such an accusation. And if we have to choose, we would rather have exaggerated a risk of war than to have underestimated it. Mistake for mistake, we prefer to have done too much for peace to not having done enough. A day will perhaps come when, confronted with an enterprise too threatening for the essential conditions of peace, we will be brought to say: "No, not that. Impossible to go any further." A day will perhaps come when we will say that, as one must say it, but in the only way in which one has the right to say it, that is, with calm and the firm resolution to accept the ultimate consequences of our speech. . . .

Responsible for the safety of this country, as long as the direction of its affairs is in our hands, our duty would be to make certain that that terrible occasion did not arise in conditions, Thorez, in which France would precisely risk being isolated, in which we would find Europe uncertain, or more uncertain, and France divided!

But he did not want to push his advantage too far in that direction and isolate the Communists. Therefore, before concluding, he extended his hand to them:

I will never allow, for my part, the communists to be forced out of the majority by any external pressure. In my eyes, the Popular Front government would lose its reason for being. It is up to it to consider whether this divergence of views must hamper the social and political work we have undertaken together during the last six months.

Jacques Duclos's reply was so harshly polemical on the subject of Spain that there was anticipation of a negative vote by the PCF, and the consequent dissolution of the Popular Front which, in Blum's terms, would have " lost its reason for being." Thorez and his friends were content to abstain. It was nevertheless the most serious challenge to the coalition that had been formed the year before. Could the cabinet survive? Jules Moch recounts the scene that followed:

Immediately after the vote, Léon Blum called us to a meeting on the premises of the Chamber. Without expressing his opinion, he asked for ours. One faction maintained that the break-up of the majority had come at a moment when the program contained in the government's declaration was entirely accomplished, and moreover after measures not in the program, but beneficial to the working class, had been carried out. In these conditions, it was better to withdraw than to become "a government like any other," without a stable majority and therefore without any effective future activity. The response to the Communists' abstention was thus the government's resignation. This argument was supported, with variations, by Maurice Violette, Vincent Auriol, Pierre Cot, Marx Dormoy, several others, and myself. Conversely, most of the Radicals and a few socialists thought that the communists' abstention would be more exploited in the country if it opened a cabinet crisis. It therefore should be considered a minor incident and we should remain in power. . . . When everyone had expressed his opinion, Léon Blum, without alluding to the debate, asked for a few minutes' recess, which he spent in an adjoining office. He returned and said to us: "I was able to reach del Vayo. Our Spanish friends strongly want us to remain in power. They think we can help them more than anyone else in their struggle. In these conditions, we will be unanimous, won't we, in drawing no conclusions from the Communists' bad mood."

"Bad mood"? This writer-premier knew how to use understatement. Concluding a declaration according to which, in spite of the Communists' abstention, the government had decided to remain in power, Blum added: "It is not a matter of overcoming a momentary difficulty but of resolving it" in order to continue "common action in conditions of confidence and trust."

Blum was again placed on the defensive when he presented a bill (finally adopted) at the Palais-Bourbon on January 15 prohibiting the departure of volunteers for Spain. He paid tribute in passing to the "free gift of the individual to an ideal, to a belief, the example of Lafayette, Byron, Garibaldi," but he nevertheless emphasized the necessity of preventing, by "measures of a general and absolute nature, Spain from being overwhelmed by alternating waves of armed migration." This was the policy of an ostrich.

Risks and Deeds

Totally blind? Totally passive? Certainly not. Within this almost suicidal framework, the Blum government constructed a policy known as "relaxed non-intervention" which rendered significant services to the Republic, services which were acknowledged by several Spanish leaders of the time, and to which we will return. But first we have to attempt to evaluate the risks of international conflagration from which Blum claimed so often—and unwarrantedly?—to have saved France and Europe.

On four dangerous occasions at least, the French government's pacifism and its permanent pursuit of conciliation manifestly helped to avoid the worst.

On August 18, 1936, the German freighter *Kamerun* was attacked by the Spanish coast guard and forbidden to dock at a Spanish port. Berlin's reaction was vigorous but did not go as far as a real reprisal. Early in January 1937, the alarm was more serious. Information reaching the Ministry of Foreign Affairs indicated that a German landing in Spanish Morocco was imminent. In Delbos's absence, Pierre Viénot handled the affair: he convened the chiefs of staff to prepare a possible military response. The Anglo-Saxon press approved the very firm warning addressed to Hitler, who asserted on January 10 that he had never contemplated a landing and that it was a matter of false rumors.

On May 29, 1937, the cruiser *Deutschland,* anchored off Ibiza in the Balearics, was attacked by Republican airplanes. At meal time, a bomb hit the sailors' mess, killing twenty-two men. Nine more died shortly afterward. Hitler flew into a rage and had the port of Almeria bombarded by his fleet, causing about twenty deaths. Anxiety ran very high; it was redoubled three weeks later, on June 19, when the *Leipzig* was in turn torpedoed by government submarines. This time, Berlin and Rome raised a storm together and withdrew from the naval organization of the non-intervention pact. It was then, on June 21, that the Blum cabinet fell. If there was a time when the socialist leader's estimates of the risks of war were confirmed, it was during those days of June 1937. The fall of a government, which in spite of everything demonstrated a spirit of anti-Fascist resistance, and its replacement by a cabinet under Radical leadership (in this case led by Chautemps, a conciliator at any cost), was sure to give Berlin and Rome ideas.

This enumeration does not include the affair of September 1936: the intelligence service of the French Defense Ministry got word of a Republican air force plan to attack the German ship entrusted by the committee of London[201] to supervise non-intervention. Daladier and Cot managed with great difficulty to dissuade their Spanish colleagues from allowing such a provocation to take place (it was never learned who had proposed it).[202] The Spanish affair was indeed full of dangerous possibilities, which avowed aid by France would obviously have aggravated. And now Salazar in Lisbon was siding increasingly with Franco.

When on September 30, 1936 Alvarez del Vayo provided direct evidence that Mussolini had never respected the "non-intervention" agreements signed in August, Blum made the decision to "relax" surveillance of the frontier and the prohibition on arms exports, measures which had been taken on August 8 and reinforced on September 7. This was what he called "elastic" non-intervention; history has retained the name "relaxed."

Let us quote the principal executor of this "relaxation," Pierre Cot:

> Relaxed non-intervention was certainly not satisfying, but at least allowed those who wished to aid Spain to do so, all the more because the Soviet Union had asked France for the right to unload its ships in the ports on the North Sea and the Channel, not wanting to risk incidents in the Mediterranean.
>
> Rarely has there been such an unusual situation. I was a member of a government which had signed the non-intervention agreements, and my role throughout the period when I was responsible for the Ministry of Aviation consisted in evading those very agreements! The whole operation depended on the Ministry of Finance, where Vincent Auriol had complete control over customs; on the hôtel Matignon, where liaison was taken care of by Jules Moch, who played one of the most important roles in the affair; and on my own cabinet department, particularly on Jean Moulin, who was my head of cabinet and took care of finding pilots. Everyone knows of the role played in the creation of the Republican air force by men like Malraux, Corniglion-Molinier, Bossoutrot, de Marnier, Major Véniel, and many others.

According to the former Minister of Aviation, the French leaders also contributed actively to the training and movement to Spain of the volunteers of the international brigades, among whom the French made up "the largest national group, approximately ten thousand men."

Pierre Cot explains that the transport of Soviet matériel unloaded in French ports was carried out by convoys of armored trucks accompanied by hand-picked customs agents, and he adds that the same "flexible" procedure was applied to French exports theoretically intended for Mexico or Lithuania, but going, in fact, to Spain.[203]

Aside from the Soviet matériel which was shipped in this way (Pierre Cot estimates that approximately 300 Russian aircraft fought in the Spanish War), we should attempt to indicate the specifically French contribution to the Republicans' struggle. We can first of all estimate that Malraux managed to get approximately twenty airplanes across the Pyrenees between July 25 and August 1, twelve to fifteen of which made up the *España* squadron. Including the thirteen Dewoitines which took off during the cabinet meeting of August 7, and those that had preceded them during the first week of the month, approximately fifty French planes had crossed the border before August 8. According to an apparently serious investigation carried out by the journalist Philippe Roland of *Le Figaro*, about fifteen more planes left Toulouse, "with Blum's approval," between August 26 and October 21.[204]

Deliveries accelerated in the spring of 1937, and again during the second Blum government of March-April 1938. The left-wing American journalist Louis Fischer, himself very involved in these operations, estimates French contributions to have been seventy planes, among them thirty-five new fighters, through the end of 1936.[205] Pierre Cot proposes a different estimate: about 120 aircraft, eighty of which were military. But he admits that the majority of these planes were out-classed models; about a half–dozen of them were 1936 models (a few Dewoitine 510 fighters and a single Bloch 210 bomber). As for Hugh Thomas, the best historian of the war, he estimates that France sup-plied approximately 200 planes to the Republic.[206]

These estimates, whatever their differences, are positive. It is never-theless fitting to correct them with an observation by General Armand Maire who, in response to an article published in *Le Monde* in Novem-ber 1975 (according to which, from 1936 to 1939, France was *supposed to have* shipped to the Spanish army more than 300 machine guns, 20,000 Lebel rifles, and forty-seven 75mm. artillery pieces) made the following correction, which is certainly to be taken into consideration:

> At the time, I worked in the artillery division of the Ministry of Defense, in charge of managing arms matériel for the army and the corresponding ammunition, and I can affirm that this report corre-sponds in no way to reality.
> Although the head of the minister's civilian cabinet did in fact several times order the head of artillery to send artillery, machine guns, rifles, and their ammunition to Spain, we barely began to prepare to follow these orders, and they were all cancelled by the head of the military cabinet before they could begin to be carried out.

It is as difficult to provide exact details about the role Blum played in the traffic he himself called "contraband" as it is to evaluate the extent of this aid. His close friendship with the three members of the govern-ment most involved in the affair—Vincent Auriol, Pierre Cot, and Jules Moch—led him to do much more than close his eyes. We have already mentioned the role played by Vincent Auriol's assistant Gaston Cusin, from the customs service ("which made me an excellent smuggler!" he commented), who paid morning visits to the Premier in order to settle the details of these operations. Sometimes Blum also entrusted him with parallel missions. Thus, an unpublished note of August 13[207] indi-cates that Blum recommended that Cusin see Maurice Thorez. Cusin reports that he made contact with the Communist leader in order to keep him informed about what was being done for Spain, but that he was rebuffed shortly afterward by the representative of the Interna-tional in France with special responsibility for aid to Spain, Giulio Ceretti, an assistant to Ercoli (Togliatti). The Italian revolutionary con-sidered contacts with his French comrades with no special mandate to be a waste of time.

Moreover, Ceretti judged Blum harshly, criticizing "his weakness and his softness, his inability to make the right decision" in the Spanish affair. He ironically quotes Blum as saying to him: "My dear fellow, go see Cusin, perhaps he may be of use to you." Or: "Talk with Auriol who likes the Spanish. . . . Not once have I had the satisfactin of being able to say: I went to see the Premier who granted me this or that."[208] But after all, Ceretti was only an unofficial agent. Was the head of government obliged to make decisions in a private conference with him? Was it so wrong to send him to the strongest supporters of Madrid?

The fact is that on a questionable strategic basis, Blum's tactical approach was clearly beneficial to the Republic, and it became more so as the months passed, even when the circumstances were very dangerous for him—as, for example, when the right-wing press obtained proof in May 1937 of the arrival in Spain of several French aircraft.

After his cabinet was brought down by the Senate, the leader of the SFIO remained very preoccupied by the Spanish situation. He later recalled that one of the few conditions he set for his participation in the Chautemps government, from June 1937 to January 1938, was the maintenance of the "relaxation" of non-intervention. When the Chautemps cabinet was formed, he demanded that a socialist Secretary of State be named as assistant to Georges Bonnet, the new Minister of Finance, for this purpose. The important thing was that Cusin be able to remain in charge of customs.

But real "relaxed non-intervention" entered fully into operation under the second Blum cabinet. In taking the post of Minister of Finance for himself—with Pierre Mendès France (an avowed pro-Republican) as Secretary of State—Blum clearly intended to maintain control over aid to Spain.[209] In fact, his aims went further. For the leader of the 1938 government was no longer as timid as he had been in 1936. What explains this evolution, which might more accurately be called a conversion? In his *Histoire du Front populaire*, Georges Lefranc has tried to analyze the reasons for it; they have to do with the setbacks experienced in 1936, the imminence of national and international tragedy, and the consolidation of his relations with President Roosevelt through Ambassador William Bullitt, who had become his friend. On this point, we should emphasize the observations made earlier on relations between Blum and American leaders, which began in 1936 and took on primary importance in 1938. The Blum of 1936, dependent on the alliance with England, felt subordinate and constrained, the Blum of 1938 felt only strengthened by the possibilities of transatlantic participation in the alliance.

Nor should we entirely neglect the role which may have been played by the replacement at the Quai d'Orsay of the timid Yvon Delbos by the expansive Paul-Boncour, who had closer ties with the Spanish

Republicans and was less susceptible (since he was not a member of the Radical party) to the pressures and manipulations of Chautemps, Malvy, and Caillaux.

In short, the second Blum cabinet proved itself determined not to pay any price for the defense of peace. This was clearly demonstrated on the third day of its existence when Blum called a meeting of the Committee of National Defense. This was shortly after the Austrian *Anschluss* which had made Hitler the master of Vienna on March 11; there was no longer time to save Austria. But Czechoslovakia might still be rescued. As for Spain, the situation was developing in a tragic manner: Aragon had just fallen into Franco's hands, and Catalonia was directly threatened.

There are several reports of this important session. Blum himself spoke of the meeting of March 15, 1938 before the Investigative Commission of 1947, indicating that on that day he and his colleagues had considered "whether it was possible, in order to save Catalonia, to carry out a military operation in the form of a rapid expedition."

But nothing can replace quotation of substantial excerpts from the minutes prepared by the Ministry of National Defense. The positions of Blum, Daladier, and the military are baldly presented:

Paris, 16 March 1938
PERMANENT COMMITTEE
of National Defense
Minutes of the Meeting (excerpts)

On Tuesday 15 March 1938, under the presidency of M. Edouard Daladier, Minister of National Defense and War, the Permanent Committee of National Defense held a meeting at the hôtel Matignon for the purpose of considering the following questions:

1) Aid to Czechoslovakia in case of German aggression.
2) Intervention in Spain.

Present:
M. Léon Blum, Premier.
M. Edouard Daladier, Minister of National Defense and War.
M. Paul-Boncour, Minister of Foreign Affairs.
M. Campinchi, Minister of the Navy.
M. Guy La Chambre, Minister of Aviation.
Marshall Pétain.
General Gamelin, Chief of Staff of the Ministry of Defense.
Admiral Darlan, Chief of Staff of the Navy.
General Vuillemin, Chief of Staff of the Air Force.
M. Alexis Léger, Secretary-General of the Ministry of Foreign Affairs.

. . .

M. LEON BLUM broached the question which he wished to ask the permanent committee:
How could we intervene in Spain?
How could we back up an ultimatum to General Franco along

these lines: "If, within twenty-four hours, you have not given up the support of foreign forces, France will resume its freedom of action, and reserves the right to take all measures of intervention it may consider useful."

He pointed out that it would be a maneuver of the same kind as the one Chancellor Hitler had just successfully attempted in Austria.[210]

GENERAL GAMELIN pointed out that the conditions were not the same.

We normally have a standing army of only 400,000 men in France, while the Germans have 900,000 men available.

If we wished to play this game, we would have to have a million men. It would therefore be necessary to organize protection, that is, to mobilize.

M. LEON BLUM summed up this part of the discussion by concluding that any operation in Spain would necessitate putting "protection" into operation.

M. PAUL-BONCOUR asked what repercussions an operation against Spanish Morocco would have in Spain. Would it provide sufficient pressure to release government forces?

GENERAL GAMELIN indicated that such an operation would have a significant effect, that it would place important centers in our hands, and that in any case it would provide an indispensable guarantee for the maintenance of the freedom of the Straits of Gibraltar.

It would necessitate the partial mobilization of Algeria.

M. PAUL-BONCOUR asked what should be thought of an operation against the Balearics.

ADMIRAL DARLAN answered that it would be a large-scale operation which would necessitate land forces the size of a division.

To a question about the comparative strength of the German and French air forces, General Vuillemin, Air Force Chief of Staff, answered that our air force would be annihilated in two weeks.[211]

MARSHALL PETAIN pointed out that in aviation, initial forces counted less than manufacturing potential. . . .[212]

M. DALADIER declared that one would have to be blind not to see that intervention in Spain would unleash general war.

M. LEGER reminded the committee that England would break with us if we abandoned non-intervention without changed circumstances.

M. LEON BLUM asked if one could, without military intervention, increase aid provided to Spain.

GENERAL GAMELIN showed that this measure would lead to disarming French forces for uncertain results, since (Spanish) government forces were tactically inept.

M. LEON BLUM indicated that he believes we have reached the point at which General Franco no longer needs foreign military aid.

GENERAL GAMELIN asked if there might not be a diplomatic means of separating him from Germany and Italy.

MARSHALL PETAIN declared that General Franco would

need English money to reconstruct Spain and that England there-fore has an effective means of action.

M. LEGER revealed that England is speculating on a xenophobic evolution in Spain which should detach Franco from Germany and Italy.

M. DALADIER asked what would be the reaction of Germany and Italy if we were to intervene in Spain.

Would it be for them, asked M. LEON BLUM, a *casus belli?*

Without doubt, answered M. LEGER.[213]

There were leaks. In his memoirs, Paul-Boncour blames Marshall Pétain's entourage. In the right-wing press these exchanges of views were suddenly and noisily transformed into a planned expedition south of the Pyrenees: a prefect even telegraphed the Minister of the Interior that filmmakers had come to Perpignan to film the entry of French troops into Spain![214]

Blum's conversion was a surprising one. Here he was replacing at one stroke unwarranted abstention with bellicose interventionism. Why? Lessons had been learned, events had proceeded, evidence had appeared. It had taken Guernica and the fall of Saragossa, it had taken the *Anschluss* above all for him to move from the desolate retreat of August 8, 1936 to this effervescent boldness. A little late? There are so many public men who remain blind to the lessons of history! He had learned, and tried to draw conclusions.

Was Blum's proposal for direct intervention more than a trial balloon? Was the leak from Pétain's cabinet[215] a warning, a countermeasure, already the establishment of a system? The camps preparing for the decisive battle for and against fascism were thus defining themselves and organizing. In any case, the debates of the Defense Committee on March 15, 1938 were not without effect: two days later, Blum gave the order to open the frontier and to authorize deliveries of French armaments to the Republic. These decisions provoked an indignant protest from the British Ambassador, a dramatic warning from Herriot, a vehement speech from Flandin.

It was too late, too late to stop Blum, but especially too late to save the Republic: Barcelona and then Madrid fell a few months later, after a final appeal to Paris by Juan Negrin, the last head of the Republican government. Non-intervention had ended, but so had Spanish democracy.

The Painful Trial

Blum's Spanish policy, from July 20, 1936 to April 8, 1938, can be put on trial on three levels, or summed up in three questions: Was non-intervention avoidable? Was the head of government personally responsible for the choice? Did the policy have a chance of success?

Most figures involved in the decisions of the summer of 1936, including those who deplored the decision made on August 7—Vincent Auriol, Pierre Cot, and Jules Moch, among others—have said, written, and repeated that Blum had been compelled by his Radical and British allies and had "resigned" himself to it. This is the argument we have accepted. But we should also quote the opinion of another participant, well-disposed toward Blum but hostile to non-intervention: Jean Zay. According to the former Radical Minister of Education, Blum did not accept it as an obligation that was imposed on him, but because he "personally considered it a good policy."[216]

In any case, recognizing the bankruptcy of the policy—obvious by the end of September 1936—Blum desperately hung on to it, trying repeatedly to demonstrate its validity. The more the audience was hostile to it, from the Luna-Park meeting to the Royan SFIO congress, the more the head of the Popular Front government claimed complete responsibility for the choice. Thus, in September 1936, when he received a delegation from the English Labour Party led by the future Chancellor of the Exchequer Hugh Dalton, he firmly claimed: "I proposed it, not Eden."

We know Blum's courage, his pride, and his persistence which could become, as André Blumel has pointed out, stubbornness. In fact, and whatever Jean Zay may have said, it is obvious that "non-intervention," so morally unworthy, so juridically fallacious, was for him only a lesser evil to be defended for want of something better.

He had no other solution. On this point we can believe the convinced interventionist Piette Cot: according to him, non-intervention was "like a lead weight on the Blum cabinet which lost its freedom of judgment and became committed to decisions that did not correspond to its leader's convictions."[217] The former Radical minister was to say later:

> I greatly regretted that the circumstances did not allow Léon Blum to adopt another policy. I say the circumstances, because I completely agree that, given the political situation, he could not have acted otherwise. What was tragic for Léon Blum was that if he had aided Spain as his sensibility, his very being urged him to, he was certain that he would be replaced the next day by a man who was much less sympathetic to the Spanish Republicans, because the government would not have survived.[218]

In his book *Souvenirs et solitude,*[219] Jean Zay asserts that "we intervened enough to earn reproaches from the enemy camp and not enough to provide effective support to the Republicans." To which Jules Moch replies:

Of course, non-intervention harmed the Republic. It prevented the defense of the Basque country in 1936, for lack of a few artillery pieces, and it later prevented the exploitation of the Ebro victory of 25 July 1938, for want of means of transport. But it preserved peace in Europe and was preferred by the three successive heads of the Republican government at war to the resignation of the Popular Front cabinet. Léon Blum knowingly took a considerable risk of unpopularity, which was thoroughly exploited by the French Communists; he was inspired by the noblest motives. As soon as Italian and German violations of non-intervention were confirmed, he did not hesitate to take another risk: that of allowing his associates to organize the "disinterested smuggling," which transported hundreds of ships, thousands of tons of goods, and tens of thousands of volunteers.[220]

The policy was "preferred by the three successive heads of the Republican government"? This is true. But is it possible to infer that cholera is tolerable because it is preferred by a sick man to the plague? If we listen to those chiefly concerned, the Spanish, we encounter at least two severe condemnations of Blum's behavior.

First, that of the Communists, expressed again by Santiago Carillo, a veteran of the 1936 war, in *Demain L'Espagne:*[221]

French responsibility in the affair was decisive, crucial—especially that of Léon Blum, because it was he who, under pressure from the English, proposed non-intervention as he shed a few tears over the corpse of the Spanish Republic. When Irun was on the point of falling into the hands of the Fascists, there were arms belonging to the Republic on French territory; these arms could have saved the city, but Léon Blum's government did not allow them to cross the border.

There is also the condemnation by Alvarez del Vayo, a left-wing socialist who was for a long time the head of Republican diplomacy. According to him, by choosing non-intervention Blum in a sense "betrayed the two proletariats," French and Spanish. He adds:

The mistakes made at the beginning had consequences which greatly troubled the socialist premier. Every time I passed through Paris, it was my duty to inform him frankly about the situation, and I saw him disturbed and in a way desperate. His despair proves his sensitivity, but it does not absolve Léon Blum from the responsibility he assumed by lending his name and that of the French socialist party to the farce of non-intervention.[222]

Other, more complex, opinions have been expressed on the Spanish side. In 1976 in Madrid, José Bergamín, who was one of the Spanish intellectuals most involved in the struggle, observed to us that "nothing less resembled the magnificent figure of Blum than the pitiful policy of non-intervention," and he added: "His hands were tied, especially by the English. He probably could not have acted otherwise. Perhaps he could have resigned." In a book published in 1976, another Republican fighter, Ambassador Azcarte, describes in detail his contacts with the leaders of the French Popular Front. Although he characterizes the attitude of Paris and London as "cowardly and humiliating," and he considers the closing of the French border in August 1936[223] a "monstrous injustice," he pays many tributes to Blum's "generosity" and the "breadth of his vision," and repeats several times that, under the circumstances, significant services were rendered. His colleague Araquistain, Republican Ambassador to Paris, asserted for his part in 1937 that "the Republic ought to win the war if non-intervention were effectively practiced."[224]

In a contribution to the 1965 conference,[225] the former Republican minister Julio Just maintained that "the idea of non-intervention was attractive and plausible, on the condition that the signatories to the agreement strictly carry out its provisions." He went on: "Premier Blum's policy toward Republican Spain involved sympathy and ideological affinity with the Spanish Republic. In Spanish government circles we knew all the difficulties Léon Blum encountered, and we felt the greatest gratitude toward [him] and those of his ministers who supported his policy in favor of the government of the Republic."

We will quote finally the opinion of Juan Negrin, the most combative of the Spanish leaders. Two years before his death, on the occasion of the centenary of the 1848 Revolution, Blum delivered a commemorative speech at the Sorbonne in which he referred to Lamartine's policy of not "intervening" in Europe to save the revolutionaries, thereby allowing the Poles and the Hungarians to be crushed. Indicating that he had criticized this policy to Jaurès, he continued, quoting his friend: "Nothing good can come from war. War is evil." This indirect apology for his Spanish policy earned the old statesman a violent uproar from the university public. The next day, Juan Negrin wrote to him to express his great indignation at these reactions, and to tell him that no one knew better than he, leader of the government at war, all that Republican Spain owed to his active friendship.[226]

Then in two letters addressed to Jules Moch, one dated June 9, 1950, the other undated but certainly later, Negrin declared himself very attached to "the memory of our great friend Léon Blum," affirming that in the summer or the winter of 1936, "the replacement of the Blum cabinet [would have been] fatal for us."

Perhaps the moderation, the leniency of some Spanish leaders of the period should be attributed to their awareness of their own mistakes, the divisions which, just as much as the failures of their friends, led to their defeat. This point of view rarely appears in the writings of Republican survivors of the war. But it is impossible not to bear it in mind. The veritable internecine wars which so profoundly weakened the Republican camp, from Barcelona during the summer of 1936 to Madrid in early 1938, weighed very heavily. One of the French leaders who was most in favor of supporting Madrid, Philippe Serre, member of the second Blum government, said in December 1976: "Whatever might be done for it, the Republic could not be saved: it committed suicide by its dissensions."

This observation only partially lightens Blum's responsibilities. Effective or not, and certainly risky, determined support for the Republican cause would have avoided a stain on French socialism and on his own name, would have deprived the dictators of an encouragement to pursue their predatory policy, and would have fortified, in Europe and elsewhere, the opponents of the Axis. But on these points, and on others, we have to allow Blum to speak. Perhaps we will find in his sometimes self-critical remarks, as in his defenses of his position, the elements of an equitable judgment.

"My torture." This is how he often characterized the Spanish conflict and the problems it posed for him. We have already referred to the various arguments he advanced to justify or explain "non-intervention." But we passed very quickly over two of them. One is formulated with particular clarity in a letter he wrote from prison in 1942 to the sister of his colleague André Blumel, Maître Suzanne Blum, who was then a refugee in the United States:

> If these possibilities had become real [intervention and its consequences], civil war in France would have preceded international war. The Spanish affair took place between the 6th of February and the armistice. It was intertwined with the social crisis. As soon as the situation had become dangerously tense, we would have had the equivalent of Franco's coup in France. Before any foreign war, France would have had civil war with little chance of victory for the Republic. That is, Spain would not have been delivered, but France would have become Fascist, probably before Spain.

The formulation is a little simplistic, a little ponderous, coming from such a subtle man. But the idea is not one that can be shrugged off. The "strong-arm" right had lost the battle of 1936. It was burning for revenge. If the aggravation of tension provoked by a clearer commitment to Spain had come about as early as the summer of 1936, it seems that, in its rising and euphoric phase, the Popular Front would have been able to deal with it. Later, after the devaluation, the "pause," after the drama of Clichy, the left had split and the right had reassembled. The possibility formulated in the letter to Suzanne Blum became plausible.

There is a final argument, that of Blum as an impassioned advocate rather than a serene jurist.

> I ask the question now: "What would intervention have been?" Intervention would necessarily have taken an armed form, and armed intervention necessarily led to war. No one ever proposed or advised intervention to me, no one in Spain nor in France, except for two men. One was a French officer who said to me one day in my office: "Sir, a King of France would have gone to war."[227] The other was a foreign diplomat who, I have reason to believe, had badly understood or badly followed the instructions of his government. Our communist comrades in the Chamber always refrained from calling for intervention, and none of them expressed himself more clearly on the subject than Maurice Thorez.[228]

It is true that the PCF was officially opposed to military intervention properly speaking, and demanded only arms deliveries—a policy which now appears to have been the best one. But in the youth movement of the party, some were arguing for direct military intervention. Gilles Martinet, who carried out a mission in Spain for the *Jeunesses communistes* in 1936, pointed out that, given the weakness of Republican troops outside street fighting, only an intervention by modern units would have been able to block the path of Franco's aggression, and then only on the condition that it were set in motion before the fall of Irun. This is the operation that was called for by militants like him.

This is also the period in which Pierre Mendès France, who is today Blum's only former close associate[229] who criticizes the basis of his Spanish policy and who believes that an alternative was possible, locates the possibilities of military aid from France to the Republic which would have been really effective, perhaps even decisive. This is to forget that at the time—July–August 1936—the Madrid leaders themselves considered the affair not very significant. We have quoted remarks by Juan Negrin asserting that he was then the only one who believed that the threat was serious and the coming struggle a long one. But Negrin was then a figure of secondary importance. Was Paris supposed to be more lucid than Madrid? When the diagnosis of French informants in Spain changed, it was to affirm—from September on—that the Republic was lost and that any effort to save it was futile. Of course, Blum and Delbos should have recalled Ambassador Herbette, who was as incompetent as he was clearly on the side of the rebels. But they did not, and the consequences were serious.

But we cannot be satisfied with an opposition between "nonintervention" and classic military intervention,[230] while three or four intermediary formulas could have been applied: simple opening of the borders to free trade, or the immediate execution of the 1935 treaties, or the establishment of "sanctuaries" similar to the sanctuaries the Tunisians and Moroccans established during the Algerian War. "Nonintervention" ought to read "abstention."

What is particularly troubling, in fact, in the expression "non-intervention" is that it seems to characterize an act of wise reserve. Since "intervention" (presumptively in the affairs of another state) is to be condemned, "non-intervention" seems to imply respect for the law. But in this case the negative prefix in reality applies to a just act. One should not speak of non-intervention, but of non-aid, non-solidarity, "non-assistance." And one should complete the formula with the usual words "to a person in danger."

To Blum's own passionate defense we should add the few self-critical notations he later occasionally expressed, both in a series of articles for *Le Populaire* in 1938 and 1939 and again in 1945 and in his deposition before the Parliamentary Investigative Commission in 1947.

> One may address all the objections one likes to this course of action. One may reproach it for lacking stature and grandeur. One may also reproach it for not having re-established real reciprocity between the totalitarian dictatorships and France, real equality between the legitimate government of Spain and the rebels.[231] One may condemn the choice which the French government made. One may consider that the former socialist ministers who participated in this choice made a mistake.
>
> The so-called non-intervention agreements, given that name because their aim was to prevent the intervention of the totalitarian dictatorships, had in reality failed in their goal, [when] intervention by Facist Germany and, in an even more pronounced way, by Fascist Italy had gradually taken on an obvious, public, almost official character.[232]

This is not much, but he did write it. One is not honest with impunity.

There are also a few undated notes, scribbled while he was a prisoner in Burassol or Buchenwald, contained in the Blum Archive of the FNSP. They, too, should be added to the dossier.

In the first, Blum recalls the reasons for which he might have resigned after three months (he seems to be alluding to the crisis of August 7–8, rather than that of July 23–24). His government had carried out most of the plans for which it had been elected. But he stayed in power, while he was tied hand and foot as far as Spain was concerned by English influence and the risks of civil war, because, he says, "I was still the man most capable of making the country understand and accept this policy which was contrary to my convictions, contrary to my instincts."

Other notes are scarcely written out. They include the word "resignation," the names Los Rios and Bouckère, and this:

> The risk. In France, what I feel today. Outside France: the *Deutschland,* the Morocco affair. What I hope: it was possible if

not for Spanish dissensions. The impossibility of intervening: to confront [them][233] with a *fait accompli,* the government at least had to be in agreement. I said to myself: never again a 7 March.[234] For once, we will confront [them] with a *fait accompli.*

The last note, also undated and written in captivity, explains:

I did not wish to risk war for Spain. I could not. But if there was anything that could have prevented it, it was the victory of the Republicans. If Spanish resistance had lasted a few more months, the German attack would have come a year later, which would have changed everything.

A remarkable statement which reveals another Blum, the one who might have been called forth by great events. To avoid general war by a Republican victory, thanks to rapid and massive assistance and a raid by mechanized units protecting at least Irun in early September 1936— this is what was perhaps very briefly possible during the first weeks, after the semi-failure of the *pronunciamento.* Between the Republican victory in Barcelona and its defeat in the Basque country five or six weeks elapsed. According to Negrin, the time the Spanish leaders thought the war would last. And afterward? Jimenez de Asua was "probably right"[235] when he pointed out to Blum (who explained to him on July 25 or August 8 the reasons for French abstention and for his remaining at the head of the government) that, by moving into opposition, the Socialist party would have more weight and would perhaps do the Spanish Republic more good.

One can indeed imagine the impact that would have been created by a Socialist party supported by the PCF, a significant fraction of the Radicals, and the CGT, if Blum, proclaiming that it had been made impossible for him to carry out in Spain the policy that was in conformity with the country's commitments, the national interest, and his own convictions, had led his comrades in a collective resignation on July 25 or August 8, 1936. A Chautemps government would have succeeded him a few months earlier than it did.[236] Would it have been able to revoke the social laws? Certainly not. Nor would it have been able to sabotage their application, confronted by a united working class. Would it have been able to follow a still more prudent policy toward Spain? The one that it did follow, after June 21, 1937, was certainly more timorous than that of the Blum cabinet. But in August, September, and October 1936, it would have been forced into more boldness by the two great parties of the left, a notable fraction of the Radical party, and the CGT, who would have harassed it, challenged it, and urged it on, still more than they harassed, challenged, and urged on Blum. One cannot dismiss the hypothesis formulated at the time by the socialist journalist Louis Lévy, who advocated this strategy and maintained that Blum would have been recalled by the masses to support the Spanish Republic openly.

Presuming, as we are inclined to, that Louis Lévy's prediction could not have been realized and that the SFIO would have remained confined to a strong opposition stance, we don't believe that the Madrid Republicans would have lost very much. One can see very clearly that the Socialist Party—and Blum himself—would have gained by it. Then, fully reexamining his arguments about fascist aggression, the spirit of resistance that was to be, was already his, would probably have ripened faster.

There is also the moral dimension of politics, the trust of a socialism understood as a culture and an ethics received from Jaurès, the vision of a legacy to be left to future generations, which he had so carefully, so jealously preserved for twenty years, rather than risk it or dilute it in ordinary electoralism. He had been able to preserve this trust until the brilliant "exercise of government" of June 1936, but he allowed it to become infected and to decay.

We have already said enough about the tragic nature of the socialist leader's position, caught between the inaccessible and the unacceptable. There are cases in which the unacceptable must under no circumstances be accepted. Cases in which a few services rendered cannot possibly balance rigidity on principles. Watching him struggle in this swamp, it is hard to resist the temptation of quoting Jaurès's appeal to Briand: "Not that, or not you!"

In concluding, "rendering a verdict," we must still take into consideration what was done and, when we speak of abandonment, abstention, betrayal, remain conscious of the realities, notably that the Franco-Spanish agreement of 1935 was in fact applied, that the "monstrosity" of which a communist spokesman like Georges Gosnat accuses Léon Blum in Verny and Santelli's film on the Popular Front was not perpetuated; juridically, the French government's promise was kept. Moreover, it is tempting to point out to those particular critics of non-intervention that they themselves, by deciding to abstain from the direct responsibilities of government in May 1936, were practicing a "non-intervention" which prevented them from acting against France's passivity in Spain. By refusing to take on governmental responsibilities, the communists condemned themselves to impotence and were thus precursors of "non-intervention" and shared responsibility for it.

Nevertheless, this does not justify the pitiful adventure of the August 1936 pact which, from late September on, called for only one decision: solemn denunciation, probably followed by the breakup of the Popular

Front government. Further persistence in the policy was a form of self-deception.

It is clear that Léon Blum's choice about Spain was the most difficult, the most painful, the furthest from his heart and his deepest desires. There is not one of his associates of the time who has not testified that he had to resign himself to acting against his most constantly proclaimed convictions. But the value of a policy cannot be judged on the basis of the suffering it inflicts on the man who conceived and practiced it.

THE GREAT RETREAT

The Wall of Money Again

Was Blum an economist? A noted jurist, an eminent business lawyer, former head of the cabinet of a socialist Minister of Public Works, surrounded by men like Auriol, Spinasse, and Jules Moch who were constantly concerned with problems of exchange and production, Blum, unlike Daladier and Herriot, was not a stranger to these questions. But he was caught in a series of contradictions which finally crushed him.

The first was the opposition between his socialist convictions and his fundamental suspicion of a planned economy. The second derived from the choice he had made to depend on the capitalist democracies to save his socialist-inspired experiment. The third was bound up with the very nature of the Popular Front coalition.

To be sure, there are forms of socialism that do not require a planned economy. There are no references to such plans in Marx, and they are rare in Jaurès. But many socialists and union members in the thirties considered the planned economy the economic framework of the doctrine. Blum took the opposite point of view, but not simply because Marcel Déat and his "neo" lieutenants were the most ardent champions of economic planning. More profoundly, it was because Blum saw in the idea of a planned economy (held by Henri de Man, for example) an "intermediate regime" between democracy and totalitarianism which risked falling into Fascism. The future was to show that this pessimism was well founded.

If there were good reasons for rejecting a planned economy, recourse to the aid of the capitalist powers was above all tied to circumstances. We have referred to the advice given by Emmanuel Monick. We must also explain the circumstances in which the devaluation of September 28, 1936 was carried out; it was less an adjustment of the relations between production and currency in France than an attempt to coordinate the French, British, and American economies.

But the most dangerous contradiction for Blum was the one between his obligations to remain within the limits of a program which protected the interests of the ruling class and the almost unanimously hostile behavior of the rich. Confronting the financial powers, the Popular Front had its hands tied by a program, that allowed it to attack only one financial fortress (the Banque de France) while the rest of the other financial powers—except for Horace Finaly, who was himself under challenge as the head of the Banque de Paris et des Pays-Bas—were animated by the most suspicious, and later vindictive, attitudes toward what the Popular Front was and what it represented.

From the beginning, the dilemma was apparently the one that Monick had outlined for Blum: either central planning and the risk of sliding toward totalitarianism, or alliance with the democratic powers, which implied the choice of liberalism for France. Liberalism? The word is a little simplistic, because social policy was after all very strongly marked by a vigorous economic framework. This too is one of the fundamental contradictions which Blum's enterprise came up against and on which it foundered; reliance on Keynesian formulas of "stimulation of consumption," and "pump-priming" provoked a growth of demand while the application of the social and labor laws[237] limited, at least in theory, the growth of production. To the left in social matters, to the right in financial ones, Blum's politics were conditioned simultaneously by the hostility of the employers, by the socialist left which persisted in demanding an acceleration of the socialization of the state and of production, by a rather naïve faith in the magical properties of Keynesian remedies, and by the vicissitudes of negotiations with London and Washington which forced France into a necessary (but belated and timid) devaluation designed not to give too many advantages to French exporters.

We have no intention of summing up Blum's economic and financial policies in a few sentences or formulas. But we can isolate, as particularly significant and consequential, three initiatives: the 40-hour week, devaluation, and the "pause" of February 1937—although the first has rather more to do with social strategy, and the other two were in response to circumstances. But, whether by free choice or adaptation, these three "moments" illustrate well Blum's and Auriol's complicated navigation between their socialist convictions and their sense of what was possible.

The 40-hour week has been the target of untold gibes, criticisms, and pessimistic analyses. Of the latter, we will refer to those by Alfred Sauvy and J.-M. Jeanneny, the first in his *Histoire économique de la France entre les deux guerres,* the second in his contribution to the conference *Léon Blum, chef de gouvernement.* For Sauvy, everything appears simple: while the Popular Front, after the devaluation of September 1936, had every possibility of bringing France out of the crisis, it was the limitation of the work week to forty hours that ruined it. The former adviser to Paul Reynaud maintains that it was the generalization of the 40-hour week in April 1937 which caused production to decline and the Blum experiment to capsize.

One of Sauvy's most forceful arguments is that the limitation of forty hours in prosperous industries meant that the others worked even less. Was this really the case? According to René Le Bras, a CGT union leader and a militant of *La Révolution prolétarienne,* discussing his experience in the meter factory where he worked, "after June '36, the work week passed from 26 or 28 to 40 hours and, with a week of five eight-hour days, the men felt as though they were working overtime. To supply orders, the assembly lines had been lengthened. For nearly two years, productivity was very high." According to Le Bras, it was the threat of war that caused production to decline in the factory.

Then should we be satisfied with global figures, like those proposed by J.-M. Jeanneny,[238] that indicated the index of industrial production was only 81 in September (it was 100 in 1928, 109 in 1929, and 87 in May 1936)? It was a period of strikes but automobile production had increased; that may make a definitive judgment impossible. As a whole, the 40-hour system functioned well. If in the end it appears to be a factor in under-production, this must be attributed in part to the renewed wave of strikes in the autumn. After all, the aim was above all a social one. The working class could not once again bear the burdens of recovery. Its past sufferings, its spirit in the spring, and the morale of the Popular Front made the law necessary. Presented in vague terms by the program of the *Rassemblement,* it was precipitated by the strikes and remains an honor to the Blum government.

We cannot say as much of the devaluation of September 1936 which, intended as a protective measure toward economic slow-down, appeared as the second defeat of the Popular Front (the first being the Spanish retreat). But, here too, it is difficult to decide; the inertia of the coalition played a large role, as did external influences and domestic sabotage. Partly because it was tied to two parties—the Radicals and the Communists—hostile to devaluation, partly because it depended in part on Western financial backing, and because it was weakened by substantial capital exports, the Popular Front delayed devaluation, and it failed. But a few suggestions of this kind are insufficient. We have to state the facts briefly.

We will again quote Emmanuel Monick, one of the protagonists of the operation. After recalling that during the electoral campaign the leader of the SFIO had sworn that under his government people would not see "the walls of Paris covered with the white posters of devaluation," Monick says:

> Our policy of deflation prevented our economic recovery. It slowed down our rearmament. It gave rise to the worst kind of social recriminations. To escape from the morass, we had to cut the Gordian knot, that is, devaluate. But public opinion was blindly attached to the gold standard for the franc. Parliament, in spite of Paul Reynaud's brilliant diatribes, had pledged itself for the length of its term to "saving" the currency, but at the same time to "torpedoing" the economy.[239]

Is it because, like Auriol, he shared this point of view that Blum called upon Monick? He was worried about the possible reactions of London and Washington. Monick replied that "a setting of the value of the franc which excluded undervaluation and consequent unwarranted competition" could be accepted by the two powers "without any economic or monetary countermaneuver." He made it clear that the case had to be presented directly to Roosevelt. "I know the President of the United States well enough to believe that he will say yes. And when President Roosevelt has said yes, the British government will not be able to say no. M. Léon Blum asked for time to think."

He waited only a few hours before sending the financial expert on an exploratory mission to Washington, where Roosevelt reacted very favorably to the French proposal of a three–power readjustment of currencies and coordination of economies. Returning to Paris, Monick received a "bittersweet" welcome from Blum, and learned from Auriol that opposition to devaluation had hardened since the formation of the government. In the Chamber on June 6, under pressure from the two allied parties (Radicals and Communists) Blum felt obliged to declare that there would be no "monetary coup d'état." He had tied his hands.

The month of August was rather calm on the financial front. But in the middle of September, the employers having worked out the details of their counter-attack, the flight of capital became alarming.[240] The hour of decision had come. It was then that the Washington negotiations, continued in London in July, took on their full meaning. The preparatory work bore fruit; the terms of the tripartite monetary agreement were worked out in ten days. Signed on September 25, the agreement was made public the next day: the French government announced that the franc was aligned with the dollar and the pound.[241]

This decision, although cleverly presented by Jules Moch as "a monetary peace treaty" (Nazi ruling circles were caused some anxiety; they saw in it the first step toward a coalition of the democracies) was very badly received. French public opinion saw in this devaluation of 29 percent a defeat of the government and a breaking of its promises. Comments from the right were virulent; from the Communists scarcely less so. "What we need," Duclos of course grumbled, "is to make the rich pay!"

Bergery's *La Flèche* did not oppose devaluation, but urgently asked the Premier to "govern France, after having governed the franc" (Francis Delaisi, October 3, 1936). *L'Oeuvre,* caustic as usual, said: "Necessity knows no law, agreed. Let us resign ourselves then, but if possible, let us not carry bad taste so far as to rejoice, like some who are closer than we to the secrets of the gods" (September 28). In the Senate, Caillaux accused Blum of having ruined the operation's chances by accompanying it "with a distribution of largesse." The Premier retorted: "Who would claim that the mission of this government is to assume the predominance of the individual property rights of industrialists over the collective interest which is called social peace?"[242]

Nevertheless, J.-M. Jeanneny points out, "from October to March there was a renewal of economic activity."[243] The index of production climbed from 81 to 93. Every branch of industry experienced a revival of production. But the deficit in the balance of payments increased and liquidity problems grew heavier. Capital inflow following the devaluation ended in December, and in February a new loan had to be floated in London.

What were the reasons for this failure? During a debate at the Ecole Normale in May 1966, Mendès France pointed out that the devaluation came much too late. Simon Nora, for his part, maintained that in 1936 "the economic policy of *reflation* and increased purchasing power made the success of devaluation impossible." How could devaluation be successfully carried out with a balance of payments that was a bottomless pit? This was the question raised in turn by Jean Bouvier, from a different angle, in his report on the debate. He explained the role of forces hostile to the Popular Front in these terms:

> One never knows exactly who builds the "wall of money." But this wall of shame nevertheless exists, clearly enough. The plebiscite of capital did not act in favor of the Popular Front. Capital flight, which to be sure antedated May 1936, increased considerably afterward. Every "technique" is also a "politics." In 1936, the technique was the surface of things. The foundation was

that the politics of June 1936 were unacceptable [to the rich]. It was child's play then to make the government capsize on the reef of the ineluctable mechanisms of capitalism, since Blum did not wish to (and could not) step outside capitalism.[244]

In short, it was with a government weakened on the economic front that Blum—whose proposal to negotiate new Matignon agreements had been refused by the employers in November—confronted the year 1937. He very soon had to decree what he called the "pause," which was to the Popular Front something like what the NEP was to the October Revolution. The "pause" was a matter, it was said in Paris as in Moscow fifteen years before, of "consolidating conquered ground." But the determination of the French socialists was not that of the Russian communists; the forces hostile to Blum were not as weak as those which had been hostile to Lenin.

In 1937, it was only a matter of "taming capital" that had been thrown into a panic by measures to control gold exchange. Three financial experts who were very "reassuring" for the right—Charles Rist, Jacues Rueff, and Paul Baudouin—were called to the aid of the Minister of Finance, and a law soon re-established free dealings in gold. Finally, on March 12, a National Defense loan was floated that included an exchange guarantee (in case the pound and the dollar were to increase in value). There was applause from the right: "The government has sacrificed the theory of purchasing power to the balanced budget," Paul Reynaud declared jubilantly. The left, of course, was angry: "We are disciplined, but not dupes," *Vendredi* commented sharply.[245] In any case, a certain revival got under way, with the support of Finaly and "Paribas."

It was then that all the obstacles and challenges of the financial, business, and political forces, whose single aim was to bring down the Popular Front, proliferated. Confidence in Blum had been withdrawn by much of the center and the left. The head of the Popular Front government had to fight without respite not only against his internal and external enemies but sometimes against his allies.

As the Rope Supports the Hanged Man

A contract between the middle class and the working class, the Popular Front was more precisely a coalition of parties, a web of currents and forces which a single deviation or withdrawal would be enough to destroy. The Communists could remain aloof in December 1936 over Spain; their parliamentary weight was not decisive. But Radical solidarity was the *sine qua non* for the survival of the cabinet.

"There is no working-class majority," Blum had asserted at the socialist congress on May 30. There was only a very ambiguous majority "of the left," in which men like Herriot and Chautemps, buttresses of the edifice, did not refrain from dreaming of alternatives like those of the legislatures of 1924 and 1932. This is why the political history of the Popular Front (which, willy-nilly, had changed from a defensive and popular anti-Fascist coalition into a parliamentary device on which everything depended) was essentially the history of Blum's efforts to maintain the Radicals as allies; just as the social history of the government was the history of Blum's steps to keep from being outflanked by the PCF or his own socialist left.

Some, like Georges Dupeux, regret that Blum made more concessions to the party of Daladier than to the party of Thorez. This is to forget that one was capable of bringing him down while the other could do nothing but cut itself off from power. As Dupeux himself explains: "the PCF had no alternative politics." The Radicals, as we have clearly seen, did.

From the very beginning things were clear: there was a threefold contract, on the bases of the program of the *Rassemblement* of January 1936, which the Radicals presented as a limit not to be exceeded, and the others, the PCF as well as the SFIO, committed themselves to respect it.

Recalling right after the devaluation that he was only the leader of a coalition charged with carrying out a program established in common, Blum explained:

> I am not a head of government who has the intention, even the secret or hypocritical one, of applying in power the doctrines of his party. Perhaps a day will come in this country when the Socialist party will be strong enough, powerful enough, when it has carried its force of penetration and persuasion far enough for other actions to be possible. We have not reached that point. That is not the role I am playing.[246]

To be sure, on the left of the Socialist party, Jean Zyromski had proclaimed on June 1, 1936, that the only objective of the new government would be to attack "the very root of the capitalist system." But Zyromski was no more Lenin than the France of 1936 was the Russia of 1917. Thorez and Blum spoke no more than Daladier did of leaving the capitalist system; the question was not of changing from one system to another but at most of adjusting the present system.

Who could be surprised that, in this respect, the Radicals behaved like incorruptible sentinels? The president of the Radical party was still Daladier, then faithful to the January 1936 alliance. But within the party, beyond Chautemps and Herriot, men like Caillaux and Malvy were active, and beyond them men like Pierre Dominique and especially Emile Roche, the faithful servant of the employers who had consolidated themselves in August-September 1936.

Radical warnings began as early as June 1936; the strikes were so many pretexts for the right of the party to denounce "Communist dictatorship." The Spanish explosion, beginning on July 18, accentuated at the same time the splits in Daladier's party between the friends of Pierre Cot, as "interventionist" as *La Bataille socialiste,* and those of Malvy, almost openly pro-Franco. In the government, Camille Chautemps was the strongest opponent of Republican aid; he even made non-intervention an implicit condition for the continuation of government solidarity.[247]

The devaluation in late September increased the gap between the government and very substantial sectors of the Radical party. Not only Joseph Caillaux and his friends in the Senate, but also important Radical spokesmen in the Chamber attacked the cabinet's decision. Georges Bonnet with formidable perfidy, said to Blum: "I am too well acquainted with your sincerity, your loyalty, and your scruples to think that you could have floated a loan, issued a moving appeal for an increase in savings deposits, at the very time that you were contemplating devaluation." In his memoirs, Paul Reynaud reports that this barb "wounded Léon Blum to the quick." In fact, who in the Chamber had not heard of the Monick mission and the exploratory talks of the summer? No insult from the right could affect Blum as cruelly as this barb from the benches of his Radical allies.

The problem of governmental cohesion had already been posed. In late October, the Radicals held a congress in Biarritz. On the eve of this confrontation between the "left" faction led by Daladier and the distinctly right-wing tendencies inspired by Emile Roche, the Radicals had put the survival of the Popular Front in doubt. Chautemps spoke of a dissolution, of a return before the electorate, and he denounced socialization: strikes were in fact resuming in many places. For the first time, on October 8, an occupied factory was evacuated by force: the right wing of the Radicals, by thus making its strength felt, gained a few points.

Nevertheless, in Biarritz the Radical party reelected Daladier and reaffirmed its adherence to a coalition of the left. But almost 30 percent of the delegates had openly called for a reversal of the majority and had booed the name of Auriol[248] if not that of Blum. From then on, it was clear that the cabinet would last only as long as its bourgeois wing was willing to support it. Thus the right of the Radical party imposed the "pause," in anticipation of tying the noose even tighter around Blum's throat, until a certain day in June 1937.

Should we, for all that, speak of Blum's "capitulation" before Radical demands, following Georges Dupeux? The word is unnecessarily contemptuous. There was a balance of power as unfavorable to Blum in parliament as in the economic arena. The socialist leader and his companions contented themselves with drawing the conclusions. Without glory? "Glory" was not their only obsession.

If he had obtained Communist participation in his government, would Blum have been hostage to such an extent to his Radical allies? The arithmetic worked against the two "working-class parties." But if they had been associated with the Communists as well as the socialists from the outset, Daladier's friends would both have better appreciated the realism and talent of Thorez and had greater fears of pushing the SFIO to the left. The absence of the Communists constantly unbalanced the team and made the Radicals Blum's critics, if not his jailers.

We have little certain information about the choice the Communist leaders made in May 1936. We have already quoted a phrase of Jacques Duclos implying that Thorez, in favor of participation, was put in the minority in the Political Bureau in May 1936. We should add that, concerning the entry of his Spanish comrades into the Madrid cabinet of Largo Caballero in September 1936, Thorez's lieutenant admits that in his opposition to such an arrangement in France he had been mistaken.

But were there really hesitations, or even deliberations within the leadership of the PCF? Not if one is to believe Annie Kriegel.[249] According to this historian of communism, it was the Seventh Congress of the International, which met in Moscow in August 1935, that had established the mandatory conditions for Communist participation in governments within a bourgeois framework. The conditions were very strict: paralysis of the bourgeois state apparatus, effective uprising of the broad masses against fascism, real support from social democracy. Since the first condition was not fulfilled, Thorez and his companions saw their impulse toward participation blocked. They presented their refusal as a reflection of their concern not to "frighten the middle classes." Prudence? Or the application of a strictly revolutionary "line"?

Was an "imminent seizure of power" on the agenda as it was at the time of the congress of Tours? Annie Kriegel is almost alone in believing so. In Moscow as in the West, it was believed that Hitler would not accept the establishment of a new Marxist power in Paris—a power capable of attacking him from that side. The time of confrontation did not seem to have come; we would be inclined to see the abstention of the PCF as a strategy of holding a force in reserve, until the moment of its full development, which could come only after the great conflict between fascism and capitalism had broken the back of the great Western powers. Nor should we forget that if the Communist leaders spoke loudly and clearly from outside the government, this was because in May 1936, for the first time in twelve years, their membership was larger than that of the SFIO: 130,000 as opposed to 125,000.

In short, from June 6 to July 18, the PCF played the game, while Jacques Duclos was simultaneously pointing out that it supported the government "*but* that beyond the confines of the Assembly, there is a whole people." On June 14 there was Thorez's famous speech ("you have to know when to end a strike"), and from the same source on July 10 a veritable hymn to the Popular Front. Support of Blum's policy could nevertheless not be taken for granted; within the PCF, a leftist faction led by André Ferrat denounced this "capitulationist" policy. Ferrat was excluded, but his arguments had had an effect.

It was the Spanish crisis which struck the first blow against the solidarity between the Communists and the new government. During the first weeks the most virulent denunciations of "non-intervention" came from the left-wing factions of the SFIO, particularly from *La Bataille socialiste*. But from August 1936 on, and even though the USSR was preparing to sign the "non-intervention" treaty, the PCF organized a verbal campaign for aid to the Spanish Republic. In this framework, the PCF carried out three maneuvers hostile to Blum: the proposal to enlarge the Popular Front into a "French Front," warnings against contacts with the Third Reich, and the struggle against devaluation.

The idea of the "French Front"—which makes Maurice Thorez in 1936 a precursor of Georges Marchais in 1977—aimed at enveloping the SFIO, indeed at outflanking the Radicals on their right by extending a hand "to all, workers, *Croix-de-feu*, national volunteers." The offer of the Secretary-General of the PCF was made on August 6 at a meeting of the Seine Communist federation and repeated on August 25: "It is possible and necessary, in the difficult moments we are going through, that those who are not in complete agreement with one point or another of the Popular Front program may be called on to cooperate in the common effort."

Blum reacted very curtly, as did the CAP of the SFIO. And by September 9, Thorez was writing to the central organ of the SFIO: "Concerned as always to say nothing and to do nothing which may affect the bonds between Communist and socialist workers, we can refrain from using the expression 'French Front.'" Was this a formal surrender? The retreat expressed the situation: the PCF certainly harassed the government, but it was still only a verbal guerilla war.

There was another skirmish in late August over Dr. Schacht's visit to Paris,[250] and the reception given him by the governor of the Banque de France. Thorez publicly wrote to Blum on August 25:

Dear Comrade,
    . . . At the moment when Hitler is accelerating the arms race,
seriously threatening world peace and the security of France, it
does not seem to us in conformity with the dignity of our people or
the cause of peace that particular honor be shown to the Director
of the Reichsbank. . . . Convinced that you share the preoccupations which lead me to address this letter to you, I remain, my dear
Blum, sincerely yours.

To which Blum responded by return mail:

My dear Maurice Thorez,
    . . . The Popular Front government will allow no attack on the
dignity of France. But [it] also knows that the desire for peace is
one of the forms of French dignity. . . . At no time does it wish to
despair of peace . . . it does not wish to reject conversations which,
either on the economic and financial plane, or on the political
plane, may facilitate a general settlement of European problems. I
am convinced, my dear Maurice Thorez, that you too share these
preoccupations, and I remain yours in friendship.

The relative and unequal cordiality of the formulas could not conceal
the irritation. It came through again a few days later in the celebrated
Luna-Park speech when the head of government, interrupted often by
the Communist slogan "Blum to action!," retorted that "if one of the
parties which adhered to the *Rassemblement populaire* from its foundation . . . considers our conduct in contradiction with mutual commitments . . . let it say so clearly. We will immediately examine together
what conclusions we should draw from this denunciation of the contract."

On November 29, in Saint-Etienne, Maurice Thorez went further.
Characterizing non-intervention in Spain as a "disastrous initiative by
our comrade Blum," he added, "We declare that the fate of the Popular
Front is tied to the existence of a government." This was clearly seen a
week later when the seventy-two deputies of the PCF broke the solidarity of the preceding seven months by abstaining on the Spanish
question, after Jacques Duclos had delivered a veritable indictment of
Blum. A motion of confidence was nevertheless passed. The cabinet
had resisted.

But the very next day, Blum reacted vigorously:

    The question has arisen for my colleagues and for me as to
    whether the deliberately aggressive terms in which Jacques Duclos
    explained his friends' abstention has made it impossible for us to
    continue our work. We have unanimously decided to remain in
    power. But the question remains. The near future will show us how
    the Communist party intends to resolve it.

There was another about-face by Thorez and his friends: two days later, they expressed their "confidence" in the government. But the consciousness of necessary solidarity had disappeared. In the Wednesday morning meetings at Blum's home exchanges remained cordial. But they constantly grew more bitter at the weekly meetings of the National Committee of the *Rassemblement populaire,* as reported by Maurice Paz, who was one of the SFIO delegates. Paz describes with some bitterness "the uninterrupted harassment by the Communist delegates, Jacques Duclos, Marcel Gitton, and Florimond Bonte. The attacks went very far, as if the Communist delegates were testing the extent of the National Committee's tolerance, or looking for the breaking point."[251]

Nor should we neglect the role played by the Moscow trials, which had been going on since August; people were not ignorant (less ignorant, in any case, than some say forty years later) of their vicissitudes, their procedure, and their scandalous anomalies. *Vendredi,* a journal most favorable to unity, published *Retour de l'URSS* by André Gide. The socialists were all the less inclined to receive lessons in virtue from the blind spokesmen of the Stalinist system.

Thus the Blum government went on until the spring of 1937, flanked on the right by Radicals half in solidarity with an enterprise which could not continue without them and which they supported only with the ulterior motive of sooner or later taking it over, and flanked on the left by a PCF which oscillated between admonition, support, and subversion, but remained incapable of offering any alternative solution.

Not a month went by in which some warning shot did not remind Blum of the precariousness of his position. In November 1936, there was the tragic death of one of his closest and most important associates, Roger Salengro; in March 1937, there was the bloody riot of Clichy; in May, there were the delays in the preparation for an international exhibition which was to be the solemn symbol of the inventiveness and the international influence of a popular government. Under repeated blows, the Popular Front was staggering.

An Assassination . . .

Roger Salengro was a deputy and the major of Lille. Along with Jean Lebas, his colleague from Roubaix, he was considered the principal representative of the key federation of the Socialist party, the Nord federation. Of working-class origin, a union man, he was at forty-six the quintessential good militant who had been repeatedly promoted for his qualities as an organizer.

In May 1936, he had appeared to Blum as a necessary choice for the

Ministry of the Interior. During the period of "social explosion" in May–June, he had in general demonstrated cool-headedness, although Blum had occasionally restrained him from harsh actions. During a morning meeting at Blum's with Thorez and Duclos the Premier had firmly reminded him that any resort to force to "break the strikes" (a possibility which Salengro had mentioned the previous evening in the Senate) was ruled out.[252] Extremely anti-Communist, Salengro had probably felt some bitterness at having thus been discreetly repudiated. (Blum alluded to this on the day of his funeral.) But the Minister of the Interior subsequently affirmed his authority, perhaps with more showiness than depth, and began to appear as one of the party's "hopes" along with Georges Monnet and Jules Moch. Was he a possible dauphin?

On July 14, 1936, an anonymous item in *L'Action française*, repeating the allegation of a Communist opponent, accused Salengro of having deserted in 1915 while he was a cyclist liaison officer. On August 20, *Gringoire*, the extreme right-wing weekly, repeated the accusation and gave details: Salengro was supposed to have been court-martialed for having "gone over to the enemy" on October 7, 1915, in Champagne.

The Minister of the Interior, who believed he had already refuted these accusations, called on Blum to create an investigative commission. Acceding to his request, the Premier and Daladier formed the commission and appointed several leaders of veterans' organizations, hardly lenient in such matters, and the Chief of Staff of the army. After three weeks of investigation, the commission published its results in early November: Salengro had advanced beyond the French lines with the approval of his superiors to bring back the body of a dead comrade; made a prisoner, he was court-martialed and—though he was absent and undefended—acquitted.

These conclusions seemed to put an end to the affair. But on November 6, *Gringoire* published an open letter from Henri Béraud to the President of the Republic, entitled "The Propengro Affair"[253]:

> Salengro has been whitewashed, and now he is Propengro! He comes out of this adventure purified, washed, cleaned of mud, scoured, sponged, and rinsed—in a word, as shiny as a new bicycle! But is that enough? No and no again! We, his friends, find that it isn't enough. . . . May the great day come, awaited by everyone, when, rising above the rolling of drums, your voice will proclaim the sacramental formula as the drums tremble: "Cyclist Propengro! In my name and in the name of the powers that are conferred upon me, I name you *chevalier* of the Legion of Honor!"

You can see the quality of what once passed for great journalism in the eyes of the French bourgeoisie.[254] But the scandal was to go further. Roger Salengro's political rival in Lille, a certain Becquart, deputy from Nord, dared to question the government again, on November 13, affirming from the rostrum of the Chamber that not only had Salengro gone unarmed toward the enemy lines but that the French positions had been bombarded shortly afterward! The matter had been pushed too far. After a vehement correction by Daladier, Blum mounted the rostrum:

> The campaign continues, the campaign is redoubled, and you know under what conditions. This campaign had become the activity and the particular property of a rag[255] which in fact I do not read, which I do not touch, of a rag whose name I do not even wish to pronounce here, but which I certainly have the right to call a loathsome rag.
>
> M. JEAN CHIAPPE: I call *Le Populaire* the same thing!
>
> M. CHARLES DES ISNARDS: *Gringoire* is a French newspaper, *L'Humanité* is Russian!
>
> M. FERNAND WIEDEMANN-GOIRAN: This is the director of a newspaper speaking like this! It's a scandal. You are carrying out a commercial operation. Hand in your resignation from the board of directors of *Le Populaire!*
>
> THE PREMIER: This rag, gentlemen, had made the campaign against Roger Salengro its property. It saw it as a weapon against him, against us, against you, and also, perhaps, as publicity for itself. Consequently, gentlemen, the rag, the loathsome rag takes pleasure in the game and carries on. It provokes all this testimony, whether consciously or unconsciously produced by the aberrations of memory, sometimes secreted by hatred.
>
> Gentlemen, there is one thing which is true, which is that Roger Salengro appeared before a court martial. It is true that he really was convicted, but it was a German court martial which judged him as a prisoner and convicted him.
>
> I have in front of me the record of the judgment rendered on 11 July 1916 by the eleventh infantry brigade of Nuremberg, in the trial conducted against the French prisoners of war of the Anberg prison camp, against Roger Salengro and thirty-nine others, for in this matter too, I am obliged to agree, Roger Salengro was a leader.
>
> What had he done? He had persuaded his comrades in captivity to refuse to work in a foundry. He had spoken in their name!
>
> . . . There are those today who are attempting to dishonor a man who, whether you like it or not, represents the French nation before the world. But wounding one's country is of little account when one can reach, through doing so, detested opponents; and one is after all a great patriot!
>
> M. GEORGES ROULLEAUX-DUGAGE: Who said once: "I hate you"?
>
> M. FRANCOIS FOURCAULT DE PAVANT: You will not give lessons in patriotism to veterans.
>
> THE PREMIER: And then, I ask you too, think of the man, for there is a man in this affair, a man with the heart of a man, a man who is your colleague, whom you all know. There is a man who, for weeks, has been frightfully tortured.

Oh, I know very well, gentlemen, and you know as well as I do, one tries in such cases to restrain one's suffering, to keep it to oneself. You say to your friends: "It's nothing, it doesn't count." And then, when your friends look closely at you, they see your face changed. Then, they feel in their friendship, in their tenderness, how far the heart of a man can be ravaged by a slander like this one.[256]

Perhaps, Roger Salengro, you are not sufficiently accustomed to this yet. You will no doubt get used to it in time. But for the loathsome creatures, this suffering inflicted on a man has no more importance than an attack against the nation.

I say all this, gentlemen, without any passion, because I have grown used to it. But I also say that it can go on no longer.

Echoes of the Dreyfus Affair? Blum certainly thought so forty years later. But this time it was not Lieutenant-Colonel Henry the forger nor the slanderers Béraud or Becquart, but Salengro who committed suicide. Four days after this moral victory in the Chamber—Minister of the Interior Salengro returned to his little apartment in Lille on the evening of November 16 and turned on the gas. Overwork and exhaustion were the generally accepted explanations. They seem inadequate. It was rather despair at having been able to get nothing more than a "vote," a "majority," but not total exoneration.

It was again Blum who provided the best explanation for the act:

As long as he had to resist, as long as he had to fight, his courage did not falter. But when the definitive victory over the lie had been won, his inner strength broke. He abandoned himself to death, as a runner collapses when he has crossed the finish line.[257]

Before killing himself, Salengro had written to the head of his party and the government:

My dear Blum, my wife died almost eighteen months ago from the slander which did not spare her and from which she suffered so much. My mother has not recovered from her operation, and the slander has cut her to the quick.

I have struggled on my side, bravely. But I've reached the limit. Although they haven't been able to dishonor me, at least they will bear the responsibility for my death, for I am neither a deserter nor a traitor.

My party has been my life and my joy.

My affection to my family, my remembrance to our comrades, and to you my gratitude.

Reprobation was vigorous throughout the country. The Anglo-Saxon press disgustedly denounced the campaign that had been conducted against the dead man. But there was a man with an honorable reputation, Henri de Kerillis,[258] to spit this at Blum on that very day: "Léon Blum bears a crushing responsibility. One does not look for ministers among men who have been court-martialled!"

On November 22, asked to deliver the farewell speech at his friend's grave, Blum intensified his tone, blending painful confession with the most direct threat:

> We spent hours, Roger and I, asking each other the question, "In the end, what can you do?" And when you suffer as he suffered, you have a choice, in this country, only between killing and dying. It is not possible for us to remain imprisoned any longer within this savage dilemma. Slander must be confounded and punished, and it will be. . . . The French people will no longer turn its citizens over to the gutter press. It will no longer stand for a situation in which, in order to satisfy their passions, their vengeance—or even their basest interests—gang leaders and mercenaries attack their honor or even their security. It will restore the national community without them. It will consolidate republican institutions against them. It will reject firmly and harshly, if necessary, their assaults against the freer and more just society which is developing. Roger Salengro would have wished for no other vengeance. . . .

Manly words! But they had little effect. A bill on the press which provided for prosecution of slanderers as well as disclosure of funds received by publications was defeated in the Senate, even though its oracle, Joseph Caillaux, had experienced the infamy of certain kinds of campaigns. The socialists were forced to recognize that Roger Salengro's death was not even "useful" to their cause, since Béraud and his ilk continued with impunity their work of denunciation and slander.

It is perhaps at this point in Blum's painful history as head of the Popular Front government, the government of the Decent Man, rather than at the moment of the social explosion of June, that one should raise the question of whether his legalism should not have given way before a reflex of collective safety. The punishments announced in the speech delivered at Salengro's grave could not await the pleasure of M. Caillaux. For Blum in late November 1936, as for Salvador Allende confronting the murderous campaigns of *El Mercurio* in Santiago during the summer of 1973, one has the right to wonder where the legitimate defense of governments begins, and whether they must depend for their survival only on the good behavior of newspapers, and on laws written by and for a class which rejects no means to preserve its interests.

Because neither the cabinet nor Blum was able to make the tragedy the occasion for passing measures of public health, because the extreme right, however dishonored it may have been, was as triumphant as it had been at the death of Jaurès, Salengro's suicide must be counted as one of the defeats of the Popular Front. The man who succeeded him, Marx Dormoy, was made of sterner stuff. But he was to come to grief over another tragedy,[259] which further precipitated the end of the Blum government: the shooting in Clichy.

Before the year 1936 ended (marked by yet another defeat—the refusal of the Communists to vote confidence at the conclusion of the great debate on foreign policy on December 5) Blum addressed the country over the radio. He launched an appeal for "amicable agreement of all social categories." So soon after the hounding which had driven poor Salengro to his death like a cornered animal? There are cases when a certain kind of moderation becomes immoderate. Too much mildness could only revive the appetites and sharpen the teeth of a certain "social category." Generous Monsieur Blum was to be forced into what he abhorred above all: resort to force against certain elements of the working class. Before summer, Blum had to have blood on his hands.

. . . And a Pool of Blood

The "leagues" had been dissolved since the summer of 1936. But some of them had been able to reconstitute themselves as political parties, like the *Croix-de-feu* which had become the French Social Party (PSF). In early March, as the government announced the floating of a second defense loan for which the experts predicted the same success as the first, this organization announced that it would hold a meeting on March 16, in the Olympia movie theater in Clichy, presided over by Colonel de la Rocque. Local officials (the mayor was a socialist, the deputy a Communist) spoke of provocation and called for the meeting to be banned. Blum and Dormoy hesitated, but the PSF was within its rights. They decided against special measures.

The parties of the left, on Communist initiative, called for a counter-demonstration. A column of Communist and left socialist[260] militants marched on the theater. The large police force sent by Dormoy attempted to block them. Shots were fired. The battle intensified. Minister of the Interior Marx Dormoy (who had never authorized the use of arms), and André Blumel, director of Blum's cabinet, hastily arrived and attempted to intercede between the police and the left-wing demonstrators (the PSF had evacuated the theater long before). Blumel was seriously wounded by two bullets. By 10 o'clock there were five dead and more than 200 wounded. One of the wounded, a young woman militant of the socialist left, died a short time later in a hospital.

Blum had been at a concert at the Opéra. He arrived at the Clichy hospital in evening dress, around 11 o'clock. The right was exultant; they would cruelly exploit this image of "blood on the shirtfront." The cartoonist Ralf Soupault, later a contributor to the Nazi press, published a drawing of Blum next to a red spot: "Who said this man has no French blood?" In the terrible portrait of Blum which he published in 1940, Maurice Thorez wrote:

Toward midnight the Premier arrived in evening dress. The assassin of the Clichy workers was coming from his box at the
Opéra, stiff in his ceremonial dress and his boiled shirt, wearing
white gloves, carrying a top hat, a cape over his shoulders. A
murmur of indignation rose from the crowd of relatives of the
wounded and workers clinging to the hospital fences.[261]

Thorez also earned a description of himself, in the extreme left press:

At 10 o'clock, Marx Dormoy arrived, pale as a corpse. "Dormoy
assassin!" "Dormoy resign!" shouted thousands of workers.
Blum's minister announced that the police would withdraw and
that everything would be settled. Immediately, pale and crushed,
the Stalinist leaders seized the occasion to shout "Disperse, comrades," "Discipline," "Long live the Popular Front!" They did not
realize that the workers of Clichy had just understood that evening
what the Popular Front was and what it was worth!
(The police charged again.) . . . At 10:45 Thorez arrived,
crushed. . . . He entered city hall. They begged him to show
himself on the balcony and to speak. He systematically refused to
speak to the disappointed workers. Before leaving, he said in a flat
tone: "Calm, calm! I'm going to ask for Dormoy's resignation."
That's all. A short time later he came back again. Near him a group
of workers chanted: "Workers militia for socialism." Thorez
turned around and angrily shouted at them: "Dirty Trotskyites."[262]

One can imagine the effect on Blum of this terrible night. Was it then
that his spirit broke, as it had for Salengro, the spirit that would have
enabled him to defend himself against the Senate three months later?
On the 17th, he declared to his friend Georges Monnet: "It is impossible for me to accept that, while I was the leader of the government,
responsible, mounted police made the blood of workers flow. Do you
want to take my place? I cannot stay"[263]

An investigation was mandatory. Blum and Dormoy shared some of
the responsibility because they allowed such a dangerous meeting to
take place. Also to blame were the *provocateurs:* "Chiappe[264] is in this,
in the ranks of the workers and also in the attitude of the police," wrote
La Révolution prolétarienne a few days later. The investigation revealed the presence in both camps of armed men with criminal records.
The infiltration had been carried out well; the date had been chosen
well, too, just at the time when the chances of economic recovery
seemed promising. According to Jules Moch, "the investigation conducted by Judge Béteille established that among the victims were
scabs. . . . The socialist federation of Nord, in particular, also recognized among the victims a well-known *provocateur* from the Lille region. . . . Also among the demonstrators were men later discovered to
be militants of *La Cagoule.*"[265]

On March 23, in the Chamber Blum did not even attempt to justify himself. Refusing to accept Dormoy's resignation or the dismissal of high-level police officers, he declared that the whole affair, the result of "the state of agitation and alarm created in the country," was "a mistake, that is, worse than a sin."[266] Strangely enough, in the days and weeks that followed, the communists did not attempt to exploit the tragedy, but rather worked to channel reactions on the left and to denounce the *"provocateurs."* Yet the shooting in Clichy, even more than devaluation or the "pause," had sounded the death knell of the Popular Front. That night the blood that had been shed was indeed the symbol of a "disagreement" with a faction of the working class which Blum on May 31, 1936, had proclaimed he "could not accept."

The death agony of the government had begun. Blum had to suffer two further defeats, one moral the other social, to complete the psychic disarmament which left him almost defenseless against the blows of his enemies in June.

Moral defeat? In fact, this is what the break with Marceau Pivert appears to have been. The leader of the "revolutionary left" had been a member of Blum's cabinet. By the end of the summer he had stopped playing the role of Blum's stage manager as he had done in June and July 1936. But he remained a kind of popular guarantee for Blum, whose policy of non-intervention in Spain he discreetly supported, because of his own pacifism. It was the "pause" of February 1937 that provoked his departure from the cabinet; his departure was, in his usual manner, dramatic: "No, I will not agree to surrender in the face of militarism and the banks!"[267]

Pivert recovered a large audience among young socialists who were irritated by the government's shift to the right. He multiplied attacks against Blum's "NEP" to such a point that the National Council of the party, meeting in Puteaux on April 18, voted to dissolve *La Gauche révolutionnaire*. It was obvious that the head of the government and of the party had done nothing to bring this about and that the initiative came from Faure; but this repressive measure, a limitation of the right to internal groups and free criticism which had always been one of Blum's proud boasts, tarnished the moral image of the orator of the Congress of Tours strapped in the uniform of power. Blum could not prevent the National Council from making the decision. Was it a maneuver by Faure against him? Personally very attached to Marceau Pivert, he felt it in any case as an attack on his personal influence.

Another image, that of both the man of culture and the popular leader, was damaged by the delays in the preparation for the Universal Exposition of Arts and Techniques, whose inauguration on May 1, 1937 was to be the triumph of a popular government, a vision of the future.

Strikes proliferated on the "expo" construction site. Some employers' groups sabotaged work. In January, Blum had asked the most efficient of his colleagues, Jules Moch, to take the matter in hand. But neither Moch nor Blum could succeed in convincing the workers that "the battle of the 'expo' is a battle of the Popular Front, that a delay in the 'expo' would be a victory for the Fascists." Carefully calculated rumors ran rampant at the site: "Take your time; afterwards, we'll be out of work."

The inauguration had to be delayed for several weeks. On May 24, 1937, rubble and scaffolds confronted the procession of notables and diplomats. The right-wing press abounded in delighted sarcasms. No subject since devaluation had so stirred the wit of the Senneps and Daudets. "A humiliating moment," wrote Jean Zay.

The Death Blow

On June 3, Blum presided over a reception on the occasion of the first anniversary of the government. He was given an amusing cartoon of himself by H. P. Gassier, but smiles were tense. Auriol had just announced to the head of government that the gold reserves were practically exhausted. The second loan, floated on the eve of the Clichy tragedy, was a failure. On the 6th, Blum declared:

> If we were to fail, one would be forced to wonder—and this is a very serious question—whether there is not a deeper vice, a congenital vice, if it is really not possible, within a legal framework, with the help of democratic institutions, to provide for the popular masses of this country the just and progressive reforms they expect.

A serious question indeed, and one which challenges almost the whole of "Blumism." He therefore turned toward a bold procedure of "full powers" which challenged neither the "legal framework" nor institutions, but was clearly aimed at getting around them.[268] On June 14, Blum presented to the Chamber a proposal according to which the cabinet would be able, until July 31, to take any measure for financial protection against speculation that it considered useful. On June 15, against Paul Reynaud (who had just said; "It is not men who are opposed to the success of your experiment. It is the facts!") Blum defended his proposal from the Assembly rostrum:

> Oh, gentlemen, I have no intention of presenting here some conspiracy out of fiction. But for the last week or ten days we have witnessed phenomena which, almost hour by hour, have taken on greater and greater seriousness: first of all, attacks on the bond

market, attacks which are, in spite of everything, political in nature, and I certainly have the right to say so. I glanced at the latest financial report in *Le Temps* and I read this, almost word for word: "In this trading session, French bonds have lost the ground they had gained in the two previous sessions, because the political situation is not developing in the direction the market had foreseen."

Speculation? For the more general and vaguer word speculation, I would like to substitute that of export of capital. That is the essential cause. M. Paul Reynaud said it on the rostrum as clearly as I am saying it myself. The cause is that a mass of capital necessary not only to the whole of the national economy, but also to the normal operations of the treasury, is lacking. It is lacking because it is not in France.

Now, after the explanations that have been provided to you and the ones I have given you in turn, you can no longer have any uncertainty about the aim of the measures we are proposing to you. We want first of all to provide immediate relief to the Treasury and to begin to carry out budgetary stabilization. We want to assure, for a sufficient period of time, the needs of the Treasury so that the market may have some respite, some rest. We also want the capital expatriated from France to return to France. Only French law is sovereign over the French, over their persons and their possessions, wherever in the world they may have chosen to conceal them. The very simple question which has been raised, which you are going to resolve in a moment, is whether we have your confidence to carry out this work!

The Chamber gave him a vote of confidence by 346 to 247. The Popular Front majority held firm, in spite of internal quarrels, although twenty Radicals voted against Blum. But the Senate placed him in the minority. The bill was returned, scarcely amended, to the Chamber which repeated almost exactly the June 15 vote. Attempting to avoid a conflict between the two Assemblies, the "delegation of the left" introduced some modifications. But the Finance Committee of the Senate tried to replace it with a bill which Blum characterized as "inert." Decidedly, he had to fight against a Senate armed with animosity and determined to defeat him. Confronting Reynaud in the Chamber, Blum had the law of numbers and an aura on his side. In confronting Caillaux in the Senate the same factors were against him. Nevertheless, his argument was stirring:

> I have never had any illusions, gentlemen, about the Senate's real feelings toward our government. It has shown for our persons a courtesy and often a kindness which we appreciate at their worth and for which I thank it. But it has always shown apprehension, not to use a stronger expression, toward the political formation which the government represents. Whether you like it or not, we are a Popular Front government, and the Senate majority is not a Popular Front majority. In fact, it has never given adhesion with-

out reservation, anxiety, or reticence to the direction we were
attempting to impart to public affairs. The Senate finds it surprising
that I am now addressing it as I do? I don't think it is surprising.

. . . We are told that we have drawn the country down the path of
bankruptcy and ruin. If it were so, gentlemen, our government
should be scorned and despised in the country. Then why is it so
strongly popular? Why has it maintained intact, in the city and in
the countryside, the confidence of the working masses of this
country? Why is it respected, and I might even say esteemed, by
international opinion? . . .

If we have failed, if our work has been disastrous, our successors will no doubt have to take the opposite tack. Is that what the
Senate wants? Does it want to revoke the laws that have been
passed, or to modify them to such a degree that their effect is
practically annulled? Does it want financial stabilization to be
achieved through the renewed rigors of deflation? Does it want the
psychological conditions of confidence to be sought in a change of
the majority, in a profound modification of relations with the working-class organizations? Does it consider that certain resistances,
de facto resistances, as the saying goes, or rather resistances of
threatened interests, should invalidate the will of universal suffrage?

But confronting Blum on the center bench was the old man with a
smooth skull, an imperious monocle, and a predator's jaw: Joseph
Caillaux. The vote was like a guillotine: 168 against, 96 for. Blum had
not asked for a vote of confidence. But this vote was a veto by the
upper chamber. What meaning should be given to it? Had the cabinet
fallen?

Blum then asked the president of the Senate, Jules Jeanneny, the
most venerable of men: "Does the Senate have the right to bring down
the government?" The President: "The Senate has the right to vote
freely, it is up to you to draw the conclusions you consider the right
ones."[269]

The problem was thus not juridical. In narrowly legal terms, the
cabinet could continue. But the Senate's verdict was received by the
Radicals as a condemnation. It was clear from then on that this essential cog in the governmental mechanism would not function, all the
more so because, as the Radical party had brought about the crisis, the
president of the Republic would offer the succession to one of its
members.

Blum was immediately assailed by contradictory appeals and pressures. If in the eyes of the Radicals he had no other solution but
resignation, there was only one goal for the left of the Socialist party:
make the Senate give in by any means possible. This is what he was
told by Jean Zyromski, who transmitted a motion from the Seine
socialist federation:

Resistance! Resistance by appealing to the masses; resistance by calling the country to action! Resistance which the government will lead. Resistance through an act like the one we performed together, with a few friends, in the name of the party, on 12 February 1934, an action which saved the Republic in this country.

The cabinet met on the evening of the 21st. Jules Moch has given a very vivid account of it:

> Several ministers having suggested that it was possible to make the Senate surrender, Léon Blum retorted: "No! Caillaux has it in hand. There is such a large majority against our bill that we may nibble at it but we will not reverse it."
>
> "Then," said someone else, "we will ask the Senate to agree to a dissolution of the Chamber.[270] The Popular Front will return with a larger majority."
>
> "If the Senate is convinced of that, it is clear that it will reject dissolution."
>
> "In that case," declared the quiet Vincent Auriol, exasperated, "we the elected officials of the Popular Front will resign alone, to let the people judge, and we will be reelected with larger majorities."
>
> At that moment, I received a note which I handed immediately to Léon Blum. He glanced at it and exclaimed: "Oh no! By no means!" I had been informed that there was great agitation in the Seine federation of the Socialist party. Marceau Pivert wanted to mobilize his TPPS (militia *"toujours prêtes pour servir"* [always ready to serve]), and Jean Zyromski thought of calling on thousands—or tens of thousands—of militants of the party and the CGT to demonstrate in front of the Senate, to win in the streets the surrender of that body to the popular forces. Léon Blum informed the ministers. It might be serious, even if the communists refused to join the demonstration. Marx Dormoy would be obliged to protect the Senate. A new "Clichy" was possible, especially if *provocateurs* of the extreme right were involved. Léon Blum refused to contemplate an adventure of that kind. He intended to remain within legality.[271]

Having persuaded his colleagues, Blum went off in the middle of the night to tender his resignation at the Elysée Palace. He immediately declared to the press: "Deprived of the means of action which we consider indispensable, we are stepping down. It is absolutely necessary that the transfer of power take place calmly and peacefully, according to republican legality."

Three weeks later, at the congress of Marseille (July 10–13), the leader of the SFIO justified his decision of June 21 before an assembly of militants who had just heard Marceau Pivert indict Blum for the resignation: "You should have held fast!":

Hold fast, what did that mean except waiting for popular demonstrations to tip the balance in favor of universal suffrage? Would
the entire Popular Front have followed us in that struggle? What
state would we have thrown the country into? You know what the
foreign news was. The crisis brewing in France was considered in
advance, in the entire hostile press, as a prelude to great social
struggles leading to a veritable civil war [which would have] eliminated France as a factor in international politics. We know what
those who love us and those who do not thought on that subject!
. . . Marceau Pivert is right to say that that struggle was necessarily
the crisis of a revolutionary offensive. Confronted with that
choice, considering the internal state of the country, its psychological state, considering the external danger, we said: "No, we do
not have the right to do that, we do not have the right vis-à-vis our
party, we do not have the right vis-à-vis our country.

"But then," said Pierre Brossolette,[272] "but then the SFIO was just a
party like the others and the government a government like the
others?" Blum's answer summed up the situation well:

In reality, even though it was carried along by an immense wave
of will and hope, well, in spite of that, it was a government that was
merely exercising power through a coalition of parties within the
framework of present society and republican legality.

Whether it was "like the others" or not, the congress of Marseille
also presented the image of a disoriented, disenchanted, and divided
party. "This is one of the most difficult and most painful moments in
our history," said Blum to his comrades. Knowing how important
friendships were to him, one can imagine how he felt watching Bracke,
his oldest companion, the former Guesdist who had stood up against
the majority of Tours and been converted by him to Jaurèsism, support
a very harsh motion opposing "the Blum line" alongside Zyromski.

This retreat in the face of the Senate's veto nevertheless appears a
little facile. On the part of a man who had clung to power even when his
personal feelings and his acute sense of the "moral" vocation of his
party and its doctrine urged him to withdraw—this kind of resignation
is surprising. René Girault seems to us to have suggested the best
explanation by considering Blum's foreign policy.[273] For several
months, since the passage of the social laws and the "pause," Blum had
turned his attention primarily in that direction. How could peace be
preserved without surrender to Hitler? Because he had for months
thought himself more capable than anyone else—notably because of
his British and American relations—of resisting the German minotaur,
Blum had hedged, compromised, surrendered in other areas.

But by late March 1937, and especially after May, all the coalitions
he had attempted to set up or to maintain were collapsing: the Italian-
Yugoslav pact decisively weakened the Petite Entente; the "appeaser"
Chamberlain was installed as the head of the British government; Dr.

Schacht returned to Paris transmitting "conditions" which indicated that Hitler had rejected any accommodation. If nothing of what he had attempted was holding up (except the re-establishment of the Entente Cordiale and its extension to Washington), Blum seemed to be no longer needed. It was just as well to "fall to the left," with a "tough" economic plan, which would serve as a prelude to the fine program of 1938. In fact, it was less Caillaux than Hitler who drove Blum from the hôtel Matignon in June 1937.

For Want of National Unity

Blum agreed, with the approval of the National Council of the SFIO, to become Deputy Premier in the government of his successor, Camille Chautemps. Chautemps, leader of the center-right faction of the Radicals, was one of the men who had carried out the most constant work of sabotage against Blum. Did Blum know that? Charles-André Julien reported that one day Blum reacted to a report about Chautemps in the following way: one of the officers of the National Police informed Blum of the hostility of the Radical Vice-President toward him, and Blum expressed doubt. The officer: "I have wiretaps which prove it!" Blum, beside himself: "You dared to do that?" In any case, the socialist leader seems to have approved the choice made by Albert Lebrun at the time.

Thus the *Rassemblement populaire* and the President of the Republic had returned to their first notion of May 1936: a coalition cabinet presided over by a Radical. It even almost came about that the new coalition was the one that Blum had foreseen fourteen months earlier. Vincent Auriol has recounted that going to the Elysée with the news that the socialists had agreed to participate in the new cabinet, he had met the Communist leaders and then heard Chautemps declare with a smile: "Thorez and Duclos have just brought me Communist participation." It was he, Chautemps, who rejected it.[274]

From June 1937 to January 1938, Blum always conducted himself as a loyal second to Chautemps. Although a number of his friends criticized him for lending his presence to a cabinet that was as ambiguous and deceitfully conservative as its leader, and although Paul Rivet and the "Committee of Vigilance of Antifascist Intellectuals" made a judgment against the new government which morally excluded it from the Popular Front, Blum refused to break with it.

His attitude on this point, expressed at the socialist congress of Marseille on July 12, 1937, was significant:

> For several days I have heard many cries of "Blum to power!"
> When people shout "Blum to power!" around me it embarrasses
> me. . . . Most of you think [that] the majority of the Chamber had

not been changed, [that] within that majority the largest and most powerful group was still the socialist group, [that] it was another socialist who should have been called to form a government.

SOME VOICES: Yes!

BLUM: Which socialist?

THE ASSEMBLY: Blum! Blum!

BLUM: I had just handed in my resignation a few hours earlier! What else could I have done? I beg you, let us take serious things seriously. You are not asking me, after a long deliberation in which we considered our resignation necessary, to accept power again a few hours later, in the same conditions?"

. . . This first experiment has just concluded after thirteen months of existence, and what months! Months in which there followed one after the other days without respite and nights without sleep, in which it seems that through some malice, some malign conspiracy of fate, all the tests, all the difficulties, those that could be foreseen and those that could not, came together at the same moment; months in which each time the telephone rang, we picked it up wondering: "What now?" Well, that ordeal is over.

In short, Blum gave a sigh of relief. But he was not content to be an ambiguous symbol, or rather a shield for ambiguities. Although he remained aloof from most of the conflicts which kept the Chautemps cabinet and Minister of Finance Georges Bonnet in perpetual uproar[275] (harshly politicized strikes at Simca, Goodrich-Colombes, and in the public services; attacks by the CSAR [the Secret Committee of Revolutionary Action—*La Cagoule*]; polemics about non-intervention; violent campaigns against Vincent Auriol's management), Blum concentrated his attention on what he saw as a fundamental problem: peace in Europe. The restoration of two-year military service in Germany, Italy's withdrawal from the League of Nations, and the continuing collapse of the Spanish Republic were all warning signs. War was approaching, and it was necessary to rearm and to bring the democracies together. He therefore shuttled between Paris, London, and Geneva. Representing the government at President Masaryk's funeral in Prague on September 21, 1937, he met not only Eduard Benes and the Czech leaders, but the leaders of Poland, Rumania, and Yugoslavia. But it was too late for coalitions.

The year 1938 began in a troubled atmosphere, and for Blum with personal anguish: his second wife Thérèse, to whom he had been married for five years, was dying in great pain. Suffering from cancer for two years, she had· become almost unrecognizable. Her sharp and charming features were hollowed and eroded by illness. She died on January 22, 1938. Blum took refuge for a few weeks with his friends the Auriols in Muret.

On the eve of this tragedy, January 14, he had been surprised by the fall of the cabinet in which he was still Deputy Premier. That day, the

Communist deputy Arthur Ramette harshly questioned the government, recalling unkept promises, working-class demands, and the urgency of democratizing taxes. Chautemps, ordinarily so bland, exploded: "I agreed to assume the leadership of a Popular Front government. But this government cannot fail to observe the most elementary dignity. M. Ramette has asked for his freedom. That is his right. I grant it to him."

This was to break with the PCF. The socialists, in spite of Blum's appeals for moderation, reacted by declaring that the Premier had stepped outside the framework of the *Rassemblement* and withdrew their ministers from the cabinet. It was a crisis. The President of the Republic called on Georges Bonnet, who asked for socialist participation. He was answered by Blum that from then on the SFIO would join no government which it did not lead. Albert Lebrun then turned to Blum, who suggested a "political Matignon," a reconciliation in order to form a national unity cabinet in the face of external dangers. The head of state objected that he was perhaps not the best man to carry out such a plan. Blum proposed that the responsibility be given to Herriot; Herriot declined. The whole imbroglio was resolved in the most banal fashion: a return to Chautemps, without the socialists. The Popular Front was no more than a shadow.

Even though it was centered on the right of the Radical party—Georges Bonnet was at the Quai d'Orsay, Marchandeau (even more hostile to the *Rassemblement* of the left) at Finance, and Albert Sarraut at Interior—the second Chautemps cabinet saw the gold reserves of the Banque de France diminish even more quickly than had its predecessors. The Premier was eager to recover the cooperation of the socialists. It was refused and, on March 9, he had to resign again, at the very moment when Chancellor Schuschnigg of Austria, threatened by Hitler, decided to organize a plebiscite for or against *Anschluss* (the absorption of his country by the Third Reich). A plebiscite, an appeal to popular judgment? The Nazis could not tolerate it. Seizing the initiative, they occupied Austria on March 10.

It was in these tragic circumstances that Blum was again called upon by Lebrun to form a government. He thought his offer of a "political Matignon" might be heard this time. With the approval of the National Council of the SFIO, where for the first time in a long time Jean Zyromski and *La Bataille socialiste* (but not Pivert and his allies) voted in his favor, he took a bold initiative with no known precedent by calling a meeting on March 12 in the Salle Colbert of the National Assembly of all the leaders of the opposition, from Reynaud and Flandin to Chiappe and Kerillis.

He confronted all those who for years had hounded and denounced him as "anti-France." There they were, suspicious or hostile, sarcastic or angry, contemptuous or jealous, professional patriots and capitalists, his enemies. Had the great lawyer ever argued before such biased judges?

> I have the feeling that an imperious duty is weighing on me, and I am determined to make every possible effort to carry it out. Some of you heard Briand say one day from the rostrum of the Chamber: "This time I'm hanging on!" This time, I, too, am hanging on to the work I have undertaken, because I believe it is salutary. . . . I beg you to believe me: I did not expect that the difficulties and resistances would come from your side. I thought the opposite. Even before the events in Austria had assumed such a dramatic form, I had consulted friends in my own party . . . the National Council of the party did not even deliberate for half an hour, and it reached its decision in a spirit of enthusiasm. The Radical party has also agreed. The Communist party has just held a meeting of its Central Committee and passed a motion of adhesion without reservations.
>
> Thus, everyone has accepted and you would refuse, it would be you who, at such a moment, would make this action impossible? It is something which I cannot believe. What determines your choice? The presence of Communists in the government? I don't ask you, I know!
>
> This morning, at a meeting of the Radical party, when the same objection was formulated, my friend Daladier, Minister of National Defense, retorted: "If the unhappy day came when France was obliged to mobilize, would we not mobilize Communist workers?" If the unhappy times forced us to return to what we have seen, to the *Union sacrée* of war, would you reject . . . the representatives of a million-and-a-half workers, peasants, small merchants . . . who would give their lives for it like the others? . . . Won't you need the cooperation of the General Confederation of Labor, if tomorrow you want greater productivity from the arms industry? Think! I beg of you. . . .
>
> You say, as I have heard it said: yes, this idea is fine, because it is necessary, because it corresponds to the reality of the moment; but it is better that it be carried out by others, that other men take the initiative. Let the idea be expressed; then we'll arrange for it not to come to fruition, so that it can be realized tomorrow or the day after in different conditions. But if the Socialist party and the Communist party and the corporate bodies of the working class were excluded from the union, what would remain? A France even more deeply divided than it is today. And that is what you wish to prepare the country for resistance? That, for the preparation of its defense? That, so that it may give the outside world a sense of its strength?

When he left the Salle Colbert, men like Kerillis and even Chiappe expressed their admiration. He thought he had persuaded them; but the right brutally indicated its rejection by 152 votes to 5 (including Reynaud). This was the "patriotic" right, blindly submissive to its two mentors: François de Wendel, leader of heavy industry, who restrained[276] its nominal leader Louis Marin from showing that he was tempted by Blum's offer; and Pierre-Etienne Flandin, the cunning giant who, six months later, after Munich, sent a congratulatory telegram to Hitler.

There was nothing left for Blum to do but express his "disappointment and sadness" to the press, and to respond to Albert Lebrun's renewed appeal that he form a government with resignation. He had just given himself entirely to his attempt at unity. This failure, coming after his wife's death, left him weakened. Moreover, he thought he saw in this new request from the Chief of State something like a trap, even a provocation. This is what Albert Blumel indicated in a contribution to the 1965 conference: "He thought that he should no longer be called, that M. Lebrun wanted absolutely to destroy the Socialist party in this adventure, and when he resigned in April 1938, he said: 'It is as though I were on the march of the Ten Thousand. I have led the party to safety and it has arrived without losses.' "[277] This was a bit too much, not on the expedition—which was in any case a retreat—but on the losses.

Retreat or expedition, he was once again in power, and once again confronted the Assembly, this time on March 17, 1938, the very day Hitler entered Vienna. He put together a government similar to that of June 1936, but with two important exceptions. The first was the substitution of Paul-Boncour for Yvon Delbos at the Quai d'Orsay; his former running mate in the socialist electoral battles of 1919–1924 demonstrated more authority than Delbos and was bolder in concealing the "relaxations" of non-intervention in Spain. The second was the replacement of Vincent Auriol at the Ministry of Finance, which was subdivided into two portfolios: one, called the Budget, which was entrusted to Charles Spinasse, and the other, the Treasury, which Blum assumed himself, despite his own well-known belief in the impossibility of the head of government taking on a portfolio.

Moreover, Blum named as his assistant in this area an Under Secretary of State, the young Radical deputy from Eure, Pierre Mendès France, whose first speeches in the Chamber on financial questions had struck him, and whose anti-Fascist attitudes were well known. Blum was thus assured that the customs problems posed by aid to Republican Spain would be resolved favorably; Spinasse, a pacifist, strongly supported non-intervention.

Aside from renewed "relaxation" of non-intervention in Spain,[278] the second Blum cabinet was marked by its attempt to accelerate rearmament—the cabinet was formed immediately after Hitler's *Anschluss*—and by the development of a still-famous economic program, which was the first great effort to organize French production in a modern manner. This program had been first outlined by a group of CGT engineers and "planners" in the Ministry of Finance under Auriol. The plan was revised, amplified, and made specific by Georges Boris, whom Blum had just made director of his cabinet at the Treasury, and by Pierre Mendès France, both of whom were convinced "Keynesians." The *Times* of April 6 described the "exposition of the reasons" for this bill as a "masterpiece."

Blum and his colleagues had been ingenious enough to present the plan as a whole in the perspective of military recovery which could or should have impressed the supposedly patriotic right:

> The measures proposed are dominated by the immense obliga-
> tion for all Frenchmen to assume the defense of the country. There
> is certainly a tragic irony in the fact that a nation deeply attached to
> peace and progress is obliged to stretch all its resources in a gigan-
> tic military effort. We did not wish for this; our thoughts turned
> away from it with horror and aversion. But we will show that free
> peoples can meet the challenge of their duties, that democracies
> are capable, thanks to freely accepted discipline, of exhibiting
> strength that is developed elsewhere only through blind obedience.
> We will proceed so that, around arms manufacture, a coordinated
> economy will be the basis of increased production in every area.

Progress *through* rearmament? This was hardly an argument characteristic of Blum. But Roosevelt and his government demonstrated a
few years later that the two requirements could come together. Yet as
far as the rearmament necessitated by Hitler's activities was concerned, he immediately came up against inflexible resistance.

On the 17th of March, in the Chamber, where he went twice to argue
for the plan developed by his associates—tax on capital, exchange
control,[279] modernization of the legal status of work, old-age pensions,
development of family allowances—he obtained a comfortable majority (311 votes to 250), reduced slightly among the Radicals because of
Flandin's virulent criticism. In fact, it was a real left program and,
explained Blum, "not the pause at all: on the contrary, a period of more
ardent life in the form of economic stimulation as well as social progress." The increased resistance was hardly surprising. Blum returned
to the rostrum:

> We have also been told and will be told again that our plan, once
> adopted, would lead this country toward an autarkic system, with
> increased constraints and generalized state control, and conse-
> quently toward dictatorship. I heard a moment ago, with horror,
> the parallel a speaker conjecturally established between the head
> of a large totalitarian state and the poor president of a republican
> government like me. At this moment we are witnessing a really
> very peculiar encounter. The same men who are secret and often
> open apologists for totalitarian regimes are criticizing us for lead-
> ing French democracy in their path. Every time democracy seeks
> to become independent and strong, the secret or open advocates of
> autocratic regimes attack it for denying and betraying itself.

We are in a Republic. I am speaking before a real Parliament, a free Parliament, where everyone says what he thinks, where everyone can do so without running the slightest risk for his life or his freedom. I am speaking before the representatives of parties which exist legally and act freely in the country. I am speaking as the head of a government formed according to a constitution where sovereignty belongs to the people, the people who are freely consulted. But if we refuse to accept a regime which resembles that of the totalitarian states, does that mean that we will refuse to profit from every experiment whose lessons we will, of course, be able to adapt to the system which is and will remain ours, the republican system? . . .

Will it be said that, in every area, the democracies will remain materially inferior to the autocracies? Will they not in the end find the means to provide for their pressing necessities, without failing, of course, in their principles, which are the very life of societies like ours? This is the ground on which we should place the problem of financial stability, financial and monetary affluence, as well as the problem of authority which is always talked about and which is rather, to use the proper term, the problem of decision.

It was not until April 8 that he confronted the Senate, this time without illusions. The reasons that had led the Senators to bring down his cabinet ten months before—their rejection of any challenge to class relations and to the distribution of the national wealth—could only be strengthened by this innovative program boldly based on centralized planning. Thus, broadening the question as he had done in the Chamber, he posed the question of the Senate's actual rights within the system of universal suffrage. After pointing out that in no country in the world was the government responsible to the upper chamber, the Premier raised in plain language

the question of the division of power between the two Assemblies, as Gambetta himself raised it more than fifty years ago. . . . The upper chamber, which is of course free to act according to its full constitutional powers, should nevertheless assign to itself only the power of supervision and moderation. I fear for republican harmony if the Senate allows itself to be drawn beyond the customs and traditions it has itself created. It is now getting ready for the second time to express, against the government representing the majority of the Chamber and the majority of universal suffrage, a decisive vote, a vote with a political direction. . . .

I bring my appeal before the Senate. Today it will go to the very limit of the power which the constitutional provisions in fact confer upon it, and it will do so, gentlemen, against the majority of the Chamber which still represents the majority of the country. It is getting ready to reject, I might say to execute—the metaphor is not mine—a plan which did not by any means deserve so much contempt and which the majority of the Chamber had adopted. I ask the republicans in this Assembly if they will not reflect.

One day I was asked: "Whom do you call a true republican?" I answered: "I call a true republican someone who would have struggled under the Empire to create the Republic and who, if the Republic were overthrown tomorrow, would struggle to restore it. It is in this sense that I am a true republican." No more than Jaurès, no more than Guesde and Vaillant, those who knew them can attest to it, have I ever separated from the Republic the present and future cause of socialism. Thus, gentlemen, it is in the name of the traditions, the spirit, and the interest of the Republic that I address to the Senate this final entreaty.

He had offered himself to the executioner's blows. As he had foreseen, he was "executed," with Joseph Caillaux hurling crudely racist barbs at him. ("You do not have enough French earth on the soles of your shoes!") As in 1937, the Socialist party reacted vigorously to this settling of scores. Marceau Pivert, secretary of the Seine federation wrote a ferocious piece attacking "that handful of hard-hearted old men, installed in their senatorial fortress for the defense of the 200 families, [who] have opposed the will of the people for eighteen months. Come to declaim your anger with us!"[280]

But this time Pivert was almost alone in advocating resistance. It was immediately felt to be impossible for Blum to "fight to the bitter end." Besides, one of the factors in the fall of the cabinet was the violent movement of strikes which had revived in the metal industry since Blum's return to power. What exactly did the Pivertists want?

The Time of Self-Criticism

This was one of the major themes of the party congress which met in Royan in early June, shortly after the fall of the government. Like the congress of Marseille, held a few days after the fall of the first Blum cabinet, this one was a congress of self-criticism and disillusionment. Even more, it was a congress of division and rupture and thereby of an even more cruel defeat for Blum.

The formation of the Daladier cabinet, in which the National Council of the SFIO had refused socialist participation, had marked the veritable breakup of the Popular Front. This time, there was not even any question of a "concentration" around the Radicals. Even though the two working-class parties still supported it with their votes, it was really a reversal of the majority: the general flavor of the government remained Radical, but from then on it was the right which played the role of indispensable support which the SFIO had played in the first Chautemps cabinet. The maneuver of a shift to the right, at which the Radicals had always excelled, had now been carried out by Daladier, leader of the left of the party since 1930 and one of the fathers of the

Popular Front, for his own benefit. What Blum had wanted so much to avert had finally come about.

How could the Socialist party not feel swindled? How could it not hold it against Blum, its navigator, who now appeared naive and foolish? Was the new failure not to be imputed to him even more than the first?

The speech Blum delivered in June at the congress of Royan was not, however, that of an accused man. To be sure, he was on the defensive when he spoke of his March 12 plan for "rallying around the Popular Front," and he was again on the defensive when he attempted to prevent the congress from declaring war on the Daladier government, and yet again when he argued against the pacifists that a military rampart should be opposed to the imperialism of the dictators. But he summed up the activity of the party in power in a tone that was, if not triumphant, at least animated by a certain pride:

> We have brought about a veritable revolution in the juridical, moral, and material condition of the workers of this country. You know, revolution is not immediately obvious. There are spectacular revolutions, and there are those which spread slowly, in the facts. There are revolutions under the lights, and there are revolutions under chloroform. And after every revolutionary change which has been brought about in the human condition—and by revolutionary change I understand a change which has suddenly accelerated, in conditions which were impossible to predict beforehand, the normal and regular course of evolution, for that is what a revolutionary phenomenon essentially is—well, after every revolution, nature, human nature resumes its rights, just as physical nature does. That is, every revolutionary change—and in this sense nature makes no leaps—is followed by a relatively long period of oscillations and stirrings whose direction is not always clearly discernible, no more than one can discern at first glance on approaching the ocean whether the tide is rising or falling. Well, we find ourselves in this period of stirrings and oscillations immediately after a revolutionary change. . . . and besides, it was perhaps more perceptible a year ago than it is today, but if you look carefully around you, it is still perceptible: I think we have rejuvenated this country. I think we have restored to it alacrity, confidence in itself, the sense of life. We have done that for the young, and we have done it for the mature. Through the very change that we have brought about in the condition of man, we have taught great masses to recover contact with nature, with the air, with the sun, with all forms of life, those that man has created with culture, art, and human knowledge of every kind. Why, speaking in the name of the party which in the end ran all the risks, confronted all the dangers, and today suffers all the attacks, why should we not express a little legitimate pride?

Where is the indispensable self-criticism? But he also had good reasons not to adopt the tone of a beaten man or a failure. Once more the unity of 1905 had been challenged—as in 1920, as in 1933—and this time on two flanks. First by the leftist faction led by Marceau Pivert, centered in the Seine federation, which had been dissolved the preceding April and was already attempting to organize itself into a dissident party. Then, and this was still more serious, by a broad pacifist faction, a faction which proclaimed that anything was better than war, anything including non-defense.

This was the argument defended from the platform of the congress by the obscure L'Hévéder. But everyone knew that it was also, especially, the argument of Faure; and the congress of Royan marks the date of the third great split of the party, between those who chose resistance to Hitler and those who chose Hitler over the resistance.

Strangely enough for him, Blum argued his case badly. He was unable to respond to those who attenuated the force of his call for struggle against Nazism by asserting that this was, after all, nothing but an echo of his call for the *Union sacrée* of 1914; between the 1914 conflict which opposed competing imperialisms, a conflict into which he had allowed himself to be drawn like so many others from Guesde to Cachin and from Bracke to Sembat; and the fundamental challenge that fascism had by 1938 launched against democracy (however imperfect and unjust it might be).

How is it that the penetrating and honest Blum was incapable of making the distinction between his adhesion to the *Union sacrée* of the first war, which was so questionable from the socialist point of view, and the basic, indispensable resistance to Nazi barbarism?

During the great crisis of 1933, he had so clearly detected the Fascist symptoms which disfigured Déat's arguments, but was incapable of demonstrating to the suicidal pacifists of 1938 that the old debates were no longer pertinent; that it was not because they had been right against him in 1917 that they were not wrong against him in 1938.

Perhaps he argued badly in the summer of 1938 because the other internal party debate obscured his vision: the one which opposed "his" majority to the turbulent Pivertist minority. Marceau Pivert—one of the few members of the party whom he called by his first name from the platform of a congress—was once again standing before him, this time in antagonism. The festivals of 1936 were over, Pivert was no longer playing the role of stage manager for the hero. This time, it was a struggle against the "father" who had been unable—or unwilling?—to exploit the chances for revolution which were supposedly great in the France of 1936, and who was presiding over a new attempt at *Union sacrée* with the bourgeoisie.

In Royan, the break came about in an atmosphere of general bitterness. The "Pivertists," a majority of whom were militants from the

Paris region, were called "Seine hoodlums" by the former minister Rivière,[281] but bravely defended by Jules Moch's wife. Faure had decided to move for their exclusion—which most of them seemed to want in any case. Zyromski himself abandoned them to their fate.

And Blum? His attitude was described by the ultra-Pivertist Daniel Guérin with customary ferocity:

> We had nothing to hope for from Blum. The conciliatory intentions which he apparently showed toward us in a circle of friends went up in smoke. He was a prisoner of his dream of national unity. By advocating amnesty for the Seine federation,[282] he contradicted himself. He struck a bargain, a horse trade, with Paul Faure: the Secretary-General, in spite of his traditional "pacifism," would deign to support the attempt at national unity, and he would support the disciplinary procedure undertaken against us. In the voice of a *mater dolorosa*, he deplored the loss of forces useful to the party. Because for him the party was like a symphonic ensemble and the orchestra should not be deprived of an instrumentalist like Marceau Pivert. Confessing aloud, he found within himself not a shadow, not the slightest trace of personal resentment against Marceau. But was it his fault that he was obliged to choose between some comrades and others? The die was cast. He had chosen Paul Faure.[283]

The "Pivertists" were excluded. Once again the SFIO was a fertile mother. After the parthenogenesis of the right in 1933, here was one of the left: on the night of June 7, the dissidents announced the creation of the "Workers and Peasants Socialist Party" (PSOP), which, not content with denouncing the "surrender" of the Popular Front, also condemned the common failure of the Second and Third Internationals and rejected any adhesion to "a ghostly Fourth International." Here were men without timidity.[284]

"A Cowardly Relief"

Since leaving the hôtel Matignon on April 9, Blum had resumed direction of *Le Populaire,* and was publishing several editorials a week. As war approached, he continued a two-fold combat: against surrender to Hitler's imperialism, and against the liquidation of the social conquests of the Popular Front.

There are few areas in which slander has pursued Blum more insidiously than in the Czechoslovakian affair.[285] Certain historians, repeating right-wing polemicists and Communist propagandists, have made Blum in this case a man of surrender, summing up his attitude by what he himself, after Munich, called a "cowardly relief."

Four quotations from *Le Populaire* will rectify these distortions. On

July 27, 1938, while London, by sending Lord Runciman to Prague, was attempting to obtain a compromise between the Sudeten secessionists of the Nazi Konrad Henlein and the Prague government, Blum warned his English friends:

> In order to arrive at an equitable transaction, it is necessary that English influence make itself felt in Berlin at least as much as in Prague. France does not intend to force Czechoslovakia into concessions which are incompatible with its political unity and its sovereignty, and consequently contrary to the true interests of peace. It does not wish the pressure of friendly powers to lead to the same results as the threat of an attack by Hitler. The fate of Czechoslovakia, and in many senses the fate of Europe, are thus dependent on the judgment of one man.[286]

On September 8, noting that the Runciman mission was merely an attempt to make Prague surrender, Blum reacted:

> It is not possible for the sovereignty and independence of Czechoslovakia now to be stripped from it piece by piece. One-sided bargaining must not go on. [It is necessary to speak] with the strong conviction that what is at stake in this case is something quite different from the condition of the Sudeten Germans, and even something quite different from the fate of the Czechoslovakian state. What is at stake is the fate of Europe, the fate of the freedom of Europe, Great Britain and France included.

On September 20 came the following warning:

> Mr. Neville Chamberlain,[287] who left to negotiate an "honorable and equitable" arrangement, returned from Berchtesgaden[288] bearing an ultimatum from the Führer-chancellor. The British government has surrendered to this ultimatum. The French government, if we refer to its official communiqué, has given its pure and simple acquiescence [to a] plan which mutilates the territory of the Czechoslovakian state, violates its sovereignty, and consequently breaks and disavows its alliances.
>
> At the moment of writing, I do not know Czechoslovakia's response. But whatever it may be, Hitler's bet against England and France has been won. His plan has become theirs. It was they who presented it to Czechoslovakia. Nothing is lacking in his success, since it seems he has even succeeded in making them accept the ouster of the USSR from the system of powers guaranteeing the mutilated territory of Czechoslovakia, and no doubt also the breaking of the Czechoslovak-Soviet Pact.
>
> Whatever may happen, the consequences will be far-ranging, in Europe and in France. War has probably been averted. But in such conditions that I, who have unceasingly struggled for peace, who for many years have sacrificed my life to it, cannot feel any joy, and I feel torn between a cowardly relief and shame.

Finally this, on September 26:

> Great Britain and France have imposed on Czechoslovakia the abandonment of the Sudetenland to the Reich. For a week, Hitler's victory over Czechoslovakia and the Western democracies has been an accomplished fact. He wanted the Sudeten Germans to be joined to the Reich. The question is now whether he will stop there, whether the sacrifice has appeased him, or whether on the contrary he will not continue to carry out the destruction of Czechoslovakia and, beyond that, his imperial conquests. The question is whether to victory he wishes to add war.

But on September 29 and October 1, at the moment the agreements were signed and immediately afterward, Blum published two surprising editorials in which he spoke of "joy" and "deliverance." This opponent of compromise with fascism resigned himself, for a few days. It was a fleeting weakness,[289] which was continued in the Chamber.

In fact, after fervently fighting against the agreement before the socialist group of the Assembly and being placed in the minority (Faure, an advocate of surrender, winning over him for the first time in ten years), Blum, as president of the group, came forward to express his party's agreement to a government foreign policy motion which implied acceptance of Munich. A pitiful tactical resignation. When the journalist had been so forceful, why did the parliamentarian humiliate himself in this way? A few friends had tried to dissuade him, among them Jules Moch, who joined him on his bench at the Assembly and told him that he had voted "against." Blum's reply was typical: "You can't do that to me!" To reverse oneself is hard. It is more cruel to do so while dragging a friend along in one's retreat.

In the social struggle, his firmness was more constant. It led him to oppose the Daladier government which, with the active support of Paul Reynaud as Minister of Finance, attempted, through extension of the work week and strike-breaking, to dismantle the whole of the social edifice constructed in June 1936. He devoted some very fine articles to the defense of the "5/8,"[290] and especially to the "test of strength" which Daladier and Reynaud imposed on the CGT.

> We finally have a government which governs—for one distinguishes the governments which govern by the way they evacuate occupied factories! For a government has authority only when it is capable of applying force. . . to the working masses, of course! The reactionaries are already showing the same inhuman satisfaction as their grandfathers at the time of the Commune or their ancestors during the June days. "It is a *Kraftsprobe,* a test of strength," exclaims M. d'Ormesson[291] in *Le Figaro.* He adjures the government, [which] surrendered in the test against Germany a month

ago, at least—in compensation—not to give in to the workers to-day. France destroyed its prestige by allowing Czechoslovakia to collapse; but it can restore it by destroying communism! A providential grace has offered it that opportunity!

Ministers of the Republic, don't you see who is pushing you and toward what? Have you forgotten that in this country it has never been possible to establish or defend free institutions without the complete support of the popular masses? Have you forgotten that France is surrounded by dangers of every kind and that everything which might set the masses of the country against the government—like everything which might divide the masses among themselves—would become a crime of *lèse-nation?* Then stop, since there is still time. But there is just barely enough time: the days are going by, and one moves rapidly down the slope you are on!

Blum repeatedly warned against the immense social reprisals unleashed by the Daladier government in December 1938. In the chamber on December 8 he tried to obtain amnesty for workers and employees dismissed for striking. He could hardly make himself heard over the interruptions.

M. LEON BLUM: Since the representatives of big capital have remained or have become, no matter, relentless adversaries of the social legislation of 1936, they have revenge to take. . .

M. XAVIER VALLAT: Let him speak: he knows the big capitalists well since he defends them.[292]

BLUM: . . . since the representatives of big capital have to avenge the possible undermining of their authority, since they also have to revenge themselves—unfortunately a very human feeling—for the fear they experienced, they had to add to this kind of fiscal oppression symbolic gestures and spectacular attacks against the forty-hour law, against the two Sundays, against collective bargaining, against the system of electing workers' delegates. This has brought about two unavoidable consequences: first, on the part of the working class, the popular masses, a movement of protest which the government was wrong, I assure you, not to consider spontaneous and natural. It was so spontaneous and natural that it occurred in every class and every region of the country, in every social category, in every political party, and even groups like veterans' associations expressed it. . .

M. GEORGES ROLLEAUX-DUGAGE: You do not have the right to speak of veterans, Monsieur Blum, because you did not fight in the war.

THE PRESIDENT: If these interruptions continue, I will adjourn the session. M. Blum's language is irreproachable. You ought to listen to him.

THE PRESIDENT: I call for order. The session is adjourned.
(The session was suspended at 12:55 and resumed at one o'clock.)

THE PRESIDENT: The assembly is in session. M. Léon Blum has the floor.

BLUM: Gentlemen, I will not finish the speech which was interrupted in the circumstances you witnessed. I have made my point sufficiently, the republicans have seen the face of the new majority.

The "new majority"? Blum was to analyze the mechanisms by which the Chamber of 1936 and the Popular Front, "his" Chamber, was converted into a reactionary and surrendering mob. In a series of articles in August 1939 which are, in the best sense of the expression, "immediate history," he described how Daladier carried out the liquidation of the Popular Front.

Asserting that the ruling classes had never considered the Popular Front victory durable and had never stopped preparing for a reversal of the majority, he pointed out that they had at first counted on "the corrosive action of financial difficulties," and had then turned to the "classic procedure of shifting the Radical party in the course of the legislature." But this time the majority of the left was stronger and more organized. Given parliamentary arithmetic, the Radicals had to

> associate not only with the republican center and parliamentary conservatives, but team up with extreme reactionaries, with the gangs of the PSF and *L'Action Française*. Although it was constructed according to the same model [as those of 1926 and 1934], the operation was therefore tougher, required greater dexterity . . . extreme precautions, the principal one obviously being the initiative, authority, and guarantee of the Radical leader. Doumergue was no longer there; nor was Poincaré; a Flandin, a Paul Reynaud, or a Marin taking open leadership of the operation would have been shattered by his first contact with the Chamber; we may even presume that their indiscreet and revealing appearance would, by an automatic reflex, have restored the old majority. . . . The operation could succeed only if the Radical party took on its ostensible leadership. . . . They had said to themselves: "Chautemps will do, because he is the most moderate of the Radical leaders, the most distant from the Popular Front contract." This was a false calculation. The operation was difficult and could be carried out only under a strong anaesthetic. To calm, lull, convince the Radical party, what was needed was the most radical of Radicals, the most intransigent, the most openly and fervently attached to the "mystique of the Popular Front." Only he could succeed, and he has in fact succeeded.

No victim of the guillotine could have better described the actions of the executioner. But this was no longer the time for analysis, still less for regrets. War was present, obvious since Hitler had annexed the surviving fragments of dismembered Czechoslovakia in March 1939, and Mussolini had imitated him in April by seizing Albania. Obvious since von Ribbentrop had gone to Moscow on August 23 to sign the German–Soviet pact with Stalin, leaving the Nazis with a free hand against the Western democracies.

"It would be futile to try to disguise my stupor," wrote Blum that very evening:

> The fact that today, in the midst of the European crisis, amid the uproar of troop movements and diplomatic preparations, while military missions from England and France are in Moscow, while we expected from one day to the next the signing of the Tripartite Pact,[293] Hitler's Reich and Soviet Russia were able to reach a political agreement is truly an extraordinary event, almost unbelievable, and we are completely stunned by it.
>
> Our astonishment is redoubled when we remember that the horror and hatred of communism are the feelings by which Hitler has claimed to justify all his recent enterprises, including the destruction of the Spanish and Czechoslovakian Republics; that anticommunist ideology is at the basis of Nazism; that the diplomatic instrument which has permitted Germany and Italy to gather their allies around them is an anti-Komintern pact. And now Hitler not only accepts, but even, to all appearances, proposes a political agreement with the Soviets.
>
> For its part, Soviet Russia has constantly stirred up anti-Fascist propaganda everywhere. Communists have constantly denounced Hitler as the public enemy of all justice, of all freedom, of all civilization. And at the most acute and dangerous moment of the European crisis, it is toward Hitler that Soviet Russia seems to lean! It would be hard to go further in audacity, fundamental contempt for public opinion, and defiance of public morality.
>
> The announcement of the German-Soviet pact had marked the real beginning of a universal state of alarm. It certainly shows that we were right to insist, as we have for months and I can say for years, on the incorporation of Soviet Russia into a defensive front for peace, for we feel today, from the void created by its absence, that its presence had real value.

Just as he had thus pointed out that everything had not been done to associate the USSR with the attempts to preserve peace, and that the "void" was not solely attributable to Stalin's Machiavellianism, so he stood up against the anti-Communist repression immediately unleashed by the Daladier government against the PCF, in which only a significant minority was courageous enough to dissociate itself from the Moscow pact.

> I know that it is tempting for a government to exploit to the full, against the party which has provoked them, the agitation and revulsion of public opinion. But I would be betraying my conscience if I did not declare to the government, on my own responsibility, that it is in the process of committing a frightful mistake. Is it in conformity with its interests to let all France believe, and especially to let foreign nations believe that the hundreds of thousands of workers grouped in Communist organizations and unions under Communist leadership are bad Frenchmen, bad patriots, toward

whom the public interest requires, at a critical moment, measures of suspicion and constraint?

We know very well that this is not so. We know very well that they will march like all the rest. Then I repeat, whom is it of interest to convince of the contrary, other Frenchmen, possible enemies, or themselves? One can understand that the pro-Hitler reactionaries in Paris would look for a diversion or an alibi in this direction, however miserable the operation may be at the present moment. But on the part of the government, I beg it to believe me, it would be a short-sighted policy devoid of real wisdom.

Three days later, the Nazis and the Soviets invaded Poland, one from the West, one from the East, an old predatory policy whereby Stalin aligned himself with Catherine II, and with Hitler.

War had come.

Part III
DEFENSE OF FREEDOM

THE TRIAL

The Collapse

Late in the afternoon of September 2, Blum left the Chamber of Deputies after voting for military appropriations which assured France's entry into the war alongside Great Britain. Poland had been invaded by Hitler (and by Stalin). Blum sat at his desk at *Le Populaire* and wrote his editorial:

> France did not want this; it did everything to prevent it. We socialists, who are struggling for peace, who, following Jaurès's sacred example, have dedicated our lives to it for the last twenty years, can bear witness to this before the world. What madness has afflicted Europe and the world? Never has history offered the slightest example of such a widespread desire for peace in the world. A single man wanted war, a single man has unleashed war.

To say that France "did everything to prevent it" was to forget some guilty retreats and to dismiss lightly the inability of several French governments to establish the great alliance in the East (which Blum himself had really attempted to do). To speak of a single man was to neglect Mussolini, the Japanese generals, the Fascists of Central Europe, and Stalin. But it was not the time for analyses or assessments. He was right to place the emphasis on Hitler; concentration of fire on the primary target is an elementary rule of strategy. This is partly why, having duly denounced Stalin's role, he later sought to attenuate the repercussions of the Georgian dictator's policy. Another reason was that Stalin's policies affected Blum's former Communist partners in the Popular Front.

He made it a rule to attenuate the rain of blows falling on the PCF not only for strategic considerations but also because he saw already that the attack on the Communists was the first phase of the right's great revenge. Anticipating the Vichy regime, which broadened and deepened the counterattack to become the "anti-Popular Front," Blum saw the tide rising. In the very heart of the government, forces aiming only for reprisals were gaining strength. It was in the name of democracy and the republican spirit that he patiently criticized the measures—banning of L'Humanité, dissolution of the PCF, impeachment of Communist legislators—which proliferated against Maurice Thorez's party.

On September 27, immediately after the decree dissolving the Communist party (which adopted the title, in the Chamber, of "workers and peasants group"), Blum wrote in Le Populaire that he considered "the dissolution a mistake." He went on:

> I remain an incorrigible republican and democrat. There are authoritarian acts with which I cannot feel in agreement. If Communists are individually convicted of treason, let them be tried and executed like all traitors!¹ But the Communist Party in itself was, in my view, subject only to the public conscience, and the only penalty it should have received was universal reprobation. That is what I think. I could not have suppressed it without committing a small act of cowardice.

Every time one of Stalin's infamies (from the occupation of the Baltic States to the invasion of Finland) was applauded by the elected officials of the PCF, he proclaimed his indignation and denounced their "absolute allegiance," their "omni-obedience." But when in January 1940 the Chamber of Deputies was considering a bill to impeach all the Communist Deputies who had not taken a position against the Hitler-Stalin pact, he protested again:

> Parliament does not have the right to impeach its members. They are not chosen by it, still less by the government; they are elected through universal suffrage. Impeachment is a sanction [which cannot] be taken without a trial, without adversary proceedings, without any possible defense.

In return, communist propaganda—which handled Hitler carefully for more than a year—made the former head of the Popular Front government its favorite target. On September 7, André Marty had sent from Moscow a "Letter to Léon Blum, conseiller d'Etat," accusing him of "justifying the war of Chamberlain, the City, Daladier, and the banks" and of being "the pope who is infallibly in error."² Maurice Thorez went much further, denouncing "Blum with his long claws, police auxiliary, informer, who combines Millerand's aversion for socialism, Pilsudski's cruelty, Mussolini's ferocity, and Trotsky's hatred for the Soviet Union."[3] These imprecations worthy of *Gringoire* conclude with the words *"Blum-la-guerre."*

This was the favorite nickname used by the militants of *L'Action Française*, who adapted the famous antimilitarist lines of the *"Internationale"* for their purposes and sang:

> *S'ils veulent, ces cannibales*
> *faire de nous des héros*
> *il faut que nos premières balles*
> *soient pour, Mandel, Blum et Reynaud.*[4]

The man who had carried pacifism so far had become, for the right and the extreme left, the symbol of war. He paid no attention. He grew closer and closer to two men who also embodied the fighting spirit: Mandel and Reynaud. Politicians of the right? Perhaps, but they were determined to fight fascism. At the time that was what counted above all.

Through Reynaud, Blum resumed contact with Colonel de Gaulle, who was champing at the bit in a secondary command in Alsace, sheltered by the Maginot Line. After a dinner together at Reynaud's, de Gaulle went home with Blum and, urging him to intervene, confessed: "I am afraid that the lesson of Poland,[5] which is really very clear, has been rejected out of prejudice. People claim that what succeeded there cannot be executed here. Believe me, we have everything left to do, and if we don't react in time, we will lose this war miserably; we will lose it by our own fault. If you are in a position to act together with Paul Reynaud, do so, I beg of you!"

Before leaving him, de Gaulle informed Blum that he would send him a note on the measures to be taken entitled "Mechanized War." Blum received it and read it at one sitting. "It was then," he wrote, "that I understood everything." The socialist leader did not have access to a very wide audience in military circles. However, he made certain that de Gaulle's note was read by General Georges, number two man in the French army. Two armored divisions were established—but on the eve of the collapse.

The interest Blum took in the war effort and the support he provided it through his advice and writing earned him bitter criticism within his own party. However great the difference between the anti-Fascist war of 1939–40 and the 1914 conflict, between resistance to Hitler and the *Union sacrée*, the debate inside the SFIO grew bitter; Paul Faure more and more took on the role of anti-Blum. By founding *Le Pays socialiste*, the secretary-general of the party made a gesture toward a kind of pacifist schism. Did he think he was back in the time of *Le Populaire du centre* of 1917? He soon rejoined *Le Populaire,* while riddling Blum with arrows and calling him "dangerous."[6]

Blum had long before judged Faure as a man judges his weaknesses. His behavior saddened him, but he was more cruelly affected by the movement in the same direction of one of his closest companions, Charles Spinasse. In the Chamber of March 12, the Deputy from Corrèze delivered an openly "defeatist" speech. Jules Moch, who heard it as he sat next to his leader, saw Blum "shudder with pain," while from the socialist benches came thunderous applause resounding like a "condemnation" of Blum's attitude.[7]

It was at this time that Assistant Secretary of State Sumner Welles, sent to Europe by President Roosevelt, visited Paris on two occasions. He particularly asked to be received by Blum, though Blum no longer occupied any official position. The two men had a conversation on March 9. Then Welles went to London. "When I returned to Paris," he relates, "my secretary informed me that while I was in London at least 3000 letters had arrived criticizing me for having gone to see Blum. Most of these letters were written in the most violent and abusive terms, and all of them criticized me—a representative of the President of the United States—for having dared to visit a Jew. Nazi ideas had penetrated and already perverted the mentality of a part of the population."[8]

On March 21, 1940, while a slanderous issue of *Gringoire* devoted to Blum was put on sale in Paris, Reynaud succeeded Daladier, who was brought down by an Assembly in which the nationalistic right reproached him for military inertia and the left, sickened by his social policies (the 40-hour law had just been practically abrogated), had withdrawn its support. The rumor circulated that Blum had directed the scheme, which was designated to bring his friend to power. The socialist leader, rather bizarrely, was campaigning instead for designation of the old President of the Senate, Jules Jeanneny.

Charles de Gaulle considered the session of the Chamber of Deputies in the course of which the new government was installed "frightful." Called on as an adviser, the author of *Le Fil de l'epée* found the Chamber "skeptical and gloomy." De Gaulle heard little in the debate but "the spokesmen of groups or of men who considered themselves wronged by the arrangement. The danger confronting the country, the necessity for national effort, the cooperation of the free world were referred to only to ornament pretention and rancor. Only Léon Blum, to whom no position had, however, been offered, spoke with nobility. Thanks to him, M. Paul Reynaud won the vote, though very narrowly."[9] (By a majority of one. Herriot, who presided over the session,

later muttered that he was not very certain about the legitimacy of that
ballot!)

Blum never spoke of this session except to wish "to abolish the
memory of it, like the memory of a bad dream." But we must quote a
bit of it to suggest the atmosphere:

> M. LEON BLUM: I have rather long experience in parliamen-
> tary life; however, the spectacle I am witnessing surprises me. I
> have not understood the personal virulence of certain attacks.
> Gentlemen, you applauded me the other day . . .
> M. FERNAND WIEDEMANN-GOIRAN: Not at all!
> M. LEON BLUM: . . . listen to me today! I have been particu-
> larly unable to understand how, in a session like this one, a kind of
> unruly atmosphere could develop . . .
> M. GASTON RIOU: Which you created!
> M. LEON BLUM: . . . in which speech seemed no longer even
> to evoke any response. I am saying to you what I feel, I am trying
> to figure out the reasons; and I confess that I don't exactly under-
> stand them.
> M. JEAN-LOUIS TIXIER-VIGNANCOUR: The atmosphere is
> the atmosphere of Good Friday!
> THE PRESIDENT: Why these interruptions? You call this na-
> tional unity!

The tenth of May was approaching, the day Hitler chose to unleash
his armored divisions on the front of the Meuse and the Ardennes.
Everyone in Paris believed they were heading for suicide. But the next
day, Jules Moch, returning full of illusions and hope from an expedition
of Allied forces in Norway, was surprised to find Blum "worried." Two
days later, Blum in turn was surprised by the anxiety of Reynaud, with
whom he dined alone before leaving to represent the SFIO at the
Labour Party Conference in Bournemouth, England. "Tell the English," Reynaud said, "to send us fighter planes. The situation is so
serious at this moment that they must not hesitate to sacrifice temporarily the protection of their own territory."[10]

At the Conference, which had decided the same day on Labour's
participation in the new Churchill cabinet, Blum launched an appeal
that has remained famous:

> I do not know what would become of capitalism if we were to lose
> the war, but I know what would happen to socialism if the Ger-
> mans were to win it. Wherever this motorized Attila has passed, all
> working-class movements have been annihilated.

But it was in London that the socialist leader heard the news that
was throwing Paris into a panic: the front had collapsed. He found a
telegram from his friend Marx Dormoy telling him that his daughter-in-

law and granddaughter,[11] without even waiting a few hours for him, had been sent to safety in the country. "I have no memory of ever having been so brutally stunned in my life," Blum wrote four months later.

In Paris, on the 17th, he thought he saw reasons to take heart. On the 21st, he attributed responsibility for spreading disaster to the surrender of the Belgian king, which was discussed with poorly documented indignation in *Le Populaire*. His optimism persisted. As late as June 10, when the Nazi tanks were in view of the Seine, *Le Populaire* published an incredible editorial by him entitled *"La Raison suprême de notre espoir."*

Of course he admitted that the situation was "particularly serious," because the Allies had "neither equivalent matériel nor an equal number of troops." But he asserted, "the men, the vital elements which make up the Allied armies, bring to this heroic struggle something which surpasses even courage: will, inner energy, indomitable determination. German force can and must exhaust itself by its every excess. Allied determination can and must come through the ordeal even more firmly and harshly tempered. That determination is what can and must compensate for the inferiority of material strength from which we are suffering today, as it can and must make the superiority we will one day enjoy irresistible." This teeters between patriotic blindness and prophetic vision: there are expressions which prefigure, almost word for word, the appeal of June 18. But de Gaulle spoke as a technician, and Blum as a naive propagandist.

Besides, when these lines appeared on the morning of June 10, Blum was no longer in Paris. For two days his friends in the government (whose departure was being prepared— to Vichy? Tours? Bordeaux?), Georges Monnet and Albert Sérol, had been begging him to leave. "And Paris? 'Our departure will change nothing,' answered Monnet, 'Paris will be defended thoroughly.' I could not manage to accept, to absorb the idea of leaving, Wouldn't it be a personal consecration of defeat?" But throughout the day of the 9th, he was repeatedly pressed. "You cannot fall into the hands of the Germans, you don't have the right."[12]

He was still hesitating when, toward eleven at night, Georges Monnet called him one last time:

> "The cabinet meeting is over," he said, "we are all leaving for Tours at this very moment, except Paul Reynaud and Mandel; the car is ready. But we cannot, we will not, leave you behind in Paris. All our colleagues think as we do and insist along with us, Reynaud first of all." Georges Monnet's wife took the phone from his hands, and she too, with tears in her voice, begged me to give her my

word. I gave in; I promised; I embraced my friends; I jumped into a car and went off into the night.[13]

When he arrived in Montluçon, where he was greeted by his friend Dormoy, mayor of the town, he learned of Mussolini's attack—and he began to regret that the Allies had not preventively brought their Mediterranean forces to bear against him. That might have disconcerted Hitler by weakening the Axis. But one is always a good strategist after a defeat. He could not stay quietly in Montluçon. What was becoming of Paris, what was being prepared there? He could wait no longer. Was it madness or boldness? On the morning of June 11, he left with Dormoy for the capital. He was perhaps the only man in France during those hours traveling in that direction. He visited the last men to be found there, the Prefect of Police Langeron, the American Ambassador William Bullitt, and General Hering, who had just been relieved of his post as Military Governor of Paris and who listened "with indulgence" to Blum's entreaties to defend the capital at all costs.[14]

Then Blum and Dormoy entered the fantastically deserted Palais-Bourbon, where they found in the security office an employee "abandoned as a hostage or a guide," the only guardian of "this necropolis." After spending an hour—the last—in his apartment on the quai Bourbon, Blum rushed back to the road, heading south. He was part of the exodus.

> I had never seen, I think, a spectacle as poignant as this immense human migration. And I imagined with horror the effect that would have been produced by a few German bombers flying over this people in flight, as they had done in Belgium and Nord. However, the mass of men, women, and children, through which our car struggled to move, and who seemed to hang onto us, showed none of the stigmata of anguish or terror. That may seem almost unbelievable, and yet it was true; this crowd was in good spirits. Casual remarks were exchanged between groups; open laughter greeted jokes or flirtations; people helped each other in innumerable little ways; a hand to replace a load that was falling off, to get an old "jalopy" running—if that's the word—again, and soon. Kindness and willingness to help were really limited only by the density of bodies and the incompressibility of objects. What an extraordinary people! I knew that the French spirit resisted everything, but these little images of the people's flight nevertheless made me understand that that spirit, at least, was not due to fear. The people had not emptied Paris out of panic, but from horror at German oppression.

On the 13th they were again in Montluçon. But the very next day, a phone call from Georges Mandel, Minister of the Interior in the government which had just barely established itself in Bordeaux, caused them to return to the road. "Come at once," Mandel said. "What is happening here is very serious." Still accompanied by Marx Dormoy, he arrived in the middle of the night in Bordeaux where, as Sembat's head of cabinet, he had already spent three months of governmental exodus twenty-five years before. He found the capital of Aquitaine in much the same state.

> Those who had fled at the first moment had already been filling it up for weeks and every hour brought, from all directions, a new wave of overloaded cars. Pedestrians covered the sidewalks, cars covered squares and courtyards, the cafés were packed. This city with such a majestic appearance seemed tainted by an atmosphere of riffraff on a spree.

Writing his *Mémoires* four months later, and then testifying before the parliamentary Investigative Commission in 1947, Blum said he was convinced that there was then a majority in the government in favor of continuing the fight from North Africa, and that it was the military leaders, Pétain and Weygand, followed by Darlan, who were responsible for shifting the decision. This is not quite the impression which Jules Moch gathered on the spot—he thinks that Blum's opinion derived from the fact that he saw hardly anyone but Mandel's entourage, the clan of the resisters.[15] Blum's narrative in any case reveals his state of mind at the time:

> It was under the authority of General Weygand that the idea of armistice was propagated. The kind of stupor I rediscover in myself when I think of those hours in Bordeaux comes from the incomprehensible character, for men arriving after barely three or four days' absence, of the assertion that was categorically stated and reiterated: "There is nothing left, there is no more army, no more resistance is possible." It seemed that in a few days a kind of decomposition, of incomprehensible volatilization had taken place. We pressed them with questions: "But it's not possible, there are men here, there are men there, there is this army and that army." "Not so, Weygand was just telling us again that there is nothing left, we couldn't assemble three intact divisions, we can no longer hold out, it's impossible." We found ourselves confronting this extraordinary situation: the men commanding the army were saying: "There is no more army, it no longer exists, nothing is left, count on nothing."

He experienced as blows of fate Reynaud's sudden resignation on the 16th, and the designation of Pétain—whom he had admired in the past, but about whom he had few illusions. Yet he believed that, though the Marshal might be obliged to remain on national soil, the state apparatus was indeed going to leave for North Africa, with Chautemps being delegated by Pétain to carry out the obligations of government there. And he, too, intended to leave, in order to represent in this exiled government a substantial political family and its principle.

With a kind of alarmed, or disgusted, humor, he has admirably recounted this false departure, the gathering of notables at night in a
Bordeaux under bombardment by the Luftwaffe, the counter-order
("We're not going to Le Verdon but to Port-Vendres"), the race toward
the Mediterranean through the Garonne valley, the sudden halt in
Toulouse where his old friend Eugène Montel transmitted the new
counter-order ("You are indeed to embark at Le Verdon!"), and the
return to Bordeaux where he learned that the *Massilia,* the ship he was
supposed to be on, had just set sail for Casablanca.

He also recognized that he had just escaped from a terrible pitfall
(premeditated by Pétain's entourage?), for the government, considering that the conditions imposed by Hitler for a cease-fire were
acceptable, was not leaving! The thirty-eight deputies who had sailed
had done so (unknowingly) not as associates of the major institutions of
the state, but as runaways, almost as deserters; and it was on this
accusation that one of them, Pierre Mendès France, was tried a few
months later. What would have been said of Blum had it been possible
to "evacuate" him in that way?

Stranded in Bordeaux, he nevertheless could not stay. The police
had informed him that they could not guarantee his safety.

> The streets of Bordeaux were in a great uproar; the old subversives
> of the 6th of February, the extreme right groups, the former
> *Cagoule* and anti-Semitic gangs were in command. I had been
> followed in my comings and goings between Herriot's hotel and
> the house where I had found shelter, spied on from every doorway;
> prudence thus required that I remain confined to my hosts' house
> to avoid a street incident. Hadn't the unpopularity which was
> gathering around my name already made my action sterile, or even
> harmful to the ideas I would have liked to support, and to the
> companions who had defended them with me? To feel oneself not
> only as a heavy burden or a dead weight, but even as a weight
> which, if it were thrown into the balance, would add to the strength
> of the opponents of what one most passionately desires to serve,
> these are cruel impressions, and they began to take possession of
> me.

Therefore, he left for the Toulouse region, where Eugène Montel's
son-in-law, Raoul Massardy, put his property "l'Armurier" at his disposal. "L'Armurier" was about 30 kilometers from Muret, the little
town of which Vincent Auriol was mayor. It was when he arrived in
Toulouse that Blum learned, on June 23 at dawn, of the armistice
conditions accepted by the Pétain government. However prepared he
may have been, the conditions astounded him:

> I can still see myself sitting in my car, picking up again the news-
> paper I had dropped on my knees, reading with an attention in

which truly all my vital strength was concentrated, and not succeeding in believing what I was reading. It was obvious: they had not bargained, or rather they had brought themselves to submit to everything.[16] Thus, in less than a week, we had just moved from the system of free negotiation—guaranteed as a need by the departure of the government and the determination to continue the war outside France—to surrender, pure and simple. The irreparable had been consummated.

The Swamp of Vichy

Thus he was installed at "l'Armurier," along with his family and the Auriols. "Leave. Leave France, you are in too great danger," they said to him. He knew that he could still embark on a British ship at Saint-Jean-de-Luz, and that he would be warmly welcomed in London or Washington. He decided to stay; he made his decision without hesitation. To his family and friends he said:

> There remains for me only one choice, only one duty, since the government has surrendered: to remain in France, here where I am to wait calmly for danger, if there really is danger, to hold myself ready to answer for my past acts in any public discussion, from the rostrum of the Chamber if I can, on the stand in a court of law if I must; to defy serenely injustice and hatred which will exhaust themselves; to preserve all the possibilities for action in France for the day, perhaps soon, when this people, crushed and stunned by disaster, will take hold of itself again. That day, my presence, or if you will, my existence will perhaps resume a meaning [although I am] rather inclined to believe that I have come to the end of my useful life.
>
> I have been and I am still a public man; I have conducted the affairs of France, that is, I have represented it in its own eyes and in the eyes of the outside world; I feel that I cannot, at will, especially at such a moment, break the bonds of solidarity which unite me to my country. I condemn everything that has happened in the last week, and I have the right to condemn: every Frenchman is a judge of the honor of France, of what honor requires and of what it forbids. I consider France dishonored. But I do not feel that I have the right to withdraw. I must accept my place in the common fate, not only in sorrow, which is relatively easy, but in shame.

"My voice no doubt broke a few times while I spoke these words, for Michelle Auriol got up and came to kiss me." One is free to smile, if one wishes, at this breaking voice and that kiss. Political sophisticates may condemn this mixture of aestheticism and moralism, seeing in it the reflection of the "politics of the just man" so brilliantly attacked by Colette Audry. It has been said, "Lenin or Trotsky would not have stayed within reach of the Nazis." Of course. It had been clear for a long time—at least since the congress of Tours—that Blum was not a Bolshevik leader. A guilty conscience? The "shame" which he wished to share in spite of everything was the word which flowed from his pen after those of "cowardly relief" at the time of Munich. Since that time he had incessantly rejected desertions and denials. But there was the Spanish Republic dying in the filthy camps where France dared to place its last defenders.

During those days after his decision had been made, when he could have devoted himself to the bitter joys of stoicism, he was once again seized by hope. His hope was nourished by General de Gaulle's first speeches, in which he rediscovered the power of imagination and reasoning of "this man all of a piece." The time of alliance between them soon arrived.

Until Berlin took full control, it was at Vichy that all decisions were then made, from the fate of *Le Populaire* (which had been banned) to the future of the regime. He hastened there on July 4. In the small Casino, where the parliament now met, he encountered the new masters, Marquet, Déat, and especially Laval, "determined to exploit to the full the fortuitous combination of circumstances which had just installed him in power. He wanted to carve out of national defeat something solid and lasting. The Republic embarrassed him; no matter, he would overthrow the Republic." Speaking to him, Pierre Laval fulminated shamelessly against the French politicians "who wanted this mad war, this criminal war."[17] As for *Le Populaire,* continued the Auvergne politician, it had no more chance of appearing than any other newspaper which "showed the slightest reticence toward my policy. I must be followed absolutely, without reservations." Blum was dumbfounded:

> I had been informally acquainted with Laval for a good twenty-five years, and I thought I knew him rather well. He had been modest in the past, and that modesty was not entirely hypocritical. He seemed to be the first to ask pardon for his success. I know how little I am worth, he seemed to say, but what do you expect? I have had luck, perhaps a little knack. Toward men in whom he sensed worthiness, culture, or dignity of character, he affected, sometimes with kindness and wit, airs of deference and subordination . . .
>
> Now, to my great astonishment, I was staring at another man. An unbelievable haughtiness had swollen his small body. He announced with a dry voice and an irritated look verdicts and orders which were not questioned. "I do . . . I want . . . I refuse . . . it is so." . . . He was obviously trying on the character of a despot and he thought he had France in the palm of his hand. His manner had something clownish about it, so great was its contrast with the pinched, bizarre, and almost repulsive ugliness of his physical appearance, but it also had something terrifying in it. It was difficult

to take it completely seriously, but it could be taken tragically. He spoke, and spoke again, with his humble and cruel gaze and his slightly singing Auvergne accent which he drew out vulgarly at the end of sentences like wooden shoes on the floor.

This is not quite Retz or Saint-Simon, his masters, but it comes close to the admirable Tocqueville of the 1848 memoirs.

The two Chambers, Laval had decided, would sit separately on the 9th of July and together on the 10th in order to "review the constitutional laws." Here and there, Blum noticed signs of resistance to the establishment of despotism. But once again it was the "resisters" whom he frequented. Shortly before the meeting, the destruction of the French fleet by the British on July 3 greatly assisted Laval's plans: "The cannon of Mers-el-Kebir would prepare and cover the assault against the Republic," wrote Blum. The session that would deliver the death blow had arrived.

The statements Laval made were unambiguous: "We want to destroy the entirety of what exists. Either you accept the model of the German or the Italian constitution, or Hitler will force it on you." Day by day Blum found the men whom he had seen determined to resist Laval's bid for power unrecognizable:

> The poison one could thus see at work was fear, quite simply, panic, fear. Laval had one by one, I won't say convinced, but infected them. One must admit in all fairness that he is unrivalled in this one-on-one manipulation and trickery.

The fear which was so cleverly propagated was that of a *coup d'état* by Weygand, or an attack by the Germans—who were camped nearby at Moulins—and, of course, also the fear of the instruments of coercion at the disposal of the new regime. Thus,

> Laval's prison came to complete the work of Weygand's sword and Hitler's boot. This panicked crowd, carried away by collective movements of terror and cowardice, avoided discussion, and even contact, with those who were already pointed at as implacable opponents, and consequently as outcasts and condemned men. The experience was obvious, since I went through it myself. A comrade who, when I entered the room, had hurried toward me with his hand extended, was obviously avoiding me an hour later and the make-up of the group in which I had seen him in the interval, speaking in a quiet voice or listening with lowered head, would have allowed me to name the agent of contamination with certainty. From moment to moment, I saw myself more alone, I felt myself more suspect . . .
> Strangely enough, the immense and echoing hall was not noisy; all this fermentation, all this festering decomposition, was almost silent, and in the silence perhaps one should see a final shred of shame. People spoke in small groups, quickly formed and dis-

persed; consultations were held in low voices, almost in whispers; as soon as someone approached, the voices became still lower, or stopped. By contrast, from outside came loud noises, for Doriot, as well as the mobile guard, was occupying the city, and as soon as one left the Casino, one had to walk past shouting crowds, hurling at the men whose faces they recognized either ferocious abuse or frenetic acclamation.

The assembly, masterfully put together by Laval and infiltrated by the friends of Tixier-Vignancour, was one great roar against those who might contest the plans to surrender all powers to Pétain. Even though he was twice provoked to speak in opposition by Laval, Blum was silent. Out of fear? If he denies it, we may believe the man who had so often confronted an outraged Chamber:

> I hadn't the slightest fear of the ferocious tumult I would unleash simply by rising from my seat or at the first sound of my voice, I had seen many others . . . [but] I could have no doubt that, in the clash that my intervention would touch off, a very large majority of my group would abandon me; indeed, a number of them would secretly join the chorus of the insulters. I did not want to offer the public spectacle of that denial. It was only that which paralyzed me, kept my mouth closed.

Blum's silence on that day is painful. A man who had been able to stand up to furious assemblies and violently hostile meetings remained silent on the day when the Republic was not only assassinated, but covered with spit—by the very men who had been his disciples, like Charles Spinasse, the Popular Front Minister who went as far that day as to denounce freedom. Must we agree with William Shirer[18] that at Vichy Blum "gave in, like Jeanneny, Herriot, and Reynaud, the pillars of the Republic"? No. Unlike the two Presidents of the Chambers, neither Blum nor Reynaud spoke a word of acceptance, and Blum voted against the bill. But from a man like Blum, one always expects more than silence, even the silence of Antigone.

The vote was a disaster, a disaster for him. The Assembly was no longer that of the Popular Front, stripped as it was of the Communist Deputies and the "travelers" of the Massilia. But all the same it contained men who had been his friends: it voted with a vast majority for the suicide of the Republic. There were only 80 representatives out of 560 who said "no" to Laval! Among those 80 there were only 35 socialists. The extent of the betrayal went beyond what he had foreseen. Leaving the meeting after voting "no," Blum encountered Camille Chautemps, still Deputy Premier, colleague and nominal equal of Laval. "Well, Chautemps, it's the end of the Republic?" Chautemps merely answered: "Yes, it is," letting his arms fall with a desolate air.

Upon returning to "l'Armurier," he learned that his son Robert, safe and sound, had been imprisoned as a result of the armistice. The first of the two.

When he found himself back at "l'Armurier" on July 12, Blum was convinced that his public life was over. He took away from Vichy the conviction that his solitude was definitive, that the Socialist party could be reconstructed only by men of another generation. Of course, after seeing Daniel Mayer (who had begged him to do everything possible to revive the party), he received the three men who had been his closest associates—Blumel, Dormoy, and Jules Moch—and also, of course, his most faithful friend and neighbor, Vincent Auriol. But confronting this last cohort of companions, he saw in operation what he called the "enterprise of Nazification" carried out by Laval and his men, two of whom—one until 1939, the other until 1938—had been among his closest disciples, Déat and Spinasse. There were also the fearful, the cowards who had abandoned him.

"History has known more frightful spectacles; I doubt that it has offered any more vile. The tyranny of the weak and the low is always more repugnant than that of fanatics," he observed, going on to note: "The country remained inert and taciturn. How long was this morbid torpor going to last?" Was this optimist by doctrine and temperament despondent or discouraged? No. For he was as much an Anglophile as he was quick to hope. And as long as Churchill and his people were continuing the fight, and Hitler could not manage to land before August 15, he observed in a burst of enthusiasm that "English resistance [may] galvanize France."[19]

Did he regret then that he had not left for London as his friends had pressed him to do? Or that Paul Reynaud was not there either?

> I have no more regrets as far as he is concerned than on my own account. The "Free French" group did not need a political government but a military leader. Since the final defeat of Germany remained the only hope for freedom, integrity, salvation, only a soldier could assert that hope was neither chimerical nor negligible. Only a soldier could preach that disobedience, practical or moral, was the most sacred of duties. This leader had already been found, and one may even say that the leader existed before the group.

Charles de Gaulle had powerfully affected him. Blum had at first fought him without knowing him; it was later that he appreciated him. In the midst of the war, de Gaulle had converted him to the mobile strategy of tanks. They had been in complicity with one another. From late 1939 on, Blum was even convinced—something which neither Reynaud nor Moch confirm in their memoirs—that on June 15 the man who was still head of the government wanted to name de Gaulle head of the army. The still-fresh memory he had of him made Blum a Gaullist from the outset. When his friends argued against him on the grounds of the danger of military power, the general's political past, and his temperament as a "strong man," Blum retorted by guaranteeing "his rectitude, his simplicity, his loyalty" and by ruling out "an adventure based on personal ambition." Blum stayed glued to the radio at "l'Armurier" every evening, deciphering through the static-filled noises coming from London the first signs of hope.

From then on, nothing could make that hope waver. For him, things very soon became clear: the two great Anglo-Saxon democracies were prepared for resistance until they could counter-attack; as for the "mysterious Stalin," the problem was to determine when his break with Hitler would take place; and as for France, at the height of the storm its affairs were in the hands of a figure worthy of assuming the role. His hope almost went as far as to be a kind of naiveté: as early as the summer of 1940, he saw France associated "wholeheartedly and passionately with the appeal launched from London by General de Gaulle"—a vision which the majority of contemporary witnesses would consider optimistic. But what is important is not the precision of the diagnosis, but the meaning of the prognosis. Blum lived with hope.

There was one ground for anxiety, however: the fate of his German comrades who were refugees in France: Breitscheid, Hilferding, Fritz Adler, Hermann Muller's daughter, all of whom came to see him at "l'Armurier." The most shameful clause of the armistice had provided that they be turned over to Hitler. He took pains to help them reach Marseille where they might have been able to embark for the United States. "We have poison, my wife and I," murmured Breitscheid.[20]

And Blum? Would the regime in process of "Nazification" respect his retirement? He could still hear Herriot telling him in Bordeaux on June 20, "If those men take power, escape from them; if you only knew the hatred they felt for you!" He didn't believe it. He learned of the indictments and arrest of Reynaud, Mandel, Daladier, Gamelin. But as a jurist he attributed these measures—which outraged him, of course—to activities directly related to the declaration, the conduct, and the outcome of the war. He had left power two years earlier—except for the brief interlude of March—in April 1938. He considered himself in the clear. How could he fail to understand that it was less any particular deed that the Pétain-Laval system was attacking than democratic practice itself? And who embodied democratic practice more vividly and passionately than Blum?

A few weeks later, he wrote, "My astonishment was complete when, on Sunday, September 15, at six o'clock . . . my servant and friend woke me and said: 'Sir, the house is surrounded by cars and there is a police officer asking to talk to you.' "[21]

Promoted to the Rank of Accused

Chazeron is a small medieval château, remodeled during the Renaissance, enlarged under Louis XIV as far as I can judge, but still stuck in a corner of the mountain above Châtelguyon. I have a spacious room, furnished with bric-à-brac reaching from Henri II style to that of the faubourg Saint-Antoine. My window is barred, but I look out over a lawn, beautiful trees, and a large patch of sky. The internal facilities are rudimentary. The château has been set up a little hastily for its new purpose as a "bastille." I can walk twice a day for an hour and a half altogether in a garden which serves as a prison yard. Supervised walks. But I have already gotten used to having armed guards at my door and I tell myself that the condition of Premier and that of "political prisoner" have some analogies! Prison was missing from my experience of life. Providence has provided it.[22]

From the beginning, he had found the tone. He never abandoned it, confronting the jailers, the judges, those who had him at their mercy—for five years, Blum was the very image of light-hearted stoicism. He was invincible, insusceptible to humiliation. On September 30, he wrote to Jules Moch who, for his part, had just been interned at Pellevoisin: "I have no doubt that you have already established for yourself a life of work and study. That is what I am doing also as well as I can."

Also interned in Chazeron were Paul Reynaud, Georges Mandel, Edouard Daladier and General Gamelin. The prisoners were forbidden to communicate among themselves, but they were allowed visitors. His daughter-in-law Renée, "Janot" (who became his third wife three years later), and a few other friends very soon helped him re-establish connections with the outside world.

His arrest had been greeted with contemptible joy by his enemies at *Le Matin* and *L'Action française*. As always, Maurras was in the forefront: "I know, I see, I have verified that it is the Judeo-Masonic politicians who have thrown us into the abyss down which we are falling."

Blum's status as a prisoner can be determined from the orders given to guard post number two which was assigned to him: "M. Blum may leave his apartment only to go to the lavatory, and in that case he will be accompanied by the civilian (!) employee as far as the door . . ." But his life was soon organized around three activities: a friendly, and soon political, correspondence with his family; the composition of "memoirs" dealing with the 1939–40 period, followed by the writing of a work of political reflections which was completed late in 1941 and published in 1945 under the title *A l'échelle humaine;* and preparation for his trial.

On October 8, a certain Cassagnau, public prosecutor for the *Cour suprême de justice* (a special tribunal which the Vichy government had just created), notified Blum of a "complementary indictment" requesting that hearings against him begin. He was referring to a law of July 30, 1940, applied to Blum retroactively. The document specified that "it appears that, in France and elsewhere,"

> 1.   Crimes and misdemeanors were committed by M. Léon Blum, former premier and former deputy premier, in the exercise or on the occasion of the exercise of his responsibilities and that he betrayed the duties of his office in the acts which contributed to the passage from a state of peace to a state of war before September 4, 1939 and in those which later aggravated the consequences of the situation thus created.
> 2.   Violations of the security of the state and associated crimes and misdemeanors were committed by the said Blum on the occasion of the acts noted in the previous paragraph.

In consideration of this a committal order was granted against the former head of government, who appeared on October 23 for an identity examination.

On the 25th he wrote to Dormoy and Auriol. To the former he announced that he had been a little delayed in answering him because he had just been "promoted to the rank of accused, a new rank [which], without disturbing me, has slightly preoccupied and distracted me, thrown me off course." To the latter, writing shortly after the Hitler-Pétain meeting in Montoire, he confessed that his spirit "shrinks, hardens," when confronted with such things.

On November 4, Blum was questioned in Chazeron on the counts of the indictment by Counselor Lesueur, a member of the *Cour suprême de justice,* whom he informed that he had chosen as defense counsel a young socialist lawyer, Samuel Spanien, who had withdrawn to Clermont-Ferrand. The first question had to do with the factory occupations of June 1936. From the very first words, the nature of the trial was revealed: it would not be military, but political, ideological. Blum was criticized above all for having embodied social democracy and having recognized the rights of the working class. His first words were to say that he had opposed any resort to force against the strikers and had been concerned "not to shed blood," to "avoid a civil war."

The second question dealt with the 40-hour law "which gave the working class a taste for less effort"(!) To which he retorted that, on the contrary, the law was designed to give the workers "feelings of confidence, and cordial cooperation with the employers and the government." Cordial cooperation with the employers? The formulation was a little exaggerated. But when the magistrate questioned him about the nationalization of war industries, which "is said to have created

serious difficulties for national defense," he exploded: "Those laws . . .
which were contained in a program approved by sovereign universal
suffrage were passed by Parliament by very large majorities. The government over which I presided demonstrated its scrupulous fidelity to
the commitments it had made to the electorate."

Five days later, there was another letter to Vincent Auriol to share
with him his joy at Roosevelt's re-election on November 5 (he wired
Bullitt: "The humanity of Washington and of Jaurès is certainly not
dead!"), to inform him about the preliminary hearings which were
aimed "at placing part of the responsibility of defeat on the policies we
pursued in government," and to describe the procedure which "is not
quite what you think. All the evidence in the dossier which may concern me is communicated to me. It is a personal communication from
which the lawyers are excluded; they have no access to the dossier and
are not present at the interrogations. I am not given a copy of each
item, but I can study them at leisure (leisure is not what I lack), copy
excerpts, analyze them, and so on. This work has kept me busy for the
last two weeks, which is a good thing, but it has distracted me from my
personal work, which was beginning to take shape."

When he wrote again, to express his sympathy for Pierre Viénot, his
former Under-Secretary of State who had just been given a prison
sentence,[23] and "for poor litle Mendès France [who] is also in the
military prison in Clermont," he had been transferred to Bourassol, "a
new residence which," he said, "does not claim to be anything but a
prison." This building in ruins, "dilapidated, without even the most
rudimentary comforts, disgustingly dirty," was not even heated, so
that water froze in the basins.[24] But Bourassol was closer to Riom, and
therefore to Renée and "Janot," who had moved into a hotel.

On December 20, in the course of another interrogation, he answered the question on the nationalization of the arms industries. It
was, he said, "demanded by a unanimous public opinion" because of
"war profits" and "the effect the private arms industry threatened to
have on war psychoses." Then the judge returned to the question of
leisure, the "lesser effort" of the working class. Blum's retort:

> I cannot possibly argue too strongly against the crude identification
> which seems to be set in some minds between laziness on one
> hand, and on the other, leisure which is rest after work. No one, I
> imagine, will dare to maintain that one harms the productive labor
> of a people by protecting the physical and psychological health of
> the individual, by developing the taste for and the practice of
> sports, by leaving more room for family life, by encouraging the
> habits of communal games and popular art.[25]

On December 28, and again on January 16, 1941, Blum boldly

counter-attacked, denouncing first of all the violations of the rights of the defense—the press had known of parts of the indictment even before the accused and his lawyers!—and then the crushing responsibilities of the military leaders, beginning with Weygand, in the preparation for and the conduct of the war. In the course of the final interrogation, to close these preliminary hearings, the former Premier made two statements:

> As it has been established by the prosecution, the dossier already permits me to show any impartial observer that no government, before the one over which I presided, had put forth a comparable effort, comparable in significance, complexity, or extent, to rebuild the military forces of France.
>
> What principle, what law can possibly allow you to attribute retroactively a criminal character to a policy demanded by the country, approved by the Parliament, and carried out with the agreement and consistent cooperation of constitutional bodies? The procedure undertaken against me could not possibly find a juridical basis except in an individual act sanctioned by a penal law. Where is that act? What is it?

He concluded:

> Illegal in principle, the trial conducted against me is therefore arbitrary in its application to my person. But, to complete my characterization of it, I insist on reminding you of a consideration which is of a still higher order in my eyes. In the Republican Constitution of 1875, sovereignty belongs to the French people. It is expressed through universal suffrage. It is delegated to the Parliament. When one accuses a man, a head of government, of criminal responsibility, without establishing, and even without alleging against him, anything to do with him personally, without producing a single fact as to probity, honor, or the professional duty of application, labor, and conscience, when he is accused only of having carried out the policies commanded by sovereign universal suffrage, supervised and approved by the Parliament as delegate of that sovereignty, then one is conducting a trial, not against that man, not against that head of government, but against the republican regime and the republican principle itself. I am proud to have to undergo this trial in the name of my life-long convictions.

Blum prepared carefully for the "trial of the Republic," to quote the title of the book Pierre Cot was writing in the United States at the time. He wrote to Jules Moch: "I have been working on my dossier as though someone else were on trial, and I feel much more like a lawyer than a defendant." This was confirmed by his lawyer, Samuel Spanien[26]:

> Léon Blum is two men in one. Léon Blum studies [the dossier] as though someone else were on trial; he assumes the perspective of an objective lawyer; his work scrupulously completed, happy, re-

lieved, he makes this admirable statement to his friends: "I've reached my conclusions." And light-hearted, alert, Léon Blum no longer concerns himself with his trial.

The preliminary hearings had been completed, but the trial was postponed to an indefinite date. On May 11, Blum sent to the Court a veritable summons to have him appear—first because he was eager to exonerate himself in the eyes of public opinion, and second because he was beginning to wonder whether it would not be made "impossible for him to plead [his case] publicly in a court room."

In March, 1941, Blum had the pleasant surprise of seeing Jules Moch, freed by Darlan, the new "director of prisons." Moch saw

> a sordid setting . . . where his little worktable sits next to a worm-eaten washstand, and where the heating is inadequate. A chamber pot in a corner accentuates the primitive character of the prison. A military bed occupies another corner. A narrow window covered with bars allows a glimpse of the interior courtyard, which has a lawn, where I can see Daladier, solitary and bent, walking up and down the gravel path. Léon Blum is wrapped up in a thick bathrobe, his neck is in a scarf, and his knees under a cover, to fight against the cold. The dossiers of his trial are piled on the table, the chairs, and the rest of the furniture.[27]

He had another pleasant surprise on April 9, 1941, his sixty-ninth birthday: a telegram from the United States with greetings from a hundred artists and writers. He thanked them through the American embassy in Vichy. The hope he had nourished to represent something for American intellectuals had thus been confirmed, and it consolidated his confidence and his courage.[28]

Gradually the world expanded beyond the walls of Bourassol. On July 16, 1941, three weeks after the beginning of Hitler's offensive against the USSR, he wrote to Dormoy:

> This attack represents the gravest of dangers for Hitler; it entails, in any case, giving up the landing in England for this year and, as a consequence, the continuation of the war in 1942, in more and more perilous conditions. Unless it is the kind of aberration which always afflicts great despotic conquerors at one moment or another, Hitler can only have brought himself to attack the USSR under pressure of an urgent domestic necessity. That necessity, it seems to me, is the approaching fuel shortage . . . . Consumption plans have been completely upset by Hitler's sense that war was necessary to avert the total collapse and perhaps the defection of Italy, to take charge of the situation in North Africa and the Balkans. The Italian-Balkan diversion had already made Hitler's final victory almost impossible and, as a direct and indirect consequence, this is what has brought about today the immense Russian diversion which makes that victory almost inconceivable. The

parallel with the Napoleonic adventure seems to me more obvious than ever. I remember with some private irony the remarks I heard and the reports I read on the value of the Soviet army, which was practically nil![29]

Not bad, for an "aesthete" distant from realities. But two weeks later, at the very moment his hope was becoming "a solid conviction," he received a blow through his correspondent: Marx Dormoy was assassinated in Montélimar by *La Cagoule,* an organization he had once pursued before it became the kernel of the Militia. Blum wrote to André Blumel, their mutual friend:

> I know what you have lost, what I have lost, what we have all lost. We had no friend who was more faithful, surer, braver, more energetic. He will not be here for the day of deliverance and victory, for the day whose coming he awaited with a confidence that nothing ever troubled. The blow was and remains very harsh. I am not consoled, but I am not shaken.

But what had become of the procedure that had been so thoroughly begun against him? On August 12, Pétain suddenly announced in a radio speech that he himself would mete out punishment to the "guilty," with the advice of a "council of political justice." What was the reason for this sudden initiative? The Nazis had intervened. Otto Abetz, Hitler's ambassador in Paris, had even indicated that if the accused were severely punished the "occupation authorities" would be more lenient toward the hostages then in their hands.[30] It was an abject bargain, to which Pétain and Justice Minister Joseph Barthelemy had agreed.[31]

Addressing the nation on October 16, the "victor of Verdun" declared out of the blue that his judgment had been made: before the trial began, the accused, Blum, Daladier, and Gamelin, were given the harshest sentence provided by Article 7 of the new constitution: life imprisonment in a fortified place. This assault against the most elementary justice skirts parody. Pétain argued that he had been unable to wait for the result of the trial because "the deliberate speed" of judicial action "was increasing the malaise afflicting the country." But the trial would still take place; convicted men would be judged. The sentence which the Marshal, in his omnipotence, imposed upon them was only a "first penalty" which could be changed to a "heavier sentence."

For, Pétain maintained, "the gravity of the deeds with which those principally responsible for our disaster are charged seems so great that it cannot possibly be marked or blinded by simple political penalties." This is what the old man proclaimed on October 16, 1941, in a language so murky that it seems barely translated from the German.

As he was listening to this verdict before the trial, Blum was presented with the "indictment" of the Court of Riom which was going to have to judge the convicted men. There were no surprises: the arguments of Counselor Lesueur, his interlocutor in Chazeron and Bourassol, were indeed reiterated—the 40-hour law, "brutal" application of the law on paid vacations, "weakness" of the government in the face of the strikes and subversive propaganda. The conclusion: "By compromising, through the unjustifiable weakness of his government, both the immediate results of production and the moral strength of the producers, M. Léon Blum, as Premier, betrayed the duties of his office."

Blum had five days to present his defense before being transferred to Le Portalet fort in the Pyrenees. On October 20, he hurled this attack at the Riom Court:

> You have asked an already convicted man, convicted under exactly the same provision of the criminal code, to answer the indictment delivered by your prosecutor. Is this anything more than a cruel mockery? In reality, your jurisdiction has been superseded; the case has been judged against you as well as against me. Ruling on the same facts, with reference to an identical indictment, are you still free to annul by your future decision the content or the basis of the verdict that has already been rendered by the supreme authority of the state? I would be ashamed to insist any further in speaking to French magistrates. I absolutely deny that the hearings conducted against me had an adversary character. The Council of Political Justice, even granted the improbable hypothesis that it had seen your dossier, therefore rendered a verdict against me although the rights of the defense were not exercised, for me or by me, in any form or to any extent whatsoever. A public man, publicly accused of having compromised by my activity in government the interests and the security of my country, I had the right to public justification and reparation. I regretfully repeat that I can no longer hope from reparation from your justice. But I maintain and demand the right to justify myself before the country, before international public opinion, and I dare to say before history.
> . . . It was possible to bring the preliminary hearings to a close without considering either of the two orders of facts irresistibly designated immediately after the defeat by unanimous public opinion, that of the soldiers as well as the citizens: on the one hand, the mistakes of the military leadership, and on the other, the suspect combination of conscious or unconscious complicities which weakened French forces in the face of the enemy, and which are generally identified by the labels "Fifth Column" and "Treason." I do not mean "betrayal of the duties of his office," but treason pure and simple.

This blow was aimed at a much higher target than the pitiful band of judges that Joseph Barthélemy had managed to assemble.

On Wednesday, November 22, an extremely cold day, the prisoners were transferred to their third place of confinement, Le Portalet fort in the Pyrenees. These were his first impressions, expressed in a letter to his friend "Cécette" Grunebaum-Ballin:

> My cell—more like a monastic cell than a prison cell—is long and narrow, painted in tempera or whitewashed, white and cream, with a vaulted ceiling and an arched window. One of the corners next to the window is taken up by a modern toilet, and there is a sink with running water (which is a pleasant change) in the room. I have moved the furniture around and put a few engravings up, and as it is now, the room is not only habitable, it has a pleasant appearance and atmosphere . . . But the journey to come to see me will be hard, through the snow and the North wind. We are really a fortress, but I prefer this fortress dilapidated by time and neglect to the run-down house in Bourassol, eaten away by avarice and filth.[32]

"Pleasant," Le Portalet? Blum fell ill there, and medical examination detected traces of uremia. But this was not the reason for which the former head of government was transferred to the Riom region: it was simply that the trial was about to begin. Scarcely had he settled in before he began to compose notes to his lawyers to help the defense.

These are luminous texts, in which he observed that the Court, "shaken as we are" by the unprecedented steps of the head of state, "has taken itself in hand" and is trying to "bring this situation into harmony with the elementary principles of every form of justice." With a kind of healthy burst of laughter, he took note of "the macabre argument" of the Minister of Justice who had explained that "symbolically, the sentence which had been pronounced was death. If it had been carried out would they be judging our memories or our shades in Riom?" Completely taken up by his magnanimous zeal to discover excuses for those who were about to judge him, he began to plead for them. The Court was given a trial in which the verdict had already been rendered. But that trial was not the one it was supposed to conduct; what the government wanted (Blum did not say: under Hitler's orders) was the trial of the "warmongering" of a few men, the Frenchmen responsible for the outbreak of the war. That, continued Blum, "was not what you wanted. Thank you. That is enough to protect your names before history. You have not prepared a trial of responsibilities for the war; you have prepared a trial of responsibilities for defeat."

On December 30, 1941, he was once again on the road, on the way back to Bourassol, where he wrote a week later to his comrade André Philip: "I am in good health, and I begin the new year with the feelings which you know and which we share. As for the trial, I have given up attempting to arrive at a reasonable prognosis." On February 10, he wrote in a melancholy vein to his son Robert, who was incarcerated in a penal colony in Germany (while his youngest brother René had been taken hostage by the Nazis): "What a strange thing, the symmetry between our two current existences. As for my particular fate, it remains bound up, like that of everyone else, with the general fate."

But he had reached his conclusions and his lawyers were at work; he could calmly await his appearance before his judges while writing what was to become À *l'échelle humaine* and accumulating reasons for hope in his heart. The *Wehrmacht* was bogged down in the Russian snow, and the United States had entered the war. He learned finally that his trial was about to begin.

Blum had devoted the greater part of his time in the château of Bourassol and Le Portalet fort to writing an essay on the responsibilities for and consequences of the disaster, and on the prospects opened by the Resistance and the coming victory of the democracies for the future of democracy and socialism in France. The work was finished late in 1941.[33]

It was not an artificial assemblage of notes put together by friends; it was an essay designed for publication. A few typed copies, given to "Janot" and Renée, circulated first; Daniel Mayer obviously took it as an inspiration for the party's reconstruction program developed in 1943. But it did not appear until early 1945 (with a preface by Bracke); Léon and Jeanne Blum were still interned in Buchenwald.[34]

"We present it as it was written," explained Bracke, "without changing a word. This is the '1941' of the captive of Vichy and Hitler's Germany, clearly set out before the Riom trial." A useful precaution. Not that the book was outdated; even the strategic views stand up very well, a third of a century later. All the same, it was the work of an imprisoned man, deprived of a good deal of information and documentation.

Reread today, in parallel with a contemporary work like Marc Bloch's *L'Etrange défaite,* this book is a little disappointing. Not so much in its historical analysis of the collapse of French society; the critique of the bourgeoisie's loss of substance and dynamism in order to take on national responsibilities which only led finally to Vichy is judicious, sometimes vigorous. It is worthy of its model, Renan's study of the defeated France of 1871, *La Réforme intellectuelle et morale.* It even contains ideas new at the time—well-designed to surprise Drieu La Rochelle or Bertrand de Jouvenel—on the deep collusion between the bourgeoisie and fascism:

> In an apparent contradition, the ruling bourgeoisie, the political expression of modern capitalism, has almost always contracted alliances with "national socialisms" which nevertheless present themselves as regimes destructive of capitalist doctrines. In Italy, it was the bourgeoisie which invented and fostered fascism before installing it in power; in France, it applauds the "National Revolu-

tion." When it is told of a classless regime, the suppression of wage-earning classes or the proletariat, a kind of social and professional unification under collective authority, it applauds wildly; for it knows what action will immediately express these "Socialist" formulas, namely the destruction of working-class organizations and institutions, the prohibition or seizure of control over unions, the annihilation of all the rights, all the laws, all the freedoms, and all the customs from which the workers drew their weapons in their now century-old struggle against capital.

What does it matter to the bourgeoisie that "national socialisms" or "National Revolutions" declaim against capital, but without attacking it in any substantial way, provided they crush the only opponent it feared. Freed from working-class socialism by nazism and its various imitations, it clearly anticipates that the movement of history will eliminate nazism in turn. Then it would find itself alone again, strengthened by a vivifying contact; it would recover, along with its still-intact economic privileges, the political power of which it had been temporarily deprived.

But, Blum continues:

This "devil's bargain" will in the end only make the bourgeoisie more debilitated, more suspect. France finds itself today at the end of a second revolution, which has in reality been going on for more than a century. The first revolution had transferred power to a rising class which was already largely in control of property. The second is excluding a fallen class, which has been capable of adjusting its acquired temperament neither to the requirements of industrial production nor to the needs of democratic government.

What is disappointing is rather the mildness of his judgment of the movements and parties which had been vainly opposing the bourgeoisie for the last half-century. The least one can say is that his self-criticism is handled with kid gloves, and that aside from criticisms of detail on everyday militant practice in the SFIO and on the destructive character which the alliance with communism had for a time, he does not dig very deeply in order to discover what had been able to undermine the trust placed in democratic socialism by the French masses.

But the real disappointment lies perhaps on another level. We know that Blum was neither a theoretician nor the creator of an ideology, but rather a very intelligent and courageous adapter; he was the first to admit it. Is it the ambitious title given to his essay by his comrades, for which he was not responsible? One might have expected—beyond some very interesting constitutional reflections[35]—a more creative reflection on the possibility of convergence between the necessity of organizing social justice and respect for liberty. Who was in a better position to do this than the orator of the Congress of Tours? There remain some good, very good passages in which he connects the demand for a "social democracy" in France to the existence of a structured international community; his evocation of the Popular Front is the most typical.

À l'échelle humaine is a book more famous than it is read. It was possible to compare,[36] even to amalgamate the *Nouvelles conversations* of 1897 to this 1941 essay; the permanence of themes and arguments is moving.

This prisoner about to be dragged before the court, this old man worn out by so many ordeals and disappointments, this man who had endured the storms of the Chamber, the shame of Vichy, this political leader who had been the most hated man in France, calmly gave his book this conclusion:

> Why should the human race and the French nation show themselves unworthy in the future of what they have accomplished in the past? The human race has created wisdom, science, and art; why should it be incapable of creating justice, fraternity, and peace? It gave birth to Plato and Homer, Shakespeare and Hugo, Michelangelo and Beethoven, Pascal and Newton,[37] all those human heroes whose genius is nothing but contact with the essential truths, the central reality of the universe. Why should the same race not engender guides capable of leading it toward the forms of collective life which are closest to universal laws and universal harmony? The social system no doubt has its laws of attraction and gravitation like stellar systems.
>
> Man does not have two different souls,[38] one to sing and to study, the other to act; one to experience beauty and understand truth, the other to experience fraternity and understand justice. Whoever considers this prospect feels inspired by invincible hope. Let man contemplate the goal, let him trust in his fate, let him not fear to wear out his strength. When man is troubled and discouraged, he has only to think of humanity.

The Barricade of Riom

It was 1:30 p.m. on Februrary 19, 1942, when President Caous, followed by nine judges, made his entry into the small room of the Court of Appeal of Riom. In front of him were seated Léon Blum, thinner but calm and sure of himself; Edouard Daladier, whose irritability here took on the colors of resistance; General Gamelin, white and pink like a doll; Comptroller General Jacomet, so banal as to be anonymous; and Guy La Chambre, Pierre Cot's successor at the Ministry of Aviation. The lawyers were seated behind their clients: Blum's were André Le Troquer, one-armed, bald, and stocky; soft-faced Félix Gouin; and Samuel Spanien, who resembled a young prophet.

Caous had the appearance and the tone of a noble father. He would not be caught engaged in open violations, like the judges of Dreyfus and Zola. He was rather ingratiating, careful to respect the rules, and he declared as he opened the trial: "Gentlemen, the judgments of which some of you have been the object and the explanations which were given when these judgments were pronounced are without value before this Court."

At first fervently wished for by Blum, the trial now seemed frightening, both to him and others. Witness this article by Jean Luchaire, Director of *Les Nouveaux Temps:* "We can never sufficiently express our regret that today's defendant was not judged within twenty-four hours, a year and a half ago, sent before a firing squad, and buried deep in a forest."

There were other methods. The Vichy censors had given their orders: they were aimed essentially at exonerating the army, at persuading public opinion that "the real trial is that of the state of affairs out of which came the catastrophe in order to permit the French people who have been thrown into misery to make a judgment about the methods of government whose victims they became," and especially at keeping the "person of the marshal" outside the whole affair. Maître Le Troquer was able to obtain this grotesque document, and he read it in front of 230 journalists, many of whom were foreign, and the few dozen diplomats and officers who were privileged to attend the trial. It was the first incident of the trial, and it was edifying.

The second incident was provoked by General Gamelin, who declared that he had decided not to "participate actively in the conduct of the trial" in order not to be forced to mention names which the interests of the country dictated should not be involved in the affair. Blum pounced:

> By his gesture, General Gamelin has identified himself with our unfortunate army. Before this trial has begun, a gaping void has opened up. You had already removed the substance, the general has removed his person. The result is that in a debate on the responsibilities for defeat the war will be absent! It is difficult to conceive of a more revolting paradox. It is you, gentlemen, who have reduced General Gamelin to silence. His silence and the respect it inspires are in reality a judgment made against you! For my part, I share that respect. But I insist on explaining why we do not share the silence.
>
> It is not that I do not feel myself affected, exactly in the same way as General Gamelin, by Marshal Pétain's sentence. When General Gamelin observes that he has been convicted even before facing his judges, he is right, but he is not the only one who finds himself in this unprecedented position. The fundamental iniquity, the original flaw, affect to the same degree all the defendants present in this court. Men whom your duty as judges obliges you to

presume innocent down to the very moment of your verdict, present themselves to you already convicted. The highest authority of the state has already declared them guilty for the same facts, under the same provisions of the penal code, and the conviction decreed by it has already been carried out. There is something in that which contradicts reason as well as written law, which breaks particularly, I may say, with the most authentic traditions of the French spirit.

The present trial is not the trial of France, but it will inevitably be the trial of the Republic. A debate on responsibilities for defeat from which all military responsibilities have *a priori* been excluded becomes, by force of circumstance, at the same time that it is a willful assault against truth, a singling out of the republican system. The Marshal's message creates the fear that this is the function you are really expected to perform. We will therefore attempt to replace this partisan attack with the serene and courageous investigation which the country expects. We will propose the means for this to you. But if we were to be denied your cooperation, we would not become discouraged, we would continue to struggle. Our duty to the country—which we, too, intend to serve—would not be changed by your refusal; on the contrary, it would be made more urgent. . . . Then it will be incumbent on us to prove to France that it is not a degenerate people which, because it believed in freedom and progress, should expiate its ideal and bend beneath punishment. If the Republic remains the defendant, we will remain at our battle stations as its witnesses and its defenders.

This was indeed a way of declaring war. The socialist leader had undertaken the trial of his judges, the regime, and their leader in stirring tones. The trial lasted seven weeks, through twenty-four sessions, and the colonized government of Vichy, panic-stricken, had to suspend it in an about-face under a threat from Hitler. Having given his word, he kept it; Blum the prisoner was more imposing than Blum the head of the Popular Front government.

From February 20 until April 11, it was no longer a trial but a duel between Blum and the eleven figures whom the Vichy government had charged with destroying him. The others—except for Daladier, who was sometimes combative—were only spectators. This seventy-year-old man, very erect, his body swimming a little in his gray suit, his hair almost white, suddenly brought together in a powerful synthesis of intelligence and sensibility the three roles that he had played for half a century: lawyer, parliamentarian, head of government. He was confronting judges, he was arguing from a platform, and he was presenting the record of a history that he had carried out. How could he not be at his peak?

His voice carried admirably—better than in the Chamber, better, of course, than at the Mutualité or in a square in Languedoc—in the little overheated room. He knew better than anyone present the substance

of the trial, and his admirable memory was precise enough to disconcert even his lawyers. He denounced the preposterous system of inves-
tigating the source of responsibilities.:

> The Court has arbitrarily chosen the beginning of the 1936 legis-
> lature. Why? Is it that the rearmament of France imposed itself as
> a duty of governmental office only after June 1936? Or else is it that
> this duty had been scrupulously fulfilled before June 1936? I will
> indicate in turn a few points of reference.
> The Nazi party took power in March 1933.
> The Third Reich left the League of Nations at the end of 1933
> and, from that time on, openly rearmed.
> On March 16, 1933, compulsory military service was re-
> established in Germany. There was at the time a *strong govern-
> ment* which possessed *full powers:* Gaston Doumergue was
> Premier, M. André Tardieu a Minister of State, and Marshal Pétain
> Minister of War. At the time, there was not the slightest trace of
> modern matériel in service in our forces. Yet what was done? How
> large were appropriations? What was the volume of actual orders?
> What work was undertaken? The duties of governmental office
> were obvious and imperious, but were they fulfilled?
> In order to answer that question, it suffices to consider the affair
> of March 7, 1936, *two years later.* Call up your memories, gentle-
> men! Remember the tone of the first words spoken publicly by the
> representatives of our government, then the collapse of the French
> position. If you were completely informed you would know the
> report of the technical ministers of the government on our military
> forces and what weight their report carried in the decision—or
> absence of decision—by the government. This incident, whose
> consequences were so serious, is enough to show the state of
> *military preparation* in which the June 1936 government found the
> army! . . . In retracing the history of the last ten years, you there-
> fore do not have the right to stop at the point you have chosen.
> Your point of departure is not justified by anything, from any point
> of view, historical or juridical. It can be explained only by a single,
> solitary reason, which I do not wish to repeat, and against which
> you will certainly wish to defend yourselves. If you were to con-
> tinue according to the pattern of the preliminary hearings, the in-
> dictment, and the judgment on venue, you would proclaim by that
> very fact that this trial is a *political enterprise,* that you are *polit-
> ical judges,* and we would only take note of the confession.

He played with the president, his dates, and the attribution of responsibilities like a cat with a ball of wool.

> M. LEON BLUM: The legislature of 1936 was divided into three
> phases: there was first a Blum phase—I am obliged to name myself
> first, chronology demands it—then there was a Chautemps
> phase . . .
> M. DALADIER: Yes!
> M. LEON BLUM: . . . which lasted for nearly a year; then there

was a Daladier phase. M. Daladier is here. I am here! And the man who was between us, I repeat, is at this moment entrusted with an official mission by the government or the head of state.[39]

THE PRESIDENT: That is of little importance. There is no question at any moment of criticizing you for M. Chautemps' actions.

M. LEON BLUM: No, Mister President. Nevertheless, I repeat that it is very important for me to emphasize this fact. M. Chautemps is definitely placed within the suspect period. Were the dangers of which you speak less in the second government, in late 1937 and early 1938? I can tell you, for example, that it was during that period that the qualitative deficiencies of our aviation matériel appeared for the first time in a completely clear and striking way. It was during that period in 1937 that the technical revolution of which one of the witnesses has spoken began to be realized in mass production.

I certainly have the right to say that the intention of the trial appears here in a particularly striking fashion. I am not at this moment asking that M. Chautemps come, that we squeeze together to make room for him here, although I was enough a friend to him to regret that he is not in our place rather than his.

But, in any case, the fact of having excluded military affairs from consideration on the one hand, and on the other the fact of artificially extracting from the period 1936 to 1939 one of the governments in power during that interval; don't these two actions demonstrate with tangible, concrete, and striking evidence, a political intention against certain men?

THE PRESIDENT: The political morality of the trial is a purely subjective question which everyone will judge in his own way. For the Court, the trial is not and never will be a political trial.

M. LEON BLUM: It is and will be in spite of you. It is by its very subject. That does not depend on the Court. But as far as I am concerned, the substance of the accusation is purely political.

. . . You said, in the course of one of the last hearings, that as far as military operations were concerned, they would be judged by the Clausewitzes and Jominis[40] after many years of archival research. Let me tell you that when you made that statement, it contained an extremely severe judgment on the very trial over which you are presiding; for if it is indeed impossible today to express a judgment on military doctrines, or on military operations which, quite obviously, were the determining factor in a military disaster, what can be meant by that except that this trial could not be conducted at the present time!

THE PRESIDENT: People are still arguing about the mistakes Napoleon may have made in the battle of Waterloo.

M. LEON BLUM: Yes, but there are other definite mistakes, if we are considering Napoleon's mistakes. That presupposes a more difficult and complicated critique, because there are comparisons which might be wounding for those compared to Napoleon!

What you have said of military operations becomes very true of a policy which was complex, which was disputed, and which had, as I indicated to you a moment ago, origins in the past and repercussions in the future, which is having repercussions even here, at the present moment.

And then, perhaps it is indeed true, as far as this policy is concerned, that we have to wait for the Tocquevilles and Taines of the future to judge it after long years of work. But that investigation, in any case, does not belong to you.[41]

So many slaps in the face. That very evening, Admiral Leaky, American ambassador to Vichy, cabled to his government that "this trial is a veritable fiasco."[42]

But these were still only skirmishes. The turn of higher figures was soon to come. For there were "higher" figures in this rump government than the protean and indestructible Chautemps. There were Darlan, Laval, and Pétain. Above them all there was Hitler. In this country occupied by an army and a police force, in this country dominated by a clique which was resigned to everything except the discovery of truth, the Jew, the socialist, proclaimed his accusations. On French soil, he spoke with the same voice as those who spoke from London.

They wanted to begin with June 5, 1936? Very well, he said in substance, let us begin there! Blum then recounted how, on June 6, he had the President of the Republic sign a decree finally organizing coordination among the different departments charged with defense, and how Daladier, leaving the Elysée, told him that with this simple document he had just "rendered more service to national defense than many of (his) predecessors over a period of many months." Then came the re-establishment of two-year military service in Germany, and the request made by Daladier: either to extend military service, or to accelerate rearmament by putting into effect the so-called program of "14 billion." What had he answered then?

> When Marshal Pétain appeared before the Senate Committee on the Army, in March 1934, and he was asked: "Is it your opinion that we should re-establish two-year military service?" (something which he probably favored at that time) he answered: "Yes, but the state of public opinion would not allow it." When M. Fabry, in 1935 went to see M. Laval and told him: "Very large appropriations are needed for national defense," M. Laval answered: "Perhaps, but the monetary situation does not permit it."
>
> I could have spoken the same language as Marshal Pétain or M. Laval. I dare assert that such language would have been less surprising coming from me than from them. If I had answered that, if I had spoken like Pierre Laval, I would perhaps have betrayed the duties of my office.[43] But no, I answered Daladier: "Count on me!" And the program "of 14 billion" was passed without the shadow of a difficulty, which is an unprecedented fact in the parliamentary history of the Republic.

Insolence can be a virtue. Blum continued hammering at his judges and those who had entrusted them with the Holy Office. It was objected that his defense expenditures had as their real objective the reduction of unemployment.

> M. LEON BLUM: I deny you the right to suspect my good faith. If I had said to the working-class organizations: "We have to rearm. These appropriations will also have the salutary effect of reducing unemployment," how would that have contradicted my good faith as a political man who had felt the necessity of rearming? But I did the opposite. Not only did I not divert toward the unemployed the appropriations voted for national defense, but I diverted toward national defense appropriations which had been authorized for the reduction of unemployment.
>
> In France, at the time of the Republic, sovereignty belonged to universal suffrage. [This "at the time of the Republic," a reminder to magistrates formed under Poincaré, must have given him great pleasure!] By carrying out the will of sovereign universal suffrage under the supervision of Parliament, I was fulfilling the first duty of the office of a republican minister. I do not believe that you can reproach me today with not having betrayed it by anticipated loyalty to another political regime already pre-formed in the designs of Providence!
>
> THE PRESIDENT: Perhaps you should change your way of thinking. But I am not a torturer, I would not like to tire you . . .
>
> M. LEON BLUM: You are not a torturer in any way. Well, we'll see!
>
> THE PRESIDENT: Don't you believe that the role of a guide is to lead and not to follow? What do you think?
>
> M. LEON BLUM: Two or three days ago, at Bourassol, I reread a collection of speeches I had delivered during the first part of my government. I would readily have dedicated a copy of this volume[44] to each member of the Court, but it has been banned and if you wish to obtain it you will have to address someone other than me. Whatever the public I was addressing—it was sometimes, as for example during the war in Spain, a public that was passionately up in arms against me—you will find the formulations which I have just recalled on the necessity of fulfilling my duty as head of government to the national community.

President Caous then referred to his responsibilities in the development of the movement of social demands in May-June 1936. Blum recounted those dramatic days: Albert Lebrun's pleas that he take hold of power, the appeal he agreed to launch on the fifth before being installed by the Chamber, the peaceful resolution of the social crisis. No one, he pointed out, had asked him to evacuate the factories by force.

> THE PRESIDENT: That assertion is contradicted by a certain number of witnesses whom we will hear . . .
>
> M. LEON BLUM: Witnesses may come to say, "No, it was nothing, it could have been resolved with a little firmness," But I affirm that no one spoke to me in those terms on June 6. No one

dared mount the rostrum to say it. In the Senate, in September,[45] in a debate about devaluation, I was attacked over the factory occupations. I recalled what had happened in June and I challenged the members of the upper chamber to cite a single instance, a single fact proving that I had been asked to use force. No one rose to contradict me.[46]

Perhaps that was what was expected of me during the debates in June. Think of it, what a windfall: A blood-letting carried out by a representative of the Socialist party in power! Or else a trick, a cruel trick played on the working class by the man in whom it had placed its confidence, whom it had wanted to be in power! I did nothing of the kind. I fulfilled the first duty of my office, which was to maintain what I called civic order.

Now, gentlemen, I come to the notorious 40-hour law. The indictment asserts that, according to me, that law did not diminish the productivity of French industry and it adds that I could not have made such an assertion in good faith . . . Is that the expression?

MAITRE LE TROQUER: "With sincerity."

M. LEON BLUM: I do not accept that judgment. What surprises me is the surprise of the government, which reveals, in industrial matters, I will not say an ignorance, but an innocence which truly astounds me. For the last century, the entire history of industry has been the continual reduction of working hours associated with a constant rise in production. There was a time when ten-year-old children worked for twelve hours a day in mines and textile mills. When attempts were made to apply the first laws providing legal protection for workers which fixed a legal maximum (which was, so they said, an assault on the freedom of labor, the freedom of the employer, and even at the height of hypocrisy, the freedom of the worker who was, so they said, entirely free to work longer if it suited him!), the employers spoke in the same terms as the government now does: "Be careful: if you reduce child labor in mines and textile mills, national production will decline!" And yet those laws were passed, and others limiting the working hours of women, of adults; they were lowered more and more, and during that time industrial productivity constantly increased. The same experience occurred in France when the 8-hour law was passed in 1919,[47] and its application did not at all reduce industrial production.

The argument grew tense over the application of the 40-hour law and overtime work, "the prosecution's great stroke of inspiration," said Blum. As far as factories working for national defense were concerned, he maintained, exemptions to the 40-hour law were always granted. Moreover, in 1938 he had obtained a kind of "concordat" from working-class organizations, increasing the work week to 45 hours in factories working, directly or indirectly, for national defense. But then the employers' organizations, through M. de l'Escaille, president of the Union of Nationalized Aviation Companies, and M. Pierre Forgeot, president of the Association of Engine Manufacturers, refused to increase the workweek to 45 hours: "Impossible," they argued, "we wouldn't know what to do with your 45 hours in aviation; we don't even have enough to keep our workers occupied for 40 hours." Blum fought hard for the 40-hour week. Why?

> The system we live in, made up for some of excessive profits, and for the great mass of others of unemployment, underconsumption, declining wages, and poverty, this kind of impious divorce between science and society, between nature and life, will not last eternally. The whole question is to determine how, through what procedures, by what means, it will change. The time will come when what is the legacy of all men will become a benefit, an advantage to every man, when everyone will receive his share, additional well-being for the same work or additional leisure for the same wages. Well, the 40-hour law had, and it still has in my eyes, the all-important significance that it represented, in the progress of civilization, the granting of that dividend to the workers. It represented a down-payment, a first installment which the workers could collect, which they could see as their legitimate share in a movement of civilization and progress which belongs to all men. This is the deep meaning of the 40-hour law, or rather the deep meaning of my attachment to it!
>
> Mister President, these are ideas which are perhaps new to the Court, but they are not outside the scope of this trial, in the sense that they were my inspiration.

"Monsieur Léon Blum," Caous said at the beginning of the next day's hearings on March 11, "I remind you that the entire political aspect of your argument is of no concern to the Court. You have forgotten it a little too often!"

The Court was judging two former heads of government and wishes for no talk of politics! Fine. Blum would talk about the nationalization of war industries. It was easy for him to demonstrate that that measure had long been required by the majority of public opinion, irritated by war profits and more and more in agreement with the idea of a state monopoly of arms manufacture. Caous was once again obliged to change the subject:

> THE PRESIDENT: Do you believe that you actively and intensely prepare the country's morale for certain dangers by speaking to it, even on the occasion of the nationalization of arms industries, about certain—how shall I say—certain dreams, like collective security . . .
>
> M. LEON BLUM: Dreams!
>
> THE PRESIDENT: . . . and gradual disarmament?
>
> M. LEON BLUM: We are engaged in a political debate!
>
> THE PRESIDENT: You're the one who started it.
>
> M. LEON BLUM: There is not a people at this moment, even those of the totalitarian countries, who can be led into or sustained in war if they are not assured that everything has been done to

preserve peace. Even the dictators are obliged to speak in these terms.[48] Today, it appears, I am a warmonger; in the past I was a pacifist, in the sense that I devoted years of effort and study to the search for means of preventing war and organizing collective security in Europe. But peace as we wanted it and as we hoped to organize it depended on the freedom of peoples and the respect for contracts. On the day when they saw the independence of nations threatened, contracts violated, and the world given over to plans for conquest and harmony, those men who were abusively called bleating pacifists realized that if peace still depended on collective security, collective security itself could no longer depend on anything but force of arms. Pacifists became so-called warmongers without having changed. It was for this reason that, as head of government, I did what I did. But I never gave up hope for disarmament, I never allowed it to be ruled out. And if, in September 1936, I entered into direct and personal negotiations with a representative of Chancellor Hitler, this was because one of the essential subjects of the conversation between us was the entry of Germany into negotiations or the general limitation and control of arms. At the same time, I was carrying out massive programs of armament, the like of which no one had done before. In one case as in the other, I fulfilled the duty of my office.

M. Caous could not stop wondering if he had done well to accept this task, or this duty. He nevertheless tried to regain the advantage:

THE PRESIDENT: Your weakness in the face of revolutionary agitation (nonetheless) led to a considerable decrease in production necessary for national defense.

M. LEON BLUM: The prosecutor threw a figure into the discussion which naturally produced a great effect because of its apparent size. He said that, according to statistics prepared by the Ministry of Labor, the crisis had brought about a loss of nineteen million hours of work.

THE PRESIDENT: 19,190,196 hours.

M. LEON BLUM: Statisticians are really admirable people! Let's say twenty million in round numbers. Twenty million hours, an astronomical number, corresponds exactly to two-and-a-half million working days. For a population of 500,000 workers of the [Paris region], that represents five days. If you apply the number to a larger population, it is approximately equivalent to one day.

There was in all of this an echo of Molière. But Blum restored full seriousness to the debate.

It is not enough to say to a man: "You have betrayed the duties of your office," you have to tell him what those duties were. I hope that you will tell me. I hope that there exists in the mind of the Court or the Prosecution a sort of Code of the duties of a political man. When you judge a murderer, it's quite simple, you have an article in the Code. He has killed. The Code says: "You shall not kill." There is no written Code for political men, Ministers, or former Ministers. You must establish one in your mind before applying it. You will have to tell me which of those duties I failed to fulfill. You will have to define my duty. If I had been mistaken, who would prevent me from saying so? What could I be afraid of? No one supposes that I have low, self-interested motives. If I did make mistakes, it was from an excess of confidence, idealism, and attachment to the working class. There is in all that nothing dishonorable for a man. My duty was clear, imperious. It was to spare France from foreign war following on civil war, not to provoke between employers and workers what the employers then feared the most, the sort of moral division which is grave and more pernicious than anything else, in a country and in a democracy. My duty was not to provoke such civil convulsions. In any case, whether I was right or wrong, my decision was made: not to use force. If I had been unable, through mediation between workers and employers, to restore civic order, republican order, I would have resigned my post and perhaps given up my life as a political man.

On March 11, 1942, he had been speaking for nearly three hours to Caous and Cassagnau. Night was falling. Like Zola, on the evening of February 23, 1898, he had a few more arrows to shoot, a few gestures of solidarity to make. Ten judges, 230 journalists, a few dozen diplomats and officers, watched in fascination as this slender old man defied a state and its foreign protector. Maître Ribet, Daladier's lawyer, wrote: "He seemed to be bringing the Gospel to the Roman procurators."[49]

I do not believe that I have evaded the prosecution in any way. But I would like to make a last effort to reach what I definitely feel to be its inner sanctum, its intention, its deepest inspiration.

For my personal use, when I take notes for my work, it is what I call "the argument of venom." The prosecution seems convinced—and it would like to convince public opinion of the same thing—that my policies injected French society, and especially the working class, with a venom, a poison, a toxic element, so toxic that its deleterious effects have continued indefinitely and are perhaps still operating today.

I think that is indeed the basis of the prosecution. I do not mean to say that it is articulated in a very precise way anywhere, but I do not think I am mistaken in asserting that this idea can be felt everywhere. I poisoned the country and I intoxicated it by what is called my weakness and my indulgence toward subversive activities and primarily, I imagine, toward the Communist party.

In a few words, without embarrassment, I would like to explain myself on my relations with the Communist party. The Communist party had entered the "Popular Front" coalition. At the end of 1935, a so-called "unity of action" pact had been signed between the Communist party and the one to which I belonged, the Socialist party. The reason for the existence of this "Popular Front" was an instinctive defense reflex against the dangers which threatened, in France, republican institutions and freedom itself.

I do not believe that the leaders of the Communist party had any particular feelings of predilection for me. But I was convinced, and I am still convinced, that it is impossible to defend republican freedoms in France if you exclude from that effort the working masses and the fraction of the working-class elite who are still grouped around the Communist idea. And I thought especially that it was an enormous result and an enormous service to have brought those masses and that elite back to feelings of love and duty toward the nation.

Having said that, the fact that there were certain difficulties between them and me no longer has any importance and, for my part, I have entirely erased them from my mind. I do not forget that, at the moment at which I am speaking, the Soviet Union is involved in the war, in the same war as we were two years ago, against the same adversaries. I do not forget that, in the occupied zone, the Communist party is providing its large, very large, share of hostages and victims! The other day, in a list of hostages given by a newspaper, I read the name of Timbaud. I knew Timbaud very well: he was a Secretary of the Federation of Metal Workers Unions in the Paris region. I saw him often and I very often fought against him. Only, he was shot, and he died singing *la Marseillaise, la Marseillaise* of Hugo "winged and singing amidst the bullets." That is how Timbaud died and how many others have died. Well, for my part, as far as the Communist party is concerned, I will say nothing more.

Is it necessary to recall Blum's situation? The situation of France? That of Europe? Blum an anti-Communist? This is what he said, in 1942, a few dozen kilometers from German tanks stationed in Moulins. He may even have known at the time that two imprisoned Communist Deputies (one of whom was François Billoux) had just asked the Riom Court, Pétain's tribunal, to be heard as *prosecution* witnesses against him!

> Gentlemen, I have finished. You may of course convict us. I believe that, even by your verdict, you will be unable to efface our work. I believe that you will be unable—the expression may appear prideful—to remove us from this history of this country, because we were a popular government; we are in the tradition of this country as it has existed since the French Revolution. We have not interrupted the chain, we have not broken it, we have restored and tightened it.
>
> Naturally, it is easy, when you have at your disposal all the means which affect public opinion, to disfigure our work, as you may disfigure our physical beings, our faces. But reality is there, and it will come to light. Freedom and justice did not make the nation an unarmed prey; with slaves, you can no more make workers than you can make soldiers. Whether it's a matter of handling a tool or handling a weapon, it is liberty and justice which engender the great virile virtues, confidence, enthusiasm, and courage. We are told: "You were wrong, you should have betrayed and broken

the will expressed by the people" We have neither betrayed it nor broken it by force; we have been faithful to it.

And, gentlemen, by a very cruel irony, it is this loyalty which has become a betrayal. And yet, our loyalty is not exhausted, it still exists, and France will reap its benefits in the future in which we place our hope, and which this very trial, this trial directed against the Republic, is helping to bring nearer!

The trial of Blum and his companions had become the trial of the Vichy regime, all the more so because these words were not confined to the little room in Riom. They were immediately circulated: "At nightfall," wrote Samuel Spanien, "in attics in Auvergne, while comrades kept watch on dark staircases, students exiled from Strasbourg typed the transcripts of the trial to make tracts. And they circulated throughout France, carrying everywhere messages of hope and unity, with a great noise of rattling chains."[50]

The Socialist action committee which had just been established on the ruins of the SFIO published a pamphlet bringing together all of Blum's interventions: "Each copy, passing from hand to hand, must reach at least a hundred readers," states the preface.[51] The radio in London gave great prominence to the voice that spoke from France with the accents of freedom.

On March 15, on the occasion of the *Heldentag,* Hitler delivered a speech in which he spewed forth his fury against the trial "in which the charges are directed, not against those who by their mad decision, are the cause of this war, but against the negligence of those who prepared it badly."[52] As a result, Otto Abetz put pressure on Pétain to suspend the trial. On April 10, Darlan was replaced as the head of the government by Laval: a guarantee that Berlin's wishes would be granted. On the 14th, a decree signed by Pétain was in fact published, announcing that the trial was "suspended" but that "the Court will complete its investigation." Another document, which Darlan had had the time to sign before his departure on April 11, specified that "the situation of the accused will remain fixed by the decision made in application of constitutional act number 7." That is, life imprisonment for Blum.

Thus this resounding moral, political, and judicial victory offered only a respite in the lives of men who had been convicted in advance. But when he was brought back to the melancholy den of Bourassol, Blum knew that these weeks of struggle had helped to change the course of events: the time for waiting had passed, the hour for fighting had arrived. He threw himself completely into the struggle.

As he returned to his melancholy cell, he found a "last summons, with charges," addressed to "M. Blum, deputy, Bourassol, from Menestrol": his taxes for the year 1941.

The Headquarters of Bourassol

A few weeks after his return to prison on May 15, Blum wrote to his old friend Suzanne Lacore, the school teacher from Périgord whom he had brought into the cabinet in 1936, and who had just congratulated him for his conduct at Riom:

> I realize the results which have been obtained and I am very pleased. The movement of solidarity and sympathy whose waves reached me has consolidated my confidence in the near future. What is absurd is that, at the precise moment when the trial was suspended, I suffered a very brutal attack of rheumatism and sciatica. I probably owe this intrusion on my life to the Riom prison. My basic health is not at all affected, but I have suffered a good deal. Long days rooted to my bed like a total paralytic.[53]

Was it because his health was faltering that he then considered leaving France? Joel Colton has published a letter which Blum had written to President Roosevelt a month earlier (April 15, 1942), transmitted through the American embassy in Vichy: "Since the Riom trial has been suspended—in itself a significant fact—I have wondered if I have not reached the limit of what it is possible to achieve from the depths of prison, and I have come to believe, for my part, that I would accomplish my tasks more successfully if I were released."[54] Did Roosevelt attempt to grant this wish? There is no trace of such an action.

Blum could have no doubts, in any case, about the sympathy and the support of American public opinion, which helped to persuade him that he had a role to play in the conflict which the United States had joined on December 7, 1941. On April 9, 1942, the occasion of Blum's seventieth birthday, the *New York Times* published a warm article entitled "For Léon Blum: As head of the government of the French Republic, M. Léon Blum may have made errors of judgment. What statesman does not? But in Riom, he showed the intelligent and heroic face of France which every human being loves and respects." In the *New Yorker* on August 1, 1942, the celebrated Janet Flanner (known as Genêt) wrote: "Thanks to him, France, although it is a prisoner, has once more become the repository of European values."

American unions organized a huge rally in his honor in New York and, as in the year before, Mrs. Roosevelt, along with a large number of celebrities, signed a telegram of congratulations "for his defense of justice and democracy," which reached him in his cell. In July he learned that his friend Maître Suzanne Blum, André Blumel's sister, had just published in Montreal a book entitled *L'Histoire jugera,* a collection of his best articles. He wrote to thank her and to tell her, referring to the trial, ". . . the press may have muddled the essential arguments, but it could not prevent a resonance, a propagation of waves which succeeded in stirring the old republican spirit throughout France. If the nation is awakening and finding itself again, as each day's events prove, our trial has had something to do with it."

From then on, he made his prison a veritable headquarters for clandestine action. Since the hearings against him and his companions were not closed, since the trial was only "suspended," he was allowed to see his lawyers, le Troquer, Gouin, and Spanien, who served as liaison agents, like Renée and "Janot," and friends like Jules Moch, Georges Buisson, and especially Daniel Mayer, his young colleague from *Le Populaire*. But he was cut off from any connection with some of those who were dearest to him: his son Robert, whom the Nazis had just interned in a camp near Lübeck, where he shared a cell with Stalin's son; and his youngest brother René, who was interned in Drancy, and was deported to Poland a few months later. He never returned.

But in all these ordeals he found new reasons for giving himself to the struggle. During the eleven months preceding his deportation he managed to get appeals and opinions to London, Washington, Paris, and to various organizations, thanks to the devotion and courage of friends and militants.

This campaign of messages and opinions consisted of ten essential documents (most of them published in *l'Oeuvre de Léon Blum*). Almost nothing written by the socialist leader presents more forcefully his political sense, his perception of reality, his capacity for synthesis, and his commanding tone, than these letters from prison. For more than two years, he had seen no more of France and the world than the patch of sky bounded by the closely set bars of his window.

We will present here only summaries of these ten messages which are too long to be reproduced in their entirety. The most important passages are quoted in full.

DOCUMENT No. 1
Letter given to the Socialist Deputy Edward Froment, on his way to London:

> Nazi Germany collapses. The Anglo-Americans land. Under what regime will France be placed?
> 1. The Vichy government and regime disappear *ipso facto*. Nothing of them must remain. We have to have a clean slate.
> 2. A new *de facto* government must be set up without delay. Any delay would bring about serious disorders, long and bloody reprisals.
> 3. National sovereignty, automatically restored, will be expressed through universal suffrage.
> 4. The provisional government can be formed around only one man, only one name, that of General de Gaulle. He was the first to call forth the will to resist and he continues to personify it.

Having set forth these principles, Blum then argued that around de Gaulle, whose taking of power should be "prompt, almost instantaneous," should gather men who represent "most publicly the resisting Republic" of the interior and those whose person and character most obviously embody republican continuity and legality"; he did not think it a good idea, even in order to display the "intrinsic nullity of the work constructed while the Republic and the law were suspended," to revive the Popular Front Chamber, the majority of its members having "signed their own disgrace"; finally, he wondered about the place that should be given to the Communists. "Their cooperation is of the greatest importance," he pointed out, but their "obedience to a foreign government" creates an obstacle to their participation in the government. He went on: "Communism will cease to be a foreign body in France to the extent that the USSR ceases to be a foreign body in Europe."

DOCUMENT NO. 2
August 15, 1942
Letter given to Daniel Mayer, on his way to London in answer to a note from the Gaullist leadership. The note has not been found but its tenor can be reconstructed from the following text.

> Agreement is complete on two points:
> —A government should be set up, almost immediately.
> —The government can have only one leader: the man who has called forth and embodied the spirit of the Resistance. Should the government immediately assure for itself a legal investiture? I do not see its necessity or appropriateness. What will forge the unity of the nation at the historic moment is the will to grasp once more its independence and freedom, and General de Gaulle personified that common will in everyone's eyes.
> The phrase that comes irresistibly to mind is what Cachin said in Strasbourg in 1918: "The plebiscite has been held."[55]
> General de Gaulle has made public and categorical commitments to democracy . . . I rely entirely on his word [as do] my friends who work most closely with him and who have come to know him best. The wisest course would be to maintain in the government established by General de Gaulle its character as a *de facto* authority, a circumstantial authority corresponding to an extraordinary situation, imposed by it and necessarily coming to an end when it does.

DOCUMENT NO. 3
August 28, 1942
Note given to Jules Moch, on his way to London, addressed to the Socialist leaders of the interior under the title "Schema of instructions for my friends, Paris-London."

> I.   The work of reconstructing the party confronts a powerful objection: "the conception of the political party is outdated." It is

true that at the present moment "the necessary action leaves no room for such competition. But liberated France will be a democracy, and there is no democracy without parties."

II.   But the Socialist Party must reconstitute itself only by "profoundly renewing itself"—since a certain number of its elements have excluded themselves from socialism.

III.   On the other hand, there is nothing to change in our socialist doctrine which has come through the ordeal immutable, intact.

IV.   Who would dare to contest the fact that the Socialist Party must play a role in the democratic France of tomorrow?

A provisional government will be established in France: General de Gaulle will be its necessary and natural leader . . . [but] for my part, I *am not calling for a good tyrant.* Nothing can make one come into contact more precisely with the necessity for political parties. Solidly organized and disciplined, nourished by the life of the people through broad areas of contact, grouped around the government, they could in a sense be champions of the people, provide guarantees, and insure the progress of its sovereignty. The Socialist Party can to a large extent bring this about, and thus its particular "mission" becomes more precise.

V.   The direction which immediate postwar action will take in France will be the one which Socialist doctrine has constantly outlined. Key industries, banking, the stock market, the distribution of raw materials and essential food supplies cannot be restored to private industry and free competition. New formulas of collective organization and cooperation must replace the gross incoherences of the present system. The Socialist Party is ready for all this work, since it continues or confirms its own work.

VI.   Finally, I would wish that—besides working for the revival of public life and even for the resurrection of other parties—the Socialist Party would prepare and negotiate a vast agreement, a *rassemblement populaire,* around a common program for immediate action. I would like the party to make a public offer of this as promptly as possible and with the widest publicity at its disposal.

DOCUMENT NO. 4

Bourassol, October 21, 1942

Letter to Félix Gouin, who had reached London, in reply to a letter from him received a few hours earlier.

After mentioning the "wave of terrorist repression" then passing over the "free" zone, and thanking his former lawyer for his letter which had "informed [him] of many facts which [he] had not yet known," Blum took up the principal problem posed by his correspondent: the divisions between socialist groups in London, some supporters of General de Gaulle (André Philip, Georges Boris), others his opponents (Louis Lévy, Georges Gombault). He warned Félix Gouin against what he called the "pathology of the emigré," and once again proclaimed his belief in "the rectitude and loyalty" of the general.

My conclusion is quite clear. Not only can there be no question, in my view, of breaking with the action organized around the General or remaining apart from it, but I would consider it a grave mistake to bring to this cooperation the slightest trace of suspicion or reserve. I understand the origin of certain apprehensions and anxieties—and you have made me understand it even more clearly. But even if one does not succeed in eliminating them from the back of one's mind, even if distressing incidents keep them alive or seem to justify them, courage and duty demand that one carry on regardless.

Here, between our comrades and the other elements of the resistance, whatever may have been the past distinctions or even oppositions between views, unity of action and confidence are complete. At the basis of this unity there is obviously—as a postulate rather than a condition—the conviction that the victory embodied by the general must restore freedom to the country at the same time that it restores independence. But this postulate is accepted by everyone as obvious.

I fully approve your suggestion that a leader of the French Communist organization take his place at the heart of the movement . . . the repercussions cannot fail to be felt on the relations between our comrades and the French Communists which unfortunately remain very troubled and very equivocal. The Communists probably consider us a defunct party which has no chance of revival. They are gravely mistaken as far as the free zone is concerned, where the organization in which you played such a large role, my dear friend, is developing in the most satisfying way. They are even more gravely mistaken about the occupied zone. Just recently I received precise information from Augustin Laurent, who had had to escape from Lille. In Nord, in Pas-de-Calais, it was *around the party,* by unanimous agreement, that the resistance was organized. Therefore, we can and we must speak to the Communists as one power to another—at least. The presence of a Communist leader in London would permit you to establish those relations in a satisfying manner.

My confidence in de Gaulle is based in large part on the certainty that he intends to set France on a new road. Neither the political system nor the social system can be a continuation or a restoration pure and simple; they must have the character of a revolutionary *beginning*. The general is certainly convinced of this. . . . The real problem, in my eyes is to determine in what conditions the general's government will be able to impart that initial drive to French life without usurping or taking precedence over democratic sovereignty.

DOCUMENT NO.5
November 1942
Letter to General de Gaulle.

In response to a request from the leader of free France, Blum sent de Gaulle a note intended for Roosevelt and possibly for Churchill. But he preceded it with a letter in which he mentioned first the Allied landing that had just succeeded in North Africa, then the "Darlan affair" and the "reaction it had provoked in France—stupor, disgust, revolt"—and finally the attitude adopted by de Gaulle—the only appropriate one ("for the sacred work of deliverance, any instrument is good. Later France will weigh and judge"). Finally, Blum spoke of his preoccupations about the relations between the Socialists and London:

> I am obliged to confess to you, with some trouble and concern, that the efforts of my comrades do not seem to me to evoke very much response from your closest friends. What is the reason for this? Does there persist in some of the circles close to you a remnant of suspicion or resentment toward socialism or rather the Socialist Party, or is it the old "Popular Front"?. . . The political parties of the old France share responsibility for the defeat only in so far as they demonstrated an egotistical and unscrupulous ambition for power. But consider carefully, France will become a democracy again, will it not? And there is no democracy without parties. They must be moralized and revived, not eliminated. A state without parties is necessasrily an autocracy. Consider also that socialism, as a doctrine, will find political expression as a party.
>
> I am sure you know that I am not speaking this way from any sectarian spirit. . . [nor] out of jealousy toward communism. I think it is mistaken to assert that only communism is organized, or to attribute automatically the label of Communist to all workers who demonstrate a will to resist. I am completely convinced that we neither can nor should keep them at a distance, quite the contrary. But it is a great mistake, which some of your direct representatives seem to me inclined to make, to consider communism as the one and only popular force. It is a great mistake to extend one's hand to the Communist party over socialism's head.

DOCUMENT NO.6

Note for Franklin Roosevelt (and Winston Churchill).

After formulating the arguments about the resurrection of democracy in France as a natural consequence of the defeat of the Axis, the impossibility of a return to the *status quo*, the urgency of a "transitional" government, the nullity of the 1940 assemblies, and the necessity of calling upon a man capable of gathering around himself all the elements of democratic France, Blum delivered to Roosevelt the "certificate" expected of him:

> Fortunately, for it is a blessing amidst so many disasters, that man exists. His authority is even now recognized. If General de Gaulle embodies unity, that is because he is to a great extent its author. It was his actions and his words which created it. Like millions of other Frenchmen, I have been a daily witness to his work. In a France battered and stunned by an incomprehensible disaster, stifled by a two-fold oppression, it was he who gradually revived

national honor, the love of freedom, and patriotic and civic consciousness. I do not make this profession of faith in my name alone, I know that I speak for all the socialists gathered together in France, in the occupied zone as well as the "free" zone; I am convinced that I express the opinion of the mass of republicans—bourgeois, workers, or peasants. One serves democratic France by helping General de Gaulle to assume, from this moment on, the attitude of a leader.

When I speak in this way, I am not thinking of throwing France into the arms of a new dictator. I am a republican and a socialist. But I am considering what the vital interests of my country will be at a moment which may soon arrive, and I cannot hesitate over my decision. It is subject to a single condition: that the provisional character of the de Gaulle government be explicitly formulated or, what amounts to the same thing, that sovereign rights remain totally and absolutely reserved. In this regard, the general has taken a categorical attitude in repeated declarations, and I trust his word.

It may be that he will increase the authority he already possesses and the confidence he inspires in public opinion, which will not challenge his position, by presenting himself under the aegis of a man who is particularly representative of the republican spirit and "the spirit of resistance." For my part, I am ready to provide, without any reservations, my personal guarantee, as I provide it now.

Blum added to this impassioned plea a harsh warning about the relations which had been established since November 8 between the Americans and Darlan:

The government of the United States must understand that France has already excluded those men from its free life in the future. Resisting France rejects, and liberated France will reject tomorrow, as a foreign body, everything which has established itself since the armistice, men as well as things and laws!

We must not forget the state to which Blum had been reduced nor the correspondent to whom he was writing—the only man in the world who might have been thought capable, taking a reasonable view, of rescuing him from death;[56] since the Riom trial, the "free" zone had in turn been occupied, and Blum was no longer the prisoner of Pétain's police alone but of Hitler's as well.

Moreover, even the circumstances in which it was written helped to heighten the tone of this message. Jules Moch has told how, in the course of composing the letter, the prisoner had stopped writing for a moment to look for the right word, when

the door of his cell was suddenly unbolted and opened by one of the guards, who stepped aside to let in two German superior officers. There were in fact rumors that, taking advantage of the disorder caused by the German advance into the southern zone, political prisoners had escaped with the complicity of French guards. Hence the order given by the enemy military authorities to visit all cells to verify the assertions of the jailers.

Imagine the scene: Léon Blum, sitting at his little table, his left hand near the letter he was writing, his right hand holding the pen in the air. He sees the two Germans. They are probably the first he has seen. Their entry surprises him. But for a moment he does not realize the risk he runs if one of them were to look at the paper. The two officers, without saying a word, take note of his presence, make a half-salute, do an about face, and withdraw, without a word being spoken. Léon Blum, having found the precise term he was looking for, lets his pen flow again on the paper intended for de Gaulle.[57]

To the dazzling testimonial which Blum had just written in his favor, General de Gaulle answered in February 1943:

We know of your admirable firmness. We are not ignorant of your struggles and your ordeals.[58] Liberation is approaching. But it will take place in equivocal and difficult conditions, as a result of our allies' policy of appeasement.[59] We hope for the formation within the country of a concrete organization grouping the representatives of the parties under the single banner of the struggle for the nation and for democracy, as long as the parties are, as parties, engaged in combat action. Their representatives would be associated with the leaders of the currently existing resistance organizations. The whole would be tied to the National Committee and would indeed constitute "fighting France."

This letter is of capital interest, and it seems to conform to the essential aspirations of Blum and his comrades. Moreover, it is almost certain that this message did not reach the prisoner until just before his deportation to Germany, and that he could not appreciate all its consequences. We should also note that de Gaulle's letter was written very shortly after Jean Moulin had parachuted into France; he was in fact going to set up an organization insprired by the one de Gaulle described to Blum.

DOCUMENT No. 7
February 5, 1943
Letter given to George Buisson, on his way to England.

A popular movement, provoked and nourished by the accumulation of German atrocities, leading toward retaliation by force or punitive cruelty inflicted on the German people, considered guilty and incorrigible. A governmental movement, with the same origins, leading not toward massive vengeance but toward systems of suspicious surveillance, a phase of supervision which would last for a rather long time, during which the victorious nations would maintain armed supervision. France would be among these victorious nations.

What do our French comrades in London think of this? Are they in contact with the Labour Party? With the exiles of the International living in London? What does a man like Louis de Brouchère[60] think of it? An international agreement among union leaders and Socialists on the conception of the peace would be an event of capital importance. Has the moment not come to act on the governments—beginning with the government of fighting France?

Faithful to his attitude of 1919–23, here Blum was already trying to avoid a new Versailles, a new revanchist strategy *à la* Poincaré. There is no such thing as a "guilty people," an "accursed race," he wrote after his deportation. Not without some merit.

DOCUMENT NO. 8
March 1, 1943
Note to the party, given to Daniel Mayer.

In this note Blum expressed the wish to maintain the title of the party—as well as the name of the Republic—but with some modifications in structure: he thought of a real executive and of "cells" inspired by those of the Communists. He did not think it urgent to fuse the organizations in the two zones. As for the representative the party was to name to the "Executive Committee," he proposed that it be Augustin Laurent, Salengro's successor in Lille, thereby representing the region where the SFIO remained the strongest.[61]

DOCUMENT NO. 9
March 7, 1943
Consultation "at a moment's notice" for the party.

Blum had just learned that the United Movements of Resistance (MUR), although they rejected contacts with the parties, had nevertheless signed an agreement with the Communists. A painful snub for the socialists. Should they withdraw from the organization? Early in the afternoon of March 7, Renée Blum brought to him in his cell a request for advice; she was supposed to bring back his answer at five o'clock. Thus, "at a moment's notice," as he said, he delivered his judgment:

> We cannot take it upon ourselves to weaken in any way the resistance organizations, either by withdrawing our friends, or by violating discipline. I am of the opinion that we should henceforth give up all demands having to do with our representation on any "executive" bodies (central resistance organization, political committees, etc.).

They want to do without us, that's clear. We are considered a
negligible element. We have only to consider it said, while we
constantly increase our strength.

Dignity—since this is the way it is, we will no longer insist, and
will work to develop our own strength.

Abnegation and feeling of our common duty as a party—the
methods used against us change—neither our often expressed
views toward de Gaulle—nor our participation in the work of resistance.

Once France has been delivered, they will see if they can indeed
do without us.

DOCUMENT NO. 10
March 15, 1943

Letter to General de Gaulle.

Written shortly after this "consultation" and the incident that called
it forth, Blum's last letter to de Gaulle—also his last before his deportation on March 31, 1943—could not fail to be marked by a certain
bitterness. We shall see that the socialist leader did not remain trapped
in melancholy and that the future had a much stronger attraction for
him than the most recent past.

This most important letter[62] can be subdivided for more clarity into
four "movements."

The first is like an overture:

At the moment I write, all France is in a state of effervescence.
Mass mobilization, daily roundups, and the continued shipment of
human material to Germany are reaching all levels of the nation
and stirring it with anguish, hope, and revolt. This is the primary
factor in the present situation, I know it and feel it like all Frenchmen. But the problems about which I have the duty and the desire
to speak to you, even if political passion and the necessities of
action have now relegated them to the background, nevertheless
remain, and will not allow themselves to be forgotten.

The second concerned the reconstruction of the Socialist party:

Some of my comrades—you have gotten to know some of them by
now—have reconstituted our party. Recruitment continues, but
the organizational work is complete. The network of our federations covers all of France. The publication of *Le Populaire* is going
to be extended to the occupied zone. This progress is so constant
and so rapid that it has really surpassed all our hopes. In order to
remake the party we have had to struggle against a very powerful
prejudice, which you yourself must to some extent have shared.
The mass of French public opinion certainly attributed a share of
responsibility for the disaster to the prewar political parties. Vichy
propaganda has spared nothing to incite it to do so, and "Gaullist"
propaganda has been indistinguishable from that of Vichy in this
respect.

Third, the limited role of the new organizations:

> I beg of you to realize very clearly that the resistance organizations
> which sprang up from French soil at the sound of your voice can-
> not to any extent replace [the parties]. When France has recovered
> its sovereignty and re-established some stability, the useful role of
> these organizations will be exhausted. This role has been of cardi-
> nal importance not only because of their decisive participation in
> the work of liberation, but through the spontaneous formation of a
> young and entirely new elite. However, the men who make up this
> elite will necessarily be led, in the new France, to redistribute
> themselves among the different parties which they will in turn
> rejuvenate and revivify, and which they will continue to instill, in
> their diversity, with a fundamental solidarity, a veritable spirit of
> "French unity." For my part, I would see only dangers, were the
> resistance organizations, once the task for which they had been
> created was accomplished, to survive in their present form. Un-
> ions of egotistical and outdated interests, like the veterans' associ-
> ations of the last war, or else paramilitary militias dangerous to any
> Republic, they could hardly choose another fate.

Finally, the fourth subject: relations between the Socialists, the
Communists, and General de Gaulle:

> You know the importance I have always attached to our relations
> and even more to your relations with the Communist party. I ap-
> preciate the role of our French Communists in the resistance. It
> would be impossible, in the world of tomorrow, to do without the
> Communist party. But on this point we must be very clearly under-
> stood. The Soviet State which the world needs is a Soviet State
> integrated into the international community; the Communist party
> which France needs is a Communist party integrated into the
> French community. And thus the difficulty becomes clear. Will the
> Soviet State agree to integrate itself into the international commu-
> nity, which implies that it henceforth give up interfering in the
> internal affairs of other states; will the Communist party agree to
> become part of French unity, which implies that it henceforth
> cease to subordinate its conduct to imperious orders from a foreign
> state? Moreover, these two questions are really one, for to obtain a
> substantial transformation of the relations of passive dependence
> which have until now subjected the Communist party to the Soviet
> State, it is obviously on the Soviet State that direct influence must
> be exercised. It was with this in mind that, in sending you my first
> note, I insisted in such an urgent manner that you establish direct
> relations with Moscow.
> 　. . . How can we obtain from Moscow a substantial trans-
> formation of the French Communist party and its sincere incorpo-
> ration into French unity, a life and death condition for any
> democratic government, if in France we encourage and reward its
> splendid isolation, if we flatter its pride, if we exaggerate its power
> to public opinion, to the point of making it appear the only orga-
> nized party and the vital center of all resistance, and finally if we

incite it in every way to preserve intact and unchanged its structure and its past tactics?

Finally, since I owe you the whole truth, I have the duty to add that my comrades, already disappointed by the silence which has been the only response to their propositions and appeals, were surprised and hurt by a step which seems to them unfriendly and unjust—with good reason. They consider it inadmissible, and I understand them, that the fact of having *en masse* joined the ranks of the resistance organizations properly speaking, while the Communists were jealously establishing their distinct action groups, exposes them today to coming under the orders of a command in which the Communist party has a substantial role and from which their party is excluded. That is enough to move—I will not say to discourage—men who feel wronged by their own abnegation, their own disinterestedness, but who are aware that they showed themselves inferior to no one in determination, contempt for danger, and the spirit of sacrifice.

. . . The situation will necessarily develop in one of the two following directions. Either my comrades will be led to follow the Communist example, that is, to create in turn Socialist action groups, which would absorb as they were established those of our men who are now participating in the various resistance organizations—all the while, of course, accepting without the slightest reservation all the systems of coordination imposed by the circumstances. Or else an agreement about command established between the resistance organizations and the Communist party will bring about a complete fusion, involving all those elements—Socialist organizations and Communist action groups—into a single and homogeneous organization. This is the solution which seems to me not only the best, but the only good one, and your authority as a leader ought to be able to prescribe it.

The staff of *Le Populaire,* half-ironically, half-deferentially, had called Blum "the general." It was, in spite of appearances, only an anticipation. Here was a very civilian prisoner who, addressing an officer of an exceptional rank with an exceptional role, seemed rather gifted for foreign and domestic strategy.

One may find his vision of the USSR and PCF armed with too much suspicion. It was only 20 months after the Soviet Union's entry into the war, at the conclusion of its long period of collaboration with Nazism; 20 months after the full entry of the PCF, as such, into a struggle that had been undertaken by a substantial number of its militants in 1940. Blum was the man whose "warmongering" toward Hitler Maurice Thorez had denounced 30 months before; Blum was the defendant against whom Francois Billoux had asked Marshal Pétain to be allowed to testify as a prosecution witness at Riom.

The guarantees and the conditions of which he spoke, with reference to Soviet Russia and its supporters in France, are moreover those which time has ripened and which international and domestic developments have made very topical today (the repercussions of the Helsinki conference, the maturity of Eurocommunism).

Deported to Buchenwald

On March 31, 1943, Blum, approaching his seventy-first birthday and his thirtieth month of captivity (the twelfth since his trial had been interrupted), was working in his cell in Bourassol. A photograph of the time shows him sitting at his work table in front of his books set out on shelves, his head resting on his right hand. A letter is spread out before him. Wearing a sweater, he is pale but not bent, and his moustache is fuller than usual.

He was writing when his door was rudely opened. A few brief sentences were spoken. He had the time to scribble hastily to "Janot": "German officers have just this instant come in. I am leaving at noon. The die is cast. I promise you I will come back in one piece."

To the Vichy government, which asked about the simultaneous seizure of Blum, Daladier, and Gamelin, Berlin replied that, having obtained proof that the Americans and the British had decided to secure these men to set up a government rivaling Marshal Pétain's, the occupation authorities were acting to forestall this operation. The Germans confirmed that the prisoners would ultimately be returned to French courts, something that was never done.

On the conditions and the circumstances of this seizure, we have some information contained in Blum's letters to "Janot," reproduced and supplemented in the clandestine *Populaire*.[63] Under the title "Léon Blum deported!" the newspaper directed by Daniel and Cletta Mayer indicates that "as of April 3, Léon Blum, Gamelin, and Daladier have joined Reynaud, Mandel, Jouhaux, and Herriot in Germany. Pierre Laval handed them over; he is the one responsible, and naturally . . . for the leader of French Socialism (following the logic of the bloody butcher across the Rhine) was born a Jew. The lives of these hostages will be paid for by those of Pétain, Laval, Bousquet, Barthélemy, Gabolde.[64] And we place the deported men under the protection of the United Nations and the Allied governments!"

Le Populaire provided further some interesting factual details. On March 15, Gestapo agents had surrounded the prison. On March 28, all visits were suspended and the prisoners placed in solitary confinement (in two of his letters, Blum expressed to "Janot" his anguish, or rather his calm certainty of the worst). On the 31st, when the operation itself was set in motion, Gamelin and Daladier were authorized to take leave of their families, but not Blum.

The prisoners were then taken to Aulnat, the airport near Clermont under the control of occupation forces. When their new guards explained to them that the operation was designed to save them from English parachutists, Daladier heaped them with sarcasms. As he climbed into the plane, Blum shouted to the small group of French troops still present: "See you soon!"

Where was he transported? At the end of March, Blum wrote to his son Robert, still interned in an *oflag*[65] with Stalin's son, that he was "lodged with General Gamelin, Daladier, and Jouhaux." The address had been crossed out by German censorship. In fact, he was very soon separated from his companions. He hardly knew where he was except that it must have been in eastern Germany, considering the length and direction of the journey, the temperature, and the type of vegetation.

He was in Buchenwald. He was not treated as an ordinary inmate— striped pajamas, incessant brutalities, inhuman work, semi-starvation, constant threat of the crematorium. Settled in a hut near the officers' quarters at the outer boundary of the camp, he did not even know that he was living in the sinister Buchenwald. The premises were clean and adequately heated. He was able to work, he had a radio, and he received newspapers: collaborationist newspapers from Paris, of course, *L'Oeuvre* and *Le Matin*. (But there are many ways of reading a newspaper.)

Blum soon discovered, with joy, that the next room was occupied by Georges Mandel, transferred a few weeks earlier from Oranienburg (where Mandel had been Reynaud's neighbor). Their meetings were practically unrestricted. They could exchange books or ideas, or play billiards. Blum and Mandel, who had been violent adversaries in political life, became friends.

Blum's life was transformed by an extraordinary gesture of the faithful and enthusiastic "Janot": "Janot" extracted from the occupation authorities the right to join Blum in Buchenwald. She had admired him since her adolescence, as a distant cousin, and she later persuaded his jailers to allow her to marry him. He thus became, in the most tragic circumstances, her third husband; she was his third wife. Jeanne Levylier had been married to the distinguished lawyer Henry Torrès, whom she had divorced; she was the widow of a big businessman named Reichenbach. For many years she lived only to add beauty and calm to Blum's life. Her devotion to him was total.

They had imagined this reunion very early on. On April 14, in his first letter from Buchenwald, Blum wrote to "Janot": "You may be able to join me." He added that she would be imprisoned, that no return would be possible, that the journey and the reunion presented the gravest dangers. While Blum sent memoranda to the camp "authorities" and to Berlin along these lines on April 14 and May 3 (in particular noting their wish to be married), "Janot" made approaches to the Paris Gestapo, pointing out that she was related to the prisoner.

The fact that the Nazis listened to her, despite her constant indignant irony—contrary to what has sometimes been alleged, she never attempted to bribe them—is one of the mysteries of this extravagant affair. The fact is that on May 3, Blum received from his daughter-in-law Renée, their enthusiastic ally, a letter saying "Janot is very hopeful."

From that point on, Blum lived in hope. His letters are full of hope, whether he was writing about Balzac and "the abandoned woman," or Luther and the problem of grace. On May 30, he wrote a long description for "Janot" of his neighbor Mandel; he admired his intellectual vigor as well as his courtesy, his spiritual strength as much as his cultivation. But he returned most often to his family's anxieties and his hope for a reunion with her.

June 5: "Thinking of your anxieties, my life is blocked. What can be said about a marriage by proxy? My God, if you could only come!"

June 11: "Yesterday I received seven letters, three of them from you. I am overwhelmed with surprise and joy. I am sending the proxy marriage authorization in the name of Sam Spanien.[66] I have confidence, Janot!"

Thus, from June 30, 1943 on, they faced the ordeal together. Nothing was the same. "My life is transformed," noted Blum. To preserve his intellectual mechanisms and his creative force, he disciplined himself to have "Janot" question him on everything, and at length. From these dialogues came notes, sometimes scribbled, sometimes developed, which make up an enlarged and spiritualized sequal to A l'échelle humaine. On occasion, he attributes to his wife his own original ideas or powerful objections: Thus, one of these minute manuscripts[67] scribbled on cards used by the mail service of the Third Reich armies and parsimoniously distributed by their guards, says: "Janot is right: the demand for repressive justice will come especially from the USSR and its friends." Another of these little notes is an homage to Pierre Mendès France, General de Gaulle's Minister of Finance, written on June 1944. Other examples:

> For political men, a single criterion: disinterestedness. One has the right to change opinions, to fight against a previously advocated reform. On one condition: that one has no personal interest in it.
>
> One is never optimistic enough, because one is enclosed in the present.
>
> To clarify is to moralize.
>
> I have tried to elevate everything, to exalt everything. Perhaps that was my mistake. If I had a gift, it was for that. Perhaps I

believed too much in virtue. To conciliate by drawing people onto higher planes. Concord, or synthesis, at the heights.

How many illusions there are in my nature. I am such a strange mixture.

My history? I have been constantly "marked out."

Sometimes, too, the prisoner took the time to give form, even a very polished form, to veritable essays, which recall both the *Nouvelles Conversations avec Eckermann* and *A l'echelle humaine*. For instance, these two passages on freedom:

> Two centuries ago, freedom appeared in human consciousness. A heroic and eloquent revolution established it. But it did not come alone. It was accompanied by equality and fraternity. The three taken together made up justice. But equality and fraternity vanished before their faces could be clearly recognized. Freedom remained alone.
>
> It remained—or it was believed that it remained—isolated. It remained—or it was believed that it remained—immutable, in a universe that was being daily transformed by another revolution, which was without heroism, and silent because it was inevitable, a revolution of coal, iron, and cement held together by human sweat. It remained—or it was believed that it remained—limited, contained within the borders of what is called a nation, while the two revolutions, the heroic and the inevitable one, the eloquent and silent one, were every day building closer ties among all the nations of the world.
>
> But freedom divested of equality and fraternity is no longer freedom but egotism. Freedom which has been blinded to the mechanical transformations of the world is no longer freedom but exploitation. Freedom enclosed within the walls of a nation is no longer freedom but war.
>
> The classical notion of freedom postulates something more than the *deciding motive* of a national or moral order particular to every deliberation. But what else does it postulate? Nothing other than the existence within us of a *general morality,* a kind of *moral army, a reserve strength* (established, as you will, by innate attributes, education, or the influence of religion and philosophy itself), able, at a critical moment of the deliberation, to come to the aid of the particular moral motive. Classical philosophy in reality defines *free will,* as the appearance at the threatened point of general morality, of the reserve army. But it is a motive like the others and of an order more essentially rational than all the others.

Speaking of a very beautiful passage from Plato on equality:

> I have a certain experience of the "people," and far from finding in them aversion for "competence," contempt for and distance from "intellectual superiority," I have always observed in the people a rather excessive respect for these qualities. Generally speaking, moreover, I believe that the worst selection technique for recruiting ruling elites in politics would be so-called intellectual superior-

ity, which would necessarily be recognized from external signs, and a mandarin system is in reality the crudest of all forms of government.

In three passages more closely connected to the events of the end of the war and the problems it posed, Blum speaks with the most authentic grandeur:

> I do not believe in fallen or damned races. I believe it no more for the Germans than for the Jews. Everything written today about the German people and its collective responsibility was said and written about the French people after Waterloo, in England as in Germany. A very slight shift of circumstances is enough to revive the beast in man, in all men. There are ages of conquerors, and ages of the conquered. The danger of ages when everyone believes himself a conqueror is greater than those when everyone feels conquered.

To members of the resistance:

> Do not be the *chambre introuvable* of the Resistance. Do not be more royalist than the king. I understand your feelings. I can even say that I share them. They are natural. They are legitimate . . . There are two kinds of émigrés: those who remain the same in the face of a country which is changing; those who, by their action, bring a country back to a common point of departure. The émigrés of 1815 were ridiculous; they returned with the jerkin of Vardes. Those of 1870 were not. You are émigrés like Hugo, not like Bonald. You are in harmony with the country, your feelings are the same. But your duty is to struggle, for the common good, against its feelings and yours.
>
> Reject from public life, and even from the life of the nation, all the unworthy, but do nothing inspired by revenge, and without considering the consecration (meaningless in my eyes) brought about by the *fait accompli* of victory; consider the state of the conscience of men who may, in good faith, have been mistaken about their duty and the interests of the country.
>
> I am not giving you this advice of an old sage—who has nothing left to give but his life, his experience, his forced meditations—out of prudence or timidity of mind. Far from it, quite the contrary. I have no hesitation about the necessity and the urgency of bold actions, going to the very heart of the country. I know that the necessity is there, the opportunity is there, that time is short and the occasion must be grasped. But to grasp it effectively, you must tap, in the country, unanimous good will, consent, and enthusiasm. Nights of August 4 are short summer nights, and afterward the moment never returns. There is your task. I am afraid that a false Jacobinism may turn you away from the true revolutionary spirit.

Speaking to the Nazis:

> You are already conquerors in this: you have succeeded in communicating your hatred and your cruelty to the entire universe. At this very moment, your hopeless resistance, in which we should

recognize heroism, appears only as the extreme limit of sadistic ferocity, as the need to push devastation and carnage to the bitter end. And we respond by conducting war like you, with exasperated rage: on both sides it has taken the form of biblical holocausts.

I deeply fear that you may also be conquerors in this: you may have spread such terror that, in order to defeat you, to prevent the return of your madness, we will see no other means but to shape the world in your image, according to your laws, according to the Right of Force. That would be a true victory. In a war of ideas, the party which triumphs is the one which has inspired the peace.

It would be interesting to compare these texts, line by line, with those published at the time by Mauriac and Camus.

Blum read also; he read a lot. Plato, Shakespeare, Gide's *Journal*. There he found the cruel passage on his "Jewish genius" written in 1914. As he was reading, his wife had seen him stoop a bit further. She knew what he had before his eyes. He was silent for a long time. Then, in an almost inaudible voice, he said, "Even so, I like André Gide very much."

But the life of Jeanne and Léon Blum in Buchenwald was not simply writing, reading, and meditative dialogue. Blum evoked their life as prisoners in a piece entitled *"Le dernier mois"*[68]:

> I arrived in Buchenwald at the beginning of April 1943 (I spent two years to the day there); my wife succeeded in joining me in the middle of the following June. We never supposed for a single minute that we would return alive to French soil. I was in the hands of the Nazis. I represented for them something more than a French political man; I embodied in addition what they hated most in the world, since I was a democratic Socialist and a Jew. But the same reasons that made me a particularly detested adversary made me a precious hostage, since I had an exchange value, not only for the French state and its allies, but also for socialism and international democracy.
>
> But what use is made of a hostage, however precious? One tries to exchange him for an appropriate equivalent value, and that kind of negotiation necessarily involves a threat—blackmail in which the life of the hostage is at stake. When you say: "I offer to exchange Mr. X, who is in my hands, for Mr. Y," it necessarily means: "If you refuse the bargain, I will do away with Mr. X." We knew perfectly well that if I was being kept with so much care, this was for a last-minute bargain. We were convinced that the Allies would reject it, and we approved their decision in advance: we understood very well that rejection would bring about the natural consequence, for me as well as for my wife, who had come to join me voluntarily and whose fate was inseparable from mine.

Death had already approached them. One morning in July, following a telephone order from Himmler, the Weimar Gestapo came to remove

Georges Mandel from the house where they had lived together for 15 months. The week before, the Paris collaborationist newspapers had brought them the news of the liquidation of Philippe Henriot by a resistance commando group. They had immediately foreseen that Darnand and his militia would demand victims in exchange. "Georges Mandel or I, perhaps the two of us together, should logically bear the cost of the sacrifice."[69]

Georges Mandel left alone. They helped him to pack his bags and his covers to protect him from a chill on the flight he had been told he would be taking. They accompanied him to the gate of the barbed-wire fence which separated them from the rest of the world. Mandel no longer had the slightest illusion about the fate that awaited him, but his companions could notice not the slightest change in the gestures of his hands, his walk, his language, or the tone of his voice. "Never had we seen him calmer, steadier, more lucid. From our window, we watched the car that was to take him to the airfield. . . . One day or another, soon perhaps, we too would follow the same road."

For two years no one entered their building but the SS on guard. The Blums never left the camp, except to go to the dentist, by car at night. They met no one on the road, encountered no one in the hospital. The twenty-five or thirty SS guarding them constantly circulated. The house was, as Blum wrote, "less a prison than a tomb or a sepulchre." Their isolation was so complete that some of their friends, who had arrived in Buchenwald before them, spent more than 18 months there without suspecting their presence.

"It is also the rigor of this isolation which explains a fact which is at first sight incomprehensible," wrote Blum,

> I mean our ignorance, which was so prolonged, about the unspeakable horrors which were being perpetrated a few hundred meters from us. The first sign we detected was the strange odor which often reached us in the evening through the open windows, and which disturbed us all night when the wind continued to blow from the same direction. It was the odor of the crematoria.

They had guessed that people were dying around them, but they did not yet know how they were dying. They understood it more clearly after the bombing of Buchenwald by the American Air Force on August 24, 1944. They saw workers enter "their" compound to carry out the most urgent repairs. "These workers were political deportees, and it was enough to see them go by, with their gaunt and deeply wrinkled faces, their bodies lost in their striped smocks, their bare feet in clogs, to understand the slow torture to which they were subjected."

Both of them rushed to the window as soon as they heard the noise of wooden shoes on the road. "They went by, yoked like draught animals to a cart overloaded with stones or sand, or else in single file, a long tree trunk weighing down their shoulders, like captives in an Egyptian or Assyrian frieze." Among them were Frenchmen and Belgians with whom, in spite of increased surveillance by the SS, they managed to exchange a few words. They were thus able to catch the names of a few of their deported friends, comrades, or colleagues. They made their presence known. They were able to gather the first precise information about the nature and length of the work, the conditions of housing and nutrition to which the inmates were subjected, and the brutality and cruelty of the guards. "But our interlocutors themselves barely suspected that, in particular sectors of the camp, where Russians, Poles, or Jews were confined, Nazi barbarism was unleashed with even more atrocious savagery." Blum observed, "It was only after the liberation of the camp by American troops, after the capture of the archives and the complete investigation of the premises, after the depositions of the surviving victims that the radio revealed to us, in all their almost insane horror, the mysteries of Buchenwald."

A Race Against Death

On Sunday, April 1, 1945, about two o'clock in the afternoon, the German prisoner who served as their orderly informed them that an officer wanted to visit them. Their fate had been decided! And yet, for the past week, "the days and nights had rushed by in a fever of anticipation and watching." The vanguard of the American Third Army had reached Eisenach, about 80 kilometers from Buchenwald. In a few hours a detachment of tanks could reach the camp. Would the American tanks arrive before an order from the Gestapo moved the captives to the mountainous retreat in the South where, it was said, the Nazis were preparing their ultimate resistance?

Blum tells how, at the height of these alternations between hope and despair, he suffered an acute attack of sciatica which totally paralyzed him. He could not be transported, but the Nazi orders were rigid. The departure would take place late in the afternoon. They should be ready to travel in a car, taking only as much baggage as would fit.

They lived in expectation for two more days. What had happened? Had Patton's tanks blocked the retreat of the SS, trapping them where they were? Was there still hope? At the end of the third day, they received confirmation of the order to leave. Blum was dressed, carried, and placed on the back seat of a small car. They went off into the night. A large bus soon appeared. They were part of a convoy. With whom were they traveling? With other prisoners who had been crowded for months into the cellars of the Buchenwald barracks, and whom they would soon recognize.

They passed through Weimar and Jena. Were they going to turn toward Nuremberg and Munich—toward the South and the Tyrolian "retreat"? No, they turned toward the east, toward Ratisbonne. They arrived at the camp in Flossenburg, near the Czech border. There a huge armored truck joined their caravan. Who could these prisoners be, carried off like that "in a cage ringed with metal"? Civilians and soldiers, they had all been arrested after the failed assassination attempt against Hitler on July 20, 1944. Among them were three generals of the highest rank: Falkenhausen, former Governor of Belgium; Halder, former Chief of Staff; and Thomas, former head of the army's economic services. To be joined with these men, whose liquidation had obviously only been postponed by the Gestapo, was a most ominous sign.

In Ratisbonne, they stopped for a rather long time at Gestapo headquarters. The driver and the officer guarding them left them alone for a moment. "Janot" turned around: there were identity cards, there was food. The Americans were not far, near Würzburg. She was about to take the wheel and escape. He objected: it was madness; they didn't speak German; all the roads were watched by the military police. "My wife answered in a serious voice and with the tone of prophetic inspiration which I have always heard from her in really dangerous circumstances: "Everything you say is perfectly reasonable. If we escape now, we have little hope of getting out of it. But I assure you, if we stay, our fate is certain: we're lost!"

Would they dare? But the officer had already returned and the convoy moved off again. It stopped at a particularly sinister prison. There several men brutally dragged Blum from the car and carried him off, alone:

> I did not cry out, but I seemed to hear behind me a shout from my wife. The door opened to let us in and closed with an inexorable noise. My thoughts were all of my wife and did not leave her. This blow would be the only one she would not have the strength to bear. Since she had joined me in Germany, we were both prepared for everything. We had always known, and we knew better than ever since we had left Buchenwald, that there was no reasonable chance that we would ever see our country again. But we wanted at least to suffer together, and if it was necessary, to die together. Separation was the only danger in the face of which we felt without courage. And now, the deed was done; I was separated from her, and separated from the world besides. Would I ever see her again? What would they do to her, who was not even a prisoner, who had voluntarily come to join me, on the basis of their promise?

But after a few hours of bargaining, "Janot" succeeded in convincing the jailers. They were reunited again.

In the cell in Ratisbonne, he was approached by a prisoner whose face was familiar. "My name is Freidrich Thyssen." Of course, he was a leader of the German Social-Democrats, a refugee in France who had been turned over to the Gestapo by Vichy.

Their journey continued to the Bavarian village of Schoenberg. They stayed there from April 5 to 16, finally getting a little rest, housed in the apartment of a Nazi functionary who pretended not to notice when they listened to the radio from London. It was there that they learned of the death of Roosevelt, "with the feeling of mourning the loss of a friendship, if not that of a friend. In fact, it was not a loss for all his friends, known or unknown, it was a loss for all mankind."

On the evening of the 16th, they returned to the road, heading toward Munich. Everywhere there was nothing but bombing, fires, and ruins. At dawn "the car stopped. Before us was a monumental gate. It was the main entrance to the camp of Dachau." They stayed there interminably; "it is almost as difficult to get into a concentration camp as it is to get out of one." During these hours of waiting they saw the prisoners leaving in groups for work:

> Their faces were ravaged and their bodies worn out by misery, but they all held their heads high. Through the car window I stared avidly at them. Perhaps I would see a comrade, a friend. Although I gave it all my attention, I recognized no one. On the other hand, many of them recognized me, and I felt a shudder run through the ranks.

They were thrown into a narrow cell whose window gave on a ditch bordered by a wall. It was worse than Buchenwald.

> A man came in. I had already seen this tall figure, his walk which was both relaxed and stiff, his reddish-brown hair. The man approached. "You don't recognize me?" I searched my memory but without success. "No, I don't recognize you." The man answered: "You must; I am Doctor Schacht!" I hadn't seen him for nine years. During the summer of 1936, while I was Premier of France and he was master of the Reichsbank and German finances, he had come to see me in Paris. He had tried to begin negotiations with me; a history I will one day write.[70] I stared at the fallen Minister: "Have you been a prisoner long?" "Since the affair of July 20.[71] When we parted for the last time at the hôtel Matignon, if someone had predicted that we would meet again in the prison of Dachau, who would have been more surprised, you or I?" Doctor Schacht smiled, showing his strong white teeth; then he explained that to welcome me to the prison we shared he had violated his orders, and he went out.
>
> He had left us only a few minutes when the door opened again

and another visitor entered the cell. "We have never met," he said, "so allow me to introduce myself: I am Doctor Schuschnigg." It was true that we had never met, but we knew each other well. In the past he had been the opponent of my friends the Austrian Socialists, and on my side I had mercilessly attacked his policies. While I was leading the French government and he was Chancellor of Austria, I had vainly tried to enlighten him about Mussolini's real intentions. I affectionately reminded him of this, grasping both hands in mine. He told me in broad outlines the history of his imprisonment.

A third neighbor presented himself, Captain Best from the British Secret Service. The Blums soon came to know other prisoners: the family of Stauffenberg who had thrown the bomb at Hitler, a nephew of Molotov—a veritable academy of anti-Nazism. Everyone came together during the alerts, which were increasing. Schuschnigg and the generals asserted that the Gestapo had received an explicit order to allow none of them to fall into the hands of the Allies alive; Best even affirmed that he had written proof, and showed Blum a copy of an order from Himmler.

Each day, one of the inhabitants of the prison disappeared without a trace. General Delestraint,[72] who was in a section next to theirs, was taken away one morning, on the pretext of a transfer. They found out that evening that he had been shot. But on the evening of the 26th, they were evacuated, along with the approximately 50,000 other prisoners in the camp.

> The SS did not drag us from our cells until nightfall. In front of us there was a moving, dark, and silent sea. Many women and children were mingled with the men. All of them had been waiting there since noon, in the sun, standing, without food. The SS made a narrow path for us through these heads, all shaved, all weather-beaten, all ravaged by suffering, through these haggard bodies who moved slightly aside. We were with them. Our advance was no longer at the edge of life and death; it was a common movement. I feel, said my wife, that we have been returned to earth.
>
> Suddenly, a shudder ran through the human sea like a wave. Men had recognized Schuschnigg, had recognized me. Our names were spoken, repeated, circulated around us. In turn, each of us murmured as we walked, as though it were our own name, the name of our country: French, Austrian, Russian, and the echo of these names murmured by other voices returned to us. The heart must steel itself or break. I felt that mine was about to break; it swelled within me; it was the clapper in a vast bell which was ringing wildly in every breast as it was in mine. Churchill said the other day in the House of Commons: this is the way all the bells will ring for victory.

They passed through the tragic ruins of Munich, taking the road to Innsbruck where there was a camp in which hundreds of illustrious victims of Hitlerism were indiscriminately jammed together, from Prince Xavier de Bourbon-Parme to Prince Friedrich of Prussia, from Pastor Niemöller to Monsignor Piguet, from a cousin of Churchill to General Garibaldi, a leader of anti-Fascist partisans. "After many siftings, this had become a kind of residue of the most hated opponents, the subjects or vassals most seriously suspected of treason. We made up the last cohort, the last battalion of enemies and hostages. They held us together, and they would never let us go."

The caravan moved off again on the road to the Brenner pass. According to Schacht, they were headed for the Dolomites, to a winter sports resort. "It seemed," observed Blum, "that for us the Gestapo had replaced the crematorium with a refrigerator." They wandered aimlessly in the mountains, and Pastor Niemöller had to take command to shelter all of them in a village called Niederdorf on April 28.

> No doubt was possible about the Gestapo's intentions for us, nor about the instructions which had been given to the SS, who had moreover been reinforced since our arrival in the Tyrol by forces stationed in the area, whose ferocious fanaticism was from moment to moment more evident. "You're taking a great deal of trouble to keep them," said an officer to one of the men, in our hearing. "Don't you have any more grenades?" The commander of the caravan was none other than Captain Stieler, head of the Dachau Gestapo, whose name will suffice for those who knew him, and he was accompanied by a confidential aide, a non-commissioned officer endowed with a reputation as sinister as his. Two or three days later, an unimpeachable witness told us of the recent statements by the gauleiter of the Tyrol, Andreas Hofer. This Nazi with an historic name[73] had declared to the Catholic Bishop of Brixen: "We can hold out for a long time in our mountains. And if we are forced to, in the end, well, we'll have some heads to throw in the Allies' faces."

But in Niederdorf, without realizing it and perhaps without their captors realizing it, they had finally moved into the sector of the German occupation army in Italy, Kesselring's army, which surrendered on April 29. "Everything happened as though we were included in the surrender." In any case, that evening the sinister Stieler called them together to elect ("Yes, to elect, as free men do!") a delegation to take things in hand. The next day, a Wehrmacht company entered Niederdorf and disarmed the SS. At its head was a Captain von Alvensleben.

> I saw this officer come into my room, erect and rigid like an officer of the old Imperial Guard. He introduced himself, saluted, inclined his head slightly, and said: "You are henceforth under the protection of the military honor of the Wehrmacht." My wife and I had sometimes wondered, as though it were a game: "If in the end we were to be saved one day, miraculously, how would it come

about?" And we tried, by a great effort of the imagination, to picture the details of the scene. We had invented quite extraordinary combinations of events, but nothing as astounding as what was in the process of taking place before our eyes.

Blum saved by the Wehrmacht, by a Prussian officer! Trucks transported them to Pragserwildsee where they were joined by a French captain named Lussac on a mission to Garibaldi's partisans; soon they saw the partisans' red shirts, followed by American helmets.

"It was Wednesday, May 4. We looked at each other, my wife and I, in a sort of ecstasy. For several days we had known that we were alive. Now we knew that we were free." They became guests of the American army. "Never was hospitality offered with such overwhelming affection and generosity. Soldiers, doctors, officers constantly asked about our needs and overwhelmed us with their offers."

On Tuesday, May 8, the day of the armistice, a U.S. Air Force plane transported them to Naples, headquarters of the British Marshal Alexander, commander-in-chief of the Mediterranean theater. There they were treated and lodged in a villa in Pausilippe.

"Finally, on Monday, May 14, an American plane set us down at Orly airport. But that is the beginning of another life."

THE LIFE OF A
SURVIVOR

The Whole Truth, Nothing But the Truth

Anew life? Rather, the life of a survivor. But he gave to the five years before his death a fullness, a power, and a vibrancy worthy of the prisoner of Bourassol, the defendant of Riom, the deportee of Buchenwald. From that point on he had placed himself at a level where nothing vile could touch him. He was out of the reach of storms of hatred.

The hundreds of faithful followers who came to greet him at Orly on May 14 saw a pale, fragile, but cheerful old man appear beside Jeanne Blum on the airplane gangway. He was seventy-three. The last few years had counted double; his health, which had been especially affected by imprisonment and his German wanderings, never fully recovered. But that was not what counted that day; he was given a hero's welcome. The new leaders of the party were there, Daniel Mayer at their head. Most newspapers spoke of a "miraculous return." The man who had provoked so much hatred was suddenly greeted as a sage, an irreplaceable unifier. It seemed the return of Solon.

He settled first in the Senate, until his wife could restore order to his house in Jouy-en-Josas, which had been pillaged by the occupation forces. He was welcomed there by his friend Felix Gouin, president of the Constituent Assembly which was meeting in the old Palais de Luxembourg. There, as a guest without a mandate, he received his first visitors. From there, too, he went to meet General de Gaulle, head of the government.

"Everything went very well. As well as possible," said Blum afterwards, laughing, to Mayer. De Gaulle offered a Ministry of State to the socialist leader, but Blum declined, "alleging his deficient health, but also his desire to devote himself entirely to his party."[74] Blum, according to the version he told to Henri Noguères, answered that he had several reasons for declining.

> "I know, General, that asserting several reasons means that they are bad ones. But in the present situation, two of them correspond to reality. First, the state of my health.[75] My active life will not last much longer. And I believe I will be infinitely more useful outside the government than in it. All my life, you know, national unity has been my essential concern. With you, France has an extraordinary chance for national unity. And I can help this chance along better by acting within the Socialist party rather than in the government." De Gaulle did not answer. Seeing that he was preoccupied, I said to him: "My refusal distresses you, I am sorry!"
> The effect of this observation was prodigious. If I had stepped on his toes he would not have reacted otherwise. His tone changed completely. With coldness and arrogance as great as the friendliness and warmth with which he had greeted me a few minutes earlier, he exclaimed: "It doesn't distress me, it inconveniences me!"

In fact, Blum had by then decided to accept no more political responsibilities, neither in the government nor in the internal organization of the SFIO. He made an exception only for *Le Populaire,* in which his first postwar article appeared on May 16. He was content with expressing the emotion he had experienced at seeing his old comrades again, and the gratitude owed to those who had been able to bring about the "regeneration" of the Socialist party and its success in the municipal elections of April–May. But the very next day, he seemed like an old man who no longer had to worry about sparing anyone's feelings:

> I am convinced that France has suffered much more from the decline of political morality than from the discrediting of institutions. I am also convinced that what was true of the nation as a whole was also true, to a greater or lesser extent, of the various political parties. I am convinced that moral regeneration is one of the conditions for the renewal of France. I will contribute to it, for my part, by forcing myself to address my readers with absolutely rigorous probity, sincerity, honesty, and frankness. I will tell them *only* what I believe to be true, which is easy. I will tell them *everything* which I believe to be true, which is more difficult.

The France to which he had returned had come out of the war without entering peace. Shortages and division were everywhere. Half a million buildings and 4000 bridges had been destroyed; only one-quarter of the energy needed for reconstruction was available; 200,000 people had been executed or deported on both sides. Summary "justice," which varied from week to week and from department to department, a revengeful ideology of "resistance" which contradicted on every point the precepts the socialist leader had set forth at Buchenwald—this France hardly resembled the purified France of which he had dreamed in his deportation.

To be sure, Blum's party patriotism found reasons for satisfaction: the SFIO, revived by the militants of *Libération-Nord,* the majority of the MLN, and a third of the membership of *Franc-Tireur,* was once again a force; it would affirm itself in the ten elections which took place in France in 1945 and 1946. The Communist party was superior to its rival in membership, organizational power, and representation in the National Assembly, and moreover it exercised decisive influence over the CGT which soon boasted nearly six million members. Nevertheless the Socialist party had become the party of government par excellence. The fact that this was its misfortune was not yet clearly apparent.

Blum glimpsed all of this. Power was there, offered along with corruption. He would have to speak. The old man, relieved of many burdens and obstacles, also knew that he would have to return to the fray, take his share of blows, make his share of mistakes, show his share of weaknesses. Had the revolution called for by the disaster and implied by the resistance already failed?

Blum delivered his first speech as a free man on May 20 in Montrouge to the secretaries of the socialist federations. *Nothing* but the truth, and the *whole* truth: militants and public opinion would have to get used to that voice. Calling on his comrades to assure both the "continuity" and the "renewal" of the party, praising those who had particularly worked for its restoration—he mentioned only "Vincent" (Auriol) and "Daniel" (Mayer)—observing that socialism had become so popular that one "might imagine that everyone in France had become a socialist, except perhaps for us," he continued, in a tense silence:

> As for the Resistance, there are many things to be said about it. I consider it the most important political phenomenon which has appeared in this country for many years; but I do not think that it has created for anyone a right to power. There is no *a priori* right to power in a democracy. The sovereign people even has the right to show ingratitude. If services rendered gave a right to power, almost all dictatorships would be justified, for there are almost none whose source is not the reality or the appearance of great services rendered to the nation. If the power which General de Gaulle is exercising today is legitimate, this is not because he was the first or the leader of the resisters, but because he was the only man who could unite the pure forces of liberated France.

This remark was already extremely bold, given the "resistance" climate which prevailed at the time. But he went further:

> Since I touched French soil again a week ago, I confess that I have been full of disappointment and concern. I have not found what I expected. I expected something which had been both purified and tempered and, in many respects, I have the impression that I am in the middle of a country which is, how shall I say, corrupt. I have the impression of a kind of tired, nonchalant, lazy convalescence, which is a medium suitable for the development of every variety of infection. With all our strength, we must work to struggle against that, to correct it, to set it right.

Reactions everywhere were vigorous. The one most affected seems to have been François Mauriac who, in *Le Figaro*, expressed indignation that one of the men who had borne some of the responsibility for the disaster was so quick to give lessons. But Mauriac was too intelligent not to realize that the Blum of 1945 could not be affected by the old arguments. He wrote to him the next day to apologize and to tell him that if he had reacted "so violently," it was because the Montrouge speech had touched on points to which he was sensitive, "the hint of dictatorship, the invitations to ingratitude"[76] (two years later, Mauriac had the opportunity to formulate the same questions about General de Gaulle).

Before the letter from the author of *Le Cahier Noir* came, Blum had received many others upon his return to Paris. From Winston Churchill, André Gide, Friedrich Adler, Roger Martin du Gard, Pietro Nenni, Henry Bernstein, there came nothing but acclamation. None of these letters touched him as much as the one he received from Jaurès's daughter Madeleine. But there were a few notes of discord; from J.-B. Séverac, former assistant Secretary-General of the party who, like his superior Paul Faure, had been excluded from the party at the Liberation for having had a hand in Vichy's plots; and from Camille Chautemps, Blum's successor at the head of the Popular Front government, who complained about the "venomous testimony" delivered against him in his *Mémoires*[77] by the leader of the SFIO. For men who had rendered such great service to Vichy, this was showing a good deal of sensitivity.

For Blum, even before direct or indirect responsibilities of power took hold of him again, the first problem to arise was that of justice concerning the two men primarily responsible for the policies of "national revolution" and the collaboration with Germany: Philippe Pétain and Pierre Laval. As a witness in Pétain's trial, and called upon to intervene after Laval was sentenced to death, the defendant of Riom found himself both judge and interested party—these were the men who had convicted him without hearing him and had turned him over to the enemy.

His deposition at the Pétain trial on July 27, 1945, is in a sense an inverse image of his testimony at the Riom trial. He had changed places, but not intellectual attitude. He no longer had to defend his life or his honor. He was not even certain that he was speaking for justice. A few months later, Jacques Duclos, in the name of the Communist party which was disappointed by the "culpable leniency" of certain courts of justice, proclaimed from the rostrum of the Chamber: "We are in the presence of crimes which can be judged only with hatred at the bottom of one's heart, a sacred hatred!" Blum responded in *Le Populaire:*

> Political justice is indeed special justice . . . [born] of the great upheavals which have shattered a people, entrusted to men moved by great collective passions, by the vigorous hatreds of which Alceste speaks. But . . . the fundamental maxim of every form of justice, political or otherwise, is that the accused is presumed innocent until the judge has decided that he is guilty. In order to decide whether the man who is brought before him is guilty or not of the crime which he hates, the judge must not and cannot hate that man. In the judge's consciousness there must coexist vigorous hatred against the crime and scrupulous impartiality toward the man accused of the crime. The terrible problem of every form of political justice lies there.

Blum entered the first chamber of the Court of Appeal in the Palais de Justice in Paris, where the High Court was meeting for the fifth day of the trial, as an expert familiar with the premises. "He gave the impression, as soon as he spoke," wrote Jules Roy in *Le Grand Naufrage,* "of extreme weakness, such vulnerability that a feather would knock him over. But he had sworn to tell the truth, and he told it with courage and serenity. Maître Isorni himself described him as a prince."

First he attacked the magistrates. Then he spoke in words which summed up the trial as a whole and even seemed to foreshadow the Court's judgment:

> To betray means to give over. In June, 1940, there was a country which I saw immobilized as though it were stunned and stupefied by the blow of its defeat, and the brutality, enormity, and incomprehensibility of that defeat, allowing itself to collapse in its stupor and despair. And this country was told: "No, no, the armistice we are offering you, which degrades you and hands you over, is not a dishonorable act, it is a natural act, an act in harmony with the interests of the nation." And a people which did not know the terms of the armistice . . . believed what it was told because the man who used those words spoke in the name of his past as a conqueror, in the name of glory and victory, in the name of the army, in the name of honor. Well, for me that is the essential thing, that kind of vast and terrible abuse of moral trust, that, I think, yes, that is treason.

When a defender said to Blum, "You judged the Marshal differently before 1940," Blum responded:

> I lived with the same illusions as the rest of France. It is precisely that fame made up of so many elements, of his bearing, the limpidity of his gaze, it is that, used to deceive France about the import of all that was presented to it wrapped up in that false appearance, that false reputation for honor while the country was being led into shame, that is for me the essential point of this trial.

Sentenced to death, Philippe Pétain was pardoned by General de Gaulle. But Pierre Laval, who was tried a month later in a climate of reprisals, could not hope for the same treatment. Even had he wished to, de Gaulle did not think he was in a position to confront the Communist prosecutors in this domain. In his prison, the former Senator from Puy-de-Dome, the former head of the Vichy government, thought of the man whom he had isolated, humiliated, and reduced to forced silence on July 10, 1940. As a last resort, on September 22, he wrote to Blum. This unpublished correspondence[78] throws both a tragic and a pathetic light on the end of this dark life.

> Mister Prime Minister,
>   I know your feelings of justice. As you have written,[79] the bars of my prison are not separated from the rest of France. You know how unjust it would be to turn me over, without sufficient defense, to jurors who will be all the harsher because they are ill-informed.
>   I send you respectful greetings from my cell.
>
>   P. Laval

On October 12, Blum received this brief message from Mme. Laval:

> Mister Prime Minister,
>   My husband may be executed this evening or tomorrow. I place all my hope in you and I cannot tell you how moved and grateful I am.

On October 14, Pierre Laval himself sent this final message, in cramped schoolboy handwriting on the coarse paper of a common prisoner:

> My Dear Prime Minister,
>   My lawyers have shown me the letter you sent them.[80] I do not believe it will be enough to save me from death. Before the irreparable, I am sending you this final appeal.
>   Will you help me, will you save me? You are the leader of the largest party in the Assembly, and de Gaulle cannot do away with a former head of government against your will.
>   A gesture from you will mean life for me. A refusal would lead me to death. Let the general commute my sentence if he does not wish to order a review of my trial. Thus, not being dead, I would

have the hope of one day explaining myself before a real tribunal, where I would not be insulted and threatened in the very course of the trial.

I believe I know your delicacy and I think that, apart from the advice given my defenders, you have acted directly. I am counting on you and this is my final hope to avoid being brought to the executioner tomorrow—and my wife and daughter will no longer have to live through such terrible moments.

What salutation can I offer you, my dear prime minister, but my hope in you and my feeling of gratitude at such a dramatic moment.

Pierre Laval

Blum could not fail to be sensitive to such a plain and simple expression of the fear of death. He immediately sat down at his desk and wrote in a few minutes this letter to General de Gaulle, which he took the trouble of copying over:[81]

My Dear General,

I have just returned to Paris and P.,[82] whom I have just called, tells me that I still have the time, barely, for a final appeal to you. I know that you are familiar with my feelings, but it is a duty for me to express them to you once again. I think that one cannot carry out a sentence of death after a trial like that.

There is no question of pardon but of a restoration of justice. No sympathy of any kind nor even any shared views has ever tied us together, and you know that I owe him no gratitude. But I administered justice in another time, and respect it, and I would like it to be respected.

Forgive me. Understand me. And believe in my feelings of deep attachment to you.

Léon Blum

P.S. I have reread this hastily written letter and I am afraid it may be ambiguous. I am not asking for a pardon but a new trial—or rather a trial.

A futile step. The very little justice that had surrounded Laval's trial was further obliterated and perverted by the repugnant death inflicted upon him: revived after trying to poison himself, he was dragged almost unconscious to the executioner's block.

Guilty of "Humanism"

The man whom Jules Roy had seen, during the Pétain trial, as "so vulnerable that a feather would knock him over," had returned to the world and to action, moving imperceptibly from the role of arbiter-witness to that of a militant. This is how the American journalist Cyrus Sulzberger described him on August 30, 1945:

> Léon Blum, who is in remarkably good spirits and radiating energy, received me in his office in the residence du Sénat where he was having tea with his wife and friends. He denied that he had committed himself not to accept the premiership if the socialists win the elections. He would take it, but would prefer not to, since he wants to retire. Says he is tired.[83]

His activity at the time was organized along three principal lines: the reorganization and intellectual revival of the Socialist party, the definition of a new kind of relationship between the SFIO and the Communists, and the development of the Constitution and the relations between the parties and General de Gaulle. These were soon supplemented by the responsibilities he took on in the creation of UNESCO and the mission he was given to the United States.

"I am proud of the doctrine I profess and the party to which I belong": Blum often repeated this sentence from a preface to a study of Jean Perrin he wrote in those months. Although the doctrine owed a great deal to him, the party had been reshaped by others, and the vigorous state in which he had found it, confirmed by a first success in the municipal elections of May, continually surprised him. But from this potential an organism had to be reconstructed, and this organism had to be given reasons for action, doctrinal perspectives. These were the tasks of the congress called for August in the Mutualité.

Blum's speech delivered at the congress on August 13, 1945, has been published under the title *"Le Socialism maître de l'heure."* It clearly sums up the evolution, begun in *A l'échelle humaine,* of a thought which was not only revisionist—what non-dogmatic thought is not constantly revisionist?—but essentially reformist, and turned toward the democratic and pluralist aspects of socialism, and even, though he refrained from using the word, toward humanism.

But first there had been the greeting offered the old leader when he appeared on the platform. Those who witnessed it will never forget the extraordinary emotional climate of the moment: the tears, the bravos, the praise. He, who had known so many reversals and betrayals five years earlier, was better prepared than anyone to resist this kind of sentimental display. But he, too, contributed his tear, although he began his speech with these words: "I am a man who has been given time to think."

He then defended the "declaration of principles" which he had just composed with the intention of reviving and rejuvenating the statutes and doctrine of French socialism. There was no question of calling Marx into question. "Then why, comrade Blum, do you speak of 'class action' rather than 'class struggle'?" asked Jean Rous. "It sounds suspicious!" "To speak of 'class action' rather than 'class struggle' is to remain faithful to the letter of Marx," retorted Blum.

What is important, moreover, is to go beyond the economic and social liberation of the individual, which is not the final goal, but the means, the necessary condition . . . for the transformations of the human condition. We must also liberate man from all the incidental and secondary servitudes created by that exploitation . . . guarantee to him, in collective society, all his fundamental rights and the full development of his personal vocation. . . The revolutionary goal is to establish harmony between the person as a social unit and collective society as a social whole. . . Our real aim, in the society of the future, is to make human beings not only more useful, but happier and better and, in this sense, socialism is more than a conception of social evolution or social structure; it is a universal doctrine, a doctrine which must impregnate hearts and minds, transform ways of life and thought, transform mores. It is in this sense that we say of our socialism that it is human, and it is not less revolutionary because of that.

He went on to suggest

. . . a synthesis between the Marxist dialectic, which I definitely do not wish to call historical materialism, and Jaurèsian idealism, which I call idealism without the slightest mental reservation. The Marxist dialectic shows us socialist society arising, I will not say inevitably, but necessarily, in the logical sense of necessity, from the evolution of capitalism itself; Jaurèsian idealism shows us Marxist socialism as the end result, the culmination of all the great movements that have swept through humanity, and human charity.

"Personalism," "humanism," "neo-Christianity." The old leader's remarks immediately provoked reservations and murmured criticisms from the Trotskyites grouped around Jean Rous and Yves Deschézelles and from the neo-Guesdists—whose leader was then an obscure deputy from Pas-de-Calais named Guy Mollet who assumed the airs of an illustrious predecessor from Arras named Robespierre. But Blum and the Secretary-General he covered with his praise, Daniel Mayer who was chiefly responsible for the reconstruction of the party during the war, were still "untouchable."

They were so no longer a year later at the 38th Congress. In the meantime, Blum had carried out a controversial mission to Washington and, on October 21, 1945, and June 2, 1946, the party had suffered two defeats in legislative elections, both times being outdistanced by the PCF. On the second occasion, it lost nearly a million votes and 21 seats in the Assembly! The electorate was making it pay for the mediocre performance of the Gouin government, which had succeeded that of de Gaulle after the latter's sudden departure of January 21, 1946. It was well-known that Blum had supported the choice of Félix Gouin by the parliamentary group and the managing committee after rejecting de Gaulle's suggestion that he himself succeed him.[84]

In June 1946, the SFIO paid the price for having been in office too long; it suffered the inevitable recovery of the right which, after sheltering some of its members under the Socialist mantle, returned to the MRP before ultimately finding refuge in the RPF. "The electorate had held us solely responsible for the tripartite system of government," Blum sadly observed in *Le Populaire* on June 3.

Their comrades in the SFIO held Blum and Daniel Mayer responsible for this setback. The left of the party was not content to attribute it to a too-prominent and continuous "participation." *La Pensée socialiste,* which expressed the ideas of Jean Rous and his comrades on the left, formulated more fundamental criticisms. It attacked a veritable doctrinal deviation. For the left, for those who had begun as Trotskyites and who were distinguished from the Communists only by their rejection of the clerical discipline which prevailed in the PCF as in Moscow, Blum and his friends were in the process of diluting the fundamentally Marxist doctrine of the party with a vaguely spiritualist, or in any case humanist, phraseology. (Some of them even went so far as to whisper that Blum had converted to Catholicism.) It was this ideological confusion which the left believed was the cause of the party's loss of prestige and authority with the electorate. It was time to rectify the political and theoretical "line" of the SFIO.

Blum responded to this campaign by publishing "Notes sur la doctrine" in *La Revue socialiste* of July 1946. It seems he intended to calm those in the party (notably the *Pensée socialiste* group) who were alarmed that he might substitute the concept of "class action" for that of "class struggle" in the party statutes, and who therefore raised the question: was the SFIO still a class party? Yes, answered Blum. He argued as follows:

> Marx teaches that to accomplish fully the definitive expropriation of capitalism which will open an entirely new era in human history, the organized proletariat can count only on its own strength. Social revolution is a logical necessity of history, but that logical necessity can nevertheless be realized only by the application of human will and, for Marx, that act of will can be nothing but the class action of the proletariat organized in a class party for the conquest of political power.
>
> The formula for class action is: "The liberation of the workers is the task of the workers themselves." It is essential to Marxism and it has become the rule for all the political parties which have come out of Marxism. It means that the proletariat can expect the revolutionary transformation of the property system neither from the justice of a good tyrant of the kind described by Renan, nor from the authority of a totalitarian dictator, nor as the result of an evangelical crusade of the Saint-Simonian variety carried out among the ruling bourgeoisie, nor from the success of a Blanquist conspiracy, nor from the proliferation of communitarian organisms on the Fourierist model within capitalist society, nor from anything but its own efforts. . .

> When a Socialist party is defined as a class party, what is meant
> in reality is that the party carries out class action. Which means
> that its goal is the conquest of political power, in the name of and
> by means of the organized proletariat which it represents; that the
> conquest of power is valuable for it as a means of and a condition
> for the revolutionary transformation of the property system; that,
> whatever the shifting and complex arrangements necessitated by
> its preliminary work within the framework of capitalist society
> (parliamentary coalitions, participation in power, exercise of
> power, and so on), whatever cooperation, sympathy, or conver-
> gent action there may be with other parties to facilitate its task, it
> nevertheless expects victory only from its particular action, or
> rather from the particular action of the organized proletariat.

A wasted effort. The "left"—in quotation marks because its leader
was Guy Mollet—was in a position of strength, for several reasons.
First, because it was based on a powerful aspiration for unity at a time
when French communism—progressing rapidly, with the halo of its
role in the Resistance—was a powerfully attractive force; second, because the old Guesdist faction, to which Mollet claimed allegiance, was
waiting for its revenge on the Jaurèsists who had so long been dominant, and who saw Blum and Mayer as their leaders; finally, what was
left of the opposition factions of the late thirties, from *La Gauche
révolutionnaire* to *La Bataille socialiste,* seized the opportunity to
make the old leader pay for what they had fought against in 1936–
1937—"non-intervention" and "pause."

On this basis, Guy Mollet, Jean Rous, Yves Deschézelles, and their
comrades presented a motion against Blum and Mayer attacking a
"succession of mistakes and failures" by the leadership of the party due
to "the weakening of Marxist thought" which had led to "submission to
de Gaulle," "indulgence toward the bourgeoisie," and "tactlessness
toward the Communist party." It was therefore necessary to condemn
the current "line" and to bring about a prompt "doctrinal and political
rectification."

This motion made immediate inroads. After two days of debate, the
congress rejected the "official report" presented by Daniel Mayer—
that is by the friends of the old leader. For the first time in the history of
the party,[85] the leadership was disarmed, the leadership embodied by
Blum, father, inspiration, martyr. It was an unheard-of failure, a devas-
tating disavowal.

But Blum was not devastated. When he mounted the platform on the
first of September, he seemed rejuvenated. Comrade Blum took the
floor:

> I have participated in our congresses for the last thirty years, and I
> have never done so with so much difficulty and worry. Something

escapes me in what is happening. I do not understand. Do the party's difficulties have their source in a doctrinal deviation?

For my part, I would be deeply happy to think that in the masses of our party there was such a passionate attachment to the doctrine, such a jealous concern for its purity. I would be happy to think that the vote for or against the official report was arrived at in our sections on the basis of doctrinal discussions on the relations between class action and class struggle, between historical materialism and dialectical materialism. I would be happy to think that, but I doubt it. And, to tell you the truth, I do not think that the doctrine of the party has ever been more coherent or more homogeneous at any moment of our history as Socialists.

Guy Mollet's motion speaks of "erroneous humanism." I can recognize myself, without excessive vanity, in this formulation, although I have never used the word humanism in that sense. I have simply pointed out that the final aim of socialism is the total liberation of the human individual.

I know very well that I have committed another heresy in the eyes of the intransigent and intolerant doctors of Marxist scholasticism, and it is the one they find least pardonable. From this very place, a little over a year ago, I tried to distinguish between the *historical materialism* of Marx and the *dialectical materialism* of Lenin and Stalin. Marx's historical materialism is, as its name indicates, a law for explaining history. I hardly need remind you that, in the movement of history, it assigns a primary, essential role to economic phenomena, all other phenomena, social first of all, and then juridical, political, moral, religious, and spiritual phenomena being determined or justified by economic phenomena and more particularly by the means of production and production relations.

Dialectical materialism, on the other hand, goes well beyond historical materialism, since it incorporates *philosophical materialism,* that is, a doctrine which presents itself not simply as an explanation of history, but as an explanation of knowledge and existence. Philosophical materialism is a doctrine which asserts that all phenomena in life and thought are reducible to biological, physical, and chemical laws, and that these laws are themselves explicable solely in terms of the qualities of inorganic matter. And the dialectical materialism of Lenin and Stalin consists essentially in maintaining that, between historical materialism, the law of history, and philosophical materialism, a theory of knowledge and existence, there exists a necessary connection.

Will you make socialism depend on a philosophy? Will you remove from your ranks a Cartesian, a Spinozist, a Kantian, a Hegelian like Marx, or even a positivist, like Littré, who would have failed the test? Will you proclaim with all the more reason that socialist convictions and membership in the Socialist party are incompatible with any kind of religious belief? You have always proclaimed the opposite. You have always said and written that socialism was independent from any philosophical or religious distinction. You have even written it in your latest statutes, and that is even one of the rare sentences not written by me!

I have heard about the superior dynamism of our opponents. Dynamism is not a pharmaceutical product or a mechanical engine. Dynamism is men. It is men's convictions. It is their self-denial and spirit of devotion. It is their faith. And if dynamism has been lacking, you must realize that this is because, in you as men, there is perhaps neither enough self-denial, nor enough self-sacrifice, nor enough faith. I am afraid that the party's difficulty, the unrest whose causes cannot be discovered by analysis, or which is out of all proportion to its causes, is essentially a matter of panic; that it expresses the complex forms of—forgive the word—fear.

I think that the party as a whole is afraid. It is afraid of the Communists. It is afraid of what the Communists will say. At every moment you anxiously wonder: "But what will the Communists do? And what if the Communists don't vote with us?" Communist polemics and Communist deformations act on you, affect you without your knowledge, and drive you apart.

You are afraid of the voters, afraid of the comrades who will or will not name you as candidates, afraid of public opinion, afraid of failure. And if there has been a change in the doctrine, a deviation, a decline, that is where they are to be found. You are afraid of novelty, of the new forces you greeted after the Liberation with reticence and suspicion. You have that same nostalgia for the past, that suspicion, almost disdain for women and the young. You make no room for women on electoral lists. You think of the young only as recruits.

The evil is in you: it is the lack of fervor, the lack of courage, the lack of faith. Do you know what passage of the Guy Mollet motion is? It is a kind of moral alibi by means of which you have attempted to deceive your bad conscience.

In *La Pensée socialiste,* organ of the victorious faction, Jean Rous responded to Blum in these terms:

Was it a situation in which we expressed fear of "what the Communists would say," vulgar discontent, or nostalgia for the past, as some men said from the platform of the congress? We do not think so. On the contrary, the concern to impose a policy of autonomy, in place of the permanent and often one-sided policy of conciliation with the center, expresses the reaction of the militants against the fear of "what people will say"—not only the Communists, but also the bourgeoisie!

The leader's failure was total. It was not only the failure of Daniel Mayer and his assistant Robert Verdier; it was also that of the representative of the powerful Nord federation, Augustin Laurent who, sponsored by Blum to succeed "Daniel," was nevertheless defeated by Guy Mollet. The party to which Blum had devoted his life, and whose idol he had been one year before, had rejected him without appeal. Several of his opponents of August 1946 came to regret it.

Stormy Dialogues with the PCF . . .

"Fear of the Communists"? Of course. Since November 7, 1917, and since the congress of Tours, how could a social-democrat define himself except by the way in which he mastered or failed to master that fear? At the Liberation, less than four years after its fall into darkness, the PCF (from then on it insisted heavily on the "F") was the dominant force in French social and political life: the largest party in Parliament, controlling production through the CGT, having at its disposal, with the "National Front," an admirably organized system of satellites, inspiring a substantial part of cultural life, based on powerful provincial strongholds, it seemed to be both a state within the state and an essential pillar of the national edifice. As Blum had pointed out in his wartime correspondence, nothing could be done without it. Could something be done with it?

As early as November 12, 1944, Vincent Auriol and Jules Moch had launched an appeal for the working-class unity which had "already been established in the Resistance." The Political Bureau of the PCF responded without warmth, but it agreed to open discussions which led in December to the creation of a "committee of national understanding," which was to prepare either the "unity of action" (coalition) or the "organic unity" (fusion) of the two parties. A common manifesto was issued on March 2, 1945.

There is a legend that Blum's return put an end to these efforts toward convergence. In fact, when the old leader returned from deportation in May 1945, confrontation had resumed between the two parties. It was the refusal of the MLN (dominated by the Socialists) to merge with the National Front (dominated by the Communists) that, by thwarting one of the PCF's essential ambitions, changed its relations with the SFIO.

But on June 12, 1945, *L'Humanité* suddenly published a plan for total unification, grouping Socialists and Communists in the "French Workers Party" (the name of Jules Guesde's old party), a plan which the PCF congress at the end of the month made more precise. In a series of articles published by *Le Populaire,* July 5 to August 7, Blum flatly rejected the idea of "organic unity," but responded favorably to the idea of a return to "unity of action." Why?

For the man who had been the spokesman of the secessionists of Tours, a return to unity basically presupposed the emancipation of the PCF from Soviet dominance. Was this the case?

> In abolishing the Komintern, Stalin was perfectly sincere, and the dissolution of the Third International is a real fact. At the present moment, the French Communist Party is no longer, directly or indirectly, in a state of organic or hierarchical dependence on the Russian state.

But what we had not foreseen, and what the Communist leaders themselves had perhaps not foreseen, is that in recovering its freedom of decision, French communism would not recover its freedom of judgment. The relationship of hierarchical dependence has been broken, the relationship of material dependence, if it ever existed, has been broken, but there remains a dependence of a psychological or affective order which is derived from both habit and passion. Their motive is not obedience or self-interest, but the perseverance of their nature and something which resembles love. If you think I am exaggerating, read through several issues of *L'Humanité* in a row, or simply read the plan for a charter of unity. After as before the dissolution of the Komintern, French communism still has its eyes fixed on Soviet Russia; Soviet Russia remains for it the permanent pole of attraction and the infallible criterion.

Observing that the policies of Stalin, "that man of genius [who] is playing his own game," were based not on proletarian internationalism but on a very comprehensible concern for security which led him to create around himself a shield of "feudatory states," Blum drew the conclusion that fusion between his unconditional supporters and the defenders of international socialism was unrealizable. He concluded:

In our national framework and at this moment, unity of action is indispensable for the political protection of the workers. But along with their capacity for and efficiency in international action, that unity would risk being damaged by premature fusion or unification. Unity of action should be conceived and practiced so that it becomes a preparation in depth for organic unity.

On this basis, the 37th congress of the SFIO in August, 1945, adopted a balanced motion, noting that the conditions for unity were "far from being realized on the Communist party's side"—every Socialist ought to "refrain from using any means which degrades the human spirit—but expressing the hope that, if the conditions were fulfilled, a "common congress" could be called.

Although the majority that emerged from the 38th congress (August–September 1946) disavowed Blum's ideological line, it did not adopt toward the PCF a strategy different from that of its predecessors. The new masters of the party, with Guy Mollet at their head, repeated the same arguments, made up of precise suspicions and vague hopes. Mollet thought of himself as a reincarnation of Jules Guesde: who had made a harsher judgment of the Bolsheviks, as early as 1919, than Jaurès's old rival?

Divided on the level of political organizations, the PCF and the PS nevertheless cooperated in government for 30 months under the direction of de Gaulle (until January 1946), Félix Gouin, Georges Bidault, and Paul Ramadier. But in May 1947 the development of the Indochina conflict and acute social tensions provoked the break-up of the

Ramadier cabinet. Fearing that it would be out-flanked on its left by the Socialist factory committee (with Trotskyite leanings) of the state-owned Renault company, the Communist party undertook a massive strike, mobilizing more than 25,000 workers of Billancourt against a wage freeze. While the party's ministers, unlike its deputies, supported the government in the Indochina affair, the ministers themselves voted against the cabinet over the Renault crisis. Ramadier took note of this break in cabinet solidarity, considering it a collective resignation, and immediately replaced the rebellious ministers. Thorez, obviously angered by the outcome of the affair, confessed to President Auriol, "I was at the end of my rope."[86]

Blum was far from pleased by the break with his old and implacable partners. He regretted that some elements of his party had "taken pointless and malicious pleasure" in provoking them and aggravating the tension. He could see, beyond the cabinet crisis, a fundamental challenge to the political balance which had been more or less stable since the Liberation. He had written a few months earlier that there was "no question of allowing the Socialist party to be trapped in an anticommunist coalition," and he was now forced to observe that the SFIO had slipped into just that position. Shortly after a session of the party's National Council, which approved Ramadier's reaction by only a very small majority, Blum wrote: "If the party has suspended the rule which requires Socialist Deputies not to participate in a cabinet from which the Communist party is absent, this is not in order to undertake or prepare for the establishment of an anticommunist bloc in France or an anti-Soviet bloc in the world."

Was the penetrating Blum playing the innocent? Was he so forgetful of the past, so ill-informed about the future? After having just carried out a long mission to the United States, could he not see the first signs of the Marshall Plan and the Atlantic Pact? We will not adopt the argument of the PCF that the dismissal of the Communist Ministers in Paris (nearly coincidental with that of their Italian comrades) was a preventive measure intended to facilitate the "Marshallization" of the two countries and the setting up of the Atlantic system. Politics is more spontaneous, complex, contingent, and day-to-day than that.

But for once, in May 1947, the old gentleman of Jouy-en-Josas preferred pious verbiage to lucidity. Whether he did not or could not see it, the dissociation between the two working-class movements had just been deepened at one blow; the situation once again recalled that at the end of 1920, with the difference that twenty-seven years earlier the Socialists, and Blum above all, denounced the anti-Soviet strategy of Paris while in 1947 they became its supporters. The formidable USSR that had arisen from the hell of war was no longer the infant workers' state of 1917.

The Communist leaders held Blum responsible for this new break.

At the Strasbourg congress on June 29, Thorez denounced "Léon Blum's infidelity to Marxism; along with Georges Izard, Maurice Schumann, and Cardinal Suhard, he would like to make the workers accept the primacy of spirit over matter." The old socialist leader thought that in a half-century of political life he had heard all the charges that could be made against a man, whether it was a matter of his origins, his features, his income, or his morality. It remained for him to be called a religious fanatic. He made fun of it the next day in an article for *Le Populaire,* denying "the tall story that since my return from Germany has presented me as a convert to Catholicism."

. . . And with de Gaulle

The stormy constitutional debate which served as the epicenter of French political life from the end of 1944 to the end of 1946 could be summed up in one question: what place can a parliamentary democracy make for an exceptional man who wishes to be considered as such? Are the system and that man compatible?

Yes, Blum had seemed to answer from prison. No, the socialist leader corrected himself, once he had returned to peace and been filled by what de Gaulle maliciously called "the poisons of the system." In any case, the debate which concluded in October 1946 with the ultra-parliamentary Constitution of the Fourth Republic was for many a debate between the two men who symbolized French public life at the time—de Gaulle and Blum—the principle of authority against the principle of equality.

Their already long-standing relations had constantly fluctuated between quarrelsome incomprehension (about the professional army) and mutual support (about the armored divisions of 1940). In an unpublished letter to Blum dated July 1945, Henry Bernstein told how he had arrived in London on June 19, 1940, and had been received by de Gaulle who had told him: "Blum and Boncour are coming. They will be my two vice-presidents." Circumstances had brought about a convergence of their aspirations in 1943. Blum's letter to Roosevelt at the time, guaranteeing the general's sincere belief in democracy, had been the gesture of a great ally. Their correspondence of the time gives evidence of much more than esteem; there was mutual admiration.

We have seen the welcome de Gaulle, head of the Liberation government had offered Blum. A few days later, on the occasion of the fifth anniversary of the London appeal, Blum, comparing June 18, 1940, to July 14, 1789, wrote with a mixture of exaltation and reserve:

> I am addressing that great spirit, whom I sense to be haughty and
> solitary. Let him have confidence in the French people; let him
> have confidence in international democracy, for confidence is con-

tagious. The man who is leading France toward a new destiny must find within himself something more than loyalty and rigid adherence to democracy, even something more than patriotic passion. To lead the people, to move them by direct influence, he needs a kind of communion with them and a kind of surrender to them.

This "surrender" was certainly the last thing of which General de Gaulle was capable. But he appreciated the tone, if not the advice. When five months later, exasperated by the demand of the Communists for one of the three "major portfolios" (Interior, Foreign Affairs, or National Defense), by the Socialists' attempt to trim the military budget, and by the plans of the Constitutional Commission (defining the powers of the future head of state, it went as far as denying him the power to pardon), de Gaulle was seriously thinking of withdrawing. He proposed that Blum succeed him:

> DE GAULLE: "You are the only man who is both familiar with the parliamentary game and capable of setting forth a vision of the whole in harmony with the grandeur of France. Take my place."
> BLUM: "I am old and ill, and I have been the most hated man in France. No."

Commenting on this exchange of views and Blum's amicable rejection de Gaulle wrote in his *Mémoires:* "I felt some sadness." A rather unusual note from him, and one which contrasts with the "It doesn't distress me, it inconveniences me!" which he had let fly six months before when Blum had refused to become Minister of State. Yet, throughout the crisis of November 1945, which was in many respects a test of strength between the Assembly and the general, Blum had been unsparing toward de Gaulle, consistently supporting the cause of the legislative body.

Two months later, the man of June 18 bade farewell to his government and to the French people. On the advice which Blum gave to de Gaulle and to his own comrades, Félix Gouin was chosen to succeed (the word went a bit beyond the reality) the general. The socialist leader did not fail to criticize the conditions of the general's departure and the good report he presented in his letter of resignation. But in concluding his article, on January 24, 1946, Blum wrote:

> The transfer of power which has just taken place is in itself a victory for democratic institutions which have allowed the replacement of a man like General de Gaulle without disturbance. But the man who has most effectively helped France to recover its democratic institutions is named precisely General de Gaulle. He did so contrary to his personal temperament, but following careful consideration, and especially in accordance with the will of the country. We would show a great deal of frivolity, or else ingratitude, if we were to forget that today.

The general would have to move quite far toward a challenge to the parliamentary system before Blum would treat him as an opponent. When de Gaulle presented his plan for a presidential Constitution in Bayeux in June 1946, Blum—not forgetting that, in *A l'échelle humaine* he had not concealed his inclination toward this kind of system—confined himself to discreet irony: "Between de Gaulle and democracy, one observes a kind of incompatibility of temperament." It was the general's brutal intervention on the eve of the October constitutional referendum (calling for a "no" vote because of the weakness of the powers granted to the head of state in André Philip's proposal) that provoked Blum's fury.

> I am not discussing the person of General de Gaulle, nor the intrinsic merits of the Bayeux Constitution. I intend to argue only on the basis of the facts. I say that the adoption of a Constitution like that of Bayeux, on the personal intervention of the general, after a campaign dominated by the person of the general, would have as its inevitable result the election of the general to the position of head of the French state and head of the French Union which he would have created according to his own measure. I say that he would be brought to that position less by the choice of Parliament than by the preceding popular vote, a vote whose character as a plebiscite could in this case not be questioned. I say that placed in such a position under such conditions, nothing would then stand in the way, neither his Ministers, nor the Chambers, of his basic conception of command. Whether you like it or not, whether you agree or not, the very reality of the Republic is therefore in question, and the question of personal power is set before the country.

There then follow from Blum's pen penetrating analyses that have been repeated for 30 years by political theorists: "He is, in the strict sense of the word, the *pretender*. He invokes a right to legitimacy on the basis of services rendered to the nation. This is why, in his heart of hearts, he considers the political bodies and the men who hold power in his place as usurpers."

He also offered literal prophecies: "The general would set up a broad sector of reserved matters, including in reality all major questions, all of high politics, which would be legally removed from the elected Assembly, practically removed from the Premier, and which the unchecked authority of the President of the Republic would alone direct." That is the whole system of the sixties.

Charles de Gaulle and Léon Blum were no longer fellow travelers. One, authoritarian by nature, had restored the Republic and democracy but had chosen to make himself the instrument for growth of power. The other, a parliamentarian by vocation, had been tempted by the notions of strengthening the executive in a presidential framework, but then had decided to block it. Plebiscite against representation, "direct democracy" against Parliament, two visions of the state and of public life confronted one another. The fact that they were incarnated in the two most antithetical types of Frenchmen produced by the twentieth century adds nothing to the significance of the debate, only to its vividness.

Blum Discovers America

De Gaulle, since Yalta, had devoted his efforts to attenuating postwar subordination to America. Blum's first official postwar effort was a U. S. visit aimed at strengthening the ties between Paris and Washington. Nothing could be more anti-Gaullist than this expedition.

Félix Gouin's term had begun badly. In his speech on assuming office on February 15, 1946, he had presented a tragic assessment of the economic situation of France; his picture was in fact a slight underestimation of the reality. Inflation was increasing at an extraordinary rate, the budget deficit had reached 300 billion francs, production was more than a third below that of 1938, war and the costs of the occupation had reduced national wealth by half—five trillion francs. There was no possible outcome but bankruptcy; unless foreign assistance was obtained.

In order to wring the best possible terms from the Americans, Félix Gouin thought of a "special mission" by Blum. On this occasion, the old leader did not need much persuasion. The mission was temporary and the urgency extreme. And to discover America! But the head of government committed the blunder of not consulting Georges Bidault, Minister of Foreign Affairs, who claimed he learned of the Blum mission "from the newspapers." This did not facilitate contact between the traveler and the Quai d'Orsay. In Washington, the choice was thought bizarre: was Blum competent? Wouldn't Bidault have been more conversant with the problems?

In short, Blum left for Washington in an atmosphere of uncertainty and reservation. Emmanuel Monick, his "secret" expert of 1936, who had become governor of the Banque de France, accompanied him. This mission's essential aim, in fact, was to obtain financing from Washington for the "Monnet plan." Very soon, in a first phase, the atmosphere improved. The naïve admiration of the old gentleman from Paris for the gigantic world which greeted him charmed the American press. His friend, William Bullitt, Roosevelt's former Ambassador in Paris, provided the best "public relations" for him.

Five days after his arrival, Blum was received with most demonstrative cordiality by President Truman, and later by Eleanor Roosevelt. The presentation he made on March 25 before the National Advisory

Board demonstrated that he was not as incapable as had been thought in manipulating figures and economic concepts.

> There is no necessary connection between the domestic system of production and exchange in a given state and the policies pursued by that state from the point of view of international transactions. England before Gladstone and France before the 1860 treaty were faithful to the most orthodox liberalism in their domestic economic systems, and nevertheless in their foreign transactions they practiced protection and even sometimes rigorous prohibition. Conversely, it is perfectly conceivable that states may apply domestically the principles of a planned or collective economy, which is now the case or the tendency in almost all the nations of Europe, while on the other hand, from the point of view of foreign transactions, pursuing a policy of international organization based on complete freedom and equality. A planned economy is no more incompatible with international economic organization than it is with domestic political domocracy. It is only under the effects of unemployment, poverty, and all their consequent material and moral disorders that the peoples of Europe might be driven to autarky and to dictatorship.

Political allusions of this kind remained discreet through the trip. But they had an effect. In his dispatches, Jean Monnet noted the psychological and political success Blum had with his interlocutors. That success culminated on April 12 with a reception in New York in honor of the French visitor on the occasion of the first anniversary of Roosevelt's death. The two ideas he elaborated at the time—the necessity of Europe, and the gratitude it owed to the dead president—produced a great effect on an audience which was dominated by representatives of the Jewish community of New York:

> Since the First World War, the position of Europe in the world seems to have gradually contracted . . . We Europeans are no longer the whole world, as we were in the earliest days of Greek and Christian civilization. We are no longer even the center of the world as we were a century ago. But if Europe is no longer the center of the world, and it knows it, it is still a part of the world. Yes, Europe is still something in the world, and you will allow me to add, without too much presumption, that France is still something in Europe.
> We should neglect nothing, no one. First of all because, in this world, states, like individuals, have duties proportionate to their power. Further, because at this moment in history prosperity has become indivisible, like justice and peace. Solidarity among nations has become a necessity of a physical order as much as a moral obligation. No nation can any longer preserve lasting prosperity in the midst of a world tormented by the spirit of hatred and conquest, just as no nation could preserve lasting freedom in the midst of a world subject to tyranny and oppression.

As for his homage to Roosevelt, it took the very personal form which Americans love. Blum told how he and his wife had learned of the president's death, in Bavaria, and how they had been devastated by it:

> We felt that the victory which was already certain, already won, would no longer be quite complete. For true victory is not only the defeat of the enemy, it is the peace which is derived from his defeat. Peace is not a test of strength, it is a test of justice and, to guide their unsteady steps toward peace, the nations needed this incomparable leader, because they all had the same confidence in his person and in his name. He was truly one of those extraordinary men who, on rare occasions, appear through the centuries, who testify in favor of humanity and offer a guarantee for the future. Let us then remain faithful to the message and the example of Franklin Roosevelt. Let us share his faith in the solidarity of men and the solidarity of peoples. Let us share his faith in the future, and we will thus bring about that future ourselves. It will not be a dream . . . if you wish it.

This eloquence in a rather Quaker style, in an almost Jeffersonian tone, was a great success. But he also had to talk figures. The reactions that his figures provoked—five billion dollars' worth of purchases on credit over five years—made Blum realize that Americans were not so eager to "auction off" their surpluses at any price to the insolvent Europeans. Was the special envoy "humiliated" by this?[87] Did he consider breaking off negotiations which were much harder and less productive than he had been led to expect?

After six weeks of bargaining, Blum signed an agreement with Secretary of State James Byrnes which can be summed up in three essential points and a significant annex. The essential was a dual American gesture—liquidation of war debts amounting to a little less than three billion dollars, and an advance of a little less than 700 million dollars (French hopes were for triple that amount). In return, France abandoned import quotas protecting French industry. The annex, introduced at the explicit request of Secretary of State Byrnes, was the abolition of most measures protecting French cinema against American competition, theaters no longer being required to show more than one French film per month. The agreement was cleverly gotten from a badly informed French delegation, and it was to have serious consequences.

Was the price paid for American aid too high? The debate is unending. The reconstruction of the French economy, largely due to the Monnet plan which needed the funds from Washington, seems to argue in favor of the negotiators of the spring of 1946. But was there not also a political bargain? Was the financing of the plan not exchanged for a limitation of national sovereignty, and paid for by an anti-Communist turn? "The negotiations concluded in Washington involved, neither explicitly nor implicitly, neither directly nor indirectly, no condition of any kind, civil, military, political, or diplomatic. I know that it is difficult to drive such an idea from some minds, but that is the way it is," declared Blum when he returned to Paris on May 31.

In a "confidential report"[88] sent to Félix Gouin toward the end of April 1946, Robert Blum indicated that certain American personalities

> have made it clear that the counterpart on the French side should be the taking of an extremely clear position in the problem which, in their eyes, dominates all others, the one in relation to which they now examine all questions, that is, the Russian-American conflict . . . In the course of a private conversation with Mr. Vinson, Secretary of the Treasury, where I was the only witness as interpreter, my father stressed very explicitly the interest he had in a rapid solution, before the French elections. The American negotiators have very clearly understood the importance of the time factor . . . Questions other than economic or financial negotiations have never been broached officially. On the German question in particular, there have been no conversations other than those concerning reparations and coal. On the other hand, in the course of a private conversation, Mr. Byrnes spoke with my father about the Spanish question.

In short, the political situation had served as a backdrop to the financial negotiations, which was inevitable. There was, on the part of "certain personalities," a tendency to situate the debate in the framework of what was not yet called the Cold War. Which was perhaps also the venial sin of Léon Blum.

Less subject to controversy and more attractive in his eyes, another task absorbed a large part of his energies: the establishment of UNESCO. Shortly after his return in September 1945 Blum had agreed to go to London to represent France in the United Nations conference for intellectual cooperation, and he had managed to have Paris selected as the headquarters of this cultural UN.

Elected president of the conference in August 1946, and re-elected in November of the same year, the old socialist leader delivered there one of his most important speeches. "The greatest war of religion of all times has showed us how education, culture, and science itself could be turned against the mutual interests of humanity . . . It is therefore not enough to develop and improve them. They must be openly directed toward the ideology of democracy and progress," an argument which he supplemented in his closing speech on December 10. He pointed out that, in this framework, "all opinions and all inclinations could enjoy equal respect."

He also sponsored a program organized in Sèvres in 1947 for the training of staff members of UNESCO, which he defined as "the best path to the superior forms of international society which we have conceived and wish to realize." He saw in this group of trainees "the outline, the microcosm of the universal cosmos we will all attempt to establish." The presidency of the French delegation to the fourth session of the General Assembly of UNESCO, in 1949, was his last public mission, performed five months before his death.

One might say, maliciously, that the convergence was only too easy between the idealist and the calmly humanistic and populist ideology of UNESCO. To correct this notion, we should recall some of the other words he spoke to the trainees of Sèvres: "Our efforts would be futile or incomplete if it only brought us contact with man in the abstract. It must allow us to touch the *real man,* like us and different."

New Year's Eve in the Government

On November 10, 1946, a new National Assembly was elected: the Communists were the largest group, with 166 deputies, ahead of the MRP. The Socialists had lost 700,000 more votes and 27 seats: the "recovery" promised by Guy Mollet had not taken place. In the name of the PCF, Maurice Thorez naturally claimed the right to form the government. He campaigned assiduously and hopefully. Blum recommended to his comrades that they support his candidacy. But all the other parties refused: the "constitutional" majority was 310 votes, and Thorez received only 259. The next day, Georges Bidault failed even more badly. At that point Jacques Duclos said to the Socialists: "Your move!"

The new President of the Assembly, and thereby the provisional head of state, Vincent Auriol, then revealed his trump card: the designation of Léon Blum. He had wanted first to obey the rules and demonstrate the incapacity of the leaders of the two principal parties to govern. But he had been thinking only of the Blum solution, in spite of the leader's friends and relatives, who were convinced that he would refuse. Accompanied by Félix Gouin and Jules Moch, he hurried to Jouy-en-Josas and pointed out to the old gentleman that it was a mission which would last for a few weeks, until the election of the president of the Republic scheduled for the middle of January. Would Blum allow the perpetuation of a stalemate which helped only Gaullist ambitions?

He accepted. Immediately, on December 12, Parliament supported him with near unanimity: 575 votes out of 583. His aim, of course, was to form a tripartite government with the Communists and the MRP. But Thorez and his comrades, as they had a year earlier with de Gaulle, demanded one of the "three major ministries," and preferably National Defense. A strong faction of the Socialists and almost the entire MRP

were opposed. In fact, Bidault and his friends were considering remaining out of power for a while in order to make their weight felt and
to leave the SFIO alone with the PCF. Blum rejected the possibility.
He, too, had a "secret plan," which he confided to Moch and Auriol on
December 13: "I will continue negotiations until noon, the final dead-
line. Meanwhile, draw up a list for a purely Socialist government which
I will name in case the negotiations fail."[89]

Established that very evening in that form, to last for a month, the
third Blum cabinet, voted in by 544 to 2, is known by the name its
leader gave it because of the date of an initiative that marked its brief
existence—"the New Year's Eve cabinet." It was the first homogeneous government in the history of the Republic, and the last provisional
government of the Fourth Republic. Blum declared over the radio on
the 16th: "We must give the country the impression that the parliamentary system is again in operation. I do not think there will be anyone in
the country who will ascribe to what I have done self-interested, personal, or partisan motives."

It was true that at the end of 1946, by taking on at his age and in his
state of health such crushing responsibilities, Blum appeared to the
public as a man with a saint's halo. While de Gaulle, who remained
furious, was in the process of being discredited, the man who had been
for so long "the most insulted man in France" advanced to a chorus of
acclamation.

Was this third government the most successful of those he presided
over? No, because it was in the course of those weeks that hostilities
broke out in Indochina that were to become a seven years' war; and
Blum, in spite of his pacifism and desire for emancipation, cannot be
exonerated from responsibility by history. But in those four weeks, the
old statesman and his comrades multiplied initiatives and demonstrated, as André Siegfried pointed out at the time, the benefits of one-
party government.

He was his own Foreign Minister, but he named a young Secretary
of State, Pierre-Olivier Lapie, as his assistant at the Quai d'Orsay. As
Ministers of State he named Félix Gouin, Augustin Laurent, and his
recent opponent Guy Mollet. Finance went to Philip, Justice to
Ramadier, Defense to Le Troquer, and Interior to Depreux. Daniel
Mayer was at Labor, Jules Moch at Public Works, Marius Moutet at
Overseas Territories; his Under Secretary of State was Gaston de
Ferre, Tanguy-Prigent at Agriculture, Naegelen at Education, and
Robert Lacoase at Industry. The Fourth Republic was calling reveille.
Blum formulated three precepts for his colleagues:

> Keep me informed of important problems, not when they are re-
> solved, but when they arise; take a position when documents are

composed, not when they are signed—otherwise it will be your departments which make decisions; and however brief the life of this government may be, you are not here to take care of immediate business. Like every government worthy of the name, this one must act under the sign of the long range, without which no impression is ever made on the future.[90]

The remarks have an almost Gaullist ring.

In less than thirty days, Blum did indeed take three initiatives which left their mark on the future, although the first and most spectacular did not last for very long: the ordering of price reductions, intended to put an end to the 50 percent rise in prices in the second half of 1946. Confronting this catastrophe, the Premier consulted his experts. Was it necessary and possible to block this wave with authoritarian measures? Jules Moch, Minister of Public Works, confessed that he did not believe in the effectiveness of price manipulation. Blum nevertheless made his decision, in agreement with unions and professional organizations. On December 31, New Year's Eve, he addressed the public:

> The wishes which the provisional government of the Republic extends to the French people this New Year's Eve are not Platonic. By accepting the temporary mission with which Parliament had entrusted us, we had assigned ourselves two essential goals: to protect the franc, and to increase the real purchasing power of the working masses. I am now in a position to inform the public that, beginning the day after tomorrow, Thursday, January 2, a first general reduction of industrial, commercial, and agricultural prices by five percent will be carried out. All bills, all price tags, every means of indicating prices at the disposal of the population must include an accurate notation of this reduction.
>
> A second stage of five percent is already scheduled for sixty days from now.
>
> For the first time in more than ten years, an act of government authority is being taken to break the spiral of rising prices and to bring its efforts to bear on the systematic lowering of prices. I call upon the country to act in a similar spirit.

Despite the skepticism of the majority of experts, the reduction was generally applied: the wholesale price index registered a decline of three percent from January to April 1947, retail prices a decline of four percent. But the concomitant wage freeze provoked harsh criticism from the Communists.

In parallel with this operation, which brought about a slight rise in the value of the franc, Blum took steps finally to give life to the Monnet plan, facilitated by the mission to Washington earlier in the year. On January 7, again addressing the country, Blum declared:

> [Since the plan is] the essential element in the economic restoration of the country, the government has decided to undertake its immediate execution.

One thing is certain: however circumstances may develop, we will need more coal, electricity, steel, cement, agricultural machinery, and means of transportation. This is why we are going to undertake immediately four-year-long precise programs in these six basic activities which are the conditions for the reconstruction of our whole economy. We also need more manpower. The workers' organizations have patriotically agreed to an effective work week of forty-eight hours. In agreement with them, we will also bring about the necessary immigration. Directly or indirectly, through consecutive orders for equipment and construction, more than 30 percent of the French economy will immediately be set on the road toward the objectives of 1950.

Having made their "mark" on prices, production, and industrial plants, Blum and his Socialist team were also to make themselves felt in foreign affairs. It is hardly surprising that the old Anglophile who directed the Quai d'Orsay for a week once again turned his eyes toward London, where, unlike 1936, there was a Labour cabinet. Strangely enough, the initiative came from the British side, Ambassador Duff Cooper having slipped this suggestion into a conversation with P.-O. Lapie on December 26: "Why not give the friendship between our two countries the form of an alliance?" The suggestion was repeated the next day in Blum's presence.

In effect, why not? Hadn't de Gaulle tied France to the USSR in the same way in December 1944? Although he and his advisers had noted that the British Ambassador's offer was a personal initiative, they easily allowed themselves to be persuaded of the necessity of signing "a treaty of alliance with the object of preventing any future aggression by Germany."

It was not Blum who signed the treaty four months later in Dunkerque, but Georges Bidault who was re-established at the Quai d'Orsay after the departure of what he called the "interim" Socialist government. In the speech he delivered on the occasion of the signing, the leader of the MRP did not even allude to the steps taken by his predecessor, which shocked the British and provoked from Blum the brief comment: "How petty."

But this one-month cabinet had done more than others do in a year; in a poll conducted in late 1947, 60 percent of those questioned placed it first among the governments since the Liberation. But this third Blum cabinet was also marked by the outbreak of the Vietnam War. No one at the time, not even the penetrating Blum, could estimate the terrible consequences of that.

It is moreover difficult not to draw a parallel between the explosion of December 19, 1946, and the event which had taken place ten years and five months earlier in Spain. In both cases, honest Blum, engaged in the positive work of reform and reconstruction, was "taken off guard" by the foreign event, with the difference that what happened in 1946 did not entirely surprise him and he had done a good deal to prevent it.

The Socialist leader in fact kept himself fully informed about Indochinese affairs. He had welcomed the agreement signed the preceding March 6 with Ho Chi Minh by Jean Sainteny, French representative in Hanoi. The agreement recognized Vietnam as a "free state within the French Union." Although this "union" remained to be defined and organized, the agreement of March 1946, in harmony with the Socialist leader's views, opened the way to the emancipation of Vietnam and seemed to be of a kind that would prevent any war of reconquest. But the failure of the Franco-Vietnamese negotiations in Fontainebleau in August, followed by the bloody incident of Haiphong in November, had shown that on both sides there were forces working stubbornly against peace.

On December 9, three days before he was offered the leadership of the government, Blum decided to publish in *Le Populaire* an appeal from Ho Chi Minh to the French public. Blum commented:

> We are perhaps on the eve of genuine war measures in Indochina. . . The French government today can choose between only two courses. Either reconquer by force of arms all or part of Indochina; or else assure the value, consistency, and duration of the agreement signed with Vietnam last March. Either use military force, or else restore friendship and confidence. This is the only choice, and I might add that I cannot conceive of any possible hesitation in the face of this choice. There is one way, and only one, of preserving in Indochina the prestige of our civilization, our political and spiritual influence, and those of our material interests which are legitimate: that is a sincere agreement on the basis of independence.
>
> It will be argued that the object of French policy is precisely the application of the agreements already concluded, and that, without a certain "firmness" on our part, they might be misunderstood or violated by the very men who signed them with us. But what exactly is meant by firmness? Haven't we given the impression that we wish to hold onto what we are giving away? I am not advocating here some thoughtless surrender. What seems necessary to me is an absolutely clear definition of our policy, which would permit no further doubt, followed by complete openness and honesty in the conduct of that policy which would permit no further ambiguity. That is where real "firmness" lies. . .
>
> The decision must lie, not with the military authorities or civilian colonists of Indochina, but with the government sitting in Paris. And when I say government I do not mean one of those interdepartmental committees who have succeeded no better in the Indochina affair than they did in the German affair, but the cabinet and the Minister responsible. The problem will arise for the new government from the very beginning. To all the reasons for hastening its formation, we must add that one.

Two days later, he was the government. He urged Marius Moutet, the Minister responsible and an old friend of Ho Chi Minh, to do everything to take charge of the situation. But when the head of the Hanoi government sent a new appeal for conciliation to Paris on the 15th, the message was "delayed" in its passage through Saigon by Admiral d'Argenlieu's services. Blum did not receive it until a week later, three days too late.

On the night of the 19th, Moutet burst in upon the head of government: "They're fighting in Hanoi!"

"I did not deserve that!" said Blum the next day to his friend Henri Noguères. But it was necessary to act. In the Chamber on the 23rd, he declared: "We were obliged to deal with violence. . . [but] the old colonial system is today a thing of the past. We will have to resume honestly the work that has been interrupted, that is, the organization of a free Vietnam in an Indochinese Union associated with the French Union."

"Free Vietnam"? He had backtracked a bit, no longer using the word independence. But by hastily sending Marius Moutet, followed by General Leclerc, on missions to Vietnam, he was attempting above all to resume negotiations. Why did he not seize the opportunity to dismiss d'Argenlieu, an acknowledged saboteur of the agreements, the man chiefly responsible for the failure?[91] To be sure, Blum offered the admiral's position to Leclerc who, with some hesitation (and probably at the urging of General de Gaulle, a supporter of d'Argenlieu), refused to accept it. But this refusal ought not to have been enough.

On the conversation between Blum and Leclerc, we have the interesting testimony of P.-O. Lapie, who was Minister for the former, and had been the latter's companion in Chad in 1940–41. In his *De Blum à de Gaulle,* the Secretary of State for Foreign Affairs in the 1946–47 cabinet describes Leclerc on his return from Hanoi with Blum in Blum's office:

> wearing a taupe velvet jacket, nothing but curves, from his shoulders to his moustache, his position somehow rounded off by the eighteenth-century chair. Opposite him Leclerc, in a khaki uniform, very straight, with a short moustache, a sharply etched profile, in his attitude a hint of stiffness. In his youth, Léon Blum must have been a bête noire for this cavalry lieutenant, from the provincial nobility, educated in Catholic schools, as he must not have been Blum's favorite kind of man. And there they were face to face after so many ordeals. "100,000 men in five years," said Leclerc, "it's a political question. . . The whole problem of the West and the East . . . A problem of government." Blum's comment after he left: "Honest, but a little laconic."[92]

Neither man—the younger died fourteen months later, long before his elder—had been able to prevent the worst. Thus opened the long-festering wound of Vietnam.

The end of this strange government, limited to one month and one party, came with the election of the President of the Republic, which signaled the official birth of the Fourth Republic. Had Blum ever allowed himself to be tempted by the highest office? No. Blum never thought of moving into the Elysée, mostly for reasons having to do with his age and his health. But perhaps in his mind, the choice of Vincent Auriol (which had been made probable by his election to the presidency of the National Assembly) was really a choice for him. Who owed him more? What personality was more closely modeled on his? What socialist attempted to reflect more faithfully his ideas and his lessons?

When the deputy from Haute-Garonne was proclaimed head of state on January 16, 1947 in Versailles (thanks to the conjunction of Socialist, Communist, and some Radical votes, reviving the Popular Front), the first to congratulate him was his mentor, his friend, and his party leader. A car carried them slowly from the palace of Versailles to the Elysée, side by side, the head of state and the head of government. We, the uninformed witnesses, crowded on the sidewalk of the place de l'Étoile, and seeing through the door of the car the delicate face of the Premier next to the round face of his friend, wondered whether a last trick of history had not justly promoted the old gentleman of Jouy-en-Josas to the post which was spontaneously conferred on him in the minds of the majority of the French.

Blum was now nothing but a Premier who had resigned. He had resisted the urgings of his friend, who naturally wished to see his mandate as head of government renewed, and returned to his country house and his office at Le Populaire—but not before indicating that the man he wanted as his successor was Paul Ramadier, a lawyer from the Midi who was nevertheless laconic, a Hellenist passionately involved in figures, a workhorse in slippers. Blum had long forgiven him for having joined the "neos" in their secession from SFIO in 1933; he had appointed him three years later as Secretary of State for Mines in the Popular Front government. It was to this man, so colorless in appearance, so awkward in his manners, that fell the "historic" task of ratifying the withdrawal of the Communists from the government.

When, after a Paris newspaper strike which lasted for more than a month, Blum resumed his function as editorialist of Le Populaire, he did so by noting that anxieties, threats, and tensions were growing worse everywhere. The lowering of prices which he had brought about was checked by the CGT's campaign against the wage freeze. In Moscow, the Ministers of the four Great Powers (USSR, USA, Great Britain, and France) found no ground for agreement about Germany. The Indochina affair was growing ugly: the Communists were ensnared in a dual attitude of protest and support, while the National Council of the SFIO came out for negotiations with Vietnam. The insurrection that broke out in Madagascar increased the arrogance of the colonial party. Finally, week by week, General de Gaulle was moving from the critique of institutions to polemical attacks on the regime.

The break between the Communist ministers and the Ramadier government posed a serious problem to Blum's party, whose new leadership had decided in principle to remain outside any government without Communist participation. On May 6, Secretary-General Guy Mollet proposed a motion to the National Council of the SFIO calling for collective resignation from the government. It was defeated, but just barely. The Socialists remained in the government, under Socialist leadership, and the Communists were thenceforth exiled from power for a long time to come.

Was this Blum's revenge on Guy Mollet? The old leader carefully refrained from presenting things in that way, and probably from seeing them that way. His editorial of May 8 emphasized the necessity for the Socialist party not to "lose contact with the mass of workers from whom it could not isolate itself without denying and destroying itself."

To this break in the working-class alliance which, despite quarrels, had been the basis of government action since the Liberation, was almost immediately added a break in the coalition of the victors over Nazism. During his journey to Washington a year earlier, Blum had been able to measure the slide of the United States from the "grand alliance" of the war, which was revived at Yalta, toward a strategy of organized suspicion, indeed of confrontation with the USSR. The failure of the Four Powers conference in Moscow in March had revealed the extent of the divergences between the Socialist camp and the Western powers, and France, gradually abandoning the strategy imposed at first by de Gaulle, joined their ranks with rather bad grace. It was a new situation from which President Truman had drawn the lessons in a very "firm" speech delivered on March 19, 1947. It can be considered the declaration of the Cold War.

Legend has it that Blum was its ideologue,[93] and that he put his admirable talent as an analyst and "leading thinker" of democratic socialism at the service of this suspect cause. But let us read what he wrote at this time:

> As for me, I liked neither the argument nor the vocabulary of [Truman's] speech, and I would hope in particular that, on the other side of the Atlantic, they would once and for all break the dangerous habit of using the same terms to designate Hitler's regime and the Soviet regime.
>
> *Le Populaire,* March 19

I do not have the qualifications to draw up, for the use of other governments, a manual of practical diplomacy with the Soviets. But I think it is not at all impossible, in relations with them, to combine openness and friendship, firmness and confidence. I believe that while using the language of "realism" with them, we must at the same time bear in mind factors of collective psychology and particularly that extreme touchiness, sometimes suspicion, which very naturally developed during the period—still quite recent—when the Soviet Union felt itself threatened by an almost universal conspiracy. All of that is difficult to handle, I realize. However, the deep wish of the Soviet Union is for peace.

Le Populaire, April 17

Blum may have changed his tone later, but we should agree that Stalin and his followers did their best to push him in that direction.

Cold War and Third Force

The year 1947, the year of Blum's seventy-fifth birthday, was decisive. It was then that political and strategic balances shifted in France and in the world. It was then that the Cold War began, then that the French Communists were removed from power and entered their career of civic dissidence, then that General de Gaulle began his long march for the reconquest of the state.

For Blum, this was thus the year of the worst ordeals. Less than two years after the end of the war and his return from deportation, he witnessed the dissolution of the "grand alliance" of the war which he had fervently supported and the dissolution of the unity of the resistance. He greeted the break between the victors of East and West over Nazism as a defeat, and all the more so because it occurred over the Marshall Plan.

The American proposal seemed to him not only an act of genuine international solidarity but the occasion on which to gather into a coherent organization all the European countries that were beneficiaries. Up until the last moment, until Soviet Minister of Foreign Affairs Molotov, who had come to negotiate the possible participation of the USSR in the operation, left Paris, Blum had hoped that the Marshall Plan would be accepted. Naïveté? The French Communist leaders also believed in it until Stalin's representative broke off the talks.

Like them, Blum had not understood that the Cold War—announced a year earlier by Churchill's Fulton speech—had begun on March 12, 1947, when President Truman solemnly made known his decision to provide military aid to the governments of Greece and Turkey to counter possible Soviet aggression. Blum had written at the time that the speech seemed to him unduly "severe and threatening." He explained that "no state, however great, had the right to deliver such a sentence on its own authority."[94] Having clearly established his distance from American political and military strategy, he considered himself all the freer, with reference to the Marshall Plan, to recommend it to all of "international socialism" and the European economic community.

What he had called "the cool and taciturn" response with which Moscow at first greeted Washington's offer had not seemed discouraging to him. but when *L'Humanité* on July 2 announced Molotov's departure and the "failure" of the Anglo-Franco-Russian conference of Paris on the use of Marshall Plan aid, Blum confessed to his "stupor" and "dismay."

He pointed out that by dissipating the chances of encouraging Europe "to form a union of complete solidarity," the Soviet reaction

> maintains the decomposition of Europe into states separated by the watertight barriers of national sovereignty, and the magnetic forces which, East and West, draw this scattering of states toward separate poles. The states on the marches of the East will find themselves pushed more thoroughly toward Soviet Russia. The states of the West may be forced to work out alone their patterns of contact with the United States. Popular opinion, in Great Britain and France, was quite prepared to say: "I decline American aid if it is deliberately refused to Russia." It is very unlikely that it will say: "I will do without American aid once Russia has seen fit to reject it for no reason."

Everything had been said. The Komintern had been resurrected at the September 1947 conference in Poland. The Atlantic Pact was created in July 1948. This did not mean that Blum was at the time determined to "lay his head on the block, like Iphegenia, for the Communist blade." Shocked by the choice the Soviet leaders made in the spring of 1947, he was on the contrary among those who denounced very early, and sometimes with a kind of prophetic exaltation, the procedures and methods of Stalinism. But there should be no mistake: for Blum, the danger was on two fronts. All his declarations of friendship and gratitude for the United States did not prevent him from assigning to France and Europe an entirely different role from that of satellites of Washington.

On February 29, 1948, just after the Communist *coup d'état* in Prague, Blum wrote with a cool-headedness which was rare at the time: "The Soviet Union has just completed, in conditions which justifiably outrage us, its system of political and territorial *defense*. But I remain convinced that it does not want war." He had the same attitude a few months later, in the spring, with the break between Belgrade and Moscow and, during the summer, over the Berlin blockade.

His major theme was not the one defined by Churchill as the "defense of the free world" against "Soviet imperialism." It was the formation of what he called the "international third force." In a speech delivered on October 18, 1947, at the Vélodrome d'hiver, Blum outlined the essential elements of the strategy:

> Whatever the mistakes and the wrongs of the Communist leaders, we refuse to cut off from the defense of the republic—as we refused to cut them off from the defense of the nation—the popular masses under Communist leadership. We want neither to be Americanized nor Sovietized. The majority of French citizens, like the majority of the citizens of the world, want to be neither American protégés nor Soviet subjects.

On January 6, 1948, the leader of the SFIO explained his point of view in *Le Populaire:*

> Between the United States, "champions of individual freedom and the rights of man," but where the capitalist economy maintains its full integrity and all its inhuman rigor, and the Soviet Union, which has destroyed private capitalist property but also eliminated all private, civic, and social freedoms, there is room for nations which want both individual freedom and a collective economy, democracy and social justice.
> This amounts to saying that between American capitalism—expansionist like all capitalisms in their rising phase—and the totalitarian and imperialist communism of the Soviets, there is room for social-democracy, room for socialism which offers what may be called the locus of European ideologies. The international third force is therefore really a force. And in order for it to act as a force, it is enough that it become conscious of itself, conscious of its nature, conscious of its immediate mission.

Was this the "neutralism" later advocated by Claude Bourdet and Hubert Beuve-Méry? Tito's "non-alignment"? Or perhaps the Gaullist arguments of the sixties? In any case, we are at some distance from the Cold War crusade for which it has been claimed Blum was a theoretician and fanatical preacher. We should not forget that this was written shortly after the failure, brought about by the Communists, of the attempt which Auriol had asked Blum to make to form a new government in November 1947.[95] France at that time was the victim of large insurrectional strikes. These strikes, in Nord, the Paris region, and Marseille, were fomented and led by the Communists according to a strategy defined by their leaders after the so-called "Warsaw" conference.

In November 1947 France found itself on the brink of civil war. While General de Gaulle's RPF which had just received 40 percent of the votes in the October municipal elections—a figure never reached by any other party—was calling on its supporters both to overthrow the "party system" and to block the Communist "separatists," who were supported by the Red Army "camped a few hundred kilometers from Paris," the PCF and the CGT called for action by the working class. The decontrol of meat prices in April had reduced the New Year's Eve policy of decreases to nothing. The purchasing power of the working class had declined by 10 percent in ten months.

In Marseilles, where the Communist municipal government had just been ousted by the RPF, a veritable battle took place at City Hall, which the supporters of the outgoing mayor took by storm. (They tried to defenestrate his Gaullist successor.) In Nord, the mines were paralyzed and management personnel sequestered. In the Paris region, the Citroën and Renault factories were occupied. Edouard Depreux, Minister of the Interior, hardly inclined to use force against the working class, was nevertheless given the mission of evacuating them. A number of veterans were recalled to duty. The state was vacillating. The Ramadier cabinet was exhausted. It was necessary to find a successor.

Farewell to Parliament

Vincent Auriol thought once again of Léon Blum. To Auriol's great surprise, the old gentleman of Jouy-en-Josas did not raise many objections; he was so worried about the future of civil peace that he found it impossible to refuse. He had only one suggestion: why not try again to form a purely socialist government? Wasn't that the formula which had produced the best results? But this time the MRP was opposed, as were the Radicals. He had to resign himself to a coalition of the incompatible.

On November 21, 1947, the day after the railway workers went on strike in response to a call by the CGT, Blum presented himself before the National Assembly to request the right to form his fourth government. Facing the socialist group that morning, he had been very discreetly warned against a unilaterally anti-Communist orientation. He could smile; whoever reads today what he wrote at the time can see that he was more preoccupied by the rise of the Gaullist wave than by the attacks unleashed by the Communist party.

He declared himself indisposed to surrender to the strikes which were spreading and intensifying. When Jules Moch, Minister of Public Works, asked him what attitude to adopt toward the pickets who were stopping the trains to Paris, Blum answered flatly: "Feeding millions of people comes before the decisions of strikers who represent only a minority."[96] Armed with this opinion, Jules Moch supported the fraction of the railway workers who not only caused the strike to fail, but who also participated in the split of *Force Ouvrière* from the CGT.

But what Blum intended to present to the Chamber was a program of "struggle on two fronts." He would be just as severe with the challenge mounted by the Gaullists against institutions as with the threats posed by the Communists to social "order." Several of his friends, among them Daniel Mayer, warned him against a strict assimilation of the two dangers: since the Communists would certainly vote against him, he would be alienating too many moderates, who might be tempted to rally to him, the wise man, by placing the Gaullist campaign and the threats of the PCF on the same level. Blum shrugged his shoulders: "Next year I will be entering on my seventy-sixth year. I must therefore expect to appear soon before the Supreme Judge.[97] Don't ask me to indulge in such cleverness."[98]

Let us quote here the account of a friendly witness of the session, Pierre-Oliver Lapie: "Herriot gave the floor to the Premier-designate. Léon Blum rose from the front bench, walking with difficulty. He moved slowly toward the steps to the rostrum, started up the president's steps by mistake, came back. He took a long time to change his glasses, and he read his declaration in a weak voice with precise articulation."

> The Republic is in danger. The Republic which, for us, is identical to the nation. Civil liberties, public order and peace itself are threatened. The danger is two-fold. On the one hand, international communism has openly declared war on French democracy. On the other hand, a party has been formed in France whose objective—perhaps its only objective—is to deprive national sovereignty of its fundamental rights.
>
> I am here to sound the alarm. I am here to attempt to rally all republicans: all those who refuse to endure the impersonal dictatorship, not of the proletariat, but of a political party: all those who refuse to seek protection against that danger in the personal power of one man.

It was at that point that the right reacted. Some Radicals, some of the MRP, and naturally those who openly or secretly supported the general shouted: "Shameful, resign!" Blum had heard worse; he didn't care. But his friends already knew he had lost the battle for refusing to play up to the right. Imperturbable, the old gentleman continued:

> We must deal with the social conflicts which are appearing and proliferating throughout the nation with firmness, that is, without making any promises which we cannot keep, and by trying not to prohibit anything which we must concede . . . We must separate, in the working-class movements, what is an enterprise of aggression and destruction directed against the institutions and doctrines of

the Republic from what is a legitimate, or at least a natural, expression of anxiety and suffering. We must seek a confident collaboration with the corporate organizations of the working class without surrendering to their control the slightest portion of the sovereignty of the democratic state. In the daily life of the unions, we must re-establish the spirit, the principles, and the habits of democracy. We must improve the condition of the working class and consequently the effective purchasing power of wages and salaries, to the very limits of the present possibilities of the French economy.

I have [told] you what I believe to be the truth, what I believe to be my duty. I ask you in return for an unequivocal and unreserved vote, and a vote which will commit you today as I have committed myself, and as the government will commit itself tomorrow. I conceal from myself neither the difficulties nor the dangers. The phrase that has been haunting me for the last few hours is Vergniand's sublime declaration: "Let our memory perish provided the Republic is saved!"

It was a revealing reference to the guillotined Girondin leader. Blum was condemned only to failure. He knew it as he left the rostrum, and he had difficulty resigning himself to it. The "imprudences" which he had just committed were not a way of extracting himself nobly from an unfortunate trap; he still considered himself useful in these days of danger. Let us quote P.-O. Lapie again[99]:

He returned to his place. How we wanted to help him, speak to him, support him, even suggest an argument to him. But, a torture invented by the Constitution, he was alone on his bench, separated from the others by the empty bench of the future ministers. I can still see that tired and slightly haggard figure, arms crossed on his desk, cheeks sunken, a certain air of one of those noble, melancholy animals who know they are close to the end. He was feeling physical weariness, no doubt, from his age and the ordeals of the past few years, but also weariness with everything, with an entire life. At that point, the disinterestedness and the elevation of the statesman which can be a source of wisdom are transformed into a source of error, since all men seem equal in their prudence or their folly.

Blum responded with ease and mastery to Jacques Duclos, who called him an American agent, and to Guy Petit, the only avowed supporter of Franco in the Chamber, who was the spokesman of the vindictive right. But he refused to alter in the slightest his condemnation of the RPF. The votes were counted. He had a majority (300 out of 560) but not the majority required by the Constitution, 314. He left, followed by the applause of his socialist friends, and in an atmosphere of general melancholy and unfocused regret. This bent and fragile figure left the Assembly forever. He supported with all the weight of his prestige the candidacy of his designated successor, Robert Schuman.

The following summer, he didn't have the courage to refuse Auriol's request that he be Deputy Premier in the cabinet of André Marie, a Radical of the kind which least appealed to him, and who had chosen as Minister of Finance the inextinguishable Paul Reynaud. Water and fire. As in June 1936, as in November 1938, as in December 1946, the two men who had been brought together by their shared horror of Nazism quarreled about social policy. Their colleague Jules Moch reports this confrontation in a cabinet meeting:

> REYNAUD: We have only to suspend the eight-hour law in the mines and extend work in the pits by two hours; we will then have enough energy.
> BLUM: Look here, Paul Reynaud, do you think it is physically possible to extend the work day of underground miners like that?
> REYNAUD: Then let's set up work with two shifts a day, and we'll get the same results.
> BLUM: Where will you find the hundreds of thousands of miners you need to make up the second shift?

For the few services he could thus render to the working class and to common sense, can we understand that Blum could have compromised his prestige and the prestige of socialism by participating in such mediocre and ephemeral cabinets? He himself provided the answer, shortly before his death, in an editorial for *Le Populaire* in February 1950:

> Since 1947, democratic freedoms have been endangered by Stalinism and Caesarism: the Socialist party must subordinate everything to the compelling duty of defending them. That is why we have moved from government to government, theoretically making our decision freely, but in reality constrained by the gravity of the circumstances and the dangers, and prisoners of our duty which is quite simply our duty as republicans.

Joel Colton judiciously sums up the situation of Blum and his companions at the time: "The Socialist Party was the prisoner of its republican duty. In order to prevent political instability from leading to the destruction of free institutions, it subscribed to an unpopular policy. For Blum, the defense of republican freedoms was the precondition for democratic socialism. But what would be left to save of socialism?"[100]

A pertinent question. It is not enough to recall that, confronting threats against the Republic from 1899 to 1905, Jean Jaurès had won agreement for a strategy of defense that was similar to Blum's strategy of the late forties: above all to save the democratic Republic, of which socialism is nothing but the supreme accomplishment. By dint of reducing the fight against the principal opponent to its simplest expression, does one not finally diminish a certain form of aspiration and weaken ideological values?

It was perhaps a question of this kind which incited Blum on February 3, 1950 to advise the collective resignation of the Socialist ministers from the Bidault government. It was the SFIO's first exile from power since the Liberation; it was significant that it began a few weeks before the old leader's death. Blum, trying to convince Jules Moch of the necessity of the withdrawal, said, "The parliamentary group must not embark on the opposition which, added to that of the 'two fronts,' would make any government impossible."[101]

Blum remained faithful to a line imposed upon him by the hierarchy of urgencies and dangers that he had fixed for himself and taught to his party. Was he a democrat, then, more than he was a socialist? In the inexhaustible debate about him, we can suggest that the first goal—the socialist goal—was dominant for him until 1933–34. He then preferred to keep the Socialist party from any participation in power, in order to preserve it for the specific tasks of the establishment of social justice. It was only later, after the consolidation of Hitler's power, that he agreed to compromise his party in a role which had become primary in his eyes, that of the republic and democracy. Thus he went on, from the Chautemps government to the Marie cabinet, serving as a noble façade for clever tacticians who had the virtue, as he saw it, of not being totalitarians.

It was while he was still a prisoner of this strategy of "republican defense" that he published in *Le Populaire* on July 9, 1948, following the 40th congress of the SFIO, the most eloquent and coherent justification for the position:

> A Socialist party cannot refuse its participation or its support—which, theoretically and practically, amount to the same thing—when it makes up the indispensable element in any possible majority. It cannot refuse it when its cooperation is indispensable to the continued existence of the democratic institutions which are the breathable atmosphere and the healthy environment which socialism needs. Or rather yes, there is a way to avoid the ordeal. But there is only one.
>
> That would be to hold ourselves entirely and rigorously outside parliamentary life, and therefore outside political life. It would mean condemning and forbidding ourselves political action in any form, electoral action as well as parliamentary action; boycotting universal suffrage as well as the Chambers; having neither electors, nor candidates, nor representatives in any kind of elected assembly. This is conceivable, arguable, and it has in fact been argued, but by socialist anarchists.
>
> To deny all value to political action—electoral, parliamentary, or governmental—in the conquest of power by the proletariat and,

in general, in the revolutionary process, is to take, I repeat, a conceivable and arguable position, but it is to place oneself resolutely and completely outside socialism and particularly outside Marxist socialism. We are Socialists and Marxists. Therefore, not that or not us.

To refer to Marx in order to defend what Lenin called "parliamentary cretinism" was an ingenious twist. Besides, the argument is attractive. At least more attractive than the politics he often justified.

The Fine Passion for Analysis

A few weeks later, Blum gave up the responsibilities of power for the last time. In November 1948, he underwent a serious operation which forced him into a silent withdrawal until late spring 1949. But before taking this long vacation, he had to surrender to the fine passion for analysis, and to fix his ideas on the dual problem of communism confused with Stalinism and the caricatural Gaullism of the RPF. After the pan-Stalinist conference of September 1947 and the success of the RPF in the municipal elections of October, he summed up the situation.

First of all, confronting Gaullism, he had to respond to the argument which presented him as a precursor of de Gaulle on the question of strengthening the executive and the "presidential system." False, retorted Blum, first because the 1941 plan did not exclude the counterweight to personal power guaranteed by political parties and because the "broad regional autonomy" which he advocated would also restrain excessive concentration of power; second, because his long visit to the United States in 1946 had allowed him to see close up the defects of the system; finally, because when he returned from deportation, he had understood that the transformation of presidential power (of the democratic variety) into personal power (of the Caesarist variety) might be impossible in the United States but it was perfectly possible in France. "I feared that by urging one in argument one would end up with the other in fact. Where did this worry come from? From the general condition in which I found the country, and also, I state it as calmly as I think it, from the person of General de Gaulle." Blum concluded:

> Yes, I placed the theory of presidential power on a back burner, I put it at the bottom of my preoccupations. Yes, I became convinced that the combination of the institution, the circumstances as a whole, and the man would represent a danger for public freedom. Parliamentarianism is not the only form, and it is not the purest form, of democracy. I have said and written it a hundred times and I will not recant now. But in the France of today, in the overcentralized France in which monarchical and Bonapartist traditions

have left so many traces, in the France from which totalitarian
poisons have not yet been eliminated, any campaign of disparage-
ment against parliamentary institutions is a Caesarist attack on
democracy.

When the moment came to define the movement as it then expressed
itself, sponsored by General de Gaulle, Blum used the cruel word
"Boulangism."

> It would be perfectly ridiculous to compare General de Gaulle to
> General Boulanger. But it is entirely natural to compare Gaullism
> to Boulangism. In both cases, it was a matter of substituting per-
> sonal power for democratic authority. No more than Gaullism did
> Boulangism have a doctrine or a program. It adopted the Napo-
> leonic devices of calling on the people and the plebiscite because
> experience had proven their usefulness: they allow one to cover a
> dictatorial construction with a vaguely popular whitewash, which
> in any case peels away quickly. But for Boulangism that was only
> one means among many others. It had only one real aim: to
> transfer sovereignty to one man, to install in a form of power of the
> same essence as monarchical authority or military command the
> man who was its leader. Without the person of Boulanger, Boulan-
> gism was nothing and could be nothing. What would Gaullism be
> without General de Gaulle? . . .
> I have said how much General de Gaulle, as a human being,
> differed from General Boulanger, and that there would be some-
> thing shocking in the comparison. But the Gaullists would be no
> less Gaullist, and in the same way, if General de Gaulle were only a
> General Boulanger. And the men capable of measuring and
> evaluating the difference are not Gaullists.[102]

Speaking of the Communists (or more precisely, of the PCF of the
1940s), Blum was no more timid. This is his reply to the report presented by Thorez to the central committee of the PCF in November
1947. Blum called it the *mea culpa* of the Secretary-General which had
been imposed on him by Zhdanov at the Polish conference of September 1947:

> Thorez confesses his treason, that is his long association with
> the Socialist party, from 1935 to 1947, from the Popular Front to
> the Resistance and the governments of the Liberation? What can
> we answer him, except that he is even more a "traitor" than he
> confesses. Maurice Thorez is today a repentant "criminal," but he
> was as hardened a "criminal" as any of his accomplices. Let us go
> back just to the beginning of this year, when the question of re-
> newal was posed for the purely socialist cabinet. Do you recall
> with what unanimity, with what conviction and energy the Com-
> munist party invoked democratic principles to call for the forma-
> tion of a coalition government in the image of the country? It called
> for one again after the government crisis last May. It called again,
> and more imperiously than ever, on the eve of the municipal elec-

tions at the precise moment when it was touched by grace, for a coalition government in the image of the country, that is, a government of friendship or alliance with the Anglo-Saxon imperialists. Yes, of course, Maurice Thorez is right to beat his breast: his friends, and he above all, are indeed guilty!

And how were they touched by grace? How did they become conscious of their sin? How was the long fabric of errors unraveled before their eyes? It is here that, in my opinion, we should find some reason to grant them indulgence. Their conversion is not the result of events; it is not a lesson from experience from which we might have profited as well as they. It is the effect of a miraculous revelation brought to Warsaw[103] or elsewhere—there is still no certainty about it—by Stalin's legates. But we were not in Warsaw. We did not participate in the miracle. It is therefore natural that we continue to think and act as Maurice Thorez and his friends have done for more than thirteen years, until the fateful moment, that is, within the framework of the reality which we know and according to that reality. Not having received the illumination of the miracle, we continue to think that they were in the truth yesterday, and that today they are deceiving themselves.[104]

This reply by Blum provoked an indignant denial in *L'Humanité*, not from Thorez but from his faithful lieutenant Georges Cogniot. Cogniot asserted that the Secretary-General of the PCF had not said *mea culpa;* he had simply said that the party "had made some mistakes." In fact, we know from the former Italian Communist leader Eugenio Reale, representative of the PCI at the meeting, that the entire strategy of the PCF since 1935 had been denounced at the Polish conference. Since Thorez had not established the distance from Moscow of his two successors, he had to give in. It is legitimate to think that the self-criticism of the PCF delegation went just as far as Blum said it did.

The most original and the most topical contribution of Blum's analysis of Communist practice did not however have to do with its clerical and dogmatic aspect but with the description of Stalin's deep designs. In a series of articles entitled "Communisme et gaullisme" in *Le Populaire* from November 3 to 5, 1948, Blum presented with impressive forcefulness an argument which can be summed up as follows: by encouraging the PCF to shift from the Popular Front strategy to a strategy of insurrectional violence, Moscow was playing the card of the establishment of a Gaullist regime in France which, however disastrous for the PCF, was most apt to damage American interests in Europe. (Who can fail to see that this prognosis was verified in 1958? In 1968? It is even tempting to reiterate it today.)

It is as though the Communist Party were determined to bring to power a personal dictatorship whose first concern would be to eliminate the party itself by any available means, a dictatorship over which the party would have no appreciable hope—at least not for a long time—of recovering the advantage by a direct confrontation. The dominant preoccupation of the Soviet leaders at the present moment is not to bring their fifth column to power, neither in France nor probably anywhere else. The only contest which concerns them and to which they are wholly committed, they, their satellites, and their fifth columns, is the worldwide contest against the United States. What can most certainly thwart American policy in all parts of the world? What can most seriously interfere with the application of the Marshall plan? . . .

If one thinks about it for a moment, the *answer to all these questions,* with respect to France, is named quite simply *de Gaulle.* It is the establishment of Gaullism in power, in France, which has the greatest chances of disturbing France's relations with Great Britain and the United States, of provoking divisions among the . . . states participating in the organization of Western Europe. . . . of muddling the application of the Marshall Plan . . . I conclude from this that if the French Communists carry on activities in France which favor de Gaulle's accession to power, and if the Moscow leaders urge de Gaulle to power, this is done knowingly and willingly, not so that a victorious counteroffensive may remove him the next day, *but in order for him to remain in power.* . . Would de Gaulle in power act in a way that favored this plan? . . . Well, he would not take a public position against "Western policy," but he would subject it to arrogant conditions which would change its spirit and would practically paralyze its execution. He would demand for France . . . primacy, military command, political leadership. He would introduce into international relations the brusque, "will to power" and the great traditions of monarchical and Napoleonic France. In a short time, he would destroy confidence, block the mechanism, in short demolish the construction which is slowly and laboriously being built up before our eyes.

By proceeding in this way, would Stalin and Moscow's leaders sacrifice the most obvious interests of the French Communist Party, and perhaps even its existence, to serve the ends of their anti-American international policy? No doubt, but does that objection invalidate the argument? What importance does the French Communist Party have for them? It is for them only a pawn on the chessboard, or if you prefer, only a regiment in the army engaged in a great battle.[105]

He had said what was, for him, essential. First, to the Gaullists, that the fate of the country could not be confused with the destiny of one man, and that, since the democratic Republic was indissociable from the existence of political parties, any regime which intended to proscribe them was condemned to Caesarism. Second, to the Communists, that the cause of the French proletariat could not be confused with the strategy—even if it were peaceful—of a Great Power, and that to claim to distinguish between socialism and freedom was to kill socialism. These were all things he had already said, either with Jaurès a half-century earlier or at the congress of Tours, but current events strongly encouraged him to repeat them.

These were the themes of the articles which he continued to publish, of the lectures he delivered (notably on the centennial of the 1848 Revolution), of the prefaces he wrote—for the *Communist Manifesto*, and for the most controversial political work of the day, *The Managerial Revolution* by James Burnham, to which we will return.

I Believe It Because I Hope for It

Sheltered but not isolated in the hermitage of Jouy, he wrote. His forehead had become a bit balder, his shoulders stooped. The house in Jouy-en-Josas was pretty but modest, one of those houses the "promoters" called a *fermette* before the word went out of fashion. It gave on the rue Calmette—now the avenue Léon Blum—in a place called Clos-des-Metz. The part one entered, through a country gate divided horizontally into two parts (for feeding animals), had three stories with four small rooms on the ground floor and two bedrooms at the top. From the little living room, whose window faced the charming garden planted with flowers and fruit trees, one opened a door on the great surprise: Jeanne Blum had made an enormous study of the old barn attached to the house. The study was furnished with only a long rough table and two or three armchairs, but there were the books, innumerable books, climbing like ivy up two of the walls. A vast bay window opened on the garden which, in summer, seemed to invade the house with its flowers, fruits and fragrances.

Blum passionately loved the house and its atmosphere. Perhaps he was never happier than during those years, in spite of the crisis of his health from November 1948 to summer 1949, which confined him for two long stays in the hospital. When he was there he saw only his wife, son, and daughter-in-law. When he recovered, he received many visitors. English statesmen, German intellectuals, socialist militants, and Egyptian or Israeli journalists took their turns in front of his large desk or next to his reclining chair. He listened and listened, enjoying other people, speaking little and briefly.

It is hard to evaluate today the intellectual authority he exercised. Any comparison to Colombey would be misleading, for there was no haughty reserve and no obsession with power. He was neither Sartre twenty years too soon nor Renan fifty years too late. In spite of his *Eckermann* it would be inappropriate to speak of Weimar.

The Cold War was raging. The Korean War would soon break out, in

June 1950. European unity was in its infancy: the Schumann Plan was exactly contemporaneous with his death. But he already found Europe quite provincial, bourgeois, and a bit fearful. It was of course a good idea to overcome Franco-German antagonism. On this level, he applauded Schumann and Monnet. But the club was rather exclusive, reserved for the rich.

The fevers of the "Empire" troubled him deeply. During those years, while the SFIO was becoming bogged down in repression overseas—1950 was the year when Bourguiba made a final effort in France to prevent the worst, and Sidi Mohammed Ben Youssef posed the problem of Moroccan independence—he was already encouraging the anticolonial activities of the same Jean Rous who had so severely attacked him at the 1946 congress. What was important was the liberation of the peoples. How could the Indochina War, which had begun when he was in power, be brought to an end?

He had become a kind of consulting doctor for politics whose advice was sought in extreme cases. But some of those close to him have indicated that he was often more than embarrassed; he was filled with anguish. Most of those whose advice he had always sought were dead. More seriously, the debates which they wanted him to judge did not directly involve him and did not make him run any risks. The role of advisor without responsibility troubled him. Therefore he "reported" as he had in the past in the *Conseil d'Etat,* competently and scrupulously but without the boldness he had demonstrated during the time of "action."

In early February 1950, P. -O. Lapie received a phone call from Blum; Blum wanted to see him in Jouy-en-Josas to speak of the work of the UN in which the visitor had just participated. This is one of the last portraits we have of Blum. " 'I'm an old codger,' he said, reclining on his bizarre chaise longue. He was worried about the fate of the government (the Socialists withdrew three days later). He still had a little gleam in his eye when he spoke of Bidault. At the name Coste-Floret,[106] he spat out: 'He's a lu-na-tic!' I had never seen him so furious."[107] They spoke of Indochina, the UN—about which Blum had too optimistic, too idealistic a vision. Lapie did not manage to draw him out on the question of Israel, which, that day at least, "he didn't want to hear about." Talking of North Africa, he vigorously criticized the "hypocrisy" and emptiness of French policy. When Lapie took his leave, he said softly, "Come again, I have time. I only need idleness."

Idleness? He was still writing several articles a week. From March 1–30, 1950, there were eleven editorials in *Le Populaire* on the British elections and on Stalinism, on various electoral methods and on Thomas Masaryk, and on the death of his friend Harold Laski[108]—

three days before his own death. There was no intellectual weakening.
One can even say that his last article, devoted to the problem of working-class wages and dated March 29, 1950, is one of his best.

> Working-class income in the France of today remains inadequate.
> It does not provide a decent life, a normal life, a human life for a
> considerable proportion of the wage-earners. The bourgeoisie
> knows that the workers are right. Their demands express their own
> needs and not the tactical maneuvers of communism. The
> bourgeoisie had a bad conscience. While the law of American
> capitalism, for example, is "Allow new businesses to come into
> being," it seems that the law of French capitalism is: "Allow old
> businesses not to die." But French capitalism cannot achieve the
> unnatural goal without the tolerance or even the active interven-
> tion of the state. This is what must change. In order to preserve
> economically weak producers, it is necessary both to set wages too
> low and to set prices too high. These privately administered rates
> are intolerable . . . Since wages and prices are set at the level of the
> economically weak, that is, wages too low and prices too high, one
> can imagine the profits of companies with modern equipment and
> organization, working in conditions comparable to those of large
> international industry. These excessive profits could be threatened
> only by foreign competition, but here, too, our monopoly capital-
> ism counts on the tolerance or the active intervention of the state.
> Does the government realize that the problem of working-class
> pay, whose solution cannot be delayed, is connected, I would say
> almost subordinate, to the problems of the organization of produc-
> tion? I hope and believe that is true. I believe it because I hope for
> it.

This article was entitled "Les Salaires et la production." On the day
it appeared, Blum had an appointment with Jules Moch, who wanted to
ask his advice about a book he was writing. But when Moch arrived in
Jouy, the former Minister found Blum stretched out as usual in his
chaise-longue and in animated conversation with Félix Gouin, who had
come unannounced to talk about the campaign being conducted against
him around the so-called "wine" affair. The petty argument had tired
the old gentleman; Blum asked Moch to postpone their conversation
for a couple of days. There was all the more reason, because later in
the afternoon Blum was to visit his old friend Oreste Rosenfeld, who
was celebrating the hundred thousandth subscription to *Le Populaire-
Dimanche*.

In this atmosphere, Blum was playful and relaxed. But in talking
with Guy Mollet, Secretary-General of the party, about the meeting of
the COMISCO (Committee of the Socialist International) which had
just been held in Hastings, he could not hide the disappointment he felt
at the slowness with which this movement, the dream of his life, was

getting underway. "It's long, it's slow," he murmured. He left his friends of *Le Populaire* around seven o'clock. Shortly after his return to Jouy, he called Robert Verdier, as he did every evening, to discuss the latest news and outline the next day's newspaper.

That March 30[109] his friends learned that he had had a bad night. But he didn't say a word about it to Verdier or Daniel Mayer. That morning, he read and signed, along with Gide, Mauriac, Camus, and Bourdet, an appeal to the head of the Italian government, de Gasperi, to prevent an "inhuman exchange" of Ukrainian and Baltic refugees in Italy for Italians imprisoned in the USSR.

During lunch, he confessed to not feeling well. But he wanted to write two or three letters on the political situation, and he sat down at the work table in the little living room, facing the rhododendrons in the garden.

Shortly before three, he felt a painful sensation weighing on him. His wife helped him to lie down on the little bed facing the window, where he often rested. He did not seem to be in pain. He murmured softly: "It's nothing. Don't worry about me."

A doctor from Jouy came first, then another from Versailles, then a third from Paris. Then his old friend Parof came. Blum was struggling against death. Shortly before four, his heart stopped beating. A coronary. Notified around three, his son and daughter-in-law had still not been able to arrive on time. A half-hour later, the stricken voice of Renée Blum was heard at *Le Populaire:* "A heart attack."

Vincent Auriol, President of the Republic, was one of the first to arrive. Subsequent visitors found him at his comrade's bedside, near Jeanne Blum, who was prostrate. Stretched out on the little bed, Blum's long body was covered with a violet blanket. The now waxy face had become still thinner, a Pascalian spareness. The sharp bridge of the nose, the powerful jaw, reminded those who saw him for the last time that this Athenian had been a fighter.[110]

Toward 7:30 in the National Assembly, Edouard Herriot, with feeling and simplicity rare for him, paid tribute to his old schoolmate who "leaves the example of a spirit who rose above all circumstance." The chamber decided that Blum would have a national funeral ceremony.

The body was removed the next day, in the presence of the Auriols and the current head of government, Georges Bidault. The ceremony was set for Sunday April 2 in the place de la Concorde. In the meanwhile, the body of the leader of the SFIO was laid out in the entry hall of the building into which *Le Populaire* had recently moved, on rue Lafayette at the corner of rue Cadet. Every quarter-hour members of the party's managing committee, his former Ministers, and his colleagues relieved each other at the coffin. A quiet crowd filed by endlessly. As a young reporter on *Combat,* brought along by a stricken Georges Altschuler, I learned what was meant by an expression of respect without ostentation.

On Sunday, a hail storm battered Paris—alternating with brief bursts of sunlight. Two platforms had been set up on the place de la Concorde, one for official and foreign personalities, the other for the dead man's companions. Between the two, there was a little dais reserved for Vincent Auriol, and Jeanne, Renée, and Robert Blum.

From *Le Populaire* to the place de la Concorde, the cortege had been preceded by a hundred miners from Pas-de-Calais, wearing their work clothes and carrying their mining lamps lit up beneath the stormy sky, and by 300 red flags draped in black. Played softly by the brass of a band from Nord, *L'Internationale* paced the march.

The speeches were heard with difficulty—Vincent Auriol more moved than moving, Daniel Mayer as moving as he was moved, Guy Mollet, Yvon Delbos, and in the name of the International, the Belgian socialist leader Louis de Brouchère. Rain and hail soon chased away those who were not bound by deep attachment.

"Then," writes P.-O. Lapie, "the soaked ambassadors went toward their cars, the Republican Guard flowed away, the immense wreath of red roses sent by Churchill shed its petals, the storm moved off toward the Arc de Triomphe, and the coffin remained alone."

Wondering at the "sudden clarification brought about by death," François Mauriac wrote the next day in *Le Figaro:* "What remains of the outrages that assaulted Léon Blum for nearly a half-century, from *L'Action Française* to *L'Humanité?*" Maurras's paper had disappeared. There remained that of Thorez, author of the abusive attack of autumn 1940. There was no point in expecting from the men of the carrefour de Chateaudun the slightest expression of fraternity, even posthumously. In a few anonymous lines, *L'Humanité* reported Blum's death "more than ever the object of the greatest praise from extreme reactionaries, [and from whom] the worst Fascists have taken the slanders launched against our party under the occupation." Evoking the dead man's career, the organ of the PCF described him as "the man of the destruction of working-class unity in Tours, 'non-intervention,' and 'the pause.'" "He still had opponents," wrote François Mauriac,

> but aside from the Communists, he no longer had enemies. He belongs to that very small number of beings whose life, when one considers it from outside, seems to be a slow rise, a constant march toward perfection. "Living degrades": the sinister quip by Henri de Régnier does not apply to Léon Blum . . . He did not leave this world in despair and overcome with horror. Léon Blum's time in power was a missed opportunity. But it is his grandeur not to have given in to bitterness nor to have concluded from

the failure of one generation that human destiny had failed . . . The example of Léon Blum reminds us that ennoblement is possible and that, despite all defeats, life is a contest which, until the end, we are free to win.

Georges Altman, editorialist for *Franc-Tireur,* organ of the socialist left which had hardly treated him gently, hailed in Blum one of the last political leaders "for whom dignity, the search for truth, human freedom, and respect for the rights of the individual cannot be separated from political struggle, even when it is revolutionary." Jean Guéhenno on the front page of *Combat:* "He had an admirable respect for the people and a horror of demagogy. The severest of dialecticians if he was speaking with men of his education, he had nothing but disgust for all the tricks, as soon as he had to do with the naïve thinking of the masses, with comrades who might have been deceived by rhetoric. It was then especially, he thought, that one must not lie. It was then that one must be absolutely truthful."

Foreign reactions ran deep. British Prime Minister and Leader of the Labour Party Clement Attlee hailed in him "the most eminent Socialist of his time and an admirable leader of free men." In Israel, the spokesman of Mapai, March Jarblum, declared: "Never since the death of Jarvis have I had such a deep feeling that humanity had just lost the man who was the expression of its conscience and that it finds itself a little more alone." The Spanish socialist leader Prieto, exiled in Mexico, wrote to *Le Populaire:* "World socialism has just lost its leader."

The body of Léon Blum had first been buried in the Montmartre cemetery, next to those of his family. It was soon transferred to the cemetery of Jouy-en-Josas where it rests in the shade of the ash trees, under a moss-covered stone on which is engraved these words: "Léon Blum, French Statesman, 1872-1950."

A CITIZEN AMONG CITIZENS

A Remarkable Power

Every public life, even one inspired only by virtue comes down in the end to the nature and use of a kind of power. From his speech as spokesman for the commission on the socialist program in April 1919 to the appeal launched from the rostrum of the Chamber on November 22, 1947, it is easy to identify in Blum the intellectual, moral, and ideological constants. It is much more difficult to discern the means by which his intelligence, sensibility, and will contributed so much to the political and social life of his time. We will attempt to break down this power into a few essential elements: an art of human relations, competence, and eloquence.

Jean Monnet, referring to negotiations he conducted with Blum in 1946 in the United States, wrote of him: "He knew how to establish contact with people, he loved them; they felt it, and there is no need to look elsewhere for the secret of the power he exercised over his contemporaries."[1] With a little exaggeration, one might be tempted to speak of a kind of strategy of empathy, but that would be rather short-sightedly cynical. We should not attribute to Blum the Franciscan benevolence of an indefatigable charmer of birds. He could be hard, biting, or supremely detached. To quote one of the people who knew him best: "He did not overestimate men. He knew them. He accepted them. Accepted in that way, everyone felt his equal."

517

It was this art of equality, it seems to us, which earned him such a broad audience, first in personal relations, and later in his role as orator. In the party, in Parliament, and at *Le Populaire*, many had long thought him haughty, locked in an ivory tower like a good intellectual. His myopia, the slightly mannered and precious character of his elegance, and his distaste for easy contact fostered this kind of misunderstanding for a long time.

He lingered seldom in the corridors of the Assembly. But as soon as a question was under debate, the attention he devoted to each objection, to every position, made barriers fall. Before being the one who proposed or replied, Blum was "the one who listens." He certainly loved to charm: but his method of doing so was simple: there is no better human contact than equal exchange.

When the moment came for a reply or a speech of his own, he could be seen armed with a few sheets of paper covered with precise notes, figures, outlines. He held them in his left hand like a player holding cards, but he almost never referred to them. His memory was prodigious. He had been thought for a long time to be absorbed by juridical, diplomatic, moral, and administrative problems. But when the occasions arose, from the Popular Front Chamber to the Riom trial, for debates on production, management, taxation, or armament, he demonstrated the same competence, the same ease.

It does not seem that Blum's authority came from seductive power, irresistible oratorical force of the kind that has been attributed to Mirabeau, Clemenceau, and Jaurès. Closer to that of Robespierre,[112] his eloquence was essentially based on the ordering and balance of ideas. He followed the precepts of Chinese grand strategy: never close the door in the opponent's face.

Earlier we referred to an observation made by Jean Guéhenno—that Blum, such a good dialectician with his peers, refrained from using his virtuosity with less-prepared audiences. This does not at all mean that he condescended, simply that he refrained from certain kinds of argument in certain situations. What characterizes Blum's discourse is its unity. Emmanuel Berl notes in his *Interrogatoire*[113] that what was surprising in the socialist leader was that he spoke to the miners of Lens in the same tone as he did to former students of the Ecole Normale or in the National Assembly. Take one of his campaign speeches in Narbonne or a study in *La Revue socialiste*. The thread of argument, the style, the eagerness to convince are the same. What bound his various listeners to him, despite all the sarcasms of conservative intellectuals about the "revolutionary in pearl-gray gloves," was the certainty these people had that Blum was speaking to them as equals.

Blum's "power" thus seems much less strange. A rational approach, not magic it is not surprising that his speech went through periods of eclipse when passion dominated reason and fear dominated logic: in March 1938 confronting the "right" in the Salle Colbert, in August 1946 at the Thirty-eighth Congress of the SFIO, in November 1947 when the Chamber of Deputies denied him office. Nothing was less "magical" than that power. Like virtue, reason had its misfortunes.

Socialism and Violence

"Léon Blum is not a socialist," wrote Alain to Mme. Halévy. "He is a Parisian radical." For others, Marx was nothing but a German bourgeois, and Proudhon the man who was capable of asking Louis Napoleon to make the police the instrument of changing the regime.

But it is difficult to say that Blum was not a socialist. To specify that he belonged to the Social-Democratic movement is to diminish him only in the eyes of those who are uninformed about the rich and progressive history of socialism. Perhaps things would be clearer if the terms were shifted and we spoke simply of democratic socialism.

What remains uncertain, even at the end of this long investigation, is the way in which Marxism informed and inspired Blum, or more precisely, how the idea of violent revolution is situated in his vision of historical development. Was Blum a Marxist? At twenty-five, he wrote in the *Nouvelles Conversations* that Marxism was losing "its armor" on all sides. In his contribution to the conference *Blum et la culture*, Louis Bodin said courteously that Blum's knowledge of Marxism was "incidental . . . more intuitive than scientific." In his preface to number 38–39 of *La Revue socialiste* (devoted to Blum), Bracke wrote: "Liking to point out that he did not have a "Marxist education," he was certain to have [with him] at difficult moments those whom the study of Marx had prepared to discern with the greatest possible clarity what divides and what unites the working class." Is this a pretty way of saying that the leader of the party often needed around him doctors of Marxism to light his path? Or that there was spontaneous agreement between traditional Marxists like Bracke and neo-Marxists like Blum?

Blum knew Marx only through Jaurès's mediation, and Jaurès had given Marxism a Gallic and idealist slant. Bracke, an old Guesdist, had read Marx "in the original," like Thucydides or the books for his *agrégation*. In the same issue of *La Revue socialiste,* Maximilien Rubel pointed out that Blum "recognized on every occasion the Marxist and Jaurèsian derivation of his doctrinal ideas." If as distinguished a Marxologist as Rubel detects a connecting thread need we be much more demanding?

It is best to refer to the texts. Not only to those which make up, according to Rubel, "the most significant contribution of post-war

French socialism to the spiritual patrimony of the international working-class movement"—the lecture Blum delivered at the Ecole Normale on May 30, 1947 and his preface to a book by James Burnham—but to the preface Blum wrote for the *Communist Manifesto* two years before his death.

Burnham's argument in *The Managerial Revolution* is fairly well known. The book was published in France in January 1947 with the title *L'Ere des organisateurs*,[114] which is a bad translation of the word "manager" (all things considered, *directeur* would have been better). The word is in the text of the book, and Blum uses it in his own argument. According to Burnham, a philosophy teacher and former Trotskyite, the approaching collapse of capitalism does not open the way for socialism but for the power of the "managers" established as a class, for a regime which today would be called technobureaucratic. Asked to write a preface for this curious work, Blum saw above all an opportunity to profess his socialist faith:

> Mr. Burnham intends to demonstrate that it is possible to destroy capitalism without establishing socialism [while] the conclusion one may legitimately draw from his analyses is less original. I would formulate it this way: it is possible to destroy capitalist property without destroying capitalism. Capitalism is not completely destroyed if the suppression of private ownership of the means of production leaves standing the set of economic and social relations which it has created: wage earning, authoritarian forms of business management, basic injustice in the distribution of wealth, the collection of profits without work or as an undue addition to the normal remuneration for work. I would even say that capitalism is not completely destroyed if the suppression of private ownership leaves standing the moral relationships derived from it, I mean the hierarchy of men corresponding to the presumed hierarchy of conditions and jobs, and which is expressed by *inequality* in all forms of human behavior. . . .
>
> The managerial regimes of Mr. Burnham, far from constituting the definitive type toward which human societies are tending, represent an "intermediate type," a transitory solution, in the movement toward socialism.

What was necessary to move from the managerial "regime" to socialism, according to Blum? After pointing out that socialism admits without reservation that the conduct of planned production following modern techniques requires an elite of "managers" (on the condition that the recruitment of the managerial elite not be nepotistic and that the patterns of transmission not be distorted by heredity and by differences in wages so great that they would undermine "a general rule of equality of conditions, ways of life, and mores"), Blum explained:

> In order for us to settle in socialist territory, it is necessary and it is enough that the discipline [required by modern production] not

depend upon hierarchical obedience but on voluntary consent, which itself has as a condition the interest and affection brought by each worker to the common task, and his initiation into all the problems of management, which corresponds in another form to the deep meaning of equality. If we imagine that these changes have been carried out, managers would be only the individuals entrusted, because they were worthy and as long as they were considered worthy, with an indispensable and fundamental duty: they would no longer make up in the slightest degree a class or a social caste. The managers as a body would possess neither the characteristics, nor the coherence, nor the permanence, nor the privileges of a class. The capitalist residue would have been eliminated. We would be in a socialist regime. I might have summed up this long argument in a sentence. In order to transform Mr. James Burnham's managerial regime into a socialist regime, what is necessary and sufficient is to introduce democracy into it. Once capitalist private property has been destroyed, the free play of democracy is necessary and sufficient to eliminate the residues of capitalism, to prevent the establishment of technical managers as a privileged class, and to assure to all collective work its essentially egalitarian character.

Blum, who was so often accused of anti-Sovietism, continued his argument by suggesting that the "managerial societies which might emerge from a period of transition and confusion would tend toward socialism under the influence of a kind of democratic attraction. Perhaps this transformation unknown to us has begun in the Soviet Russia which Mr. James Burnham considers the model of the managerial societies of the future." (This was written in 1947, on the eve of the declaration of the cold war; the "managers" were Malenkov, Kruschchev, Kosygin, and Brezhnev.) Blum concluded:

I feel enlightened and strengthened in one [of the ideas] most dear to me, that the revolutionary transformation of the system of property and production is not an end in itself, but the necessary means and the indispensable condition for the liberation of the individual, which is an end in itself and the ultimate goal of socialism.

A few months later, in May 1947, Blum was invited to address the socialist student group at the Ecole Normale Supérieure. On that occasion, in a speech of a very human and touching spontaneity (of which we have only a stenographic report), he refined the famous distinction between the exercise and the conquest of power to which his name was attached, this time referring to Marx's teaching:

Revolutionary conquest by the working class conditions social transformation, that is the revolution [but] is not by and in itself the revolution [for it is possible that] the working class may seize control of the totality of political power by force, that it may be absolute master of state power, and yet that the control of the state not allow it, because of economic or other kinds of obstacles, to carry out the revolutionary transformation, [that is] not only the destruction of the juridical system of ownership, but the destruction of all the social, moral, and cultural relations and also all the international constraints which capitalism had created.

The "conquest" of political power does not answer all questions, to be sure. But is the simple "exercise" of power within the framework of capitalist society not more weighed down with insoluble problems than the bearer of social improvements—even if those "improvements" lead toward the socialist society of tomorrow?

We have two realities to reconcile. We are established in power within the framework of capitalist society, and we are obliged to exercise leadership faithfully, not only because of a rule of moral probity, but because it is quite obviously in our collective interest as a party and in the interest of the working masses of which we are the political expression. The Communists have always declared that as managers of capitalist society by the operation of democratic law, they would act in full conformity with the collective interest. One might support more subtle tactics which would consist of taking on the exercise of power in order to occupy with more ease positions which would facilitate the final destruction of the capitalist framework. But I do not want to attribute to anyone intentions other than those they express.

We therefore have to manage honestly and faithfully the society which has been placed in our hands, it is our duty as the holders of power. At the same time, we are socialists, and our actions, whatever they may be, tend toward social transformation and therefore toward developments and improvements which necessarily lead the capitalist society of today toward the social system of tomorrow. . . .

It often happened, considering the difficulties of the exercise of power which I witnessed and in which I was sometimes even more intimately involved, that I wondered who had been right: Proudhon and Bakunin, or Marx; however, I think it was Marx who was right: I think that a proletarian party which had repudiated political action,[115] which had grown silently, waiting for its hour, reserving itself entirely and in all its policies for that work, I believe that that party would have gradually lost the capacity and the taste for action. I believe that there is an impetus toward action which is necessary for the health of proletarian parties; I believe that political action was necessary for the political education of the masses.

. . . The contradiction which socialists experience from the exercise of power does not now present itself in the same conditions as in earlier periods of the capitalist system. I am not among those who say that the revolution has already begun in France, because capitalist property persists in its essential aspect of indefinite transmissibility and because the wage relationship persists in all its rigor. I do not think that we are in a revolutionary phase, but conversely, revolutionary problems have appeared, in the sense that a two-fold contradiction is becoming more and more acute: it is obvious that capitalism is less and less capable of organizing the productive forces from which it has arisen, and it is seeing the [democratic] institutions which it created moving away from it. The modern state is gradually moving away from capitalism, and this is why it is possible for socialist parties to manipulate it without mastering it, and with all the more reason without becoming enslaved by capitalism. They take possession of power by using it as an instrument in the struggle against capitalism, that is, by using the authority of the state to create conditions favorable to the advent of socialism.

Two years before his death, Blum was asked to write a preface for *The Communist Manifesto,* published a hundred years before. The tribute he paid to Marx—if not to all the Marxists—was without reservation. Having first emphasized the immense influences of this little book, which he could compare only to that of *The Social Contract,* he maintained that "after the test of a century, Marxism is more vital, more active, more influential than it ever was. The doctrinal foundations of Marxism [have been] consolidated rather than weakened by time."

> If something today could throw a shadow or a doubt on Marxism, it would be the very excess of spiritual devotion professed by some of its disciples; it would be the proliferation, around the literal texts of Marx, of fanaticism or idolatrous fetishism analogous to those which the Holy Scriptures or the works of Aristotle inspired in the scholastics of the Middle Ages. But this idolatry is in reality a heresy. In Marx, it is the spirit that counts, not the letter, and Marx's entire work is a permanent appeal to free criticism and to reason. . . . The entirely original contribution of the *Manifesto,* and Marx's true creation of genius, what has made one the point of departure of modern socialism and the other its uncontested master, is that he transformed the ideas of his precursors by introducing the concepts of class and class action, that he established in principle and in practice that the substitution of collective and common appropriation for capitalist ownership, which is the essence of the social revolution, could be achieved only by the workers themselves, internationally organized into a class party.
>
> Before Marx, there had been socialist thinkers, socialist schools, but there had been no socialism, and there were no socialist parties before him. . . . Marx's genius was to have been the first to assert that social transformation would be the deed neither of an indoctrinated bourgeoisie, nor of a democratized state, but that the liberation of the workers would be the action of the workers themselves . . . a class action by the proletariat [which] is the consequence of class antagonism, the law of history.
>
> In the current state of economic evolution, the exploiters are the owners of the means of production, the exploited are the wage-earners, the proletarians. The strength of the proletarians lies in

their constantly growing numbers. The initial revolutionary task will therefore be the bringing together of the largest possible proporton of the proletarians and their organization into a class party for the purpose of conquering political power. For the conquest of power, Marx does not rule out legal means; class action, when it is exercised within a democratic state, is thus extended into electoral and parliamentary activities. Grouping the mass of the workers, extending class action into the political domain, using universal suffrage to win legal majorities, these are the points of connection between socialism and democracy, and this is the way in which Marxism is democratic.

It is also international, asserted Blum; the founder's action of creating the International Workingmen's Association not as a successor to preexisting organisms but as a point of departure from which "will develop the various national parties" was exemplary. "The whole history of international socialism is outlined there in advance, in a prophetic anticipation."

> Marxism is in no way a fatalism: it involves on the contrary incessant stimulation of human will. But it inspires in men the exalting certainty that their effort is carried by the movement of history, that force of circumstances serves as a support, an ally, and a guide to their will. The dialectical process of the *Manifesto* shows the realization of socialism not only as the goal, but as the conclusion and the reason for being of human evolution.

In the conclusion, he expressed both his critical faith and his vigilance as a responsible political leader:

> The capitalist system probably has more strength of resistance than any of its predecessors in history. But Marx has shown us why it contained within itself the causes and the conditions logically necessary for its own disappearance. I also know that democratic socialism, that is, Marxist socialism, is dangerously compromised by the doctrinal and tactical deviations of Leninist-Stalinist communism. But I believe that Marx will prevail over his wandering or perverted disciples. Force of circumstances is there. Only the reason and the will of men could be lacking. It depends on each one of us that they function and that they triumph.

There are many ways of being a Marxist. One can be so as Mgr. Dupanloup was a Christian, M. de Polignac a royalist, and Marshall MacMahon a soldier: by seeing it as a solid, uncracked pillar to which one may lash one's total faith. One can also be a Marxist in the manner of Rosa Luxemburg or Antonio Gramsci—finding in it a system of questions and answers related to the anguish of being responsible for a society which is and will long remain unjust.

Trotsky made little of Blum's Marxism, asserting to his young disciple Fred Zeller[116] that there was "nothing Marxist in an article by

Blum." But considering the analysis of French society in 1936, it is legitimate to ask who was more Marxist—that is, who was the observer more aware of the real relationships between social and economic forces, the more exact analyst of collective tensions. Would Marx have dared to assert in 1936, like Trotsky, that "the French revolution has begun" because, confronting an intact state apparatus, a capitalism in a state of rapid change but vigorous nonetheless, and a class of employers temporarily disconcerted by lost elections, hundreds of thousands of workers camped in their factories? Marxism is first of all the knowledge and critique of reality.

Was Blum more a Marxian than a Marxist? Perhaps. He was certainly closer to the young Marx—analyst, historian, sociologist, journalist—than to the majestic leader of the International. Brought to Marxism by the Hegelian Lucien Herr, confirmed in his attachment by the idealist Jaurès, maintained in his faith by the free spirit Bracke, Blum could not use Marxism as armor. Given that class antagonism is the motor of history, that capitalism bears within itself the seeds of its own destruction, but that this operation must be carried out by the workers organized into a party and thoroughly prepared to exercise power, Blum, believing all this, took it for granted that he was a Marxist. Was this an abuse of language? Let us observe that he especially laid claim to the title when there was danger in doing so—notably under the occupation.

Yet there is a point on which his writings, and even more his career, make him diverge strongly from the teachings of the philosopher of Trier: the question of the recourse to violence. Not that one made it a necessary precondition for revolution, not that the other ever ruled it out. On this point we have quoted, from the speech of 1919 to that of the 1946 congress, dozens of Blum's texts admitting that no socialist worthy of the name can confine himself to legality and non-violence. But he placed so many conditions on the passage to armed struggle, he was so suspicious of "Blanquism," he criticized "putschism" in such detail, he was so intent on winning the battle without firing a shot, that one may wonder where he located the qualitative strategic change, the passage from "maturation"—a word which he held dear—to the break.

In his strategy, almost everything depends on the brains of headquarters, little on the infantry, nothing on the cavalry. But from the fact that Sun Tse delivered precepts for winning wars without fighting, the laws of "non-battle,"[117] must we conclude that Sun Tse was antimilitarist? Marx was not in favor of illegality on principle. He certainly believed that violence was a midwife of societies. But he tends to advocate the "break." Let us say that Blum emphasized rather the work of maturation which precedes that break, and the process of assimilation which follows it.

On "His" Jewish Question

Shortly after Blum's death, André Blumel[118] published a pamphlet entitled *Léon Blum, juif et sioniste*. The formulation is a bit heavy-handed.

Léon Blum was of Jewish origin—his mother was attached to the religion of her ancestors; the study of Judaism played a role in his youth; he grew up in a neighborhood that had a large Jewish population and in a mainly Jewish social and professional environment. But from the age of seventeen, even before his entry into the Ecole Normale, we can say that the young man placed himself outside any religion. Not that he ever stopped showing the deepest attachment to his family or that he did not, once a year, and on the occasion of certain bereavements, make his way to the synagogue. But those are only signs of solidarity and family loyalty. His agnosticism and religious neutrality were fundamental.

His education had very little to do with Judaism. His Protestant friends, Gide among them, were struck by his ignorance of the Bible. The only Jewish philosopher whose teaching had influenced him was Spinoza. It can be said that he lived in a very Jewish milieu—his wives; most of his doctors (Bernard, Weil, Paraf); his friends (Porto-Riche, Bernard, Natanson, Paul Dukas, Romain Coolus, Grunebaum-Ballin). But the two friends who had the greatest influence on his life were Herr and Jaurès; and he was a close friend of Gide and the Berthelots, of Bracke and the Auriols. Did the Dreyfus Affair, through the shock of its injustice, awaken his Jewish consciousness? He himself said how reserved the Jewish bourgeoisie had been during the first phase of the Affair, when those who were leading him into battle were Herr, Clemenceau, Péguy, France, and Jaurès.

There is a very curious passage in the *Nouvelles Conversations avec Eckermann* in which the young Blum attributes to the Jewish "race" a specific revolutionary role. Recalling the origins of Marx and Lassalle, he maintains that the Messiah of the Jew "is nothing but the symbol of eternal justice" and that "the Bible says: 'a just man' when the Gospel says: 'a saint.'" But generalizations of that kind are not unusual for twenty-year-olds. What is striking in this passage of *Nouvelles Conversations* is less the role attributed to the Jews than the "distancing" of the essayist. He has little of the apologetic tone Nietzsche or Péguy would have adopted in dealing with the same subject.

To anti-Semitic slurs Blum responded either with silence or, when the attacks were public as in the Chamber, with vigorous words. To Léon Daudet and company, who jeered heavy-handedly at his Jewishness, he said: "I have already said and I will repeat as many times as I must that I take pride in it and that no one wounds me by recalling my origin." He reacted with more bitterness to an attack from Xavier Vallat; Vallat called him a "subtle Talmudist" on June 5, 1936, the day Blum was presented to the Chamber as Premier. Blum would have left the Assembly had his friends not held him back. Blum was a Jew, as Sartre would have it, because he saw himself as a Jew in the eyes of others. But then with firmness, ardor, and sympathy for his people.

In a message he addressed to a French Zionist organization in 1950 Blum said: "I have often been asked if there is a Jewish race. Scientists say not. But Hitler has given an incontestable definition of it. The Jewish race includes the men, women, and children whom Hitler condemned to total extermination."[119] There is also, it will be said, the passage from Gide quoted earlier,[120] in which Blum's former schoolmate at the lycée Henri IV attributes to the author of Stendhal a passionate belief in the superiority of the Jewish race and a systematic predilection for Jewish art and literature. Gide tried later, and badly, to explain the passage when Maurras had seized upon and thrown it in the face of the leader of the Popular Front. The fact that Blum overestimated Porto-Riche and Coolus is obvious. But is that a racist matter? He also overestimated France and Hervieu, and he always preferred, baptized or not, Jules Renard and Claudel.

Blum has been reproached for the choice of his closest collaborators in the party, on Le Populaire, and in the government. In the SFIO, his chief lieutenants, aside from Faure and Séverac, whom he had not chosen, were Auriol, Bracke, and then Monnet, Dormoy, Salengro, and Spinasse. On Le Populaire, Rosenfeld, despite his name, was not Jewish, and chief contributors included Dunois, Bidoux, and Verdier, in addition to Louis Lévy, Georges and Charles Gombault, Salomon Grumbach, and Daniel Mayer. In the Popular Front government there were no more Jewish ministers than in the cabinets that preceded or followed. There were indeed a number of Jews in his immediate circle, but hardly more than in all the other high level organisms with great technical demands in contemporary France. One can say, too, that the policy of the state was not influenced by that fact.

What is also surprising is the infrequency of his oratorical references to the great moments of biblical history and to the unifying force of the Jewish religion. When he spoke of socialism as a "religion," notably in his pamphlet of 1919, it was in reference to Medieval Christianity not to the Hebrew Scriptures. When he spoke of the care he had taken to protect his party from the worst ordeals in order to bring it safely to port—whether after the long period of non-participation from 1924 to 1934, or after the experience of the Popular Front—he did not refer to Moses but to the "retreat of the 10,000" and to Xenophon. His allusions and his eloquence were almost always Greek and Christian. Compared to a speech by Attlee, for example, a speech by Blum is notable for the absence of Biblical references. His style, more ordered than resonant, more insistent than attractive, really owes nothing to Judges or Kings. Sending him his latest book, Saint-John Perse inscribed it to "Léon Blum, quintessentially French writer."

From certain writings of the end of his life, notably the homage to Chaim Weizmann, some commentators—particularly André Blumel—have drawn conclusions about Blum's Zionism which seem unwarranted. Can one be a Zionist when one appears on every occasion as a pure product of the policy of assimilation which was one of the master strokes of the French Revolution? Can one be a Zionist when, as a deportee, one dreams and hungers only for French soil? Given the friendship he felt for Chaim Weizmann, his cordial relations with Marc Jarblum, and the ties between the movement and the Second International, Blum's tribute does not seem to warrant all the fuss. On September 1, 1947, commenting on the odyssey of the *Exodus* passengers who had been driven off on London's orders, Blum wrote: "Jews, a century-and-a-half ago, had no homeland anywhere in the world, no more than the proletariat did when Marx wrote his *Communist Manifesto,* but the free democracies made a home for them. I was born a Jew; for the last twenty-five years, I have done my best to help in the establishment of the "Jewish national home" in Palestine, and I never dreamed of leaving France." The parallel between the situation of the nineteenth-century proletariat and that of twentieth-century Jews was bold but significant. He believed that the discovery of a homeland created among proletarians duties of defense, without turning them away from the duties of internationalism; he considered that his French citizenship did not prevent him from helping other Jews to discover and solidify their own national foundations.

There were times when he saw excesses in Zionist nationalism, something "fierce and elemental"; he came to "condemn without reservation Palestinian terrorism" against the British authorities.[121] As for Bernard Lazare a half century earlier, something too nationalistic troubled him in the doctrine and strategy, as it also troubled Martin Buber, as though it were the reduction of a spiritual message to a political and military function, with the fanaticism that sometimes comes in its wake. But he never argued against the Zionist movement or the state of Israel. In 1929, he participated, along with Albert Einstein, in a conference of the Jewish Agency in Zurich. Immediately after the First World War, at the request of Zionist leaders, he interceded with his friend Philippe Berthelot to remove French opposition to the British mandate in Palestine—the condition for the creation of the "Jewish national home". The Balfour Declaration had in fact just made London the guarantor of the survival and development of Zionism. In 1937, he agreed to give his name to a colony (Kvar Blum) created in Palestine by an American Jewish association that made clothespins. In November 1938, at the request of Zionist organizations, he delivered at a meeting of the League against anti-Semitism (LICA) an attack against Hitlerism as "idolatrous fanaticism." After the Liberation he fervently pleaded the cause of Jewish "displaced persons" to his English Labour Party friends.

At the time of the creation of the state of Israel, he again intervened with the British leaders, his friends Attlee and Bevin, to weaken their opposition. Learning that the French delegation to the United Nations had received an order from Paris to abstain in the debate on partition—which implied the creation of the Jewish state—he wrote an urgent letter to Georges Bidault: "A strong majority in favor of the plan could frustrate Arab threats. Will we dissent on the only problem over which the USSR and the US are finally in agreement? It would be a failure of courage. Think again!"[122] He was the recipient of untold requests to act in this way: many Jews wrote to him to criticize his indulgence toward British policy. A certain M. Perez from Tunis wrote: "Finally be a good Jew, M. Blum, that is the only thing that counts!"

As an advocate of the Zionist state, he recognized in contemporary Arab reactions only unfounded rancor and the greed of petty tyrants. But we should not see in his sympathy for Israel a specifically Jewish attitude. This was the attitude expressed and demonstrated at the time by all the representative figures of French parliamentary democracy, from the Christian socialists to the Radicals, from the Gaullists to the social democrats—even including the PCF: the Soviet Union had just fully supported the creation of the Jewish state. Was it a simple reaction as a French Socialist Democrat? Hardly. Neither Herriot, nor Philip, nor Schumann could have signed the tribute to President Weizmann Léon Blum sent to Tel Aviv shortly before his death:

> A French Jew, born in France from a long line of French ancestors, speaking only the language of my country, nourished chiefly by its culture, having refused to leave it at the very moment when I was in the greatest danger, I nevertheless participate with all my heart in the admirable effort—miraculously transported from the realm of dreams to that of historical reality—which henceforth guarantees a dignified, equal, and free nation for all Jews who have not had, as I did, the good fortune to find it in their native country. I have followed this effort since President Weizmann explained it to me. I have always felt, and I feel so more than ever, in solidarity with it.

One may make allowances for friendship and circumstances. One may locate this text at its date and at its moment in Léon Blum's life. But one must nevertheless conclude that it is eloquent and significant. Hardly Jewish, Blum's politics were strongly pro-Zionist, and this at a time when he was also calling for the recognition of Arab rights in North Africa and the Near East. Perhaps Blum would have been surprised if he had been told that one day he would have to choose between the policy of the Franco-Syrian treaty and his encouragement of the Jewish state. He did not live to see that.

For the Emancipation of Peoples

What would socialism be if it were confined to a single country, aiming only to bring justice to the working class of one nation? Nothing was further from the vision of Jaurès. Blum was in good hands. What there was in him that was incurably Parisian and insidiously bourgeois did not however prepare him for the warm and multifarious vigilance which made for Jaurès's greatness. But if Blum was not always capable, as theater critic, of seizing the opportunities to denounce injustices of every variety, Jaurès's death seemed to awaken in him that kind of political sensibility. On July 14, 1920, in fact, he wrote in *Le Populaire:*

> A certain number of Tunisians have just addressed to the French people an appeal which cannot be read without emotion and without shame. They demand from the old nation of the Declaration of the Rights of Man a written Constitution, the guarantee of civil rights and liberties, the complete participation of the people, without racial or religious distinctions, in the government of the country, "to the extent compatible with its international obligations"— that is, with French sovereignty. . . . What can one reply to that? Why should the diplomatic fiction of the "Protectorate" maintain under a pure tyranny men who can also claim the right of peoples and who have shown themselves worthy of freedom?

Seven years later, Blum again made an assault on colonialism, in a series of articles written for *Le Populaire* on a book by the excellent journalist Georges Le Fèvre, *L'Epopée du caoutchouc.* What is the share of the indigenous population in this wealth, product of "a soil which is theirs and of labor which is also theirs?" Blum asked firmly. He went on:

> In Indochina, where almost all goods are produced by something approaching slave labor, our work of colonization, of civilization, is being carried out in such conditions that we feel it is at the mercy of the first cry of revolt. We risk turning against ourselves both what remains of the barbaric in the natives and what is developing in them of the nobly human, I mean the spirit of hatred and the spirit of justice, the call of conscience and the call of vengeance. There is the real danger. Will we guard against it by attacks or speeches.[123]

Blum, in search of colonial targets, moved from Le Fèvre's book to one by Victor Augagneur, *Erreurs et brutalités coloniales,* all the more significant in his eyes because "the author is not, as we are, an opponent of colonial conquest, and what he deplores is not the injustice that has been done but the way in which it has weakened the willingness to work on the part of the natives of Africa and Madagascar, who were already so 'indolent.' "

Then Gide published *Voyage au Congo:* it was a perfect opportunity to extend a little further his reflections on the colonial system and its economic infrastructure imposed by the large concessionary companies. Blum's meditation extended Gide's observations; the indictment was broadened and deepened:

> We are still living with a set of ideas which have, in reality, changed very little since the time of slavery. The Black seems to us to have been created and placed on earth in order to work for the White, in order to provide profit for the White. The White can legitimately requisition the Black for his service, pay miserably for his work, and deprive him of the goods he produces for purely nominal pay. Where does he get this right? From the difference of colors, cultures, religions; from our innate belief in a system of human castes. Everything comes from that. . . . "The less intelligent the White," says Gide, "the more stupid the Black seems to him." . . . Nothing useful will be done as long as we have not attacked the notions which are at the basis of colonization, and above all the idea of the natural inferiority of races justifying dependence and subordination.[124]

Until 1936, however, Blum devoted his attention only sporadically to questions of the emancipation of the people. When the moment for the exercise of power arrived in June 1936, he chose well the men who were entrusted with changing the relations with overseas peoples: to the Ministry of Colonies he named Marius Moutet, an old Jaurèsist who had saved the Vietnamese patriot Phan Chu Trinh from death and thereby earned the friendly gratitude of the future Ho Chi Minh; to Mediterranean Affairs, he appointed Pierre Viénot and Charles-André Julien; to prepare a change in the status of Algeria, he put in Maurice Violette, who had been the governor in Algiers most hated by the "ultras." We have indicated the meager results of the Popular Front's colonial policies. But from the Franco-Syrian treaty to the institution of the Labor Code in Indochina, we cannot neglect what they tried to do.

It was after the Second World War that Blum was confronted most harshly with the problems of colonization. There is no doubt that his convictions had remained unchanged in this area. He believed more than ever in the necessity for the emancipation of dominated people.

Thus he unreservedly supported the constitutional proposals of his friends Pierre Cot and André Philip which were leading toward the construction of the French Union.

On the question of anticolonialism during those years, he was consistently on the left of the party. He clearly supported the anti-imperialist "line" of Jean Rous, whatever their other disagreements. When the leader of the Trotskyite faction asked him to help create the "Congress of Peoples against Colonialism" in 1949, alongside revolutionaries as militant as Messali Hadj, Blum did not hesitate to stand by them at the opening of the first session.

But during these years events constantly blocked his plans for colonial liberation. He had carefully followed the development of the situation in Indochina. He had approved the bargaining between Jean Sainteny and Ho Chi Minh, and the agreement that had come from it, recognizing Vietnam as a "free state within the French Union." A free state. He himself would have preferred the word independence—and the reality.

When the Vietnamese delegation designated to negotiate with its French counterpart in Fontainebleau arrived in Paris (soon joined by Ho Chi Minh) in July 1946, Blum greeted them cordially. His friend Oreste Rosenfeld brought "Uncle Ho" and Blum together for lunch. The two antagonists of Tours[125] greeted each other warmly. We know from a guest at the meal, Tran Ngoc Danh, that at one moment Blum turned to Ho Chi Minh and said: "I will be there at difficult moments. Count on me." Armed with this confidence, Ho declared to his young comrades when he left Paris on September 15: "Have confidence in Léon Blum, whatever may happen."[126]

In Vietnam, however, the attempt at a peaceful resolution suddenly halted. In late November, the bombardment of Haiphong ruined the negotiators' hopes. From Hanoi on December 7, Ho Chi Minh sent to Parliament and the government an urgent warning against the rising dangers: *Le Populaire* was almost alone in publishing it. They accompanied it with an editorial by Blum which was an ardent appeal for peace, on the basis of Vietnamese independence.[127] A week later, on December 17, he was designated as head of government, assisted by Moutet, Philip, and Depreux: how could war take place? Two days later, however, hostilities broke out in Hanoi; on both sides, there were men who were determined to prevent the peaceful meeting of minds about to take place between Ho and Blum.

When Blum presented himself before the National Assembly on December 23, battles were raging. A message sent to him by Ho Chi Minh had been held up in Saigon. Blum asserted that the government had been "obliged to confront violence" but that "the old colonial system which based possession on conquest and its maintenance on force, which fostered the exploitation of the conquered lands and peoples, is today a thing of the past," and that the government's only aim remained "the organization of a free Vietnam in an Indochinese Union associated with the French Union."

Six months later, no longer in power, Blum received a very curious letter from Ho Chi Minh:

> Mister Prime Minister and esteemed comrade,
>
> War has been making my country bleed for five months now. It is very painful for me to observe that this war [was] unleashed immediately after the adoption of the new French Constitution which condemns imperialism, that this war [was] unleashed and continued under a socialist government. Our friends the minister Eugène Thomas and Doctor Boutbien[128] have probably reported to you what they saw in Indochina: tens of thousands of young Frenchmen and Vietnamese killed and wounded; French business reduced to zero; dozens of cities, thousands of villages, railways, and roads destroyed.
>
>   . . . The only possible policy is the one you defined in *Le Populaire* on 12 December 1946: a policy of friendship and trust based on the unity and independence of Vietnam within the French Union. I hope that you will make efforts to bring into being this wise and generous policy which is yours.
>
> Affectionate respect to Mme Blum. Greet our friends Bracke, Lussy, and Rosenfeld. I embrace you fraternally.
>
>   Ho Chi Minh.[129]

In *Le Populaire* on August 6, Blum launched another appeal for peace:

> Yes, we must put an end to it . . . now that "peaceful order" has been sufficiently restored in Indochina, which was the only preliminary condition. Yes, we must speak as one people to another, not as the victor to the vanquished. Yes, we must negotiate with the authentic and qualified representatives of the Vietnamese people, whoever they may be, with no exceptions on personal or political grounds. Yes, Ho Chi Minh, who is not dead despite rumors to the contrary, who is very much alive, with whom M. Paul Mus [130] has spoken, from whom I received a personal message a few days ago through perfectly official channels, remains the authentic and qualified representative of the Vietnamese people. There is a glow in Indochina, and this glow must become dawn and then daylight.

This article provoked a reaction which strikingly illuminates the relations between Blum and the leaders of the Vietminh. On August 13, Blum received from Tran Ngoc Danh this message, which is typical of a certain Vietnamese romanticism.

> Mister Prime Minister, I have read and reread your editorial of 6 August, and it has moved me to tears. Everything in you shines. I see in you an arbiter, a benefactor to my country. May I be permitted to call you 'my father,' and to call Mme Blum 'my dear mother,' if you will allow it.

Such effusions show that Blum's moral authority remained very strong. Did he make all the use of it which one might hope from him? It is striking in any case that at moments when almost everyone gradually surrendered to the droning on of the ideological war and pretended to believe in the "Bao Dai solution," his voice was raised in 1949 to recall that the declaration recognizing the independence of Vietnam addressed to the former sovereign could just as well apply to Ho Chi Minh. A few months later he pointed out that the arrival of the Chinese Red Army on the Vietnamese border made "military action in Indochina even more problematic."[131]

In late 1949, he followed with the most ardent concern the attempt by Alain Savary, then a member of the Assembly of the French Union, to establish contact with Ho Chi Minh, and hailed the numerous efforts of his young comrade to prepare the way for political negotiations with the Vietminh. Two months before his death, on January 24, 1950, Blum launched this appeal: "Since the bases for peace are now established, let us make peace!"

The old socialist leader also sensed that in North Africa, and especially in Algeria, the general degradation of the system of domination called for a reshaping of Franco-Maghreb relations. Defending the status proposed for Algeria in 1947 by Edouard Depreux, Minister of the Interior (which the Assemblies of Algiers and Paris refused to pass), he described it as an attempt to "share between the two peoples (Muslims and Europeans) the free government of the land of Algeria" by finally breaking with "the chimera of assimilation." Admitting that the plan was "timid," he saw it as the "last recourse to preserve on Algerian soil the moral influence and political presence of France." Should we, in our turn, find him "timid"? Let us make the effort to situate this statement in 1947, two years after the massacres of Kerrata and Sétif. Let us note, at the end of his article, the formula of Algerian "self-government," which went well beyond the views of the authors of the 1947 plan[132] and was received with hope by young Algerian intellectuals.

Blum defended every inch of the way the UN's right of supervision over "non-autonomous" territories, French or not, and repeated a few weeks before his death, in *Le Populaire*[133]:

> Colonization, the maintenance of domination by force, the exploitation of men and wealth by constraint, all of that is disavowed

by modern law and morality, all that belongs to a past period in human history. Possession of territories which were colonized in the past cannot be continued against the will of the colonized people.

A Socialist Democrat

Legend has it that Blum was fragile and wavering, sinuous, feminine, yielding, specious. He was tall, strongly built, fond of the open air, devoted to physical exercise. A hearty eater, a respectable drinker of Burgundy, he was a man who made his decisions quickly, and held to them with a determination approaching stubbornness. Loving the company of women, like his masters Retz and Stendhal, he practiced friendship with delight, although his true friends were not always the ones who thought they were.

Very secretive about himself, Blum was passionately attached to his family. But of all the legends that were propagated about him, from that of his "golden dishes" to that of his effeminate tastes, none was more absurd than the one that accused him of taking steps to facilitate his son's career—unless one thinks it possible to use the presidency of the socialist parliamentary group to assure a young man's entry into the Ecole Polytechnique.

Shaped by Hellenism, imbued perhaps to excess with the lessons of the French seventeenth and eighteenth centuries, thirsting for "balance" and "rationalism," but convinced with Pascal that a man is admirable only in so far as he possesses contrasting virtues, Blum was above all an intellectual. A jurist, a moralist? Law was his profession, and he was permanently marked by it. In the legalistic, cautious, sometimes formalistic character of his behavior in Parliament and especially in government, there is reason to see a lawyer's reflexes: when he rejected Daladier's proposal to dissolve Parliament on February 7, 1934; when he refused even to consider advancing the date of taking on governmental responsibilities in May 1936; when he hastened to give in to the Senate's veto in June 1937; when he voted, in the name of his group (he was opposed), for the bill which accepted the Munich agreements. The concept to which his name will remain attached more than to any other, the "exercise of power," is profoundly marked by respect for the "contract."

A less juridical cast of thought would probably have led a pure politician, Marxist or not, to the same conclusions; the fact remains that Blum's behavior in the face of power was essentially legalistic.

This is why Blum's name and career are so readily associated with the formula of the "social contract." Rousseau revived the law with everything in society that was associated with the vital principle, and he thereby reinvented democracy. Blum could not lay claim to the same creative imagination: but we should not forget that he never ceased being an interpreter of the law, and that his decisions on the *Conseil d'Etat* were all marked by a boldly evolutionist spirit. His arguments were always based on social movement, on the fertility of communal life. Thus citizens have an obligation to obey the law only in so far as it reflects the evolution of society.

A jurist or a moralist? The socialism he had inherited from Benoît Malon and Jean Jaurès, themselves interpreters of Proudhon and Marx, was first of all a morality. This is where he joins or reflects Jaurès, in whose eyes socialism was not only the "inevitable" product of the contradictions of capitalism, as Marx had demonstrated, but also the desirable, the delectable fulfillment of human aspirations. Thus it was also a utopia. Thus Blum, addressing his constituents for the last time on the eve of the 1936 election, said to them with some irony: "I am not describing a utopia to you."

But it was less into institutions than into social practices that Blum the moralist projected his will. It is not a matter of indifference that he was the only French public man of his time to have attempted to modify the basic social unit—the couple. Nor is it a matter of indifference that he considered the fundamental work of the Popular Front to be the passage of measures introducing "democracy into the workplace," by breaking down the fundamental isolation of the wage-earner from the all-powerful employer. Taking as a priority intervention in social relations, he was thus less concerned with production relations than with the moral health of the group, and perhaps even went so far as to consider the latter autonomous from the former. A strange socialist? Fourier was no less socialist than Lassalle. Yet if there was an element lacking in Blum's education it seems to be Machiavelli—and Blum did not have the audacity to consider himself anti-Machiavelli. Not to mention Clausewitz. The extreme case, in Blum's career is of course the "non-intervention" affair. To claim to perform an action in order to attempt to persuade an adversary to imitate it—an adversary whose ideology and interest are based on contrary premises—amounts to acting like the sheriff locking himself in jail in the hope that the gangster will join him there.

"A man who wishes to do good in all things," writes Machiavelli, "must fail amidst so many others who live in evil." Blum would not have agreed. The figure in French history whom he denounced with the greatest fury was "the frightful Talleyrand."

This is not enough to make of him the model of the intellectual in politics. In an essay on the subject, James Joll compares Léon Blum to Walther Rathenau (whom the socialist leader deeply admired), and to the Italian futurist Marinetti, to formulate a kind of law of the pattern of failure of the intellectual involved in public affairs. These three careers, writes Joll, raise the question of determining to what extent "a man endowed with exceptional intelligence, sensitivity, originality, and independence can face up to the violence of the brutal political machinery of the twentieth century, whether the intellectual confronted with political life is not doomed to failure because of his very qualities."[134] For Rathenau, the "failure" consisted especially in being assassinated by precursors of Nazism for having been the signatory of the November 1918 armistice which put an end to the suffering of the German people. Marinetti's failure was a kind of political idiocy: plunging into the moral void of fascism.

The "failure" of Léon Blum, head of the Popular Front government, is more indicative of the failure of "the intellectual in politics," although we must note that it was less due to the person and the decisions of the statesman or the socialist leader than to the structure of a government within which its ideological opponents occupied key positions, and whose political allies had preferred to remain aloof from responsibilities—and to external factors which made the Spanish Civil War and the continual harassments by the Axis powers the backdrop against which the second phase of the history of the 1936–37 cabinet unfolded.

Most leaders of working-class movements or revolutionary parties were and are intellectuals. These men are not the only ones capable of considering society badly made; but it is their role, once they have discovered that fact, to seek the means to change it, to develop alternative theories, and (less frequently) to put into practice the conclusions at which they have thus arrived.

Is the intellectual condemned to the role of Hamlet? Giving great importance to analysis, is he condemened to devote too much time to it? Are non-adhesion to the Third International, non-participation in government from 1924 to 1936, and non-intervention in Spain three phases, or three faces of non-action, of a strategy of doubt which makes Blum the symbol of the non-active intellectual?

Colette Audry's argument, which structures her penetrating study *Léon Blum ou la politique du juste,* is well known. For her, who at the time was expressing the leftist theories of the *Rassemblement démocratique et révolutionnaire* of Sartre, Rousset, and Rosenthal, Blum was the archetype of the "guilty conscience" who sought, at the expense of the collective interest, his own solitary "salvation."

Blum's behavior in public life does not seem to us to conform to this pattern. Even in his unfortunate choice of non-intervention in Spain, and the justifications that he tried to provide for it, he was constantly looking for the "line" most likely to assure, not his glory, but the safety of the party over which he had assumed responsibility, and of the country in which that party inevitably played a role.

Blum's "realistic" politics were not precisely the ones dictated by his temperament, his education, or his noble vision of socialism. Nor was it fearful behavior: Blum's physical courage, from the violent days of February 1934 to the sinister time of deportation, from his wanderings in the provinces between June 10 and 25, 1940 to the Riom trial, is as obvious as his civic courage. Blum's defects were not cowardice or excessive flexibility, but rather a kind of temerity and an obstinate determination to stick to the decisions he considered good.

But is a public man whose declared program consists of changing the social order "by every means, even legal means" in a position to display such disgust for violence? We have quoted many of his writings which do not rule out any possibility. But one must grant more importance to deeds than to words. Blum's deeds were constantly denials of violence—I mean, of revolutionary violence.

This is not the place where he will be reproached for not having bourgeois blood on his hands. but his almost instinctive rejection of the possibility of mass violence—the demonstrations called by his friends in June 1937 and March 1938, his "Oh! no, not that!" addressed to Zyromski or Pivert—is a kind of infirmity. It is true that the "indulgent" also have their place in revolutionary pantheons. Camille Desmoulins survives Collot d'Herbois in men's memories, and no one becomes a Thermidorean more quickly and maliciously than a great leader of purges.

Blum's "indulgence" could be more certainly laid to his credit if it had not shown itself at times when horror was the rule. This is perhaps the fundamental reservation that historians will have when the time for definitive judgments has come: Blum, so great in his generosity, talent, character, education, and his desire for the common good, was an anachronistic figure. He was not perhaps a man for the time of assassins. Let us try to imagine Pericles at the time of the Barbarians, in the Rome of the fifth century, or Gladstone confronting Napoleon. Was this highly civilized man in the wrong role at the wrong time, marching for the *Fête de la Fédération,* for February 1848, for Bandung? Let us not dream. Blum would have been more appropriate at the time of the Antonines, the Encyclopedia, or John XIII. But it is perhaps his "inappropriateness" which makes him indispensable.

What accounts for the "weakness" is to be found less in Blum himself than in the framework of his life—social-democracy more dreamed of than experienced. Recently, defining the social-democratic concept of the state, Nicos Poulantzas saw it as an all-powerful subject, endowed with a specific rationality, incarnated by its ruling elites whose will alone determines the relations of the state to the bourgeoisie—a state in which an elite of the left would occupy the ruling positions, would keep the bourgeoisie in line, and "would lead to socialism by a kind of parthenogenesis."[135]

This specific rationality incarnated by ruling elites leading toward a socialist parthenogenesis refers less to Blum's vision than to the vision others have of him. As it has been practiced in Great Britain, Germany, and Sweden, social-democracy has its strength, its social truth. It is a style of life, a conception of the world. In France, there are survivals of it, which will perhaps soon be considered pioneering experiments, in Nord and Pas-de-Calais, and also, in a way, in the municipalities that have long been governed by Communists, the Paris region and Le Havre.

Blum had only a marginal role in the reality of social-democracy. To be sure, his attachment to men who expressed it and lived it, like Jean Lebas and Augustin Laurent, brought him close to it. But we should see in Blum less a social-democrat, a practitioner of social-democracy in its contingency, than a socialist democrat; that is, a man attached above all to preserving or promoting popular sovereignty, with a view toward assuring its extension in socialism.

Was this fundamental "democracy" experienced in the party? However ingeniously diversified the structures of the SFIO may have been, the party of Jaurès and Blum remained a pyramid, elitist, and voluntarist. There is no comparison, of course, with the automatic majorities of the neighboring party. Control by the militants remained a reality, initiatives could come from the rank and file. But, true and sincere a democrat as Blum was, devotee of egalitarianism as he may have been, he had been unable to extend democracy beyond its narrow borders, which explains why after his death, and for a long time, it was the hour of the bureaucrat.

Even if the rank-and-file militants had been granted total and immediate attention by the "elites" of the party, the contradictions in which French social-democracy is exhausting itself would have bound Blum. How can one preserve the integrity of the republican state while calling into question the economic system at its foundation, or destroy a system of production relations while maintaining the public order which conditions that system, or defend a panoply of freedoms that also serve as an alibi for the perpetuation of injustice? And how can this be done when these contradictions, also experienced in Great Britain, Germany, and Sweden, are worsened and accentuated in France by the existence of a social-bureaucracy more closely tied to the working class?

Until a genuine, reshaped, and enriched "common program" permitted the attenuation of this "contradiction in the contradictions," the

French social-democratic project was (remains?) for many a nostalgic dream in which Blum bravely lived and died.

Blum, more than any other man of his time, attempted to reconcile the conquest of justice and the defense of freedom. The fact that the balance between the two is constantly unstable, that whatever is lost by one is not necessarily gained by the other, that nothing which is conquered on one front allows one to turn away from the other—all of this Blum knew well. He had paid the price for that knowledge. But he never stopped fighting to unify the two hopes.

Justice was the great cause of his life—he called it socialism. And it remained his cause after he recognized that fascism and Stalinism could confiscate freedoms that had been won and condemn the "dis-alienated" working class to a new oppression.

Blum was the man most hated by the French bourgeoisie and by international fascists. After the congress of Tours, he was the favorite target of the spokesmen of dogmatism armed with the "Marxist" vulgate. But he also knew that even within the barbed wire of Dachau, one can talk to other men. He believed that, provided one does not despise, lie, ridicule, one can persuade.

This passion, this hope of persuading, is perhaps what is most exemplary about him. He was the man who believed he could change life by the force of words. He was the man who believed it possible to establish a politics on esteem, respect for the other, on the hope of convincing reasonably.

He desperately refused the mortal choice between the constraints of justice, the weight of "order," and the demands for freedom. He refused to choose one over another, and thus attempted to avoid transforming a question into conflict. He chose, for his last written words, these: "I believe it because I hope for it."

He did not believe in the political virtue of evil.

NOTES

Part I

1. Against the *communards* in 1871.
2. Notably Joel Colton, *Blum.*
3. Conversation with Mme. Lancrey-Javal, Lucien Blum's daughter, September, 1975.
4. Gregh, *L'Age d'or.*
5. Lévy, *Comment ils sont devenus socialistes,* p. 53.
6. Preserved in the Archives Nationales.
7. At night the calm water of pools / in the light of vague reflections / forms imaginary waves / and fantastic designs / there are bizarre cushions / embroidered with necklaces and rings / horsemen drawing their swords / flowers as large as breasts . . .
8. Gregh, *L'Age d'or,* p. 51.
9. Blum, *Souvenirs sur l'affaire.*
10. Vaillant, *Derrière le miroir.*
11. Fraser and Natanson, *Blum,* p. 56.
12. Benda, *La Jeunesse,* pp. 122–123.
13. Lévy, *Comment ils sont devenus socialistes,* p. 56.
14. Gregh, *L'Age d'or,* p. 114.
15. Audry, *Blum ou la politique du juste,* pp. 28-29.
16. According to François Mauriac, Blum's commentary on Jane Austen predicted the evolution of the novel over the succeeding half-century: "The characters are never expressed from the inside, through reasoning or psychological analysis, but entirely through attitudes, speech, gestures, and characteristic acts in the choice of which the novelist seems not to have intervened." "Bloc-Notes," *l'Express,* May 27, 1954.
17. The real Goethe, three-quarters of a century before Blum's Goethe, in the real conversations with Eckermann, spoke of him as a "powerful precursor," animated by a "vocation for the universal."

18. Lefranc, *Jaurès et le socialisme*, p. 89.
19. He registered at the bar in 1919, when his political commitment removed him from the *Conseil d'Etat*.
20. Charmes is Barrès's native village.
21. *Vendredi*, June 5, 1936.
22. Gide, *Journal*, p. 15.
23. Ibid., p. 228.
24. *Le Mercure de France*, July 1895.
25. *La Revue blanche*.
26. Bourgin, *L'École normale et la politique*, pp. 107–109.
27. Lévy, *Comment ils sont devenus socialistes*, p. 59.
28. Ibid., p. 22.
29. Unpublished letter, archives of the *Foundation Nationale des Sciences Politiques* (FNSP).
30. Andler, *Lucien Herr*, p. 107.
31. *Nouvelle revue socialiste*, July–August 1926, quoted by Ziebura, *Blum et le Parti socialiste*, p. 33.
32. Now the rue Guynemer.
33. Three years later, having become a general, he was almost carried to the presidency by Paul Deroulède who needed a uniform.
34. A local telegram or *pneumatique*.
35. Blum's hypothesis (1935) was verified by the later revelations of the Italian military attaché Panizzardi. According to the assertions of the great English journalist Wickham Steed in his *Memoirs,* this officer made very precise accusations against Colonel Henry, who, in concert with Esterhazy, had transmitted seventy documents to Schwarzkoppen. Since then there has been the publication of *Journal de l'affaire Dreyfus* by Maurice Paléologue, according to whom, in the period from 1894 to 1896, acts of treason must be charged to "an officer of very high rank who had for several years occupied very high positions in the Ministry of War." Was his target General Saussier, military governor of Paris, or General Rau, cabinet secretary of the Minister of War? Henri Guillemin has taken this position, with verve, but without being completely convincing. Léon Blum's hypothesis is more admissible.
36. A veritable call for murder.
37. It was an "Allemanist" journalist, Maurice Charnay, in *Le Parti ouvrier,* the organ of the movement, to which Lucien Herr was a contributor, who first called the validity of Dreyfus's conviction into question.
38. As though to justify the notions of his over-cautious comrades, he had been beaten at Carmaux.
39. Then head of the government.
40. The first one had convicted Dreyfus in 1894; the second one had acquitted Esterhazy in 1898.
41. In charge of the investigation against Dreyfus from September 1894 on.
42. Then Minister of War.
43. His successor.
44. Chief of the General Staff, and his adjutant (in charge of intelligence matters), respectively.
45. Maître Demange was Dreyfus's lawyer. Besson d'Ormescheville was the officer entrusted with drawing up the indictment in the first trial.
46. A lawyer to whom one of the members of the 1894 court-martial had confided as much.

47. During a recess in the trial, in the witness room in the Palace of Justice, Major Ferzinetti, seeing Captain Lebrun-Renault, had said to him: "You told me that Dreyfus had never confessed. Now you say the opposite. You are a liar." Lebrun-Renault was at a loss for an answer.
48. Former Minister of Justice, a Dreyfusard, who founded at the time the *Ligue des droits de l'homme*.
49. "The question will not be asked . . ." repeated the president.
50. Jaurès and Guesde had been defeated, but the socialists had tripled their representation.
51. A letter from Colonel Picquart, denouncing the forgery of the documents, had also alerted Cavaignac.
52. Among them Paul Valéry!
53. Malraux's novel had appeared eighteen months earlier.
54. Ziebura, *Blum et le Parti socialiste*.
55. He had lost his seat, as we have seen, in 1898, and won it back in 1902.
56. "Conférence sur Jean Jaurès," Théâtre des Ambassadeurs, February 16, 1933.
57. Ibid.
58. Alcibiades, as we have seen, was Clemenceau's nickname for Blum.
59. "Rencontre de Léon Blum et de Jaurès," *La Nef*, May 1950.
60. "Conférence sur Jean Jaurès." Blum on one occasion perceived the same "seal" in the gaze of Jean Perrin.
61. Ibid.
62. Quoted in Fraser and Natanson, *Blum*.
63. An article on Anatole France in 1904, *"En Lisant,"* in Blum, *Oeuvre* (1891–1905), p. 88.
64. See on this point Ziebura, *Blum et le Parti socialiste*, p. 58.
65. Marx's son-in-law was from Bordeaux.
66. Quoted in Goldberg, *Jaurès*.
67. The article was not published. (Was it too committed?) It is included in Blum, *Oeuvre* (1891–1905), pp. 493ff.
68. Auclair, *Vie de Jean Jaurès*, p. 294. Six francs in 1900 are worth about 100 francs in 1977.
69. Ibid., p. 297.
70. Renard, *Journal*, p. 897.
71. July 29, 1905. Unpublished letter, Fondation Nationale des Sciences Politiques.
72. Held at the Senate in March 1975, under the sponsorship of *La Société des amis de Léon Blum*.
73. Leader of the antimilitarist extreme left.
74. Revolutionary syndicalist leader, ardently internationalist pacifist.
75. In the index of the complete works, *La Colère* is called a "play in two acts."
76. Renard, *Journal*, p. 762.
77. He shared this signature with other contributors, but Louis Faucon has succeeded in identifying his articles. See Blum, *Oeuvre* (1891–1905).
78. Jean Jaurès had also fought duels, once with Déroulède on the Isle of Pheasants on the Bidassoa.
79. *Excelsior*, May 1, 1912. Quoted by Madeleine Rebérioux, "Blum et la production culturelle (1903–1914)" conference of March 1975.
80. Gide, *Journal*, p. 209.
81. Ibid., p. 228.

82. Rebérioux, "Blum et la production culturelle."
83. Ibid.
84. Robert Blum, who was a discreet colleague and adviser to Léon, and a loyal socialist militant, possessed, like his father, exemplary moral elegance. He died in December 1975. He provided us with innumerable details and suggestions.
85. Annette Vaillant, *Pain polka*, pp. 49–50.
86. Ibid.
87. Renard, *Journal*, pp. 528–529.
88. Le Bargy, *Sous de nouveaux soleils*, p. 76.
89. Renard, *Journal*, p. 520.
90. Blum, *Oeuvre* (1905–1914), pp. 6–7.
91. Unpublished, in the archives of the Fondation Nationale des Sciences Politiques.
92. Vichniac, *Blum*, p. 90.
93. Blum, *Oeuvre* (1905–1914), p. 163.
94. Ibid., p. 164.
95. See the catalogue of the exhibition at the Archives de France.
96. Statement of Paul Grunebaum-Ballin in Logue, *Blum: The Formative Years*.
97. It is also amusing to consult *Réponse au livre de M. Blum intitulé "Du mariage,"* a pamphlet published in Lyon in 1937, with a red, white, and blue cover, under the patronage of the "école des chefs," by a certain Max Bridge, the pseudonym of a lady who concealed neither her advanced age nor the horror created in her by the work of an author who was guilty of attacking the "beautiful French Race . . . Queen-mother of all human races!"
98. Jubilee volume of the *Conseil d'Etat*.
99. "Le Conseil d'Etat à travers les documents d'époque," *Histoire de l'administration française*, p. 704.
100. Logue, *Blum: The Formative Years*, p. 79.
101. *Recueil Lebon* (1911), pp. 139–140.
102. It asserted a political role in the course of the thirties.
103. Blum, *Oeuvre* (1905–1914), p. 596.
104. The trial of the wife of Minister of Finance Joseph Caillaux, for the murder of Calmette, director of *Le Figaro*, which was conducting a campaign of slander against her husband.
105. Blum, *Oeuvre* (1905–1914), p. 588.
106. Ibid., pp. 520–521.
107. *Stendhal et le Beylisme*, in Blum, *Oeuvre* (1905–1914).
108. Eight or nine current francs.
109. Ludovic Frossard, *De Jaurès à Lénine*, p. 10.
110. Soon after the crime, the comtesse de Martel, known as "Gyp," wrote that the killer, inspired by *L'Action française*, had done "fine work."
111. Goldberg, *Jaurès*.
112. du Gard, *Été 1914*, p. 303.
113. Barrès, *Mes Cahiers*, p. 735.
114. "Conférence sur Jean Jaurès," p. 9.
115. Fraser and Natanson, *Blum*, p. 133.
116. Rabaut, *Jaurès et son assassin*, p. 180.
117. Unpublished document, Blum archive of the FNSP.
118. Of whom Joseph Caillaux says in his memoirs that he was more intent on seizing occasions to fight than on listening to arguments for peace.

119. Frossard, *De Jaurès à Lénine*, pp. 11–12.

120. Ibid.

121. Caillaux, *Mémoires*, vol. 3, p. 198.

122. Fraser and Natanson, *Blum*, p. 118.

123. Ziebura, *Blum et le Parti socialiste*.

124. Preserved in the Léon Blum archive of the Fondation Nationale des Sciences Politiques.

125. Caillaux, *Mémoires*, Vol. 3, p. 197.

126. It was republished in 1936, shortly after Blum's accession to power. It can be found in Blum, *Oeuvre* (1914–1928), pp. 507–574.

127. Blum had already formulated the idea in the *Nouvelles Conversations*, twenty years before.

128. November 1917.

129. Ziebura, *Blum et le Parti socialiste*, p. 143.

130. From Marxist orthodoxy to the "realism" inspired by Kautsky.

131. The militantly pacifist left.

132. Paul-Boncour, *Entre deux guerres*, p. 18.

133. Frossard, *De Jaurès à Lénine*, pp. 39–40.

134. Notably in two editorials on July 6 and 23.

135. In his earliest analyses, Blum spoke of only nine, then seventeen "conditions": the twenty-one were not known, and then only by a few, until the eve of the congress of Tours.

136. He had the support of 10,000 volunteers.

137. Kriegel, *Congrès de Tours*.

138. Frossard, *De Jaurès à Lénine*, p. 162.

139. Destroyed by German bombs in 1942.

140. Of Vaillant's Blanquist "Central Revolutionary Committee."

141. This was the case for Marcel Cachin, who did not utter a word about this in his entire speech.

142. Regretfully, we can quote only substantial excerpts from it.

143. Kriegel, *Congrès de Tours*, p. 195.

144. Two years after this courageous speech, Frossard left the party, and later moved to the right.

145. *Le Populaire*, January 2, 1921.

146. Audry, *Blum ou la politique du juste*, p. 54.

147. Ziebura, *Blum et le Parti socialiste*, p. 167.

148. Julien left the PCF three years later, joined the SFIO, and became one of Blum's closest collaborators during the Popular Front.

Part II

1. Judt, *Reconstruction*, p. 20.

2. Paul Faure, *Le Populaire*, February 14, 1921.

3. Paul-Boncour, *Entre deux guerres*, p. 65.

4. "Reconstruction," for them, meant reconstruction of the International.

5. Blum is analyzing Rosa Luxemburg's last pamphlet.

6. She had been assassinated a year earlier in Berlin by the counter-revolutionary *Freikorps*.

7. The elections of 1924.

8. *Le Populaire*, July 15, 1922.

9. Barrès, *Mes Cahiers,* p. 851.
10. Judt, *Reconstruction.*
11. Fraser and Natanson, *Blum,* p. 170.
12. See Part 1.
13. See Gravitz, *Blum.*
14. Révelin died prematurely in 1922, having played a discreetly active role in support of Blum and at the head of the party.
15. Parliamentary victory of the *Cartel des gauches* in 1924.
16. Quoted in Ziebura, *Blum et le Parti socialiste,* p. 240.
17. Ibid., p. 276.
18. Reorganizing reparations as a function of German production.
19. The expression became famous and was often used against Blum by the right.
20. Annie Kriegel, *Preuves,* April 1966.
21. This "war-mongering" was that of 1939—resistance to Nazism.
22. *Le Populaire,* April 28, 1928.
23. Duclos, *Mémoires* Vol. I, p. 303.
24. Shot by the Nazis in 1943.
25. On this subject, see Depreux, *Souvenirs.* Although very favorable to Blum, Duclos declared himself opposed to his candidacy in the second round. Daniel Mayer, himself a member of the twentieth section, reports that Blum did not wish to contest the second round, in order not to be in the position of eliminating a Communist with votes from the right. It was the electoral tacticians of the party, like Fiancette, who carried off his consent.
26. Prélot, *Evolution politique,* p. 263.
27. Ziebura, *Blum et le Parti socialiste,* p. 305.
28. Account established by a conversation on October 15, 1976, between the author and one of the Socialist militants of Narbonne who contributed the most to establishing Blum in Aude, from 1929 to 1940.
29. With Sembat, from 1914 to 1916.
30. Signs and portents proliferated: this was also the time when Ludovic-Oscar Frossard, the one-man band of the majority of Tours, rejoined the SFIO.
31. Which Blum had refused to do a few months earlier.
32. Although Marquet distinguished himself as Minister of Labor in 1934 by a significant attempt at paramilitary conscription of the unemployed.
33. Déat, Montagnon, and he.
34. Bernstein, *Le 6 fevrier 1934.*
35. Ibid., p. 129.
36. The chief of staff, also known for his extreme right-wing opinions.
37. Ziebura, *Blum et le Parti socialiste,* p. 239.
38. Quoted by Bernstein, *Le 6 fevrier* p. 242.
39. Labrousse, ed., *Blum, chef de gouvernement.*
40. In another article, after the November 1932 elections, Blum wrote that Hitler's "hopes for power were dashed."
41. He was assassinated by the militia in 1944.
42. Depreux, *Souvenirs,* pp. 91–92.
43. Chavardès, *Été 36:,* pp. 16–17.
44. A "civil" cermony, as the leaders of *L'Action française* had been excommunicated by Rome.
45. Quoted in Touchard and Bodin, *Front Populaire,* p. 31.

46. But the newspaper continued its work.
47. It was that very year that the Narbonne rugby club won the championship of France.
48. Fernand-Laurent preferred to let the matter drop, and the "idiotic legend" persisted, like the one that attributed the entry of his son Robert into Hispano-Suiza to an intervention of the shady banker Oustric.
49. But only 31 percent of its inhabitants were younger than twenty.
50. Because of naturalizations, which had been made easier.
51. Dubief, *Déclin de la Troisième République*, p. 97.
52. Ibid., p. 101.
53. The SFIO had gotten the right for the opposition parties also to have some speeches rebroadcast.
54. Blum, *Oeuvre* (1934–1937), p. 235.
55. Lefranc, *Front Populaire*, pp. 96–97.
56. Quoted in Bodin and Touchard, *Front Populaire*, p. 47.
57. G. Lefranc, Bodin and Touchard, G. Dupeux, among others.
58. *L'Echo de Paris*, March 23, 1936.
59. Eliminated in the first round in Valence by a Radical, Moch was elected in Sète two years later.
60. On these assimilations, I agree with the point of view of Georges Lefranc rather than with that of Georges Dupeux, who attributes their votes to the Radicals.
61. Malraux, *La Fin et le commencement*, p. 16.
62. "Joshua grew pensive and pale,/For he had been chosen by the Lord." (tr.)
63. *L'Oeuvre*, May 5.
64. Moch, *Rencontres avec Blum*, p. 136.
65. Ibid., p. 136.
66. The expression is sometimes attributed to Paul Reynaud.
67. A sequence used by J. -N. Jeanneny in his excellent film, *Léon Blum ou la fidélité*.
68. The German Social-Democratic Minister of the Interior who savagely repressed the Communist movement known as the "Spartakist" movement (led by Rosa Luxemburg and Karl Liebknecht).
69. In an article in *Preuves* in 1960.
70. Duclos, Vol. 2, pp. 147, 177. The same information is provided by various spokesmen of the PCF: for example, by Laurent Salini in the film by Verny and Santelli already mentioned. Salini, judging from the perspective of forty years later, considered the refusal a mistake. Aragon made a similar judgment in a radio interview in 1971.
71. Leader of the Austrian anti-Nazi right.
72. Guilloux, *Batailles perdues*, pp. 494–497.
73. Two bankers who were considered suspect and a millionaire friendly to the Radicals.
74. Quoted in Bodin and Touchard, *Front Populaire*.
75. It was in 1924.
76. Danos and Gibelin, *Juin 36*.
77. The word "slapped" has a more negative and humiliating connotation.
78. June 13, 1936.
79. June 25, 1936.
80. Danos and Gibelin and Jean Lhomme, *Juin 1936*, p. 340. There were 12,000 strikes in May–June, 1936, 9,000 of them with factory occupations.

81. Frossard was former Secretary-General of the PCF, Déat leader of the dissident "neos."
82. *L'Echo de Paris*, June 12, 1936.
83. *La Révolution proletarienne*, July 1936.
84. Gide, *Correspondence*, p. 74.
85. Quoted in Lefranc, *Juin 36*.
86. June 17, 1936.
87. A future Vichy minister.
88. Letter to Georges Lefranc of August 29, 1965, quoted in Lefranc, *Juin 36*.
89. Lefranc, *Front Populaire*.
90. Conversation of Daniel Mayer with the author, November, 1976.
91. Labrousse, ed., *Blum, chef de gouvernement*.
92. *La Révolution prolétarienne*, June 10, 1936.
93. Deposition at the Riom trial, February 1942.
94. Speech in the Senate, July 7, 1936.
95. In order not to break up artificially the narrative of the great social movement of May–June, we will anticipate here by watching Blum act as head of government before we have seen him installed.
96. Jules Moch in a conversation with the author, October 1976.
97. Danos and Gibelin, *Juin 36*, p. 125.
98. The future *Confederation nationale du patronat français* (CNPF).
99. Toward the resumption of work and the evacuation of the factories.
100. André Delmas, quoted by Lefranc, *Juin 36*, p. 150.
101. Writing on June 14 to Roger Martin du Gard, André Gide noted: "The night before last, I thought things were going to turn bad; there was a sense of a storm in the air and you could see suspicious groups circulating trying to stir up trouble. Tension relaxed rather quickly; for the moment at least."
102. For peasant strikes broke out again. Not to mention the resumption of the movement in September.
103. Leon Trotsky sent his contribution from Norway.
104. *Le Populaire*, May 27, 1936.
105. *L'Humanité*, May 29, 1936.
106. From the beginning of May to the middle of June, perhaps.
107. Labrousse, ed., *Léon Blum, chef de gouvernement*.
108. Blumel, *Léon Blum*, p. 46.
109. Doumergue and Flandin had done as much before him.
110. *Front populaire, réevolution manquée*. One document remains from Marceau Pivert's work as Blum's theatrical director: photographs of the meeting at the Vélodrome d'Hiver on June 7, used in the film by Verny and Santelli.
111. The program spoke only of a "reduction in work time without a reduction in wages."
112. Who should not be confused with figures like Déat or Doriot: he was deported under the occupation for acts of resistance.
113. Which, according to André Blumel, soon had 50,000 secret and well-organized adherents.
114. Conversation of Jules Moch with the author, October 1976.
115. Labrousse, ed., *Léon Blum, chef de gouvernement*, p. 166.
116. *Gringoire*, May 29, 1936.
117. Moch, *Recontres avec Blum*, p. 171.
118. *Le Populaire*, July 7, 1936.

119. *Le Temps,* July 28, 1936. Barthélemy reappeared under Vichy as Minister of Justice, shamelessly violating the law.
120. *Vendredi,* July 17, 1936.
121. "L'idéalisme dans la conception de l'histoire," 1894.
122. Gladstone. It would be interesting to explore the parallel between him and Blum.
123. Conversation of Jules Moch with the author, October 1976.
124. Conversation with Madeleine Lagrange.
125. Quoted by M. Chavardès, pp. 262–263.
126. Conversation with Gaston Cusin, November 1976. See next chapter.
127. Vol. 2, *Aux jours ensoleillés du Front populaire,* p. 163.
128. Reynaud, *Mémoires,* vol. 2, pp. 62–64.
129. Conversation with Renée Blum, April 1977.
130. Note by Admiral Abrial, March 8, 1936, Archives of the Ministry of the Navy. At the time, Blum was still recovering from the attack on the boulevard Saint-Germain, and was necessarily isolated and silent.
131. Deposition before the Investigative Commission, August 8, 1947, Blum, *Oeuvre* (1937–1940).
132. 1934–35.
133. Eden, *Facing the Dictators,* pp. 429, 431.
134. Monick, *Pour mémoire,* pp. 44–47.
135. I would like to thank René Girault, a remarkable observer of the diplomacy of the Popular Front, for having drawn my attention to this episode.
136. Gamelin, *Servir,* vol. 2.
137. Dreifont, *Yvon Delbos.*
138. Colton, *Blum,* p. 161, n.4.
139. Quoted in Colton, *Blum.*
140. Blum's deposition before the Investigative Commission, August 8, 1947, Blum, *Oeuvre* (1937–1940), p. 367.
141. Ibid., p. 368.
142. Cot, *Le Procés de la République,* pp. 343–344.
143. Labrousse, ed., *Léon Blum, chef de gouvernement,* p. 348.
144. Note from Ambassador François-Poncet to the Quai d'Orsay, May 21, 1936.
145. Papers of Ambassador Fouques-Duparc, quoted by Renouvin in Labrousse, ed., *Blum, chef de gouvernement.*
146. Blumel in Labrousse, ed., *Léon Blum, chef de gouvernement.*
147. Dispatch from François-Poncet to Delbos, June 19, 1937.
148. Matteotti, Italian Socialist leader and friend of Blum, had been assassinated by the Fascists. In the notes he took during his confinement in Buchenwald, Blum evokes this tragedy in a few words, and concludes, in capitals: "THE HORROR!"
149. Blumel, *Léon Blum, chef de gouvernement,* p. 360.
150. Blum, *Oeuvre* (1940–1945), p. 114.
151. An air force officer during the war, Pierre Mendès France explains the backwardness of the French air force by the generally recognized pre-eminence of the British in this area.
152. Delmas, *A gauche de la barricade,* p. 110.
153. Bowers, *Mission to Spain.*
154. It should be noted that the Giral government at the time included neither Socialists nor Communists.

155. André Géraud, known as Pertinax, one of the most celebrated journalists of the period. He was then the special correspondent of *l'Echo de Paris* in London.
156. July 25th.
157. Pierre Cot was Minister, Jean Moulin head of his cabinet.
158. Twenty aircraft from this (nationalized) firm had been promised.
159. Del Castillo. He had distributed a letter saying that he was resigning in order not to be involved in a sale of arms which were going to kill his compatriots.
160. At least two of the Radical Ministers, Pierre Cot and Jean Zay, were in favor of aiding the Republic.
161. Leader of the Socialist right.
162. The visit of July 23–24.
163. Emphasis in the manuscript.
164. *Le Populaire,* October 15, 1945.
165. Zay, *Souvenirs,* p. 114.
166. Letter to the author, May 17, 1975.
167. Dreifort, *Yvon Delbos,* p. 206 n.
168. As though by accident, through the intermediary of Corbin.
169. Moch, *Recontres avec Blum,* p. 195.
170. Reported by Pierre Cot.
171. According to Jules Moch.
172. According to Jules Moch, who in this case, exceptionally, is speaking only from hearsay.
173. Jules Moch, interview with the author, November 1976.
174. Blum confused the First Sea Lord, the military title of Chatfield, with the First Lord of the Admiralty, that is, Minister of the Navy.
175. Investigative Commission, 1947, I, p. 218.
176. Dreifort, *Yvon Delbos,* p. 45.
177. Ibid., p. 47.
178. Ibid., p. 52.
179. Hart, *Memoirs,* vol. 2., pp. 127–128.
180. Deposition before the Investigative Commission, *Oeuvre* (1937–1940), p. 378.
181. Through Germaine Moch, who was in Bordeaux.
182. Interview with the author, November 1976.
183. These last five were socialists.
184. See Pierre Renouvin's contribution to Labrousse, ed., *Léon Blum, chef de gouvernment,* p. 335.
185. *L'Humanité,* August 10, 1936.
186. Archives of the Ministry of Foreign Affairs.
187. Chavardès, *Été 36,* p. 276.
188. A Socialist, who obtained Communist participation.
189. Discovered in the Wilhelmstrasse archives, this document, among others, corresponds to remarks by Hitler which show him as being little concerned with the Spanish affair.
190. The Marceau Pivert faction was divided between interventionists and pacifists.
191. Eden, *Facing the Dictators,* p. 450.
192. Pike, *Guerre d'Espagne,* p. 144.
193. Ibid., p. 137.
194. Proposing the non-intervention pact.

195. A German ship attacked two weeks earlier, August 18, by the Spanish Republican navy.
196. He referred to this argument addressing the judges in Riom.
197. A remark which provided Henri Bérard with the occasion for vulgar sarcasm in *Gringoire*.
198. May 10, 1936.
199. An "example" given to a Hitler or a Mussolini, who were supposed to be "stirred by honor"? Spain was involved, but to confuse the dictators with the characters of *Le Cid?*
200. Editorialist for *L'Humanité* and deputy in the PCF.
201. Known as the "Non-Intervention Committee."
202. Conversation of Pierre Cot with the author, November 1976.
203. Conversation of Pierre Cot with the author, December 1976.
204. *Le Figaro,* November 15, 1936.
205. Fischer, *Men and Politics,* p. 448.
206. Thomas, *Spanish Civil War,* p. 980.
207. Provided by M. Cusin.
208. Ceretti, *A l'ombre des deux T,* pp. 131–32. (The two Ts are Togliatti and Thorez.)
209. Interview of Pierre Mendès France with the author, July 1976.
210. A strange assimilation.
211. Astounding frankness.
212. In that case, why hurry to prepare?
213. Gamelin, *Servir,* vol. 2, pp. 323–326.
214. Lefranc, *Front Populaire,* p. 417.
215. Blame has been placed particularly on Major Loustaunu-Lacan, then a sympathizer of *La Cagoule,* who later joined the resistance.
216. Zay, *Souvenirs et solitude,* p. 114.
217. Cot, *Le Procès de la République,* vol. 2, p. 306.
218. Labrousse, ed., *Léon Blum, chef de gouvernement,* pp. 369–70.
219. P. 115.
220. Moch, *Rencontres avec Blum.*
221. Seuil, 1975, p. 67.
222. Del Vayo, *Freedom's Battle,* (E. E. Brooke, 1940), pp. 65–70.
223. Azcarate, *Mi Emajada en Londres durante la guerra civil espanola,* pp. 253–55.
224. Letter from Massigli to Léger, January 23, 1937, archives of the Quai d'Orsay.
225. Labrousse, ed., *Léon Blum, chef de gouvernement,* pp. 374–375.
226. Unpublished letter, Léon Blum, archives of the FNSP.
227. We already quoted this remark of Colonel Morel.
228. *Le Populaire,* October 15, 1945.
229. He was a member of his second government in March–April 1938.
230. Which Blum himself proposed, as we have seen, on March 15, 1936.
231. An "equality" which was already perfectly scandalous.
232. *Le Populaire,* June 29, 1938.
233. Presumably the English.
234. 1936: Hitler's coup in the Rhineland.
235. The formula, as we have seen, is Blum's own.
236. Chautemps took over the government in June 1937.
237. Particularly the 40-hour law.
238. Labrousse, ed., *Léon Blum, chef de gouvernement,* p. 218.

239. Monick, *Pour mémoire*, pp. 48–49.
240. According to Sauvy, *Histoire economique*, vol. 2, gold exports, which were estimated at 3.3 billion francs in May 1936, slowed in June to 1.2 billion. They increased later.
241. Monick, *Pour mémoire*, p. 57.
242. Parliamentary debates, Senate, October 1, 1936.
243. Labrousse, ed., Blum, *chef de gouvernement*, p. 220.
244. Bouvier, in *Le Mouvement social*, January–March 1966.
245. March 12, 1937.
246. Debate in the Senate, October 1, 1936.
247. See the preceding chapter.
248. Lefranc, *Front Populaire*, p. 209.
249. Labrousse, ed., *Léon Blum, chef de gouvernement*, p. 130.
250. See above, "Popular Front."
251. *Preuves*, 1960.
252. Duclos, *Mémoires*, vol. 2.
253. "Propre" means "clean" here.
254. The author, who was a naïve reader of the article, can testify as much.
255. *Gringoire*.
256. It is hard not to hear this as a kind of confession.
257. Speech at Salengro's funeral, November 22, 1936.
258. Who became one of the most ardent critics of Nazism from 1938 on.
259. The militia assassinated him in Montélimar in 1942.
260. Among whom the Trotskyites were the most dynamic element.
261. *Oeuvres* (Editions Sociales, 1965), vol. 5, p. 43.
262. Thorez in *La Lutte ouvrière*, March 19, 1937, quoted in Rioux, *Révolutionnaires du Front Populaire*, p. 295.
263. Quoted by Lefranc, *Front Populaire*, p. 123.
264. The prefect of police, who had been fired just before February 6, 1934, and had become one of the leaders of the right, had maintained contacts in the police.
265. Moch, *Recontres avec Léon Blum*, p. 225. It was *La Cagoule*, the kernel of Darnand's militia, which assassinated Marx Dormoy seven years later.
266. A curious allusion to Talleyrand's quip on the part of a moralist in politics who was very hostile to the man of the Congress of Vienna.
267. Lefranc, *Front Populaire*, p. 233.
268. This was the expression Blum used on the rostrum of the Chamber.
269. Labrousse, ed., *Léon Blum, chef de gouvernement*, comment by François Goguel, p. 168.
270. According to the Constitution, the Chamber could be dissolved only with the approval of the Senate.
271. Moch, *Recontres avec Blum*, p. 235.
272. Who died at the hands of the Gestapo.
273. Conference at Nanterre, March 18, 1977, published in *Les Cahiers Léon Blum*, 1977.
274. Lefranc, *Front Populaire*, p. 257.
275. Paul Claudel, an implacable opponent of the Popular Front, wrote at the time to Paul Reynaud: "Georges Bonnet is in the process of making us miss Vincent Auriol!" (quoted by Georges Lefranc).
276. In his book about François de Wendel (Paris: Seuil, 1976), Jean-Noel Jeanneny qualifies this point of view, attributing to the industrialist-parliamentarian a more "passive" role.

277. Labrousse, ed., *Léon Blum, chef de gouvernement,* p. 162.
278. See preceding chapter.
279. Which the American government, a signatory of the tripartite agreement of September 1936, had recognized as being necessary.
280. Quoted by Lefranc, *Front Populaire,* p. 513.
281. Who was a minister again under Pétain.
282. Broadly speaking, the "Pivertists."
283. Guerin, *Front populaire, révolution manquée,* p. 201.
284. A boldness which paid very few "dividends" in recruitment: the PSOP contained between four and five thousand members.
285. After annexing Austria in March, during the summer of 1938 Hitler attempted to take from Czechoslovakia, an ally of France, the Sudetenland, more than half of whose population was of German origin.
286. *Le Populaire,* July 27, 1938.
287. British Prime Minister.
288. Hitler's residence.
289. Which has led a historian like J. Bariéty to call him an "appeaser."
290. The week of five days, eight hours work.
291. Uncle of the director of the 1970s.
292. A traditional accusation of the right: Blum was a counsel to large companies—notably the Galéries Lafayette. He appeared in court very rarely.
293. Anglo-Franco-Soviet.

Part III

1. Which the PCF did not fail to do itself, notably liquidating its former Secretary Marcel Gitton shortly before the liberation.
2. André Marty, in *Cahiers du bolchevisme,* November 1939.
3. The authenticity of this text, first published in German, has been questioned. But it is included in volume 5 of Thorez's complete works.
4. "If those cannibals want to make heroes of us, our first bullets must be for Mandel, Blum, and Reynaud." (tr.) In the revolutionary hymn, of course, the last line is "for our own generals."
5. The lightning victory of the German tanks.
6. A year later he found himself in Vichy as a member of Pétain's "National Council."
7. Moch, *Rencontres avec Blum,* pp. 257–58.
8. Welles, *Time for Decision,* p. 130.
9. De Gaulle, *Mémoires de guerre* p. 25.
10. Blum, *Oeuvre* (1940–1945), p. 7.
11. Renée and Catherine Blum. Robert Blum was an artillery officer at the front.
12. Blum, *Mémoires,* in *Oeuvre* (1940–1945), p. 22.
13. Ibid., p. 23.
14. Confronting the judges in Riom, this officer, who was reputedly an honest man, and had been called as a witenss by Blum, claimed to remember this conversation only very vaguely.
15. In his *Mémoires,* Paul Reynaud published the facsimile of a note drawn up on June 15 at 4 p.m., which summed up the relative strength of the factions of the cabinet in these terms: Against armistice: Rio, Marin, Del-

bos, G. Monnet, Rollin, Serol. For armistice: Bouthillier, Pétain, Ybar-negaray, Frossard, Pomaret, Chautemps, Chichery, Pernot, Baudouin, Queuille, Eynac, Julien.

16. Including the most dishonorable clause, the one which obliged France to turn German political refugees over to Hitler—as Stalin was returning to him Communists who had taken refuge in the USSR.
17. Blum, *Mémoires,* in *Oeuvre* (1940–1945), p. 68.
18. Shirer, *Collapse of the Third Republic,* p. 942.
19. Blum, *Mémoires, in Oeuvre* (1940–1945) pp. 101–3.
20. Blum, *Mémoires,* in *Oeuvre* (1940–1945), pp. 127–28. Breitscheid did not succeed. He and Hilferding were assassinated by the Gestapo.
21. Ibid., p. 131.
22. Letter to Mme. Grunebaum-Ballin, September 24, 1940, in *Oeuvre* (1940–1945), p. 141.
23. Viénot later joined de Gaulle in London, where he died in 1944, as Ambassador of Free France.
24. "Archives de France," p. 70.
25. Blum, *Oeuvre,* (1940–1945), p. 158.
26. At Blum's request, Spanien had been joined by his comrade André Le Troquer.
27. Moch, *Rencontres avec Blum,* p. 286.
28. Colton, *Blum.*
29. Blum, *Oeuvre* (1940–1945), p. 178.
30. Reynaud, *Au coeur de la mêlée,* p. 986.
31. Barthélemy was a Professor of Law in Paris, A violent opponent of the Popular Front—see chapter 7—he presided over the creation in Vichy of the "Special Section," the most illegal judicial institution in contemporary French history, which was the subject of a film by Jorge Semprun and Costa-Gavras.
32. Blum, *Oeuvre* (1940–1945), p. 200. In spite of the hard journey, Renée and Janot visited several times.
33. Draft notes written in captivity. Blum initially thought of using an exchange-of-letter or a dialogue form, similar to the form of *Eckermann.* Archives of the FNSP. Preface by Bracke, *Oeuvre* (1940–45), p. 408.
34. See below pp. 00ff.
35. Blum, *Oeuvre* (1940–1945), pp. 444–449. He declared himself in favor of the American presidential system, but later repudiated that choice.
36. Raffalovitch, *Des "Nouvelles Conversations" a "A l'échelle humaine."*
37. In the draft, the list of these heroes also includes the names of Spinoza and Einstein, later crossed out.
38. This last paragraph is a repetition, with minor differences, of a passage from the *Nouvelles Conversations.*
39. Chautemps was then Vichy's Ambassador to Washington.
40. Swiss military historian, a specialist in Napoleon's campaigns.
41. Hearing of March 10.
42. Colton, *Blum.*
43. This was the chief count of the indictment, thus turned against Pétain and Laval.
44. Blum, *L'Exercice du pouvoir.*
45. The great fear had subsided.
46. Yes. Léon Blum was forgetting a Count Louis de Blois, who is known for nothing else.

47. Under the Clemenceau government.
48. Hitler had demanded the Riom trial in order to demonstrate that it was French politicians who started the war.
49. Ribet, *Riom*, p. 170.
50. Blum, *Oeuvre* (1940–1945), p. xv.
51. "Archives de France," p. 74.
52. Aron, *Histoire de Vichy*, p. 114.
53. Blum, *Oeuvre* (1940–1945), p. 358.
54. Colton, *Blum*.
55. Cachin (still a social-patriot for a few more months) was prompted to say this by the popular enthusiasm at the entry of French troops into Strasbourg.
56. In fact, nothing was done, neither by Roosevelt nor by de Gaulle, to attempt to rescue Blum from prison or concentration camp.
57. Moch, *Rencontres avec Blum*, p. 297.
58. The "we" seems to refer to the committee of Free France, not the general himself.
59. In English in the text. De Gaulle sometimes spoke "franglais."
60. The (Belgian) President of the Second International.
61. Augustin Laurent did not accept the nomination. André Le Troquer was chosen, and replaced after his departure for London by Daniel Mayer. The Executive Committee became the CNR (National Council of the Resistance).
62. Blum, *Oeuvre* (1940–1945), pp. 397–399.
63. April 1943, No. 11.
64. Chief of police in Vichy, Justice Minister, and Minister of the Interior, respectively.
65. Camp for officers. But this one, a "punishment" camp, was reserved for members of the Resistance and Jews.
66. One of Léon Blum's lawyers in Riom.
67. In the Blum Collection of the FNSP. The notes are often barely legible. I believe I have reproduced them accurately.
68. Blum, *Oeuvre* (1940–1945), pp. 513–544. The quotations on the following pages are taken from this beautiful memoir.
69. "The assassination of Philippe Henriot on 28 June . . . had produced among the ultra-collaborationists a thirst for reprisals. The German government, perhaps under pressure from Brinon's clan, proposed the return of hostages to France . . . the first to be handed over were to be Mandel, Léon Blum, and Reynaud. . . . Laval vacillated, and then refused. . . . It was too late, Mandel was already in France." (Favreau, *Mandel*, p. 249.) Léon Blum, for his part, was convinced that he was a hostage for Pétain, his life depending on Pétain's.
70. He did not write it.
71. Stauffenberg's assassination attempt against Hitler, in which the Gestapo implicated him.
72. One of the military leaders of the French Resistance.
73. The name of a leader of the German resistance to Napoleon, who was shot.
74. de Gaulle, *Mémoires de guerre*, vol. 3, p. 258.
75. Blum had returned from captivity and deportation "weakened" in no way. His doctors, and those who knew him well before and after his ordeals, strongly confirm this. But from time to time he had circulatory problems,

diagnosed by the American doctors who had examined him in Naples in early May 1945, which showed themselves by imperceptible absences, a very brief "power failure." For the most part, except when he underwent two serious surgical operations (1948–1949), he remained perfectly himself for these five years.

76. Unpublished letter, Léon Blum Collection, FNSP.
77. Then being published by *Le Populaire*.
78. Léon Blum Collection, FNSP.
79. In an article in *Le Populaire* a week earlier.
80. A letter we have not been able to find.
81. We present the text of this copy.
82. Probably Gaston Palewski, the general's cabinet chief.
83. Sulzberger, *A Long Row of Candles*, p. 266.
84. Gouin was chosen over Auriol because the Communists were much less hostile to him than to the former Finance Minister of the Popular Front.
85. With the exception of the minor episode of November 1918 at La-Grange-aux-belles.
86. Auriol, *Journal du septennat*, vol. 1, p. 210.
87. Elgey, *La République des illusions*, p. 139.
88. Revealed by Georgette Elgey in *La République des illusions*, pp. 140–141.
89. Moch, *Rencontres avec Blum*, p. 315.
90. Lapie, *De Blum à de Gaulle*, p. 24.
91. We can point to this note by Pierre Nora: "The fact that Léon Blum did not take this step toward which he was led by both the Leclerc mission and his declaration of December 23, 1946, is explicable only by the climate of insecurity created by the December 19 attack and the personal temperament of the great old man" (in Vincent Auriol, *Journal du septennat*, preface, p. xxxix).
92. Lapie, *De Blum à de Gaulle*, p. 111 ("Laconic" seems inappropriate for Leclerc. "Simple" would have been better, and "clear" better still.)
93. "In the beginning, we approved the Marshall Plan," declared Jacques Duclos to Georgette Elgey fifteen years later. (Elgey, *La République des illusions*, p. 336.)
94. *Le Populaire*, May 23, 1947.
95. See below p. 000
96. Moch, *Rencontres avec Léon Blum*.
97. An expression which should not be made to say too much.
98. Elgey, *La République des illusions*, p. 347.
99. Lapie, *De Blum à de Gaulle*, p. 128.
100. Colton, *Blum*.
101. Moch, *Rencontres avec Blum*, p. 333.
102. *Le Populaire*, January 1948.
103. The mysterious conference of Slklarska-Poreba was still thought to have taken place in Warsaw.
104. *Le Populaire*, November 5, 1947.
105. *Le Populaire*, November 4–5, 1947.
106. Directly in charge of the government's Indochina policy.
107. Lapie, *De Blum à de Gaulle*, pp. 265–266.
108. Who was to the Labour Party what Bracke was to the SFIO.
109. Most of the details which follow are taken from *Le Populaire* of March 31.
110. "The conquest of such a face is the meaning of socialism," said François Mitterand twenty-five years later. He had been a visitor that day, still young and in search of a doctrine (speech in Lille, April 13, 1975).

111. Monnet, *Mémoires,* p. 301.

112. Minus the Roman side, of course.

113. Conversations with Patrick Modiano, Gallimard, 1976.

114. Paris, Calmann-Lévy, 1947, in the collection "Liberté de l'esprit," edited by Raymond Aron.

115. "Political" or governmental action? In this case, Blum seems to be bending Marx for his purposes.

116. Zeller, *Trois points.*

117. To quote the title of a book by Guy Brossolet.

118. He was also named Blum, and had changed his name to avoid confusion. His sister, Maître Suzanne Blum, kept hers.

119. Blumel, *Blum, juif et sioniste* (Ed. Terre retrouvée, 1951), p. 5.

120. *Journal* (quoted above p. 499).

121. *Le Populaire,* August 1, 1947.

122. Letter of November 26, archives of the FNSP, Paris.

123. *Le Populaire,* June 7, 1927.

124. *Le Populaire,* July 5, 1927.

125. See above, "Ordeal by Fire."

126. Letter from Tran Ngoc Danh to Léon Blum, August 11, 1947, collection of the FNSP.

127. See above p. 536.

128. Two important figures in the SFIO, the second a leader of the most anti-colonialist wing, who later supported *Algérie franç̣aise.*

129. Léon Blum collection of the FNSP. Charles Lussy was one of the leaders of the left wing of the SFIO.

130. The great orientalist who had just carried out a mission to contact Ho Chi Minh.

131. *Le Populaire,* December 10–11, 1949.

132. If not beyond the personal views of Edouard Depreux.

133. *Le Populaire,* December 5, 1949.

134. Joll, *Intellectuals in Politics,* p. 2.

135. But is this not also a possible definition of the state in a "people's democracy"?

BIBLIOGRAPHY

As Léon Blum was first and foremost a writer, the most important research source is his own work. Most of it has been collected in the nine volumes published by Editions Albin Michel between 1954 and 1966, under the direction of Robert Blum, assisted by Daniel Mayer, Oreste Rosenfeld and Robert Verdier. Although certain important articles do not appear in this collection, it is nevertheless an incomparable research tool for the historian. The fifth volume, covering the war years 1940–1945, is especially valuable, for it contains previously unpublished letters concerning the captivity and resistance of Blum, as well as most of the transcripts from the Riom proceedings.

Beyond the numerous articles, speeches, and pamphlets published in *La Revue blanche, L'Humanité, La Revue socialiste, Le Populaire,* and *Le Populaire-Dimanche,* the main works of Léon Blum are:

Nouvelles Conversations de Goethe avec Eckermann, Editions de *La Revue blanche,* 1901

Les Congrès ouvriers et socialistes français, Bibliotheque socialiste, 1901

En lisant: réflexions critiques, P. Ollendorf, 1906

Au théâtre, 4 vol., P. Ollendorf, 1906–1911

Du mariage, P. Ollendorf, 1907

Stendhal et le Beylisme, P. Ollendorf, 1916

Lettres sur la réforme gouvernementale, Grasset, 1918

Pour être socialiste, Editions socialistes, 1919

Les Problèmes de la paix, Stock, 1931

Souvenirs sur l'Affaire, Gallimard, 1935

L'Exercice du pouvoir (discours de 1936–1937), Gallimard, 1937

L'Histoire jugera, recueil d'articles rassemblés par Suzanne Blum, Éd. de l'Arbre, Montréal, 1943

A l'échelle humaine, Gallimard, 1945

A special issue of *La Revue socialiste* in June–July, 1950 should be added to this list. It is a collection of "selected writings" by Blum. Another work which must be set apart from the many books about Blum is a small volume published

559

without the author's name and entitled simply *Léon Blum, 9 avril 1872–30 mars 1950*. This is the work of his third wife, Jeanne.

Besides the above sources, this book was written with the help of many other works, foremost among them being *Léon Blum, chef du gouvernment (1936–1937)*, the transcript of a symposium held in 1965 and published by Armand Colin in 1967, under the direction of Ernest Labrousse. Also important are the catalogs of two exhibits about Blum, one at the Bibliothèque Nationale, one at the Archives de France. The most important articles about Blum are cited in the Notes. In addition to the following list of written works on Blum, two films should be mentioned: Jean-Noël Jeanneney's *Léon Blum ou la fidélité* and Claude Santelli and Françoise Verny's *Le front populaire ou la mémoire des peuples*.

Alain. *Correspondence avec Florence et Elie Halévy*. Paris: Gallimard, 1958.

Alvarez del Vayo, Julio. *Freedom's Battle*. New York: E. E. Brooke, 1940.

Andler, Charles. *Vie de Lucien Herr*. Paris: Rieder, 1938.

Aron, Robert. *Histoire de Vichy*. Paris: Fayard, 1954.

Auclair, Marcelle. *Vie de Jean Jaurès ou la France avant 1914*. Paris: Le Seuil, 1954.

Audry, Colette. *Léon Blum ou la politique de juste*. Denoel, 1970. (First edition, Paris: Julliard, 1955).

Auriol, Vincent. *Journal du septennat, 1947*. Paris: Gallimard, 1970.

Azcarate. *Mi Emajada en Londres durante la guerra civil española*. Madrid, 1976.

Beauchard, Philippe. *Léon Blum, le pouvoir pour quoi faire?* Paris: Arthaud, 1976.

Benda, Julien. *La Jeunesse d'un clerc*. Paris: Gallimard, 1936.

Berl, Emmanuel. *La Politique et les partis*. Paris: Rieder, 1932.

Bernstein, Serge. *Le 6 février 1934*. Paris: Julliard ("Archives"), 1975.

Bloch, Marc. *L'Étrange Défaite*. Paris: Société des editions Franc-Tireur, 1946.

Blum, Léon. *L'Oeuvre de Léon Blum*. Paris: Albin Michel, 1891–1950.

———. *Nouvelles Conversations de Goethe avec Eckermann*. Paris: Editions de La Revue blanche, 1901.

———. *Les Congrès ouvriers et socialistes français*. Paris: Bibliotheque Socialiste, 1901.

———. *En lisant: reflexions critiques*. Paris: P. Ollendorf, 1906.

———. *Au théâtre*. Four volumes. Paris: P. Ollendorf, 1906–1911.

———. *Du mariage*. Paris: P. Ollendorf, 1907.

———. *Stendhal et le Beylisme*. Paris: P. Ollendorf, 1916.

———. *Lettres sur la réforme gouvernementale*. Paris: Grasset, 1918.

———. *Pour être socialiste*. Paris: Editions Socialistes, 1919.

———. *Les Problèmes de la paix*. Paris: Stock, 1931.

———. *Souvenirs sur l'affaire*. Paris: Gallimard, 1935.

———. *L'Exercice du pouvoir* (discours de 1936–37). Paris: Gallimard, 1937.

———. *L'Histoire jugera* (recueil d'articles rassembles par Suzanne Blum). Montréal: l'Arbre, 1943.

———. *A l'échelle humaine*. Paris: Gallimard, 1945.

Blumel, André. *Léon Blum, juif et sioniste*. Paris: Terre retrouvée, 1951.

Bodin, Louis and Touchard, Jean. *Front populaire*. Paris: A. Colin ("U"), 1972.

Bourgin, Hubert. *L'Ecole normale et la politique, de Juarès à Léon Blum*. Paris: Fayard, 1938.

Bowers, Claude. *My Mission to Spain*. New York: Simon and Schuster, 1954.

Broué, Pierre and Temine, Emile. *La Révolution et la Guerre d'Espagne*. Paris: Ed. de Minuit, 1961.

Caillaux, Joseph. *Mes Mémoires*. Paris: Plon, 1947.

Ceretti, Giulio. *A l'ombre des deux T*. Paris: Julliard, 1973.

Chavardes, Maurice. *Été 36: la victoire du Front Populaire*. Paris: Calmann-Lévy, 1966.

Clemenceau, Georges. *La Mêlée sociale*. Paris: Fasquelle, 1895.

Colton, Joel. *Léon Blum*. Paris: Fayard, 1966.

Cot, Pierre. *Le Procès de la République*. New York: Maison française, 1944.

Danos, Jacques and Marcelin Gibelin. *Juin 36*. Paris: Editions ouvrieres, 1952.

de Gaulle, Charles. *Mémoires de guerre*. Paris: Plon, 1955.

Déat, Marcel. *Perspectives socialistes*. Paris: Librairie Valois, 1930.

Delperrie de Bayac, Jacques. *Histoire du Front Populaire*. Paris: Fayard, 1972.

Depreux, Edouard. *Souvenirs d'un militant*. Paris: Fayard, 1972.

Desgranges (Abbé). *Journal d'un prêtre-député*. Geneve: La Palatine, 1960.

Dreifort, J. E. *Yvon Delbos at the Quai d'Orsay*. Lawrence: University of Kansas Press, 1973.

Droz, Jacques. *Histoire générale du socialisme*. Vol. 2, article by M. Reberioux, PUF, 1974.

Dubief, Henri. *Le Declin de la III*e *Republique*, in *Nouvelle histoire de la France contemporaine*. Paris: Le Seuil, 1976.

Duclos, Jacques. *Mémoires*. Especially Vol. 2, *Aux jours ensoleillés du Front Populaire*. Paris: Fayard, 1970.

Eden, Anthony. *Facing the Dictators*. Boston: Houghton Mifflin, 1962.

Ehrenbourg, Ilya. *La Chute de Paris*. Paris: Hier et Aujourd'hui, 1945.

Elgey, Georgette. *La République des illusions (1945–1951)*. Paris: Fayard, 1965.

Fauvet, Jacques. *Histoire de la IV*e *République*. Paris: Fayard, 1959.

Favreau, Bertrand. *Georges Mandel*. Paris: Pedrone, 1969.

Fischer, Louis. *Men and Politics*. New York: Duell, Sloan and Pearce, 1941.

Fraser, Geoffrey and Thadée Natanson. *Léon Blum, Man and Statesman*. London: Lippincott, 1937.

Frossard, Ludovic. *De Jaurès à Lénine*. Paris: Bibliotheque de documentation sociale, 1930.

Gamelin, Maurice. *Servir*, Vol. 2. Paris: Plon, 1947.

Gauthier, Robert. *Dreyfusards*. Paris: Julliard ("Archives"), 1965.

Gide, André. *Correspondence*. Paris: Gallimard, 1939.

———. *Journal*. Paris: Gallimard ("La Pléiade"), 1939.

Goldberg, Harvey. *The Life of Jean Jaurès*. Madison: University of Wisconsin Press, 1962.

Gravitz, Madeleine. *Léon Blum*. Paris: Sirey, 1956.

Gregh, Fernand. *L'Age d'or*. Paris: Grasset, 1947.

Guérin, Daniel. *Front Populaire, revolution manquée*. Paris: Maspero, 1970.

Guilloux, Louis. *Les Batailles perdues*. Paris: Gallimard, 1960.

Halévy, Daniel. *Pour l'étude de la III*e *Republique*. Paris: Grasset, 1937.

Hart, Liddell. *The Liddell Hart Memoires*, Vol. 2. New York: Putnam, 1966.

Herr, Lucien. *Choix d'écrits politiques*. Paris: Rieder, 1932.

Joll, James. *Three Intellectuals in Politics*. New York: Harper, 1971.

Judt, Tony. *La Reconstruction du Parti Socialiste* (1921–1926). Paris: Presses de la FNSP, A Colin, 1976.

Julliard, Jacques. *La IV*e *République*. Paris: Calmann-Lévy, 1968.

Kayser, Jacques. *L'Affaire Dreyfus*. Paris: Gallimard, 1946.

Kriegel, Annie. *Le Congrès de Tours*. Paris: Julliard ("Archives"). 1964.
———. *Les Communistes français*. Paris: Le Seuil, 1968.
———. *Aux origines du communisme français*. Paris: Flammarion, 1970.
Labrousse, Ernest, ed. *Léon Blum, chef de gouvernement*. Paris: Colin, 1967.
Lapie, Pierre-Oliver. *De Blum à de Gaulle*. Paris: Fayard, 1971.
Le Bargy, Simone. *Sous de nouveaux soleils*. Paris: Gallimard, 1957.
Lefranc, Georges. *Juin 36, l'explosion sociale*. Paris: Julliard ("Archives"), 1966.
———. *Jaurès et la socialisme des intellectuels*. Paris: Aubier, 1968.
———. *Histoire du Front Populaire*. Paris: Payot, 1965.
Lévy, Louis. *Comment ils sont devenus Socialistes*. Paris: *Populaire*, 1931.
Logue, William. *Léon Blum: The Formative Years (1872–1914)*. De Kalb: Northern Illinois University Press, 1973.
Malraux, Clara. *La Fin et le commencement*. Paris: Grasset, 1976.
Maxence, Jean-Pierre. *Histoire de dix ans*. Paris: Gallimard, 1939.
Martin de Gard, Roger. *Les Thibault, Été 1914*. Paris: Gallimard-Folio.
Mayer, Daniel. *Pour une histoire de la gauche*. Paris: Plon, 1969.
Mendès France, Pierre. *Choisir*. Paris: Stock, 1974.
Michel, Henri. *Les Courants de pensée de la Résistance*. PUF, 1962.
Moch, Jules. *Recontres avec Léon Blum*. Paris: Plon, 1970.
———. *Le Front Populaire*. Perrin, 1971.
Monick, Emmanuel. *Pour mémoire*. Paris: Grasset, 1971.
Monnet, Jean. *Mémoires*. Paris: Fayard, 1976.
Noguères, Henri. *Histoire de la Résistance*. Paris: Laffont, 1973.
Paul-Boncour, Joseph. *Entre deux guerres*. Paris: Plon, 1945.
Philip, André. *Les Socialistes*. Paris: Le Seuil, 1967. (new edition, 1977).
Pike, David. *Les Français et la Guerre d'Espagne*. Paris: PUF, 1976.
Prélot, Marcel. *Evolution politique de socialisme français* (1789–1934). Paris: Ed. Spes, 1939.
Quillot, Roger and Claire Quillot. *L'Homme sur le pavois*. Paris: Gallimard, 1976.
Raffalovitch, Olga. *Des "Nouvelles Conversations avec Eckermann" a "A l'échelle humaine"*. Paris: Albin Michel, 1957.
Rebérioux, Madeleine. *La République radicale,* in *Nouvelle histoire de la France contemporaine*. Paris: Le Seuil, 1973.
Remond, René. *La Droite en France, de 1815 à nos jours*. Paris: Aubier, 1963.
Renard, Jules. *Journal*. Paris: Gallimard ("La Pléiade"), 1967.
Reynaud, Paul. *Mémoires,* Vol. 2, *Envers et contre tous*. Paris: Flammarion, 1963.
———. *Au coeur de la mêlée*. Paris: Flammarion, 1951.
Rioux, Jean-Pierre. *Révolutionnaires du Front Populaire*. Paris: Plon ("10–18"), 1973.
Rosmer, Alfred. *Le Mouvement ouvrier pendant la Première Guerre Mondiale*. Paris: Mouton, 1959.
Rous, Jean. *Itinéraire d'un militant*. Paris: Jeune Afrique, 1968.
Sauvy, Alfred. *Histoire économique de la France entre les deux guerres*. Paris: Fayard, 1965.
Shirer, William. *The Collapse of the Third Republic*. New York: Simon and Schuster, 1969.
Sulzberger, Cyrus. *A Long Row of Candles*. New York: Macmillan, 1969.
Tardieu, André. *La Note de semaine, 1936*. Paris: Flammarion, 1937.
Thomas, Hugh. *The Spanish Civil War*. New York: Harper and Row, 1977.

Touchard, Jean. *La Gauche en France depuis 1900.* Paris: Le Seuil, 1977.

Vaillant, Annette. *Derrière le miroir.* Paris: Mercure de France, 1874.

Verdier, Robert. *PS-PC: une lutte pour l'entente.* Paris: Seghers, 1976.

Vichniac, Marc. *Léon Blum.* Paris: Flammarion, 1937.

Welles, Sumner. *The Time for Decision.* New York, 1944.

Wickam, Henry Steed. *Mes souvenirs.* Paris: Plon, 1926.

Winock, Michel and Jean-Pierre Azema. *La IIIe Republique.* Paris: Calmann-Lévy, 1970.

Zay, Jean. *Souvenirs et solitude.* Paris: Julliard, 1946.

Zeller, Fred. *Trois points, c'est tout.* Paris: Laffont, 1976.

Ziebura, Gilbert. *Léon Blum et le Parti socialiste.* Paris: Cahiers de la FNSP, A. Colin, 1967.

INDEX OF PRINCIPAL NAMES

Delmas, André, 239, 305.
Depreux, Édouard, 160, 491, 501, 532, 534.
Déroulède, Paul, 50, 51, 207.
Doriot, Jacques, 172, 186, 214, 272, 280.
Dormoy, Marx, 262, 268, 287, 309, 314, 323, 328, 342, 374, 375, 376, 377, 381, 407, 409, 410, 416, 419, 422, 527.
Doumergue, Gaston, 170, 211, 397, 431.
Dreyfus, Alfred, 4, 10, 12, 13, 21, 27, 31, 32, 35–52, 63, 64, 66, 70–1, 74, 80, 95, 206, 207, 230, 299, 373, 429, 526.
Duclos, Jacques, 178, 183, 186–7, 209, 241, 250, 266, 276, 285, 340, 341, 363, 367, 369, 370, 371, 383, 471, 503.
Dunois, Amédée, 98, 99, 108, 117, 151, 527.

Eden, Anthony, 290, 292, 297, 298, 308, 318, 319, 326, 332, 334.
Einstein, Albert, 57, 528.
Engels, Friedrich, 66, 157.

Faguet, Émile, 10, 76, 84, 92.
Faure, Paul, 10, 102–3, 106, 109, 115, 124, 126, 130, 132–3, 142, 147, 149, 150, 151, 160–3, 168, 171, 172, 189, 196, 202, 213, 226, 244, 268, 284, 310, 328, 377, 392, 393, 395, 405, 470, 527.
Fénéon, Félix, 10, 20.
Ferrat, André, 109, 110, 115, 125, 213, 368.
Ferry, Abel, 48, 115.
Finaly, Horace, 231, 360, 364.
Flandin, Pierre-Étienne, 270, 294, 299, 349, 385, 387, 388, 397.
Fourier, Charles, 12, 59, 82, 536.
Frachon, Benoît, 179, 262, 263, 264, 266.
France, Anatole, 11, 13, 14, 20, 27, 32, 40, 62, 67, 157, 526, 527.
Franco, Francisco, 315, 316, 319, 320, 323, 325, 331, 333, 334, 335, 347, 353, 503.
Frossard, Ludovic-Oscar, 117, 123, 125, 126, 127, 130, 132, 133, 142, 143, 151, 170, 220, 257, 260, 261.

Gambetta, Léon, 3, 19, 389.
Gamelin, Maurice, 272, 291, 295, 347–8, 417, 418, 423, 428, 429, 453, 454.
Gaulle, Charles de, 300, 301, 321, 405, 408, 413, 416–7, 442–3, 444–5, 447–8, 450–1, 455, 468, 469, 470, 472–3, 474, 475, 481, 483, 484, 485, 486, 490, 491, 493, 495, 497, 500, 506, 509.
Gide, André, 7, 8, 10, 12, 14, 17, 19, 22–4, 30, 32, 55, 57, 71–2, 75, 76, 77, 80, 81, 90, 95, 161, 252, 257, 370, 458, 470, 513, 526, 527, 531.
Giral, José, 306, 311, 313, 325, 333.
Giraudoux, Jean, 234, 282.
Gitton, Marcel, 265, 276, 285.
Gombault, Charles, 228, 527.
Gombault, Georges, 228, 444, 527.
Gouin, Félix, 428, 442, 444, 467, 475, 481, 484, 486, 489, 490, 491, 512.
Gramsci, Antonio, 157, 524.
Gregh, Fernand, 9, 12, 83.
Grumbach, Salomon, 527.
Grunebaum-Ballin, Cécile, 231, 335, 425.
Grunebaum-Ballin, Paul, 231, 262, 279, 335, 526.
Guéhenno, Jean, 267, 277, 515, 518.
Guérin, Daniel, 46, 51, 181, 254, 264, 266, 269, 284, 393.
Guesde, Jules, 15, 20, 30, 41, 55, 59, 60, 64, 65, 67, 68, 97, 98, 102–3, 105, 130, 132, 137, 147, 157, 158, 159, 162, 166, 168, 178, 230, 268, 390, 392, 480, 481.
Guilloux, Louis, 233, 251.

Hahn, Reynaldo, 78, 157.
Halévy, Daniel, 63, 67.
Henriot, Philippe, 209, 228, 241, 349, 459.
Henry (Lt colonel), 37, 42, 50, 373.
Herr, Lucien, 7, 11, 16, 28–33, 35, 37, 38–9, 40, 49, 51, 53, 54, 55, 56, 60, 62, 67, 68, 71, 80, 81, 90, 97, 100, 105, 107, 134, 150, 157, 183, 231, 525, 526.
Herriot, Édouard, 165, 170–2, 175, 176, 181, 182, 183, 192, 197, 198, 207, 210, 218, 228, 234, 236, 245, 251, 268, 271, 287, 317, 319, 323,